Baedeker's

FRANCE

Imprint

326 colour photographs, 58 town plans, 21 general maps, 20 drawings, 12 ground plans, 1 large map of France (see list of maps at end of book)

Text: Rosemarie Arnold, Gisela Bockamp, Birgit Borowski, Madeleine Cabos, Dr Gerhard Eckert, Rainer Eisenschmid, Werner Fauser, Angelika Frank, Carmen Galenschovski, Prof. Wolfgang Hassenpflug, Anja Schliebitz

Editorial work: Baedeker Stuttgart (Anja Schliebitz)

English language edition: Alec Court

Design and layout: Creativ GmbH, Ulrich Kolb, Stuttgart

General direction: Dr Peter Baumgarten, Baedeker Stuttgart

Cartography: Gert Oberländer, Munich; Christoph Gallus, Hohberg-Niederschopfheim; Mairs Geographischer Verlag GmbH & Co., Ostfildern-Kemnat (large map of France)

English translation: James Hogarth

Source of illustrations: Abend (90), Air France (1), Anthony/Jogschies (1), Baedeker (1), Bahon (1), Baumgärtner (2), Bernard (1), Bouhot (1), Bruguière (1), Cabos (47), Chastel/Courtois (1), Choisnet (2), Delvert (1), dpa (1), Eisenschmid (7), Explorer (4), Maison de la France (58), Goélette (1), Griffith (1), Historia (2), IFA/COMNET (1), Joudrier (1), Kugler (1), Lade (3), Laiter (1), Laubier (2), Les Editions Albert René/Goscinny-Uderzo (1), Messerschmidt (1), Müller (1), Musée Unterlinden Colmar/O. Zimmermann (1), Nahm (62), Schliebitz/Schleicher (65), Sindicat d'Initiative Andorra la Vella (1), Schneiders (2), Schuster (7), Steffens (7), Stetter (4), Thomas (3), Transglobe (6), Ullstein (7), Wyrwich (3), ZEFA (2)

To make it easier to locate the various sights listed in the "A to Z" section of the Guide, their co-ordinates on the large map of France are shown in red at the head of each entry.

Following the tradition established by Karl Baedeker in 1844, sights of particular interest are distinguished by either one or two asterisks.

Only a selection of hotels, restaurants and shops can be given: no reflection is implied, therefore, on establishments not included.

In a time of rapid change it is difficult to ensure that all the information given is entirely accurate and up to date, and the possibility of error can never be completely eliminated. Although the publishers can accept no responsibility for inaccuracies and omissions, they are always grateful for corrections and suggestions for improvement.

English edition
Reprinted 1994 with revisions

Prentice Hall General Reference
US and Canadian edition

Distributed in the United Kingdom by the Publishing Division of The Automobile Association, Fanum House, Basingstoke, Hampshire, RG21 2EA.

A CIP catalogue record for this book is available from the British Library.

Licensed user:
Mairs Geographischer Verlag GmbH & Co., Ostfildern-Kemnat bei Stuttgart

Printed in Italy by G. Canale & C. S.p.A. – Borgaro T.se – Turin

ISBN 0–671–89309–2 US & Canada
0–7495–0792–6 UK

Contents

The Most Important Places of Tourist Interest at a Glance

Continued on page 638

Preface

This guide to France is one of the new generation of Baedeker guides.

These guides, illustrated throughout in colour, are designed to meet the needs of the modern traveller. They are quick and easy to consult, with the principal places of interest described in alphabetical order, and the information is presented in a format that is both attractive and easy to follow.

The present guide covers the whole of France, including the Mediterranean island of Corsica, but also includes the principality of Monaco on the Mediterranean coast and the small independent state of Andorra in the Pyrenees.

The guide is in three parts. The first part gives a general account of the country, its geography, climate, flora and fauna, population, education system, government and society, economy, transport and tourism, history, culture and art. The second part describes the places and features of tourist interest – cities and towns, regions and provinces, river valleys and islands. The third part contains a variety of practical information. Both the sights and the practical information are listed in alphabetical order.

The Baedeker pocket guides are noted for their concentration on essentials and their convenience of use. They contain numerous specially drawn plans and colour illustrations; and at the end of the book is a large map making it easy to locate the various places described in the "A to Z" section of the guide with the help of the co-ordinates given at the head of each entry.

Facts and Figures

Not so long ago France's principal attractions for visitors were Paris and the Riviera, and relatively few holidaymakers explored the rest of the country. Nowadays things are very different. The Mediterranean resorts still attract their devotees, but visitors now also realise how much the rest of France has to offer. Its historical monuments range from the prehistoric cave paintings and drawings of Périgord by way of the Greek and Roman settlements on the Mediterranean coast, the Romanesque and Gothic churches of the medieval period and the palaces of the absolute monarchy to the buildings of the present day. And no less varied than the architecture are the landscapes of France – the rugged coasts of Brittany, the gentler shores of the Mediterranean, the wide valley of the Loire with its châteaux, the volcanic terrain of Auvergne with its extinct volcanoes, the splendours of the Alps and the Pyrenees.

General

Area

France is the largest country in Europe (excluding the former Soviet Union), though only a fourteenth of the size of the United States. It has a total area, including Corsica but excluding the overseas départements, of 547,026 sq. km/211,207 sq. miles – more than twice the area of the United Kingdom.

Situation

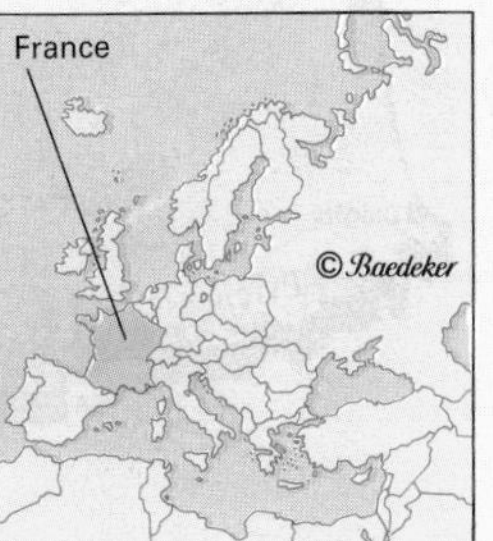

France's most northerly point is near Dunkirk (latitude 51°), its most southerly point Cerbère on the Mediterranean coast (latitude 42°30′). Its greatest extent from north to south is thus some 955 km/593 miles. From west to east it extends for 1315 km/817 miles, from Le Conquet (longitude 4°70′ west), to the most easterly point in Corsica (4°30′ east). France has the general form of a hexagon, with boundaries which are almost entirely natural. It is bounded on the north by the North Sea, on the west by the Atlantic, on the south by the Pyrenees and Andorra and, between Perpignan and Menton, by the Mediterranean. Altogether it has a sea-girt coastline of 3120 km/1939 miles. In the east the frontier follows a range of well-wooded hills, the Alps and the Jura, along the borders of Italy and Switzerland. The frontiers with Germany, Luxembourg and Belgium are less clearly marked out by geography, except along the Rhine valley. In the extreme south-east, the tiny principality of Monaco, with an area of only 1.95 sq. km/¾ of a square mile, forms an enclave within French territory, as does Andorra in the eastern Pyrenees (464 sq. km/180 sq. miles). The island of Corsica also belongs to France, as do a number of overseas départements and territories which ae not covered by this Guide.

Geography

France is made up of three main landscape units: the plains (the Paris Basin, the Aquitanian or Garonne Basin and the Rhône–Saône Depres-

◀ *In the Dordogne valley*

Basins, Mountains and Rivers in France

sion); the "old" mountains, much eroded ranges of medium height (the Massif Central, the Vosges and the Ardennes); and the higher "young" mountains (the Pyrenees, the Alps and the Jura). The landscape pattern does not consist, as in central and eastern Europe, of successive zones ranging from north to south, but is a patchwork of spacious basins, plateaux, hill ridges and ranges of mountains.

The heartland of France – in historical and economic as well as geological terms – is the Paris Basin or Seine Basin, with the country's capital in its centre. It covers a large area, taking in the Ile de France, Champagne, Lorraine, Burgundy, Picardy and eastern Normandy. In the south-west of the country is the Aquitanian or Garonne Basin with its limestone plateaux and fertile valleys. The third of the three great basins, the Rhône–Saône Depression, opens out on to the Mediterranean in the south.

The French Alps near Bourg-St-Maurice

The Paris Basin is surrounded by four old mountain ranges, the Vosges, the Ardennes, the Armorican hills of Brittany and, to the south, the Massif Central. This is a scantily wooded upland region covering an area of some 85,000 sq. km/32,800 sq. miles. Most of it consists of plateaux slashed by numerous gorges, but there are also large areas of volcanic terrain. Its highest point is the Puy de Sancy (1886 m/6188 ft).

In the extreme south and south-east France is separated from its neighbours by two ranges of mountains. The frontier with Spain is formed by the Pyrenees, extending for 450 km/280 miles from east to west and reaching heights of around 3000 m/9900 ft. The frontiers with Switzerland and Italy, between Lake Geneva and the coast of Provence, are protected by the even mightier range of the Alps, reaching 4807 m/15,770 ft in Europe's highest peak, Mont Blanc.

In the north-west the hills of the Armorican massif (Brittany, the Cotentin peninsula, parts of Maine and Anjou, and Vendée) reach heights of no more than 400 m/1300 ft. Round the coasts the jagged cliffs and numerous offshore islands and reefs bear witness to the powerful action of the waves.

An intermediate stage between the upland regions and the high mountains is formed by the (Swiss) Jura, a range of folded hills lying below the arc of the Alps and reaching a height (in France) of 1718 m/5637 ft.

To the east, rising above the rift valley of the Rhine, are the wooded Vosges, reaching a height of 1424 m/4672 ft in the Grand Ballon. The Ardennes, also well wooded, are mainly in Belgium, with foothills extending into France.

The coastal regions of southern and south-western France are, geologically, the youngest parts of the country: the alluvial land and lagoons of Languedoc in the west and, to the east of the Rhône delta, the Camargue, the rocky and much indented coast of Provence and the Côte d'Azur.

Corsica

This beautiful and mountainous island is separated from the French mainland by the Ligurian Sea and from its neighbouring island of Sardinia by the Strait of Bonifacio, which is only 15 km/9 miles wide. Its highest peak is Monte Cinto (2710 m/8892 ft). There are numerous bays and inlets on the

The Pointe de Penhir, Brittany

west side of the island; on the east side there is only a narrow coastal strip.

Origins of the landscape

The topography of France reflects its geological history. It has no counterpart to the plains of northern Central Europe, opening out towards the east and owing their topographical variety to the work of the ice. In France the higher mountains were ice-capped, but the glaciers and the deposits they carried with them never extended far into the lower slopes, and the advancing ice masses from Scandinavia stopped short of the territory that is now France.

The topographical pattern of France is determined by four groups of ancient rocks, which were consolidated in very early geological times and later only locally fragmented, thrust upwards and displaced by subsequent movements in the earth's crust.

Between these four ranges (the Armorican massif, the Massif Central, the Vosges and the Ardennes) lie extensive basins of lower ground. Since their formation over a period extending from the Triassic to the Tertiary (roughly 225 to 60 million years ago) they have undergone only slight folding and displacement as a result of later movements in the earth's crust, particularly during the formation of the Alps. As a result they lie closely together, mostly level or with only a moderate slope, so that the transition from the Paris Basin to the Aquitanian or Garonne Basin is barely perceptible. This basin contains deposits of detritus from the Pyrenees, which were built up at an earlier stage than the Alps and were raised to their present height in the Tertiary era.

Raw materials

The large depressions between the ranges of older hills and the younger folded mountains of Alpine type are economically of great importance, since in these areas the geological conditions, in their different ways, promoted the formation of deposits of valuable raw materials. In the depressions bordering the Variscan massif and in the ranges of folded hills in the interior of France are seams of hard coal and in some areas also ore-bearing strata. These deposits provided the basis for the older indus-

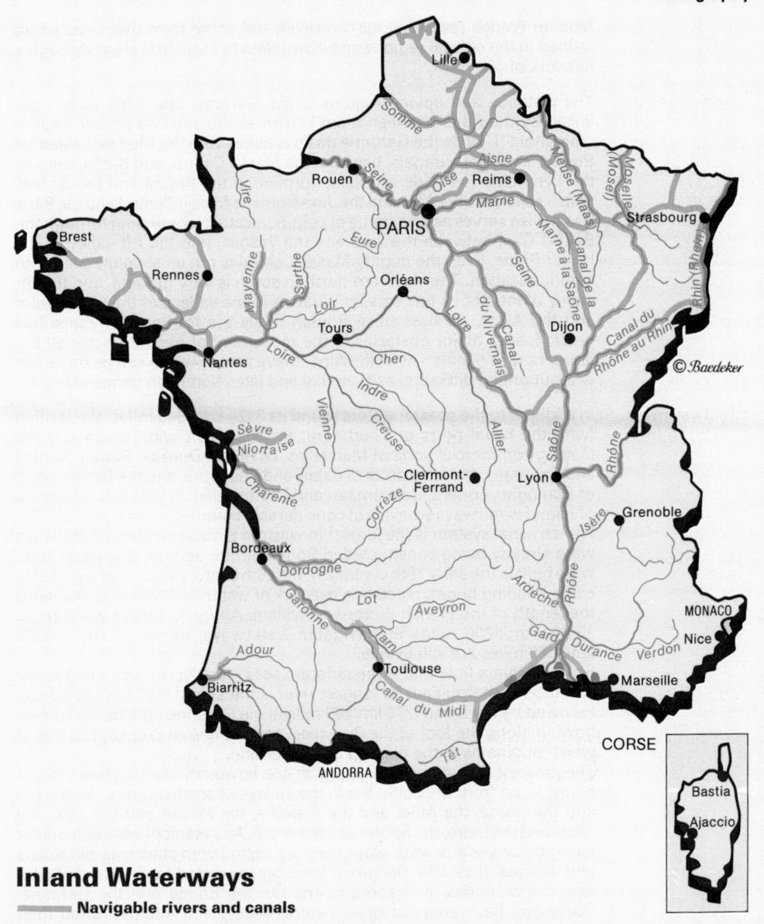

trial areas, such as the industrial region of northern France, with the Artois coalfield and the iron ores of Lorraine, and the industrial region of Lorraine, with the continuation of the Saar coalfield on the eastern edge of the Paris Basin and the phosphorous ores in the limestones of the Moselle hills. The industries of St-Etienne and Le Creusot in the Massif Central are also based on local deposits of coal, while at Caen the ores of the Armorican massif are worked, though on a relatively small scale. More recently, the working of fairly numerous deposits of uranium has favoured economic development in areas without much industry.

In the Garonne Basin geological conditions have promoted the formation of deposits of natural gas and oil, and the predominant share of French production now comes from installations at the foot of the Pyrenees; the main centres are Lacq (gas), St-Marcel (gas) and Parentis (oil). Oil is also extracted to the south of Paris (Coulommes, Cahilly, Châteaurenard, etc.).

Most of French requirements, however, still come from overseas, being refined in the coastal regions and distributed to industrial areas through a network of pipelines.

Communications

The plateaux and upland regions of the Garonne and Paris Basins are linked by the ridge between them known as the *seuil de Poitou (seuil* = "threshold"), while the Garonne Basin is linked with the Mediterranean by the low *seuil* of Lauragais, between the Massif Central and the foothills of the Pyrenees. The wide rift valley formed by the Rhône and the Saône, which separates the Alps and the Jura from the Massif Central and the Paris Basin, also serves as an avenue of communication, continuing through the Belfort Gap, between the Jura and the Vosges, into the rift valley of the Upper Rhine. Even the mighty Massif Central is not an absolute barrier to communication. The rise from north to south is very gradual, and the rift valley of the Rhône has smaller parallels in the valleys of the upper Loire and the Allier. At least since Roman times the territory of France has presented no major obstacles to the movement of peoples, since all the larger ranges of hills – even the Alps – have passes which can be traversed without undue difficulty, as Hannibal and later Napoleon demonstrated.

Inland waterways

In addition to the coastal waters round its 3120 km/1940 miles of coastline (with the naval ports of Cherbourg, Brest, Lorient and Toulon and the leading commercial ports of Marseilles, Le Havre, Dunkirk, Rouen, Nantes and Bordeaux, the ferry ports of Calais and Boulogne, and the fishing ports of Boulogne, Lorient, Concarneau and La Rochelle), France has a network of inland waterways which is of considerable commercial importance. The French canal system is the largest in western Europe. Artificial waterways were already being constructed in Roman times, and the first canal locks were built in the early 16th century. In the 18th century there was a veritable canal-building boom, creating a network of waterways which is still twice the length of the French motorway system. Altogether there were about 13,200 km/8200 miles of navigable waterways, of which some 6500 km/4000 miles are still usable.
France's rivers flow into three different seas – the North Sea, the Atlantic and the Mediterranean. Its longest river is the Loire (1020 km/630 miles), followed by the Seine (770 km/480 miles), the Garonne (650 km/400 miles) flowing along the foot of the Pyrenees, and the Rhône (522 km/324 miles) which originates in the glaciers of Switzerland.
The greatest attractions for visitors do not, however, lie along these major rivers, apart from the Loire, but in the valleys of smaller rivers like the Lot and Dordogne, the Allier and the Ardèche, the Meuse and the Tarn, the Aude and the Indre, the Saône and the Aisne. As a result of early settlement along these various waterways they are dotted with charming old towns and villages; they offer delightful landscapes created by the hand of man over the centuries, and some rivers, like the Rhône and the Garonne/ Dordogne, have areas of great natural beauty and interest round their deltas and estuaries (the Camargue, the Gironde).

Climate

France can be broadly divided into three climatic zones, Atlantic, Continental and Mediterranean.
The low-lying regions near the sea in western and northern France have a temperate maritime climate with small seasonal differences of temperature and rainfall in all four seasons, reaching a maximum in autumn. Along a narrow coastal strip in Brittany the winters, under the influence of the Gulf Stream, are as mild as on the Mediterranean coast.
Inland the climate becomes more continental in type. In central France rainfall is lower, but in the east the moist air masses coming in from the Atlantic are compelled by the mountains to rise, and the resultant cooling of the air leads to the discharge of rain on the windward side.

In southern France the climate is determined by the Mediterranean, with mild winters and dry, hot summers, but also with heavy falls of rain, usually in the form of thunder showers. The abundance of sunshine is one of the region's great tourist attractions, and the dryness of the air makes the high summer temperatures tolerable.

Mistral

A major element in the climate of southern France is the *mistral*, a gusty cold north wind in the Rhône valley which may on occasion reach the dimensions of a storm wind. It may blow up at any time of year, but particularly in winter and spring. It occurs when air is drawn southward by a depression in the Golfe du Lion, south of the Rhône delta. Cold air from the Massif Central then surges down over the Cévennes and down the Rhône valley between the Cévennes and the Alps, increasing in speed as it is funnelled down the valley. In the area subject to the mistral Mediterranean vegetation cannot develop fully; wind-breaks and hedges provide only a measure of protection.
Sirocco-like south winds – which may be either hot and dry or close and sultry – may also sometimes blow up the Rhône valley as far as Lyons.

Flora and Fauna

Flora

France was once covered by dense forests, but now these account for only about a quarter of the country's area. The vegetation zones of France show great variety, depending on the size of the area, the climate and the altitude. The flora is also affected by the work of man (forest clearance, cultivation) and, in southern France, by forest fires.
In northern France, Normandy and Brittany the woodland consists predominantly of oaks. Where the forest has been cleared there may be a vegetation of heather, broom and gorse (the type of area known as *lande* or *bruyère).* Farther inland there are mixed deciduous forests of beech, hornbeam, lime or ash. In the hills the vegetation varies with altitude, deciduous trees giving place higher up to conifers, with Alpine meadows above 1700 m/5500 ft.
In the Aquitanian Basin Mediterranean plants such as holm oaks and maritime pines occur. In the Mediterranean south there are evergreen oaks and stone pines, which in the hills give place to sweet chestnuts and pines. The olive-tree, one of the most typical Mediterranean plants, was brought into France from the eastern Mediterranean by the Greeks 2500 years ago and spread into the Rhône valley. Also characteristic of the Mediterranean flora are the hard-leaved evergreens, well adapted to arid conditions, and the plant communities of the maquis and garrigue.

Maquis

The maquis (Italian macchia) is a scrubland of trees and shrubs, ranging in height up to 2 metres (6 feet) or more, which flourishes on silicaceous soil. It usually develops on ground which has been cleared of its original cover of oak-trees. The species found in the maquis include holm oaks, kermes oaks, brooms and gorse, Judas trees, myrtles, tree heaths and heathers, and aromatic shrubs and herbs like rosemary, carob-trees and butcher's broom.

Garrigue

The garrigue (Provençal *garoulia)* is frequently found on rocky limestone soils. It rarely grows higher than about half a metre and usually consists of a thorny scrub, including box, thistles, kermes oaks, gorse and aromatic plants like thyme, lavender, sage and rosemary, together with hyacinths, irises, tulips and orchids.

A colourful display in the Nice flower market

In Auvergne

Parc National de la Vanoise

Fauna

The fauna of France is basically that of Central Europe, but as a result of the French enthusiasm for fishing and shooting the country's stock of game animals is much reduced. In less easily accessible areas, particularly in southern France, there are large numbers of reptiles and insects – tortoises, lizards, geckos, adders and vipers, etc. Much sought after by anglers are trout, pike, perch and fresh-water crabs. In coastal waters there are shellfish, molluscs, crustaceans and various species of fish (although fish stocks in the Mediterranean have been much reduced by intensive fishing and by pollution). In the Camargue there are half-wild horses and colonies of flamingoes, now a protected species.

Protection of nature

France's six National Parks (Vanoise, Port-Cros, Western Pyrenees, Cévennes, Ecrin and Mercantour) seek to provide conditions in which rare plants and animals can live and flourish in protected conditions. There are also 21 regional nature parks more concerned with the presentation than the protection of native plants and animals. (See Practical Information, National Parks.)

Population

Settlement

The early settlement of France took place along the four river valleys which reach far into the interior of the country – the valleys of the Rhône, the Garonne, the Loire and the Seine – and most of France's larger towns (with populations over 200,000) are to be found in these valleys. Other areas of settlement in northern and north-eastern France developed only with industrialisation in the 19th century. There is still a great concentration of population around the country's main economic centres: the conurbations of the three great cities of Paris, Lyons and Marseilles, with respectively 8.7, 1.2 and 1.1 million inhabitants, contain some 20% of the total population – as many people as the whole of south-western France.

Population density

France has a population of 55.5 million, representing 7% of the population of Europe, on an area of 547,026 sq. km/211,207 sq. miles. With 102 inhabitants to the sq. km (264 to the sq. mile) it has the lowest density of population in the European Community apart from Ireland (51 to the sq. km/132 to the sq. mile) and Greece (76 to the sq. km/197 to the sq. mile).

Some 75% of the French population live in towns, though only 40 of these have a population over 100,000 and only 17 more than 250,000. There is a correspondingly high proportion of small towns. Thus in spite of the concentration in and around Paris (where a sixth of the population lives) France is much less urbanised than other European countries like Britain or Germany. 78.6% of all French communes, accounting for some 17% of the population of France, have fewer than 1000 inhabitants, and only half the population live in towns of over 10,000 inhabitants. Census figures show that there is a movement of population away from the cities and that only communes with populations under 20,000 are still growing.

Population growth

It is estimated that around A.D. 500 the territory of present-day France had a population of around 3 million. By 1800 the figure had risen to 27.5 million, and by 1866 to 38 million. By 1950 it had risen only slightly, to 41.6 million. It was only after the Second World War that the population began to show a substantial increase as a result of a more active family policy, the repatriation of French citizens from the former colonies of Indochina and North Africa (1.5 million), and an influx of foreign workers. There are now some 2.8 million foreigners (5% of the total population) living in France, mainly in the Paris area, the Rhône–Alpes region and the Provence–Côte d'Azur region. Of these 20.8% are Portuguese, 21.6% Algerians, 11.7% Moroccans, 9.1% Italians, 8.7% Spaniards, 5.1% Tunisians, 3.4% Turks and 1.8% Yugoslavs.

Foreigners

The present annual growth rate is 0.4%.

Population

Population

The population in 1987 was 55.5 million (27 million males and 28.5 million females).

Working population

The working population amounts to 43.3% of the total population, and 41.8% of the working population are women. The most striking change in the labour market since the end of the Second World War has been the fall in the number of people working in agriculture (in 1946 40%, in 1988 only 7%). Over the same period there have been considerable increases in the numbers engaged in service industries, commerce, transport and the public service (63%). Some 30% of the working population is now employed in industry.

Unemployment

10.25% of Frenchmen are at present unemployed. One major cause of unemployment has been the restructuring of the economy – for example the reduction of capacity in the steel industry. Young people are particularly hard hit: just under half the unemployed are young people under 25, and women.

Religion

Although church and state have been separated since 1905, 76.5% of French people are Roman Catholics. The church is now financed by collections and offerings and by its landed property, as well as by its own commercial activities. The state makes no contribution to the expenses of the church and has no influence on the teaching of religion. The Roman Catholic church is, however, the largest provider of private schools, which feature prominently in the French educational system. Other religious denominations – some 180,000 Orthodox Christians, 600,000 Jews and 2.8 million Muslims – play a relatively minor role in public life. The churches of Alsace and Lorraine have a special status of their own, reflecting their different history.

Language

France's various population minorities, almost all living in peripheral areas of the country, differ in customs, traditions and above all in language.
The modern French language came into being in Paris and the Ile de France: it was the language of the king and, from the 12th century, of the royal administration. Its extension to the rest of France was closely bound up with the growth of state authority over the provinces.
French developed out of the Vulgar Latin spoken by the Celtic peoples of Gaul after the Roman conquest and which preserved its Romance character in spite of its adoption of many words of Celtic and later of Germanic origin. For many centuries it was the most important Romance language, widely used by educated people and in diplomacy.
Although the regional languages were subject to a ban which was at times rigorously enforced, they survived in stories and tales, autobiographical accounts, songs and legends. Since the 1970s there has been a revival in these languages, accompanied by the promotion of local and regional cultural traditions, in which young teachers and school-children have taken a leading part. In southern France there is the Occitanian language or *langue d'oc,* the number of speakers of which it is difficult to estimate; in the far west Breton (Brezonnek), spoken by about a million people; in French Flanders Flemish (*c.* 400,000); in Roussillon Catalan (*c.* 200,000). The Basque language (Euzkara) – the only non-European language to have survived – is spoken by around 200,000 French Basques as well as by 2 million Spanish Basques. Elsässerditsch, an Alemannic dialect of German, is spoken by about a million people in Alsace and part of Lorraine, and on the island of Corsica another million people speak Corsican, a dialect of Italian. In recent years demands for recognition of the various regional languages have been linked with movements for greater regional independence of the central government in Paris. A number of groups, particularly in Corsica and Brittany, also seek to achieve political autonomy for their linguistic region. The increased interest in regional cultures and languages also finds expression in demands for these languages to be optional subjects in schools.

Education

The French educational system was completely reformed after the Second World War. Since 1959 school attendance has been compulsory up to the age of 16, and education in state primary and secondary schools is free and non-denominational. Some 15% of all school-children, however, go to private schools which are mostly run by religious bodies. The whole educational system, from the kindergartens to the final classes, is based on all-day schooling. The system is centrally organised, and teachers have the status of public officials.
The school system consists of a number of different stages, in which vocational training is included.

Ecole maternelle

The *école maternelle* caters for children between two and six. Attendance is not compulsory, but in practice 65% of three-year-olds, 90% of four-year-olds and 100% of five-year-olds attend these schools.
For children under two there are crèches, though not enough to meet the demand. There is also a government-organised child-minding system.

Ecole primaire

The *école primaire* (primary school), attendance at which is compulsory, caters for children between six and eleven.

Collège

The *collège* (secondary school) takes children between eleven and fifteen. In addition to the basic subjects the curriculum includes economics and science. Pupils who leave school at 16 are offered vocational training courses. This first stage of secondary education leads to a certificate known as the BEPC *(brevet d'études du premier cycle)*, first introduced in 1981.
Beyond this point the school system, hitherto unified, divides into two: the general or grammar school *(lycée d'enseignement général)* and the vocational school *(lycée d'enseignement professionnel)*.
At present 42% of each year group obtain, after 12 years' schooling, a certificate entitling them to university admission (though some certificates give admission only to a technical university or college). Under a major reform introduced in 1989 it is planned to raise this proportion to 80%, while the remaining 20% will receive a certificate admitting them to vocational courses.

Higher education

Since 1968 French universities have been independent and self-governing. Other forms of higher education are provided by technical colleges *(instituts universitaires de technologie)* and the famous *grandes écoles*. These are elite schools with highly selective admission procedures which leads to careers in the higher reaches of the public service, education, the armed services, industry and commerce. The most prestigious are the Ecole Nationale d'Administration (ENA: for top posts in public administration and business), the Ecole Normale Supérieure and the Ecole Polytechnique.

Government and Society

République Française

France became an independent state in 843 under the treaty of Verdun, and Hugues Capet was crowned as the first king of France in 987, a date now regarded as marking the birth of the French nation. After the abolition of the monarchy in 1792 the First Republic was founded, followed in 1848 by the Second, in 1870 by the Third and in 1946 by the Fourth. The present Fifth Republic was established in 1958.
The national flag is the famous red, white and blue *tricolore*. In 1789, during the turmoil that led to the storming of the Bastille, the members of the Paris electoral assemblies formed a new "municipality" with its own citizens' militia under the leadership of the Marquis de Lafayette. The militia wore arm-bands which combined the colours of Paris, red and blue, with the

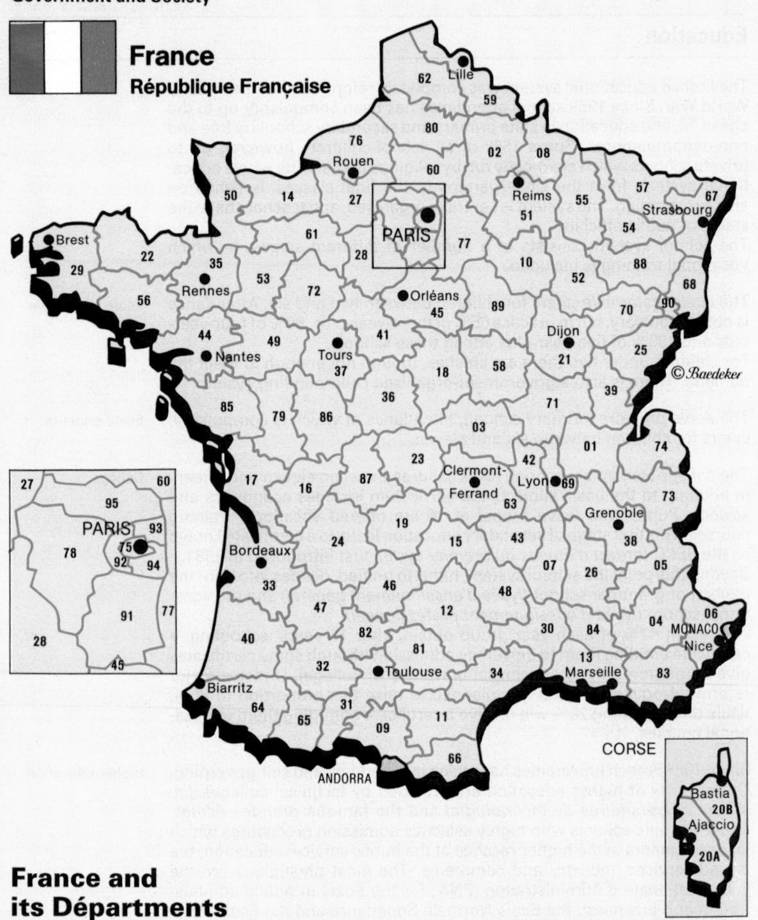

France and its Départments

white of the royal fleur-de-lis banner; and a red, white and blue cockade became the symbol of the Revolution and the model for the French national flag.

Since 1870 France has had no official heraldic emblem. The emblem now used consists of the symbols of the Revolution surrounded by the chain of the Légion d'Honneur, with the motto "Liberté, Egalité, Fraternité".

Marseillaise

The French national anthem, the Marseillaise, was composed by Rouget de Lisle in Strasbourg in 1792 as a marching song, and was adopted as a national anthem in 1795: "Allons, enfants de la patrie, le jour de gloire est arrivé; contre nous de la tyrannie l'étendard sanglant est levé . . ." ("Come, sons of the fatherland, the day of glory is here; the bloody standard of tyranny is raised against us . . .").

No.	Name	Area (sq. km)	Population	Chief town
01	Ain	5,756	443,100	Bourg-en-Bresse
02	Aisne	7,378	535,500	Laon
03	Allier	7,382	365,000	Moulins
04	Alpes-de-Haute-Provence	6,944	122,400	Digne
05	Hautes-Alpes	5,520	107,000	Gap
06	Alpes-Maritimes	4,294	894,800	Nice
07	Ardèche	5,523	271,600	Privas
08	Ardennes	5,219	299,100	Charleville-Mézières
09	Ariège	4,890	134,700	Foix
10	Aube	6,002	292,100	Troyes
11	Aude	6,232	286,000	Carcassonne
12	Aveyron	8,735	277,900	Rodez
13	Bouches-du-Rhône	5,112	1,740,900	Marseilles
14	Calvados	5,536	604,300	Caen
15	Cantal	5,741	160,400	Aurillac
16	Charente	5,953	341,600	Angoulême
17	Charente-Maritime	6,848	519,500	La Rochelle
18	Cher	7,228	322,500	Bourges
19	Corrèze	5,860	242,000	Tulle
20A	Corse-du-Sud	4,013	113,300	Ajaccio
20B	Haute-Corse	4,555	135,400	Bastia
21	Côte-d'Or	8,765	482,600	Dijon
22	Côtes-du-Nord	6,878	544,500	Saint-Brieuc
23	Creuse	5,560	136,800	Guéret
24	Dordogne	9,184	380,100	Périgueux
25	Doubs	5,228	468,900	Besançon
26	Drôme	6,525	404,000	Valence
27	Eure	6,004	486,500	Evreux
28	Eure-et-Loir	5,876	378,800	Chartres
29	Finistère	6,785	840,500	Quimper
30	Gard	5,848	558,100	Nîmes
31	Haute-Garonne	6,301	851,500	Toulouse
32	Gers	6,254	173,000	Auch
33	Gironde	10,000	1,116,400	Bordeaux
34	Hérault	6,113	745,200	Montpellier
35	Ille-et-Vilaine	6,758	774,200	Rennes
36	Indre	6,778	238,800	Châteauroux
37	Indre-et-Loire	8,124	520,900	Tours
38	Isére	7,474	980,600	Grenoble
39	Jura	5,008	245,500	Lons-le-Saunier
40	Landes	9,237	302,900	Mont-de-Marsan
41	Loir-et-Cher	6,314	301,800	Blois
42	Loire	4,774	738,800	Saint-Etienne
43	Haute-Loire	4,965	207,100	Le Puy
44	Loire-Atlantique	6,894	1,029,700	Nantes
45	Loiret	6,742	561,600	Orléans
46	Lot	5,228	156,700	Cahors
47	Lot-et-Garonne	5,358	302,300	Agen
48	Lozère	5,168	73,500	Mende
49	Maine-et-Loire	7,145	700,100	Angers
50	Manche	5,938	473,400	Saint-Lô
51	Marne	8,163	550,800	Châlons-sur-Marne
52	Haute-Marne	6,216	210,200	Chaumont
53	Mayenne	5,171	276,700	Laval

No.	Name	Area (sq. km)	Population	Chief town
54	Meurthe-et-Moselle	5,235	711,700	Nancy
55	Meuse	6,220	198,200	Bar-le-Duc
56	Morbihan	6,763	604,600	Vannes
57	Moselle	6,214	1,009,100	Metz
58	Nièvre	6,837	236,100	Nevers
59	Nord	5,738	2,505,300	Lille
60	Oise	5,857	688,800	Beauvais
61	Orne	6,100	295,200	Alençon
62	Pas-de-Calais	6,672	1,421,900	Arras
63	Puy-de-Dôme	7,955	601,900	Clermont-Ferrand
64	Pyrénées-Atlantiques	7,683	566,500	Pau
65	Hautes-Pyrénées	4,507	227,100	Tarbes
66	Pyrénées-Orientales	4,087	349,100	Perpignan
67	Bas-Rhin	4,787	937,900	Strasbourg
68	Haut-Rhin	3,523	661,700	Colmar
69	Rhône	3,215	1,460,900	Lyons
70	Haute-Saône	5,343	237,700	Vesoul
71	Saône-et-Loire	8,565	571,000	Mâcon
72	Sarthe	6,245	511,500	Le Mans
73	Savoie	6,036	333,200	Chambéry
74	Haute-Savoie	4,391	522,000	Annecy
75	Ville de Paris	105	2,127,100	Paris
76	Seine-Maritime	6,254	1,206,300	Rouen
77	Seine-et-Marne	5,917	976,200	Melun
78	Yvelines	2,271	1,267,700	Versailles
79	Deux-Sèvres	6,004	344,600	Niort
80	Somme	6,175	549,200	Amiens
81	Tarn	5,751	339,700	Albi
82	Tarn-et-Garonne	3,716	194,500	Montauban
83	Var	5,993	754,900	Toulon
84	Vaucluse	3,566	439,700	Avignon
85	Vendée	6,721	499,700	La Roche-sur-Yon
86	Vienne	6,084	377,900	Poitiers
87	Haute-Vienne	5,512	357,000	Limoges
88	Vosges	5,903	393,700	Epinal
89	Yonne	7,425	317,200	Auxerre
90	Territoire de Belfort	610	133,800	Belfort
91	Essonne	1,804	1,027,000	Evry
92	Hauts-de-Seine	175	1,363,100	Nanterre
93	Seine-Saint-Denis	236	1,332,200	Bobigny
94	Val-de-Marne	244	1,182,600	Créteil
95	Val-d'Oise	1,249	973,800	Pontoise

Overseas Départements

No.	Name	Area (sq. km)	Population	Chief town
97-1	Guadeloupe	1,780	335,300	Basse-Terre
97-2	Martinique	1,106	328,600	Fort-de-France
97-3	Guyane	91,000	89,000	Cayenne
97-4	Réunion	2,511	564,600	Saint-Denis

Collectivités Territoriales

Name	Area (sq. km)	Population	Chief town
Mayotte	375	52,000	Dzaoudzi
Saint-Pierre-et-Miquelon	242	6,300	Saint-Pierre

Overseas Territories

Name	Area (sq. km)	Population	Chief town
Nouvelle-Calédonie	19,058	145,000	Nouméa
Polynésie Française	4,000	184,600	Papéete (on Tahiti)
Wallis et Futuna	255	14,000	Mata Utu (on Ueva)
Terres Australes et Antarctiques Françaises	432,000	200	

The French Regions

Regions

Name	Area (sq. km)	Population	Chief town
Alsace	8,310	1,599,600	Strasbourg
Aquitaine	41,407	2,718,200	Bordeaux
Auvergne	25,988	1,334,400	Clermont-Ferrand
Bourgogne	31,592	1,606,900	Dijon
Bretagne	27,184	2,763,800	Rennes
Centre	39,061	2,324,400	Orléans
Champagne – Ardenne	25,600	1,352,200	Châlons-sur-Marne
Corse	8,681	248,700	Ajaccio
Franche-Comté	16,189	1,085,900	Besançon
Ile de France	12,001	10,249,700	Paris
Languedoc – Roussillon	27,448	2,011,900	Montpellier
Limousin	16,932	735,800	Limoges
Lorraine	23,540	2,312,700	Metz
Midi – Pyrénées	45,382	2,355,100	Toulouse
Nord – Pas-de-Calais	12,376	3,927,200	Lille
Basse-Normandie	17,583	1,372,900	Caen
Haute-Normandie	12,258	1,692,800	Rouen
Pays de la Loire	32,126	3,017,700	Nantes
Picardie	19,411	1,773,500	Amiens
Poitou-Charentes	25,790	1,583,600	Poitiers
Provence – Alpes – Côte d'Azur	31,436	4,058,800	Marseilles
Rhône-Alpes	43,694	5,153,600	Lyons

Form of government

France is a democratic parliamentary republic headed by a powerful President.

Government and policy

The history of France since the end of the Second World War has been eventful and full of vicissitudes. The foundation and collapse of the Fourth Republic were followed by the birth of a new political system (the Fifth Republic), bloody colonial wars and a grave social crisis (May 1968), together with fundamental changes in economic and social structure. The election of the socialist François Mitterand as President in 1981 was seen as an event of historic significance which it was feared might split the country into two opposing camps. In fact Mitterand, who was re-elected in 1988 for a second seven-year term, has beaten all records for popularity and to that extent has made good his claim to be President of all the French. In 1984 and 1986 explosive protest movements against plans for school and university reform brought down two governments.

Fifth Republic

The Fifth Republic was established in 1958, when General de Gaulle became prime minister with special powers to repress the military rising in Algeria. A new constitution approved by a national referendum came into effect on October 6th 1958, strengthening the power of the state and its political institutions and giving the President (who, after another referendum in 1952, became directly elected for a seven-year term) increased powers which made him the dominant political authority in government. Under this constitution the President is head of state and supreme commander of the armed forces, with authority to activate France's nuclear forces. He appoints the prime minister and can dissolve Parliament (as has

already happened four times). In the event of a national emergency the President has sole power of decision.
This hybrid between a parliamentary and a presidential system, originally tailored to the personality of de Gaulle, who served as President from 1959 to 1969, was taken over by his successors, Georges Pompidou (1969–74), Valéry Giscard d'Estaing (1974–81) and François Mitterand (from 1981).

Administration

Until 1982 government and financial authority in France rested mainly with the central government in Paris. The regions (formed in the post-war period by combining several départements) had for all practical purposes no independent authority of their own; and the départements (the main local units of administration, established during the Revolution) and communes had insufficient resources to cope with their increasing responsibilities.

Faced with a series of urgent problems – the creation of a modern infrastructure for the communes, the correction of over-dependence on a single industry (e.g. steel in Lorraine), the drift away from the land and soil erosion in the Massif Central and other areas, the recognition and restoration of regional cultural traditions in Alsace, Flanders, Brittany, Occitania, the Basque country and Corsica – all political parties agreed that existing legislation on the structure of local government, dating from 1884, was in need of reform. One of the major reforms introduced by the government of the Left, therefore, was the decentralisation of government authority. This was achieved by a series of laws promulgated from 1982 onwards. The position of the regions as independent territorial authorities was strengthened by a redistribution of powers between the central government, the regions, the départements and the communes and finally by a reform of communal finances.

France is now divided into 22 regions, which since 1982 have had a real function as administrative authorities and since 1986 have had directly elected parliamentary representation. These in turn are divided into 95 départements (the most important territorial authority between the central government and the communes, with elected assemblies), which themselves are divided into 322 arrondissements, 3208 cantons and 35,600 communes. Corsica enjoys special status.

Overseas départements and territories

The national territory of France also includes four overseas départements, two *collectivités territoriales* and four overseas territories *(territoires d'outre-mer)*, together with a few islands in the Indian Ocean (in the Mozambique Channel between Madagascar and the African mainland) with no permanent inhabitants. France also claims Adelie Land in Antarctica.

Parties

The French parties are given no special status in the French constitution, and it was only in 1988 – following earlier mistrust of the party state – that the state began to make contributions to party finances in elections.
Although France has long been regarded as having a multi-party system of government, election on the "first past the post" principle (proportional representation having been adopted only once, in 1986) has led to the emergence of two parties of roughly equal strength: on the right the Gaullist groupings, the Rassemblement pour la République (RPR) and the liberal conservative Union pour la Démocratie Française (UDF), formed in 1978 by the amalgamation of the parties supporting the former President Giscard d'Estaing, and on the left the Parti Socialiste (PS) and the Parti Communiste Français (PCF). These two camps, however, are not by any means stable political blocs but rather combinations of competing tendencies. With the emergence since the early eighties of the extreme right-wing Front National (FN) the situation of the parties of the right has become more difficult, while on the left the Socialist Party outstripped the Communists, with whom they had had electoral agreements since the mid sixties, for the first time in 1978.

There are also a number of smaller parties, of no significance politically or numerically, such as the conservative-liberal Republicans (Parti Républicain), the Radicals (Parti Radical, France's oldest party, founded in 1901) and the Christian Democratic Centre des Démocrates Sociaux. Others are the left-wing liberal Mouvement des Radicaux de Gauche (MRG), the left-wing Parti Socialiste Unifié (PSU), the Trotskyite Ligue Communiste Révolutionnaire (LCR) and Lutte Ouvrière, and two extreme right-wing parties, the Front National and the Parti des Forces Nouvelles.
Although the French Green party, les Verts, sent nine members to the European Parliament after the 1989 elections they have so far been unable to achieve similar success in French parliamentary elections. This is due partly to the long-standing disunity within the ecological movement and partly to the different view taken in France of such traditional "green" causes as the emancipation of women and nuclear energy (including the nuclear strike force): thus nuclear energy is still seen by many people, whatever their party allegiance, as a symbol of national independence. The successes of the Greens in recent communal elections and the European elections, however, show that concern with the protection of the environment is growing in France.

Trade unions

There is no all-embracing trade union body in France corresponding to the British TUC. The French unions tend to reflect different political trends and to compete with one another for members.
The most important trade union organisations are the communist CGT (Confédération Générale du Travail, founded in 1885), the FO (Force Ouvrière), which split off from the CGT in 1948, the Christian CFTC (Confédération Française des Travailleurs Chrétiens, founded in 1919) and the socialist CFDT (Confédération Française Démocratique du Travail), which broke away from the CFTC in 1964. All these unions take members from any trade or profession. Unions representing particular professions are the CGC (Confédération Générale des Cadras, founded in 1944), which represents managers and executives at all levels, and the FEN (Fédération de l'Education Nationale, founded in 1947), which represents teachers.
The influence of the various unions is measured mainly by the number of joint production committees *(comités d'entreprise)* which they establish in particular enterprises with members elected by the workers for a two-year term.

Employers' organisations

The CNPF (Conseil National du Patronat Français, founded in 1940) is the principal employers' organisation, with some 900,000 members. Small and medium-sized firms and agricultural enterprises have their own organisations.

Constitution

The constitution of the Fifth Republic, now in force, was promulgated on September 28th 1958 and amended in 1962.

Head of state

The President of the Republic is directly elected for a seven-year term. He cannot be deposed during his term of office, but can dissolve Parliament (as happened in 1962, 1968, 1981 and 1988), can call a national referendum and has wide powers as head of the executive.

Prime minister

The prime minister, although formally responsible to Parliament, is in practice subordinate to the President and dependent on him.

Parliament

The French Parliament consists of two chambers, the Assemblée Nationale and the Sénat.
The 577 members of the National Assembly are directly elected for a five-year term. If no candidate obtains an absolute majority in the first ballot there is a second ballot in which only a relative majority is required.
The 317 members of the Senate are indirectly elected by an electoral college for a nine-year term. One-third of the members retire from office every three years.

The two chambers play an equal part in legislation, but if there is disagreement between the two the National Assembly has the final word. Only the National Assembly can overthrow the government by a vote of no confidence. The Senate has only a right of veto which gives it power to delay legislation.

Law

French law is based on the Napoleonic codes promulgated in 1811, including the Code Civil and the Code Pénal. which have been much amended over the years. Thus the provisions for divorce introduced in 1792 were repealed in 1816 and reintroduced in 1884, and the death penalty was abolished in 1981. By the end of 1992 the Napoleonic penal code was replaced by an entirely new code.

Foreign policy

France is a member of the United Nations and its subsidiary organisations, the European Community, Western European Union, the Council of Europe and OECD. It was also a founding member of NATO, though some features of its foreign policy differ from those of its partners in the western alliance. In the late fifties and early sixties, against the background of the political and social stabilisation of France after such major problems as the process of decolonisation and the wars in Indochina and Algeria, de Gaulle put forward a programme for making France an "independent world power". In order to achieve this aim of greater political independence France set out to become a nuclear power (as it did by 1960) and in 1966 opted out of the military side of NATO.
France is a permanent member of the UN's Security Council. In addition Paris is the seat of international organisations such as UNESCO and the OECD, and has been the scene of important international conferences, including the Vietnam peace negotiations.
The overriding aim of French foreign policy is national independence. This is reflected, for example, in the fact that France advocates close cooperation between the countries of western Europe in order to achieve an independent Europe but rejects the "supra-national" solution of a European federal state. France's adherence to the Atlantic alliance has never been in question, but it dislikes American dominance in NATO: hence its withdrawal in 1966 from NATO's joint military command.
On the basis of its earlier colonial responsibilities France maintains wide-ranging relations with the countries of the Third World, particularly in Africa and the Mediterranean, where this concern is sometimes expressed in a military presence.

Recent developments

In recent years there has been an increasing polarisation in French domestic politics. In the 1970s this was between the right-wing majority and the left-wing opposition. President Giscard d'Estaing, elected in 1974 with only a bare majority, sought to meet this challenge by a liberal reforming policy, but was unable to prevent a further advance of the left in by-elections and communal elections. Only the collapse of the alliance of the Left destroyed their prospect of victory in the 1978 parliamentary election. The inability of the government of the Right to solve the country's economic and social problems, however, gave the Left a majority in 1981, when the socialist François Mitterand was elected President and the socialists and communists won two-thirds of the seats in the National Assembly. The new government, conscious of the high expectations of the population, introduced a series of major reforms (notably the decentralisation of government), but soon, like its predecessor, came up against the limitations of the French economic system and lost much of its support among the electorate. Far-reaching social plans were abandoned and the government, which the communists left in 1984, concentrated its efforts on traditional policies designed to bring about an increasing modernisation of French economic structures. The 1986 parliamentary election brought back a conservative majority, leading to the period of "cohabitation" when a socialist President had to live with a parliamentary majority of the right. When

Mitterand was re-elected President in 1988 he brought forward the date of the parliamentary election in the hope of securing a socialist majority.

1988 election

The election held in June 1988 made the socialists the largest party in the National Assembly, with 209 seats, but still left them without an absolute majority. The Gaullist Rassemblement pour la République (RPR) had 150 seats, the Union pour la Démocratie Française (UDF) 127. The Communists and National Front had 35 seats each, and there were 21 independent members (14 on the right, 7 on the left). Mitterand invited Michel Rocard, the former minister of planning and agriculture, who was widely respected for his social-democratic views, to form a minority government. The Rocard government, which includes a few politicians of the centre, has a flexible policy; among its declared aims is the improvement of the international competitiveness of French industry. For this purpose the government has introduced tax concessions for industry and is encouraging the establishment of new enterprises and take-overs of ailing companies, while state-owned industries are to be privatised.

Anniversaries

Two important anniversaries were celebrated in 1987 and 1989. In 1987 there was the thousandth anniversary of Hugues Capet's coronation as the first king of France on July 3rd 987, a date which is held to mark the birth of the French nation; then in 1989 there was the 200th anniversary of the French Revolution, which was the occasion for even more splendid celebrations.

Economy

General

France is now the fifth largest commercial and industrial nation and the fourth largest exporting country in the world. In 1988 it had just under 24 million people in employment, or some 43% of the population. Of these 7% worked in agriculture, 30% in productive industry and 63% in the service sector.

Development of industry

During the 19th century French industry at first developed relatively slowly in comparison with other European countries. In the first half of the century the low rate of population growth held back the expansion of the domestic market, French industries were hampered by the demands of the money market, and the traditional attachment to small-scale production limited the scope for the expansion of large modern companies and the amalgamation of smaller ones.

Structural changes

After the Second World War, however, the French economy underwent a fundamental structural change – from a basically agricultural country to one of the leading industrial nations of the western world – and began to achieve rapid growth. Among the most important stages in the country's recent economic development have been the reconstruction and modernisation of the economy promoted by state intervention (nationalisations, particularly of transport, energy, banking and insurance, and the car industry; planning, with the introduction of five-year plans), a carefully planned industrialisation policy aimed at the concentration and modernisation of industrial enterprises, and – from the early sixties – the promotion of high-tech industries. Since the seventies the main emphasis has been on the leap forward into the technological age and preparations for the single European market in 1992.

Economic situation

In 1988 France had an inflation rate of 3.25% and a growth rate of 3.7%. Industrial production accounted for 31% of the gross domestic product.
Among the leading branches of industry are machinery and vehicle production, steel manufacture, chemicals, electrical apparatus and appliances and textiles. Also of great importance are foodstuffs and tobacco, the manufacture of cosmetics and the armaments industry. Among top

growth-oriented sectors are telecommunications and information technology, bio-technology and other high-tech developments. Many French firms are among Europe's leading industrial enterprises, like the car manufacturers Renault and Peugeot-Citroën and the aircraft firms Dassault and SNIAS. In the field of space travel the European satellite programme, Ariane, is under French direction, and Framatome is one of the world's largest constructors of nuclear reactors.

Problems

At the present time France's major problems are – as in most European countries – increasing unemployment (more than 2.5 million unemployed in 1988, or some 10.8% of the working population, women and young people being particularly affected), regional differences in growth rate, a balance of trade deficit (30 billion francs in 1989) and increasingly intense competition from foreign suppliers, big deficits in social insurance funds and a weak currency. Since the limited success of the socialist government's attempt in the early eighties to find a way out of the crisis by nationalisation and government promotion of growth, modernisation and adaptation to the free world market and to the new technological challenges are once again in the forefront of the programme for dealing with France's economic problems.

Agriculture

A characteristic example of the economic changes which have been taking place in France is agriculture, which in spite of the small contribution (barely 4%) which it makes to the gross domestic product is economically of great importance. And although the traditionally high proportion of the working population engaged in agriculture has now fallen steeply (from 21.3% in 1960 to 7% in 1988) it is still higher than in Britain and Germany. France, together with the Netherlands, ranks as the world's largest exporter of agricultural produce after the United States.
30% of all the agricultural land of the European Community is in France. 57.8% of its area is in agricultural use (57% arable, 38% pasture, 4% orchards and vineyards). France also has the largest area of forest of any country in continental Europe (around 14 million hectares/35 million acres).

The drastic reduction in agriculture after the Second World War was accompanied on the one hand by a massive drift away from the land, which is still continuing, and on the other by a thorough modernisation of the country's farms, improved methods of cultivation, redistribution of land, mechanisation and a consequent increase in productivity.

Among the consequences of the drift away from the land were soil erosion and the abandonment of cultivated land, and attempts have been made to remedy this by a government programme of reafforestation. Another result was to provide manpower required by the rapidly expanding service trades (the tertiary sector).

The very varied pattern of French agriculture is the result of different geographical situations, soils and climates. Northern France with its medium-sized units (arable and stock farms) produces high yields of wheat, barley, oats, maize, potatoes and sugar-beet. With only 15% of France's agricultural land and 19% of its population, this region produces 40% of the country's wheat and oats and over 90% of its sugar-beet, together with large quantities of milk and meat. In western Normandy, Brittany, the Vendée and the country extending south to the fringes of the Massif Central fodder crops are grown and stock farming is the principal activity. Almost half France's butter and a third of its beef come from here. This is the *bocage* country, a patchwork of fields enclosed by hedges, which provide shelter from the wind, mark property boundaries and serve to keep the stock from straying. The *bocages* also supply wood in a region with little woodland.

The Paris Basin is an area of large farms (usually over 200 hectares/500 acres) growing cereals and maize. A distinctive pattern of agriculture is found in an area extending from the southern slopes of the Massif Central to the Mediterranean and also in some Alpine valleys. In these areas crops of Mediterranean type are grown – originally vines, cereals and olives but now also fruit and flowers, tobacco, rice and tomatoes. The mulberry trees which were formerly common, providing food for silkworms, are now much rarer. Here and in the hills are stock farms (cattle, sheep), with the stock alternating between summer and winter pastures or spending the summer in the upland meadows and the winter under cover. The use of mountain pastures which was once the normal pattern in the Alps and Pyrenees is now declining and the Alpine meadows are being abandoned.

Stock farming

More than half of France's agricultural output is accounted for by stock farming, which yields meat (mainly beef, poultry and mutton), milk and milk products, and wool, skins and hides.

Wine

A high degree of specialisation on wine-production predominates in Languedoc, with vineyards of all sizes. Depending on the abundance of the crop, France is either the largest producer of wine or the second-largest (after Italy). The main wine producing areas are Burgundy, south-western France around Bordeaux, the Rhône and Loire valleys, the Mediterranean area, Champagne and Alsace.

Problems and prospects

The development of French agriculture is closely bound up with the European Community agricultural market and the common pricing policy. Two-thirds of France's agricultural exports – principally cereals, milk products, fruit, vegetables and wine – go to its Community partners (Germany 14%, Benelux and Italy 10%, Britain 10%). The high expectations that were

A farm in Calvados

Charolais cattle

A vineyard in Beaujolais

attached to French agriculture as an earner of foreign currency have so far been only partly fulfilled, since the progress of modernisation and the development of marketing arrangements are still inadequate and France lacks efficient foodstuffs industries. The southward extension of the Community to take in Spain and Portugal has also produced problems in relation to specifically Mediterranean agricultural produce.
Attempts are being made, through a comprehensive policy for restructuring agriculture, to make French agriculture more efficient, for example by reducing over-capacities (cereals) and seeking to exploit gaps in the market (e.g. medicinal herbs, spice plants).

Fisheries

Although France has fishing rights in extensive fishing grounds it ranks only sixth in Europe and 23rd in the world in terms of annual catch. Since 1983 the same regulations and quotas within the 200-mile zone apply to all fishermen within the European Community. The main centres of the French fisheries are on the Atlantic and Channel coasts. Fish and seafood of all kinds (shellfish, oysters, crustaceans) play an important part in French cuisine, and demand is steadily rising.
The most important French fishing harbours are Boulogne-sur-Mer, Lorient, Concarneau, La Rochelle, Cherbourg and Dieppe.

Minerals

France has deposits of iron ores and of coal (though this is gradually being worked out), reserves of uranium and bauxite, and a few other minerals. Sulphur is produced as a by-product of the natural gas industry, and considerable quantities of salt are harvested from seawater. Otherwise France has to import most of its raw materials.

Energy

Given its geological structure, France requires to import much of its energy requirements from other countries. In 1982 it met only 34.7% of its own needs; it is planned to increase this figure to 51% in 1990. The high costs of energy imports (around 39 billion US dollars in 1984) are a heavy burden on the balance of trade, and accordingly self-sufficiency and economy in the use of power have become major themes in French energy policy.

Coal

In spite of an increase in production under the aegis of the European Coal and Steel Community (established 1952) the French coal-mining industry has been unable to compete effectively with cheaper imported coal and with oil and natural gas. France now imports 60% of the coal it uses. The strong competition from foreign producers and other sources of energy has compelled the French coal corporation Charbonnages de France (CDF) to invest large sums in transport and in mining and processing technology.

Oil

French oil production, centred at Parentis in the Landes, still meets less than 1% of the country's requirements; and the reserves at Lacq (worked by Elf-Aquitaine) are now almost exhausted. Accordingly Elf-Erap and the Compagnie Française des Pétroles (CFP) are intensifying their foreign activities (drilling, extraction, refining), and prospecting is being concentrated on offshore projects (drilling from platforms near the coast).

Natural gas

The proportion of gas requirements met by home production, which was 11.7% in 1983, is due to rise shortly to 15%. Gaz de France (GDF) is responsible for both the extraction (at Lacq) and the import of gas.

Atomic power

The grounds for the ambitious nuclear programme which has been pursued by Electricité de France (EDF) since 1973, with the help of government subsidies, were on the one hand the desire to relieve the balance of trade of the cost of importing energy and on the other the lower costs of atomic power and France's relatively large resources of uranium. With an installed capacity of almost 25 gigawatts and 53 nuclear power stations on stream, supplying 38.7% of its requirements of energy, France is now the world's largest producer of atomic power after the United States.
Indeed it now has a considerable excess of capacity, and in 1987 a number of atomic power stations were taken out of production. It is hoped, therefore, that after 1992 France will be able to export power to other European countries, in particular to Germany.

Reprocessing of nuclear fuel

There are at present two nuclear fuel reprocessing plants in France. The first (UP1) was built at Marcoule, near Avignon, in 1958; the second (UP2), at La Hague, came into operation in 1966. Since 1982 Cogema (Compagnie Générale des Matières Nucléaires), still looking towards the expansion of nuclear power, has been constructing UP3, and at the same time the capacity of UP2 is to be doubled. In order to relieve the financial burden on the French electricity industry, already heavily in debt, reprocessing capacity is hired to foreign operators. Some 80% of all used fuel elements in the western world are reprocessed at La Hague. Here again the French atomic industry is threatened with over-capacity. In the meantime, too, with a ten-year time lag, popular unease about the nuclear industry has reached France, as the electoral successes of the Greens in 1989 demonstrated.

Industry

French industry accounts for some 27% of the gross domestic product, and in 1988 30% of the working population were employed in industry.

Recent developments

Intensive economic planning and an industrial policy involving government subsidies to promote development, accompanied by comprehensive modernisation of the industrial structure, have provided a powerful stimu-

lus to the whole economy. Progressive branches of industry, particularly the capital goods industries (mechanical engineering, car manufacture and the electrical industry) and innovative consumer durables have achieved the highest growth rates, while the traditional consumer goods industries have shown a steady decline. As a result of the government's policy of promoting the amalgamation of smaller firms the predominance of small and medium-sized family businesses – long characteristic of France's economic structure – has been steadily reduced, and their place has been taken by the large enterprises and huge state-subsidised concerns which now play such a large part in the French economy (with around 3% of businesses employing more than 50% of the working population).
Within the last decade, however, there has been a marked trend towards smaller businesses, due mainly to the increasing importance of the service trades.

Tertiary sector

The service or tertiary sector is now the largest sector of the French economy, employing 63% of the working population and in 1987 accounting for 65% of the gross domestic product. This is a growing sector of the French economy, while agriculture is shrinking and industry has also been been declining since the 1970s.

The Paris region

The leading French industrial region is the area round Paris (Ile-de-France), in which 21% of the working population live. A retrospective look back to the early 19th century reveals the industries that were already established there: for example 65 carpet factories, 70 cabinetmakers, 166 watchmakers, 108 perfume factories, 72 factories making artificial flowers. Present-day Paris is France's largest producer and consumer of goods, with a particular concentration on modern growth industries (electronics, electrical engineering, aircraft and car manufacture) and service industries (banking, commerce, insurance). Many branches of industry, from clothing, fashion jewellery, perfumery and printing and publishing to leather goods, are now mainly concentrated in and around the capital.

Other areas

The second most important industrial area is the Rhône–Alpes region, with energy production, metal-processing, textiles and chemicals as its major industries.
Like the region of Lorraine in eastern France (coal, steel, textiles), the Nord–Pas-de-Calais region (textiles, coal, steel, engineering) suffers from a preponderance of traditional industries which, as in the rest of Europe, are in a state of crisis. Efforts are being made to improve the economic structure and create new jobs by extensive assistance towards re-training and the establishment of modern industries.
In western and south-western France the sharp decline in agriculture after the Second World War and the absence of alternative employment led to a drift away from the land and an aging of the remaining population, accompanied by the decay of the already weak infrastructure. The principal task in this huge area, therefore, was to remedy its economic under-development. Thus in the Midi–Pyrénées region important aircraft and armaments industries were established at Toulouse, and the extraction of natural gas gave Lacq a fresh lease of life.
In the Pays de la Loire region (in which are Nantes and St-Nazaire) and Brittany (Rennes) also, new industrial centres have been developed.

Problems

One of the main problems of the French economy is the continuing imbalance between Paris and the provinces and between the various regions: it has been predicted that in the nineties 80% of jobs in the service sector will be in the Paris region. The problem is aggravated by the fact that Paris enjoys a political and cultural as well as an economic predominance. This overwhelming importance of the capital is challenged only by a few other industrial centres such as the Marseilles region, and there are many under-developed regions, including the whole of western and south-western France. In these traditionally agricultural crisis areas the government is

The TGV, France's high-speed train

trying to promote the establishment of new industries by tax inducements; the decentralising reform initiated in 1982 gave the regions new independent responsibilities in developing regional economic policies.

The public sector

As a result of government credits and government orders, combined with the extensive nationalisation programme of 1982 (mainly affecting key sectors like energy, transport, the large banks and insurance corporations), the public sector of the French economy has again increased substantially. In 1984 joint-venture industrial concerns, mostly export-oriented, accounted for around 32% of turnover, 24% of jobs and 59% of investment in the industrial field.

The extended public sector includes mainly energy supply, transport and communications, almost all credit agencies and insurance corporations, motor vehicle and aircraft production, the armaments industry, iron and steel, aluminium production (with French bauxite), the electrical and electronics industries, chemicals, computers and glass manufacture. In 1986 the conservative Chirac government brought forward a number of denationalisation measures, including in particular the phased privatisation of enterprises nationalised in 1982, but was unable to achieve any major change of direction. The socialist government which returned to power in 1988 has been able to exert a strong influence on private companies by its control of the nationalised insurance groups, two large banks and a powerful savings bank. The ruling principles might be stated as a mixed economy, state enterprises as auxiliaries and state influence in support of threatened private firms.

Transport and Tourism

General

The pattern of French communications, predominantly centred on Paris, is conditioned by the size of the country, regional imbalances and the coun-

try's centralised system of government. In spite of some notable developments, there are high concentrations and overloads of traffic in the large conurbations, particularly in the Paris region, while large areas in the provinces are still relatively ill provided with roads.
In spite of increases in the price of petrol and the steady development of public transport the French still prefer to travel by car, and every year almost 2 million new cars are registered in France. There are now 394 vehicles per 1000 inhabitants. The movement of goods by road also continues to increase, and now accounts for about 56% of total traffic.

Roads

The French road network is one of the best in the world, with about 15 km/9 miles of road per 1000 inhabitants. The total of 804,650 km/499,985 miles includes 34,000 km/21,125 miles of *routes nationales,* 347,000 km/215,600 miles of *routes départementales* and 421,000/261,600 miles of communal roads. The 6150 km/3820 miles of motorway (mostly subject to toll) have been developed mainly within the last twenty years; in 1966 there were only 789 km/490 miles.

Railways

The French rail system, run by the SNCF (Société Nationale des Chemins de Fer Français, formed in 1938 by the amalgamation of a number of separate companies), is one of the most modern in the world, and has responded to the growing demand with increased comfort and higher speeds. Of the total network of 34,600 km/21,500 miles about 30% were electrified by 1982. The SNCF runs 13,000 trains and carries some 2 million passengers every day. The fastest trains are those from Paris along the routes of the TGV (see below), notably to Lyons, Marseilles, Bordeaux, Lille and Calais.

TGV

The celebrated Train à Grande Vitesse (TGV) came into service in 1981. It links Paris with the south of France (TGV Sud-Est), with a number of towns and cities on the Atlantic coast (TGV Atlantique), and with Lille and Calais (TGV Nord Europe) connecting with the Channel Tunnel services beginning

Toulon harbour, with the car ferry to Corsica

in 1994. On some stretches it reaches speeds of 300 km/186 miles per hour, cutting journey times considerably. Further developments are planned, and a link between Paris, Brussels, Cologne and Amsterdam is due to come into operation before the end of the century.

Shipping

The French merchant fleet consists of just under 400 vessels, including around 100 tankers, and ranks eleventh in the international league. The principal French ports are Marseilles, Le Havre, Dunkirk, Rouen, Nantes–St-Nazaire and Bordeaux.

Inland navigation

France has 6658 km/4137 miles of inland waterways, but only a quarter of this total can take vessels of over 300 tons. The most important waterways are the Seine between Paris and Le Havre, the Rhône and the Alsatian section of the Rhine-Rhône Canal.

Air services
International

With its three national airlines – Air France, Air Inter and TAT (Transports Aériens Transrégional) – France takes fifth place in world ranking. The largest of the three airlines is the semi-nationalised Air France, which carries around 11.6 million passengers (1983) annually to 73 countries.

Domestic

France has a dense network of domestic air services, flown by Air Inter, TAT and other airlines.

Tourism

The tourist trade is the most important branch of the French economy in the service sector. In 1988 it had a net revenue of 30 billion francs – more than the whole of the car industry. In 1986 France had over 36.1 million foreign visitors, who spent an average of 8.2 days in the country.
The government is making great efforts to promote the tourist trade, and under the arrangements for decentralising government the regional tourist authorities are to be given greater independent responsibility.
The development of the road system helps to foster the tourist trade, as does the wide range of leisure and cultural activities on offer and the variety of accommodation available for visitors, from first-class luxury hotels to modest farmhouses and *gîtes,* catering both for the individual traveller and those who prefer holiday clubs or the large new holiday centres on the Languedoc–Roussillon coast and in Aquitaine.

Winter sports

New winter sports centres have mushroomed in recent years. In the Savoy Alps huge skiing areas have been developed, but there are also excellent facilities for winter sports in the Southern Alps and the Pyrenees.
Some places in France are almost obligatory Meccas for visitors: Paris, of course, the French Riviera, Provence. But there are also great attractions, and many discoveries to be made, in remoter areas off the beaten tourist track. It is unrealistic, in any event, to try to get any general or complete impression of France in a single visit: it is too large, too varied and too rich in treasures of all kinds.

Gastronomy

France is, of course, famed for its food and drink, which are an essential element in its culture, appreciated by all classes of the population. With all its varied attractions France is also the land of *savoir vivre,* the art of living, of which good food and good wine form a necessary part.

Language

Increasing numbers of French people, particularly young people, speak at least some English, and in hotels, restaurants, etc., catering for visitors the staff will usually be able to understand what is required. Visitors need not, therefore, know French well to enjoy a holiday in France; but it will add to the enjoyment, and enable them to get to know French people better, if they have at least some knowledge of the language.

History

Prehistory and the Early Historical Period

The territory of France was settled in prehistoric times, and has yielded much evidence of the earliest human cultures.	*c.* 10,000 B.C. to 5th c. A.D.
Later Palaeolithic. Cave paintings in southern France (figures of animals, including mammoths and reindeer).	10,000 B.C.
Megalithic culture. In the late Neolithic and early Bronze Age monumental graves and cult structures are built (e.g. in Brittany).	2700–1600 B.C.
Foundation of the colony of Massilia (Marseilles) by Greek traders (Phocaeans).	c. 600 B.C.
Celts, led by their chieftains and priests (druids), advance into France from the east. In southern France the Iberians (north of the Pyrenees) and Ligurians (on the Mediterranean coast) remain independent.	from 500 B.C.
The Romans establish the Provincia Gallia Narbonensis (Provence) to protect the land route between Italy and Spain.	121 B.C.
The Germanic Cimbri and Teutons move into Provence.	109 B.C.
The Roman general Marius defeats the Teutons at Aquae Sextiae (Aix-en-Provence) and the Cimbri at Vercellae (Vercelli) in northern Italy.	102–101 B.C.
Caesar conquers Gaul (giving an account of his victories in "De Bello Gallico"), and the country is put under Roman civil administration. The process of linguistic and cultural Romanisation begins; the population, now known as Gallo-Romans, adopt the language of the conquerors, the Vulgar Latin which later develops into French. Towns are founded, stone buildings replace wooden huts and well-made roads replace the older tracks. Remains of fine public buildings can be seen in Nîmes, Arles, etc.	58–51 B.C.
Economic upsurge (agriculture, metalworking, textile production, pottery) and cultural flowering in Gaul.	1st–3rd c. A.D.
The Christianisation of Gaul begins.	2nd c. A.D.
The towns are surrounded by new walls. Lutetia (Paris) becomes the occasional residence of Roman emperors.	*c.* 300 A.D.
The great migrations reach Gaul.	300–600 A.D.
Visigothic kingdom in southern Gaul, with its capital at Tolosa (Toulouse). The Franks drive the Visigoths out of France into Spain.	418–507 A.D.
The Burgundians, after their defeat by the Huns on the Middle Rhine, establish a kingdom (Burgundy) in the Rhône valley under Roman protection. The southern part of their former territory, round Worms, is occupied by the Alemanni, the northern part, extending as far as Mainz, by the Franks.	443 A.D.
Celts, driven out of Britain by the Jutes, Angles and Saxons, settle in Brittany, giving it its present name.	from 449
In the battle of the Catalaunian Fields, near Troyes, the Huns, led by Attila,	451

are defeated by the Romans and their auxiliaries (Visigoths, Franks, Burgundians), and thereafter withdraw to Hungary.

The Frankish Kingdom under the Merovingians and Carolingians

400–800 A.D.	The Frankish kingdom, the most important Germanic state of the early medieval period, provides the basis for the political, social and cultural development of Western Europe, particularly France and Germany.
from 400	Franks settle in Gaul as far as the Seine and Loire.
482–511	The Merovingian king Clovis I unites the Franks, conquers Gaul and thus becomes the founder of the Frankish kingdom.
496	The Franks defeat the Alemanni, become Catholic and thereafter receive the support of the Church.
from 511	Three new kingdoms emerge as a result of successive partitions of the Frankish kingdom – the Germanic Austrasia, with its capital at Reims (later Metz), Neustria, with Paris as its capital, and Burgundy (capital Orléans).
687	The Carolingian Pépin of Herstal, "mayor of the palace" in Austrasia, rules over the whole Frankish kingdom.
732	Pépin's son Charles Martel (the "Hammer") defeats the Arabs advancing from Spain in the battle of Poitiers. Close association between Aquitaine, Burgundy and the Frankish kingdom.
751	Pépin the Short is proclaimed king by an assembly of dignitaries at Soissons and anointed by the papal legate, Archbishop Boniface (Pope Zacharias having agreed to the deposition of the last Merovingian king).
754	Pope Stephen II asks Pépin for help against the Lombards and puts Rome under the protection of the Frankish king. Pépin and his sons are granted the style of "Patricius Romanorum". He cedes to the Pope the territories conquered from the Lombard king Aistulf (the Pentapolis, the exarchate of Ravenna).
772–814	Charlemagne enlarges the Frankish empire by the addition of northern Italy and the territories of the West Germanic peoples (Saxons and Bavarians). The empire is divided into counties ruled by counts, and the frontiers are protected by border marches; the imperial strongholds become economic and cultural centres.
800	Charlemagne's authority in western Europe is confirmed by his coronation as emperor in Rome.

From the Rise of France to the Age of Absolutism

843–1600	The French kingdom, supported by the Church and the towns, steadily consolidates its position, establishing itself as a hereditary monarchy in spite of the existence of numerous independent fiefs and territories and defending its frontiers against foreign enemies, particularly England.
843	Under the treaty of Verdun the Frankish empire is partitioned. Charles II, the Bald, receives the western part, whose eastern boundaries remain in all essentials the frontier between France and Germany until the late medieval period. Carolingian kings rule in France until 987.

Norsemen (Normans) raid the western Frankish kingdom and plunder Paris.	857
In the absence of any strong central authority a number of large regional units come into being – Francia, Champagne, Aquitaine, Gascony, Toulouse, Gothia, Catalonia, Brittany, Normandy, Flanders.	from 888
Charles III grants the Normans the duchy of Normandy.	911
The Capetians rule France in the direct line until 1328, and in collateral lines until 1848 (with the exception of 1792-1814).	987–1328
Hugues Capet (from *cappa,* "little cloak") possesses only his family territory, the duchy of Francia (the area round Paris, extending to Orléans). Although the king's authority is still weak in face of his powerful vassals, he gains the support of the Church. The Capetians re-establish the hereditary character of the monarchy. The literature produced from the 11th century onwards reveals the differences between the *langue d'oil* of the north, subject to Frankish influence, and the *langue d'oc* of the south, which remains closer to Celto-Romance.	987–996
William, Duke of Normandy, conquers England.	1066
France plays a leading part in the Crusades. The way is prepared by the monastic orders and the Church, and the leaders are mainly French princes and nobles. The abbey of Cluny in Burgundy (founded in 910) becomes a centre of monastic and ecclesiastical reform. The Carthusian order, an eremitical order, is founded in the mountain valley of Cartusia, near Grenoble (the Grande Chartreuse). The Cistercian order, centred on the abbey of Cîteaux (1098), promotes scholarship and architecture and pursues the Christianisation and colonisation of the eastern German territories. A Cistercian abbot, Bernard of Clairvaux, is one of the leading scholars of his day. The campaigns of conquest in the East, and the consequent contacts with the advanced culture of Islam, make possible the political, economic and cultural rise of France in the 12th century. The French nobility set the pattern of European chivalry, and the Gothic architecture and courtly literature of France exert a lasting influence throughout Europe.	1096–1270
Louis VI, the Stout, subdues his rebellious vassals and founds the fortunes of the Capetian dynasty.	1108–1137
Under Louis VII the conflict with England begins. Henry II, a vassal of the French crown, possesses more than half of France.	1137–1180
Philippe Auguste recovers from 1202 onwards all the French possessions of the English king except Guyenne and Gascony.	1180–1223
Philippe Auguste defeats the English and their ally Otto IV of Germany in the battle of Bouvines, strengthening the French consciousness of national identity.	1214
Albigensian wars in southern France. The French crown takes part in the repression of the Albigensian sect (named after the town of Albi) and in 1229 acquires Languedoc, bridging over the antagonism between the Frankish northern part of France and the Romance southern part.	1209–1229
Under Louis VIII France becomes a hereditary monarchy, and Reims becomes the place of coronation of the French kings.	1223–1226
Robert de Sorbon founds a theological college, the Sorbonne, the nucleus of the University of Paris.	1253

1226–1270	In the reign of Louis IX (St Louis) Henry III of England loses all the English possessions in France north of the river Charente and does homage to the French king for the duchy of Guyenne. The Parlement de Paris is established as the country's supreme court.
1285–1314	Philippe IV (Philippe le Bel) acquires the county of Champagne and the archbishopric of Lyons.
1302	The States General meet for the first time.
1309–1377	The "Babylonian captivity" of the Popes in Avignon.
1328	The crown passes to the house of Valois, a collateral line of the Capetians (until 1498).
1333	Edward III of England claims the French crown.
1339–1453	The Hundred Years War between France and England. Heavy defeats and grave social tensions between the nobility and the townspeople. The royal authority is shaken by peasant risings and fighting between rival groups of nobles.
1348	The heir to the French throne inherits the Dauphiné, and thereafter is known as the Dauphin.
1356	Edward III's son Edward, the Black Prince, defeats and captures king John II, the Good, at Maupertuis, south-east of Poitiers.
1360	Treaty of Brétigny: Edward III gives up his claim to the French crown and receives in return Calais and south-western France.
1363	John II gives the duchy of Burgundy to his son Philip the Bold.
1369	Charles V, the Wise, resumes the war against England and reduces English-held territory to a few bases.
1380–1422	Under Charles VI (who becomes insane in 1392) the conflict between the Dukes of Burgundy and Orléans becomes increasingly bitter.
1415	Henry V of England defeats a French army at Agincourt and, with the support of Burgundy, occupies Paris and the whole of northern France.
1429	Joan of Arc compels the English army to raise the siege of Orléans, and accompanies Charles VII to his coronation in Reims.
1430	Joan of Arc is captured by the English and burned at the stake as a heretic in Rouen on May 30th 1431. (Canonised in 1920).
1438	The Pragmatic Sanction secures the independence of the French church from the Papacy: establishment of the French national Gallican Church.
1439	A new system of taxation, the *taille royale,* makes possible the formation of a standing army.
by 1453	England loses all its possessions on the Continent except Calais.
1461–1483	Louis XI finally establishes the authority of the centralised monarchy over the great nobles.
1470	The first French printing press is established in Paris.
1477	On the death of Charles the Bold the duchy of Burgundy and Picardy pass to the French crown, while his other possessions fall to the Habsburg

Emperor Maximilian I: beginning of the conflict between France and the Habsburgs.

The French crown acquires Anjou (1480), Maine, Provence (1481) and Brittany (1491). — 1480–1491

Reign of Charles VIII, who claims the kingdom of Naples as heir to the House of Anjou but is able to retain it only for a short period. — 1483–1498

Meeting of the States General in Tours, with all the French provinces represented for the first time: the representatives of the towns are recognised as the Third Estate. — 1484

Louis XII conquers the duchy of Milan, but is compelled to give it up after his defeat at Novara (1513). — 1500

François I recovers Milan after his victory over the Huguenots at Marignano. — 1515

François I seeks to obtain the German imperial crown, but in spite of papal support is unsuccessful. — 1519

François I fights four wars against the Habsburg Emperor Charles V. France loses Milan and is driven out of Italy. — 1521–1544

Henry II, having married Catherine de Médicis, persecutes the Huguenots, occupies the German bishoprics of Metz, Toul and Verdun (1522) and takes Calais (1558). After Henry's death Catherine gains increasing influence on French policy. — 1547–1559

Franco-Spanish war. France renounces its claims to Italy and Burgundy. — 1556–1559

The spread of Calvinism among the middle classes and some of the nobles is followed by religious wars between Catholics, led by the Dukes of Guise, and Protestants, led by the Bourbons. — 1562–1598

In the St Bartholomew's Day massacre (Aug. 24th) the Huguenot leader Admiral de Coligny and thousands of his supporters are murdered on the orders of Catherine de Médicis. — 1572

After the murder of Henri III the Bourbons succeed to the throne (until 1792). — 1589

In order to secure peace within France Henry IV of Navarre becomes a Catholic ("Paris is worth a Mass"). He restores the royal authority: the great nobles are forbidden to maintain their own private armies, the administration is centralised, the country's finances are established on a sound basis and the economy recovers. In 1600 Henry takes Marie de Médicis as his second wife. — 1593

The Edict of Nantes grants Huguenots limited freedom of religion and equal civil rights. — 1598

Establishment of the first French colony in Canada. — after 1603

From the Age of Absolutism to the End of the First Empire

The age of absolutism brings the royal authority to its peak, but leads to economic and social changes which destroy the existing social structure. The basic ideas of the Enlightenment, which the French Revolution seeks to put into practice, do not yet produce a stable system of government but point the way towards 19th century Europe. — 1610–1815

1624–1642	In the reign of Louis XIII Cardinal Richelieu becomes the king's chief minister and establishes the absolute authority of the crown.
1628	After the conquest of La Rochelle Richelieu puts an end to the special political status of the Huguenots but does not interfere with their freedom of worship. He suppresses the opposition of the great nobles and appoints Intendants to control the administration of the provinces.
1635	Foundation of the Académie Française to promote art and learning.
1635	France becomes involved in the Thirty Years War.
1643–1661	Cardinal Mazarin governs France during the minority of Louis XIV.
1648	Under the Peace of Westphalia France acquires the Habsburg possessions in Alsace.
1648	Outbreak of the Fronde, a rising by the great nobles, the Parlement and the people of Paris against the absolute power of the crown; it is crushed in 1653.
1659	The Treaty of the Pyrenees ends the war with Spain. Spanish power is broken, and France becomes a European great power.
1660	Louis XIV marries the Infanta Maria Teresa.
from 1661	Louis XIV reigns alone as the "Roi Soleil" (Sun King). The absolute monarchy reaches the height of its power in both domestic and foreign affairs, and the court at Versailles becomes the model for courtly and aristocratic life throughout Europe. There is a flowering of Baroque art (Palace of Versailles, etc.), classical French literature (Corneille, Racine, Molière, La Fontaine), philosophy (Descartes, Pascal) and painting (Poussin, Watteau). The financial and economic policy of Colbert (mercantilism) and the reorganisation of the army by Louvois make possible Louis XIV's wars of conquest. Vauban develops the art of fortification and siege warfare.
1664	Foundation of the French West India Company.
1667–1668	War of conquest against Spain and the Spanish Netherlands. Under the treaty of Aix-la-Chapelle France acquires Lille and other fortified towns in the Low Countries.
1672–1678	War with Holland. Under the treaty of Nijmegen the Franche-Comté and certain frontier areas in the Low Countries are ceded to France.
1679–1681	Annexation of Alsace (Strasbourg occupied 1681).
1685	The revocation of the Edict of Nantes leads half a million Huguenots to leave France. Persecution of the Jansenists.
1688–1697	War of the Grand Alliance. The Palatinate (Heidelberg, etc.) is devastated by the French.
1701–1714	War of the Spanish Succession. France suffers heavy defeats at the hands of the Grand Alliance (the Emperor and the German princes, Spain, Sweden, Britain, Holland, Savoy).
1713	Peace of Utrecht. Philip V, Louis XIV's grandson, is recognised as king of Spain; France and Spain never to be united.
1715	Death of Louis XIV. Years of war and an extravagant court result in the economic ruin of the country, a huge national debt and the impoverishment of the peasants. France is no longer a great power.

The storming of the Bastille

During the reign of Louis XV the Scottish-born financier John Law and Cardinal Fleury seek in vain to redress the financial situation by currency speculation. — 1715–1774

Through its participation in the War of the Polish Succession France acquires the right of succession to the duchy of Lorraine, which falls to France in 1766. — 1733–1738

The king under the influence of his mistresses (Mme de Pompadour, Mme du Barry). — from 1743

In the colonial war with Britain and the Seven Years War (1756–1763) France loses its colonies in North America and almost all its bases in southern and eastern India. — 1754–1763

Genoa sells Corsica to France. — 1768

Attempts at reform by Louis XVI's finance ministers (Turgot, Necker, Calonne) founder on the resistance of the privileged classes (the nobility and clergy, who are represented in the supreme courts and the Parlements). — 1774–1789

Outbreak of the French Revolution. The collapse of the "Ancien Régime" results from the weakness of the absolutist system. The decline in the authority of the crown under the incapable Louis XV, failures in foreign policy and extravagant expenditure lead to criticism of the monarchy, and the outdated feudal order (exemption of the nobility and clergy from taxes, etc.) produces social tensions. The well-to-do middle classes, demanding greater political rights, take up the fight against feudalism and the Church. Industrial crises resulting in high unemployment and agrarian crises caused by crop failures lead to the impoverishment of the lower middle classes and peasants. The opposition to the Ancien Régime is influenced — 1789

	by the ideas of the Enlightenment (the "Encyclopédie", Voltaire, Montesquieu, Rousseau, etc.) and by the American War of Independence. In order to make good the deficit Louis XVI summons the States General (May 5th), which had not met since 1614.
	The Third Estate (the ordinary people as opposed to the nobility and clergy) declares itself a National Assembly (June 17th) and takes the "Oath of the Tennis Court" to produce a constitution (June 20th). Storming and destruction of the Bastille, the state prison in Paris (July 14th: now the French national holiday). The nobility begin to leave the country. Abolition of feudal rights and liberation of the peasants (Aug. 4th–5th). Declaration of the Rights of Man (Aug. 26th). The Paris mob compels Louis XIV and the National Assembly to move to Paris (Oct. 5th).
	Formation of political clubs: the radical Jacobins (named after the monastery where they met: Robespierre, St-Just) and Cordeliers (Danton, Desmoulins, Marat), the moderate Feuillants (Bailly, Lafayette), etc. Nationalisation of church property (Nov. 2nd).
1791	Louis XVI attempts to flee (June 20th). New constitution (Sept. 3rd) establishing a constitutional monarchy.
1791–1792	Legislative Assembly, with a majority of moderate Girondins but an increase in the number of radicals.
1792	Establishment of the First Republic. With the declaration of war on Austria (April) the Revolutionary Wars begin. Storming of the Tuileries: the royal family are imprisoned in the Temple (Aug. 10th). "September massacres" of suspected anti-revolutionaries. At the battle of Valmy the "cannonade of Valmy" routs the Prussian army. Revolutionary armies conquer Belgium and occupy the left bank of the Rhine.
1792–1795	National Convention, with a radical majority (Robespierre, Danton, etc.).
1793	Execution of Louis XVI (Jan. 21st).
Mid 1793 to 1794	The Terror, under Robespierre and the Committee of Public Safety. A revolutionary tribunal condemns Queen Marie-Antoinette, the Girondins and many others to death, and promulgates radical laws. Bloody suppression of risings in Vendée, Brittany and some cities. After military defeats Carnot forms a people's army (the *levée en masse)* for the defence of France.
1794	Fall and execution of Robespierre (July). End of the Terror.
1794–1795	Reconquest of Belgium. Holland is declared a "Batavian Republic".
1795–1799	The Directory, a governing body of five, is too weak either to deal with the economic and financial crisis or to prevent risings of the right (royalists) and the left (an early communist movement led by Babeuf).
1796–1797	Napoleon Bonaparte defeats the Austrians in northern Italy and conquers Lombardy. Establishment of the Cisalpine Republic (Milan) and the Ligurian Republic (Genoa).
1798–1799	Switzerland becomes the Helvetian Republic, the Papal State the Roman Republic and Naples the Parthenopaean Republic. In his Egyptian expedition Bonaparte defeats the Mamelukes in the Battle of the Pyramids, but the French fleet is annihilated by Nelson in the Battle of the Nile.

After an adventurous flight from Egypt Bonaparte overthrows the Directory in a coup d'état and is elected Consul for a ten-year term in a plebiscite. He centralises the administration, encourages the return of many émigrés and signs a Concordat with the Pope (1801).	1799
Peace of Lunéville between France and Austria. The left bank of the Rhine remains French; the subsidiary republics established by France are recognised.	1801
Under the Peace of Amiens between France and Britain the British give up most of their overseas conquests with the exception of Ceylon and Trinidad, while the French evacuate Egypt. In a further plebiscite Bonaparte is made Consul for life.	1802
Napoleonic Wars with the European powers.	1803–1815
At a meeting of the Imperial Diet in Regensburg, strongly influenced by Bonaparte, the old Holy Roman Empire is reorganised.	1803
Napoleon Bonaparte is crowned Emperor of the French as Napoleon I. French civil law is codified in the Code Civil ("Code Napoléon").	1804
Napoleon crowns himself king of Italy in Milan. Nelson destroys the French fleet in the battle of Trafalgar. Napoleon wins a decisive victory over the Russians and Austrians at Austerlitz (the "Battle of the Three Emperors").	1805
Establishment of the Confederation of the Rhine under Napoleon's protection. Napoleon defeats the Prussians in the double battle of Jena and Auerstedt. While in Berlin he decrees the "Continental Blockade" of Britain.	1806
Defeat of the Russians at Friedland. Establishment of the kingdom of Westphalia, with Napoleon's brother Jérome as king, and the Grand Duchy of Warsaw.	1807
National risings in Spain against the French occupying forces.	from 1808
Rising in Austria. Popular rising in Tirol, led by Andreas Hofer, against the French and Bavarians.	1809
Napoleon marries the Austrian Emperor's daughter Marie Louise.	1810
Napoleon's Russian campaign turns to disaster after the burning of Moscow and the early onset of winter.	1812
Wars of liberation by various European peoples against Napoleonic domination. Napoleon is defeated in the "Battle of the Nations" at Leipzig (1813).	1813–1815
The Allies enter Paris; Napoleon abdicates and is given Elba as a principality. The Bourbons, in the person of Louis XVIII, return to the French throne. The first Peace of Paris (May) confines France to its 1792 frontiers.	1814
Napoleon returns to France for the "Hundred Days". He loses the decisive battle of Waterloo against the British and Prussians, and is exiled to the British island of St Helena in the south Atlantic (where he dies in 1821). In the second Peace of Paris (November) France is returned to its 1790 frontiers.	1815

From the Restoration to the First World War

The history of France during the 19th century is mainly determined by the effects of the French Revolution and the industrial revolution. The revolutions of 1830 and 1848 give rise to movements which reshape the political	1815–1914

situation not only in France but in most other European countries. After 1850 France increasingly participates in the imperialist and colonialist policies of the European great powers.

1814–1815	Louis XVIII promulgates the Charte Constitutionelle, which gives France a new constitution. Persecution of Jacobins and Bonapartists.
1825	Compensation granted to émigrés. Louis Braille devises his script for the blind.
1830	The abolition of the freedom of the press and a change in electoral law lead to the July Revolution and the abdication of Charles X. The liberal-minded Louis-Philippe, Duc d'Orléans, is proclaimed King of the French (the *roi citoyen* or citizen king). Early socialist ideas are propagated by Fournier, Proudhon, Blanc and Blanqui.
1830–1847	Conquest of Algeria.
1843–1848	Karl Marx living in Paris.
1848	February Revolution in Paris, as a result of discontent with the bourgeois monarchy and the property qualification for voting. Louis-Philippe abdicates and France becomes a republic (the Second Republic). First election to the National Assembly by popular vote (April). The closing down of the uneconomic "national workshops" leads to a workers' rising in Paris, which is ruthlessly repressed (June). Prince Louis-Napoléon (nephew of Napoleon I) is elected President of the Republic.
1851	Coup d'état by Louis-Napoléon. He is given a ten-year term as President in a plebiscite.
1852	After a further plebiscite Louis-Napoléon becomes Emperor of the French as Napoleon III. Supported by the army and the Catholic church, he pursues an economic and social policy (creation of employment by large-scale public works) and supports nationalist movements in Italy, Germany and the Balkans.
1854–1856	France takes part in the Crimean War against Russia.
1859	France and Sardinia at war with Austria. Napoleon allows Sardinia to take Lombardy, while France acquires Nice and Savoy (1860).
1859–1867	France extends its colonial possessions in South-East Asia.
1859–1869	Construction of the Suez Canal by Ferdinand de Lesseps, with French support.
1861–1867	The "Mexican expedition". The Mexican empire established by Napoleon III for Maximilian of Habsburg falls to pieces as a result of American opposition.
1870–1871	Franco-Prussian War. Napoleon III is taken prisoner after his defeat at Sedan, and a republic is proclaimed in Paris (Sept. 4th).
1870–1940	Third Republic. Thiers, who had been prime minister in the time of Louis-Philippe, becomes President (until 1873).
1871	The Paris Commune, a rising by socialists and communists, is repressed by MacMahon (March–May). Under the treaty of Frankfurt France cedes Alsace and Lorraine to Germany. Hostility between the two countries increases.

The French Socialist Workers' Party is founded by the Marxists Guesde and Lafargue.	1879
Extension of France's colonial possessions: parts of Central Africa (1879–1894), Tunis (1881), Indochina (from 1887), Madagascar (1896).	from 1879
On the centenary of the French Revolution an International Exhibition is held in Paris; the French contribution is the 300 m/985 ft high Eiffel Tower. Foundation of the Second International in Paris (May 1st: now celebrated as Labour Day).	1889
The "Panama scandal": bankruptcy of a company founded by Ferdinand de Lesseps.	1892–1893
Military alliance between France and Russia.	1892
Lumière invents the first cinematograph.	1894
Foundation of the Confédération Générale du Travail, a trade union organisation.	1895
The Dreyfus Affair: a Jewish officer, Alfred Dreyfus, is condemned on the basis of forged documents and rehabilitated only in 1906.	1896–1906
The Fashoda incident, when France and Britain come into conflict in the Sudan. France is compelled to abandon any idea of extending its North African colonial empire to the Upper Nile.	1898–1899
Secret treaty with Italy over Tripoli.	1902
The Entente Cordiale between Britain and France: recognition of Britain's supremacy in Egypt and France's in Morocco.	1904
Law on the separation of Church and State. The French section of the Workers' International (SFIO) becomes the PSU (Parti Socialiste Unifié).	1905
First Moroccan crisis: Germany protests against French intervention in Morocco.	1905–1906
The Entente Cordiale is extended to include Russia in the Triple Entente.	1907
Blériot becomes the first man to fly the English Channel.	1909
Second Moroccan crisis: Germany recognises the French protectorate over Morocco in return for compensation in the Cameroons.	1911
Franco-Russian naval treaty.	1912

From the First World War to the Present Day

France is a major theatre of war in both world wars. After the Treaty of Versailles it recovers its position as a European great power, but the desire for security prevents the development of any peaceful policy for the revision of the treaty. The Second World War alters the balance of power in Europe in favour of the United States and the Soviet Union. In consequence French policy is aimed at strengthening France's position within Europe and breaking free from United States leadership.	from 1912
The president of the Socialist Party, Jean Jaurès, is murdered (July). Truce between the government and the socialists during the First World War (August).	1914

1914–1918	First World War. The immediate occasion is the assassination of the heir to the Austrian throne and his wife in Sarajevo (June 28th 1914); the causes are conflicts between European states based on considerations of power politics (including France's desire to recover Alsace and Lorraine), competition in armaments, the difficulties of the multi-national Austro-Hungarian state, Russia's Balkan policies and over-hasty mobilisations and ultimatums. On Aug. 3rd 1914 Germany declares war on France. In the battle of the Marne a French counter-attack holds up the German advance (Sept.). The war of movement develops into trench warfare.
1916	The battle for Verdun (Feb. 21st to July 21st). The French retake the Verdun defences (Oct. 24th to Dec. 16th).
1917	German withdrawal between Arras and Soissons to the Hindenburg or Siegfried Line.
1918	Allied counter-offensive under Marshal Foch (July). Franco-German armistice at Compiègne (Nov.).
1919	France becomes a founder member of the League of Nations. Under the Versailles treaty France recovers Alsace and Lorraine and also secures mandates over Syria and Lebanon, large parts of the Cameroons and Togoland, economic control of the Saar, the occupation of the Rhineland for a period of 15 years and the major share of German reparations. Election victory of the National Bloc (Clemenceau, Poincaré) over the Cartel of the Left under Herriot.
1920	Military convention with Belgium and alliances with Poland (1921), Czechoslovakia (1924) and Romania (1926). The Communists break away from the Socialists.
1923	Occupation of the Ruhr ordered by Poincaré in spite of British resistance.
1924	Election victory of the Cartel of the Left. France gives diplomatic recognition to the Soviet Union.
1925	Locarno Pact: Germany guarantees the inviolability of France's eastern frontier.
1925–1926	Rising in Morocco.
1927	Repression of independence movement in Alsace.
1929	The French foreign minister, Briand, agrees to the evacuation of the Rhineland and to the Young Plan for the reduction of German reparations. Construction of the Maginot Line.
1931	The world economic crisis hits France.
1932	Non-aggression pact with the Soviet Union.
1934	The continuing financial crisis is accompanied by a crisis of the parliamentary system and the growth of radical opinion on both left and right.
1935	Colonial agreement with Italy. Mutual assistance pact with the Soviet Union.
1936	The German army marches into the demilitarised Rhineland; neither France nor Britain takes any military action.

Victory of the Popular Front (Communists, Socialists, Radical Socialists) in a general election. The government led by Léon Blum (1936-1937) carries through progressive social legislation (40-hour week, holidays with pay).

1938 Munich agreement: Prime Minister Daladier agrees to the cession of the Sudeten German areas of Czechoslovakia to Germany.

1939 Franco-British guarantees to Poland (Mar. 31st), Romania and Greece (Apr. 13th).

1939–1945 Second World War. After the German attack on Poland France declares war on Germany (Sept. 3rd 1939).

1940 Beginning of the German campaign in the west (May 10th), which leads to the collapse of the French army. Paris is occupied without a fight (June 14th). Armistice signed at Compiègne (June 22nd): France is divided into an occupied (northern and eastern France) and an unoccupied zone. The government of Marshal Pétain moves to Vichy (July 1st); end of the Third Republic. General de Gaulle forms a government in exile in London and continues the war along with Britain. Within France resistance groups are formed and carry on the fight against the German occupying forces and French collaborators.

1942 The Allies land in French North Africa (Nov.); German troops then march into the unoccupied parts of France.

1943 De Gaulle sets up the National Liberation Committee in Algiers, which is recognised by the Allies.

1944 The liberation of France begins with the Allied landings in Normandy (June 6th) and southern France (Aug. 15th), supported by armed French resistance groups. De Gaulle and the Allies enter Paris (Aug. 25th). A government of national unity is formed by de Gaulle and the Resistance (Aug.): Fourth Republic.

1944–1945 Trials of collaborators and supporters of the Vichy regime.

1945 France obtains a seat on the Security Council of the United Nations and occupation zones in Germany and Austria.

1946 De Gaulle (head of government since Nov. 1945) resigns. A new constitution comes into force (Dec. 24th): the Fourth Republic. The French colonial empire becomes the Union Française.
Economic crises (inflation, strikes), the growing strength of the Communists and the radical right and controversy over Algerian policy lead to frequent changes of government.

1946–1954 War in Indochina.

1947 De Gaulle founds the Rassemblement du Peuple Français (RPF), a political movement of the right.

1948 France receives aid under the Marshall Plan.

1949 France joins NATO and the Council of Europe.
The first World Peace Congress meets in Paris.

1954 War in Algeria.

1954–1956 Loss of Indochina, Tunisia, Morocco, French West Africa and French Equatorial Africa.

1956	France is involved, along with Britain and Israel, in the abortive Suez war. Gaullists and the army seize power in Algeria.
1957	France becomes a member of the European Iron and Steel Community, Western European Union, the European Economic Community and Euratom.
1958	Putsch in Algiers (May 13th). President Coty declares a state of national emergency and appoints de Gaulle prime minister with special powers. A new presidential-type constitution is approved in a national referendum: the Fifth Republic.
1959	As President of the Republic de Gaulle carries through a series of firm economic and financial measures. The Union Française becomes the Communauté Française, and the colonies are granted internal self-government or independence.
1960	First French atomic bomb exploded in the Sahara.
1962	The Evian Agreement grants Algeria independence. De Gaulle proposes a confederation of Western European states. Amendment of the constitution: the President of the Republic to be directly elected by popular vote.
1963	France gives diplomatic recognition to the People's Republic of China.
1966	France withdraws from NATO and builds up a national nuclear strike force, the *force de frappe* (later renamed the *force de dissuasion)*.
1968	Strong economic growth and social injustices lead to student unrest, particularly in Paris, and a general strike (May). The weakness of the French franc leads to an international currency crisis (Nov.).
1969	De Gaulle steps down from the Presidency and is succeeded by Georges Pompidou, who continues de Gaulle's foreign policy.
1971–1974	Two-tier exchange rates introduced in an attempt to resolve the world currency crisis. The parties of the left agree on a common programme for government. (The Union of the Left breaks up in 1977 and is not re-established until 1981.)
1974	Valéry Giscard d'Estaing becomes President of the Republic. The governments of Jacques Chirac and Raymond Barre (1974–1976 and 1976–1981) are supported in the National Assembly by a majority of Gaullists (who in 1976 combine to form the RPR) and parties of the Liberals, Centre and moderate Right (who in 1978 form an electoral coalition, the UDF).
from 1974	Steep increases in oil prices lead to a world-wide energy crisis and economic recession. Fall in imports and exports; increased unemployment, inflation. Statutory restrictions on the use of energy.
from 1975	Violence, particularly in Corsica, by pro-independence groups.
1976	France leaves the European "currency snake" and allows the franc to float. Domestic political tension (strikes and demonstrations).
1977	General strike against the government's economy programme (May 24th). Agreements on cooperation with the Soviet Union signed during a visit to Paris by the Soviet head of state, Mr Brezhnev (June 22nd). Violent demonstration by anti-nuclear protesters at Creys-Malville (July 31st).
1978	Heavy pollution of the northern coast of Brittany after the wreck of a giant oil tanker (Mar. 17th).

In a controversial military action French and Belgian troops clear rebel forces out of the copper province of Shaba (Katanga) in Zaire in order to permit the evacuation of Europeans.
Increasing resistance to Prime Minister Barre's stringent measures designed to secure stability (June).
Bomb attack on the Palace of Versailles by Breton separatists (June 26th).

1979 Fight against inflation and unemployment.
In consequence of the difficult position of the steel industry the government decides to close steel works; this leads to mass demonstrations in Paris (March).

1980 Taking of hostages by Corsican nationalists in Ajaccio (Jan.). Bomb attack on a Paris synagogue by supporters of the extreme right (four dead).
The Franco-British condominium of the New Hebrides becomes independent.

1981 Presidential election (May), won in the second ballot by François Mitterand, with 51.75% of the votes. Dissolution of the National Assembly and formation of an interim government led by Pierre Mauroy.
Parliamentary elections give the Socialists an absolute majority; Communists join the government. Reform programme: improvement of living and working conditions, abolition of the death penalty.
Nationalisation of the Usinor and Sacilor-Sollac steel groups.
Inauguration of the super-express train (TGV, *train à grande vitesse,* with a top speed of 260 km/160 miles an hour) between Paris and Lyons.

1982 New tax to relieve unemployment. Nationalisation of industrial concerns (5), banks (39) and holding companies (2). Comprehensive regionalisation programme. Wage and prices freeze.

1983 Celebration of the 20th anniversary of the Franco-German treaty of friendship.
Restriction of currency for foreign travel (2000 francs).
Franco-African summit in Vittel (including negotiations on Chad).

1984 Resignation of the Mauroy government. The government's economy programme (delays in development of social services, attempts to bring private schools into the national educational system) gives rise to domestic political tensions. The Communists leave the government. Laurent Fabius becomes prime minister.
New policies designed to achieve economies and the reduction of inflation.
The Alpine passes are blockaded by lorries in a protest against clearance procedures at the Italian frontier. Dispute with Spain over fishing rights in European Community waters.
Franco-German frontier agreement (abolition of controls on passenger and goods traffic).
Jacques Delors becomes President of the European Community.

1985 The French secret service explodes a bomb on the Greenpeace ship "Rainbow Warrior" in a New Zealand port.

1986 In a parliamentary election in March the ruling Socialist Party is defeated, giving the Right (RPR and UDF) a clear majority. For the first time France has a socialist President and a conservative prime minister (Jacques Chirac of the Gaullist RPR) and an opposition majority: "cohabitation". Immediate devaluation of the franc; liberalisation of currency controls and prices; planned reprivatisation of nationalised undertakings (41 banks, 2 holding companies, advertising, industrial and armaments firms, the Elf-Aquitaine oil corporation, television channels). Highest priority is given to the fight against inflation.

France and Britain sign an agreement on the construction of a rail tunnel under the Channel, due to be opened to traffic in 1993.
All foreigners (except nationals of European Community countries and Switzerland) required to have visas for entry to France.
The Cattenom nuclear reactor comes on stream.
Great demonstrations (Dec.) against proposals for university reform (increases in fees, tighter rules on admission). Social unrest over the government's inflation policy (Dec. 1986/Jan. 1989).

1987 Celebration of the thousandth anniversary of France as a nation.
In a referendum in New Caledonia the majority of the population vote to remain part of France.

1988 Mitterand is re-elected President (Apr./June) and appoints Michel Rocard prime minister. In a parliamentary election, brought forward to June, neither the Socialists, the Gaullists (the URC, Union du Rassemblement et du Centre) nor the parties of the centre gain an absolute majority.
Serious disturbances in New Caledonia, followed by military intervention by France. Political agreement between the pro-independence and "loyalist" parties on a ten-year period of transition followed by a referendum on independence.

1989 Two hundredth anniversary of the French Revolution.
Introduction of a statutory minimum income of 2000 francs, the *revenu minimum garanti.*

1991 Prime Minister Rocard resigns, and is succeeded by Edith Cresson, the first woman prime minister in France's history.

1992 The XVI Winter Olympics are held in Albertville and Savoy in February.

1993 Communal and regional elections are held in March, and Parliamentary elections in June.

Culture and Art

French Culture

More than in any other country the visitor to France, wherever he goes, will be confronted with the fact that culture and art have from time immemorial played a central role in life. Not only in Paris and the large towns but also in tiny villages and remote corners of the country evidence of an active cultural consciousness can be found. French art finds expression in the caves of south-western France, in the Romanesque churches of Burgundy and the cathedrals of the Ile de France, in the châteaux of the Loire valley and other regions of France, in countless museums and art galleries, and in literature, from the 15th century poet François Villon to André Gide, François Mauriac, Albert Camus, Saint-John Perse, Jean-Paul Sartre and André Simon, France's six Nobel Prize winners of the post-war period.

It is part of the accepted image of France that in this country culture and art are elements in the framework of life for a broad stratum of the population. The intellectual *homme de lettres* does not stand outside everyday life but is part of it. The artist is respected and honoured, not smiled at as a phenomenon out of the ordinary. The painting of the Fauves in the early 20th century, the architecture of Le Corbusier, a French-speaking Swiss, and the music of the Basque composer Maurice Ravel have exerted powerful influences on the art and culture of our day. Impressive as the artistic achievements of the past have been, France's contribution to the culture of the 20th century has been no less remarkable; and this is the result to some extent of the unspoken consensus of a whole people with its artists and thinkers – even when it does not always understand them at first sight.

Art

Any journey in France should therefore also be, in greater or lesser degree, a cultural journey. Often art forms a counterpoint to the landscape: one can be enjoyed without neglecting the other. It is clearly impossible in a visit of only a week or two to get even a cursory view of French art: it is a good idea, therefore, for visitors to limit their horizon, either to a particular region or to a particular field of interest. Even a visitor who limits himself to Burgundy cannot hope to cover the whole range and variety of Romanesque architecture. A pilgrim to the masters of modern painting would have to travel from the Pyrenees to Provence and visit numerous museums and galleries, large and small, to get a view of changing styles and schools. Gothic buildings, too, extend over the whole country from Amiens to Perpignan; and who is to say whether Quimper Cathedral is more important than the Palace of the Popes in Avignon, or vice versa? To get any real impression of French art and culture many visits to the country are required.

Prehistory and the Early Historical Period

Cave art

The roots of art, which in its early stages is bound up with religion and myth, reach far back into the past. The first evidences of French art are found in caves, in the form of naturalistic paintings and incised drawings of animals with which the men of the Palaeolithic era (*c.* 15,000 B.C.), known in France as the Magdalenian, hoped by magical means to gain power over their prey. In Périgord, in the valley of the Vézère and round the village of Les Eyzies-de-Tayac, are a number of caves with paintings and drawings of

this kind, the most important of which is the one at Lascaux, discovered in 1940 but now unfortunately closed because of damage to the paintings by algae; instead visitors must be content with a painstaking reproduction of the cave and its paintings. Other caves can still be visited, however: the Font-de-Gaume cave in the Vézère valley, the Grotte de Niaux near Tarascon-sur-Ariège, Pech-Merle near Cabrerets (east of Cahors), Cougnac (north of Gourdon), the Mas d'Azil (north-east of St-Girons). In the Grotte du Tuc d'Audoubert (also near St-Girons) two figures modelled in clay were found, and early examples of sculpture were found in caves near Montespan.

Stone structures

The famous stone-settings in Brittany, particularly round Carnac, date mainly from the Neolithic (7000 B.C.); they served as funerary monuments or for some religious purpose. A distinction is made in French terminology between dolmens (table-like megalithic structures, originally tomb chambers), menhirs (standing stones, with some cultic significance) and cromlechs (stone circles). In the Cévennes there is evidence of a megalithic culture in the form of stone-settings, erected by the Ligurians at the beginning of the metal age.

Ornamental art

Excavations at Bibracte and Vix in the Côte-d'Or have brought to light other artistic achievements – Celtic ornaments and Greek bronze and pottery vessels. Those interested in the art of the pre-Roman period in France should go to St-Germain-en-Laye, near Paris, to see the Musée des Antiquités Nationales in the 16th century château, which has works of art (including some replicas) of the prehistoric and early historical periods, as well as Gallic, Roman and Frankish antiquities.

The Roman heritage

Between the 2nd century B.C., when the Romans first penetrated into France by way of Massilia (Marseilles), and the great migrations of the 5th and 6th centuries A.D. the country was under Roman administration and under the influence of Roman culture, which left their mark on the architecture, the language and the people of France. Most of the surviving remains of Roman art and architecture are to be found in Provence, the Roman Provincia, but there are also notable remains in the Pyrenean foreland as well as farther north. Although the amphitheatres of Arles and Nîmes, the well-preserved theatre of Orange, the triumphal arches of Orange and St-Rémy and the temples of Nîmes and Vienne are well known, few visitors to France realise that there are also important Roman remains to be seen in Toulouse, Besançon, Reims and Bordeaux. The most visited Roman sites are still Arles, Nîmes, Orange and the Pont du Gard. Smaller objects are displayed in many museums.

Museums and collections

The leading French museum is, of course, the Louvre in Paris, which possesses a fine collection of Roman antiquities. There are other important museums with Roman material at Bordeaux, Toulouse, Arles, Nîmes and Vienne. The Musée des Beaux Arts in Lyons has sculpture and mosaics. There are also numerous regional and local museums containing finds from the five centuries of Roman occupation. The closeness of past and present is demonstrated by the fact that the old Roman baths, partly preserved, at Aix-les-Bains (between Geneva and Grenoble) and Plombières (Vosges) are still in use.

Carolingian Art

Influence of Christianity

With the end of the Roman period art in France came under Christian influences, which made their way into the country from Italy and led to the building of the first churches in Lyons and Vienne. Often pagan temples were converted into Christian churches: a typical example of this is at Nîmes. Some of the early churches had a crypt, which housed the relics of

◀ *Roman triumphal arch, Orange*

the saint to whom the church was dedicated but also served other purposes (a meeting-place for the community, a mausoleum). Examples of such crypts dating from the 7th century can be seen in Jouarre Abbey, near Metz, and the church of St-Laurent in Grenoble. Another important feature of these early churches was the baptistery, in which new Christians confessed their faith; the church of St-Jean in Poitiers has a late 7th century example. During this period, too, increased importance was given to the area in a church where the nave and transepts met at the crossing, which now became the spiritual and religious centre of the church, separating the most sacred area from the body of the church. Although the church at Vignory (on the Marne) was consecrated only in 1052 and thus belongs to a later period, it gives a very clear idea of this development. It was bound up with the emphasis given to the longitudinal axis of the church – the nave, leading to the altar – which was, as it were, made narrower by the use of piers or walls to separate the aisles. Vignory is a characteristic example of this, as are the churches at Tournus and Nevers.

Monasteries

Although important monasteries were founded during the Carolingian period (from the middle of the 8th to the end of the 9th century), the original buildings were replaced in later centuries by new construction, so that only fragmentary remains of the original structure can be detected by a trained eye. Nevertheless the church of St-Germigny-des-Prés, near Orléans, still shows, in spite of later rebuilding, how the original cruciform church (consecrated in 806) was planned. In the dome of the choir chapel are old mosaics depicting angels bearing the Ark of the Covenant – an example of Carolingian wall decoration going beyond the typical interlace ornament. Although the church of St-Pierre-aux-Nonnains ranks as the oldest French church (probably 7th century) it survived only in a state of ruin and was completely rebuilt in the Gothic period.

Manuscripts

Manuscripts of this period are mostly to be seen in the Bibliothèque Nationale in Paris.

Romanesque

Characteristics

Between the early 11th century and the middle of the 12th the Romanesque style of church architecture came into being, with marked regional differences. The style is known as Romanesque because its new features, such as the twin-towered west front and the stepped choir or ring of chapels, were based on Roman, late antique or Byzantine and eastern traditions. Nevertheless Romanesque architecture amounted to a new creation, expressed in the planning of space, the importance given to the façades and the disposition of doorways, which developed a remarkable range of variations in France.

Romanesque was the first truly monumental style since the architecture of antiquity, a style in which the Christian West achieved an architectural unity. Later Romanesque art also contrived to combine this monumentality with a whole range of decoration, in the form of friezes on walls, doorways and windows and an extraordinary variety of ornament on the capitals of columns. Although essentially a religious style, Romanesque contains many secular elements.

Architecture

Characteristic features of Romanesque churches are barrel, groin or ribbed vaulting, round domes (sometimes the central feature of a circular building) and round-headed arches, with the dome over the crossing as the central point of the church. They have a basically cubic structure, soaring up in a succession of stages into a kind of pyramidal form. In southern France the churches (for example the domed churches of Aquitaine) remain closer to late antique and Roman/Byzantine traditions, while in the north the archaic character of the architecture – reflecting Burgundian, Frankish and Norman influences – and the conflict between Christianity

Sainte Foy of Conques

The Virgin of Orcival

and late antique spiritualisation express very strikingly the double aspect of the style.

Burgundy

The Romanesque style thus did not develop in the same way throughout France. Its finest flowering, however, is to be found in Burgundy. Here the twofold nature of medieval art is expressed to perfection: monkish asceticism and Christian renunciation of the world in their most refined forms side by side with the assertion of an imperious existence, a well regulated way of life and physical strength. These characteristics gave the Cluniacs their preponderant authority. In Burgundy the Romanesque style is expressed in "the rigid centralisation of the structure round the crossing tower, the chapels grouped round the choir, the vertical and longitudinal form of the aisles, the uniform articulation of the walls and the strict linking of the whole structure by the barrel vaulting" (Hamann).

Stylistic variety

The variations in the Romanesque style in different parts of France are less evident in the great churches, which learn from one another and thus show closer resemblances. Thus the churches of St-Etienne and Ste-Trinité in Caen, St-Sernin in Toulouse, St-Gilles in Provence and Ste-Foy in Conques show a community of style, with supra-regional, "inter-provincial" features. Small country churches, on the other hand, reveal more of the life and strivings of the men and artists who created them.

Normandy

The strict articulation of the walls with their galleries and engaged columns found in the Romanesque churches of Normandy (St-Etienne, Caen) already points towards Gothic. To the south, in the Poitiers area, the hall-church developed, still preserving all the Romanesque architectural forms but with nave and aisles of the same height.

Languedoc Périgord

In Languedoc and Périgord, centred on Périgueux, Byzantine origins are evident. St-Front in Périgueux, though much altered in the 19th century, is a faithful imitation of St Mark's in Venice, which itself was modelled on the church of the Holy Apostles in Constantinople; the succession of domes creates something of the effect of a tent. Angoulême Cathedral forms a kind of transition: the centralised layout reappears in the disposition of the domes from west to east, with a dome in front of the choir which was evidently seen as the central feature.

Provence

Still farther south, in Provence, the sacred area under the dome gives place to a meeting-house for the community which is almost secular in feeling – Rome rather than Byzantium. A good example is the 12th century chapel of St-Gabriel near St-Rémy (north of Fontvieille).

Sculpture

The sense of plastic form expressed in the architecture also led to a revival in the art of sculpture. Small-scale sculpture was predominant: the capitals of columns became a riot of tiny human and animal figures, fabulous creatures and plants modelled in almost full relief. Some of the finest work of the period is seen in the tympana of doorways and in the draped figures flanking them. In these figures in particular – which at St-Denis and Chartres almost take on the form of columns – France prepared the way for Gothic sculpture.

Burgundy

In Burgundy the elongated animal and human figures give expression to ideas about virtue and vice, heaven and hell, while the mystical representations of the Last Judgment, brotherly community and a merciful God reflect a spiritual movement.

Southern France

In southern France the sculptural ornament on the façades of churches shows a preference for figures of Christ and his disciples. A typical transitional form is seen at Moissac, where Burgundian influence is more strongly evident. Here the Last Judgment shows only Christ with the Elders of the Apocalypse, standing as a King above the kings. In Poitou and Languedoc Christ's Ascension becomes the dominant theme on church façades. The archaic sculpture of southern France, as seen for example in Toulouse, is more closely related to the art of antiquity. This is seen still more clearly in Provence. The façade of St-Gilles, undoubtedly the finest in southern France, renounces the miraculous: it tells a story, in which the Apostles come closer to the spectator and the miracle of the Ascension is less important than the narrative of the Passion.

Cluny

The Romanesque period in France was also the period of the Cluniac reform. The church built by Abbot Majolus in the second half of the 10th century, which was the model for a smaller counterpart in Normandy (Bernay), departs from the previous basilican form. The transept is emphasised and there is a tower over the crossing; the aisles are continued eastward into the side chapels round the choir; there is no crypt; at the west end the atrium becomes a porch.
Cluny was the model for the churches of Paray-le-Monial, La Charité and Fleury (St-Benoît) and also for churches in Normandy (for example, Jumièges). Cluny itself, demolished after the French Revolution, was the most magnificent as well as the largest Romanesque church in France.

Cistercian architecture

In Burgundy the Cistercians, with St Bernard of Clairvaux, were also active builders. Their churches were cruciform in plan, without towers and without decoration. The style can be seen in the monasteries of Fontenay and Pontigny.
Other glories of Romanesque architecture are the numerous cloisters, among the finest of which is St-Trophime in Arles.

Painting

The predominant form of painting in the Romanesque period was wall painting. The churches were decorated by itinerant painters with scenes from the Old and New Testament and the legends of saints. The church of St-Savin-sur-Gartempe, near Poitiers, begun about 1080, has its walls and barrel-vaulted ceiling covered with frescoes of grest expressiveness but strict stylisation.

A scene from the Bayeux tapestry

Impressive ruins: Jumièges

Notre-Dame, Paris

The finest examples of stained glass are to be seen in the cathedrals of Le Mans, St-Pierre in Poitiers, Angers, St-Denis and – last, but certainly not least – Chartres. The mystical illumination provided by the carefully articulated stained glass windows was also to be characteristic of the new stylistic language of Gothic.
Related to painting are the arts of tapestry and embroidery, as in the famous Bayeux Tapestry (in fact a work of embroidery).

Chartres

Although Chartres Cathedral is commonly regarded as one of the great achievements of Gothic architecture, it also retains some Romanesque features. With the technical resources available to the Middle Ages the building of churches and cathedrals might take many years or even centuries; and a church begun in the Romanesque period might well be still under construction in a later period when new forms and features had come into fashion. At Chartres the west doorway was built in 1145 in pure Romanesque style, salvaged from the ruins when the cathedral was burned down in 1194 and incorporated in the new Gothic structure begun in 1195. The figures flanking the doorway are stiff but the heads express life and individuality; the figures in the tympanum are similar in style. Here, living happily together, are Gothic architecture and Romanesque sculpture.

Gothic

Although the term Gothic is now purely descriptive, it was originally used by Italian artists (probably Raphael in particular) as an abusive description of an incomprehensible new style which they compared to the barbaric work of the Goths. Indeed, it was believed until the 17th and 18th centuries that the Gothic style had been created by the Goths and then imported into France.

Origins

The first Early Gothic building is the abbey of St-Denis in the Ile de France, and French art historians like to refer to this style, developed in northern France before 1150, as the "Style français". For almost four centuries the Gothic style dominated church architecture in France, reaching its peak in the 13th century, when most of the great Gothic cathedrals (Chartres, Reims, Amiens, Beauvais, the Ste-Chapelle in Paris) were built.
As these names indicate, Gothic architecture was predominant especially in northern France, though it also produced the cathedrals of Clermont-Ferrand, Albi and Narbonne. In the south there was a preponderance of fortress-like structures, the best examples of which are at Carcassonne, Avignon (Palace of the Popes) and Aigues-Mortes.
Burgundy and Champagne also have important Gothic churches (Dijon, Nevers, Auxerre, Semur-en-Auxois, Troyes).
In Anjou, under the influence of the Plantagenets, Gothic architecture took a particular form. Here the Romanesque dome of Byzantine origin was combined with ribbed vaulting, as in Angers Cathedral. Poitiers Cathedral and churches in Périgord, the Vendée and Limousin show the same influence.

Flamboyant style

The Late Gothic of the 15th and 16th centuries is also known as the Flamboyant style after its profusion of flame-shaped ornament.

Gothic style

While the Romanesque style was still under the influence of ancient models, Gothic broke completely with the past and created a new and logically conceived structural system. There was now a new feeling for space: the architectural masses were no longer earthbound but soared upwards.
The flowering of architecture, sculpture and painting in the Middle Ages would have been impossible without the profound piety of the men and women of the period, which led towns and villages all over France to incur the enormous cost of building their churches and cathedrals. It has been estimated that the building of Notre-Dame in Paris cost the equivalent of

120 million gold francs – a horrendous sum in view of the wage levels of the time, particularly when it is remembered that the whole population, from nobleman to peasant, contributed personally to the work (as we know, for example, from accounts of the building of Chartres Cathedral).

Characteristics

The mysticism which developed as a reaction against dogmatic scholasticism led to a upward striving towards the infinite, the life hereafter, and this striving was reflected in the architecture of churches. The architectural means of achieving this upward movement were provided by four basic elements: the pointed arch, groin vaulting, buttresses and the triple doorways of the façade. The combination of these elements achieved a lightness of structure unattainable in Romanesque architecture. The groin vaulting directed all the stresses outwards; the mass of the building and its supports were now quite distinct from one another in the eyes of the beholder, as they had not been in the buildings of antiquity and their derivatives. The vaulting in the interior of the church now directed the eye ever upwards (in the unfinished Beauvais Cathedral to a height of almost 50 metres/165 ft), whereas in the domed Romanesque church the eye was drawn round and down.

This produced an entirely different impact, as the cubic monumentality of Romanesque gave place to the active upward movement of Gothic. There were now two towers rather than one, enclosing a central bay in which was the doorway. The whole of the west front became in effect a monumental entrance portal, with the central doorway into the nave and the flanking doorways into the aisles forming a unit. In order to direct the eye upwards, into the world beyond, the church itself rose out of the huddle of low houses surrounding it. It was by deliberate intention that the view of the church from the streets around it was blocked. The faithful were not to see it as a two-dimensional building on the ground but as a line soaring upwards towards heaven. Although later clearances of encroaching buildings may have improved the view of the medieval cathedrals they have falsified the effect originally intended.

The walls of Gothic churches were no longer solid areas of masonry. The new building techniques made it possible to replace them by windows of brilliantly coloured glass, creating new light effects in the interior which had an almost magical impact. The most striking examples of this were the rose windows on the west front which became one of the regular characteristics of the style.

Development of Gothic

During the centuries of predominance of Gothic the style underwent changes – not always for the better. In France four main phases can be distinguished.

Early Gothic

The first period saw the building of the magnificent cathedrals of Laon, Paris, Amiens, Reims, Chartres, Bourges, Strasbourg and Beauvais, which represent a high point of Gothic architecture. This period includes Early Gothic (from the second half of the 12th century, with features transitional between Romanesque and Gothic, to the first quarter of the 13th) and High Gothic (to the end of the 13th century), which strove for an impression of lightness and space, producing churches whose successive levels draw the observer's eye steadily upward.

High Gothic

In the 14th century the cathedrals begun earlier were completed, in what is known as the Rayonnant style. This development continued in the 15th century; pillars gave place to columns, which merged into the arches without an intermediate capital. During the 16th century the interior of the church was conceived as a single picturesque whole, and accordingly the hall-church was preferred to the basilican type. Characteristic of Late Gothic is the Flamboyant style with its intricately patterned flame-like tracery. The church at Brou (near Bourg-en-Bresse), the Palais de Justice of Rouen, the choir of Albi Cathedral and the north and south fronts of Senlis, Beauvais, Sens and Limoges cathedrals belong to this fourth phase.

Rayonnant

Late Gothic

Town development

During the Gothic period towns began to be seen as an architectural whole. Their development reflected the growing self-confidence of the rising middle class.
In southern France some medieval towns (Aigues-Mortes, Carcassonne) have survived almost unscathed, though restored in later centuries. They demonstrate that Gothic architecture could give life to secular as well as religious buildings. Many examples of such buildings have survived – castles, town halls, law courts, the Hôtel-Dieu in Beaune and many houses built by prosperous citizens.

Sculpture

The doorways of the churches are given additional importance by rows of sculptured figures very different from those of the Romanesque period. Although they are still linked with the architecture they are carved fully in the round. Female figures play a more prominent part than before, as can be seen, for example, at Reims, Paris and Amiens. The Virgin becomes a lady, smiling and dignified. Unfortunately the figures on Notre-Dame in Paris were destroyed during the Revolution (fragments in the Cluny Museum), but other doorways of this type with a full complement of figures can be seen at Amiens, Bourges, Auxerre, Le Mans, Rouen and – though dating from the early 15th century, after the High Gothic period – Strasbourg. The new style is very evident in Chartres Cathedral, where the Gothic doorways in the transepts (1200 onwards) contrast sharply with the severe, almost stiff, Romanesque figures on the west front. The Gothic figures reflect an inner life, and the heads and limbs are gracefully disposed. The greatest sculptor of the Late Gothic period was a Breton, Michel Colombe, whose masterpiece is the tomb of Duke François II of Brittany and his wife in Nantes Cathedral. Also very fine, but on a smaller scale, are the ivory carving and goldsmith's work of the period, of which there are examples in all the larger museums and in church treasuries.

Chartres

Thanks to its complete preservation and its wonderful stained glass, Chartres Cathedral – which ranks with Strasbourg Cathedral as the most visited of the great churches of France – gives the best general impression of the characteristics of French Gothic. This is true both of the exterior, with its sculpture and its transepts, and the richly articulated interior with its three-aisled nave, five-aisled choir and girdle of chapels, all of which had a far-reaching influence on French and German architecture of the 12th and 13th centuries.

Painting

Visitors interested in the Gothic influence on painting might feel a certain disappointment in France were it not for the altar paintings of the 15th century (which can be seen in the Louvre and in Beaune) and the splendid examples of book illumination. This is found mainly in the Books of Hours (prayer-books) which were particularly popular in the 14th and 15th centuries, decorated by Dutch masters working in the spirit of French Gothic. Examples are to be seen in the Bibliothèque Nationale in Paris and the Musée Condé in Chantilly.
The Gothic period also produced fine work in the form of tapestries. There are magnificent examples – showing a neglect of perspective but nevertheless achieving astonishing realism – in the Louvre and at Angers ("Tenture de l'Apocalypse", 14th c.).

Renaissance

Architecture

In France the "rebirth" of antiquity in the 16th century, the age of humanism, the Reformation and the great discoveries which marked the beginning of the modern world, found its principal expression not in churches but in secular buildings, particularly in châteaux. Francis I and his sister Margaret of Angoulême, later queen of Navarre, were great patrons of the arts. Francis had his tomb in St-Denis designed by Philibert de l'Orme in the form of a Roman triumphal arch; he completed the châteaux of Chaumont, Langeais and Amboise, which had been begun in the reign of Charles VIII,

St-Eustache, Paris's first Renaissance church

and built those of Châteaudun, Chenonceaux, Blois (with its famous spiral staircase), Chambord and Azay-le-Rideau; and he attracted foreign artists, in particular Leonardo da Vinci, to his court. Church building declined in importance compared with secular building, and kept aloof from the new trend.

Characteristics

The finest examples of the new style are the châteaux in the Loire valley with their clear lines and simple geometrical forms. In the architecture of the Renaissance the pointed arch gives place to the round-headed or basket arch, groin vaulting to coffered ceilings. Whereas the castles of the early medieval period were designed for defensive strength and were often of massive bulk (like the keeps of Langeais, Montrichard, Montbazon and Beaugency), in the Gothic period the towers took on rounder forms and the style of building gradually became less austere. In the 16th century there was a major change, with a reversion to ancient models (as described, for example by Vitruvius). The dominant influence of Italy, which provided architectural models (e.g. in the form of staircases), gave a stimulus to the creation of specifically French traditions and the emergence of a new national consciousness.

Louvre

Most of the Renaissance châteaux were laid out round a rectangular courtyard and had steeply pitched roofs and pavilions (towers) at the ends of the wings. The architects responsible for these châteaux set out to alter the Italian model and give their buildings a distinctive character of their own. One of the great works of the Renaissance is Pierre Lescot's new Louvre, much altered though it was in the course of the following two centuries. The building of the Louvre began in 1546 with the wing facing the Seine and the adjoining half-wing at the west end, and the work was continued by Henry II, his widow Catherine de Médicis, Henry IV and Louis XIII.
Around Paris are two other Renaissance châteaux, St-Germain-en-Laye and Fontainebleau. On a more modest scale there is the Place des Vosges in Paris, a square built to a uniform design in the reign of Henry IV.

Versailles illuminated

Classicism

Louis XIV

While in Italy and Germany the architectural development was from Renaissance to Baroque, France preferred the stricter forms of neo-classical architecture. This did not, however, involve a mere imitation of ancient models, and motifs from classical antiquity were used merely as supplements to the architecture. A typical example is the main front of the Louvre. For this project Louis XIV employed Bernini, the leading European architect of the day, who had left a decisive mark on the Baroque townscape of Rome; but his intention of completing the Louvre in Roman Baroque style did not appeal to Louis, and it was completed in 1670 with a massive colonnade designed by Claude Perrault, a doctor by profession. The architectural style of late antiquity, rediscovered by Palladio, had won the day.

Rococo

In Louis XIV's later years and in the reign of Louis XV the Rococo style developed in reaction against the official classical style. This was the preferred decorative style of the noble families of Paris, characterised by asymmetrical shell-like ornament. From France it spread all over Europe until displaced about 1765 by the Louis XVI style, which returned to ancient models.

Versailles

The construction of the palace of Versailles had begun in 1626, in the reign of Louis XIII, but at first had made slow progress. Louis XIV provided the impetus for its enlargement, by the addition of side and transverse wings, to the considerable length of 580 m/635 yds. From the outside, with the chapel and the Hall of Mirrors, the palace still has a classical appearance; in the other rooms Charles le Brun gave free rein to his passion for decoration; the total effect was completed by the gardens laid out by Le Notre. The result was a magnificent palace which was imitated by rulers all over Europe.

The Rococo style finds its most characteristic expression in the Cabinet du Conseil. The walls are covered with elegant tracery, alternating with wreaths and garlands, so that the ceilings seem to bear heavily down on the apparent lightness of the walls.

The culmination of French Rococo is seen in the Hôtel de Soubise in Paris with its magnificent circular hall, which seems both enclosed and open at the same time, with decorative and representational painting contributing to the total effect.

Painting

The rise of the middle classes and the falling off in the artists' commitment to the nobility and the church led to a revaluation of what had been regarded as inferior forms of art, like the genre painting in which Watteau mirrored the life of his time; the work of Boucher, who painted Madame de Pompadour and designed beautiful tapestries; and the paintings of Nicolas Poussin, the leading painter in a classical style which pointed the way towards the pastoral scenes of the Rococo period.

Return to the Past

French art was torn between classicism and romanticism until well into the 19th century. An attempt was made to achieve new artistic forms by a return to the classical ideas which had been repressed during the Rococo period. Characteristic of this neo-classical style are colonnaded façades and triumphal arches in the antique manner.

Architecture

The architects of the Revolutionary period (C.-N. Ledoux, E.-L. Boulée) sought to return to the severer style of antiquity, to pure geometry, to cubes, balls and cones. The disturbed conditions of Napoleon's reign, however, were not favourable to the development of this architecture.

Empire

The Empire style was the art of the Napoleonic period. Although the style is mainly identified with furniture and interior decoration it has also left its mark on Paris in a number of buildings: the Arc de Triomphe de l'Etoile (designed by Chalgrin), the smaller Arc de Triomphe du Carrousel (by Percier and Fontaine) in the outer courtyard of the Louvre, the church of the Madeleine and the Panthéon.

Romantic art

The revival of classicism was accompanied by a Romantic movement which enthusiastically favoured the Gothic style, now regarded as a French creation. This had the rather dubious consequences that neo-Gothic buildings began to be erected from the turn of the century onwards, none of which were of any merit, and that genuine Gothic buildings suffered from unsatisfactory restorations or extensions. The glories of the past, genuinely French though they had been, could not be brought back to life.

Painting

The most fertile achievements of this period were in painting. Jacques-Louis David, the founder and leading member of the French classical school, expressed the ideas of the French Revolution in subjects taken from classical antiquity, though he abandoned his classical austerity in his monumental representation of Napoleon's coronation. He was also a portrait painter of outstanding quality. His pupil Jean-Dominique Ingres surpassed him in posthumous fame, as the Ingres Museum in his home town of Montauban suggests. He painted mythological and religious subjects and also portraits of women, which place him alongside the great masters.
The monumental classical style was given a fresh lease of life by the frescoes of Puvis de Chavannes, most notably in the Panthéon in Paris; his work can also be seen in various museums.
French painting too had a Romantic school. Romantic painting was brought to France by Goya after his expulsion from Spain; but the principal representative of the Romantic school in the first half of the 19th century was Eugène Delacroix, whose work is partly explained by his own remark that true antiquity is to be looked for among the Arabs. He followed Ingres in depicting great events, but also went in for genre painting. He took up a stance against classicism and saw himself as a practitioner of naturalism;

Claude Monet, "Argenteuil"

August Renoir, "Ball at the Moulin de la Galette"

but the nature he depicted was classical in spirit, and what he represented was beauty of costume rather than nature itself.
As well as Ingres there was Honoré Daumier, who achieved world fame as a caricaturist but was also a considerable painter.

Transition to the Modern World

Architecture

From the end of the classical period to the beginning of the 20th century architecture was content to imitate older styles. This "Historicism" produced Charles Garnier's sumptuous Paris Opéra in Renaissance style, and the neo-Byzantine Sacré-Cœur in Montmartre.
During the Second Empire the town-planning ideas of Haussmann produced great changes in Paris. Much of the old city was destroyed and replaced by broad boulevards, spacious squares and parks. Around the middle of the 19th century France took over the techniques of building in iron and steel from Britain and developed them further. Notable examples of this are the Bibliothèque Ste-Geneviève and the Eiffel Tower.

Sculpture

In the field of sculpture two names stand out above all others: those of Auguste Rodin and Aristide Maillol, two artists whose work overlapped from the 19th into the 20th century.
Rodin, whose work can be seen in the museum in Paris which bears his name, is one of the truly great figures in French art. It has been said of him that he is the only 19th century master who can be set beside Michelangelo. Maillol, who survived Rodin by 27 years, achieved a new form of classicism in his figures of women.

Painting

French painting was a dominant influence on European and world art in the 19th century. The Romantic period gave place to a new realism, and Camille Corot's landscapes and portraits of young girls formed a link between the 18th and 19th centuries. Daumier had already discovered a new subject, the life of ordinary people; particularly famous was his "Washerwoman". Jean-François Millet followed a similar course with his "Man with a Hoe", "Gleaners" and "Winnower". Gustave Courbet, the leading representative of the French realist school, painted his "Stonebreakers" in 1851. All this work mirrored the age, with themes that were totally French. They gave expression to social concern, often depicting the poorest of the poor. Colouring and mood, however, were usually determined by the light in the painter's studio.

Photography

Corot, Millet and Courbet remained attached to a form of realism which it was left to the following generation to transcend. In 1837 Daguerre had invented photography, and the development of the new art, which continued throughout the 19th century and into the 20th, confronted painters with completely new assumptions and new possibilities. Pure representation could now be achieved by photography: it was for the painter to contribute emphasis and interpretation.

Impressionism

This was the task of the next generation of French painters. Edouard Manet, an observant practitioner of naturalism, developed the symbolic value of objects and the application of colour. Edgar Degas went one stage farther: although originally a follower of Ingres, he later joined the Impressionists. Impressionism was inspired by a soberly realist view of the world. Subjects taken from everyday life were interpreted as a subjective perception, an "impression", with particular effects of light and colour. Characteristic members of this school were Claude Monet, Camille Pissarro and Alfred Sisley, together with Pierre Bonnard and Edouard Vuillard.
Other painters close to the Impressionists included Auguste Renoir, Paul Cézanne, Vincent van Gogh and Henri de Toulouse-Lautrec, the painter of the *vie de Bohème* and an influential practitioner of the art of the poster; a collection of his works can be seen in Albi.

Paul Cézanne, "L'Estaque"

Pointillism and Neo-impressionism

While the Impressionists were still active a new school of painting came to the fore in which representational forms became more abstract, with the disintegration and application of colour in accordance with a new scientific theory. Pissarro, who, like Sisley, concentrated on landscapes, had begun to apply paint in small dots of colour, and this technique was carried further by Georges Seurat and Paul Signac under the name of Pointillism (from *point* = "dot"). The "impression" was now created by the interplay of a myriad coloured dots.

The Nabis

A small group of painters known as the Nabis (in Hebrew "Prophets") reacted against these views, painting in flat, pure colours and attaching importance to subject-matter. The leader of the group was Paul Sérusier, and other members included Pierre Bonnard and Edouard Vuillard.
Soon a new generation of artists came forward, who sought to break even more radically with the past. The Symbolists, among whom were Paul Gauguin, Gustave Doré and Gustave Moreau, dealt with irrational themes and painted fantastic visions with strong contrasts of light and shade.
Paul Cézanne achieved a very individual presentation of his subjects and created a new reality in his portraits, landscapes and still lifes through his identification of theme and colour. He was a powerful influence on modern art and particularly on Gauguin, in whose paintings colour was even more dominant. His work, matured during his stay in the South Seas, left a decisive mark on Expressionism. The townscapes and landscapes of Vincent van Gogh, who stood close to Gauguin, take their appeal from their radiant colours.

Musée d'Orsay

The works of the French Impressionists are well represented in the Musée d'Orsay in Paris.

Jean Tinguely and Niki de Saint-Phalle, Igor Stravinsky Fountain, Paris

Twentieth Century Art

Painting

At the beginning of the 20th century two fundamental innovations in representational technique were introduced by the "Fauves" with their expressive use of colour and, even more notably, the Cubists with their analytical and symbolic depiction of objects. The starting-point of contemporary art was marked by the paintings exhibited at the Paris Salon d'Automne in 1908 by a group of artists to whom an art critic gave the name of the Fauves ("wild beasts").

The Fauves

The members of the group – who were strongly influenced by Gauguin and Van Gogh – included Matisse, Rouault, Vlaminck, Derain, Dufy and Braque. Common to them all was a style which laid the main emphasis on pure colour in reproducing the "impression" made by their subjects. Matisse was the central and most creative figure of the movement. Although as a stylistic movement it lasted only a very short time it exerted considerable influence, particularly on German Expressionism.

Cubism

The Spanish painter, sculptor, graphic artist and potter Pablo Picasso, a Frenchman by choice, is recognised as the most important artist of the modern age, a powerful influence for more than eight decades on the art of our century. With his epoch-making work, the "Demoiselles d'Avignon" (1907), he laid the foundation which enabled him, along with Georges Braque, to found the Cubist movement, to which Juan Gris and, for a time, Fernand Léger later belonged.

Surrealism

Surrealism, which was originally initiated by writers (André Breton, Guillaume Apollinaire) and took over many ideas from Dadaism, rapidly developed into an international movement and has remained influential to the present day. In contrast to the anarchy of Dadaism, however, Surrealism is based on certain principles. The Surrealists' aim is to explore hitherto untouched regions of the unconscious, which they believe is revealed in dreams and in automatism. The most important exponents of Surrealism were Francis Picabia, Marcel Duchamp, André Masson, Yves Tanguy, Jean Arp, René Magritte, Max Ernst, Salvador Dali and Joan Miró.

Paris as an art centre

From 1924 onwards, with many foreign artists living and working in the city, Paris became the art capital of the world, the centre of the Surrealist and Constructivist movements and, from 1931, of the "Abstraction-Création" group, which after 1945 established itself as the Informal Art movement, paving the way for the development of Op Art. Around 1950 the Ecole de Paris became the leading exponents of Informal Art, and in particular of Tachisme.

Nouveau Réalisme

The group known as Nouveau Réalisme was founded in 1960 as a counter-movement to Informal Art. In many respects it can be seen as paralleling the British and American Pop Art movement. Its common feature was a new attitude to reality (Y. Klein, B. Vautier). Commonplace everyday objects like watches and spoons replaced canvas, paint and paint-brushes (Arman, César). Art and life were to be brought together again (action painting).

The Eighties

In the 1980s a group known as "Figuration Libre" or as Neo-Expressionism came to the fore (Robert Combas, Hervé di Rosa, J.-C. Blais). All the trends of the eighties, however, are reflected in the work of Le Gac, Boltanski and D. Buren (Place du Palais-Royal, Paris).

Museums and galleries

All over France visitors will find museums and galleries displaying interesting work by contemporary artists, from the little Musée de l'Art Moderne in Céret by way of museums in St-Etienne, Bordeaux and many other towns to the Musée d'Art Moderne in Paris.
The most important displays of 20th century art in Paris are in the Musée d'Art Moderne (the Cubists, the Fauves, the Ecole de Paris), the Musée Picasso (drawings, prints, ceramics, collages, reliefs, sculpture and paintings from all Picasso's different periods) and the Musée National d'Art Moderne (Musée d'Orsay), in which all the 20th century schools are well represented.
At present there are 186 new museums under construction in France, reflecting the efforts at present being devoted to expanding France's museum resources.

Architecture

After the First World War modern building methods, using glass, steel and concrete, increasingly came into use, with widespread application of concrete- and steel-framed construction, man-made materials, prefabrication and standardisation.
Tony Garnier produced epoch-making designs for industrial buildings, particularly in Lyons, and this development was carried on by Auguste Perret (Théâtre des Champs-Elysées, Paris; reconstruction of Le Havre) and Eugène Freyssinet (bridges, airship hangars).
The dominant figure in world architecture was Le Corbusier (born Charles-Edouard Jeanneret), from French-speaking Switzerland, who after the First World War, together with Amédée Ozenfant, founded a much respected review, "L'Esprit Nouveau". His constructional system, based on a limited number of supports, made bearing and enclosing walls unnecessary and allowed great freedom in planning. Such buildings as his pilgrimage chapel at Ronchamp, the "Cité Radieuse" complex of flats in Marseilles and the miners' town of Firminy near St-Etienne exemplify his very individual plastic architectural style and were much imitated.

New towns

Modern developments like the Grande Motte holiday centre on the Languedoc coast with its challenging series of pyramids illustrate the quest for new architectural forms to meet contemporary requirements, and the building of "new towns" round Paris which began in the mid sixties gave a fresh impetus to government policies on town development. Examples of these are La Défense on the western outskirts of Paris and the Galerie des

The favourite genres were short verse tales and animal fables. Some of these works were satirical, others moralising; some were joyously secular, others were religious.
The "Roman de la Rose", the first part of which was written in the first half of the 13th century and the second part about 1275-1280, remained popular into the 16th century. The (unfinished) first part is still inspired by the ideal of courtly love, while the second part takes a very much more realistic view of love and suggests that men's actions should be governed by reason.
In the 14th and 15th century poetical forms such as the ballade were popular. One of the great practitioners of the ballade was François Villon, author of cynical but shatteringly honest poems inspired by his adventurous and disreputable life. In his "Petit Testament" (1456) and "Grand Testament" (1461) he strikes a new lyrical note, reflecting the ups and downs of existence, joy in life and fear of death, all ruthlessly displayed. His themes are love, mortality and death.

Modern French literature

The turn of the 15th and 16th centuries was also the turning-point between the Middle Ages and modern times. First the writers of classical antiquity were rediscovered and translated into French, and then the voyages of discovery and the invention of printing led to a revision of traditional views and provided means for the diffusion of new ideas.
Under the influence of the Italian Renaissance the first French sonnets were written. In "Gargantua" and "Pantagruel" François Rabelais successfully combined medieval traditions of story-telling with the ideas of humanism.

Joachim du Bellay

In his "Défense et illustration de la langue française" (1549), which became the manifesto of the group of poets known as the Pléiade, Joachim du Bellay gave the French language new self-respect and confidence. He argued that it could be developed into a poetical instrument worthy to stand beside Italian and the classical languages by borrowing from Latin and Greek and creating new words to meet its needs.

Montaigne

Between 1580 and 1590 Michel de Montaigne created a new and independent literary form with his "Essays" on a wide range of personal, moral and philosophical themes. Even in our own time his relativist and sceptical philosophy has lost none of its relevance.

The century of classicism

A turning-point in French literature came when François de Malherbe was summoned to the court in 1605. He rejected the ideas of the Pléiade, the use of foreign words, dialectal expressions and Latinisms, and recommended instead *le bon usage,* logic, clarity and discipline, laying down a set of rules based on reason which thereafter governed the classical theatre.

The salons

The salons of the Marquise de Rambouillet and Mademoiselle de Scudéry now became influential in promoting polite manners and a culture which became steadily more refined. They evolved an affected manner of speaking, full of metaphors and circumlocutions, which was caricatured by Molière in his "Précieuses ridicules".

Académie Française

The French Academy was founded by Richelieu in 1635, with the prime task of formulating rules for the French language.
In 1674 Boileau's "Art poétique" prescribed the "three unities" (of time, place and action) for classical French drama, the observance of which was strictly monitored by the Academy. Linguistic guidelines were laid down by Claude Fabre Vaugelas in his "Remarques sur la langue française" (1647), setting up the language of the court and the style of good authors as the models which must be followed.

Corneille, Racine, Molière

The court and the salons were the dominant influences on the literature of the 17th century, the commanding personalities in which, during the high classical period, were Corneille, Racine and Molière.
Pierre Corneille began by writing comedies ("La Place royale", 1634), but

after 1637, following the criticism of his play "Le Cid" for its failure to observe the rules, wrote important classical tragedies ("Cinna" and "Horace", 1640; "Polyeucte", 1642) in sublime and heroic vein.
Jean Racine achieved an internalised expression of human passions in the spirit of Greek mythology ("Andromaque", 1667; "Iphigénie", 1675; "Phèdre", 1677).
Jean-Baptiste Poquelin (1622-1673), known as Molière, was a master of comedy. Starting from farce, with elements of the Italian commedia dell'arte, he developed a comedy of character and manners. "Tartuffe" (1664), "Don Juan" (1665) and "Le Misanthrope" (1666) are still played in all the great theatres of the world.

La Fontaine

At the end of the 17th century Jean de la Fontaine gave fresh life to the fable as a combination of fairytale charm and instruction. His fables, suggesting the need to recognise reality and the natural order, come close to the work of the moralists.

Moralists

The analysis of human nature and the study of man in society were the principal themes of the 17th century French moralists, the most important of whom were François de la Rochefoucauld and Jean de la Bruyère.

Letters and memoirs

The literature of the period also includes some notable letter-writers (Guez de Balzac, Mme de Sévigné) and authors of memoirs.

Philosophy

The philosophy of René Descartes (1596–1650: "Cogito, ergo sum"), advocating rational thought as the means of approaching truth, influenced the whole of his century.
While Descartes' dualist view of the world freed knowledge from theological ties, Blaise Pascal (1623-1662) combined Christian piety with philosophical and scientific rationalism.

The Enlightenment

During the 18th century the salons, clubs and coffee-houses became the focus of literary life. They provided a forum for criticism of absolute rule and dogmatic attitudes, which found expression in such works as the "Lettres persanes" (1721) and "L'Esprit des lois" (1748) of Charles-Louis de Montesquieu and Voltaire's "Lettres philosophiques" (1734). Montesquieu's and Voltaire's criticisms of French public and religious life were influenced by their visits to Britain. Many critical works of this kind, however, could be published only anonymously or abroad.

Rationalism and tolerance now became the guiding themes of French literature, which found an enthusiastic audience throughout Europe. Thus Denis Diderot, editor-in-chief of the "Encyclopédie" (published from 1751 onwards), spent some time at the court of Catherine the Great of Russia, while Voltaire (1694-1778; real name François-Marie Arouet) was summoned to the court of Frederick the Great of Prussia. Jean-Jacques Rousseau's "Contrat social" (1762), which called for the restoration of the natural equality of man, pointed towards the ideas of the French Revolution.

Criticism in literary form

After Marivaux's psychological comedies of love ("La Surprise de l'amour", 1722) came the bourgeois dramas of Diderot ("Le Père de famille", 1757), which had a moral under-current; and the comedies of Beaumarchais ("La folle Journée, ou le mariage de Figaro", 1784) laid bare the social injustices of the Ancien Régime. The novel ranged from picaresque stories of social criticism to Voltaire's philosophical tales ("Micromégas", 1752), Diderot's dialogues and novels of manners ("Le Neveu de Rameau", 1805) and Marivaux's analytical depictions of character ("Le Paysan parvenu", 1735), and by way of the deliberately amoral work of the Marquis de Sade to the sentimental stories of the Abbé Prévost and Bernardin de Saint-Pierre ("Paul et Virginie", 1787), and so to the beginning of the Romantic movement.

The French Revolution

Few of the patriotic works written during the French Revolution have survived. André Chénier, who wrote during this period, was perhaps the most important lyric poet of the 18th century. The parliamentary rhetoric of the revolutionary leaders is at any rate of value for the light it throws on the events of the time.

Romanticism

The French Revolution established a new social as well as political order, and this brought the old aristocratic salon culture to an end. The subsequent period saw a whole succession of different literary schools succeeding one another and competing with one another – Classicism and Romanticism, Positivism, Realism, the Parnasse, Symbolism, Naturalism. Among the most important writers of the period were Chateaubriand, Lamartine, Victor Hugo, Stendhal, Balzac, Flaubert, Baudelaire, Verlaine, Rimbaud and Mallarmé.

Sensibility

François-René de Chateaubriand and Madame de Staël ("De l'Allemagne", 1810) brought back the sensibility which had been repressed during the reign of deism and rationalism, and from 1820 onwards Alphonse de Lamartine reintroduced sensibility to lyric poetry. In his novel of self-analysis "Adolphe" (1816) Benjamin Constant describes a split personality involved in a tragic love affair. Simultaneously with the emergence of Romanticism the hierarchy of the literary genres was abolished and verse became freer – a consequence of the demand by Victor Hugo in 1827 for greater artistic freedom.

Cénacles

The ideas of Romanticism were developed in the coteries of like-minded people known as *cénacles* and were given expression in the dramas of Alexandre Dumas the Elder ("Henri III", 1829), Alfred de Musset ("Lorenzaccio", 1834) and Victor Hugo ("Hernani", 1830).

The novel

The novels of the Romantic generation were characterised by lyrical elements, autobiographical features and historical subject-matter. The weltschmerz of the time was expressed in Senancour's "Obermann" (1804), Mme de Staël's "Corinne" (1807) and Benjamin Constant's "Adolphe" (1816), but the greatest Romantic novel was Victor Hugo's "Notre-Dame de Paris" (1831). Stendhal (Henri Beyle) exposed in his novels ("Le Rouge et le Noir", 1830) the most intimate impulses of his heroes. Honoré de Balzac ("Illusions perdues", 1839) was already moving in the direction of Realism. Other works of this period were Prosper Mérimée's colourful short stories ("Colomba", 1840), George Sand's novels of passion and social criticism, the historical novels of Alexandre Dumas the Elder ("Les trois Mousquetaires", 1844) and Eugène Sue's novels of adventure and manners.

The Parnasse

Theophile Gautier ("Emaux et Camées", 1852) rated aesthetic form higher than content ("l'art pour l'art", "art for art's sake"), pointing the way towards the impersonal poetry of the "Parnassiens".

Symbolism

A significant precursor of the Surrealists was Gérard de Nerval ("Aurélia", 1855). From Charles Baudelaire ("Les Fleurs du mal", 1857) and Paul Verlaine (1844–1896) the development of poetry moved on to Symbolists such as Arthur Rimbaud and Stéphane Mallarmé, who did away with the dividing line between the idea and the word.

Realism

As with lyric poetry, the development of narrative prose writing involved a rejection of Romanticism. A new impulse was brought to the novel by Gustave Flaubert with his dispassionate scientific presentation of external circumstances and psychological processes in "Madame Bovary" (1857), which amounted to an advance towards Realism. He sought to overcome his revulsion against human existence by rigorous artistic discipline.
The brothers Jules and Edmond Goncourt also presented examples of contemporary states of mind in their novels, which they called "documents humains".

Literature

Naturalism

Auguste Comte's positivism and sociological ideas ("Cours de philosophie positive", 1830–1842) and Hippolyte Taine's determinist theory of the milieu provided the philosophical backing for Emile Zola's "experimental novels" of social criticism, particularly in the Rougon-Macquart series (1871–1893), the major achievement of Naturalism.
The stories of Alphonse Daudet are full of humour as well as realism. Guy de Maupassant, the master of the short story ("Yvette", 1884), gives point and wit to ordinary life in a terse narrative style. Joris-Karl Huysmans' "A Rebours" (1884) was the most important example of the literature of decadence which was a deliberate reaction against the nationalistic trend of literature after the Boulanger and Dreyfus affairs.

The theatre

The "boulevard" style was now dominant in the theatre. Alfred Jarry's "Ubu roi", in a very different tone, is regarded as the first example of the theatre of the absurd.

Some 19th century writers continued writing well into the 20th century, including the Nobel Prize winner Anatole France ("Thais", 1890), Pierre Loti, Romain Rolland, Paul Bourget and Maurice Maeterlinck, whose works reflect the gradual dissolution of the bourgeois life-style.

20th century

The variety of 20th century styles and trends is almost endless. The horrors of the First World War were realistically presented by authors such as Henry de Montherlant and Henri Barbusse, but great international events (the Russian Revolution, the Spanish Civil War, the rise of the Third Reich) had little resonance in French literature with the exception of André Malraux's "La Condition humaine" (1930) and Georges Bernanos' "Les grands cimetières sous la lune" (1938).

Renouveau Catholique

One of the leading representatives of the "Renouveau Catholique", which sought a renewal of literature and society on the basis of religious faith and which left its mark on many genres, was Paul Claudel ("L'Echange", 1901), whose profound symbolism is nourished by the certainties of the Catholic faith.

Unanimism Populism

Two significant 20th century literary schools were Unanimism (Jules Romains, Georges Duhamel, etc.) and Populism (Marcel Aymé, "La Jument verte", 1933; Louis-Ferdinand Céline, "Voyage au bout de la nuit", 1932).
In contrast to the psychological novel, Unanimism sought to capture the group and community soul and total reality. Populism was a reaction against the society novel.

Surrealism

The only movement of literary origin which achieved a new overall conception of human behaviour was the avantgarde Surrealist movement which came into being after 1921, originally as a branch of Tristan Tzara's Dadaism, with writers such as André Breton, Louis Aragon, Guillaume Apollinaire and Paul Eluard. In opposition to traditional values, Surrealism was influenced by the psychoanalysis of Sigmund Freud and sought insight and the sources of artistic inspiration in the pre-rational depth strata of the consciousness; literature, in the Surrealist view, should articulate the unconscious as a spontaneous act. Surrealist influence can also be detected in the work of René Char, Jean Cocteau and Blaise Cendrars.

The theatre

The traditional boulevard theatre was transformed by Jean Giraudoux with his witty and poetically ironical plays ("La Guerre de Troie n'aura pas lieu", 1935). New impulses were also given to the theatre by Jean Anouilh ("Antigone", 1946), Henry de Montherlant, Albert Camus ("Les Justes", 1949) and Jean-Paul Sartre ("Les Mouches", 1944).

Individuals

Among the great individuals who cannot be immediately assigned to any particular school is the lyric poet Paul Valéry, who against a background of nihilism sought a pure spiritual reality ("Charmes", 1921).

Marcel Proust's great novel cycle "A la Recherche du temps perdu" (1913–1927) contains autobiographical elements, social analysis and subtle psychology, with much sensory detail and interior monologue. He inaugurated a new epoch in the novel by his "discovery" of a new dimension – time. Although his novels have a beginning and an end, they represent merely an extract from the duration of existence, and the action is as open-ended as is time.
In "Les Faux-monnayeurs" (1925), written in an experimental technique, André Gide ironically blurs the dividing line between reality and fantasy. The novels of Raymond Radiguet ("Le Diable au corps", 1932), Colette ("Chéri", 1920), Jean Giono ("Regain", 1930) and Antoine de Saint-Exupéry ("Vol de Nuit", 1931) also describe very personal worlds. Saint-Exupéry expresses social criticism in "Le petit Prince" (1943), depicting a world from which poetry and love have disappeared.

Existentialism

The Second World War brought profound changes in literature as in much else. The unity of the Resistance, which had brought together people of many different backgrounds and beliefs, fell apart after the war as political and ideological differences surfaced again.
The works of Aragon, Eluard and Vercors reflected the experience of the Resistance. Jean-Paul Sartre developed the doctrine ("L'Etre et le néant", 1943) that if there is no God man cannot have been created by God and therefore exists without purpose or intention. He then must realise himself by action, and the choice he makes not only shapes his own existence but creates human values. Sartre's works, expressing atheistic and nihilistic and later Marxist views, found a wide audience.
Simon de Beauvoir was concerned, from an existentialist and emancipatory point of view, with the social situation of women ("Le deuxième sexe", 1949). Her novel "Les Mandarins" (1954), for which she received the Goncourt Prize, is a *roman à clef* on the world of the left-wing intellectuals of the postwar years.

The Absurd

Albert Camus perceived the absurdity of life in a different way from Sartre. For him this absurdity resulted from man's confrontation with the world; and since there is no place in Camus' thought for religious belief man is driven back on himself alone. His works ("La Peste", 1947) were concerned with the human aspects of men's solidarity in their revolt against the absurdity of existence, for example in the fight against the injustice of the world. Camus received the Nobel Prize in 1957.

The modern theatre of the absurd is based on similar views. Samuel Beckett ("Waiting for Godot", 1953), Eugène Ionesco ("Le Piéton de l'air", 1962) and Jean Genet ("Le Balcon", 1957) took over and adapted to their own purpose elements from the grotesque and surrealist theatre in order to reveal the absurdity of man's existence in the ordinariness of daily life and normality.

Nouveau roman

After the Second World War Paris became the literary centre of the West. Never before had so many novels been written, and many new literary ideas had their origins in Paris. Among the pioneers of the *nouveau roman*, the "new novel", were Nathalie Sarraute ("Les Fruits d'Or", 1961), Michel Butor ("Mobile", 1962), Alain Robbe-Grillet ("Les Gommes", 1953), Claude Simon ("Le Vent", 1957; Nobel Prize 1985) and Marguerite Duras ("India Song", 1973). Although the nouveau roman derived from existing literary traditions it led to a radical transformation in narrative technique; its ideal was that the manner of writing should influence the manner of thinking of its readers and should thus indirectly lead to action. Thus the traditional characters of the novel were dispensed with; the presentation was purely descriptive and there was no narrator. Frequently reflection on the novel became the principal theme.

The theatre after 1968

A new committed theatre developed in France, particularly from the sixties onwards, using a variety of media and stage effects and also involving the audience. A prominent place was taken in this movement by the Théâtre du Soleil, directed by Ariane Mnouchkine.

Future prospects

The novel continues to develop, with experiments in various directions. Well-worn subjects retain their attraction, so long as they can be related to current problems and contemporary conditions. Representatives of current trends are Françoise Sagan, Jacques de Bourbon Busset, Marguerite Yourcenar (who in 1980 became the first woman member of the Académie Française), Michel Tournier, Giono, H. Cixous and C. Rochefort. At present French literature is receiving important new impulses from literary criticism; time will tell what new lands may be discovered in future.

Music

In serious music, although it has a great tradition behind it, France tends to be overshadowed by Germany and Austria. Nevertheless much orchestral and chamber music and a number of operas have survived the test of time and are established in the repertoire of concert halls and opera houses throughout the world.

Origins

After the origins of French music in the 9th century and the gradual development and refinement of polyphony, Josquin des Prés (*c.*1440–*c.*1521) broke out of the old structures and created a new musical language. He is the earliest French composer whose works are still regularly performed.

17th and 18th centuries

In the 17th century French music enjoyed a great flowering in the work of Jean-Baptiste Lully (1632–1687), who composed ballets and operas, initiating a tradition which has continued into our own day, Marc-Antoine Charpentier ("Te Deum", with the "Eurovision" fanfare) and François Campra. The decades after Lully's death were dominated by Jean-Philippe Rameau (1687–1764), whose theory of harmony became the basis of all modern harmonic theory, and François Couperin (1626–1661). Between the death of Rameau and the first works of Berlioz French music merely marked time.

The musical scene in Paris was dominated by foreign composers living in the capital, including Christoph Willibald Gluck, a German, Luigi Cherubini, an Italian, and the Belgian-born André Grétry (1742–1813).

The Romantic period

The Romantic period began with the work of Hector Berlioz (1803–1869), one of the founders of programme music. His "Symphonie Fantastique", "Harold in Italy" and "Romeo and Juliet" choral symphony are still among the most popular works in the symphonic repertoire.
Berlioz's operatic works ("The Damnation of Faust", "Benvenuto Cellini", "The Trojans", "Beatrice and Benedick"), however, are rarely performed. A similar fate has befallen the once highly praised operas of Spontini, Auber, Halévy and Meyerbeer.

Comic opera

The comic operas of Esprit Auber ("Fra Diavolo") and Adolphe Adam ("Le Postillon de Longjumeau", "Si j'étais Roi") have had rather more success. The best known French opera of the 19th century is "Carmen" (1875), by Georges Bizet (1838–1875), which is still one of the most popular.

Lyric opera

The lyric/tragic operas of Charles Gounod ("Faust", "Mireille"), Jules Massenet ("Manon", "Werther"), Ambroise Thomas ("Mignon"), Léo Delibes ("Lakmé"), Gustave Charpentier ("Louise") and Edouard Lalo ("Le Roi d'Ys") are – with a few exceptions – little known outside France.

Operetta

Operetta developed during the reign of Napoleon III. Jacques Offenbach (1819–1880), a native of Cologne, became the very symbol of French *esprit* and Parisian *joie de vivre* ("Orpheus in the Underworld", "La Vie parisienne", "La Périchole").

Dance and ballet

Since the time of Lully and Rameau the French have had a particular affection for dance and ballet. In the 19th century imperishable contributions were made to the repertoire by Léo Delibes ("Coppélia", "Sylvia") and Adolphe Adam ("Giselle").

Instrumental music

In instrumental music the leading names are the Belgian-born César Franck (1822–1890), who established a school (d'Indy, Chausson), and Camille Saint-Saëns (symphonies, piano concertos, violin and cello concertos, "Carnival of Animals", "Samson and Delilah").

Impressionism

At the beginning of the 20th century French musical life was dominated by Claude Debussy (1862–1918; orchestral works: "La Mer", "Printemps", "Jeux", "Nocturnes", "Images"; piano works: "Préludes", "Estampes", "Images"; chamber music; opera: "Pelléas et Mélisande") and Maurice Ravel (1875–1937; orchestral works: "Boléro", "La Valse", "Daphnis et Chloé"; piano concertos; piano and chamber music). Gabriel Fauré (1845–1924) composed chamber music and church music ("Requiem"). Albert Roussel (1869–1937) is remembered mainly for his magnificently orchestrated ballet "Bacchus et Ariane", Paul Dukas for his symphonic poem "L'Apprenti sorcier" and ballet "La Péri".

Groupe des Six

Around 1920 the Paris Groupe des Six, whose principal representatives were Erik Satie, Francis Poulenc, Darius Milhaud and the Swiss-born Arthur Honegger, reacted against the influence of Impressionism.
Notable among contemporary composers are Olivier Messiaen (piano and organ music, song cycles, exotic-sounding orchestral music), Henri Dutilleux and André Jolivet.

Serial music

The principal representative of serial music in France is the composer and conductor Pierre Boulez (b. 1925), who also directs the Institut de Recherche et de Coordination Acoustique/Musique (IRCAM) in Paris, which is concerned with experimental music.

Folk music

Every French region has its own folk songs and dances, often centuries old, and the old tunes are still played and sung at folk festivals and on certain family and religious occasions. This folk music shows an extraordinary variety in its rhythms and melodies and in the instruments used – from the brass bands of Alsace to the farandole of Provence, from the Basque male voice choirs to the Celtic music of Brittany (often with bagpipes), from the Catalan sardana of Roussillon to the songs and dances of Auvergne.

Literary chansons

In the field of light music France has developed the chanson as an important genre in its own right, with origins which can be traced back to the troubadours of medieval Provence. Among singers who have achieved reputations extending beyond the bounds of France are Edith Piaf, Jacques Brel, Georges Brassens, Yves Montand, Gilbert Bécaud, Charles Aznavour, Juliette Gréco, Jacques Higelin and Renaud. A Festival of the French Chanson has been held annually in Bourges since 1977.

SANDWICHS
BAR

France from A to Z

Aix-en-Provence N11

Region: Provence–Alpes–Côte d'Azur
Département: Bouches-du-Rhône
Altitude: 177 m/581 ft
Population: 155,000

Situation and characteristics

Aix (pronounced "Ex"; Provençal Ais), the old capital of Provence (see entry), lies 30 km/20 miles north of Marseilles in a fertile plain surrounded by hills. Many old palaces, principally dating from the 17th and 18th centuries, as well as the art treasures in the museums and churches bear witness to the glorious past of the town, which is still the intellectual heart of Provence, the see of an archbishop and the seat of a university. Apart from the thermal springs (recommended for vein disorders, stomach complaints, nervous and gynaecological conditions), which have been frequented since Roman times, and its attractions as a tourist centre, Aix's economy depends on the processing of almonds for use in cakes and confectionery. An international music festival takes place in July/August every year.

History

Aix-en-Provence, the first Roman settlement in Gaul, was founded by Caius Sextius soon after the destruction in 121 B.C. of the Celto-Ligurian settlement at Entremont, just north of the town, and was given the name of Aquae Sextiae. Twenty years later, near the town, the Roman general Marius routed an army of Teutons who were advancing on Italy. Thanks to its thermal springs and to its situation on the Via Aurelia, the main road to Spain, the town prospered.
After suffering severely during the great migrations and from Saracen raids Aix became capital of the County of Provence and, particularly in the reign of the cultivated and art-loving René of Anjou (1409–1480), a centre of Provençal literature and poetry. The University was founded in 1409. In 1481 the town passed to the French crown. It suffered severely during the 16th c. wars of religion.
Aix was given its distinctive architectural aspect by much building activity in the 17th and 18th centuries. The Revolutionary statesman Mirabeau (1749–1791) had close associations with the town, as had the painter Paul Cézanne (1839–1906), who was born and died here. Picasso lived in the Château of Vauvenargues from 1958 to 1961 and is buried there. The rise of Marseilles in the 19th c. led to a temporary decline in the importance of Aix.

Sights

*Cours Mirabeau

The Cours Mirabeau, a broad avenue laid out in 1651 and shaded by old plane-trees, runs between the old town of Aix and the newer districts to the north. On the avenue are three fountains. The middle one, the Fontaine Chaude, dispenses water from the thermal springs. In Place du Général-de-Gaulle, at the west end of the avenue, is the large Fontaine de la Rotonde. The Cours Mirabeau is lined with handsome buildings, like the Hôtel des Villiers (No. 2; 1710), the Hôtel d'Isouard de Vauvenargues (No. 10; 1710), the Hôtel d'Arbod Jouques (No. 19; early 18th c.), the Hôtel de Forbin (No. 20; 1656) and the Hôtel de Maurel de Pontèves (No. 38; 1647–1650). At the east end of the Cours is the Fontaine du Roi René, by David d'Angers (19th c.). Also at the east end is the Chapelle des Oblats (part of a Carmelite convent), built by a pupil of Pierre Puget and renovated about 1700.

◀ *Impressive château in Fougères*

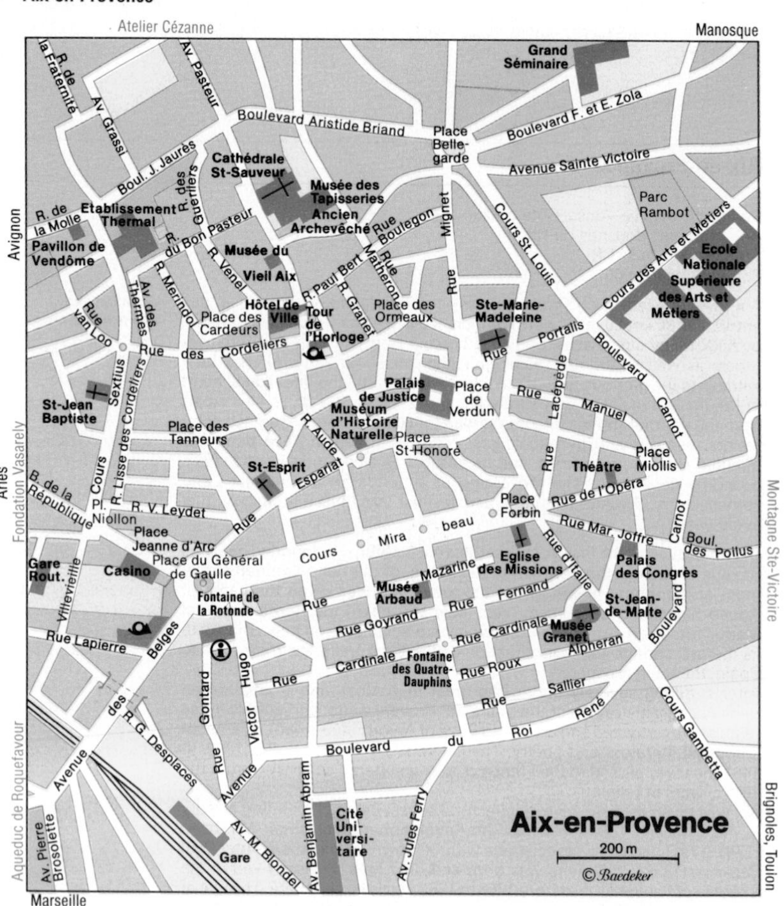

North of the Cours Mirabeau, extending to the Hôtel de Ville (Town Hall), is the old town of Aix. Much of it is now a pedestrian zone.

Muséum d'Histoire Naturelle

From the Cours Mirabeau Rue Clemenceau runs north to the Place St-Honoré. Off this to the left is Rue Espariat, in which is the Natural History Museum, housed in the late 17th c. Hôtel Boyer d'Eguilles. A particularly notable exhibit is the clutch of dinosaur's eggs found in Provence.

Palais de Justice

North-east of this are the Palais de Justice (Law Courts) and the church of Ste-Marie-Madeleine, which has an "Annunciation" of about 1440. The church's Renaissance-style façade dates from 1860; the church itself was rebuilt in 1905.

Place de l'Hôtel-de-Ville

The Place de l'Hôtel-de-Ville, the central feature of the old town, has a fountain of 1755, round which the daily flower market is held. In the square is the old Halle aux Grains, built in 1759–1761, with a magnificent triangular gable and sculptural decoration by Jean-Pancrace Chastel (18th c.). It now houses the Post Office.

Hôtel de Ville and Tour de l'Horloge

Pavillon de Vendôme

Hôtel de Ville

On the west side of the square is the Hôtel de Ville (Town Hall), with a central courtyard; built in 1652–1668, it is in Italian Baroque style. The wrought-iron grille on the balcony and a fine doorway date from the 17th c. On the first floor are the Bibliothèque Méjanes (18th c.; 350,000 volumes) and the Fondation Saint-John Perse, commemorating the diplomat and writer of that name, winner of the Nobel Prize for Literature in 1960.

Tour de l'Horloge

Adjoining the Hôtel de Ville on the right is the Tour de l'Horloge (Clock-Tower; 1510), one of the old town gates, built on Roman foundations. The astronomical clock was installed in 1661.

Musée du Vieil Aix

In Rue Gaston-de-Saporta, which runs north from the square, are a number of other old noble mansions. The Hôtel Estienne de St-Jean (17th c.) is now occupied by the Musée du Vieil Aix, museum devoted to history of the town.

*St-Sauveur

In the north of the old town is the Cathedral of St-Sauveur, built in several phases between the 12th and 17th centuries. In the Late Gothic doorway are fine carved walnut doors by Jean Guiramand (1508–1510); on request the verger will open the protective shutters,

The Cathedral is entered through a Romanesque doorway. Immediately on the right is the Early Christian baptistery (6th c.; renovated 1577), with antique columns. In the nave, on the right, is a triptych (Mary in the Burning Bush) by Nicolas Froment (1435–1485), with the figure of Roi René in the left-hand panel. In the central and right-hand aisles are Flemish tapestries (scenes from the life of the Virgin and the Passion; 1511). Behind the high altar is the Chapelle de St-Mitre (5th c.). On the south side of the church is a small Romanesque cloister (11th c.).

*Musée des Tapisseries

Adjoining the Cathedral is the former Archbishop's Palace, which now houses the Musée des Tapisseries, with 17th and 18th c. Beauvais tapestries.

During the summer there are concerts in the courtyard of the Museum.

Etablissement Thermal

Rue du Bon-Pasteur runs west from the Cathedral to the Etablissement Thermal (Spa Establishment), which is built on Roman foundations. The water (temperature 36° C/97° F) is used for both drinking and bathing, especially for metabolic and circulatory disorders, nervous diseases and post-operative complaints.

Pavillon de Vendôme

West of the Etablissement Thermal, set in a small park, is the Pavillon de Vendôme, built in 1664–1667 (when it was outside the town walls) and remodelled in the 18th c. It contains 17th and 18th century furniture and paintings.

Atelier Paul Cézanne

To the north of the old town, in Avenue Paul-Cézanne, is the studio of the famous Impressionist, a native of Aix. In addition to mementoes of the painter it offers an informative audio-visual display.

Quartier Mazarin

The Quartier Mazarin, to the south of the Cours Mirabeau, was built in the 17th c. on the initiative of Michel Mazarin, brother of the Cardinal, who was Archbishop of Aix. Laid out on a rectangular plan, it is bounded on the south by the Boulevard du Roi-René and on the east by the Boulevard Carnot, part of which follows the line of the old town walls. The central feature of the quarter is the Place des Quatre-Dauphins, with the Fontaine des Quatre Dauphins (1667: figures of four dolphins).

Musée Paul Arbaud

The 18th c. Hôtel d'Arbaud, to the north of the fountain, is one of the handsomest old mansions in the quarter. It houses the Académie d'Aix and the Musée Paul Arbaud (faience, pictures), with an extensive library.

*Musée Granet

The Musée Granet (Musée des Beaux-Arts et d'Archéologie), to the east of the Fontaine des Quatre Dauphins, is one of the finest museums in Provence. It occupies the former Palais de Malte, a commandery of the Order of Malta built in 1671. The nucleus of the museum was the collection of the painter François-Marius Granet (1775–1849). The exhibits include Celto-Ligurian sculpture from the oppidum of Entremont (a native settlement destroyed by the Romans), Greek reliefs, Roman fragments, an Early Christian sarcophagus, medieval sculpture and works by European painters (including Jost van Cleve, Hans Holbein the Younger, Rubens, Rembrandt, Cézanne and Pissarro).

St-Jean-de-Malte

Adjoining the Musée Granet on the east is the church of St-Jean-de-Malte, which belonged to the old commandery. Built in the late 13th c. (with 17th c. extensions), it is the town's earliest Gothic building, with a 14th c. bell-tower. It contains notable tombs and pictures.

Cité Universitaire

The University City, originally founded in 1409, in the reign of Louis II, is now in the Quartier des Fenouillères, south of the Boulevard du Roi-René.

Bibliothèque Méjanes

The valuable collection of 181th c. books, comprising 350,000 volumes, of the Bibliothèque Méjanes is housed in an old converted match factory in Rue des Allumettes, in the west of the town. The building also contains the Fondation Saint-John Perse, in memory of the diplomat who was awarded the Nobel Prize for Literature in 1960.

*Fondation Vasarely

The Fondation Vasarely is in the Jas de Bouffan district, in the west of the town. This unconventional modern building, 87 m/286 ft long, contains numerous works by the Hungarian-French painter Victor Vasarely (b. 1908), one of the originators and leading exponents of abstract constructivist painting and Op Art.

*Oppidum d'Entremont

The excavated remains of this Celto-Ligurian settlement lie to the north of Aix (reached on road D14), in a magnificent strategic situation. Some 4 hectares/10 acres of the site, which consists of an upper and a lower town, have been excavated. Fragments of pillars indicate the layout of individual buildings and houses. A mosaic pavement and the remains of what seem to have been charnel-houses provide evidence of a sanctuary situated on the highest point of the hill which was destroyed in 123 B.C.

Surroundings of Aix-en-Provence

Vauvenargues

D10 runs north-east from Aix and continues along the north side of the artificial Lac de Bimont, through beautiful scenery. Above the river which supplies this reservoir, 12 km/7½ miles from Aix, is the village of Vauvenargues, in an area noted for its abundance of game. The village church dates from the 12th and 16th centuries. The Renaissance château, in which the 18th c. Marquis de Vauvenargues wrote his famous "Maxims", was bought in 1958 by Picasso, who is buried in the park together with his second wife, Jacqueline Roque (no public access).

**Croix de la Provence

South of Vauvenargues is the Montagne Ste-Victoire, one of Cézanne's favourite subjects. From the hamlet of Les Cabassols, on the west side of the hill, an attractive path runs up to the Croix de la Provence (945 m/3100 ft), from which there are panoramic views, extending from the Camargue in the west by way of the Massif des Maures to the Alps in the east.

Ventabren

Ventabren, 15 km/9 miles west of Aix, is a hilltop village – also known as a "Nid d'aigle" (eagle's nest) – dominated by a ruined castle, situated high above the valley of the Arc. The parish church of St-Denis dates from the 11th–12th c. and from the castle ruins there is a magnificent view of the Etang de Berre and the town of Martigues on its south side.

*Aqueduc de Roquefavour

The Roquefavour aqueduct, a 19th c. counterpart of the Pont du Gard, was built to supply water to Marseilles. It is three-storeyed, 83 m/272 ft high and 375 m/410 yds long.

Roquepertuse

West of Ventabren in the valley of the Arc is this Celtic rock shrine, reached on a path which runs south from the junction of the D65 and D10. Finds from the site are mostly in the Musée Borély in Marseilles (see entry).

Les Milles

To the south-west, in Les Milles, is an 18th c. château built by L'Enfant, set in a beautiful park.

Ajaccio

Q13

Region: Corse (Corsica)
Département: Corse-du-Sud
Altitude: 0–18 m/0–60 ft
Population: 55,000

Situation and characteristics

Ajaccio (pronounced Azhaksió in French, Ayácho in Italian), the largest town in Corsica (see entry), lies half-way down the west coast of the island in the Gulf of Ajaccio, surrounded by mountains which have a covering of snow right into summer.
The town was founded by the Genoese in 1492, and is the capital of Corsica. Its harbour is second in size only to that of Bastia (see entry) and it also has an airport.
Its situation, beautiful beaches and mild climate (average winter temperature 13.3° C/56° F) attract large numbers of visitors.

Sights

Hôtel de Ville

Opening out from the harbour is the Place du Maréchal-Foch, studded with palms and plane-trees. On the north side of the square is the Hôtel de Ville (Town Hall, 1826), which houses the Musée Napoléonien, containing mementoes of the Bonaparte family, mainly pictures and a collection of orders and medals.

Maison Bonaparte

Not far to the south, in Rue St-Charles, is the Maison Bonaparte, in which Napoleon was born on August 15th 1769, the son of a family which originally came from Lombardy and Tuscany. The house contains furniture of the period, weapons, portraits and family documents.

Cathedral

The Cathedral of Notre-Dame de la Miséricorde, dedicated to the town's patroness, known as La Madunuccia, was consecrated in 1593. In the first chapel on the left is a painting by Eugène Delacroix (1796–1863), "Du Sacré Cœur".

Place de Gaulle

The real centre of the town is the spacious Place de Gaulle, with an equestrian statue of Napoleon and his four brothers (1865 by Viollet le-Duc); there are fine views from the terrace. Running north from the square is Ajaccio's main shopping street, the Cours Napoléon.

Palais Fesch

In Rue Fesch, which runs parallel to the Cours Napoléon on the east, is the Palais Fesch. In the Imperial Chapel is the mausoleum of Napoleon's mother and other members of the family and also that of Cardinal Fesch (1763–1839).

* Musée Fesch

On the first floor is the Musée Fesch, which houses a collection of 14th–19th c. Italian paintings. The Baciocchi Collection contains works by Dutch, Flemish and French painters.

Musée A Bandera

In Rue General Levie lies the Musée A Bandera, a museum which illustrates the eventful and warlike history of Corsica and other Mediterranean islands.

Surroundings of Ajaccio

Cap de la Parata

* Punta de la Parata

A beautiful coast road runs west from Ajaccio for 2.5 km/1½ miles to the Chapelle des Grecs (1632), and then passes a cemetery containing numerous small domed tombs (a type reminiscent of Moslem models) belonging to leading citizens of Ajaccio. At the end of the road is the Punta de la Parata, with the Tour de la Parata, one of the 90 or so Genoese watch-towers scattered round the island. From the tower there are magniificent views, particularly of the four uninhabited islands known as the Iles Sanguinaires.

Château de la Punta

From Ajaccio a road runs north over the Col de Pruno (217 m/712 ft), passing a memorial chapel and the Tours des Monticchi, the ruins of a medieval castle before arriving at the Château de la Punta (1886–1894; furniture and pictures).

* Golfe d'Ajaccio

It is worth taking a trip down the coast road to the south of the town to view the beautiful Gulf of Ajaccio.

Albi

K11

Region: Midi–Pyrénées. Département: Tarn
Altitude: 174 m/571 ft. Population: 50,000

Situation and characteristics

Albi, the chief town of the département of Tarn, lies above the left bank of the river Tarn some 80 km/50 miles north of Toulouse. Its most striking features are its massive medieval brick buildings, in particular the

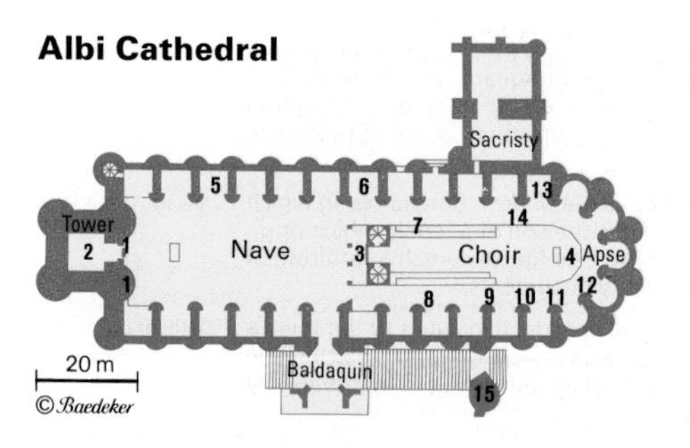

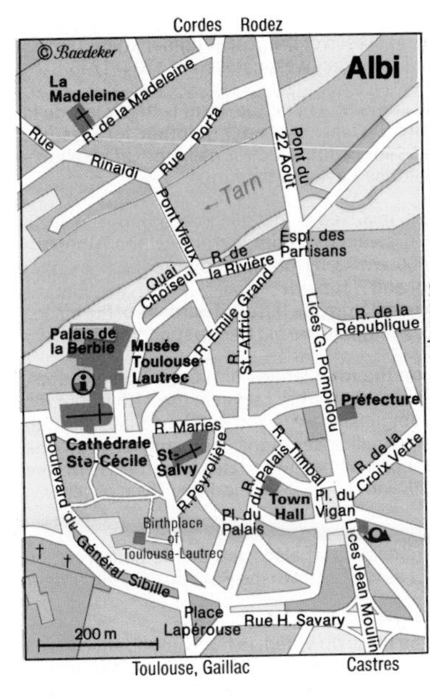

Albi Cathedral

Cathedral and the Archbishop's Palace. Albi is a commercial and industrial town, with an old-established glass industry.

History

The town's name is of Celtic origin, and there was a Civitas Albiensium here before the Christian era. After suffering many vicissitudes under the Romans, the Visigoths and the Saracens Albi passed into the hands of Charles the Bald in 843. In the 13th c. it gave its name to the Albigensians, a heretical Christian sect (also known as Cathars) which was almost completely wiped out in the Albigensian wars of 1209–1229. Thereafter the country of Alby was annexed by the French king. In 1678 the town became the see of an archbishop.
Albi was the birthplace of the painter Henri de Toulouse-Lautrec (1864–1901).

Sights

** Cathedral

The dominant architectural feature of the town is the fortress-like Cathedral of Ste-Cécile, one of the great achievements of the brick-built Gothic of southern France, which was begun in 1282, on the site of an earlier church, and completed in 1480. The nave is almost 100 m/330 ft long, 20 m/65 ft wide and 30 m/100 ft high; its defensive walls tower to a height of 41 m/135 ft. The massive tower was increased in height in the 15th c..
The Cathedral is entered through the south doorway and a richly decorated porch known as the Baldaquin. The aisleless nave is separated from the choir by an elaborately carved French rood screen of about 1500, unfortunately almost all the statues which were on it have been lost. Along the north and south sides are a series of square chapels separated by projecting piers, which appear on the outside of the building as small engaged round towers. The choir has rich sculptural decoration, with angels on the inside and Old and New Testament figures on the outside; Burgundian influence is evident in the carving.

On the inside of the west front is a fresco of the Last Judgment (late 15th c.; damaged in 17th and 18th c.). The organ was installed in 1734–1736.

*Palais de la Berbie

To the north of the Cathedral, standing above the Tarn, is the Palais de la Berbie (from a Romance word *bisbia,* "bishop"), another fortress-like structure built in the 13th and 14th centuries. Originally the archbishop's palace, it now houses the Toulouse-Lautrec Museum.

*Musée Toulouse-Lautrec

The Toulouse-Lautrec Museum, installed in the Palais de la Berbie in 1923, contains numerous pictures, drawings and lithographs by the Albi-born painter, together with over 400 works by his contemporaries (including Degas, Rodin, Matisse, Maillol and Rouault).
From the second Lautrec Room and from the terraced gardens of the palace there are fine views of the Tarn valley and the old bridge spanning the river.

St-Salvi

The church of St-Salvi, built on the foundations of a Carolingian church, and the monastery to which it belonged were begun in the 11th c., but the work was interrupted by the Albigensian wars and continued into the 13th c. A number of capitals and the small apses in the choir still date from the Romanesque period. The lower part of the tower dates from the 11th c., the upper part, which shows Gothic influence, from the 14th. The cloister was added in the 13th c.

Other sights

A good general view of the Archbishop's Palace and the Cathedral can be had from the Pont Vieux (1035) as well as from the Pont du 22-Août farther upstream.

Place du Vigan

The real centre of the town is the Place du Vigan. In Rue Timbal, which runs north-west from the square, is the Hôtel Reynès (1530), a handsome Renaissance mansion built by a wealthy merchant family, with fine busts of Francis I and Eleanor of Austria in the courtyard. Facing it is the Pharmacie des Pénitents, a typical 16th c. building. To the west of the Place du Vigan is the 16th c. Hôtel de Ville (Town Hall).

Birthplace of Toulouse-Lautrec

A little way south-west of the Hôtel de Ville is the handsome 18th c. mansion in which Toulouse-Lautrec was born. It contains a few mementoes of the painter and works by him.
Adjoining the Toulouse-Lautrec mansion is a Wax Museum, with displays illustrating local history.

Surroundings of Albi

St-Michel, Lescure

5 km/3 miles north-east of Albi, in Lescure, is the 11th c. Benedictine church of St-Michel, with a finely carved doorway. It now houses a postcard museum.

*Cordes

Perched on a hill 25 km/16 miles north-west of Albi is the town of Cordes (pop. 1000), which enjoys the picturesque style of Cordes-sur-Ciel. This little walled medieval town was founded by the Count of Toulouse in 1222, and with its towers, embrasures, numerous 13th and 14th c. buildings, market hall of 1352 and other features it is a museum of secular medieval architecture.

Porte de l'Horloge

The Escalier du Pater Noster in the west of the town, with exactly as many steps as the Lord's Prayer has words, leads up to the picturesque Porte de l'Horloge, which was probably rebuilt in the 16th c. The Maison du Grand Fauconnier, now the Mairie, takes its name from the figures of falcons on the façade. Carefully restored by Viollet-le-Duc in the 19th c., it has a fine 15th c. spiral staircase and houses the Musée Yves-Brayer, with work by the painter of that name (d. 1970).
In the Grand'Rue are the Maison du Grand Veneur and the Maison du Grand Ecuyer (14th c.). Also of particular interest are the market hall (1352),

with stone pillars and a fine timber roof structure, a well over 100 m/330 ft deep and the church of St-Michel, with a 13th c. choir and transept.

Alsace

O/P 6/7

** Situation and characteristics

The historical region of Alsace extends to the west of the Upper Rhine. The two départements of Bas-Rhin (chief town Strasbourg) and Haut-Rhin (chief town Colmar) approximately correspond to the areas traditionally known as Lower and Upper Alsace. The region has an area of 8300 sq. km/3200 sq. miles and a population of 1.5 million. Its capital and economic centre is Strasbourg.

** Vosges

Above the Rhine plain rise the hills of the Vosges (see entry), with their magnificent forests and high pastures, numerous ruined castles and their spas. The west side of the range lies in the départements of Vosges, Meurthe-et-Moselle and Moselle. Along the eastern fringes of the hills, which provide shelter from wind and rain, is a climatically favoured zone, a region of vineyards dotted with picturesque little wine towns and villages.

Topography

The landscape of Alsace is the mirror image of the other bank of the Rhine in Germany, with the Black Forest corresponding to the Vosges. The Rhine plain is a large rift valley which has been filled up by deposits from the Rhine and its tributaries. The Vosges and the Black Forest are the relics of a great mountain massif whose central section fell in at some time during the Tertiary era. The Alsatian plain, a tract of sands and dry gravels which for the most part is broader than its counterpart on the right bank of the river, is flanked by rolling country, particularly around Saverne, in an area of very varied geological structure, and in the Sundgau in southern Alsace. Beyond this again is a zone of low hills, mostly built up from light-coloured limestones but in some places from variegated sandstones, and largely

Alsation wine grapes

Kayersberg

forest-covered, like Mont Ste-Odile. The region owes its fertility to the great expanses of loess and loess clay.
The Vosges resemble the Black Forest in structure, with their more steeply scarped slopes facing the Rhine. The Southern or High Vosges rise to 1423 m/4669 ft in the Grand Ballon and 1245 m/4085 ft in the Ballon d'Alsace, the Central Vosges to 1008 m/3307 ft in Mont Donon, the Northern Vosges to only 581 m/1906 ft in the Grand-Wintersberg.
Extending into southern Alsace are the Sundgau uplands, rising to 350–400 m/1150–1300 ft, and the Alsatian Jura.

History

The Upper Rhine Plain was settled by man many thousands of years before our era. Around 1000 B.C. Celtic influence began to make itself felt; a massive relic of this period is the Mur Païen on Mont Ste-Odile. Caesar's victory over Ariovistus and his Suevi at Cernay in Upper Alsace in 58 B.C. made Alsace part of the Roman province of Germania Superior. The Roman peace, inaugurated by Augustus in 17 B.C., afforded the region 500 years of quiet development. Around A.D. 300 the Romans introduced the vine into Alsace and began to produce wine. In the 5th c. the name Alsace (Elisaza, "those who live over the Rhine") came into use. The name was applied to the Alemanni, who had advanced from this region and were subjugated by the Franks in 496. Alsace became part of the Frankish kingdom, and between 640 and 740 it was an independent duchy, which under the Carolingians was divided into the two counties of Sundgau and Nordgau. After Charlemagne's death the Frankish kingdom fell apart into three separate kingdoms, and under the treaty of Verdun (843) Alsace became part of the central kingdom of Lotharingia under Lothair I. In 870, however, on the death of the heir to that kingdom, it was divided between the eastern and western kingdoms and Alsace fell to the eastern kingdom. In 925 it became part of the duchy of Swabia. The duchy passed in 1079 to the Hohenstaufens, for whom it became a favoured place of residence and a central element in their dynastic possessions. After the death of the last Hohenstaufen in 1268 the duchy fell to pieces and Alsace broke up into numerous small lay and ecclesiastical lordships, some of which retained links with the territories on the right bank of the Rhine. The landgraviate of Lower Alsace fell into the hands of the bishops of Strasbourg, while most of Upper Alsace came under Habsburg control.

Imperial cities

The free imperial cities (cities directly subordinate to the Holy Roman Emperor) bcame increasingly important, and in 1354 ten imperial cities in Alsace, excluding Strasbourg and Mulhouse, formed themselves into a league. From 1520 onwards the Reformation came to Alsace, largely through the imperial cities. This was followed soon afterwards by peasant wars and in 1586 by the Catholic Counter-Reformation. Under the Peace of Westphalia (1648) after the Thirty Years War the Sundgau and the ten imperial cities passed to France, followed 25 years later by the whole of Alsace except Strasbourg and Mulhouse. In 1681 Strasbourg, except for its German university, was annexed to France by Louis XIV. Mulhouse remained within the Swiss Confederation, to which it had been admitted in 1515.
The French Revolution, by creating the départements of Bas-Rhin and Haut-Rhin, bound Alsace more firmly to France, and it was in Strasbourg that Rouget de Lisle composed the "Marseillaise". In 1798 Mulhouse also became part of France.
After the Franco-Prussian War of 1870–1871 Alsace was incorporated in the German Empire. After the 1914–1918 war French troops moved into Alsace, and under the treaty of Versailles it was returned to France. Between 1940 and 1944, during the Second World War, Alsace was incorporated in the German Reich, but thereafter again became French. It had thus changed its nationality four times within 75 years.
Alsace is now no longer a frontier territory as in the past, but, as the seat of the Council of Europe (since 1949), the European Parliament (since 1958)

and other European institutions, has taken on a new role in the move towards European unity.

Language

French is the official language of Alsace, but many of its inhabitants also speak a dialect of German. Since 1972 German has been an optional subject in schools from the fourth year onwards. In 1978 Alsace became the first French region to be granted a degree of cultural autonomy.

Economy

Agriculture is a major activity in the Rhine plain. On the fringes of the hills vines are grown and wine is produced. In the hills themselves the predominant activity is forestry, but there is also pastoral farming on the upland meadows in areas cleared of forest; one of the products is the famed Munster cheese.
The traditional textile industry of the region is now declining, and since 1945 metal-processing has become the most important branch of industry.

Art

Since the Middle Ages Alsace has played an important role in the development of art. Romanesque architecture is represented by a relatively small number of churches (Wissembourg, Andlau, Murbach Abbey, Lautenbach, etc.). Strasbourg Cathedral, recognised as a masterpiece of Gothic, was begun in Romanesque style (the crypt), but from the end of the 12th c. onwards came increasingly to show Gothic features (the transept), a process which reached its full expression with the building of the nave around 1250. The numerous castles in Alsace (Haut-Kœnigsbourg, Fleckenstein, Ortenberg, Hohenbourg, Ribeauvillé, Kaysersberg, Drei Exen, Landskron) are also important examples of medieval architecture; many of them date from the period of Hohenstaufen rule.
Other examples of Gothic art in Alsace apart from Strasbourg Cathedral are to be seen at Thann, Molsheim and Colmar. During this period the art of sculpture flourished in Strasbourg and radiated from there. The great church-building period was also the age of great painters and sculptors like Matthias Grünewald (Isenheim Altar, 1512–1515), Martin Schongauer ("Madonna of the Rose-Garden") and Hans Baldung Grien (1485–1545).
While Romanesque and Gothic art mainly found expression in religious buildings, the Renaissance produced much secular architecture – guild houses, burghers' houses and handsome town halls (Mulhouse, Obernai) which bear witness to the increasing prosperity and self-confidence of the towns.
There are few Baroque churches in Alsace, but important Baroque palaces can be seen in Strasbourg and Saverne.
Among the major attractions of Alsace, to be set alongside such masterpieces as Strasbourg Cathedral and the Isenheim Altar, are the many little towns and villages which have preserved their medieval aspect, such as Colmar, Riquewihr, Hunspach, Kaysersberg, Turckheim, Obernai.
The successful graphic artist and illustrator Gustave Doré (1832–1883) and the sculptor Frédéric-Auguste Bartholdi (1834–1904) in the 19th c. and Hans (Jean) Arp in the 20th were natives of Alsace.

Wines

Alsace is famed for the wines (mostly white wines) grown on the eastern slopes of the Vosges. Seven types of grapes are used – Sylvaner, Pinot Blanc (Weissburgunder), Riesling, Muscat d'Alsace (Tokay), Pinot Gris (Grauburgunder/Ruländer), Gewürztraminer and Pinot Noir (Spätburgunder) – producing six white wines and one rosé, all with *appellations controlées*. The wines are dry and fruity, with a strong bouquet. They are grown round Riquewihr, Ribeauvillé, Hunawihr, Sigolsheim, Kaysersberg, Ammerschwihr, Turckheim, Katzenthal, Guebwiller and Thann, all of which lie on the Route du Vin (see below).

Beer
Fruit brandies

Alsace has numerous breweries, which produce more than a third of the beer drunk in France. Also excellent are the clear fruit brandies, mostly produced in small distilleries.

Route du Vin

An attractive way of getting to know Alsace is to follow the Route du Vin, the Alsatian Wine Trail, which runs west, parallel to N422, from Marlenheim (west of Strasbourg) via Obernai and Colmar to Thann (west of Mulhouse), passing through a series of picturesque Alsatian wine villages, with plenty of opportunities for looking round the wine-making establishments and sampling the product; almost all the producers sell direct to the public.
The main trunk road which runs over the Rhine plain from Strasbourg to Colmar and Mulhouse is to be recommended only to travellers in a hurry.

Along the Route du Vin

Since the Route du Vin along the eastern fringes of the Vosges is the most popular tourist route in Alsace, the main features of interest are described here in geographical order from north to south along this route. Some places which lie within easy reach of the Route du Vin are also described. Places north of Strasbourg are covered in the description of the Route des Vosges du Nord (page 98).

Strasbourg

See entry

Molsheim

The little town of Molsheim (pop. 7000) has preserved remains of its medieval walls, old houses and fountains. In the market square are an old guild house, the Alte Metzig (16th c.), and a fountain of the same period. The Alte Metzig houses a museum displaying material of the prehistoric and early historical periods and documents on the history of the town; a section is also devoted to the Bugatti car works, formerly in Molsheim.
The Jesuit church (1617) is one of the finest examples of Jesuit architecture.

Nideck

Near Molsheim is the ruined castle of Nideck.

Rosheim

*St-Pierre-et-St-Paul

The old wine town of Rosheim (pop. 3900) was a member of the Decapolis, the league of ten free imperial cities in Alsace. Its medieval walls and towers and many half-timbered houses are well preserved. The church of St-Pierre-et-St-Paul is one of the finest Romanesque churches in Alsace; the church is first mentioned in 1051, but the present building dates from 1150-1160. Particularly charming are the friezes round the exterior and the unusual animal and human figures in the pediments.
The 12th c. Heidehuss (Heathen House) is the only stone-built house of the Renaissance period in Alsace. The Town Hall and the fountain in the market square date from 1775.

Obernai

*Townscape

Obernai (pop. 10,000), at the foot of Mont Ste-Odile (see Vosges), is an old imperial city which has preserved its picturesque aspect, with part of its town walls, narrow lanes, old burghers' houses and a handsome Town Hall. The market square, with the 15th c. Cornmarket, the Renaissance fountain of St Odile, the Town Hall (15th–16th c.) and old Gothic and Renaissance houses, has a particularly attractive old-world air. The Town Hall, with its decorated balcony and council chamber of 1608, was restored in the 19th c. Another prominent landmark is the Tour de la Chapelle (13th and 16th c.). In front of the Hôtel de la Cloche is the Puits des Six Seaux (Six-Bucket Well) of 1579, and to the north of the large neo-Gothic church (1873) is another picturesque spot, the Place de l'Etoile with its angular half-timbered houses and storks' nests on the roofs, set against a background of vine-covered hills.

Mont Ste-Odile

See Vosges

Ottrott

At the foot of Mont Ste-Odile lies Ottrott (pop. 1390), with the ruins of its two castles, the Lutzelbourg (12th c.) and Rathsamhausen (13th c.). In the lower part of the town is a small Romanesque chapel.

Barr

This little town (pop. 4700), set amid vineyards at the foot of the Vosges, has a Renaissance Town Hall (1640), charming burghers' houses (14th–15th c.), some in Gothic style, and the Musée de la Folie Marco (furniture), in an 18th c. house. The tower of the Protestant church dates from the 12th c. An important wine market is held here in July.

Andlau

The beautifully situated town of Andlau (pop. 1750) has many half-timbered houses and an abbey founded for Benedictine nuns in 887 by Richardis, the discarded wife of Charles the Fat. The church, which dates from the 11th and 12th centuries, has fine reliefs on the façade and doorway, and, in the choir, a 14th c. reliquary of the foundress. Above the town (alt. 475 m/1560 ft) are the ruins of a 13th c. castle, the Spesbourg.

Dambach-la-Ville

This little town of wine-growers and farmers (pop. 2000) has preserved parts of its walls, three 13th c. gate towers and many half-timbered houses, particularly in the market square. Amid the vineyards is the 11th c. chapel of St-Sébastien, with a Romanesque tower, a Gothic choir and a beautifully carved and decorated Baroque altar of the late 17th c.

Châtenois

The name of the town (pop. 3000) refers to the chestnut-trees that grow here. It has a 15th c. tower, the "Witches' Tower", a relic of the town's defences, a church dating from 1760 with a Romanesque tower (12th c.) and a Town Hall (1493–1496). Some distance outside the town, looming picturesquely over the old village of Kintzheim, is the fine castle of Kintzheim (13th and 15th c.; alt. 320 m/1050 ft), with residential quarters of the 13th c. and a Late Gothic chapel. In the village are a park with storks, an aviary in which eagles fly freely and a monkey-house with over 300 animals.

Kintzheim

From Kintzheim an excursion can be made to the Haut-Kœnigsbourg (see Vosges).

St-Hippolyte

This little village (pop. 1200), picturesquely situated at the foot of the Haut-Kœnigsbourg, has preserved its medieval aspect, with a Gothic church (14th–15th c.) and remains of its walls.

Haut-Kœnigsbourg

See Vosges

Sélestat

Sélestat (pop. 15,000) lies on the river Ill, roughly on the border between Upper and Lower Alsace. In the 8th c. it was a Carolingian stronghold, and between 1217 and 1648 it was a free imperial city, a member of the league of ten Alsatian cities from 1354. In the 15th and 16th centuries it was an important centre of early humanism, with its "Latin school" (grammar school) and its Literary Society.

*Ste-Foy

In the centre of the old town is the Hôtel de Ville (Town Hall), and a little to the east is the three-towered church of Ste-Foy, a Late Romanesque building (11th–12th c.) with rich external ornament, a porch of typical Alsatian type and a handsome octagonal tower over the crossing. Notable features of the interior are the capitals and the crypt.

*St-Georges

North of Ste-Foy is the church of St-Georges, one of the largest Gothic churches in Alsace (early 13th c.), with a richly carved pulpit (1619), old stained glass and a modern work by Max Ingrand. The Municipal Library, founded in 1452 in the abbot's lodgings of the nearby abbey of Ebersmünde, recalls the town's great days as a centre of humanism; it possesses valuable manuscripts ranging in date between the 7th and the 16th c., 530 incunabula and 2000 printed works of the 16th c. Sélestat has also preserved two fine old towers, the Witches' Tower, a relic of the old fortifications restored by Vauban, and the Clock-Tower (14th and 17th c.).

***Ribeauvillé**

*Townscape

Ribeauvillé (pop. 5000), whose Alsatian name is Rappschwihr, is a little wine town at the foot of famous vineyards with a picturesque aspect and many old half-timbered houses. Above the town are three ruined castles dating from the 11th–14th centuries, Girsberg (528 m/1732 ft), St-Ulrich

The fortified church of Hunawihr, surrounded by vineyards

(530 m/1739 ft) and Haut-Ribeaupierre (642 m/2106 ft). In the Middle Ages the town was held by the Count of Ribeaupierre (Rappoltstein), "king" of all the strolling musicians and singers of the Upper Rhine, who paid dues to him for his protection and gathered annually at Ribeauvillé for "Pfiffertag" – a festival which is still celebrated every year on the first Sunday in September.
In the Grand' Rue (No. 14) is the Pfifferhaus, and farther along the street is the main square, with the Town Hall (1773-1778), a Renaissance fountain (1536) and a Late Gothic monastic church (1412). Parts of the old town walls have been preserved, including the Tour des Bouchers (Butchers' Tower, 13th–16th c.) and other defensive towers.

Hunawihr

The wine village of Hunawihr (pop. 600), situated amid vineyards, has a picturesque Late Gothic fortified church (15th c.) and a fortified churchyard. Until 1789 it was a fief of the ducal house of Württemberg.

****Riquewihr**

The old wine town of Riquewihr (pop. 1100) is one of the most popular tourist attractions of Alsace and one of its most charming and unspoilt towns, with its well preserved walls and towers and its many Gothic and Renaissance houses (beautiful courtyards). The castle (1539) of the Counts and later Dukes of Württemberg-Mömpelgard (Montbéliard) now houses a Postal Museum. The main street, Rue du Général-de-Gaulle (no cars allowed in summer) is lined by fine old houses and at the upper end is the Dolder, a gate tower of 1291 which now houses a local museum. Beyond it is the Obertor (Upper Gate), with portcullises, machicolations and loop-holes. On the fountain are the arms of the Dukes of Württemberg-Mömpelgard.
To view the town from outside, take a path running through the Schœnenberg vineyards from the Tour des Voleurs (Thieves' Tower; 1300), which contains a torture chamber.
The main events of the year in Riquewihr are the Riesling Festival in August and the Vintage Festival on two weekends in September,

Kientzheim

Kientzheim (pop. 1000) was one of "three towns in one valley" (the others being Ammerschwihr and Kaysersberg). It has preserved its medieval walls, two castles and numerous half-timbered houses. On the Untertor (Lower Gate) is a curious grotesque face, looking towards the traditional "enemy" town of Sigolsheim. In the 15th c. parish church (to the left) is the gravestone of Marshal Lazarus von Schwendl (1552-1584), a German officer in the service of the Emperor who is said to have brought the Tokay grape to Alsace from Hungary during the Turkish wars. Some 16th c. votive tablets can be seen in the Lower Church. The imposing castle of Reichenstein near the Untertor (15th c., enlarged by von Schwendl in the 16th and 17th c.) has an interesting wine cellar and wine museum.

Kaysersberg
*Townscape

This old imperial city (pop. 2700), beautifully situated at the mouth of the Weiss valley, was acquired by the Hohenstaufen Emperor Frederick II in 1227. Above the little town loom the ruins of an imperial castle with a circular keep (destroyed during the Thirty Years War). Kaysersberg has preserved remains of its medieval fortifications, an old fortified bridge over the Weiss (15th–16th c.), and handsome Gothic and Renaissance burghers' houses. The Town Hall was begun in 1521, in early Renaissance style, and enlarged in 1605 (council chamber with rich carved decoration). The chapel of St-Michel has well preserved frescoes of 1464. The house in which Albert Schweitzer (1875–1965) was born now contains a small museum.

This old imperial city (pop. 1700) is a well-known wine village, with remains of its walls, two towers, the Obertor (Upper Gate) and the 16th c. parish church of St-Martin.

Turckheim

Turckheim (pop. 3500), at the entrance to the Munster valley, is another old imperial city, which became a member of the league of ten Alsatian cities in 1354. Still partly surrounded by walls, it has preserved its old-world aspect,

A picturesque street in Riquewihr

Tour des Fripons, Ammerschwihr

Marmoutier Abbey

with Late Gothic stone-built and half-timbered houses (17th c.). The Renaissance Town Hall dates from the early 17th c.

Munster

Munster (pop. 4700), the chief town in the Munster valley, grew up round a Benedictine abbey founded in the 7th c. which was dissolved in 1790. It became an imperial free city in the 13th c., and in 1354 joined the league of ten cities. The town is now well known for its textile industry and famed for its cheese and its *tourte* (a kind of meat vol-au-vent). The Town Hall dates from 1555, the Laub (market hall) from 1503. Munster is a good base for excursions into the Vosges (see entry), and the starting-point of the Route du Fromage (Cheese Trail).

Les Trois-Epis

Les Trois-Epis, a place of pilgrimage since 1491, has a 17th c. chapel (pilgrimages in May and August). It is now also a popular holiday place, commandingly situated high above the Rhine plain.
In Niederhaslach is a church which was rebuilt in the 13th c. by the son of the architect of Strasbourg Cathedral, Erwin of Steinbach.

Lac Blanc
Lac Noir

Farther into the Vosges, surrounded by coniferous forests, are two picturesque crater lakes, the Lac Blanc and Lac Noir; they were linked by a pressure pipe in 1930 and the water is used to generate electricity.

Colmar

See entry

Neuf-Brisach
*Fortifications

Neuf-Brisach (pop. 2200) was built for Louis XIV by the great military engineer Vauban in 1699-1703. It is a characteristic example of his work, octagonal in shape with four gates, one of which, the Belfort Gate houses a Vauban Museum. Some 17th c. burghers' houses have survived.
To the east of the town is the Colmar–Neuf-Brisach port on the Rhine.

Eguisheim

This ancient little wine town (pop. 1500) has preserved its picturesque lanes and fountains and its attractive half-timbered buildings (16th–17th c.), including several tithe barns which belonged to monastic houses. In the

centre of the town is an octagonal stronghold, the enclosing walls of a small moated castle of the Hohenstaufen period, originally founded in the 8th c. (rebuilt in 1903). Within the walls is a chapel built in 1889 in honour of Pope Leo IX, who was born here in 1002.
Above the town rise the Trois Tours d'Eguisheim or Drei Exen, belonging to the ruined castle of Haut-Eguisheim.

Pfaffenheim

Pfaffenheim, 4 km/2½ miles before Rouffach, has a beautiful pilgrimage church with a Romanesque choir.

Rouffach

*Notre-Dame

Rouffach (pop. 5000), a town of wine-growers and farmers, has remains of its old town walls and many handsome old burghers' houses. The church of Notre-Dame de l'Assomption, built between the 12th and 14th centuries, shows the transition from Romanesque to Gothic; its three towers were restored in the 19th c. Opposite the church is the Renaissance Town Hall (16th c.), and adjoining this are the Tour des Sorcières (Witches' Tower) and the Cornmarket. North of the town, on the Rehberg, is the castle of Isenburg, built in 1880 on the foundations of a stronghold of the Merovingian and Frankish kings.

Guebwiller

*St-Léger

Guebwiller (pop. 11,000), situated at the mouth of the Lauch valley, known as Florival ("Valley of Flowers"), now an important wine town, developed in the 8th c. around a grange belonging to Murbach Abbey. The Romanesque and Gothic church of St-Léger, which dates from the Hohenstaufen period, has fine sculpture on the central doorway. The church of Notre-Dame (18th c.) is one of the few Baroque churches in Alsace and has fine carved woodwork. The Dominican church (14th c.) has a cycle of frescoes, and there is a museum in the choir.
The atomic physicist Alfred Kastler (Nobel Prize 1966) was born in Guebwiller.

Murbach

*Abbey church

North-west of Guebwiller is the famous Romanesque Benedictine abbey of Murbach, which in the 8th and 9th centuries was the cultural centre of Upper Alsace and one of its most powerful lordships. All that survives is the towers, transept and choir of the abbey church, which ranks with Marmoutier and Rosheim as one of the oldest and most important monuments of Romanesque architecture in Alsace.

Lautenbach

The village of Lautenbach, near Guebwiller, also has a Romanesque church, with a fine pulpit, richly carved choir-stalls and beautiful windows (16th c.). Adjoining the church is a 16th c. cloister.

Thann

*St-Thiébault

Thann (pop. 8000), at the southern end of the Route du Vin, attracts many holidaymakers with its beautiful situation at the mouth of the narrow Thur valley. Although an industrial town, it is also famed for its wine made from grapes grown on Mt Rangen. In the centre of the town is the church of St-Thiébault, the most important Gothic building in Alsace after Strasbourg Cathedral. The very fine tower, 76 m/250 ft high, is modelled on the tower of Freiburg Cathedral (south-west Germany). On the west front is a large double doorway (14th–15th c.) with rich sculptural decoration, and the north doorway (15th c.) also has fine sculptured work. The interior is notable for its 16th c. carved woodwork, 15th c. stained glass and richly carved choir-stalls.
Other features of interest in Thann are its old half-timbered houses, remains of its walls, the Witches' Tower (Tour des Sorcières) and the Storks' Tower (Tour des Cigognes). The old Cornmarket, a handsome 16th c. building, now houses the Museum of Alsatian History.

Mulhouse

Mulhouse (pop. 114,000) is the second largest town in Alsace and the industrial metropolis of Upper Alsace. The warehouses on the river port north-west of the town are among the largest in the world.
From 1308 to 1515 Mulhouse was a free imperial city and a member of the

league of ten Alsacian free cities. Thereafter, until 1648, it was Swiss; between 1798 and 1871 it was French, from then until 1918 it was German, and then returned to France. It lies between the Vosges and the Black Forest at the point where the Upper Rhine plain merges into the uplands of the Sundgau, and is traversed by the rivers Doller and Ill and by the Rhine-Rhône Canal. It now has a university, founded in 1969.

Place de la Réunion

In the centre of the old town is the market square, the Place de la Réunion, with the Town Hall (1552), a handsome Renaissance building with mural paintings on the façade and a double external staircase. The council chamber has 16th and 17th c. stained glass, and the Town Hall houses a Historical Museum. Opposite is the 15th c. Maison Mieg. The church of St-Etienne has fine 15th c. windows and 17th c. choir-stalls. Other buildings of interest are the Pharmacie au Lys (1646), the Cour des Chaînes (converted into a dwelling-house in the 16th c.), the Tour du Diable and the 13th c. chapel of St-Jean.
In the Place de l'Europe is the 31-storey Tour de l'Europe, with a revolving restaurant at the top.

Museums
*Musée National de l'Automobile

The town has a number of museums and a Zoological and Botanical Garden. The most unusual of the museums is the Musée Nationale de l'Automobile in the Avenue de Colmar, which developed out of the private collection of two Swiss brothers named Schlumpf. It contains around 450 vintage and veteran cars from many different countries, including 122 Bugattis as well as Rolls-Royces and Panhards. In the suburban district of Dornach is the French Railway Museum, with locomotives and rolling-stock from 1844 to the present day. There are other museums concerned with the history of fire, printed fabrics, wallpaper, art and mineralogy.

*Railway Museum

Ecomusée d'Alsace

In Ungersheim, 15 km/9 miles north of Mulhouse, is the Ecomusée d'-Alsace, an open-air museum with 20 traditional half-timbered houses from the Sundgau.

Altkirch

South of Mulhouse is Altkirch, the old capital of the Sundgau, with a small museum of history and art, and the pilgrimage church of St-Morand, which contains a fine Romanesque high-relief.

Route de la Carpe Frite

There are a wide range of possible excursions from Mulhouse. The Route de la Carpe Frite (fried carp being a local speciality) is a good introduction to the beautiful scenery of the Sundgau.

***River Rhine**

The Rhine is Europe's most important waterway. With a total length of 1320 km/820 miles, it is an international river traversing six countries, including France. Between Basle and Strasbourg the main shipping channel is the Grand Canal d'Alsace, which runs parallel to the river and has a link with the Rhine–Rhône Canal (Canal du Rhône au Rhin). The Grand Canal du Rhin is 51 km/32 miles long and between 110 and 140 m (360 and 460 ft) wide. In the southern section, which is wholly canalised, there are four dams and hydroelectric stations (at Kembs, Ottmarsheim, Fessenheim and Vogelgrün) and the total fall is 140 m/460 ft.

Route des Vosges du Nord

The features of interest north of Strasbourg lie on the Route des Vosges du Nord, and are described here in geographical order, starting from Strasbourg.

Strasbourg

See entry

Haguenau

Haguenau is the fourth largest town in Alsace (pop. 25,000) and has a varied range of industry. In 1354 it became the chief town of the league of

ten Alsatian imperial free cities. After frequent destruction in the course of its history (burned down by the French in 1677, badly damaged in 1944-1945) Haguenau has preserved only a few old buildings.
The Romanesque and Gothic church of St-Georges (originally 12th–13th c., later enlarged) possesses a colossal wood figure of Christ (1488) and the oldest bells in Alsace (1268). On the northern edge of the old town is the Gothic church of St-Nicolas (13th–14th c.), with beautifully carved 18th c. choir-stalls. The Historical and Alsatian Museums have interesting collections of material on early history and the region of Alsace.

Soufflenheim

Soufflenheim (pop. 4500), 14 km/9 miles east of Haguenau, is the centre of the Alsatian ceramic industry.

Sessenheim

5 km/3 miles south-east of Soufflenheim is Sessenheim (German spelling Sesenheim; pop. 1500), scene of Goethe's love affair with the local pastor's daughter Friederike Brion in 1770–1771. In the Auberge du Bœuf is a small Goethe Museum.

Wœrth

The little town of Wœrth, on the river Sauer, was the scene of bitter fighting during the Franco-Prussian War of 1870–1871. It has a Renaissance château (16th c.) with a 14th c. tower. In front of the Town Hall is a Roman altar with reliefs of Mercury, Hercules, Minerva and Juno.

Niederbronn-les-Bains

Niederbronn-les-Bains (pop. 4500) is an important spa and climatic resort, situated at the entrance to the beautiful Falkenstein valley, and a good base for walks and climbs in the hills. Its brine springs, which were already known to the Romans, and chalybeate springs are used in the treatment of a variety of complaints. There is a museum containing prehistoric and Roman material.

Wissembourg

The picturesque holiday resort of Wissembourg (pop. 6600), surrounded by vineyards, grew up around a Benedictine abbey founded in the 7th c., and was a member of the league of ten imperial free cities in Alsace. The Town Hall, in the market square, was built in 1741–1751. The church of St-Pierre-et-Paul, the largest church in Alsace after Strasbourg Cathedral, has medieval stained glass and a crown-shaped chandelier. The Romanesque west tower dates from 1070, the beautiful cloister from the 14th c. The Westercamp Museum has a collection of archaeological material and documents on the history of the town.

*St-Pierre-et-Paul

Fleckenstein Castle

Fleckenstein Castle (alt. 370 m/1215 ft), built in the 12th c. but now a ruin, is partly built into the sandstone crag on which it stands.

La Petite-Pierre

This little town (pop. 700), still partly surrounded by walls, is charmingly situated on the slopes and crest (wide views) of the Altenberg. The church has 15th c. frescoes in the choir.

Bouxwiller

Bouxwiller (pop. 400) lies at the foot of the Bastberg (320 m/1050 ft). The Renaissance-style Town Hall, built in 1659 as the chancellery of the Count of Hanau (restored 1909), has a very handsome doorway.

Saverne

Saverne (pop. 10,500), the Roman *Tres Tabernae,* chief town of the Vosges region in the Middle Ages and from 1414 to 1789 a residence of the bishops of Strasbourg, lies at the point where the river Zorn and the Rhine–Marne Canal enter the Alsatian plain. The neo-classical Château Rohan, the palace of the bishops of Strasbourg, was built in 1779–1789 on the site of an earlier castle. It now houses museums of archaeology, art and history and the Louis Weiss Museum. In the Grand' Rue are a number of fine Renaissance houses; the 17th c. Maison Katz has richly carved half-timbering. To the west of the Town Hall (1900) is the former Franciscan church (14th c.), with a Gothic cloister.

*Maison Katz

Marmoutier
*Abbey church

Marmoutier (pop. 2000) has one of the most beautiful churches in Alsace, the abbey church of St-Maur (see illustration on page 96), which belonged to a Benedictine abbey founded in 724. The present church, of dark red sandstone, was built in the 12th and 13th centuries. Its main features of interest are the curious animal figures on the Romanesque façade, the ancient foliage capitals in the porch, a Silbermann organ of 1709 in the Gothic nave and beautifully carved stalls in the 18th c. choir.

Route des Villages Pittoresques

The Route des Villages Pittoresques offers an attractive trip from Wissembourg via Oberseebach, Hunspach, Hoffen, Leiterswiller, Oberrœdern, Hatten, Rittershoffen, Betschdorf and Surbourg, returning by way of Soultz-sous-Forêts. The route runs through a series of picturesque little villages of half-timbered houses where the old traditional costumes can sometimes be seen.

Amboise

I7

Region: Centre
Département: Indre-et-Loire
Altitude: 60 m/200 ft
Population: 11,000

Situation and characteristics

The old town of Amboise lies 25 km/15 miles east of Tours on the left bank of the Loire (see Loire Valley), which here flows around the long, narrow Ile St-Jean. To the south, between the Loire and the Cher, extends a large area of forest.

History

The town, recorded in Roman and Merovingian times under the name of Vicus Ambaciensis, passed from the control of the French kings into the hands of the Counts of Anjou, and from the 12th c. until 1431 it was the seat of the Anjou family. When Louis d'Amboise fell into disfavour with King Charles VII, however, the town was confiscated by the crown. Thereafter the château was enlarged and sumptuously decorated as befitted a royal residence. Leonardo da Vinci died here in 1519.
In 1560, in the Conspiracy of Amboise, a group of Huguenots called for freedom of worship and tried to counter the influence of the Catholic family of Guise on King Francis II. The plot miscarried and the conspirators were ruthlessly punished; it is said that 1200 of their supporters were hanged from the iron railings on the balcony of the château.
In 1563, however, the Edict of Amboise granted the Huguenots limited freedom of worship.

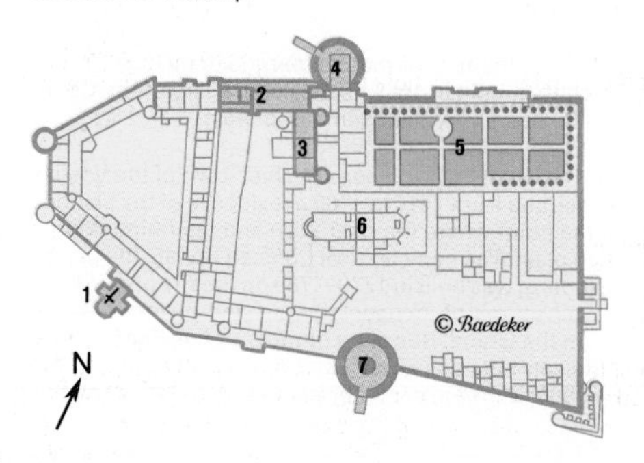

Amboise
Château

1 Chapelle St-Hubert
2 Gothic Wing
3 Renaissance Wing
4 Tour des Minimes
5 Garden
6 Chapel
7 Tour Hurtault

50 m

Château d'Amboise

Sights

*Château

Only part of the château, which was originally four times its present size, has been preserved. On the north side, facing the river, the building is supported by massive buttresses, above which rises the richly articulated façade of the château with the iron railings of the balcony, flanked by two imposing round towers, the Tour des Minimes (with a spiral ramp up which horses could be ridden) and the Tour Hurtault.

*St-Hubert

The Chapelle St-Hubert, which stands on the curtain wall, was built around 1491 by Charles VIII and his wife Anne de Bretagne. It is a fine example of Gothic architecture. On the doorway is a relief representation of the legend of St Hubert, and in the tympanum is a 19th c. figure of the Virgin flanked by Charles and Anne. The roof and roof turrets were restored in the 19th c. In the left-hand transept is a tablet commemorating Leonardo da Vinci, who is believed to have been buried here.

Logis du Roi

On the north side of the terrace are the two surviving wings, at right angles to one another, of the Logis du Roi (King's Lodging). The wing parallel to the river is Gothic, the other one Renaissance. The difference in style is clearly seen in the form of the dormer windows.

Interior

In the Salle des Gardes are arms and armour, Aubusson tapestries and Gothic furniture, in the Renaissance wing more tapestries and Gothic and Renaissance furniture. Visitors can also see the large Salle de Justice, in which the Huguenot conspirators were tried and condemned, and the Balcon des Conjurés, where many of them were hanged.
The gardens and terraces of the château are also worth seeing.

Clos-Lucé

South-east of the château of Amboise is the manor-house of Clos-Lucé, in which Leonardo spent his last years. In the basement are models of machines and machinery constructed on the basis of his drawings.

From the cellar of Clos-Lucé an underground passage once ran to the château of Amboise, 500 metres away.

Other sights in Amboise

In the lower town is the 16th c. Hôtel de Ville (Town Hall), which houses a small museum (manuscripts, pictures, etc.). Opposite it is the 15th c. church of St-Florentin, with a Renaissance steeple.
On the Loire embankment is an unusual fountain (1968) by Max Ernst, who lived for many years in France.

St-Denis

The church of St-Denis, on the outskirts of the town to the south-east, is a fine example of Romanesque architecture with Angevin features. It has finely decorated capitals and contains the marble tomb (16th c.) with what is said to be a likeness of "la belle Babou", a mistress of Francis I.

Forêt d'Amboise
Pagode de Chanteloup

In the Forêt d'Amboise, a former hunting reserve of the French kings to the south of the town, is the 44 m/144 ft high Pagode de Chanteloup, built in the late 18th c. – all that remains of a large Baroque château which was built in 1715 but later demolished and used as rubble.

Amiens K5

Region: Picardie. Département: Somme
Altitude: 27 m/90 ft. Population: 136,500

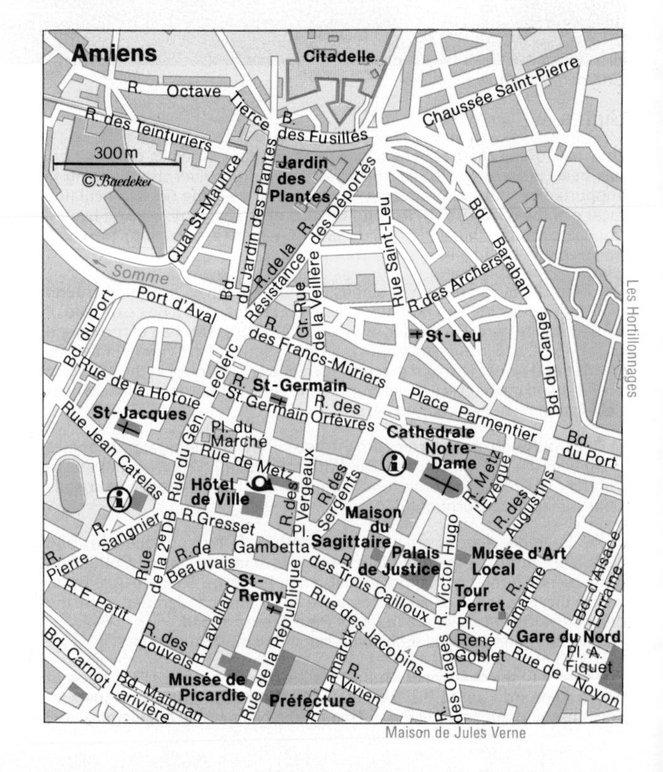

Amiens Cathedral

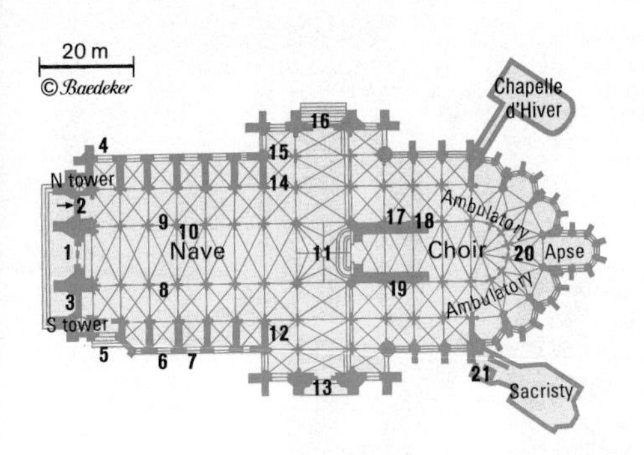

1 Portail du Beau Dieu
2 Portail de St-Firmin (entrance)
3 Portail de la Vierge
4 Charles V
5 St Christopher
6 Annunciation
7 Marchands de Waide
8 Geoffroy d'Eu
9 Evrard de Fouilloy
10 Maze
11 Transept
12 St James the Great defeating the sorcerer Hermogenes
13 S doorway
14 Christ with the merchants in the Temple
15 Font
16 N doorway
17 Choir-stalls
18 St John
19 St Firmin (Firminus)
20 Weeping angel
21 Treasury

Situation and characteristics

Amiens, lying 130 km/80 miles north of Paris on the left bank of the Somme, here divided into a number of branches, is the old capital of Picardy (see entry) and now the chief town of that region and of the département of Somme, the see of a bishop and a university town.

Situated at the intersection of trunk roads linking Paris with northern France, Britain, the Benelux states and Germany, Amiens is a busy town and popular tourist centre, rebuilt after suffering heavy damage during the Second World War, which fortunately spared its magnificent cathedral.

Amiens has long been famed for its linen, wool, cotton and jute industries.

History

As Samarobriva ("bridge on the Somme") Amiens was the chief town of a Celtic tribe, the Ambiani, until their conquest by Caesar. Under the Romans it flourished, thanks to its situation on the Roman road to the north.

The town was Christianised by St Firmin (Firminus) in the 4th c., and the existence of a bishopric is recorded in 511.

In the 9th c. Norman raids wrought great devastation. At the end of the 12th c. the county of Amiens became subject to the French crown. As a fortified town defending the approach to Paris from the north Amiens was the scene of numerous conflicts with the house of Burgundy and later with the Spaniards.

In 1802 the treaty which brought a temporary peace in the Napoleonic wars was signed in Amiens.

Sights

Place Gambetta

The hub of the city's life is the Place Gambetta. From here the busy main street, the Rue des Trois-Cailloux, runs east to the Gare du Nord, on the wide boulevard which follows the line of the old town walls.

Hôtel de Ville

A little way north-west of Place Gambetta is the Place Leon-Debouverie, in the centre of an area which was totally destroyed during the Second World War and has now been almost completely rebuilt. In this square is the Town Hall (17th–20th c.).

****Cathedral**

To the east of the Town Hall is the Cathedral of Notre-Dame, the largest in France in terms of area (7700 sq. m/9210 sq. yds) and in ground-plan and construction a classic example of French Gothic (which also provided the model for Cologne Cathedral).

Built to replace an earlier cathedral destroyed by fire in 1218, it was begun in 1220 by Robert de Luzarches, Thomas de Cormont and his son Regnault,

and was practically complete by 1264; the façade was built in the 15th c. The two dissimilar towers on the west front barely rise above roof level; the south tower dates from 1366, the north tower from the early 15th c. The tower over the crossing was added in 1529.

Façade

The three doorways on the west front, which was strongly influenced by Notre-Dame in Paris, are decorated with a profusion of statues, mostly of Old and New Testament figures, which are among the earliest masterpieces of Gothic cathedral sculpture. Particularly fine is the figure of Christ in the attitude of blessing (the "Beau Dieu d'Amiens", c. 1240) on the middle pier of the central doorway. On either side are apostles and prophets, and in the tympanum is a representation of the Last Judgment. The right-hand doorway is dedicated to the virgin, the left-hand one to St Firmin, patron saint of Picardy. Above the doorways runs a gallery of 22 statues of French kings, and above this again is a magnificent rose window 11 m/36 ft in diameter.
Also of note is the doorway of the south transept, mainly devoted to the life of St Honoré (Honoratus), a later bishop of Amiens. On the central pier is the famous Vierge Dorée (so called because the figure was formerly gilded), a much imitated masterpiece of Gothic sculpture.

Interior

The 42.3 m/139 ft high interior, with its 126 pillars, is one of the world's supreme achievements in the organisation of space and shows the High Gothic architecture of northern France in its greatest perfection. In the nave are the 13th c. tombs of Bishop Evrard de Fouilloy (d. 1222) and his successor Geoffroy d'Eu (d. 1236).
In the five-aisled choir, enclosed by a magnificent wrought-iron grille (18th c.), are choir-stalls carved by various local artists between 1508 and 1518, with no fewer than 3650 figures in some 400 scenes from the most varied fields of religious and secular life. On the choir screen (14th–15th c.) are very fine painted and gilded carvings in high relief (scenes from the life of St Firmin, John the Baptist, etc.). Behind the high altar is the tomb of a canon named Lucas, by Blasset (1628), with a famous weeping angel. In the left-hand transept is a much venerated relic (part of John the Baptist's head). The pulpit is Baroque.

*Musée de Picardie

A little way south of Place Gambetta, in Rue de la République, is the Musée de Picardie, housed in a Second Empire building (1855–1867) with large murals by Puvis de Chavannes in the stair-well. It is one of the ten largest provincial museums in France, with archaeological material (prehistoric, Gallo-Roman, Egyptian and Merovingian) from the region and from the Mediterranean area, works by the Puy Notre-Dame d'Amiens, a pious confraternity (15th–16th c.), works of the Flemish and Dutch schools of the 17th–19th centuries and the 18th c. French school, 19th c. sculpture and a small collection of modern art (Manessier, Hélion, Dubuffet, Jorn, etc.).

Other sights

To the north of the cathedral, beyond the Late Gothic church of St-Leu (timber roof structure with carved beams), is a district traversed by numerous canals, like a miniature local Venice. On the southern edge of this area is the city's river harbour, the Port d'Aval.

Musée d'Art Local

In the Hôtel de Berry, an elegant 1634 mansion full of period furniture, is a museum of regional history. Behind the Hôtel de Ville is the old Bailliage, with a Renaissance façade (restored). The church of St-Germain has a 15th c. doorway and a curious lopsided tower. In Place Parmentier there is a water market every Saturday.

Centre Jules Verne

In the house in which Jules Verne lived for many years visitors can see the room where he worked and wrote. He is buried in the romantic Cimetière de la Madeleine.

◀ *Amiens Cathedral*

Surroundings of Amiens

Hortillonnages

It is well worth taking a trip round the "Hortillonnages", a curious market-gardening region immediately east of Amiens in which fruit and vegetables are grown on land irrigated by countless little channels *(rieux)* carrying water from the Somme. Nowadays they are mostly used for recreation and can only be reached by water.

Samara

10 km/6 miles west of Amiens is Samara, a large leisure park and exhibition complex with a variety of entertainment facilities, including "Riddles of the Past" and "Visions of the Future", an archaeological trail and a botanical garden.

St-Quentin

See Picardy.

Andorra

I12

Flag of Andorra

State: Principality of Andorra (French Principauté d'Andorre, Catalan Principat d'Andorra, Spanish Principado de Andorra).
Capital: Andorra la Vella
Area: 464 sq. km/179 sq. miles
Altitude: 900-3000 m/2950-9850 ft
Population: 47,000

*Situation and characteristics

The little principality of Andorra lies in the eastern Pyrenees between Spain and France. The main settlements are scattered about the high valleys of the river Valira and its two source streams, the Valira d'Orient and the Valira del Nord.

Andorra became accessible from Spain only in 1913 when a pass road was opened up. It is reached from France by the road over the Port d'Envalira (2408 m/7901 ft), built in 1931. Like some other small states, Andorra is famed as a tax haven. It also attracts increasing numbers of visitors (13 million in 1984) as a duty-free area under its customs union with France. Stock-farming, once Andorra's principal source of revenue, now takes second place to tourism. Other contributions are made to the country's economy by its two radio stations, the export of electricity to France and the sale of Andorran stamps to collectors.

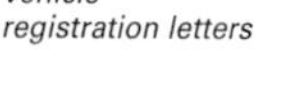

Vehicle registration letters

Some 12,000 of the inhabitants of Andorra are Catalans, around 27,000 come from Spain, 3000 from France and a few from Portugal. The language of Andorra is Catalan, but most Andorrans also speak French and/or Spanish. There is no independent Andorran currency, and both French francs and Spanish pesetas are in circulation.

History and Administration

Arms of Andorra

Archaeological finds in Andorra show that the high valleys were inhabited in the Bronze and Iron Ages. Legend has it that Andorra was founded by Charlemagne. It is first mentioned in a document of 839 recording the consecration of the cathedral in the Spanish town of Seo de Urgel (Catalan La Seu d'Urgell) as belonging to the county of Urgell. In 1133 the territory came into the hands of the bishop of Urgell, who granted it as a fief to the Caboet family. When Andorra passed by marriage to the Counts of Foix this gave rise to a dispute over sovereignty with the bishop of Urgell, which was eventually settled by an agreement *(pareatge)* signed in 1278 and a further agreement ten years later. Under these agreements, which remain in force to the present day, Andorra is under the joint protection of the Count of Foix and the Bishop of Urgell as representatives of the Pope. It is thus, legally, still a medieval feudal state, though in practice sovereign. In 1419 the Andorrans were granted the right to establish a council (the Consell de la Terra) to deliberate on their own affairs, and this still operates under the name of Consell General. Universal suffrage was introduced only in 1970.

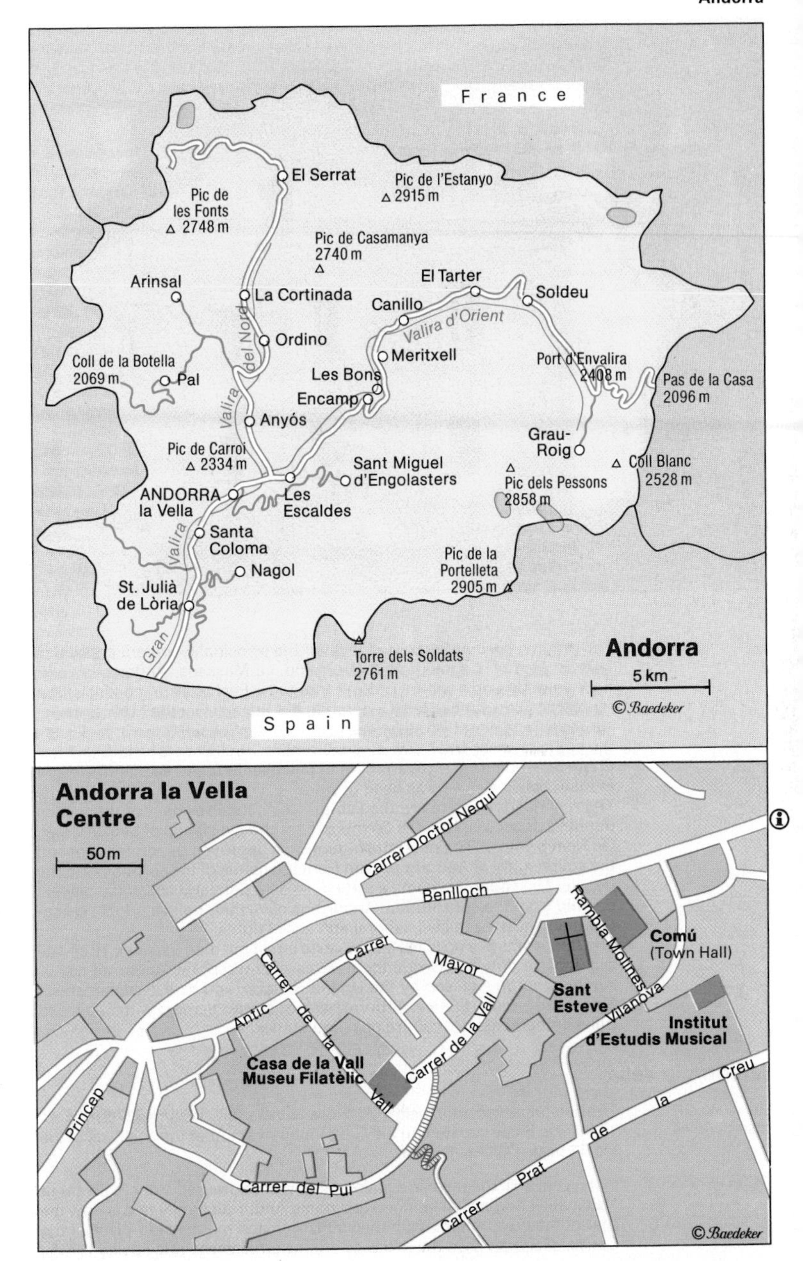
France
El Serrat
Pic de l'Estanyo 2915 m
Pic de les Fonts 2748 m
Pic de Casamanya 2740 m
El Tarter
Soldeu
Arinsal
La Cortinada
Canillo
Valira d'Orient
Ordino
Meritxell
Coll de la Botella 2069 m
Pal
Valira del Nord
Les Bons
Port d'Envalira 2408 m
Pas de la Casa 2096 m
Encamp
Anyós
Grau-Roig
Pic de Carroi 2334 m
Sant Miguel d'Engolasters
Coll Blanc 2528 m
Pic dels Pessons 2858 m
ANDORRA la Vella
Les Escaldes
Santa Coloma
Valira
Nagol
Pic de la Portelleta 2905 m
St. Julià de Lòria
Gran
Torre dels Soldats 2761 m
Andorra
5 km
© Baedeker
Spain
Andorra la Vella Centre
50 m
Carrer Doctor Nequi
Benlloch
Rambla Molines
Comú (Town Hall)
Carrer Mayor
Carrer de la Vall
Sant Esteve
Vilanova
Antic
Institut d'Estudis Musical
Casa de la Vall Museu Filatèlic
Carrer de la Vall
Princep
Carrer Prat de la Creu
Carrer del Pui
© Baedeker

Casa de la Vall

The original six communes (valleys) of the principality were increased in 1978 to seven – Canillo, Encamp, Ordino, La Massana, Andorra la Vella, Sant Julià de Lòria and Escaldes-Engordany. Each commune elects four representatives (Consellers General) to the Consell General. Under a constitutional and administrative reform in 1981 the Consell General was given the right to elect the head of government (President of the Executive Council), who forms a government of between four and six members and in many fields also acts as head of state.

The real heads of state are the "co-princes", the President of the French Republic as successor to the Counts of Foix and the bishop of Seo de Urgel. On March 14th 1993 a new constitution was approved by referendum and the sovereignty of Andorra passed from the hands of the co-princes to the people. The country became a state in its own right and has equal powers derived from the constitution. Andorrans have their political rights recognised and also claim civil, laboral and social rights.

The Andorrans pay no taxes and have no army, but men between 16 and 60 are under a duty to provide themselves with weapons. Andorran sovereignty is not recognised by the United Nations, and its external interests are looked after by France. Andorra has a postal agreement with Spain and trade agreements with both Spain and France.

Andorra la Vella

Situation and characteristics

The capital of the principality, Andorra la Vella (alt. 1029 m/3376 m; pop. 16,000), is finely situated on the Gran Valira river under the east side of the Pic d'Enclar (2317 m/7602 ft).

*Casa de la Vall

In the centre of the town is a plain building of undressed stone built about 1580 which originally belonged to a noble Andorran family and is now the seat of the government, with the courtroom and the meeting-place of the Consell General. Over the entrance are the arms of the principality (1761), with the mitre and crosier of the bishop of Urgell, the four pales of Catalonia, the three pales of the Counts of Foix and the two oxen of the Counts of Béarn in its four quarters. The reception room on the first floor has 16th c. wall paintings. In the council chamber (Sala de Sessions) is the "cupboard of the seven keys", to which each of the seven communes has a key. It contains the archives of the principality, including documents which are said to date from the time of Charlemagne and Louis the Pious. Before every meeting of the Council the councillors attend a service in the Capilla Sant Ermengol. The large kitchen with its old utensils gives an impression of domestic life in the 16th c.

Museum of Philately

The Casa de la Vall also houses the Museum of Philately (Museu Filatèlic), with displays of the stamps which are an important source of revenue for the principality.

Sant Esteve

The church of Sant Esteve, the town's principal church, dates from the 12th c.; it was enlarged in 1969 and has some fine carved woodwork.

Duty-free shops

The main street of Andorra la Vella is lined with shops selling hi-fi equipment, cameras, tobacco goods, spirits and perfume in which visitors (mostly day-trippers) can stock up with duty-free goods.

Valira d'Orient Valley

Les Escaldes

From Les Escaldes (alt. 1105 m/3626 ft), north of Andorra la Vella on the road to the French frontier, a narrow and winding road leads up to the Capilla de Sant Miquel d'Engolasters, a typical example of the Pyrenean churches in Lombard Romanesque style which probably dates from the 12th c. From here it is possible to walk to the Estany d'Engolasters, an artificial lake created by a dam.
Les Escaldes was the home of the Catalonian sculptor Josep Viladomat, many of whose works are displayed in the Josep Viladomat Museum.
Other features of interest in the village are the ruined Capilla Sant Romà and an old bridge, the Pont dels Escalls, while a museum houses scale models of Andorra's Romanesque churches.
Les Escaldes is also a popular spa (sulphurous water).

Encamp

The village of Encamp (alt. 1315 m/4319 ft) has an old Romanesque church in addition to the parish church.
The National Automobile Museum (Museu Nacional de l'Automòbil) displays 200 old cars, motorcycles and bicycles, and also has a collection of miniature china cars.

Les Bons

Near Encamp, huddled round a ruined castle, is the village of Les Bons, with the chapel of Sant Romà de Les Bons (consecrated 1164).

Meritxell chapel

North of Encamp, on a hill to the right of the road, is the chapel of Our Lady of Meritxell. The old pilgrimage chapel was burned down in 1972, and in its place was built a modern chapel designed by Ricardo Bofill (consecrated 1976). In the new chapel each of the seven Andorran communes is represented by a likeness of its patron saint, and there is also a 12th c. statue of the Virgin of Meritxell, patroness of Andorra since 1873.

Sant Joan de Caselles

A little way north of the old-world little village of Canillo, which has Andorra's tallest church-tower, is the chapel of Sant Joan de Caselles, one of the finest Romanesque chapels in the principality, dating from the 11th–12th c. Notable features of the interior, which is decorated with frescoes, are a retablo of 1525 ("St John and the Apocalypse"), the choir grille and a Romanesque stucco figure of Christ on the Cross, surrounded by polychrome painting.

Valira del Nord Valley

A road runs through the valley of the Valira del Nord, ending in the mountains in the north-west of the principality.

Anyòs

After passing a medieval bridge, the Pont de Sant Antoni, the road comes to the picturesque village of Anyòs, with the Capilla de Sant Cristofor.

Ordino

The chief place in the valley is Ordino (alt. 1305 m/4282 ft), the most interesting feature in which is the Casa Plairal d'Areny de Plandolit. The house, originally built in 1633, was rebuilt in the mid 19th c. by its then owner, the Baron de Senaller, initiator of the "New Reform" of 1866, which gave heads of households, for the first time, a limited right of election to the Consell General. The house, which has a magnificent wrought-iron balcony of 1843, is now open to the public. The tour begins in the hall, which contains a reproduction of the original "cupboard of the six seals". On the ground floor are store-rooms for wine, oil and meat and a blacksmith's shop. On the upper floor are the old armoury, now the principal room in the house, with a large barrel-organ, the kitchen and the dining room, in which the baron's Limoges and Sèvres dinner services (the latter a gift from the Austrian Emperor), bearing the family arms, are displayed. Other interesting rooms are the library (with the coats of arms of related families), the music room (with a copy of the original version of the Andorran national anthem), the private chapel and a bakery. In the garden are displayed old stone blacksmith's hammers.

La Cortinada

In La Cortinada, a village surrounded by fields of tobacco, is the church of Sant Martí de la Cortinada, with Romanesque frescoes, a charnel-house and a beautiful old dovecot.

El Serrat

At the end of the road is the magnificently situated mountain village of El Serrat (alt. 1540 m/5053 ft).

Gran Valira Valley

Between Andorra la Vella and Les Escaldes the Valira d'Orient and Valira del Nord join to form the Gran Valira river, which flows south towards the Spanish frontier.

Santa Coloma

On the right of the main road to Spain, in the little village of Santa Coloma, is a fine Romanesque church with a round three-stage tower very different from others in the principality. It contains a much venerated 12th c. statue of the Virgin of Coloma. On the arched entrance are Mozarabic frescoes. The church has a notable medieval font.
Above the village is the 12th c. castle of Sant Vicenç, built by Roger Bernat, Count of Foix.

Sant Julià de Lòria

The road continues past another medieval bridge, the Pont de la Margineda, to Sant Julià de Lòria (alt. 939 m/3081 ft), from which a narrow road winds its way up to the church of Sant Cerní de Nagol, which has fine Romanesque frescoes. The church of Sant Julià de Lòria has a Romanesque bell-tower, a figure of the Virgin of the same period and a 17th c. crucifix.

Sport

Andorra offers endless scope for hill walkers. For anglers there are the mountain streams and lakes, with an abundance of trout. Popular winter sports resorts are Pas de la Casa–Grau Roig, Soldeu–El Tarter, Arinsal, Pal and Arcalís.

Angers

G7

Region: Pays de la Loire
Département: Maine-et-Loire
Altitude: 20 m/ 65 ft
Population: 142,000

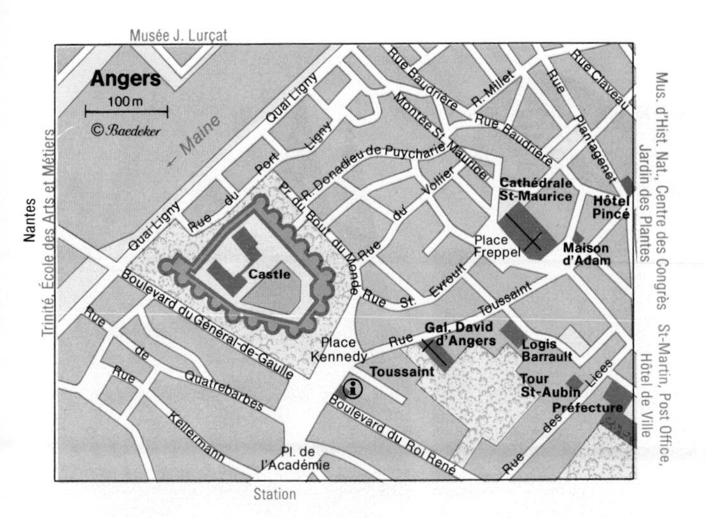

Situation and characteristics

Angers, once capital of the county of Anjou (see entry) and now chief town of the département of Maine-et-Loire, the see of a bishop and a university town, lies half way between Tours and Nantes straddling the river Maine, 8 km/5 miles above its junction with the Loire.
Slate-quarrying is an old-established industry in the surrounding area, and the wines of Anjou are famous. Other important industries are textiles and electrical apparatus and appliances.

History

In Gallo-Roman times Angers was the centre of a territory inhabited by the Andecavi, and after the Roman conquest a fort was built above the river at this point. In the 9th c. the Normans occupied the town but were driven out by Charles the Bald. With the rise of Foulques dynasty, who were at first Viscounts and from around 950 Counts of Anjou, the town flourished, along with the rest of Anjou. In the time of Foulques Nerra (987–1030) in particular many defensive and religious buildings were erected. Geoffroy V (1129–1151) was the first of the line to bear the name Plantagenet (after his crest, a stylised broom bush *(genista)*, and his son was the first Plantagenet king of England as Henry II. In the 12th c., therefore, Anjou became an English possession.
Charles of Anjou was given the throne of Naples and Sicily by the Pope, but his ambitious political plans were shattered by the Sicilian Vespers (1282), when 6000 Frenchmen were killed by the Sicilians.
The best known figure in the history of Angers is Duke René I, "le bon Roi René". As a ruler he was unsuccessful (losing the last remaining Italian territories held by Anjou), but as a man he was highly cultivated, a patron of the arts, and made his capital a great cultural centre. After his death in 1481 Anjou passed to the French crown.
In 1940 the provisional government of Poland was based in Angers.

Sights

*Castle

On a 32 m/105 ft high crag above the left bank of the Maine is the castle, surrounded by stout defensive walls with 17 round towers which now stand 40–60 m/130–200 ft high. The castle was originally built by Foulques Nerra in 1230–1240 and renovated by Louis IX of France (St Louis) later in the 13th c.

Angers castle, the original gateway

Maison d'Adam

During the 16th c. wars of religion Henry III ordered the towers to be pulled down, but in the end only the tops were destroyed.
Of the castle's two gates only the one on the north side, the Porte de Ville, can be used. The south gate, the Porte des Champs, is half way up the outer wall between two towers.
From the walls (along considerable stretches of which it is possible to walk), from two truncated towers and from the wall-walk there are fine all-round views.
In the castle courtyard are the Gothic chapel, the Logis Royal and the Logis du Gouverneur. In both the Royal and the Governor's Lodgings are tapestries of the 14th to 18th centuries.

** Tenture de l'Apocalypse

A specially built modern glass gallery houses one of the great masterpieces of medieval tapestry, the Tenture de l'Apocalypse, woven by the Paris weaver Nicolas Bataille in 1375–1380 after drawings by Hennequin of Bruges. 168 m/550 feet long and 5 m/16 ft wide, it originally consisted of seven parts, of which seventy complete scenes have survived. The theme is the Revelation of St John. The gallery also displays reproductions of the scenes and the relevant passages from the Bible.
At the far end of the exhibition hall, below floor level, the apse of a Romanesque church has been exposed.

* Cathedral

In the Place du Ralliement, in the old town, is the Gothic Cathedral of St-Maurice (12th–13th c.), to which a handsome ramp and staircase lead up from the banks of the Maine. On the doorway are sculptured figures with remains of their original colouring; in the tympanum is Christ enthroned, surrounded by the symbols of the four Evangelists, and above this are eight statues of knights (16th c.). The façade has three towers; the central tower was built in the High Renaissance period.

Interior

The interior is impressive, with fine stained glass (12th, 13th and 15th c.) depicting scenes from the life of the Virgin and the martyrdoms of St

Catherine of Alexandria and St Vincent, tapestries and a richly decorated 18th c. organ gallery. In the cathedral treasury is an antique marble bath converted into a font.

Treasury

Immediately behind the apse of the cathedral is the Maison d'Adam, a handsome and well preserved half-timbered house (15th–16th c.).

Maison d'Adam

The 15th c. Logis Barrault, a handsome burgher's house in which Mary Queen of Scots and Catherine de Médicis once stayed, is now occupied by the Musée des Beaux-Arts, with works by Raphael, Murillo, Ribera, Philippe de Champaigne, Watteau, Chardin, Boucher, Fragonard, David, Ingres, Delacroix and Corot.

*Logis Barrault

In the little Gothic church of Toussaint (All Saints) is an exhibition of the complete work of David d'Angers (1788–1856), consisting partly of originals and partly of copies.

Galerie David d'Angers

A little way east is the Early Gothic bell-tower of St-Aubin.

Tour St-Aubin

The Hôtel Pincé (1523–1530), the finest private mansion in the town, now houses the Musée Turpin de Crissé (enamels, prints and drawings, masks, Oriental and East Asian art, Greek vases).

*Hôtel Pincé

The Lurçat Museum, housed in the old Hôpital St-Jean (12th c.), displays works by the painter Jean Lurçat (1892–1966), best known as the renewer of the art of tapestry. In the large Gothic hall, originally the hospital ward, hangs a cycle of ten tapestries woven in Aubusson, the "Chant du Monde", depicting the problems of mankind in our day and thus in a sense forming a counterpart to the "Apocalypse" (see above).
The hospital complex also includes a Romanesque cloister and a chapel, as well as a small wine museum.

Musée Jean Lurçat

The Pont de Verdun, the middle bridge of the three in the town centre, leads over the Maine into Rue Beaurepaire (houses with beautiful courtyards). At the far end of this street is the Romanesque church of La Trinité, which belonged to Ronceray Abbey (17th c.). The abbey now houses the Ecole Nationale des Arts et Métiers (public not admitted).
The Pont de la Haute-Chaîne leads by way of Boulevard Ayrault and Avenue M.-Talet to the church of St-Serge, which has a fine Angevin-style choir (13th c.). To the south-east is the Jardin des Plantes.

Other sights

Surroundings of Angers

7 km/4 miles south of Angers is the town of Les Ponts-de-Cé, built on islands in the Loire, with seven bridges over the arms of the river.

Les Ponts-de-Cé

In the little town of Brissac, 16 km/10 miles south-east of Angers, is a château set in a beautiful park, built in the early 17th c. on the site of an earlier building of the 13th–15th centuries. The interior is particularly fine and includes some interesting tapestries.

Brissac

The château of Le Plessis-Bourré, 20 km/12 miles north of Angers, has scarcely changed since it was built in the 15th c. It is a rectangular structure with round corner towers surrounded by a wide moat, which is crossed by a 40 m/130 ft long bridge. There are a number of rooms with period furniture and, on the upper floor, an unusual painted wood ceiling with allegorical representations.

Le Plessis-Bourré

The castle of Le Plessis-Macé, 15 km/9 miles north-west of Angers, was originally founded in the 11th c., and owes its present aspect mainly to the 15th c. Particularly notable are the inner courtyard and the Flamboyant (Late Gothic) chapel.

Le Plessis-Macé

Serrant

The moated château of Serrant, 18 km/11 miles south-west, is a sumptuous Renaissance building (16th–18th c.) flanked by corner towers and set in a beautiful park. The exterior shows a charming contrast between light and dark-coloured masonry. The château (open to visitors) contains numerous works of art, tapestries and pictures and a library.

Anjou

G/H7

Situation and characteristics

This delightful region in western France, lying on both sides of the Loire, is now the département of Maine-et-Loire, with Angers (see entry) as its chief town. It bears the name of an old county which in 1360 became a duchy.
This region offers excellent conditions for the growth of flowers and fruit, and in particular for the production of the famed wines of Anjou. Along the banks of the Loire and the other rivers in the region (the Mayenne, the Sarthe, the Loir, the Layon) and in the surrounding area are the numerous châteaux and churches which give Anjou its special charm.

Route du Vin

The most important town after Angers is Saumur, farther up the Loire valley. The Route du Vin d'Anjou (speciality: rosé and sparkling wines) runs from Angers to Chalonnes, Thouarcé, Doué, Montreuil-Bellay, Saumur, Gennes, Brissac and back to Angers. The varied character of Anjou's scenery was expressed by René Bazin in the words: "Anjou is not made all of a piece – it is composed of a hundred different landscapes."

Haut-Anjou

Haut-Anjou (Upper Anjou) is the area north of Angers centred on Le Lion d'Angers.

History

In the Middle Ages, under the Foulques dynasty, Anjou developed into one of the most important French feudal states, which considerably extended

The church . . .

. . . and kitchen, Fontevraud

its territories by conquest and dynastic marriage, acquiring in this way Touraine, Maine and parts of Aquitaine. Geoffroy V (1128–1151), Count of Anjou, the first of his line to bear the name Plantagenet, conquered Normandy for his son Henry, later Henry II of England, and he in turn acquired Aquitaine by his marriage with Eleanor of Aquitaine. With the destruction of the Angevin kingdom by Philip II of Spain Anjou passed to the French crown (1204). Thereafter the title of Duc d'Anjou was borne by princes of the French royal house. At the end of the 18th c. Anjou was the scene of the Vendée rising against the French Revolution.

Sights

Baugé

In the 15th c. Baugé was the favourite residence of Yolande of Aragon, mother of the future Roi René, who also liked to hold court here. The château of Baugé, which has an elegant spiral staircase, now houses the Town Hall and a small museum (china, weapons, old coins). In the Chapelle des Filles du Cœur de Marie is the Croix d'Anjou (Cross of Anjou), a precious relic brought from Constantinople in the 13th c.

*Croix d'Anjou

In 1421 a joint French and Scottish army defeated the English in the battle of Baugé.

***Fontevraud-l'Abbaye**

The little town of Fontevraud or Fontevrault (pop. 1500), famed for its abbey, lies half-way between Chinon and Saumur a few kilometres south of the Loire.

Abbey

The great abbey of Fontevraud was founded in 1099 by a preacher named Robert d'Arbrissel. It was occupied by monks and nuns who lived under the strict rule of the Benedictine order. The abbey was dissolved during the French Revolution, and from 1804 to 1963 served as a prison. It is now a conference centre.
The church dates from the first half of the 12th c. It contains the tombs of members of the Plantagenet house (which favoured the Benedictine order), in particular of Henry II of England, his wife Eleanor of Aquitaine and Richard Cœur-de-Lion – fine examples of 13th c. sculpture.
On the south side of the church is the Cloître Ste-Marie, off which opens the Chapterhouse; both were rebuilt in the 16th c. in typical Renaissance style. Adjoining is the Cloître St-Benoît, which is open on one side; it was partly restored in the late 17th and early 18th c. The best known of the conventual buildings is perhaps the kitchen, with its striking conical roof. Round the octagonal interior are five apses (before the refectory adjoining the kitchen was built there were eight), each with its own chimney hood, which join in the middle in a single large chimney. A low door (usually closed) leads into the rib-vaulted refectory.

St-Michel

The village church of St-Michel (13th–15th c.) has a fine high altar and contains art treasures from the abbey.

Montsoreau

The 15th c. château of Montsoreau, between Fontevraud and Saumur, has preserved its fortress-like character. It contains the Musée des Goums, with mementoes of the conquest of Morocco. (The Goums were Moroccan units incorporated in the French army.)
Alexandre Dumas immortalised one of the châtelaines of Montsoreau in his novel "La Dame de Montsoreau".
1.5 km/1 mile south is the 15th c. Moulin de la Herpinière.

Le Plessis-Bourré

See Angers, Surroundings

Saumur

The medieval town of Saumur, half-way between Angers and Tours, lies on the left bank of the Loire amid the smiling countryside of Anjou. On the outskirts of the town are numbers of wine-cellars hewn from the limestone rock. This is also an important mushroom-growing centre: three-quarters

Château and church of St-Pierre, Saumur

of all the *champignons de Paris* produced in France come from the cellars of Saumur.
In 1763 Saumur became the depot of the French cavalry, and the National Cavalry School is still based here.

*Château

Saumur has one of the finest of the Loire châteaux, built in the 14th c. on a hill high above the Loire. King René called it the "castle of love". At the end of the 16th c. it was converted by its Protestant owners into a fortress, and it still retains its defensive character.
The château, laid out round three sides of a courtyard open on the north-west, is entered through a large and imposing doorway. Obliquely opposite the entrance is a Late Gothic staircase tower housing a spiral staircase. The Tour du Guet, which towers over the south-west wing of the château, can be climbed by way of a series of spiral staircases and passages, and affords fine views of the château courtyard, the roofs of Saumur and the Loire valley.

Museums

The château contains two museums, the Musée des Arts Décoratifs (decorative arts) and the Musée International du Cheval (the horse).

Other sights

On the south side of the Place de la République, which lies on the bank of the Loire, are the two buildings of the Hôtel de Ville; the one on the left dates from the 16th c., while the one on the right-hand side of the square is the neo-classical Theatre. North-west of the square, in the complex of buildings occupied by the Cavalry School, is the Cavalry and Armoured Forces Museum.
In the south of the town, west of the Jardin des Plantes (Botanic Garden), is the beautiful Romanesque church of Notre-Dame de Nantilly (12th c.; rebuilt in 17th c.), with an aisle in Flamboyant (Late Gothic) style and fine capitals. The church of St-Pierre is also Romanesque, with a 17th c. façade. Both churches have fine Aubusson tapestries (15th–17th c.).

Bagneux

At Bagneux, 2 km/1½ miles south-west of Saumur, is one of the most impressive megalithic tombs in Europe.

Brézé

11 km/7 miles south-east of Saumur is the Château de Brézé, a Renaissance moated castle (restored).

Cunault

13 km/8 miles north-west of Saumur is the beautiful Romanesque abbey church of Cunault (11th–13th c.), with an interior notable for its clarity of form. There are remains of Romanesque and Gothic frescoes in the domes of the apses.

Antibes P11

Region: Rhône–Alpes–Côte-d'Azur
Département: Alpes-Maritimes
Altitude: sea level
Population: 63,000

Situation and characteristics

Antibes lies east of Cannes at the west end of the Baie des Anges with the seaside resorts of Cap d'Antibes and Juan-les-Pins within the area of the town. Flower-growing is an important element in the economy of the surrounding area.

History

Ancient Antipolis (that is, the city opposite Nikaia Polis, or Nice) was founded by Phocaeans in the 5th c. B.C., and later became a Roman base. From the 14th c. onwards it was a frontier town between Savoy and France; then in 1481 it passed to France along with the rest of Provence. Later the town's fortifications were reconstructed by Vauban and the Fort Carré (end of 17th c.), of which only a few remains survive, was built. The château in the old town was for many years the seat of a bishop and a residence of the Grimaldi family.

Sights

Château
*Musée Picasso

The old Grimaldi château (16th c.) stands to the south of the cathedral and houses the Picasso Museum, a collection of modern and contemporary art which includes works by de Staël, Ernst, Miró, Calder, Léger, Hartung, Atlan, Richier, Adami, Modigliani, Saura, Cesar, Arman and Alechinsky. The first floor is devoted to Picasso himself, with pictures, ceramics and sculpture which he created during a six months' stay in the château.

Archaeological Museum

The seafront promenade runs south to the Bastion St-André, a relic of Vauban's fortifications. It is now occupied by the Musée d'Archéologie Terrestre et Sous-Marine (Museum of Terrestrial and Submarine Archaeology).

Cap d'Antibes

Plateau de la Garoupe

The Cap d'Antibes is the tip of a peninsula jutting out into the Mediterranean from Juan-les-Pins and Antibes. Its highest point is the Plateau de la Garoupe (78 m/256 ft), with a lighthouse from which there are views of the town and the coast, with the offshore Iles de Lérins, the Massif de l'Esterel and the Maritime Alps beyond.
The old pilgrimage chapel of Notre-Dame de la Garoupe (13th and 16th c.) has frescoes, two statues of gilded wood and numerous ex-votos.

Jardin Thuret

The Jardin Thuret, which contains a wide range of subtropical plants, is named after the scientist of that name who began to plant exotic species here in 1856.

Musée Naval et Napoléonien

At the tip of the cape, in the Tour Grillon, a relic of an old fort, is the Naval and Napoleonic Museum.

Juan-les-Pins

Juan-les-Pins, a busy and fashionable resort, lies on Golfe Juan, the bay which extends between Antibes and Cannes (see entry), in a situation commanding extensive views.

Surroundings of Antibes

Marineland

The road to Biot (north of Antibes) runs past Marineland, a marine zoo which offers among its attractions trained dolphins, sea-lions and killer whales.

Biot

Biot, once the capital of a Ligurian tribe, is now a town of craftsmen in which old techniques (e.g. of glass-blowing) are being revived. The church of Ste-Madeleine has two fine altarpieces of the Nice school and a Madonna of the Rosary by Louis Bréa.

* Musée Léger

20 minutes' walk away, just outside the town, is the Léger Museum, with a monumental mosaic by Léger on the outside wall. The museum, established by his widow Nadya, displays work from his various creative periods. The wire portrait of the artist in the stair-well is by Alexander Calder.

Arles M11

Region: Provence–Alpes–Côte-d'Azur
Département: Bouches-du-Rhône
Altitude: 10 m/33 ft
Population: 51,000

Situation and characteristics

The old city of Arles lies on the Rhône, just south of the point where it divides into two arms, the Grand Rhône to the east and the Petit Rhône to the west. The two arms of the river enclose the Camargue (see entry), a region of lakes and lagoons, before flowing into the Mediterranean.
Arles preserves impressive remains of its Roman and medieval past, and has many associations with the painter Vincent van Gogh, who lived here in 1888 and 1889.

History

Arles (Arelate, the "town in the marshes") was originally a Greek settlement. In 46 B.C. it became a Roman colony, and thereafter competed with Massilia (Marseilles) as a port on the Mediterranean coast of Gaul. There was a Christian community here at an early period, and in 314 the first church council in the Western Empire was held at Arles. In 406 the town became the administrative centre of the whole of Gaul. From the 10th c. it was part of the kingdom of Burgundy, and in 1481, along with the rest of Provence, passed to France.
Arles is now the largest commune in France, with an area of more than 750 sq. km/290 sq. miles (compared with Paris's 105 sq. km/40 sq. miles).

Sights

** Arènes

The Roman amphitheatre, known as the Arènes, which is believed to date from the early 2nd c., is the largest ancient structure in Arles. Oval in shape, measuring 107 m/350 ft by 136 m/445 ft, it was one of the largest in Gaul, with room for 26,000 spectators in its 34 tiers of seating. It became a fortress in the Middle Ages, when three square towers were built and the arches (of which there were originally three tiers – now only two) were

Bird's eye view of Roman amphitheatre and theatre, Arles

blocked up. From the top of the towers there are marvellous views over the roofs of the town and the surrounding area.
The amphitheatre is now used for bullfights and other events.

The van Gogh Foundation

The van Gogh Foundation was installed in the Palais de Luppé in 1984. On display are works by a number of artists which are dedicated to van Gogh.

Theatre

The ancient theatre, built in the time of Augustus, was as large as the one in Orange (see entry), with accommodation for an audience of 8000 in its 33 tiers of seating. From early medieval times it was used as a quarry of building material for the construction of the town walls and other purposes. It preserves the semicircular tiers of seating, orchestra, pit for the curtain and remains of stage (two columns and a few column stumps).

Place de la République

To the west of the theatre is the Place de la République, with an ancient granite obelisk 15 m/50 ft high. On the north side of the square is the Hôtel de Ville (Town Hall) of 1673–1675.

*St-Trophime

On the east side of the square is the former cathedral of St-Trophime, dedicated to the Greek apostle (Trophimus) who Christianised Provence. In its present form (1152–1180) it is a Romanesque church of basilican type, the interior of which already shows Gothic influences.

Façade

St-Trophime has a magnificent doorway with fine sculptured figures, which was incorporated in the existing Carolingian church in the 12th c. On the piers are figures of saints: centre, left, St Trophime being crowned by angels with a mitre; right, the stoning of St Stephen. In the tympanum are scenes from the life of Christ and a Last Judgment (on the left the elect, on the right the damned), and on the capitals below this the Annunciation (left) and the Nativity of Christ (right).
The side doorways, which are smaller than the main doorway, date from the 17th c. The interior of the church shows the transition from Roman-

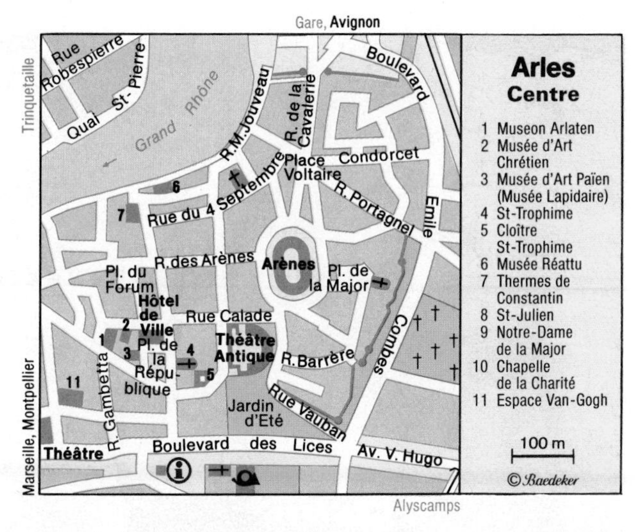

esque to Gothic (the transepts 11th c., the high, narrow nave 12th c., the choir and ambulatory 15th c.).

Cloister

The cloister which adjoins the church on the south-east is half Romanesque and half Gothic; the north and east sides date from the 12th c., the south and west sides from the 14th. Pillars and coupled columns alternate, with delicately carved capitals depicting Biblical scenes. The chapterhouse contains tapestries and, in the gallery, a small lapidary museum.

Musée d'Art Païen (Musée Lapidaire)

This museum of pagan art, in the church of Ste-Anne (1630), displays Roman and Hellenistic antiquities, mainly from excavations in Arles and the surrounding area.

*Musée d'Art Chrétien

A little way north-west, in the former Chapelle des Jésuites (17th c.), is the Museum of Christian Art, with Early Christian sarcophagi. The Cryptoporticus is entered from the museum; this is a vaulted hall (89 × 59m/290 × 194ft) dating from *c.* 40 B.C. under the ancient forum, probably a store room or granary.

Musée Arlaten

The Museum of Arles, founded by the Provençal poet Frédéric Mistral (Nobel Prize 1904) and housed in the 16th c. Hôtel de Laval-Castellane, has a large and important collection of material on Provençal folk art and traditions.

Espace van Gogh

The Dutch painter Vincent van Gogh (1853–90) spent fifteen productive months (1888/9) in Arles, some of them in this former hospital. The 16th c. building has now been made into a culture centre.

Thermes de Constantin

The Baths of Constantine, built in the 4th c. A.D., are near the banks of the Grand Rhône. All that survives of this once palatial complex is the caldarium (hot bath) and parts of the system of hypocausts (under-floor heating) and tepidarium (warm room).

Musée Réattu

The Musée Réattu, housed in a former commandery of the Order of Malta dating from the 15th–16th c., has pictures and drawings of the Provençal school (18th and 19th c.), a collection of contemporary art, including drawings presented by Picasso, and a collection of photographs.

St-Trophime, doorway . . .

. . . and cloister

Alyscamps

Beyond the wide Boulevard des Lices, on the south-eastern outskirts of the town, are the Alyscamps ("Elysian Fields"), an extensive Roman burial-ground which was later consecrated as a Christian cemetery and during the Middle Ages was widely famed. Thereafter it fell on evil days, and the sarcophagi were given away, sold or destroyed; the most important of those that survived are now in the museums of Arles and in St-Trophime. Along the atmospheric Allée des Tombeaux there are now only undecorated sarcophagi of the early medieval period. At the end of the avenue is the church of St-Honorat (originally 12th c.), of which only the choir and the chapels (added between the 15th and the 18th c.) have survived.

Pont de Langlois

This canal bridge, made famous by van Gogh's paintings, lies outside the town to the south.

Musée Camarguais

This museum, housed in a former sheepfold 11 km/7 miles south-west of Arles on D570, with a 3.5 km/2 mile long ecological trail, will give visitors an idea of what life in the Camargue (see entry) is like.

Surroundings of Arles

Arles is the starting-point for a trip to the Camargue (see entry).

St-Gilles

St-Gilles (pop. 11,000), the gateway to the Camargue, lies 20 km/12 miles west of Arles, on the edge of the Camargue.

Church

The church of St-Gilles, in the centre of the old town, was built in the 12th c., destroyed during the 16th c. wars of religion and rebuilt on a smaller scale in the 17th c.

*Façade

The façade (1180–1240), with its three doorways, is one of the masterpieces of Romanesque sculpture in Provence. The three-aisled interior is Gothic.

Château du Roi René, Tarascon

In the crypt, which has pointed vaulting, is the tomb of St Gilles (11th c.). In the ruins of the old choir, which was destroyed in the 17th c., is the Vis de St-Gilles ("St Gilles's Screw"), a stair-well with a spiral staircase, now standing by itself.

***Alpilles**

The Alpilles (Provençal Aupiho) are a 25 km/15 mile long range of hills on the east side of the Rhône running from St-Rémy in the north to Les Baux in the south. The first deposits of bauxite, which is used in the manufacture of aluminium, were discovered here in 1822. The rugged limestone cliffs of the Alpilles yield a building stone which was already being used in Roman times. The quarrying of the stone leaves underground chambers resembling rock-cut tombs. From the highest point in the range, Mt Caume (383 m/1257 ft) there are fine panoramic views extending to the mouth of the Rhône and the Camargue in the west and Mont Ventoux and the Durance valley in the east.

Tarascon–St-Rémy–Les Baux–Montmajour (60 km/37 miles)

Tarascon

Tarascon (pop. 11,000) lies on the left bank of the Rhône. According to the local legend this was the home of man-eating monsters called *tarasques* which were tamed by St Martha: hence, it is said, the name of the town. The tarasque now appears in Tarascon's coat of arms.
Tarascon has been given wide fame by the hero of Alphonse Daudet's novel "Tartarin of Tarascon" – the French equivalent of Baron Münchhausen.

*Castle

The formidable castle of Tarascon, which is open to the public, occupies the site of a Roman castrum and was built in the late 14th c. by Duke René of Anjou, "le bon Roi René", and soon became a centre of Provençal culture.

"Tomb of the Julii" and triumphal arch, St-Rémy

View of lower town, Les Baux

From the terrace there are magnificent views of the Alpilles, the Rhône, Beaucaire and Tarascon.
Just to the east of the castle is the 17th c. Hôtel de Ville (Town Hall).

Ste-Marthe

The church of Ste-Marthe, which served as the castle chapel, was built in the 12th c. and altered in the 14th and 15th. The doorway on the south side is Romanesque. The church contains a number of pictures and in the crypt is the sarcophagus of St Martha.

Beaucaire

On the right bank of the Rhône opposite Tarascon is the little town of Beaucaire, in the Languedoc–Roussillon region. It was once known throughout western Europe for its market, first held in 1217.
Features of interest are the Town Hall (by J. Hardouin-Mansart, 1679–1683), the ruins of the medieval castle (11th and 13th c.; fine views), the chapel of St-Louis (1254) and the Musée de la Vignasse.

St-Rémy

*Glanum

*Triumphal Arch

At the foot of the Alpilles, 1 km/¾ mile south of St-Rémy (pop. 8500, and the birthplace of Nostradamus in 1503), are the remains of the Greek and Roman settlement of Glanum (2nd c. B.C. and 1st–3rd c. A.D.), which was destroyed by the Visigoths in 480. The most prominent monuments are the Roman triumphal arch and tomb known as Les Antiques. To the right is the triumphal arch, which has a frieze of relief carving round the outside of the arch and coffered vaulting on its under side, to the left the 18 m/60 ft high "Tomb of the Julii", which has reliefs on the lower part and an upper section in the form of a temple. Both of these monuments date from the 1st c. A.D. Beyond them, on the left of the road, is the entrance to the excavation site, with foundations and walls of the Hellenistic, Roman and Gallo-Roman periods. The forum, baths, temples, houses and a nymphaeum are among the remains that have been identified.

St-Paul-de-Mausole

To the east of the excavations is the former monastery of St-Paul-de-Mausole, now a psychiatric hospital, with a church and a small cloister (Romanesque). Vincent van Gogh was a patient here in 1889–1890.

**Les Baux

This town of ruins lies on the ridge of the Alpilles in the extreme south-west of Provence. Here in 1822 a French scientist discovered bauxite, the raw material used in making aluminium, and named it after the find-spot.
The site of Les Baux (Provençal Li Baus, "the rocks") was occupied by man in the Neolithic era. In the 12th and 13th centuries it was the capital of a county, with a population of over 3000, famed for its "court of love", the meeting-place of troubadours and a centre of courtly poetry. During the reign of Louis XIII it was a Huguenot stronghold and was destroyed in 1632. In 1642 Les Baux was presented to the Grimaldis, but handed back by them in 1791.

Lower town

Upper town

In the lower town, now taken over by souvenir shops and restaurants, there are numbers of handsome houses of the 14th–16th centuries. In Place St-Vincent (fine view) is the 12th c. church of St-Vincent. From here a steep lane leads up to the upper town, which is entered through the Musée Lapidaire (grave goods from a nearby Celtic cemetery, other archaeological material, displays illustrating the working of bauxite). From the bare rocky plateau, surrounded by almost vertical cliffs (unprotected edges), there are superb views of the Rhône valley, the Crau plain (known to the Romans as Campus Lapideus or Cravus; a stony tract formed by Ice Age detritus brought down by the Durance) and the Alpilles. There are impressive ruins of the castle of Les Baux.

*Montmajour

5 km/3 miles north-east of Arles, prominently situated on a crag, are the ruins of the Benedictine abbey of Montmajour, an important place of pilgrimage throughout the Middle Ages. The monastic buildings, of which substantial remains survive, date from the 12th–14th and 18th centuries.
The church of Notre-Dame is entered through the Romanesque crypt (12th c.). South-east of the church is the cloister, over which towers a battle-

Montmajour, the cloister

Moulin de Daudet, Fontvieille

mented keep. Some 200 m/220 yds east of the abbey is the little 12th c. chapel of Ste-Croix (Holy Cross), which was the abbey's cemetery chapel.

Fontvieille

North-east of Montmajour, at Fontvieille, is one of the most popular tourist sights of the area, the mill once occupied by the 19th c. writer Alphonse Daudet – though his famous "Lettres de mon Moulin" (1869) were actually written in Paris. The mill contains a small museum.

Auvergne

K/L 9/10

**Situation and characteristics

Auvergne, one of the historic provinces of France and since 1960 an administrative region, lies in central France, extending over much of the Massif Central, and takes in four départements (Allier, Cantal, Haute-Loire and Puy-de-Dôme). Its chief town is Clermont-Ferrand (see entry).
With its distinctive volcanic cones, its ranges of hills rising to almost 1900 m/6200 ft and the valleys between them, varying in form according to the extent of erosion, this is one of the most interesting parts of France. Less developed for tourism than some other regions, it has much to offer the visitor – large nature reserves, thermal springs emerging from the volcanic soil, numerous lakes either volcanic or artificial, rivers and mountain streams, the sources of the Loire, the Allier, the Lot and the Dordogne, excellent winter sports facilities, numbers of fine churches in the characteristic Auvergnat Romanesque style.

Economy

From the economic point of view Auvergne is one of France's problem areas. Its plateaux, largely deforested, are suitable only for extensive agricultural use (dairy farming, producing such well-known cheeses as Fourme d'Ambert, Cantal and St-Nectaire). In the few larger towns like Clermont-Ferrand, St-Etienne, Le Puy, Rodez, Aurillac and Tulle, which lie in a ring

The Puys (volcanic cones)

around the region, there is some industry namely metal-processing, pharmaceuticals, uranium mining and coal. Clermont-Ferrand has been a centre of the rubber industry since 1832 (Michelin works).

History

In pre-Roman times the people of Auvergne, the Arverni, occupied a leading place among the Gallic tribes, and it was the Arvernian chief Vercingetorix who led the fight against the Romans (52 B.C.). In 471–475 the region was conquered by the Visigothic king Eurich. From the early 11th c. it was a county owing allegiance to France, and the Counts of Auvergne were at times also Margraves of Septimania and Dukes of Aquitaine. In the middle of the 12th c. Auvergne was divided into two: one part, which the king had taken into his own hand in 1213 and made a duchy, passed to the Bourbons by marriage in 1425 and to the crown in 1527, while the county, held by the La Tour family from 1422, passed by inheritance to Catherine de Médicis in 1524 and later to Louis XIII.

Topography

Monts Dômes

In northern Auvergne, to the west of Clermont-Ferrand, is a sparsely forested plateau in the Massif Central, lying at over 600 m/2000 ft, known as the Chaîne des Puys or Monts Dômes – a 30 km/20 mile long chain of some 60 extinct volcanic cones *(puys,* from Latin *podium),* the best known and highest of which is the Puy de Dôme (1465 m/4807 ft).

Monts Dore

To the south of the Monts Dômes are the Monts Dore, a very much older (3 million years) volcanic range, shaped by Ice Age erosion, which reaches its highest point in the Puy de Sancy (1886 m/6188 ft). Perhaps the finest part of this range is the area round the spa and winter sports resort of Le Mont-Dore (pop. 2400) with its valleys, waterfalls and lakes.

Monts du Cantal

Farther south again are the Monts du Cantal, the ruins of a huge volcano which was the oldest part of the whole massif (around 20 million years old). Lava from the volcano, which was originally 3000 m/10,000 ft high, extended over a radius of 70 km/45 miles, breaking down into a soil which nourishes fertile pastureland. The highest peak in the range is the Plomb du Cantal (1858 m/6096 ft).

Monts d'Aubrac

In the extreme south of Auvergne, between the valleys of the Truyère and the Lot, are the Monts d'Aubrac, a range of basaltic hills.

Limagne

North of Clermont-Ferrand lies the Limagne basin, a valley of non-volcanic origin traversed by the Allier, with many mineral springs.
The plateau is cut by numerous valleys, which form deep gorges like the Gorges de la Sioule, the Vallée des Couzes, the Gorges de la Rhue, the Gorges de l'Allagnon, the Gorges de l'Allier and the Gorges de la Truyère.

Nature parks in Auvergne

The Parc Régional des Volcans, the largest regional nature park in France, with an area of 345,816 hectares/854,165 acres, lies in the heart of Auvergne. The object of this park and of the recently (1984) established Parc Naturel Régional Livradois–Forez is to ensure that the native flora and fauna are not endangered by the increasing numbers of visitors in both summer and winter.

Sights

Spas

In northern Auvergne, on the very edge of the region, is Vichy (see entry), its only major spa, which had its greatest days in the 19th c. and for a brief period during the Second World War played a political role. By far the most important tourist resort in the hills is Le Mont-Dore, lying at an altitude of 1050 m/3445 ft below the Puy de Sancy. Other resorts are Châtel-Guyon (a mineral and thermal spa), Bourbon-l'Archambault (thermal spa), Néris-les-Bains (thermal spa), Chaudes-Aigues (thermal spa), Royat–Chamalières (thermal spa), La Bourboule (thermal spa, with baths for children) and St-Nectaire (thermal spa).

Aurillac

The old capital of Auvergne (pop. 35,000) has a picturesque old town which grew up round the abbey of St-Géraud, founded in the 10th c. and rebuilt after its destruction in the mid 17th c. The first French Pope, Silvester II (Gerbert; 10th–11th c.), came from its monastic school. The church of Notre-Dame-des-Neiges (14th c., restored in 17th c.) has a fine 17th c. Black Virgin. The 19th c. Château St-Etienne, which has a wing dating from the 11th c., now houses the Maison des Volcans, with a collection of minerals and displays illustrating volcanic activity.

Château d'Alleuze

The ruined castle of Alleuze (13th c.) lies south of St-Flour in a setting of great beauty.

***Bort-les-Orgues**

The little town of Bort-les-Orgues (pop. 5000), prettily situated in the Dordogne valley, has a church of the 12th–15th centuries. Near the east end of the church are remains of the old town walls. 3km/2 miles to the south-west are the "organ-pipes" from which it takes its name – massive columns of phonolite 80–100 m/260–330 ft high extending for some 2 km/1½ miles. The Barrage de Bort pounds water from the Dordogne and its tributaries, forming a reservoir with a capacity of 477 million cu. m (105 billion gallons). On the bank of the lake (water-sports) stands the 15th c. Château de Val.

***Gorges de Dordogne**

Bort is also a good setting-out point for the Dordogne Gorges as far as the Barrage de l'Aigle, a reservoir some 85km/53 miles south-west.

Brioude

Brioude (pop. 8000) lies in the plain of the Allier. The Basilique St-Julien (11th–12th c.) is the largest Romanesque church in Auvergne, with multi-coloured masonry, frescoes in the porch and the nave, and richly decorated capitals. Also in the town is the recently opened Maison du Saumon, a large salmon aquarium.

Ste-Foy, Conques

St-Austremoine, Issoire

La Chaise-Dieu

Between Le Puy and Thiers is La Chaise-Dieu (from Latin Casa Dei, the House of God), with the most celebrated church in Auvergne. A monastery was founded here in the 11th c. and rapidly grew. The three-aisled church of St-Robert, built in the 14th c., has a Gothic cloister. The interior, with shallow vaulting, is divided into two by a Late Gothic rood screen (15th c.). The choir, which has carved oak stalls (15th c.), contains the tomb of Pope Clement VI. The church also has fine early 16th c. Brussels and Arras tapestries and a famous wall painting, 26 m/85 ft long, of the "Danse Macabre" (15th c.).

Clermont-Ferrand

See entry

Conques

The little walled town of Conques (pop. 500), on the south-western borders of Auvergne, is huddled around the beautiful Romanesque church of Ste-Foy (11th–12th c.); see Lot Valley.

Issoire

In Issoire is the church of St-Austremoine (12th c.), the largest Romanesque church in Auvergne after St-Julien in Brioude. The choir has polychrome mosaic and sculptural decoration.

Moulins

The town of Moulins (pop. 27,000), which grew up in the 10th c. around a castle, takes its name from the many mills which once lined the Allier. In the 14th c. it became the chief town of the district of Bourbonnais, which was raised to the status of a duchy.

In the centre of the picturesque old part of the town is the Place de l'Hôtel-de-Ville, in which is the Belfry (1455), with a remarkable *jacquemart* ("Jack-o'-the-clock", a clock with animated figures). The Musée de Folklore et du Vieux Moulins displays old craftsmen's tools, a model of a peasant's house, traditional costumes and furniture.

Cathedral

The Cathedral of Notre-Dame has a late 15th c. choir in Flamboyant style and a 19th c. nave. The ambulatory has fine 15th and 16th c. stained glass, and in the sacristy is the famous triptych by the Master of Moulins (late 15th c.). Opposite the cathedral is the Tour Mal Coiffée, the keep of the old ducal castle, of which the Pavillon d'Anne de Beaujeu on its north side was also a part. The Pavillon now contains an interesting museum of art and archaeology. To the north of the cathedral is the mausoleum of Duke Henry II of Montmorency (1653).

Orcival

25 km/15 miles south-west of Clermont-Ferrand, between the Monts Dômes and the Monts Dore, is the village of Orcival, which grew up round the church of Notre-Dame, founded by the abbey of La Chaise-Dieu in the 12th c. and partly rebuilt in the 15th and 19th centuries. This is one of the finest Romanesque churches in Auvergne. In the choir is a much revered 12th c. statue of the Virgin enthroned (see illustration on page 57).
Near the village is the château of Cordes (15th and 17th c.), with gardens laid out by Le Nôtre.

Le Puy

See entry

****Puy de Dôme**

The best known peak in the Monts Dômes is the Puy de Dôme (1465 m/4807 ft), the central feature of the range, whose volcanic nature was discovered only in 1751. It was a sacred mountain both to the Gauls and the Romans, and during the construction of the observatory on its summit (1872) remains of a Roman temple of Mercury were found.
A toll road opened in 1926, with a gradient of 12%, runs up to the summit, from which there are breathtaking views. The summit can also be reached on a path from the Col de Ceyssat (1078 m/3537 ft).

Puy de Sancy

The highest peak in Auvergne and in the Massif Central, the Puy de Sancy (1886 m/6188 ft), can be reached with the help of a cableway, from which it is a 20 minutes' climb to the summit (wide-ranging views). The Dordogne rises in the Puy de Sancy massif.

Riom

The old town of Riom (pop. 18,000), on the western edge of the fertile Limagne basin, was for many years capital of Auvergne, and is still one of its major towns.
In the north-west of the old town, now ringed by boulevards, is the Palais de Justice (Law Courts), on the site of the old castle of the Dukes of Berry. The Sainte Chapelle (1382–1388), all that survives of the castle, has three fine 15th c. windows in the choir.

Sainte-Chapelle

North-east of the Palais de Justice is the Musée Régional d'Auvergne (folk art, everyday objects, furniture). The town's main street is the Rue de l'Hôtel-de-Ville, in which are a number of handsome old houses and the Musée Mandet (1640), with a collection of pictures. The 16th c. Hôtel de Ville (Town Hall) has a beautiful courtyard and contains memorabilia on the history of the town, and the Maison des Consuls (1530) has a richly sculptured façade. Near the Carrefour de Taules, the main street intersection, are a clock-tower (15th and 16th c.) and the 16th c. Hôtel Guimoneau, which has an attractive courtyard.

St-Amable

The church of St-Amable has some Auvergnat Romanesque features (nave and transepts; 12th c.) and Gothic elements in the choir (13th c.). The façade was added in the 18th c.
The church of Notre-Dame du Marthuret (14th–15th c.), to the south of the old town, has fine 15th and 16th c. windows. In a chapel on the south side of the church is the "Virgin with the Bird", a fine piece of 14th c. sculpture.

Mozac

1 km/¾ mile west of Riom is Mozac, with a fine 12th c. church in Auvergnat Romanesque style which belonged to a Benedictine abbey, and a beautiful Black Virgin (12th c.).

St-Flour

This old fortified town (pop. 9200) lies at an altitude of 881 m/2890 ft on a petrified lava flow. The impressive Gothic Cathedral of St-Pierre-et-St-

Flour, built of black basalt, was founded by the abbey of Cluny in the 11th c. It possesses a large crucifix of black wood (13th or 15th c.) known as the "Beau Dieu Noir".

Viaduc de Garabit

This iron viaduct spanning the Truyère, to the south of St-Flour, was built by Gustave Eiffel in 1884, and the experience he gained here no doubt stood him in good stead a few years later when he built the Eiffel Tower.

St-Nectaire

Above the spa of St-Nectaire is one of the finest Romanesque churches in Auvergne (12th c.), with over a hundred capitals depicting Old and New Testament scenes. The church has a rich treasury, including a gilded copper bust of Ste-Baudine (12th c.).

Salers

This little medieval town (pop. 500), picturesquely situated at an altitude of 951 m/3120 ft, has preserved its old walls, many old gabled and tower houses and some Renaissance houses. The 15th c. church of St-Matthieu, which preserves a Romanesque arch, has old Aubusson tapestries and a Holy Sepulchre of 1495. The Maison des Templiers contains a small exhibition on the history of Salers and some material illustrating the folk traditions of the area.
The Grande Place is one of the finest squares in France.

Vichy

See entry

Avignon M11

Region: Provence–Alpes–Côte-d'Azur. Département: Vaucluse.
Altitude: 19 m/62 ft. Population: 93,000.

Situation and characteristics

The one-time Papal residence of Avignon, today the chief town of the département of Vaucluse and the see of an archbishop, lies on the left bank of the Rhône, which here divides to enclose the island of Barthelasse. The town is situated at the foot of a 58 m/190 ft high limestone hill on which are the Palace of the Popes and the cathedral.
Among the attractions which draw large numbers of visitors to Avignon every year are its monuments of art and architecture, its convenient situation as a base from which to explore Provence and its many festivals, including the annual drama festival held in July/August.

History

In Roman times Avignon *(Avennio)* was a thriving provincial town. Later it fell into the hands of the Burgundians and then the Franks. In the 13th c. it passed to Charles of Anjou along with the rest of Provence. In the Albigensian wars Avignon supported the Counts of Toulouse and the Albigensians, and in consequence was captured by Louis VIII of France in 1226. In 1348 it was purchased by the Pope. During the "Babylonian captivity" (1309–1377) Avignon was the residence of the exiled Popes Clement V, John XXII, Benedict XII, Clement VI, Innocent VI and Urban V, until Gregory XI's return to Rome brought the period of exile to an end. Later, during the Great Schism, the Antipopes resided in Avignon until 1403. During this period Avignon became a flourishing centre of the arts with the Italian artists who worked for the Popes here (in particular Simone Martini) stimulating the development of an important Avignon school of painters.
The town and surrounding area remained in Papal hands until it was reunited with France during the French Revolution.

Sights

*Town walls

The whole of the old town is surrounded by a complete circuit of walls 4.8 km/3 miles long, with eight gates and 39 towers. The walls, built between 1350 and 1368, were heavily restored in the 19th c.

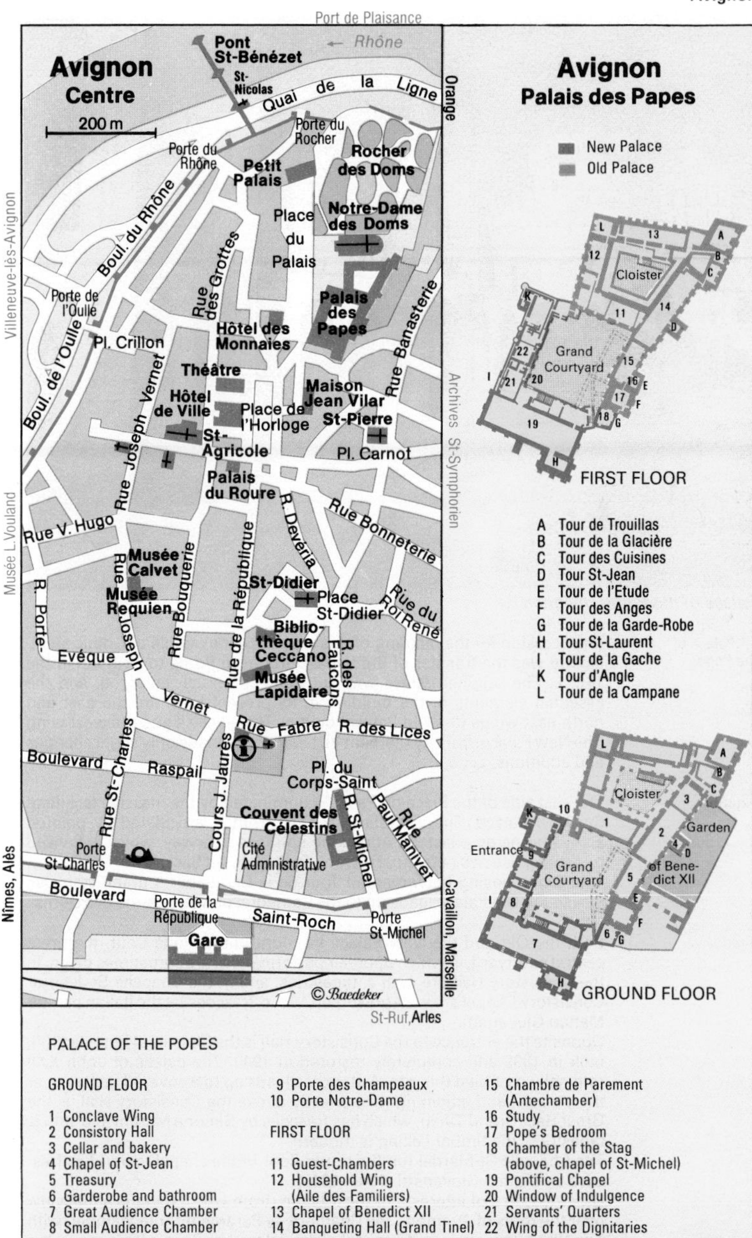
Port de Plaisance
Rhône
Avignon
Centre
200 m
Pont
St-Bénézet
St-Nicolas
Quai de la Ligne
Orange
Porte du Rocher
Porte du Rhône
Petit Palais
Rocher des Doms
Place du Palais
Notre-Dame des Doms
Boul. du Rhône
Rue des Grottes
Palais des Papes
Rue Banasterie
Porte de l'Oulle
Boul. de l'Oulle
Pl. Crillon
Hôtel des Monnaies
Théâtre
Rue Joseph Vernet
Hôtel de Ville
Place de l'Horloge
Maison Jean Vilar
St-Pierre
St-Agricole
Pl. Carnot
Palais du Roure
R. Devéria
Rue Bonneterie
Rue V. Hugo
Musée Calvet
Musée Requien
Rue Joseph Vernet
Rue Bouquerie
Rue de la République
St-Didier
Place St-Didier
Rue du Roi René
R. Porte-Evéque
Bibliothèque Ceccano
Musée Lapidaire
R. des Faucons
Rue Fabre
R. des Lices
Boulevard Raspail
Rue St-Charles
Cours J. Jaurès
Pl. du Corps-Saint
Couvent des Célestins
R. St-Michel
Rue Paul Manivet
Cité Administrative
Porte St-Charles
Boulevard Saint-Roch
Porte de la République
Porte St-Michel
Gare
© Baedeker
Villeneuve-lès-Avignon
Musée L. Vouland
Nîmes, Alès
Archives St-Symphorien
Cavaillon, Marseille
St-Ruf, Arles
Avignon
Palais des Papes
New Palace
Old Palace
Cloister
Grand Courtyard
FIRST FLOOR
A Tour de Trouillas
B Tour de la Glacière
C Tour des Cuisines
D Tour St-Jean
E Tour de l'Etude
F Tour des Anges
G Tour de la Garde-Robe
H Tour St-Laurent
I Tour de la Gache
K Tour d'Angle
L Tour de la Campane
Cloister
Garden of Benedict XII
Entrance
Grand Courtyard
GROUND FLOOR
PALACE OF THE POPES
GROUND FLOOR
1 Conclave Wing
2 Consistory Hall
3 Cellar and bakery
4 Chapel of St-Jean
5 Treasury
6 Garderobe and bathroom
7 Great Audience Chamber
8 Small Audience Chamber
9 Porte des Champeaux
10 Porte Notre-Dame
FIRST FLOOR
11 Guest-Chambers
12 Household Wing (Aile des Familiers)
13 Chapel of Benedict XII
14 Banqueting Hall (Grand Tinel)
15 Chambre de Parement (Antechamber)
16 Study
17 Pope's Bedroom
18 Chamber of the Stag (above, chapel of St-Michel)
19 Pontifical Chapel
20 Window of Indulgence
21 Servants' Quarters
22 Wing of the Dignitaries

Palace of the Popes, Avignon

** Palace of the Popes

The occasion for the building of this magnificent example of Gothic architecture was the transfer of the Papal Curia from Rome to Avignon in the 14th c. The original palace was subsequently much enlarged, and the essential elements of the building in its present form are the east and north-east wings (the Old Palace) built by Benedict XII and the west wing (the New Palace) built by Clement VI. Later Popes made only slight changes and additions.

Exterior

The east side of the Place du Palais is dominated by the massive façade of the New Palace. The irregularly shaped front is articulated by pointed arches borne on pilasters. Above the entrance doorway, which is flanked by turrets, rise two octagonal towers. To the left, set back, is the Old Palace, with the imposing battlemented Tour de la Campane. A grand staircase beside the Old Palace leads up to the Cathedral of Notre-Dame des Doms.

Interior

Both the Old and the New Palace lie round the Grande Cour, the great central courtyard, in which open-air performances are sometimes given. In the Consistory Hall are 17th c. tapestries, and in the Chapelle St-Jean or Consistory Chapel are well-preserved 14th c. frescoes by the Italian painter Matteo Giovanetti.
Opposite the entrance to the Consistory Hall is the Cloister of Benedict XIII, built in 1339 and completely restored in 1940. The palace of John XXII originally occupied this site. A staircase leads up to a covered gallery over the cloister, and adjoining this, directly above the Consistory Hall, is the Great Hall (Grand Tinel), which has frescoes by Simone Martini and 18th c. tapestries; the timber ceiling is modern.
The Chapelle St-Martial (on the upper floor of the chapel tower) has frescoes by Matteo Giovanetti (1344–1345).
Other features of interest are the Kitchen (from which there is a fine view over the roofs of Avignon), the Chambre de Parament (Antechamber, with two 18th c. tapestries and a model of the palace, the Pope's Bedroom in the

Pont St-Bénézet, known from the song "Sur le Pont d'Avignon . . .

Tour des Anges and the Chambre du Cerf (Chamber of the Stag), so named after the hunting and other secular scenes in the wall paintings. A staircase leads to the North Sacristy, in which are numerous plaster replicas of the tombs of church dignitaries. Then follows the Grande Chapelle or Chapelle Clémentine, with many Baroque paintings. To the right of the altar is the entrance to the South Sacristy, which also contains replicas of tombs. Then through the Loggia and down a broad vaulted staircase to the ground floor and the Grande Audience, the two-aisled Audience Chamber, which also has frescoes by Matteo Giovanetti (1352).
From here the Corps du Garde (Guard Room) leads back to the entrance.

Notre-Dame des Doms

Immediately north of the palace is the Cathedral of Notre-Dame des Doms (originally 12th c.; enlarged in 14th–16th c.). The two tympana of the doorway have remains of frescoes by Simone Martini. The church contains a 12th c. bishop's throne in white marble and the Late Gothic tomb of Pope John XXII in the fourth chapel on the south side. At the entrance to the baptistery are early 15th c. frescoes.

*Pont d'Avignon (Pont St-Bénézet)

The Pont d'Avignon or Pont St-Bénézet, which reaches out into the Rhône below the Rocher des Doms, must be the best known bridge in France, familiar to children from the old nursery song "Sur le pont d'Avignon, l'on y danse tous en rond". It was built in 1177–1185, but was partly destroyed in 1668. Of its original 22 arches there survive only four. At the near end is the Romanesque chapel of St-Nicolas (restored in the 19th c.).

Musée du Petit Palais

On the north side of the Place du Palais is the Petit Palais (14th c.), a fortress-like Gothic building which was once the bishop's palace. It now houses the important Campana Collection of 13th–15th c. Italian masters and a collection of work by painters of the Avignon school, which was influenced by Simone Martini and Matteo Giovanetti.
A little way north of the Petit Palais is a gate in the walls, the Porte du Rocher, which gives access to the Pont St-Bénézet.

Hôtel des Monnaies

Opposite the entrance to the Palace of the Popes is the Hôtel des Monnaies, the old Mint (17th c.), now the Conservatoire. The façade, which is decorated with figures of animals, bears the arms of Pope Paul V, of the Borghese family.

St-Symphorien

To the east is the church of St-Symphorien, which dates mainly from the 15th c. It contains 16th c. statues and a number of pictures.

Place de l'Horloge

In the busy Place de l'Horloge are the Hôtel de Ville (Town Hall; 1845) and the 14th c. clock-tower.

St-Pierre

To the east of the square is the church of St-Pierre (1356; enlarged in 15th c., restored in 19th c.), with a handsome façade and carved wooden doors of 1550. The choir is sumptuously decorated in 17th c. style.

St-Agricol

South-west of the Town Hall is the church of St-Agricol, a three-aisled basilica without transepts built in the reign of Pope John XXII (14th c.) and later enlarged.

St-Didier

The 14th c. church of St-Didier, with a Late Gothic façade, has one of the earliest works of art of the Renaissance, "Road to Calvary" by the Italian painter Francesco da Laurana (1478–1481), and 14th c. wall paintings.

Other places of interest

*Musée Calvet

Avignon's most important museum is the Musée Calvet, housed in the Hôtel Villeneuve-Martignan, south-west of the Place de l'Horloge. It has large collections of antiquities, sculpture and pictures.

Musée Requien

The Musée Requien has geological and botanical collections and a large natural history library.

Musée Lapidaire

The Musée Lapidaire is housed in a Baroque Jesuit church which is linked by a bridge with the former Jesuit college founded in 1564 (now a grammar school). The collection includes Roman mosaics, fragments of a triumphal arch, reliefs and antique sculpture.

Couvent des Célestins

This church (originally a 14th c. Celestine convent) boasts a magnificent apse by Perrin Morel.

Bibliothèque Ceccano

The Ceccano Library occupies a recently restored 15th c. building.

Palais du Roure

The Palais du Roure contains a library of Provençal history and a collection of antiquities and ethnographic material.

Maison Jean Vilar

The Maison Jean Vilar houses both permanent and special exhibitions on the history of the Avignon Drama Festival and the work of the director Jean Vilar (1912–1971), who ran the Festival from 1947 onwards.

Musée Louis Vouland

The Musée Louis Vouland (near the Porte St-Dominique, on the west side of the old town) displays French furniture (mainly of the 18th c.), pictures, tapestries and china.

Surroundings of Avignon

*Pont du Gard

See Nîmes

Villeneuve-lès-Avignon

From Avignon a bridge leads over the south end of the island of Barthelasse to the little town of Villeneuve-lès-Avignon, originally built by the French king Philippe le Bel to watch over the Papal town on the opposite bank.

*Fort St-André

On the banks of the Rhône, opposite the Pont St-Bénézet, is the Tour Philippe-le-Bel (1307). This tower and the 13th c. Fort St-André with its two round towers are relics of the old fortifications of Villeneuve. From both of

Harbour, Bastia

these vantage-points there are fine views of Villeneuve, Avignon, Mont Ventoux, the Montagne du Lubéron and the Alpilles.
The church of Notre-Dame (consecrated 1333) has a number of panel paintings and a notable treasury. Farther north are the ruins of the Chartreuse du Val de Bénédiction (14th c.), with a large cloister (14th c., restored in 17th and 18th c.) and a 14th c. church containing the tomb of Pope Innocent VI; the Papal chapel has important frescoes.

Bastia

R12

Region: Corse (Corsica)
Département: Haute-Corse
Altitude: 15–70 m/50–230 ft
Population: 50,000

Situation and characteristics

Bastia, chief town of the département of Haute-Corse and Corsica's principal port, lies at the northern end of the east coast, at the base of the Cap Corse peninsula. Founded by the Genoese in 1380 and protected by a mighty bastion, Bastia was capital of Corsica until 1811, when, on Napoleon's orders, this distinction was transferred to his birthplace, Ajaccio.

Sights

Place St-Nicolas

The central feature of the town is the Place St-Nicolas, a large square shaded by plane-trees and palms with a marble statue of Napoleon. The square is bounded on the east side by the quay along the Bassin St-Nicolas. To the north is the New Harbour, to the south the old town.

*Old town

The Terra Vecchia, the old fishing village, is a maze of narrow lanes and tall, closely packed houses. The former Cathedral of St-Jean-Baptiste (16th c.) with its twin towers dominates the Place de l'Hôtel-de-Ville. The chapels of the Immaculate Conception (1611) and St-Roch (1604) are sumptuously decorated. On a spur of rock to the south of the picturesque Old Harbour is the Genoese Citadel, within the walls of which are the palace of the Genoese governor and many old houses.

Citadel

The building of the Citadel began in 1378 and was completed about 1530 with the construction of the bell-tower at the entrance. The inner courtyard is surrounded by two-storeyed galleries. Also within the Citadel are the church of Ste-Marie (begun around 1495, consecrated in the early 17th c.) and the chapel of Ste-Croix, built in 1547 to house a wonderworking crucifix, the "Christ des Miracles", recovered from the sea by fishermen in 1428. Here too are the interesting Museum of Corsican Ethnography, with material on the history of the island, and a Military Museum.
The Citadel quarter is known as the Terra Nuova, the new town, as opposed to the Terra Vecchia, the old town.

Surroundings of Bastia

*Cap Corse

See Corsica

*Castagniccia

Some 20 km/12 miles south of Bastia is the hilly region of Castagniccia (named after the chestnut-trees which grow here). The chief place in Castagniccia is Piedicroce d'Orezza, a good base from which to climb Monte San Pietro (1766 m/5794 ft; about 2½ hours).

Belfort

O7

Region: Franche-Comté
Département: Territoire de Belfort
Altitude: 358 m/1175 ft
Population: 55,000

Situation and characteristics

The town of Belfort on the river Savoureuse, capital of the Territoire de Belfort, was an important fortress controlling the Trouée de Belfort, the Belfort Gap, a key-point on the route between the Vosges and the Jura. Until 1870–1871 it belonged to the département of Haut-Rhin (see Alsace). Belfort has important textile and engineering industries.

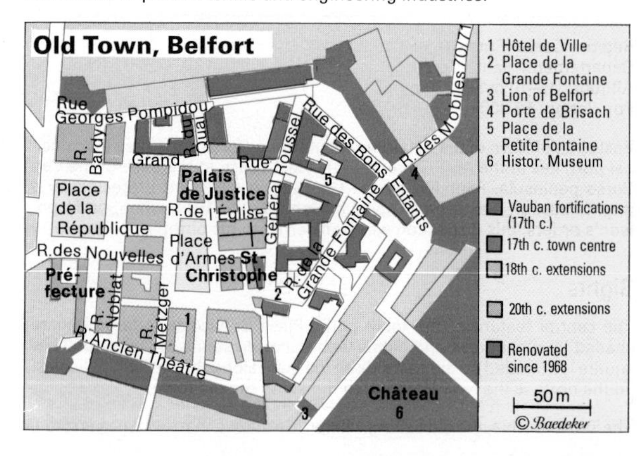

The Lion of Belfort

History

For many centuries the destinies of the town turned on its geographical situation. Until the 14th c. it belonged to the Counts of Mömpelgard (Montbéliard). From 1350 to 1639 it was held by the Habsburgs; then in 1648, under the Peace of Westphalia, it was assigned to France. Vauban surrounded the town with fortifications which helped it to withstand a 103-day siege during the Franco-Prussian War of 1870–1871.

Sights

Place de la République

The present-day town is divided into two parts. The central feature of the old town, on the left bank of the Savoureuse, is the Place de la République, with the large Monument des Trois Sièges by the Colmar sculptor A.-F. Bartholdi (completed in 1904 by his pupils), commemorating the three sieges of 1813–1814, 1815 and 1870–1871.
On the north side of the square is the Palais de Justice (1901), on the south side the Prefecture.

St-Christophe

To the east, in the Place d'Armes, are the parish church of St-Christophe (1725–1750), with a beautiful interior, and the Hôtel de Ville (Town Hall) of 1784.

Musée d'Art et d'Histoire

On a 70 m/230 ft high crag is a 13th c. castle, rebuilt by Vauban as a citadel, much of which was pulled down in the 19th c. The surviving part, known as the Château, now houses the Musée d'Art et d'Histoire, with an important collection of material on local history (Bronze and Iron Age weapons, Neolithic, Gallo-Roman and Frankish jewellery and ornaments), a collection of pictures (including works by Signac, Vlaminck, Utrillo, Courbet and Rodin) and models of the Vauban fortifications. From the Château there are extensive views over the Jura and the Vosges.

Porte de Brisach

North-east of the Museum is the Porte de Brisach (1687), a relic of the old fortifications.

*Lion of Belfort

From the Porte de Brisach a street runs round the ramparts to the imposing Lion of Belfort hewn from red Vosges sandstone by Bartholdi in 1875–1880 to commemorate the siege of 1870–1871.

Surroundings of Belfort

Ronchamp

See Jura

Besançon O7

Region: Franche-Comté
Département: Doubs
Altitude: 246 m/807 ft
Population: 120,000

Situation and characteristics

The old city of Besançon, picturesquely situated in a bend on the Doubs, on the north-western fringes of the Jura, is the chief town of the département of Doubs, a university town and the see of an archbishop. It is the centre of the watchmaking industry established by immigrants from the Swiss Jura, and since the late 19th c. has also produced artificial silk (rayon).
The poet and novelist Victor Hugo (1802–1885) and the brothers Auguste and Louis Lumière, inventors of the cinematograph, were born in Besançon.

History

Besançon was the capital *(Vesontio)* of a Gallic people, the Sequani, who are mentioned by Caesar in his account of the Gallic War. In the Middle Ages it was for long the chief town of the Franche-Comté (the "free county" of Burgundy). In 1032–1034 it passed into the hands of the German kings. From the 13th c. it was a free imperial city under the name of Bisanz; then in 1678, under the treaty of Nijmegen, it became French.
The town was given its present character in the late 17th c., when Vauban pulled down the old upper town, including the cathedral, to make room for the Citadel.

Sights

Citadel and museums

South-east of the old town, 118 m/387 ft above the Doubs, lies the Citadel, with an elaborate system of fortifications which was largely the work of Vauban. It now houses a number of interesting museums – the Musée Agraire, the Musée Populaire Comtois, the Musée de la Résistance et de la Déportation and the Musée d'Histoire Naturelle, together with an Aquarium and a Zoological Park.

*View

From the Citadel there are fine views of the town and the river.

Old town

The central feature of the old town is the Place du 8-Septembre, with the church of St-Pierre and the Hôtel de Ville (Town Hall; 16th c.). To the rear of the Town Hall is the Palais de Justice (Law Courts; also 16th c.), once the seat of the Parlement of Franche-Comté. The town's main street is the Grande Rue, which follows the line of a Roman road, the Vicus Magnus. The sober regularity of the house fronts (the result of uniform standards laid down by Vauban), is relieved by the imaginative design of the entrances; a particularly striking example is at No. 67. Victor Hugo was born in No. 140. In the Square Archéologique A.-Castan (after the archaeologist of that name) are remains of an ancient theatre and cistern, with eight Corinthian columns as relics of former architectural splendour.

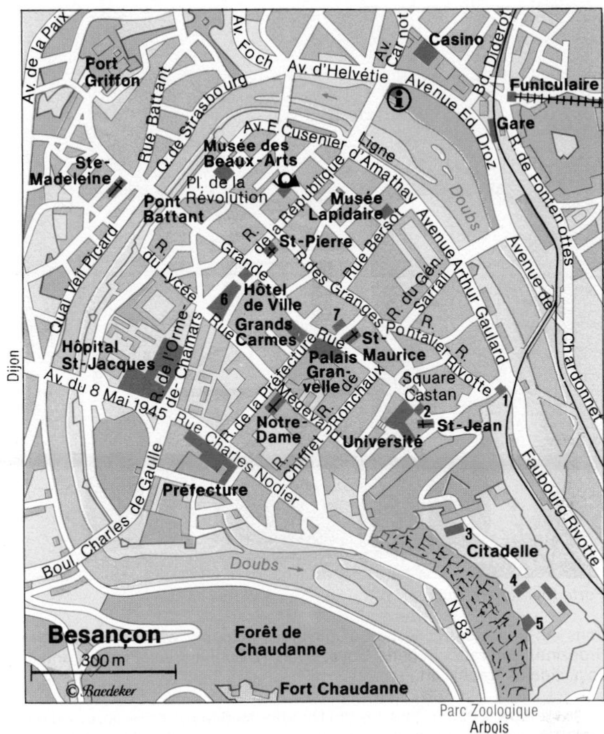

1 Porte Rivotte
2 Porte Noire
3 Musée de l'Agriculture Traditionnelle
4 Musée Populaire du Folklore Comtois
5 Musée de la Résistance et de la Déportation
6 Palais de Justice
7 Bibliothéque

Cathedral

Below the Citadel is the Cathedral of St-Jean (11th–13th c.; choir 18th c.), with a large nave between two choirs. It has a number of valuable paintings, including a "Virgin and Child with Saints" by Fra Bartolommeo (1518). In the belfry is an astronomical clock by A.-L. Vérité (1860), with thousands of moving parts which come into action at certain times of day.

Porte Rivotte

Porte Noire

To the east of the cathedral is the 16th c. Porte Rivotte, with two round towers; the passages for pedestrians were inserted in the 19th c. To the west is the Porte Noire, a triumphal arch of the 2nd c. A.D. with rich sculptural decoration.

Palais Granvelle

In the centre of the old town is the Palais Granvelle, built in the 16th c. by Cardinal Granvelle, chancellor of Charles V, which has a fine colonnaded courtyard. It is now occupied by the Musée d'Histoire et d'Ethnographie de la Franche-Comté. The exhibits include tapestries portraying the life of Charles V, as well as memorabilia of Victor Hugo and the Granvelle family. The theatre, in Rue Mégévand, was designed by the Revolutionary architect Claude Ledoux.

*Musée des Beaux-Arts et d'Archéologia

North-west of the Place du 8-Septembre, near the Doubs, is the Musée des Beaux-Arts et d'Archéologie, housed in a former granary which was rebuilt by L. Miquel, a pupil of Le Corbusier's. It has large archaeological collec-

Porte Rivotte, Besançon

tions, an important collection of pictures, including works by Cranach, Bronzino, Tintoretto, Rubens, Goya, Courbet, Bonnard and Picasso, and a collection of graphic art.

Quartier de Battant

On the left bank of the Doubs is the Quartier de Battant, once occupied by the wine-growers whose vineyards were on the surrounding hills; the large cellar doors of the houses are a reminder of those days. The church of Ste-Madeleine (18th c.) was designed by Nicolas Nicole.
Along the left bank to the east is the Promenade de Micaud, with fine views of the Citadel.

Surroundings of Besançon

Belvédère de Montfaucon

The best view of Besançon and the Jura hills is from the Belvédère de Montfaucon, 3 km/2 miles away.

Champlitte

This château (16th–18th c.) lies 66km/41 miles to the north-west and houses a good folk-lore museum.

Notre-Dame-des-Buis

There are still wider views from the hill of Notre-Dame-des-Buis (460 m/1510 ft), 5 km/3 miles south-west, which is crowned by a statue of the Virgin erected in 1945.

Biarritz

F11

Region: Aquitaine. Département: Pyrénées-Atlantiques.
Altitude: 40 m/130 ft. Population: 28,000.

Situation and characteristics

Biarritz, situated on the Atlantic coast in the Gulf of Gascony (Bay of Biscay: see Côte des Basques), in the south-west corner of France, is one of the world's most celebrated coastal resorts. Its magnificent situation on a much indented, surf-beaten coast, its beautiful sandy beach, brine springs and mild maritime climate favoured the rise of this former fishing village, and its prosperity was ensured when the Empress Eugénie built a palace here (now the Hôtel du Palais) for herself and her court.
Handsome mansions decked with turrets and oriel windows are reminders of Biarritz's 19th c. splendours. Present-day holidaymakers are catered for by two casinos, three beaches, beautifully situated golf-courses and abundant facilities for water sports.

Sights

Place Georges-Clemenceau

The hub of the town's life, at the meeting of its principal streets, is the elongated Place Georges-Clemenceau. From here it is a short distance to the sea by way of the Place Bellevue, with the Casino Bellevue to the left and the Casino Municipal to the right.

Biarritz's magnificent situation and the beauty of the coastal scenery can be appreciated in a walk along the seafront promenade. To the north-east the popular Grande Plage (heavy surf) extends to the Pointe St-Martin, with a 73 m/240 ft high lighthouse from which there are wide views. Beyond this is the Plage de la Chambre d'Amour, another very beautiful beach; bathers should beware of strong currents and high waves.

* Fishing harbour

Boulevard Maréchal-Leclerc runs west from the Casino Bellevue above the picturesque little fishing harbour, nestling in a steep-sided rocky inlet between the Rocher du Basta and Cap Atalaye, and through a tunnel to the Esplanade de la Vierge. A narrow iron bridge built by Gustave Eiffel leads to the Rocher de la Vierge, a long, narrow ridge of rock from which there is a magnificent view extending from the mouth of the Adour to the Spanish frontier.

Rocher de la Vierge
* View

Musée de la Mer

Opposite the Rocher de la Vierge is the Musée de la Mer (Museum of the Sea), with a salt-water aquarium and rich natural history collections.

Plage des Basques

Farther along the coast is the rocky inlet containing the Port Vieux (Old Harbour), with a beautiful sheltered beach. From the adjoining Esplanade du Port-Vieux and, better still, from the Miramare viewpoint there is a magnificent prospect of the cliff-fringed Plage des Basques, exposed to the full force of the breakers, and beyond this the first hills of Spain.

Thermes Salins

To the east of the town are the Thermes Salins (brine springs), which are effective in the treatment of anaemia, metabolic disorders and gynaecological conditions.

Surroundings of Biarritz

Biarritz is a good base for excursions in the surrounding area. To the south is the Côte des Basques (see entry), with such attractive towns as Bayonne, St-Jean-de-Luz and Hendaye, to the north Labenne, Hossegor, with the world's highest dune (see Gascony), Capbreton and Seignosse.

Ascain

South of Biarritz, inland, is the little town of Ascain, with pretty Basque half-timbered houses.

Blois

I7

Region: Centre. Département: Loir-et-Cher
Altitude: 72 m/236 ft. Population: 52,000

Situation and characteristics

Picturesquely situated on two hills above the right bank of the Loire, Blois, dominated by its famous château and its cathedral, is the chief town of the département of Loir-et-Cher and the see of a bishop. It lies in the centre of a rich agricultural area and is noted for its electrical and leatherworking industries. Denis Papin, inventor of the pressure cooker and the autoclave, was born in Blois in 1648.

History

Blois was the Roman settlement of *Blesum,* and in the Middle Ages the chief town of the County of Blésois or Blaisois. In 1397 it passed to Louis of Orléans when it became a royal residence, and in the reigns of Louis XII and Francis I played a similar role to that of Versailles in the reign of Louis XIV. During the 16th c. wars of religion, in 1588, the château was the scene of bloody events. The Duke of Guise, Henry II's rival and leader of the Catholic League, had compelled the king to call a meeting of the States General in Blois. His object was to dethrone the king, but Henry anticipated him and had him murdered on the morning of December 23rd. Eight months later the king himself suffered the same fate.

Sights

**Château

In the centre of Blois is the spacious Place Victor-Hugo, with the 17th c. church of St-Vincent and the Pavillon d'Anne de Bretagne, set against the majestic backdrop of the château with its loggias and galleries and oriel windows.

The château, built in stages between the 13th and the 17th c., reflects changing architectural styles over five centuries. It is laid out around a large central courtyard, partly open only on the south-east side. The château is entered through the Louis XII wing (1498–1503), built in red brick and natural stone. Over both the large and the small doorway appears the crowned porcupine, the emblem of Louis XII, and above the large doorway, framed in Late Gothic ornament, is an equestrian figure of Louis, a 19th c. copy of the original.

The interior of the Louis XII wing is supported on arcaded walkways, with winding stairways in staircase towers to left and right. On the right, after such a projecting tower, is the Salle des Etats, a remnant of the 13th c. castle. Adjoining this is the Francis II wing (1515–24), a masterpiece of Renaissance architecture, with the famous richly decorated octagonal staircase. Around the corner (opposite the entrance) lies the south-west wing, built between 1635 and 1638 by François Mansart for Louis XIII's brother Gaston d'Orléans. Parts of the Francis I wing had to be removed in order to construct it. However, the three-storey building remains unfinished; it now houses the library and municipal festival hall.

St-Calais

In the south-east the Louis XII wing is followed by the Galerie Charles d'Orléans, with the Late Gothic chapel of St-Calais. In front of the chapel is a lookout terrace from which there is a fine view of the lower town, with the church of St-Nicolas in the foreground.

Francis I wing

The Francis I wing (Aile François I) contains a series of handsome state apartments, the decoration of which, however, mostly dates from the 19th c. The tiles still show traces of coloured glazing. On the massive and richly decorated chimneypiece in the Salle d'Honneur on the first floor can be

Blois
Centre

1 Château
Musée des Beaux-Arts
2 Church of St-Nicolas
3 Cathedral and Bishop's Palace
4 Church of St-Vincent
5 Pavillon d'Anne de Bretagne
6 Musée d'Art religieux et Musée d'Histoire naturelle

200 m
© Baedeker

seen the salamander of Francis I and the ermine of Anne de Bretagne. Adjoining are the apartments of Catherine de Médicis, who was banished to Blois by her son. On the second floor are the apartments of Henry III. Between the Francis I wing and the Louis XII wing is the Salle des Etats-Généraux (Hall of the States General; 30 m/98 ft long, 18 m/60 ft wide and 12 m/40 ft high), with huge 17th and 18th c. tapestries depicting the exploits of Louis XIV and episodes from the life of Constantine the Great.

Louis XII wing

Along the inner wall of the two-storey Louis XII wing, built of red brick and light-coloured stone, runs an arcaded gallery, at each end of which is a staircase tower containing a spiral staircase at each end. On the ground floor is the Musée des Arts Religieux with a collection of medieval and Renaissance sculptures and religious items, on the upper floor the Musée des Beaux-Arts (pictures, including works by Solario, dell'Abbate, Caron, Vignon, Bowdon, Boucher, Ingres, David and Fromentin; china, ceramics and musical instruments of the 18th c.

Museums

Gaston d'Orléans wing

The three-storey classical-style Gaston d'Orléans wing (unfinished) on the south-west side of the courtyard was built in 1635–1638 by François Mansart, the leading French exponent of this style. Its construction involved the demolition of part of the Francis I wing.

*St-Nicolas

To the south of the château is the former Benedictine church of St-Nicolas (12th and 13th c.), which has fine capitals and a 15th c. reredos.

Cathedral

The Cathedral of St-Louis stands on high ground in the old town, north-east of the château. There was a church on this site in early Christian times which was rebuilt and altered in the 12th, 15th and 16th centuries. The church was destroyed in the 17th c., apart from the apse, the tower and the west front, and was then rebuilt. The crypt dates from the 10th and 11th centuries.

Hôtel de Ville

Immediately east of the cathedral is the 18th c. Ancien Evêché, the former Bishop's Palace, now the Hôtel de Ville (Town Hall). There are fine views from the adjoining gardens.

Old town

The old town of Blois, with a number of interesting old burghers' houses, lies to the south of the cathedral.

Notre-Dame-de-la-Trinité

North-east of the town centre is the modern church of Notre-Dame-de-la-Trinité, consecrated in 1949. It has a very fine interior, notable particularly for the stained glass and the Stations of the Cross. From the top of the tower there are fine panoramic views.

Château doorway with statue of Louis XII

The famous staircase of Blois

Surroundings of Blois

Château-Renault

In the little town of Château-Renault, 34 km/21 miles west, are the ruins of a 14th c. castle, with a keep which is even older. There is a small Leather Museum in the castle grounds.

Ménars

6 km/4 miles north-east of Blois on the right bank of the Loire is the village of Ménars. Amid beautiful terraced gardens stands a château of the mid 17th c. which was acquired by the Marquise de Pompadour in 1716 and enlarged by the court architect Gabriel. In the 18th c. extensive changes were carried out. It is one of the few classical-style châteaux in the Loire valley.

Bordeaux G10

Region: Aquitaine. Département: Gironde
Altitude: 5 m/16 ft. Population: 246,000

Situation and characteristics

Bordeaux, chief town of the region of Aquitaine and département of Gironde and the commercial and cultural centre of south-western France, lies on the left bank of the Garonne, which a short distance upstream joins the Dordogne to form the wide funnel-shaped estuary of the Gironde and, 90 km/55 miles farther on, flows into the Atlantic. Bordeaux is France's sixth most important port, the see of an archbishop and a university town. As well as the traditional wine trade, shipbuilding, the chemical and foodstuffs industries and oil-processing (refineries at Ambès, Pauillac and Le Verdon) make major contributions to the economy.

History

The Roman *Burdigala,* an important port and commercial centre, was one of the leading cities of Gaul and became capital of the province of Aquitania. Wine-growing was introduced to the area by the Romans. In the 4th c.

the town became the see of a bishop, and in the Middle Ages it alternated in allegiance between the Duchy of Aquitaine and Gascony. For three centuries, from 1154 to 1451/1453, it belonged to England, and during that period its extensive trade made it a major economic and cultural centre. The city centre, with its streets and squares along the Garonne, is a magnificent example of 18th c. urban architecture.

Sights

Place de la Comédie
*Grand Théâtre

The hub of the city's life is the busy Place de la Comédie, on the site of the Roman forum. In this square is the Grand Théâtre, one of the finest theatres in France, built by Victor Louis in 1773–1780. It has a colonnaded front with twelve Corinthian columns topped by a balustraded gallery bearing twelve statues of Muses and goddesses. The main house, the staircases, foyers and smaller halls are splendidly decorated.

Esplanade des Quinconces

North of the theatre is the Esplanade des Quinconces, the largest square in Europe (12 hectares/30 acres), laid out in 1818–1828. In the square are a monument to the Girondists (1895) and statues of Montaigne and Montesquieu. To the north-west is the Jardin Public, with the Botanical Garden and Natural History Museum.

Palais Gallien

On the far side of Rue Fondaudège is the only relic of ancient Burdigala, the "Palais Gallien", the entrance to an amphitheatre of the 3rd c. A.D. which could accommodate 15,000 spectators.

*St-Seurin

Some 500 m/550 yds south of the Palais Gallien is the church of St-Seurin (12th–15th c.; façade 19th c.). On the south side, under a protective porch, is a doorway (13th–14th c.) richly decorated with statues. The entrance to the church is on the west front, which has an 11th c. porch preserved from an earlier building. In the choir are a stone abbot's throne and fine stalls, both

Porte Cailhau

St-André

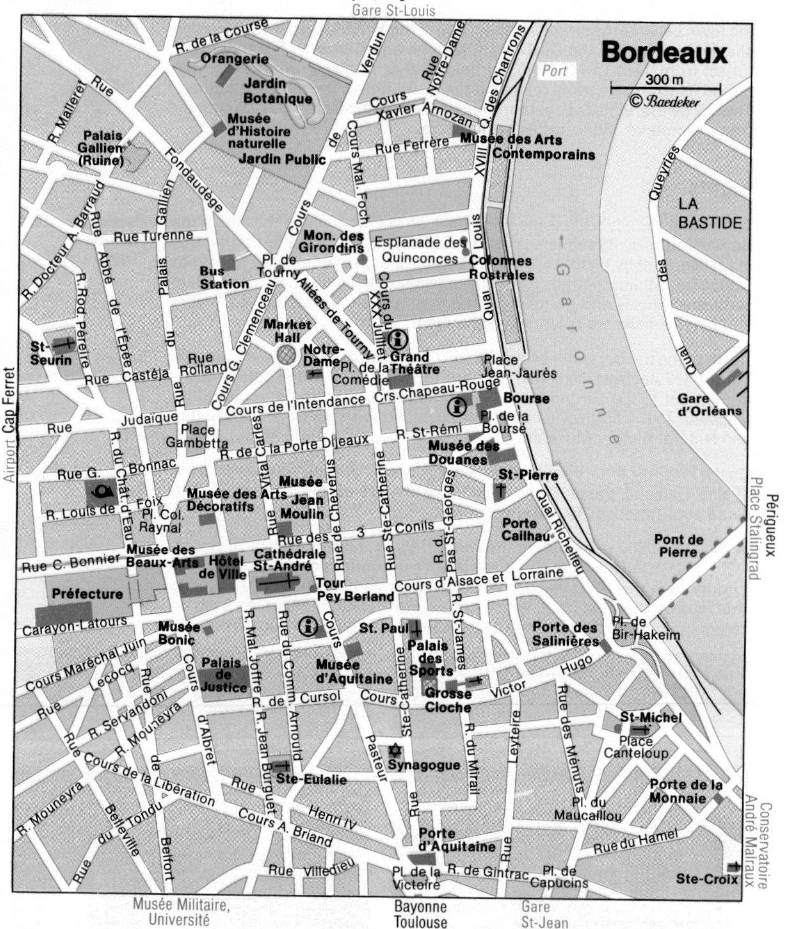

dating from the 14th and 15th centuries. The left-hand choir chapel has a large Late Gothic reredos with twelve alabaster reliefs and a 14th c. Virgin. In the 11th c. crypt are reliquaries and sarcophagi of the 6th and 7th centuries.

* Place de la Bourse

To the south-east, on the banks of the Garonne, is the Place de la Bourse, built between 1730 and 1755 by members of the Gabriel family of architects. The square is flanked by two pavilion-like buildings, the Bourse (Stock Exchange) and the Musée des Douanes (Customs Museum: history of the port of Bordeaux, with ship models and nautical instruments, etc.). In the centre of the square is the Fountain of the Three Graces.

Cathedral

In the south of the old town is the Cathedral of St-André, which is comparable in size with Notre-Dame in Paris. The nave, built in the 12th c., was

Place de la Bourse

altered in the 13th and 15th centuries; the choir and transepts date from the 14th c. The west front is plain, since it was too close to the town walls. The finest feature of the exterior is the north doorway, richly decorated with sculpture (Last Supper, Ascension, Christ in Majesty) and flanked by two tall towers. Also on the north side is the Porte Royale, with fine 13th c. sculptural decoration (five figures of Apostles on each side of the doorway, Resurrection of the Dead on the lintel, Last Judgment in the tympanum).

*Porte Royale

Beside the cathedral is a richly decorated free-standing tower, the Tour Pey Berland, built by the archbishop of that name in the 15th c. On the top of the tower (extensive views) is a 19th c. statue of Notre-Dame d'Aquitaine.

Tour Pey Berland

Opposite the west front of the cathedral is the former Archbishop's Palace (18th c.), now the Hôtel de Ville (Town Hall), with a handsome staircase hall and finely appointed rooms.

Hôtel de Ville

The Musée des Beaux-Arts, in the Jardin de la Mairie (behind the Town Hall), has a collection ranging in date from the 15th to the 20th c., including pictures by Titian, Perugino, Veronese, Van Dyck, Brueghel, Rubens, La Tour, Delacroix, Renoir, Corot, Kokoschka, Rouault, Vlaminck, Bissière and Masson and sculpture by Rodin, Barye and Zadkine. The adjoining Galerie des Beaux-Arts puts on exhibitions of contemporary art.

*Musée des Beaux-Arts

The Museum of Decorative Art, in the Hôtel de Lalande (by Etienne Laclotte, 1779), displays furniture, ceramics, glass, jewellery, everyday objects and luxury articles from the 16th to the 18th c.

Musée des Arts Décoratifs

The Museum of Aquitaine vividly illustrates the history of the city and the region from prehistoric times to the present day.

Musée d'Aquitaine

Other sights

*Pont de Pierre

The 486 m/530 yd long Pont de Pierre (1813–1821) spans the Garonne with its 17 arches. At its west end is the 18th c. Porte de Bourgogne or Porte des

Cathedral and Bishop's Palace, Bourges

Salinières. Still farther west is the Grosse Cloche, a gate tower of the 13th and 15th centuries. To the south of the bridge is the Gothic church of St-Michel (14th–16th c.), with a free-standing belfry (1472–1492) 109 m/ 358 ft high, from the top of which there are fine views of the city.

Centre Jean-Moulin

The Centre Jean-Moulin is a small museum telling the story of the Resistance movement in Bordeaux during the Second World War.

Surroundings of Bordeaux

Wine tour

The vineyards from which come the famous wines of Bordeaux begin just outside the city. The oldest of the estates *(châteaux)* go back to the 17th and 18th centuries, when they belonged to noble families. Most of the large estates are now owned by businessmen.

The system of classification *(classement)* of Bordeaux wines was introduced in 1855 on the occasion of the Paris International Exhibition. For the red wines of Bordeaux (clarets) the best sixty châteaux were placed in five classes or growths *(crus)*, while for the white wines there were two growths (plus a special category, "first great growth", for Château Yquem). The original classification is still in force with only slight modifications. Some wine-producers not included in the scheme have devised categories of their own, like *cru bourgeois, cru bourgeois supérieur* and *cru exceptionnel.*

Among the best known wine-producing areas are, on the left bank of the Gironde to the north of Bordeaux, the Médoc (mainly red wines, e.g. Château Lafite, Château Latour, Margaux), farther south the great red wines of St-Emilion (see Poitou–Charentes–Vendée), Pomerol, Graves and Sauternes (also white wines), and, between the Garonne and Dordogne, the Entre-deux-Mers area (mainly white wines).

Château Labrède

To the south of Bordeaux is the Château Labrède, in which Montesquieu was born in 1689. South-east of Bordeaux, in Cadillac, is the Château d'Epernon (16th–17th c.), with eight monumental chimneypieces.

Bourges

K7

Region: Centre
Département: Cher
Altitude: 130 m/530 ft
Population: 80,500

Situation and characteristics

The old ducal city of Bourges, now chief town of the département of Cher, the see of a bishop and a university town, lie at the confluence of the Yèvre and the Aveyron in the fertile province of Berry, which claims to be the heart of France. In addition to its famous cathedral it preserves many remains of its past, including old palaces and burghers' houses.
The principal industries of Bourges are armaments, engineering, car manufacture and tyres.

History

Bourges, the Gallic town of *Avaricum,* was conquered by Caesar in 52 B.C.. In the early Middle Ages it was the chief town of a county, and later it became the residence of the Dukes of Berry, under whom it prospered economically and culturally, acquiring a university at which Jean Calvin, the future Reformer, was a student around 1530. During the wars of religion the town, which was captured by the Protestants in 1562, was largely destroyed.

Sights

**Cathedral

On the east side of Rue Moyenne is the Cathedral of St-Etienne, one of the most splendid of French cathedrals. It was built in two stages, the apse and

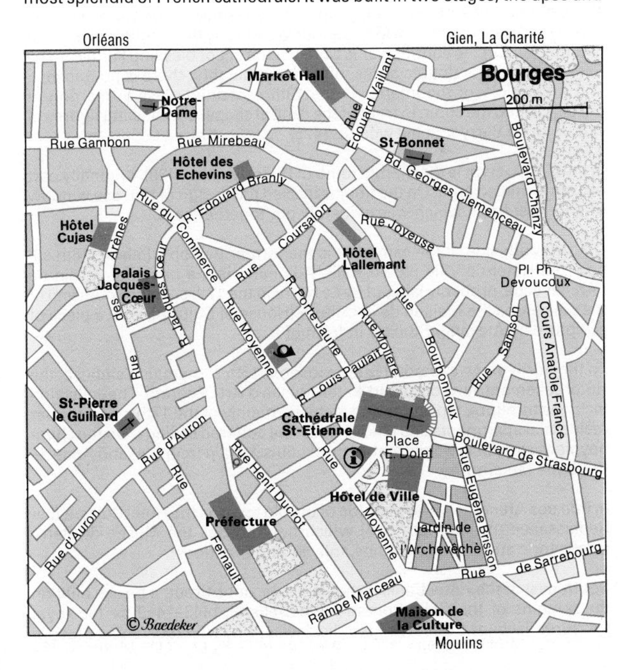

Bourges Cathedral
Kathedrale St-Etienne

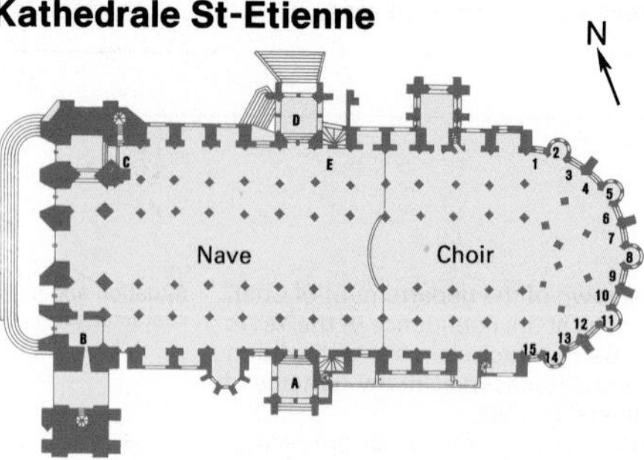

A S doorway
B Sacristy
C Ticket office
Entrance to tower
D N doorway
E Entrance to crypt

STAINED GLASS
1 The rich man and Lazarus
2 Mary Magdalene, St Nicholas and St Mary of Egypt
3 Legend of St Stephen
4 The good Samaritan
5 St Dennis (Dionysius) of Paris, St Peter, St Paul, St Martin
6 Parable of the prodigal son
7 The Old and the New Covenant (Abraham, Isaac, Moses, David and Jonah)
8 Life of the Virgin
9 Last Judgment
10 Christ's Passion
11 St Lawrence, St Stephen, St Vincent
12 Apocalypse
13 St Thomas
14 St James the Great, St John the Baptist and St John the Evangelist
15 Joseph in Egypt

30m

choir (over an undercroft) between about 1195 and 1215, the nave and west front between 1225 and 1260. The magnificent west front, flanked by massive towers has five doorways with rich sculptural decoration and a beautiful 14th c. rose window. In the tympanum of the central doorway is a fine representation of the Last Judgment. A fire in 1986 caused considerable damage.

The original north tower collapsed in 1506 and was rebuilt in Flamboyant style; from the top there are fine views. The south tower, which was given added support by a massive buttress in the early 14th c., is of severer form and was left unfinished.

Interior

The cathedral is entered through the Romanesque south doorway, over which is a figure of Christ in Majesty, surrounded by the symbols of the four Evangelists. On the central pier is Christ in the act of blessing (13th c.). The nave is flanked by double aisles, of different heights; there is no transept. The great glory of the interior is the 13th c. stained glass in the ring of chapels round the choir. In front of the central chapel are kneeling figures of Duc Jean de Berry and his wife (*c.* 1425).

Crypt

In the Gothic crypt is the marble tomb of Duke Jean (*c.* 1430), originally part of a large mausoleum. On the floor is incised the design of the rose window on the west front, which was evidently put together here.

Hôtel de Ville

On the south side of the cathedral is the former Bishop's Palace (16th c.), now the Hôtel de Ville (Town Hall). Adjoining is the beautiful Jardin de l'Archevêché, probably laid out by Le Notre in the 17th c. At the south end of the gardens is the Maison de la Culture (House of Culture), with a piece of sculpture by Alexander Calder in front of it.

Hôtel Lallemant

To the north of the cathedral is a handsome 16th c. merchant's house, the Hôtel Lallemant, now occupied by the Musée d'Art Décoratif. The collection includes furniture, tapestries and pictures, mainly of the 17th c. The former residential apartments and chapel have fine coffered ceilings. On the chimneypieces are the heraldic emblems of Louis XII (a porcupine) and Anne de Bretagne (an ermine).

Hôtel Cujas
Musée du Berry

In Rue des Arènes, on the west side of the old town, is the Hôtel Cujas, a fine Renaissance mansion (*c.* 1515) which now houses the Musée du Berry (prehistoric and Roman remains, folk art and traditions).

*Palais
Jacques Cœur

South-east of the Hôtel Cujas is the Palais Jacques Cœur, a palace built on the remains of the Gallo-Roman town walls in 1443–1453 by the royal treasurer Jacques Cœur. His heraldic device, a heart *(cœur)* and a scallop-

Sancerre and its vineyards

shell *(coquille St-Jacques)*, recurs all over the building. The palace, picturesquely grouped round a courtyard, is one of the finest examples of a Gothic mansion built by a member of the prosperous middle class. In the courtyard, which is partly surrounded by arcades, are three richly decorated staircase towers leading to the upper floors.

Interior

In the Great Hall are fine pieces of 15th and 16th c. sculpture, including ten weepers from the tomb of Duc Jean de Berry. The chapel has colourful ceiling paintings of 1488. In spite of the absence of furniture the rooms, with their richly decorated chimneypieces and doors, give a good impression of the living conditions of a prosperous 15th c. household.

Other sights
Notre-Dame

The church of Notre-Dame, to the north of the old town, was built in the 15th c. and, after being destroyed in a great fire in 1487, rebuilt in 1520–1523. It thus illustrates the transition from Gothic to Renaissance style.

Hôtel Pelvoisin

To the south is the Hôtel Pelvoisin (15th–16th c.), said to have been occupied by the master builder who built the cathedral.

Hôtel des Echevins

South-east of the church of Notre-Dame is the Hôtel des Echevins (late 15th c.), the meeting-place of the town's mayor and magistrates, with a beautiful courtyard. Notable features are the octagonal staircase tower in Flamboyant style and the Renaissance gallery, built only twenty years later. The house is now occupied by the Musée Maurice-Estève (20th c. painting and graphic art).

Surroundings of Bourges

Château de Bois-Sir-Aimé

10 km/6 miles south of Bourges are the ruins of the Château de Bois-Sir-Aimé, in which Charles VII's mistress Agnès Sorel lived. Beyond this, on the road to St-Amand-Montrond, is the Château de Meillant (late 16th c.),

which resembles one of the Loire châteaux in its architecture and sumptuous decoration.

*Noirlac

Farther south-west, on the right bank of the Cher, is the Cistercian abbey of Noirlac (restored), which was rediscovered by Prosper Mérimée in 1838. The abbey, which was founded in 1150, is one of the best preserved examples of Cistercian architecture with an arcaded cloister dating from the 13th and 14th centuries. The large dormitory was divided into separate cells in the 17th c.

St-Amand-Montrond

South of Bourges, farther up the Cher valley, is the little town of St-Amand-Montrond, in an area where the famous white Charolais cattle are bred. In the south-east of the town is the Romanesque church of St-Amand (12th c.). 16 km/10 miles north are the ruins of a 14th c. castle which belonged to Duc Jean de Berry.

Nohant

6 km/4 miles north of La Châtre is Nohant, with a small château in which the novelist and feminist George Sand (1804–1876) was brought up and lived for many years. There is a small George Sand Museum in the keep of the old castle of La Châtre.

Sancerre

50 km/30 miles north-east of Bourges is the old-world little town of Sancerre (pop. 2500), famed for its wine, picturesquely situated on a hill in rolling country covered with vineyards. An old defensive tower (1509) now serves as the belfry of the church of Notre-Dame. In the park surrounding the château is the Tour des Fiefs, a 14th c. keep which is all that remains of a castle of the Counts of Sancerre.

Brest

See Brittany

Brittany

D-G 6/7

**Situation and characteristics

Brittany (Bretagne), the most westerly part of France, a peninsula 255 km/155 miles long and 100–150 km/60–95 miles wide reaching out into the Atlantic, was once a mighty range of mountains up to 4000 m/13,000 ft high which in the course of some 60 million years was worn down to a granite base no more than 400 m/1300 ft high. Brittany is the land between *ar mor,* the sea, and *ar goat,* the forest. Armor, the land on the sea, was the name given by the people of Gaul to this region with a tidal movement of up to 18 m/60 feet and a much indented coastline of 1100 km/685 miles, a region of rocky promontories affording magnificent views of the ocean and cliff-fringed inlets with a scatter of islands, of little fishing towns and popular seaside resorts. Inland Brittany – Argoat, the land of the forest – is a region of lonely moorland and heath, with scattered settlements and fields enclosed by hedges.
Among the charms of the coastal regions are the islands, which are particularly numerous off the south-west coast. The most important is Belle-Ile (area 84 sq. km/32 sq. miles). The principal ports are Brest and Lorient.
Brittany holds out a whole range of attractions to visitors – its variety of scenery, its seaside resorts, its castles, churches and museums, its megalithic stone-settings and other monuments, and the lovingly preserved customs and traditions – which make it a popular and much frequented holiday area.

Population

Brittany is thinly populated, with some 3.5 million people living in an area of 27,208 sq. km/10,505 sq. miles. The administrative region of Brittany takes in the départements of Ille-et-Vilaine, Côtes-du-Nord, Morbihan,

Pointe de Penhir and Tas de Pois

Finistère and Loire-Atlantique. The largest town, with a quarter of a million inhabitants, and the historic capital of the region is Nantes (see entry), but the real capital and cultural centre of present-day Brittany is Rennes (see entry).

History

Brittany, then occupied by a Celtic population, was conquered by Caesar in 56 B.C.. For four centuries it was part of the Roman Empire under the name of Armorica, belonging to the province of Lugdunensis (Lugdunum = Lyons). From around 460 it was settled by Celtic immigrants from Britain, driven out by the Angles and Saxons. The incomers called their new country Little Britain, which then became known as Brittany. Unlike the earlier Celtic population, which was now completely Romanised, the new arrivals retained their own language and culture, and the Breton still spoken today is a Celtic language related to Gaelic.

In 799 Brittany became part of Charlemagne's Frankish kingdom, but remained relatively independent. After suffering from raids by the Normans (Norsemen), Brittany came under Norman–English control in 1113. In 1213 it passed by inheritance to Pierre Mauclerc, Count of Dreux, a scion of the Capet family, whose grandson Jean II was created duke in 1297. Finally in 1532 Brittany fell to the French crown.

In subsequent centuries disputes about rights and privileges led to repeated risings against the French crown. During this period the port of Brest was built by the royal military engineer Vauban.

During the French Revolution Brittany was the scene of a civil war between townspeople of republican views and the country people (Chouans) whose sympathies were with the royalists.

In the early days of industrialisation there was a movement of population out of Brittany which was halted only with the establishment of industry in Brittany itself and the development of agriculture.

Economy

The main element in the Breton economy is agriculture – meat, dairy products, vegetables, poultry (half the eggs eaten in France come from

Brittany). Second to agriculture are the fisheries (barbels and soles, cod and sardines, lobsters and crabs, the famed Belon oysters, scallops and other shellfish, molluscs, algae). Industry plays a smaller role (cars and tyres, Citroën and Michelin, shipbuilding, electrical products, electronics, precision engineering). A leading place is now taken by the foodstuffs industries, in particular the canning and preserving industry.
Tourism is playing an increasingly important part in the economy, helped by the development of good communications with Paris. It is, however, confined to the summer season, between late spring and early autumn.

Current developments

In the early 20th c. regionalist movements began to develop in Brittany, followed after the First World War by movements seeking self-government, which on occasion resorted to militant action.
There is now a well developed regional consciousness in Brittany, which finds expression, for example, in the preservation and development of the Breton language, which is now spoken at home by over a million Bretons. There are now numerous institutions concerned with the study and preservation of the language, which is seen as the symbol of an independent Breton culture.
Various organisations reflect varying regionalist, ecological and political attitudes. Information can be obtained from the Union Démocratique Bretonne (UDB), which is represented in most communal councils and publishes its own journal, "Le Peuple Breton"; its headquarters are in Brest.

Art

Breton art begins with the cult monuments of the 3rd and 4th millennia B.C., the menhirs (standing stones), dolmens (megalithic chamber tombs), and stone-settings, either in groups (cromlechs) or in rows (alignements), which feature prominently in the landscape in certain areas (more than 3000 in the Carnac area alone): silent witnesses to a long vanished culture, probably associated with some form of solar cult. Apart from Carnac, other important sites are Er Lannic, on a small island in the Gulf of Morbihan, Erdeven, St-Just, Lagat-Jar, Camaret-sur-Mer, Locmariaquer and Commana.

Enclos paroissiaux

The *enclos paroissiaux* of Brittany are walled enclosures with a monumental entrance, within which are the church and churchyard, a charnel-house *(ossuaire)* and an elaborate Crucifixion group *(calvaire)* carved from the local granite. The best known are those of St-Thégonnec, Guimiliau, Lampaul-Guimiliau, Pencran, La Martyre, Sizun, Pleyben and Kergrist-Moëlon.

Folk traditions

Brittany is a land of ancient myths and legends which have survived in varying degrees in the life and customs of the people. Here Parsifal is said to have come in quest of the Holy Grail; here the wizard Merlin fell in love with the fairy Morgan le Fay; here the city of Ys sank into the sea after the king's daughter, Dahut, became involved with the Devil, and still, as the fairy Marie-Morgane, lures seamen to their doom at the bottom of the sea. Another well known Breton legend is the tale of Tristan and Isolde, which inspired Wagner's opera. In Christian times the Breton belief in wonders was transmuted into a fervent reverence for the saints, in which ancient Breton beliefs fused with the teachings of Christianity. St Yves is the most celebrated Breton saint, and St Anne is honoured along with the Virgin as the protectress of mothers.

Pardons

The Breton pilgrimages known as *pardons* are religious festivals with processions in which the participants, many of them wearing traditional costumes, beg for forgiveness of their sins. Of medieval origin, they begin with a pilgrimage, which is followed by the celebration of mass and then by a popular festival *(fest noz)* which has no religious content. On these occasions music is provided by bands playing traditional instruments like the *bombarde* (a kind of oboe) and the *biniou* (the Breton bagpipes). The most important pardons take place between May and September; the exact dates can be obtained from local tourist information offices.

Port de Recouvrance, Brest

Brittany has a rich variety of traditional costumes, but nowadays these are mostly to be seen in local museums and only occasionally in pardons or other festivals.

Coasts of Brittany

Brittany has a very beautiful coastline of around 1100 km/685 miles. There are numerous attractive seaside resorts, both on the cliff-fringed north coast and on the gentler south coast with its long sandy beaches and numerous islands.

Sights of Brittany

La Baule

La Baule, situated on the estuary of the Loire, was founded only in 1879, and now has a population of some 15,000. It lies to the west of Nantes, halfway between that city and the island of Belle-Ile. It ranks along with Biarritz as one of the leading resorts on the French Atlantic coast, with a very beautiful beach several kilometres long. A seafront boulevard runs along above the beach, with numerous hotels and guesthouses and the Casino, set in beautiful gardens. Around the town are salt-pans and pine-woods planted to stabilise the dunes. Adjoining it is the smaller resort of La Baule-les-Pins, to the east of which is the Parc des Dryades, an interesting botanical garden.

Guérande

6 km/4 miles north of La Baule, amid extensive salt-pans, is the little town of Guérande, still surrounded by its medieval walls. The church dates from the 12th–16th centuries. The Porte St-Michel, one of the old town gates, contains an interesting museum of regional history. Also worth a visit is the Presqu'Ile de Guérande, a peninsula jutting out into the Atlantic on the south side of a cove which is now silted up and covered with salt-pans.

* **Belle-Ile**

Off the south-west coast of Brittany, 16 km/10 miles south of Quiberon, is Belle-Ile, the largest of the Breton islands (17 km/10½ miles long, 10 km/

6 miles wide), with a population of 4500. There are boat services from Quiberon; the crossing takes an hour.
The island was frequently attacked by the British and Dutch, and between 1573 and 1761 it was held by Britain.
The chief place on the island is Le Palais. Above the harbour is a citadel originally built in 1549 and strengthened in the following century by Vauban. For many years it was a prison and later, until 1961, a barracks. It now houses a museum on the history of the island.

Circuit of the island
* Aiguilles de Port-Coton
** Grotte de l'Apothicairerie

From Le Palais the route runs south-west across the island to the rugged Côte Sauvage, passing a large lighthouse, and comes to the Aiguilles (rock pinnacles) de Port-Coton. It then continues to the north of the island, where a visit must be paid to the Grotte de l'Apothicairerie (so called because the cormorants' nests in its walls resemble the compartments for bottles in an old-fashioned pharmacy). South-east of Le Palais is the Plage des Grands Sables, the island's most beautiful beach.

Ile de Bréhat

Off the north coast of Belle-Ile is the Ile de Bréhat (3.5 km/2 miles long), which actually consists of two small islets, with handsome red granite cliffs.

Brest

Brest (pop. 160,000), the third largest town in Brittany, lies at its western tip. From the 12th c. it was France's leading naval port; it now takes second place to Toulon. During the Second World War it was an important German submarine base. It is now a considerable commercial port.

Sights

Tour de la Motte

* Musée de la Marine

From the Place de la Liberté, in the centre of the city, Rue de Siam runs south-west to the Pont de Recouvrance (1954), a massive drawbridge 64 m/210 ft high spanning the river Penfeld and linking Brest with the outlying district of Recouvrance. In the Tour de la Motte-Tanguy (14th c.) is the Musée du Vieux Brest. South of the Pont de Recouvrance is the château (13th c., altered by Vauban in 17th c.), with massive round towers; it now houses the Préfecture Maritime and the Musée de la Marine. To the east of the château, running along the old ramparts, is the Cours Dajot, which offers the best view of the extensive Rade de Brest, one of the finest and best protected anchorages in the world.

Océanopolis

On the south-eastern outskirts of the town, at the Port de Plaisance du Moulin Blanc (a marina), is Océanopolis, a high-tech sea-life centre containing Europe's largest marine aquarium.

Carnac
** Megaliths

Carnac (pop. 4000), on Quiberon Bay in southern Brittany, lies in an area with an extraordinary assemblage of standing stones and other megalithic monuments which attract large numbers of visitors. The name of the town comes from the Celtic word *carn,* meaning a stone monument.

* Musée de la Prehistoire
* Ménec

Near the 17th c. church of St-Cornely, notable particularly for its porch, is the Musée de la Prehistoire, with an important collection of material illustrating the development of mankind between 450,000 B.C. and 800 A.D.

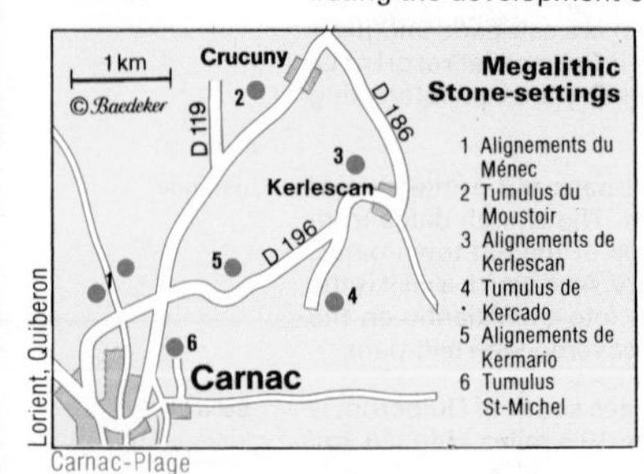

On the west side of Carnac is the starting-point of the Circuit des Alignements, which takes in the stone-settings and other megalithic monuments of Carnac, Ménec, Kermario and Kerlescan. These consist of menhirs (standing stones, which may be up to 6 m/20 ft high), either free-standing, in rows (alignements) or in circles (cromlechs), dolmens (from a Celtic word for "stone table"), which were originally tombs, and tumuli containing tomb chambers – evidence of a prehistoric culture of which almost nothing is known. It is estimated that the oldest stones date from the Neolithic

Standing stones, Carnac

(about 3500 B.C.). The function of the stones has been the subject of much speculation. One suggestion is that they may have served some calendrical purpose, but there is no agreement among experts on when and why they were erected.

Tumulus St-Michel

This tumulus, which is 125 m/410 ft long and 60 m/200 ft across and contains a number of tomb chambers, is topped by a small chapel. From the top of the mound a number of megaliths can be seen. There are others in the surrounding area, at Locmariaquer, Kermario, Kerlescan, Kercado and Moustoir.

Concarneau

Concarneau (pop. 18,500), at the mouth of the river Moros, is France's third largest fishing port, an important tunny fishing and commercial centre with numerous fish-canning plants.

Ville Close

The "closed city" is a 14th c. stronghold enclosed by massive granite walls and towers which was enlarged by Vauban in the 17th c.
The former Arsenal is now occupied by the Musée de la Pêche (Fisheries Museum) which illustrates the history of the port and displays the various species of fish, the best known of which can be seen, live, in an aquarium.

Cornouaille

*Port-Musée

**Pointe du Raz

In the Middle Ages the district of Cornouaille in south-western Brittany was a duchy with Quimper as its capital. Its most striking features are two rocky peninsulas, Cap Sizun and Penmarc'h. It has a number of attractive seaside resorts like Tréboul and the fishing port of Douarnenez, with Port-Musée, a maritime conservation area featuring the large Musée du Bateau (Shipping Museum). The Pointe du Raz, a promontory 70 m/230 ft high reaching far out into the Atlantic, is the most westerly point in Brittany. A good path runs to the tip of the promontory, from where there are magnificent views.

***Côte d'Emeraude**

The "Emerald Coast" runs along the north coast of Brittany from St-Malo and Dinard to Cap Fréhel. Along this stretch of coast are numerous seaside

Pointe de Penhir

resorts like Dinard, Paramé, Servan-sur-Mer, Rothéneuf, St-Briac, St-Lunaire, Lancieux, St-Jacut, St-Cast et Cancale (oyster-beds), all linked by a coast road. The most striking feature is Cap Fréhel, which rears to a height of 72 m/236 ft above the sea, affording fine views of the coast. It can also be reached from Dinard by boat. Inland from the coast are Dinan, Fougères and Combourg, with a château which was the family home of the 19th c. writer and statesman René de Chateaubriand. At Essé, south-east of Rennes (see entry), is the Roche aux Fées, a megalithic chamber tomb.

*Cap Fréhel

****Crozon peninsula**

The rocky promontories on the much indented Crozon peninsula, north of Cornouaille and the Pointe du Raz, offer the most splendid views in Brittany. Along the peninsula are a number of seaside resorts like Morgat, Camaret and Roscanvel. The Pointe de Penhir rises to a height of 70 m/230 ft above the sea, with impressive views, particularly of the isolated crags known as the Tas de Pois (illustration, page 153), and a memorial to Bretons who fell in the Second World War. To the north is the Pointe des Espagnols, with a view of Brest, to the south Cap de la Chèvre. Between the Pointe de Penhir and Cap de la Chèvre is the Pointe de Dinan, from which there is a fine view of a rock known as the Château. A little way inland is the viewpoint of Ménez-Hom (orientation table).

*Pointe de Penhir

*Tas de Pois

*Pointe de Dinan

**Ménez-Hom

Daoulas

See Plougastel-Daoulas

***Dinan**

The town of Dinan (pop. 14,500), still surrounded by its old walls, lies on a hill above the left bank of the Rance, which from here to its mouth, between Dinard and St-Malo, widens into a fjord-like inlet. The old town with its 15th and 16th c. houses (particularly in Rue du Jerzual) and the castle of Anne de Bretagne with its massive 14th c. keep 34 m/110 ft high preserve something of Dinan's medieval atmosphere. The castle now houses a historical museum. The church of St-Sauveur (12th–16th c.) is also worth a visit. To the west is the 15th c. Tour de l'Horloge. An attractive excursion from Dinan is a boat trip down the river to Dinard or St-Malo.

*Castle

Cobac Park

Cobac Park is a leisure park (area 8 hectares/20 acres) with a restaurant, a zoo, facilities for riding and a pleasure lake.

*Dinard

Opposite St-Malo on the other side of the Rance estuary, here 2 km/1½ miles wide, is Dinard (pop. 10,000), which ranks along with La Baule as the most elegant of the Breton resorts. Mimosas and camellias flourish here under the influence of the Gulf Stream. To the north of the town is the Grande Plage, a beautiful bathing beach 500 m/550 yds long. On the Promenade du Clair-de-Lune (Moonlight Promenade) is the Musée de la Mer (Museum of the Sea), with an aquarium.

*Le Folgoët

In this little town (pop. 2900) is the important pilgrimage church of Notre-Dame (14th–15th c.), whose north tower is one of the finest in Brittany. Notable features of the interior are the antechamber to the Chapelle de la Croix and the magnificent granite rood screen (15th c.).

Fougères

Fougères (pop. 25,000), 50 km/30 miles north-east of Rennes, has long been noted as a centre of shoe manufacture, and has an interesting Musée de la Chaussure (Shoe Museum). Nowadays, however, it is mainly an agricultural town, with the largest cattle market in Europe. Once a fortified town, it still preserves its massive castle (11th–15th c.), with 13 towers around its circuit of walls. The courtyard of the castle is used as an open-air theatre. To the south is the church of St-Sulpice (15th–18th c.), with a beautiful interior. The Hôtel de Ville (Town Hall) dates from the 14th and 15th centuries. In an old half-timbered house (16th c.) adjoining the Town Hall is the Musée Emmanuel de la Villéon, an Impressionist painter (1858–1944) born in Fougères.

*Castle

*Golfe du Morbihan

The Golfe du Morbihan, connected with the Atlantic only by a narrow channel, is an attractive inland sea with numerous small islands which is one of the most popular places in Brittany. On the island of Arz there are a number of standing stones, and on Gavrinis an 8 m/26 ft high tumulus. The largest and most populous of the islands is the Ile aux Moines (Monks' Island), which once belonged to a monastery.

*Tumulus

*Guimiliau

This little village in north-western Brittany, south of Roscoff, has one of the finest *calvaires* (Crucifixion groups) in Brittany (1581–1588), with more than 200 figures in scenes from the life of Christ. The 16th c. church and a charnel-house of 1648 are also worth seeing.

Josselin

*Château des Rohan

Josselin, north of Vannes, has numbers of old houses (16th–17th c.), some of them with half-timbering and caryatids. The façade of the residential wing of the Château des Rohan (14th–16th c.) is particularly fine. The Late Gothic church of Notre-Dame-du-Roncier has impressive gargoyles.

Montagnes Noires

The Montagnes Noires (Black Mountains), along with the Monts d'Arrée, form the backbone of the peninsula, rising to just over 300 m/980 ft. In recent years there has been extensive reafforestation.

*Monts d'Arrée

The Monts d'Arrée, in western Brittany, are the highest hills in the peninsula, rising to around 400 m/1300 ft. They have some of the finest scenery in inland Brittany, with a variety of fine viewpoints, like the Montagne St-Michel (382 m/1253 ft).

Nantes

See entry

*Ile d'Ouessant

The island of Ouessant (in English traditionally Ushant), 7 km/4½ miles long by 4 km/2½ miles across, lies north-west of Brest, surrounded by treacherous cliffs, dangerous currents and a ring of lighthouses. The Phare de Créac'h on the rugged north-west coast is a lighthouse which is passed by about 30,000 ships every year, marks the entrance to the English Channel. There are ferries to the island from Brest and Le Conquet.

***Plougastel-Daoulas**

The *calvaire* of Plougastel-Daoulas, with more than 180 figures, is one of the finest in Brittany (illustration, page 160). It was erected after an epidemic of plague in 1602–1604.

Daoulas

To the east is the little town of Daoulas. Its *enclos paroissial* is entered through a handsome 16th c. porch. The abbey church dates from the 12th c., the charnel-house from the 16th. The chapel of Ste-Anne has a 17th c. doorway, and the Romanesque cloister which adjoins the church was built in 1167–1173.

Quiberon

The Quiberon peninsula, 8 km/5 miles long by 1–1.5 km/¾–1 mile across, was originally an island but was joined to the mainland by the accumulation of soil washed up by the sea. Its varied scenery – particularly impressive along the Côte Sauvage on its western side – attracts many visitors. There are boat services from the town of Quiberon to Belle-Ile.

Quimper

Quimper (pop. 60,000), in the early medieval period capital of Cornouaille and now chief town of the département of Finistère, lies in south-western Brittany at the confluence of the Steir and the Odet. In the centre of the town is Place St-Corentin, named after the first bishop of Quimper. The Gothic Cathedral of St-Corentin (13th–15th c.) has a richly decorated west doorway. Between the two 76 m/250 ft high towers, which date only from 1856, the legendary figure of the founder, King Gradion, watches over the town. The most notable features of the interior are the numerous tombs and the magnificent stained glass, some of it dating from the 15th c. In the Town Hall is the Musée des Beaux-Arts, with pictures by French and foreign painters, drawings and manuscripts of the poet Max Jacob and pictures of the Pont-Aven school. South of the cathedral, in the former Bishop's Palace is the Musée Breton, with a collection of regional folk art. In the old part of the town are many handsome old houses with oriel windows and richly decorated façades.

*Cathedral

*Musée des Beaux-Arts

Locmaria

Locmaria, on the left bank of the Odet, has a beautiful Romanesque church.

Rennes

See entry

Roscoff

A little way north of St-Pol-de-Léon (see below) is the little seaside resort of Roscoff (pop. 4000). The church of Notre-Dame de Kroaz-Baz has a beautiful 16th c, belfry with superimposed balconies and lanterns; fine reredoses in the interior. The Musée Océanologique has an interesting sea-water aquarium.

St-Malo

See entry

St-Nazaire

The important port and industrial town of St-Nazaire (pop. 70,000) lies at the mouth of the Loire. During the Second World War the town was almost completely destroyed. It is now the outer port of Nantes (see entry). From the viewing platform between the Bassin St-Nazaire and the Loire there are good views of the harbour and the Second World War submarine base. West of the town, near the road to Guérande, is the prehistoric burial mound of Dissignac.

Loire Bridge

At the mouth of the Loire the river is spanned by a road bridge built between 1972 and 1975. 2.6 km/1½ miles long and up to 61 m/200 ft high, it is a fine example of modern functional architecture. There is a beautiful view from the top of the bridge.

Grande Brière

20 km/12 miles north is the Grande Brière nature reserve, an area of marshland and moorland which has been partly drained.

***St-Pol-de-Léon**

This former episcopal city lies in a fertile area on the north-western coast of Brittany. Its Cathedral of St-Pol, which was modelled on Coutance Cathedral (see Normandy), was begun in the 13th c. on the site of an earlier

◂ *Calvary, Plougastel-Daoulas*

church and completed in the 16th c. It has fine stalls (16th c.), beautiful 16th c. windows and a 15th c. rose window. A Romanesque sarcophagus serves as a holy water stoup. The Chapelle du Kreisker, to the south of the cathedral, dates from the 14th and 15th centuries; its imposing tower was imitated in many Breton churches.

***St-Thégonnec**

This little town (pop. 2200) is famed for its magnificent *enclos paroissial* (16th–17th c.). It is entered through a monumental gateway (1587). The burial chapel *(chapelle funéraire)* (1676–1682), one of the finest Renaissance buildings in Brittany, contains an "Entombment" of painted wood by Jacques Lespaignol (1699–1702) and a valuable treasury. The *calvaire* (1610) has three crosses with scenes from Christ's Passion. The church dates from the 16th c. but was much altered in the 17th and 18th; the belfry was built in 1563. The main features of the interior are the pulpit (1683) and the carved woodwork of the apse and transepts (17th and 18th c.).

Vannes

Vannes (pop. 44,000) lies between Nantes and Brest on the Gulf of Morbihan, with which it is connected by the Rivière de Vannes. The interesting old part of the town grew up within the walls and round the Cathedral of St-Pierre (13th–19th c.), which has an external chapel in Italian Renaissance style in the form of a rotunda and contains fine 17th c. tapestries and a valuable treasury. From the Promenade de la Garenne there is a good view of the cathedral and the Tour du Connétable (14th–15th c.). The Château Gaillard (15th c.) is now occupied by an archaeological museum.

Vitré
*Castle

Vitré (pop. 13,000), east of Rennes on the left bank of the Vilaine, has preserved its original townscape almost unchanged. The massive castle on a spur of hill, built on the remains of an earlier stronghold, dates from the 14th and 15th centuries, and now houses various museums. At the foot of the castle is the old town with its medieval lanes and half-timbered houses. The most picturesque street is Rue Beaudrairie, once the quarter of the saddlers *(baudroyeurs)*. The Gothic church of Notre-Dame (15th–16th c.), with an external pulpit and a fine interior (triptych consisting of 32 panels of Limoges enamel), seems entirely in place against the background of the old town walls and towers.

*Château des Rochers

7 km/4 miles south-east of Vitré is the Château des Rochers (14th c., rebuilt in 17th c.), which features in the celebrated letters of Madame de Sévigné.

Burgundy (Bourgogne)

L/M 7/8

**Situation and characteristics

Burgundy, in the narrower sense of the term the territory of the old Duchy of Burgundy, is a region of passage between the Paris Basin and the Rhône valley and between the upper Rhine and the Loire valley, and is accordingly, from the point of view of history and culture, one of the most interesting parts of France. Taking in the four départements of Saône-et-Loire (chief town Mâcon), Côte-d'Or (Dijon), Nièvre (Nevers) and Yonne (Auxerre), it has a total area of 31,582 sq. km/12,194 sq. miles and a population of around 1.6 million.

Lower Burgundy

Lower Burgundy, the northern part, is a plateau of Jurassic limestones dissected by the river Yonne and its right-bank tributaries the Cure, Serein and Armançon which in the north gradually merges into the Paris Basin. It is an area famed for its wines.

Upper Burgundy

To the south of Lower Burgundy is Upper Burgundy, which is of more interest scenically and greater importance historically. The heart of the region is the fertile basin of the Saône.

Bresse and Dombes

East of the Saône is the old county of Bresse, a wooded upland region with many lakes (poultry rearing). South of this are the Dombes, a plateau formed from Ice Age detritus with innumerable lakes which falls steeply down to the Rhône valley. West of the Saône is a Jurassic plateau which rises to around 600 m/2000 ft in the famed wine region of the Côte d'Or. The Autun basin, with iron and coal, has developed into an important industrial region centred on Le Creusot.

Morvan

In the heart of the Monts du Morvan, a northern spur of the Massif Central, lie a series of enchanting lakes. At higher altitudes in these granite hills are areas of agricultural land intersected by hedges (the typical *bocage* landscape) and expanses of magnificent forest. Farther south are the uplands of the old county of Charolais or Charollais, mostly covered with pasture, with the Monts du Mâconnais to the east. Still farther south are the Monts du Beaujolais, another renowned wine-growing area.

Economy

Agriculture (cereals, stock farming) still plays an important part in Burgundy, and in this well wooded region forestry also makes a considerable contribution to the economy. A special position, however, is occupied by wine production.

Burgundy wines

Three of France's best wine-growing areas, with something like a hundred *appellations controlées,* are in Burgundy – Chablis in the north, the Côte d'Or in the middle and Chalonnais, Mâconnais and Beaujolais in the south. The four main types of grape used are Pinot Noir and Gamay for red wine, Chardonnay and Aligoté for white wine.

Waterways

Burgundy's 1200 km/750 miles of waterways (principally the Seine, Loire and Rhône, the Canal de Bourgogne, the Marne–Saône Canal and the Canal Latéral de la Loire), mostly regularised or developed during the 18th and 19th centuries, are now little used by commercial traffic, but offer excellent facilities for holidays afloat (see Practical Information, Canal and River Cruising).

History

The oldest traces of human habitation in Burgundy date back 100,000 years. As an area of passage, a transit route, Burgundy has yielded only modest evidence of early human settlement (see Beaune, Archéodrome). Between 60 and 50 B.C. Caesar's forces pushed into Burgundy, and in 52 B.C. the Romans broke the stubborn resistance of the Gallic chieftain Vercingetorix at Alesia (Alise-Ste-Reine, north-east of Semur-en-Auxois). In subsequent centuries Roman civilisation and the Christian faith gradually spread throughout the region. In the 5th c. the Burgundians migrated from the Middle Rhine into the Saône plain and gave their name to this new home. In 534, however, the Burgundian kingdom was conquered by the Franks. When the Frankish kingdom was divided under the treaty of Verdun (843) two independent kingdoms came into being in the eastern part of its territory. In 934 these were combined to form the kingdom of Burgundy, which in 1032, in the reign of Emperor Conrad II, was incorporated in the German Empire (the "Holy Roman Empire"). The western part of the territory then passed to the West Frankish kingdom and developed into the independent duchy of Burgundy – the region now known as Burgundy – which became a pillar of the Christian church. Here Bernard of Clairvaux (1091–1153), fighting against the pomp and magnificence of Cluny, established his position as the strongest and most influential figure in the West. When Burgundy passed in 1363 from a collateral line of the Capetians to Philip the Bold of Valois this marked the beginning of a brilliant period of expansion towards the North Sea and the Jura. Then, with the death of Charles the Bold in 1477, the Duchy of Burgundy passed to France, of which it has now been part for more than five centuries.
Numbers of magnificent and well preserved buildings erected by the ecclesiastical and secular authorities in Burgundy still bear witness to a power and prosperity which was brought to an end by the French Revolution. The wealth of Burgundy depended on the building timber and the wine which could be sold to the court or to the city of Paris, then steadily growing in size – the transport problems being eased by the canals which were now

being constructed on an increasing scale.

Art and architecture

Although Burgundy has a few remains of Roman art and architecture, its great period of artistic achievement began in the 11th c. with the flowering of Romanesque architecture, sculpture and painting. It is as if, around the year 1000, a new impulse came into Christian art in this region. Burgundy's numerous Romanesque village churches for long remained unnoticed, and it is only within recent decades that art historians have fully realised and appreciated their importance. There are something like 350 churches in Burgundy, of which, with the best will in the world, the ordinary visitor can see no more than a handful. Cluny, Vézelay, Tournus and Paray-le-Monial are perhaps the best known and most visited, but the less obvious churches like those of St-Etienne, La Charité-sur-Loire, Semur, Autun, Saulieu and Fontenay ought not to be neglected.

Cluny

The name of Cluny is a reminder that the church reform movement which started there developed its own version of Romanesque architecture and influenced many religious houses both in Burgundy and elsewhere in Europe. The Benedictine monks of Cluny built what was until the 16th c. (when St Peter's in Rome was built) the largest church in Christendom. Without the example of Cluny many of the churches of Burgundy could not have been conceived. Art historians are still at a loss to explain this great creative flowering of architecture and sculpture in Burgundy over the space of a century and a half; they cannot say what impulse set this great building programme in motion or how, with the material resources available, it was successfully carried through.
It is not surprising that, after such an apotheosis of art and architecture dedicated to the glory of God, the Gothic style which about the middle of the 12th c. began to radiate from the Ile de France made only slow progress in Burgundy and is represented by a relatively small number of buildings – small, at any rate, in comparison with the numbers of Romanesque churches. Examples of Gothic churches are Notre-Dame in Dijon and the cathedral of Auxerre. The Flamboyant (Late Gothic) style of the 14th c. made even less impact in Burgundy, and Renaissance influence is also limited: Burgundy has few châteaux comparable with those of the Loire valley.

Sights

Ancy-le-Franc
*Château

The village of Ancy-le-Franc (pop. 1200), which lies to the east of Auxerre on the Canal de Bourgogne, has a late 16th c. château designed by Francis I's court architect Serlio, set in a large park. The interior is sumptuously decorated in Italian Renaissance style (by Primaticcio and Niccolò dell' Abbate of the school of Fontainebleau). The old working-quarters now house a motor-car and coach museum.

Autun

Autun (pop. 22,000), south-west of Dijon, is called the "gateway to Morvan". On the east side of the town are a number of important Roman monuments, including the largest Roman theatre in Gaul, with seating for 20,000 spectators, two town gates (the Porte d'Arroux and the Porte St-André) and the imposing remains of a temple of Janus.

**Cathedral

Autun's most important building is the Cathedral of St-Lazare, one of the finest examples of Cluniac architecture, built between 1120 and 1130. It has a ground-plan in the form of a Latin cross, an aisled nave, a plain transept and a three-stage choir with a semicircular end. The spire was built by Cardinal Rolin in the 15th c.

Tympanum

In the tympanum of the Romanesque main doorway is a superb Last Judgment by a sculptor named as Gislebertus. The medallions round the tympanum and the capitals of the three columns are also masterpieces of medieval sculpture.

Interior

The cathedral contains a profusion of figural capitals. Some of these have been replaced by copies, the originals of which are displayed in the chapterhouse. The chapels are also richly decorated; the third one on the left contains a "Martyrdom of St Symphorien" by Ingres (1834).

Musée Rolin

The Musée Rolin, in the 15th c. Hôtel Rolin, has prehistoric and Gallo-Roman sections and a particularly fine medieval collection.

Auxerre

Auxerre (pop. 40,000), a busy commercial centre and chief town of the département of Yonne, lies 150 km/90 miles north-west of Dijon on two hills rising above the left bank of the Yonne.

Old town

The old part of the town has preserved its old-world aspect, within its ring of boulevards with charming old houses in Rue de l'Horloge (clock-tower of the late 15th c.), Rue de Paris, Rue Joubert and Place Charles-Surugue. The oldest of Auxerre's three notable churches is the abbey church of St-Germain, which has a Carolingian crypt and 9th c. frescoes around the tomb of St Germain. The church of St-Eusèbe has a beautiful Romanesque belfry with a 15th c. octagonal spire.

Musée Leblanc-Duvernoy

The Musée Leblanc-Duvernoy, housed in an 18th c. mansion, displays furniture, china, Beauvais tapestries and pictures of the 17th–20th centuries.

*Cathedral

The Cathedral of St-Etienne (13th–16th c.), the fifth church on the site, was built on the foundations of a Romanesque cathedral, of which the crypt (11th c. frescoes) survives. The north tower is 65 m/215 ft high. The west front, which was richly decorated with sculpture, was destroyed during the 16th c. wars of religion; the sculpture on the three doorways dates from the 13th c. The interior is very fine, with short transepts, a choir with a semicircular apse, a beautiful ambulatory (13th c. triforium), richly carved capitals and fine 13th c. stained glass in the ambulatory. In the cathedral treasury are liturgical utensils, reliquaries with Limoges enamel decoration, ivory statuettes and manuscripts.

Avallon

Avallon (pop. 8900) is beautifully situated above the valley of the little river Cousin, 15 km/9 miles east of Vézelay. The old town centre is still surrounded by walls. The Romanesque church of St-Lazare (12th c.) has two richly decorated doorways on the west front, fine examples of Burgundian Romanesque. The choir is on a lower level than the three-aisled nave. A door in the south aisle leads into the chapel of St-Pierre, a 15th c. parish church. In the Grande Rue is a town gate of 1460 (clock-tower). The Musée de l'Avallonnais, in the Ancien Collège (1653), contains material on the history of the region and a small art collection.

*Doorways

Montréal

12 km/7½ miles north-east is the old-world little town of Montréal (pop. 200), its main street lined with 15th and 16th c. houses. The 12th c. collegiate church, restored by Viollet-le-Duc in the 19th c., is a fine example of Early Gothic architecture. Notable features of the interior are a 15th c. altar with scenes from the life of the Virgin and choir-stalls of 1522, with New Testament scenes.

Beaune

The old town of Beaune (pop. 20,000), on the Bouzaise, lies amid the vineyards which produce the celebrated wines of the Côte d'Or. Originally a Roman foundation *(Belna* or *Belena),* it was a residence of the Dukes of Burgundy. Apart from its wines, Beaune's great attraction for visitors lies in its numerous medieval houses. The old town walls now accommodate wine-cellars.

Sights

The central feature of the town is the Place Monge, with a tower of the 13th/14th c., which now houses a museum of archaeology and natural history, and the Hôtel de la Rochepot (16th c.), which has beautiful court-

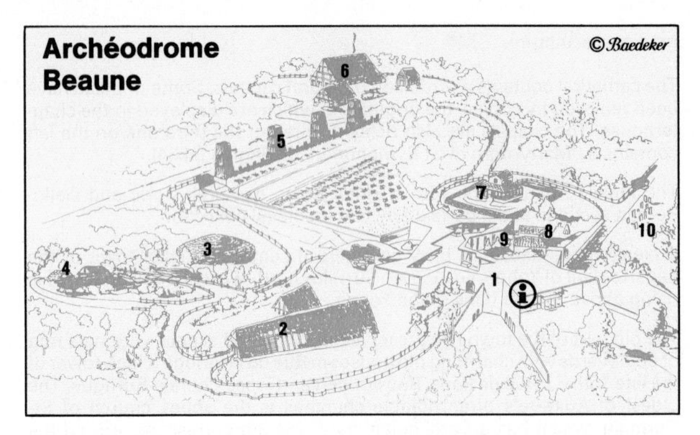

1 Information
Exhibitions
Air photography in archaeology
2 Neolithic longhouse (c. 4000 B.C.)
3 Tumuli (burial mounds) of c. 6000–900 B.C.
4 *Eperon barré* (defences of a settlement on a spur of hill)
5 Roman fortifications (reconstruction of fortifications round Alesia, c. 52 B.C.)
6 Gallic farmhouse
7 Fanum (Gallo-Roman temple) of c. 2nd c. A.D.
8 Potter's workshop
9 Remains of Gallo-Roman villa
10 Gallo-Roman cemetery (1st–4th c. A.D.)

yards.

**Hôtel-Dieu

Beaune's main sight is the famous Hôtel-Dieu, a hospital for the poor built by Chancellor Nicolas Rolin and his wife in the mid 15th c. This is a typical example of Flemish Gothic (architect Jacques Wiscrère), a long half-timbered building with a colourful roof of glazed tiles laid in geometric patterns and a picturesque courtyard surrounded by two tiers of galleries. In the courtyard, in front of the main hospital ward (which remained in use until 1971), is a wrought-iron well-head.
The Hôtel-Dieu now houses a museum, notable particularly for a large polyptych of the Last Judgment by Rogier van der Weyden (between 1442 and 1450) and a number of tapestries. Visitors can also see the old hospital ward, the chapel, the kitchen and the pharmacy, still with their medieval furnishings.

Notre-Dame

North of the Hôtel-Dieu is the Romanesque church of Notre-Dame, a three-aisled basilica in Cluniac style with transepts, a choir ending in a semi-circular apse and a square tower over the crossing. As a result of later extensions the exterior of the church is largely Gothic. The interior (modelled on Autun) has fine 15th c. stained glass, medieval frescoes and 15th c. tapestries.

Museums

Visitors interested in wine will want to see the Museum of Wine in the old Hôtel des Ducs de Bourgogne, the town house of the Dukes of Burgundy which later passed into the hands of the French kings. The Musée des Beaux-Arts, housed in part of the 18th c. Town Hall (originally an Ursuline convent), displays archaeological finds from the surrounding area, French and Flemish paintings of the 17th–19th centuries and the apparatus used by a scientist named Etienne-Jules Marey (1830–1904), a native of Beaune who invented "chronophotography", a predecessor of the cinematograph.
Beaune has a number of 16th c. houses, particularly in Rue de Lorraine, which are now owned by the municipality.

Archéodrome

The Archéodrome, situated near the motorway junction on the east side of Beaune, is an open-air museum illustrating the development of human settlement in Burgundy from the time when men first began to make tools until the end of the Roman period.

Hôtel-Dieu in Beaune

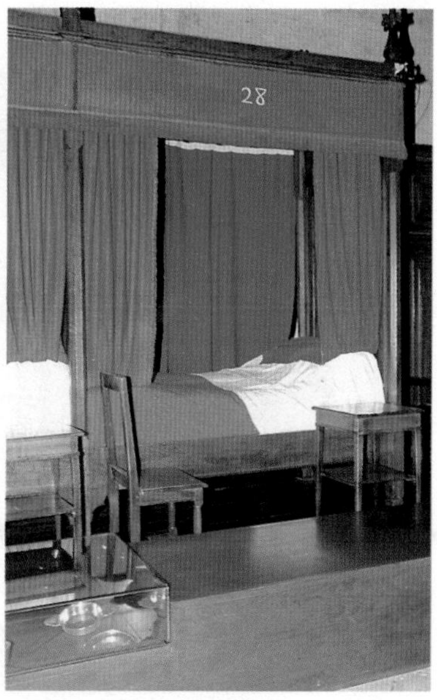

Hospital ward in the Hôtel-Dieu

Bourg-en-Bresse

Bourg-en-Bresse (pop. 45,000), the old capital of the district of Bresse, lies in south-eastern Burgundy, on the western fringes of the French Jura. It is noted not only for the famous *poulets de Bresse* which are reared in this area but for a jewel of Gothic architecture, the monastic church of Brou. The monastery of Brou, which stands a little to the east of the church of Notre-Dame (15th–16th c.; beautiful carved choir-stalls), was begun in 1506, and the church was built between 1513 and 1532 by the Brussels architect Louis van Bodeghem for Margaret of Austria.

*Eglise de Brou

Interior

*Tombs

In the harmonious interior, which is entered through a richly decorated Renaissance doorway, are a magnificent rood screen and beautiful old stained glass. The choir has 74 fine carved oak stalls (1530–1532) and contains three tombs (in the centre Duke Philibert II of Savoy, d. 1504; on the left his wife Margaret of Austria, d. 1530; on the right Margaret of Bourbon, d. 1483) and fine stained glass. On the left of the choir is the Chapelle de la Vierge, with a marble altar decorated with scenes from the life of the Virgin.

Museum

The cloisters and monastic cells now house a folk museum.

Bourg was also the birthplace of the astronomer Gérome Lalande (1732–1807) and the historian Edgar Quinet (1803–1875).

Museum

Situated on the right bank of the Saône, this town (pop. 60,000) is an important traffic centre and industrial town, as well as being the birthplace of Nicéphore Niepce (born 1775), a pioneer of photography who has a museum named after him. There are some interesting old half-timbered houses in the old town, and at the north-eastern end stands the former St-Vincent cathedral (13th–15th c. with a modern front). The Musée Denon contains archaeological finds and an art collection.

La Charité-sur-Loire

The little town of La Charité-sur-Loire (pop. 6400) grew up round a monastery founded in the 11th c. on the gently rising right bank of the Loire.

Romanesque arches, La Charité

St Pierre and St Paul

Tour Fabry

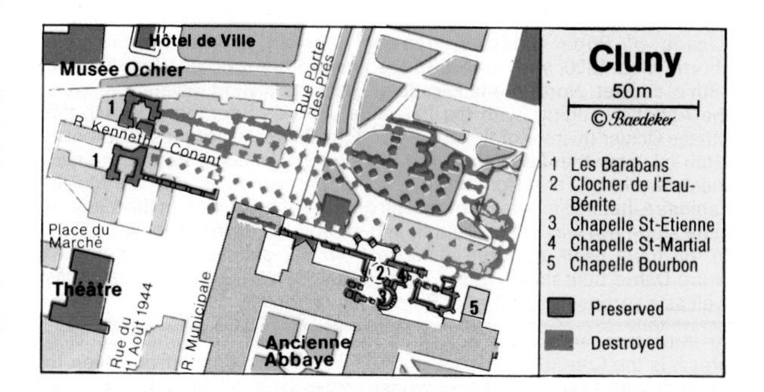

Notre-Dame

Although the church of Notre-Dame has suffered damage over the centuries, it is still a remarkable example of Burgundian Romanesque architecture.

Charlieu

Situated near the Loire in the extreme south of Burgundy, Charlieu (pop. 5000) has a Benedictine abbey, only part of which has been preserved. The main features are the narthex of the 12th c. church, the north wall of which is decorated with figures (the rest of the church has been destroyed), and the late 15th c. cloister. Also worth seeing is the cloister of a Franciscan friary, some distance away. Around Place St-Philibert are a number of handsome old houses of the 13th–16th centuries, including the Maison des Armagnacs and the Maison des Anglais.

Cluny

The quiet little town of Cluny (pop. 4400), north-west of Mâcon, grew up round the celebrated Benedictine abbey, mother house of the reforming Cluniac order.

History

The abbey of Cluny (Cluniacum) was founded in 910 by Duke William of Aquitaine on the site of a Franconian estate, and became from its earliest years the starting-point and centre of a great reform of the church which set out to effect a revival of monasticism, which had entered a state of crisis and to promote monastic life in accordance with the rules laid down by St Benedict. The impulse that went out from Cluny led to the reform of existing monastic houses and the foundation of new ones, until there were some 2000 Cluniac houses all over western Europe. New architectural ideas were also developed at Cluny in order to give monumental form to the spiritual strivings of the order. The first church on the site (Cluny I), erected soon after the foundation of the order, was replaced by Cluny II (consecrated 981), a columned basilica with transepts and a type of choir (a main choir flanked by two subsidiary choirs) which found imitators in northern France and Germany. This in turn gave place in 1089 to the largest and most magnificent church of its time (Cluny III), a huge pillared and vaulted basilica 171 m/560 ft long consisting of a three-aisled ante-church with a twin-towered west front, the five-aisled main church, a large transept with five towers, a smaller transept with a roof turret and a choir with a semicircular end, an ambulatory and a ring of chapels. During the French Revolution the abbey was closed down, and thereafter was sold for the sake of its stone and demolished. Only a few fragments survive.

*St-Pierre-et-St-Paul

Around the former monastery were fortifications of which only three of the towers (Tours des Fromages, Tour Fabry, Tour Ronde) and the Porte des Jardins still remain. The south transept with the Clocher de l'Eau Bénedite and the lower Clocher d'Horloge (clock-tower) are all that remain of the abbey church. On the way to the Musée Ochier (where tickets can be purchased and the tour begins) the visitor will pass over the site where the giant abbey church Cluny III once stood. The deeper, excavated parts formed part of the ante-church. The double gateway somewhat higher up was once the main entrance to the abbey. On Place du 11 Août stands the

Façade of Pope Gelasius

Façade of Pope Gelasius, heavily restored in the Gothic style shortly after 1300, with access to the enclosed monks' quarters and the 18th c. cloister. North of the Façade of Gelasius, a short distance away, is the Abbot's Lodging, with the Palais de Jean de Bourbon (15th c.), the Musée Ochier (history of the abbey) and the Palais de Jacques d'Amboise (16th c.), now the Town Hall. The church's magnificent figural capitals, masterworks of Early Romanesque sculpture, can be seen in the Musée Lapidaire, housed in the old monastic granary, the Farinier. In the 19th c. a state stud-farm was set up on the land around the former abbey.

*Musée Lapidaire

In the town itself, at some distance from the abbey, is the church of Notre-Dame, built shortly after 1100 and later remodelled in Gothic style, as well as a surprising number of Romanesque houses.

Côte d'Or

An important part of Burgundy, famed as one of the major wine-producing areas, is the Côte d'Or, a ridge of low hills which extends from Dijon to Chagny, with a series of villages whose names are a roll-call of the wines of Burgundy – Chenove, Brochon, Gevrey-Chambertin, Vougeot, Vosne-Romanée, Nuits-St-Georges, Aloxe-Corton, Pommard, Volnay, Meursault, Puligny-Montrachet, Santenay.

Dijon

See entry.

***Fontenay**

The well preserved old abbey of Fontenay, situated in wooded country north-west of Dijon, gives a vivid impression of life in a 12th c. Cistercian house. The church, founded by Bernard of Clairvaux, is one of France's oldest surviving Cistercian churches, with a magnificent cloister.

Morvan

The Monts du Morvan (a name of Celtic origin meaning "black hill") are a range of hills of medium height between the Loire and the Saône rising to 900 m/3000 ft in the peak of Haut-Folin. On Mont Beuvray (821 m/2694 ft) Vercingetorix, Caesar's most dangerous adversary in Gaul, summoned an assembly of Gallic chieftains in 52 B.C. to secure their agreement to a common effort against the Roman invaders.

For centuries Morvan was the sole supplier of wood to Paris, and the Canal du Nivernais was built in 1842 to provide a convenient means of transport; 178 km/108 miles long, it has 110 locks and three tunnels. The granite hills of Morvan have now been replanted with trees, and the Morvan Nature Park, established in 1970, takes in 173,000 hectares/427,000 acres of the hills, with the valleys and gorges, the streams and the numerous lakes which pattern the landscape.

Nevers

Nevers (pop. 50,000), the old capital of the Nivernais, lies on the right bank of the upper Loire. The settlement was of Celtic origin, and in Roman times became an important supply base. The town is famed for its faience, which has been made here, following Italian models, since around 1575. The factories can be visited.

Cathedral

The Cathedral of St-Cyr-et-Ste-Juliette shows a whole range of architectural styles, from the 10th to the 16th c. The Romanesque west choir has remains of a 12th c. fresco, and in the crypt under it is an early 16th c. "Entombment" in polychrome stone. In the south transept are a doorway with fine sculptural decoration and a Renaissance spiral staircase. The imposing Porte du Croux (14th c.), a gate tower which was part of the town's circuit of walls, now houses the Musée Archéologique du Nivernais (antique and Romanesque sculpture).

*Palais Ducal

The Palais Ducal (15th–16th c.), once the residence of the Counts of Nevers, is a fine example of Renaissance secular architecture. The most striking feature of the front facing the Loire is the central staircase tower, with relief decoration between the windows. At each end of the façade is an octagonal tower.

*St-Etienne

In the north-east of the old town is the church of St-Etienne, a purely Romanesque church of 1097, with three Merovingian sarcophagi in the choir.

Palais Ducal, Nevers

Paray-le-Monial

Paray-le-Monial (pop. 11,000), on the river Bourbince, is still a much frequented place of pilgrimage. The town grew up around a Benedictine abbey founded in 973. This was the place of origin, in the 17th c., of the cult of the Sacred Heart, inspired by the visions of Marguerite-Marie Alacoque (1647–90, a nun who was subsequently canonised), which spread throughout the whole Catholic world in the 19th c.

*Notre-Dame

A massive steeple draws attention to the church of Notre-Dame, one of the most important Romanesque churches in Burgundy, built in the 12th c. on the model of the abbey church of Cluny and dominated by the massive octagonal tower over the crossing. On the river front are three round-headed doorways. Adjoining the church are the neo-classical conventual buildings, which contain a museum of ceramics.
To the north of the church is the neo-Romanesque Chapelle de la Visitation, which is decorated with mosaics and frescoes. It is built on the spot where Marguerite-Marie Alacoque had her visions; her glass sarcophagus is in a side chapel on the right.

Other sights

Other features of interest in Paray-le-Monial are the Hôtel de Ville (Town Hall), a striking Renaissance building (1515) with a superb façade, and the Tour St-Nicolas, originally the belfry of a church. North of the Chapelle de la Visitation is the Musée du Hiéron (Italian, French and Flemish pictures of the 16th–18th c.).

La Rochepot

Near the south end of the Côte d'Or is the castle of La Rochepot (12th and 15th c.; extensively restored in 19th c.), looming over the village of that name (pop. 200). The beautiful courtyard and the interior can be visited.

Semur-en-Auxois

The little town of Semur-en-Auxois (pop. 5300), situated on a rocky ridge above the river Armançon, north-west of Dijon, has preserved much of its medieval aspect, with remains of a castle, the 15th c. Porte de Sauvigny, one of the old town gates, and many handsome old houses. On the highest point is the Gothic church of Notre-Dame (13th–14th c.), which was re-

Notre-Dame

stored by Viollet-le-Duc in the mid 19th c. Notable features of the church are the tympanum of the north doorway, an "Entombment" of 1490, a rich treasury of works of art and beautiful 14th c. stained glass. The old Jacobin convent (17th c.) now houses the Municipal Library and Museum. The Tour de l'Orle d'Or, a remnant of the old castle, contains geological material, archaeological finds and folk art.

Château de Bourbilly

9 km/6 miles south-west is this handsome 14th c. castle (restored in the 19th c.).

Sens

Sens (pop. 27,000), in north-western Burgundy, was the chief town of a Gallic tribe, the Senones, and later the capital of a Gallo-Roman province. In 1627 it became the see of an archbishop. The doctrines of Abelard were condemned at a church council held here in 1140, and Louis IX (St Louis) was married in the cathedral in 1234. Thomas Becket lived here during his exile from England.

* Cathedral

The construction of the Cathedral of St-Etienne, one of the largest and finest Gothic buildings in France, was begun in 1140 and completed about 1500. Most of the rich sculptural decoration of the west front was destroyed during the French Revolution: all that survives is the figure of St Stephen on the central doorway, the representation of his legend in the tympanum (*c.* 1200), the legend of John the Baptist on the left-hand doorway (also *c.* 1200), the Doorway of the Virgin on the right (early 14th c.) and a Flamboyant doorway in the north transept. The beauty of the spacious three-aisled interior with its bold vaulting is enhanced by the fine stained glass (12th–17th c.). The cathedral treasury is one of the richest in France (ecclesiastical vestments, tapestries, etc.).

* Stained glass
* Treasury

The 15th c. Palais Synodal, restored by Viollet-le-Duc in the 19th c., now houses a Musée Lapidaire. The Municipal Museum has a fine collection of Gallo-Roman antiquities. The church of St-Pierre-le-Rond (13th–15th c.) has good stained glass. The church of St-Savinien dates in part from the 11th c.

Sully

The château of Sully (15 km/9½ miles north-east of Autun) was built in the 16th c. on the site of a medieval castle. Marshal Mac-Mahon, Duke of Magenta and President of France from 1873 to 1879, was born here in 1808. The château is surrounded by a large park.

* **Tanlay**

Tanlay, situated on the Canal de Bourgogne and the river Armançon in northern Burgundy, has a magnificent Renaissance château (16th–17th c.). During the Huguenot wars it was a centre of Protestant resistance. In the Tour de Ligue can be seen ceiling frescoes portraying gods and goddesses from ancient Olympus representing those involved in the religious wars of the period.

Tournus
* St-Philibert

Tournus (pop. 7000) lies on the right bank of the Saône, to the north of Mâcon. The former abbey church of St-Philibert (11th–12th c.) has a large porch and an impressive interior. In the apse is the reliquary of St Philibert and under the choir is a large 10th c. crypt with well preserved capitals. The Musée Bourguignon Perrin de Puycousin and the Eglise de la Madeleine (15th c.) are also of interest.

Vézelay

* Ste-Madeleine

Vézelay (pop. 600), beautifully situated on a hill above the river Cure, possesses one of the great masterpieces of French Romanesque architecture in the basilica of the Sainte-Madeleine which crowns the summit of the hill. Believed to be the resting-place of the relics of Mary Magdalene, the church (meticulously restored by Viollet-le-Duc in the 19th c.) was one of the greatest places of pilgrimage in Christendom. In 1146 Bernard of Clair-

Paray-le-Monial ▶

vaux proclaimed the Second Crusade here. Built in the 11th–13th centuries as the church of an abbey founded in 864, the basilica is the largest monastic church in France. It is notable particularly for its richly carved doorway and the fantastic profusion of its figured capitals on both Biblical and secular themes. Under the Early Gothic choir (rebuilt 1190–1220) is a handsome crypt. From the terrace outside the church and from the tower there are wide-ranging views.
Vézelay also has many picturesque old houses, remains of its 12th c. walls (over 2.5 m/8 ft thick) and the Porte Neuve (14th–16th c.) with its two massive towers, once the main entrance to the town.

Caen G5

Region: Basse-Normandie
Département: Calvados
Altitude: 8 m/26 ft
Population: 121,000

Situation and characteristics

Caen, situated on the river Orne 14 km/9 miles above its outflow into the Channel, is the chief town of Lower Normandy and the département of Calvados and the seat of a university. Although three-quarters of the town was destroyed during the Allied landings in June–July 1944, it is still, after large-scale reconstruction and with its magnificent churches which were almost entirely unscathed by the war, second only to Rouen as one of the main tourist centres of Normandy. The port to the east of the town is one of the most important in France. Caen also has iron and steel, engineering and electrical industries.

History

There was originally a Gallo-Roman settlement on the site. Later the town developed into the administrative centre of Normandy, ranking alongside Rouen. It first became French in 1204, and was finally incorporated in France in 1450.

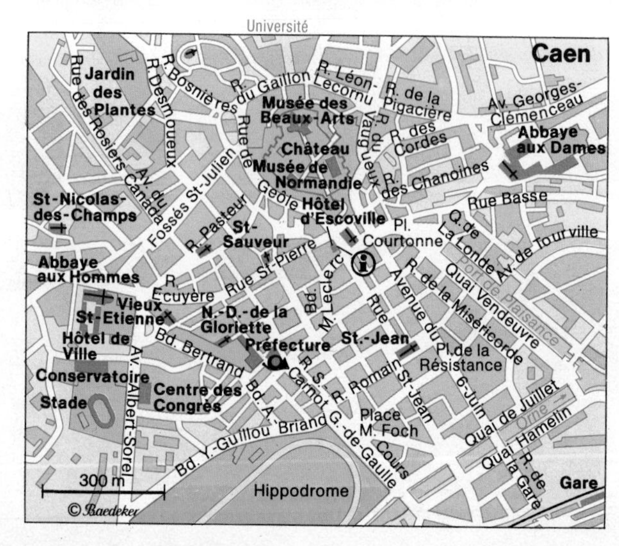

Sights

*St-Pierre

The central feature of the town is the Place St-Pierre, with a monument to Joan of Arc (1964). Here too is the church of St-Pierre (13th–14th c.), with a 75 m/245 ft high tower (1308), whose boldly soaring spire was destroyed in 1944 and subsequently rebuilt. The interior is notable for a magnificent Renaissance apse, with rich decoration and unusual stalactitic vaulting. Opposite St-Pierre, to the west, is the Hôtel d'Escoville, a Renaissance mansion of 1538 (restored) with a beautiful courtyard.

Château

Occupying an extensive area on the hill which rises immediately to the north of Place St-Pierre is a castle built by William the Conqueror (1060; enlarged in 13th–15th c.), now laid out in gardens, which is entered through the 14th c. Porte des Champs on the east side. From the terrace and from the castle walls there are fine views of the town.
In Rue de Geôle, which runs along the west side of the castle, is the Maison des Quatrans (No. 31), a handsome half-timbered house built in 1381. Within the precincts of the castle are the chapel of St-Georges (12th and 15th c.), with a Romanesque nave; the Musée des Beaux-Arts (1960), with pictures by Rogier van der Weyden, Tintoretto, Rubens, Courbet and Boudin and faience from Rouen, Nevers and Strasbourg; the Musée de Normandie (a museum of regional interest, with exhibits illustrating the history of Normandy); and the Salle de l'Echiquier, a splendid Romanesque building in which the Council of Normandy used to meet.

*Musée des Beaux-Arts

*Musée de Normandie

North of the castle are the imposing new buildings of the University. A short distance west is the church of St-Julien, on an elliptical plan, built in 1958 on the site of a church destroyed in 1944.

*La Trinité

To the east of Place St-Pierre, at the end of Rue des Chanoines, is the Place de la Reine-Mathilde, in which is the magnificent Romanesque abbey church of La Trinité or of the Abbaye-aux-Dames, built by William the Conqueror's wife Matilda in 1062 to expiate the offence of marrying her

St-Etienne, Abbaye-aux-Hommes

cousin. In the impressive interior is the queen's tomb, and beneath this is a crypt. Adjoining the church, on the site of a Benedictine abbey founded by Matilda, is the Hôtel-Dieu, a hospital built in the 18th c.

St-Jean

South of Place St-Pierre is the St-Jean district, rebuilt after wartime destruction, with the church of St-Jean (14th–15th c.; badly damaged in 1944 but since restored) and the broad Avenue du 6-Juin (D-day 1944), which runs south over the Orne to the railway station.
Some 1500 m/1600 yds south of the station is the Château d'Eau de la Guérinière (by G. Gillet, 1957), a water-tower in the shape of a top.

Old town

Rue St-Pierre, the main street of the old town, runs south-west from Place St-Pierre. 200 m/220 yds along this street, on the right, are two handsome half-timbered houses (Nos. 52 and 54). Farther along, also on the right, is the church of St-Sauveur (14th–15th c.), with a beautiful tower and a richly decorated apse of 1546. Rue St-Pierre continues past the church through a part of the town which escaped destruction during the last war and ends in Place Malherbe. A little way south is the Jesuit church of Notre-Dame de la Gloriette (1684).

Mémorial

The Mémorial, to the north-west of the town centre, is a modern Peace Museum, built of light-coloured sandstone in the form of a square block (architect Jacques Millet). Its themes are the two world wars and the means of ensuring and preserving peace.

Jardin des Plantes

To the west of the castle is the Jardin des Plantes, a beautifully laid out botanical garden.

*St-Etienne

From Place Malherbe Rue Ecuyère runs west to Place Fontette, with the 18th c. Palais de Justice (Law Courts). From here Rue Guillaume-le-Conquérant continues west to the imposing abbey church of St-Etienne or of the Abbaye-aux-Hommes, built by William the Conqueror in 1066 in Romanesque (Norman) style, together with an abbey of which little now remains, in expiation of his sin in marrying within the prohibited degrees. The choir and towers, in Early Gothic style, were added in the 13th c. The façade of St-Etienne is particularly fine. In the impressive interior a stone in front of the high altar marks the position of William the Conqueror's tomb, destroyed by Calvinists in 1562.
Adjoining the church on the south are the abbey buildings, largely rebuilt in the 18th c., which were occupied for many years by the Lycée Malherbe and now house the Town Hall. Richly decorated interior (beautiful wrought-iron banisters, fine panelling, large refectory). From the Romanesque cloister there is a fine view of the church towers.

St-Nicolas

A little way north-west of St-Etienne, on the south side of an attractive churchyard, is the disused church of St-Nicolas (1083–1093), with a fine Romanesque porch and a beautiful apse facing towards the churchyard.

Abbaye d'Ardenne

6 km/4 miles north-west of the town centre are the ruins of the Premonstratensian abbey of Ardenne (12th–13th c.).

Calais

See Picardy

Camargue M11

Situation and characteristics

The district of the Camargue (in Provençal Camargo) in southern France, which takes its name from a Roman senator named Camar, includes Grande Camargue, an area of some 720 sq. km/280 sq. miles of alluvial land

Gipsy pilgrimage, Stes-Maries

Flamingoes in the Camargue

lying between the Grand Rhône and the Petit Rhône, the two arms of the Rhône which separate a short distance above Arles, and also Petite Camargue, an area of 200 sq. km/77 sq. miles west of the Petit Rhône. The western arm, the Petit Rhône, here forms the boundary between the regions of Provence–Alpes–Côte d'Azur and Languedoc–Roussillon (see entries).
Since the medieval period the Camargue has been mainly agricultural. Rice-growing is believed to have been introduced in this marshy terrain by the Arabs, coming from Spain towards the end of the 13th c. With the draining of the marshland the growing of rice declined, but in recent years it has again increased, making intensive use of irrigation, which is seen as the only means of counteracting the increasing salinity of the soil. Other contributions to the economy of the region are made by horse and cattle rearing, wine-growing and, increasingly in recent years, tourism.

**Topography

The Camargue is a region with a very distinctive landscape of its own, much of it – in spite of the increasing numbers of visitors – still lonely and remote. Over many centuries the Rhône has been depositing soil in its delta, which has thus gradually been advancing into the sea. As a result the old port of Aigues-Mortes in the western Camargue is now silted up. But what the sea has lost in the west it has gained in the south-eastern Camargue, where Saintes-Maries-de-la-Mer, in the Middle Ages an inland town, is now a seaside resort.
The younger part of the Camargue, on its seaward side, flanking the large Etang de Vaccarès, consists mainly of shallow coastal lagoons and reed-fringed marshland or barren salt-pans and dunes with occasional umbrella pines, junipers and tamarisks.
The Camargue is the home of large numbers of waterfowl, and in recent years also of colonies of flamingoes, herons and birds of prey. It is also the habitat of turtles and beavers. The pastureland is grazed, particularly in winter, by half-wild herds *(manades)* of sheep, small black bulls and small white or light-grey horses, who are looked after by mounted herdsmen.

Town walls and Tour de Constance, Aigues-Mortes

The famous Camargue horses are sold as riding horses, and during the holiday season can be hired in many places for pony-trekking trips *(promenades à cheval).*

Parc Régional de Camargue

The Camargue regional nature park was established in 1970. It covers an area of 820 sq. km/317 sq. miles, roughly the whole of Grande Camargue. The southern part, the Etang de Vaccarès together with the adjoining coastal area, has been a nature reserve since 1975.

*Round the Camargue

Musée Camarguais

10 km/6 miles south-west of Arles on D570 is the Mas du Pont de Rousty, an old sheep-farm now occupied by the organisation for the protection of nature and the Musée Camarguais, which gives an introduction to the history of the Camargue.

Etang de Vaccarès

Near Albaron the D37 branches off from the D570. Beyond Méjanes it leads past this coastal lagoon, surrouonded by reeds, the largest in the Camargue, with an area of some 6000 hectares/15,000 acres, but with an average depth of only 50 cm/20 inches. Near Villeneuve the D36B branches off to the south. The lighthouse known as the Phare de la Gacholle can only be reached on foot. From there a path leads via the Digue à la mer (a dyke) to Ste-Maries-de-la-Mer. On the Etang de Ginès, a small coastal lagoon 4 km/2½ miles north of Saintes-Maries-de-la-Mer, is a Centre d'Information (origins of the Camargue; its flora and fauna).

Bird Park

A little way to the south an area of 12 hectares/30 acres has been made into a Bird Park (Parc Ornothologique), where visitors can see large numbers of native and migrant birds.

Aigues-Mortes

Aigues-Mortes (pop. 4500), on the western edge of the Camargue, owes its name ("Dead Waters") to the marshes and shallow lagoons amid which it lies. It is linked with the sea, 6 km/4 miles away, by four navigable channels. The port, now silted up, was founded by Louis IX (St Louis), who set out from here in 1248 on the First Crusade.

*Town walls
*Tour de Constance

The town was surrounded by Louis and his son Philip the Bold with massive walls and towers. The mightiest of the towers is the Tour de Constance, at the north corner of the circuit of walls, which was used for several centuries as a prison. The 54 m/177 ft high tower, once topped by a beacon or navigational light, affords fine views of the surrounding area. There is a fascinating walk round the walls.

Salin-de-Giraud

Near Salin-de-Giraud lie giant desalination parks where sea-water is gradually evaporated to provide salt, which is then processed in chemical factories to produce bromide and magnesium salts.

St-Gilles

See Arles, Surroundings

Saintes-Maries-de-la-Mer

The best known place in the Camargue is Saintes-Maries-de-la-Mer (pop. 2000), near its western edge. It owes its name to the legend that the three Marys (Mary Cleophas, sister of the Virgin, Mary Salome, mother of James and John, and Mary Magdalene) landed here, coming from Palestine, in A.D. 40, accompanied by their black maid Sarah, who became the patron saint of gipsies.

*Church

The fortress-like church of the Saracen period in the centre of the town (now very much a tourist resort) dates from the 10th, 12th and 15th centuries. It contains a well, enabling it to withstand a siege. In a chapel above the apse are the relics of the first two Marys; those of their servant Sarah are in a crypt. Large numbers of gipsies come in pilgrimage to honour the relics. From the roof of the church there are fine views.

Musée Baroncelli

The Musée Baroncelli, in the former Town Hall, has a collection of material on the history of the town and local folk traditions.
On the southern outskirts of the town is the bullring, which is used for bullfights and similar events.

Musée Tsigane

The 1000-year history of the city of Rome is portrayed in this open-air museum situated to the north.

Cannes P11

Region: Provence–Alpes–Côte d'Azur. Département: Alpes-Maritimes
Altitude: sea level. Population: 73,000

Situation and characteristics

The fashionable resort of Cannes lies in a sheltered situation on the wide Golfe de la Napoule, off which lie the Iles de Lérins. The town is fringed by a semicircle of hills dotted with villas. With its exceptionally mild climate, its rich subtropical vegetation and its beautiful bathing beach, Cannes is one of the most visited resorts on the Côte d'Azur (see entry).

History

Evidence of an early settlement on the Mont Chevalier is provided by finds dating from the Celto-Ligurian period. The Romans are believed to have built a fort here, under the name of Castrum Marsellinum, in the 2nd c. B.C. In the 11th c. a watch-tower was built, around which a small walled town later grew up. In the 14th c. the town came under the control of Provence, and in 1481, along with the rest of Provence, became French. The town's development into a famous seaside resort began with the discovery of its amenities by the British statesman Lord Brougham (1778–1868), who took refuge in Cannes from a cholera epidemic raging in Nice. The harbour was built in 1838, and the construction of the seafront promenade began thirty years later.

Boulevard de la Croisette

Cannes is now the scene of the International Film Festival, held annually in April–May.

Sights

Old town

Musée de la Castre

The old part of Cannes, the district of Le Suquet, is built on the slopes of Mont Chevalier. On the summit of the hill is an 11th c. watch-tower from which there are magnificent views. A little to the south is the Musée de la Castre, with collections of Egyptian, Phoenician, Etruscan, Greek and Roman antiquities and Far Eastern and Central American art. Nearby is the Late Gothic church of Notre-Dame de l'Espérance (1521–1648).
The Boulevard Jean-Hibert runs westward along the seafront to the Square Mistral, beyond which the Boulevard du Midi runs below the Quartier Anglais with its sumptuous villas to join the Corniche de l'Esterel (Corniche d'Or).

*Vieux Port

To the east of the old town is the Vieux Port or Old Harbour, also known as Port Cannes, on the north side of which is the Gare Maritime (Marine Station, 1957). The harbour area is bounded on the north by the beautiful Allées de la Liberté, shaded by plane-trees, in which a colourful flower market is held in the mornings. Immediately west is the Hôtel de Ville (Town Hall, 1874–1876). Running parallel to the Allées on the north is the Rue Félix-Faure, the town's principal shopping street.

*Boulevard de la Croisette

The busy centre of the town's life is the Boulevard de la Croisette, which runs east from the Palais des Festivals (see below) along the Baie de Cannes (beautiful sandy beach), lined by luxury hotels and shops, with magnificent views of the Golfe de la Napoule and the Iles de Lérins. In the boating harbour is the pirate ship "Neptune", once the setting of a pirate film.

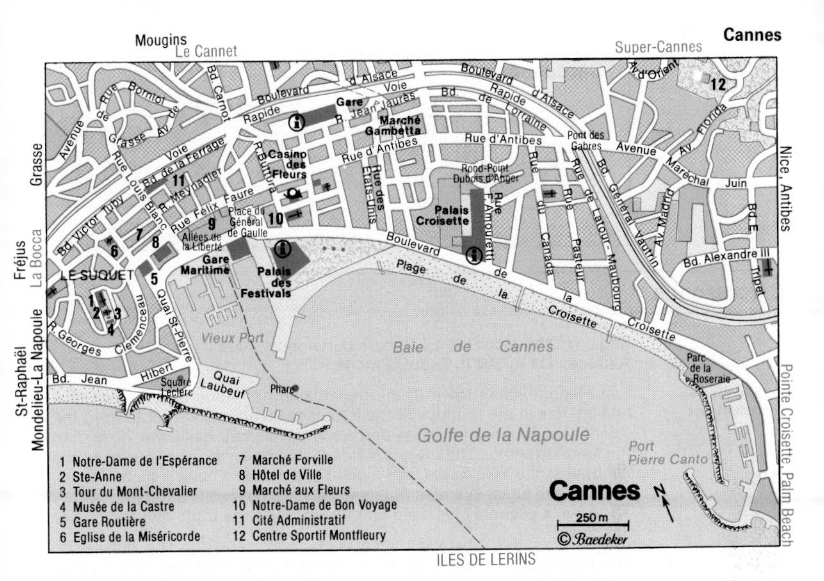

The Palais des Festivals, opened in 1982, is an imposing complex of buildings which includes three large concert or function halls, eleven conference rooms, two exhibition halls, a gaming casino, a night club and a restaurant.

Palais des Festivals

Surroundings of Cannes

North-east of Cannes is the charming suburb of La Californie, with the Observatoire de Super-Cannes. From the lookout tower, situated at a height of 325 m/1065 ft, there is a superb view.

La Californie
* View

4 km/2½ miles south-east of Cannes lie the Iles de Lérins. The largest of this group of islands is the Ile Ste-Marguerite, which is covered by forests of eucalyptuses and pines. On its north side is a 17th c. fort designed by Vauban, long used as a prison. Among those confined here was the mysterious figure known as the "man in the iron mask", whose identity is still unknown.

* Iles de Lérins

Some 700 m/750 yds farther south is the smaller island of St-Honorat, on the south side of which is the Abbaye de Lérins, a fortified religious house said to have been founded by St Honoratus, bishop of Arles (d. 429). On the coast to the south is the Château St-Honorat, a tower built in the 11th c. as a refuge from pirate raids and later altered, with beautiful cloisters on the ground and first floors (fine views).

5 km/3 miles west, at the foot of the Massif du Tanneron, is the seaside resort of La Napoule-Plage, above which is a rebuilt 14th c. castle (art exhibitions).

La Napoule-Plage

5 km/3 miles north-east is the famous potters' town of Vallauris, which once belonged to the monks of Lérins, along with its vineyards and orange-groves. Here in 1946 Picasso made the acquaintance of the potters Suzanne and Georges Ramié, and took with enthusiasm to the new material. In the beautiful crypt of a Romanesque chapel belonging to the priory of Lérins is his painting "War and Peace" (1952–1959). The fortified priory, founded in the 12th c., was destroyed in 1569 and rebuilt during the Renaissance; it now houses the Musée National Picasso. In the town square is a bronze by Picasso, the "Man with a Sheep".

* Vallauris

Carcassonne

K11

Region: Languedoc–Roussillon. Département: Aude
Altitude: 111 m/364 ft. Population: 46,000

**Situation and characteristics

Carcassonne, chief town of the département of Aude and the see of a bishop, lies in the foothills of the Pyrenees on an ancient route from the Atlantic up the Garonne valley and along the present-day Canal du Midi to the Mediterranean. The town is divided into two by the river Aude: on the left bank is the Ville Basse, and high above the right bank is the old town, the Cité, the finest example of the medieval art of fortification in Europe. The town's economy is based on tourism, the wine trade and the rubber industry.

History

The little market town of Carcasso, lying on the road from the Atlantic to the Mediterranean, was built and fortified by the Romans in the 1st c. B.C. In the 6th c. A.D. the Visigoths erected defensive towers which still survive. In the 8th c. the town was captured from the Arabs by the Franks and during

1 Porte Narbonnaise
2 Notre-Dame des Voyageurs
3 Tour du Trésor
4 Tour du Moulin du Connétable
5 Tour de Vieulas
6 Tour de la Marquière
7 Porte du Bourg
8 Tour de Samson
9 Tour du Moulin d'Avar
10 Poterne d'Avar
11 Tour de la Charpenterie
12 Tour de la Chapelle
13 Tour Pinte
14 Poterne Pinte
15 Tour de Justice
16 Porte d'Aude
17 Tour Wisigothe
18 Tour ronde de l'Evêque (Tour de l'Inquisition)
19 Tour carrée de l'Evêque
20 Tour de Cahuzac
21 Tour Mipadre
22 Tour du Moulin de Midi
23 Tour St-Nazaire
24 Tour St-Martin
25 Tour des Prisons
26 Tour du Castéra
27 Tour du Plo
28 Tour de Balthazar
29 Tour de Davejean
30 Tour St-Laurent
31 Tour du Trauquet
32 Tour du Sacraire St-Sernin
33 Barbacane de l'Est
34,35 Tours de la Porte orientale
36 Tour des Casernes
37 Tour du Major
38 Tour du Degré
39 Tour de la Poudre
40 Tour St-Paul
41 Barbacane d'Aude (Barbacane de l'Ouest)
42 Outwork
43 Barbacane St-Louis
44 Tour de Bérard
45 Tour de Bénazet
46 Barbacane Notre-Dame (Poterne Notre-Dame)
47 Tour de Moreti
48 Tour de la Glacière
49 Tour de la Porte Rouge
50 Echauguette de l'Ouest
51 Tour du Petit Canissou
52 Tour du Grand Canissou
53 Tour du Grand Burlas
54 Tour d'Ourliac
55 Barbacane Crémade
56 Poterne du Razès
57 Tour Cautière
58 Tour Pouleto
59 Echauguette de l'Est
60 Tour de la Vade
61 Tour de la Peyre

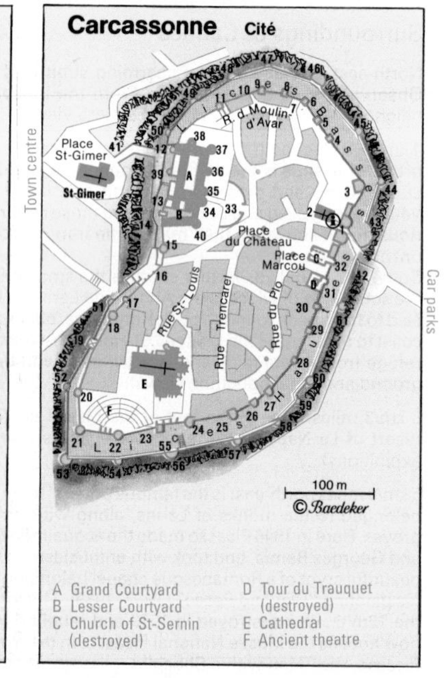

the Albigensian wars it was taken by Simon de Montfort. In 1229 the town, along with the county, fell to the French crown. The stronghold was enlarged by the Counts of Carcassonne, Louis IX (St Louis) and Philip the Bold, and was considered to be impregnable. It was restored by Viollet-le-Duc in the mid 19th c.

Sights

Ville Basse

Two bridges (one of them the 13th c. Pont Vieux) lead to the Ville Basse or lower town, which is laid out on a regular grid and ringed by boulevards. The central feature is the Place Carnot, in which is the Neptune Fountain (1770). To the north is the Gothic church of St-Vincent (14th c.), with an unfinished tower and a beautiful main doorway. To the south is the Cathedral of St-Michel (13th c., restored), with fine 14th c. windows and a treasury.

Musée des Beaux-Arts

South-east of the Place Carnot is the Musée des Beaux-Arts, which contains works by Chardin, Gamelin, Rigaud, Constant and others and a ceramic collection.

**Cité

The Cité, the fortified upper town, lies at a height of 148 m/485 ft. Elliptical in plan, it is surrounded by a double circuit of walls with 54 towers. The fortifications, dating in part from the Visigothic period and strengthened in 1170, by Louis IX in 1250 and by Philip the Bold in 1280, remained unscathed until the French Revolution.

*Porte Narbonnaise

There are only two entrances to the town, the twin-towered Porte Narbonnaise and the Porte d'Aude. The interior is a maze of winding lanes. On the west side is the Château Comtal, originally built about 1125 and enlarged in the 13th c.; it abuts on the inner circuit of walls and could be defended on its own. It now houses a museum on the history of the stronghold, with a small lapidary collection. From the battlements there are wide views.

*St-Nazaire

Within the Cité is the former Cathedral of St-Nazaire, built between the 11th and 14th centuries and later extensively restored. The west front was once part of the Visigothic fortifications. The Gothic choir (13th–14th c.) contains 22 statues, 14th–15th c. windows and a number of important tombs, including that of Simon de Montfort.

Surroundings of Carcassonne

Castelnaudary

Castelnaudary, on the road to Toulouse, has the 14th c. church of St-Michel. 8 km/5 miles beyond this is St-Papoul, once the see of a bishop, with the beautiful former cathedral (14th–16th c.) and cloister.

Castres

*Musée Goya

56 km/35 miles north, on the road to Albi, is Castres, an old textile town. The former Bishop's Palace (designed by Jacques Hardouin-Mansart, 1675), with gardens laid out by Le Nôtre, is now occupied by the Musée Goya, with an outstanding collection of the painter's pictures and drawings. The 17th

c. Hôtel de Ville (Town Hall) was also designed by Jacques Hardouin-Mansart.

Les Corbières

See entry

Pic de Nore

North-east of Carcassonne is the Montagne Noire, an outlier of the Cévennes, with the industrial town of Mazamet (47 km/29 miles from Carcassonne), a good starting-point for the ascent of the Pic de Nore (1210 m/3970 ft).

Cévennes

L/M 10/11

* Situation and characteristics

The Cévennes, known to the Romans as Mons Cebenna, form the south-eastern section of the Massif Central, lying between the valleys of the Ardèche and the Hérault and falling steeply down to the Rhône basin. This beautiful range of hills has an average height of around 1500 m/4900 ft, rising to 1702 m/5584 ft in Mont Lozère (Pic de Finiels). The hills consist mainly of slate and the plateaux of limestone. Between the sharp-edged hill ridges *(serres)* are canyon-like gorges, the best known of which are the Gorges du Tarn (see entry).

Climate and vegetation

The Cévennes form the climatic boundary between the mild Mediterranean region and the harsher Massif Central, so that they have a varied pattern of vegetation. The forest clearance which took place in the 18th and 19th centuries to supply the charcoal needed by the numerous glass-blowing establishments gradually came to an end around a hundred years ago, and since then much reafforestation has been carried out. The varied landscape of the Cévennes, alternating between areas of forest, barren grassland, bare moorland and deeply indented valleys, offers a haven of solitude and tranquillity. The National Park of the Cévennes was established in 1970 to protect the typical fauna and flora of the region.

Corniche des Cévennes

The Corniche des Cévennes is a beautiful scenic road running through the hills for some 50 km/30 miles between Florac to the north-west and St-Jean-du-Gard to the south-east, offering views of the two highest peaks in the range.
The foreland region to the south-east, an area transitional to Provence and Languedoc, already has a Mediterranean climate in which olives, vines and mulberry trees extend far into the hills.

Economy

The coal mined round Alès has made possible the development of iron-working and chemical industries.

History

During the 16th c. wars of religion, and after Louis XIV's revocation of the Edict of Nantes, these inaccessible mountain regions offered a place of refuge for the Huguenots. The persecution of Protestants led to the Guerre des Cévennes (1702–1710), a rising by the Huguenots, who became known as the "Camisards" from the shirts they wore. Finally the killing was ended by an amnesty. The descendants of the Huguenots still meet annually at the famous Musée du Désert in commemoration of these events. The population of the Cévennes is still largely Protestant, even though Protestants were not granted equal rights in France until 1804, under the Code Napoléon. The clearance of the Cévennes forests was halted by a series of well conceived measures introduced by Georges Fabre, director of forestry, from 1875 onwards.

Sights

* **Mont Lozère**

Mont Lozère is a granite hill reaching its highest point in the Pic de Finiels (1702 m/5584 ft), accessible only on foot, which offers magnificent views of the whole Cévennes region. To reach it, drive from Le Bleymard in the direction of Le Pont-de-Montvert; the starting-point of the climb is the Col de Finiels (1540 m/5050 ft).

*Mont Aigoual

Mont Aigoual (1567 m/5141 ft) rises to the south-east of Meyrueis (see Gorges du Tarn). On the summit is an observatory, established in 1887. There are impressive all-round views, extending in favourable conditions to the Alps, the Pyrenees and the Mediterranean, and sometimes to Mont Blanc and Maledetta.

Anduze

Anduze, south-east of St-Jean-du-Gard, was around 1625 a base of the Protestant forces led by the Duc de Rohan. The picturesque old town, with a clock-tower of 1320, is, with the nearby pass, the Porte des Cévennes, a good starting-point for trips into the hills.

Gorges du Tarn

See entry

Chamonix

O9

Region: Rhône–Alpes
Département: Haute-Savoie
Altitude: 1035 m/3395 ft
Population: 9000

*Situation and characteristics

Chamonix (officially known as Chamonix-Mont-Blanc), situated at the foot of the highest peak in the Alps, is a climatic and winter sports resort and a climbing centre of international reputation. The resort area, which extends for 23 km/14 miles along the Vallée de Chamonix between Les Houches and Argentière, also includes the smaller resorts of Les Bossons, Les Praz de Chamonix, Les Tines and Argentière.
Chamonix was host to the first Winter Olympics in 1924. The Mont Blanc road tunnel (11.6 km/7¼ miles long) links Chamonix-Mont-Blanc with the Italian resort of Courmayeur in the Aosta valley.

Topography

The high valley of the Arve, flanked on the south-east by the Mont Blanc chain with its mighty glaciers and on the north-west by the Aiguilles Rouges, does not quite equal the Bernese Oberland in scenic beauty, but vies with Zermatt in the magnificence of its glaciers and possesses in the Aiguilles a series of mountain pinnacles which are unique in their rugged grandeur. From 1091 the valley, under the name of Campus Munitus, belonged to a Benedictine priory. From the mid 18th c. onwards it became more widely known through the writings of the English travellers Pococke and Windham and the Genevese scientists Saussure and Bourrit.

Sights

Chamonix

The central point of Chamonix is the intersection of the main street (Rue Dr-Paccard and Rue J.-Vallot), which runs along the whole length of the town, with the Avenue de la Gare (formerly Avenue Foch). Near the junction is the Hôtel de Ville (Town Hall). A little way south, on the banks of the Arve, is the Saussure Monument (by J. Salmson, 1887), commemorating the first scientific ascent of Mont Blanc in 1786; it shows the guide, Jacques Balmat, pointing out the route to Saussure.
The Musée Alpin illustrates the history of the valley and its development by man.

Mountain Railways and Cableways

*Montenvers

A rack railway (lower station opposite the railway station; May-Oct. only; journey time 20 min.) runs up to the summit of Montenvers (1913 m/6277 ft;

restaurant with extensive views). From this mountain there is a magnificent view of the Mer de Glace ("Sea of Ice"), a river of ice 7 km/4½ miles long and 1-2 km/¾-1½ miles wide formed by three converging glaciers. Immediately opposite is the overhanging west wall of the Aiguille du Dru (a difficult rock climb); beyond it, to the left, is the Aiguille à Bochard; to the right the Aiguille du Moine, farther back the Grandes Jorasses, and far right the Aiguille des Grands Charmoz. From the upper station of the rack railway there is a cableway (2 min.) down to a 100 m/330 ft long tunnel driven into the glacier. For experienced climbers with a good head for heights there is a good return route by way of the Chapeau to Les Tines (2½ hrs): across the Mer de Glace to the right-hand lateral moraine (3–4 hrs), then the "Mauvais Pas" up a steep rock face (¾ hr) to the Chapeau (1601 m/5253 ft; inn), a projecting crag at the foot of the Aiguille à Bouchard (2669 m/8757 ft), with a magnificent view of the lower reaches of the Mer de Glace, and from there on a mule-track (¾ hr) to the Hôtel Beau-Séjour (1243 m/4078 ft); then left to Les Tines (20 min.).

**Aiguille du Midi

There is a cableway (5.4 km/3½ miles) from the Praz-Conduit station (1040 m/3412 ft), on the south-west side of the town, by way of an intermediate station at Plan de l'Aiguille (2308 m/7573 ft), with fantastic views en route, to the upper station (3790 m/12,435 ft; 20 min.), under the summit of the Aiguille du Midi (3842 m/12,606 ft; chair-lift to top), with a view of Mont Blanc.
From the upper station there is a cabin cableway (5 km/3 miles; 20 min.) by way of the Gros Rognon (3533 m/11,592 ft) and the Punta Helbronner (3462 m/11,359 ft; passport control) to an Italian mountain hut, the Rifugio Torino (3322 m/10,899 ft; views), below the Col du Géant (3369 m/11,054 ft); then a third cableway leading down by way of the Pavillon del Monte Frety (2130 m/6989 ft) to the Italian town of Entrèves (1306 m/4285 ft; station in La Palud district). The whole trip from Chamonix to Entrèves (*c.* 15 km/9 miles) takes about 1½ hours and offers a memorable experience.

**Brévent

A cableway installed in 1926–1930 (lower station in La Molaz or La Molard, 1090 m/3576 ft) ascends in 15 min. to the top of Le Brévent (2525 m/8285 ft). From here it takes 8 min. to reach the intermediate station of Planpraz (1993 m/6539 ft), where it is necessary to change. The upper section, 1350 m/4430 ft long, climbs in 7 min., without any intermediate supports, to the upper station (2505 m/8219 ft), just below the summit (restaurant). From here there are breathtaking views of the Mont Blanc group immediately opposite, the Bernese Alps to the north-east and the mountains of Dauphiné to the south-west.

Flégère and Col du Fout

Cableway up Flégère and from there to the Col du Fout: see below under Walks and Climbs.

Bellevue

Cableway from Les Houches to the Pavillon de Bellevue.

Nid d'Aigle

Rack railway (the "Tramway du Mont-Blanc") from Le Fayet to the Nid d'Aigle.

Walks and Climbs

Glacier des Bossons

From Les Bossons (4 km/2½ miles south-west of Chamonix) in ¾ hr (chair-lift available) to the Pavillon des Bossons (1298 m/4259 ft; restaurant), on the left-hand lateral moraine of the Glacier des Bossons, with a fine view of the glacier and Mont Blanc du Tacul (4248 m/13,938 ft) looming over it; to the left the Aiguille du Midi and Aiguille du Plan (3673 m/12,051 ft).

*Flégère

There is a cableway from Les Praz (2205 m/2410 yds long; lower station 1509 m/4951 ft, upper station 1894 m/6214 ft). The bridle-path (2½–3 hrs)

Chamonix and the Mont Blanc massif ▶

leaves the road to Argentière on the left 800 m/½ mile above the Chamonix church and in 1 hr reaches the Chalet de la Floriaz (1337 m/4387 ft), from which there are fine views. From here it is 1½–2 hrs to the Croix de la Flégère (1877 m/6158 ft), a projecting spur of the Aiguilles Rouges, with magnificent panoramic views almost as fine as those from Brévent. From Flégère there is a cabin cableway (the Télécabine de l'Index) to the Col du Fout (2385 m/7825 ft).

Col du Fout

**Mont Blanc

Mont-Blanc (4807 m/15,772 ft), the highest peak in the Alps, over which the French-Italian frontier runs, was first climbed in 1786 by a village doctor named Michel Paccard with Jacques Balmat of Chamonix, and in the following year by the scientist Horace-Bénédict de Saussure with Balmat and 16 porters. To experienced climbers with a guide the climb offers no particular difficulties, but it is extremely strenuous. From Les Houches the climb takes 10–12 hrs, taking the cabin cableway to the Pavillon de Bellevue and the "Tramway du Mont-Blanc" to the Glacier de Bionnassay and continuing on foot to the Chalet-Hôtel de Tête-Rousse (3167 m/10,391 ft; 2 hrs). From there it is 3 hrs to the Refuge de l'Aigle du Goûter (3817 m/12,524 ft), and another 5 hrs to the summit. The fantastic panorama which can be enjoyed from the summit rewards the effort of the climb.

Mont Blanc Tunnel

Of great importance to tourist traffic is the Mont Blanc road tunnel, constructed in 1958–1964. It begins above the hamlet of Les Pèlerins at an altitude of 1274 m/4180 ft and runs through the mountain for a distance of 11.6 km/7¼ miles to Entrèves (1381 m/4531 ft). The tunnel (toll charge), which is open all year round, shortens the distance from northern and central France and western Switzerland into Italy during the period when the high Alpine passes are closed (October–June) by several hundred kilometres.

Champagne

L–N 5–7

*Situation and characteristics

Champagne extends to the east of the Ile de France, between the upper Oise (near St-Quentin) and the Yonne (near Sens), approximately as far as the upper Meuse. The former province includes the present-day départements of Marne, Haute-Marne, Aube, Yonne and Ardennes. The main industrial towns in addition to Reims (see entry) are Châlons-sur-Marne and Troyes (see entry).

Champagne Crayeuse

The western part of Champagne, round Reims, Epernay, Châlons, Ste-Ménehould and Vitry-le-François, is known as Champagne Crayeuse ("Chalky Champagne"), a region of dry soil consisting of permeable chalk which during the First World War was also called "Champagne pouilleuse" ("lousy Champagne"). The gently undulating plain, widely used as pasture for sheep, gives only scanty yields; on the sunny slopes of the valleys, however, the deeply rooted vines produce the renowned wine which takes its name from the region.

Champagne Humide

The adjoining region known as Champagne Humide ("Wet Champagne") forms an arc to the east of Ste-Ménehould and Vitry. It consists of sandy and clayey strata of the Lower Cretaceous and is a wooded and well watered cattle-rearing region with many individual farms.

Ardennes

In north-eastern Champagne are the Ardennes, a gently rolling and well wooded region with hills rising to just over 500 m/1640 ft through which flow the Meuse and the Semois. The Ardennes are noted mainly for their forests of beeches and firs and their abundance of game. The region can be explored either on foot or on horseback; horses can be hired in Charleville-Mézières .

History

Much of the history of France has been written in Champagne. When Caesar conquered Gaul in 57 B.C. he made the chief town of a Belgic people, the Remi, a local capital under the name of Durocortorum, since eight trading routes met here. After the collapse of the Roman Empire in the early 5th c. the Frankish king Clovis was baptised by Archbishop (St) Remi in Reims in 496, establishing the city as the place of coronation of the French kings. In subsequent centuries authority lay in the hands of the Archbishops of Reims and the Counts of Champagne.
During the Middle Ages Champagne, within which important trade fairs were held (dealing mainly in luxury wares like silk and spices), enjoyed great prosperity – a prosperity which was reflected in its architecture. In 1147 St Bernard launched his call for the Second Crusade in Châlons. The region's prosperity began to decline in the 13th c. as a result of the increasing centralisation of authority and the devastation wrought by the Hundred Years War. In 1361 Champagne finally came under the control of the French crown.
In 1429 Joan of Arc crowned Charles VII in Reims. Two leading 18th c. figures, the philosopher Denis Diderot (1713–1784) and the Revolutionary politician George-Jacques Danton (1759–1794) came from Champagne. In 1792 French Revolutionary forces won their first victory at the mill of Valmy.
The economic revival which began in the 19th c. was interrupted by the three wars with Germany. Like Lorraine to the east, Champagne saw much

fighting during these wars. Notable events in the 1870–1871 war were the battles for Sedan and Metz (in Lorraine). The fighting round Reims in the First World War has left its mark in the remains of trenches and numerous military cemeteries. The Maginot Line is a relic of the Second World War.

Champagne – the Wine

(Note that in French *la Champagne* is the region, *le champagne* the wine).

Champagne owes its particular qualities to a combination of circumstances: the local chalky soil, a statutorily limited growing area, a particular climate, "noble" types of grape (Pinot, Chardonnay; blending of red and white wine grapes, except for Blanc de Blancs), pruning of the vines to reduce the number of clusters and limitation of the quantities harvested and pressed. The grapes are carefully selected at the vintage, a second fermentation is induced, and there is a long period of maturation in cool chalk cellars.

History

The production of wine in Champagne has been carried on with only brief interruptions since Gallo-Roman times. St Remi, Archbishop of Reims, refers in his will (533) to the vineyards of the region. During the Middle Ages wine production was mainly in the hands of religious orders, and the fame of their wines was spread through the trade fairs of Champagne.

Dom Pérignon

It was not until the late 17th c., however, that Dom Pérignon, cellarer of Hautvillers Abbey, succeeded in achieving a natural fermentation in which the wine effervesced but still preserved its clarity. With the help of the *cuvée* system, blending grapes of different kinds, the champagne was given a richer bouquet. Thereafter it succeeded malmsey and sherry as the favourite drink of the European aristocracy. It still remained to solve the technical problems of making the bottles strong enough to resist pressure and finding the right kind of cork, but this was achieved in the time of Napoleon, who made a personal visit to Champagne in 1807.

Champagne today

After the Napoleonic wars the great days of the champagne export trade began, as millions of bottles went out from Reims and Epernay to countries all over the world. The wine-growing area of Champagne, however, extends only over a strip of hilly country 150 km/95 miles long and between 300 m/330 yds and 2000 m/2200 yds across – only a fiftieth of France's total wine-growing area. In Champagne, too, only the finest kinds of grapes (small ones with few pips) are used; and no wine can be called champagne unless it comes from certain statutorily defined areas with a particular quality of soil. These requirements were incorporated in the treaty of Versailles (1919) and the Madrid agreement of 1932.

Vin mousseux

Sparkling wines from other parts of France may only be designated *vins mousseux;* if they are produced in accordance with the classic champagne method.

Méthode champenoise

Champagne is produced in a special process known as the *méthode champenoise*. From each 4000 kg/8818 lb of grapes 2666 litres/704 gallons of must is pressed, of which about 2000 litres/440 gallons of the highest quality is processed into champagne. After the first fermentation various wines are blended with wines of earlier years, depending on their quality. The wine is then bottled and an exactly calculated quantity of sugar solution is added. Then in the hermetically sealed bottles a second fermentation begins, the so-called "bottle fermentation". The resulting sediment is made to collect at the cork by setting the bottles on the slant and regularly shaking them; and when fermentation is complete the sediment is removed along with the cork in the process known as *dégorgement*. The small amount thus lost is made good by the addition of a solution of sugar in old champagne, the concentration of which determines the nature of the wine *(brut* = very dry, *sec* = dry, *demi-sec* = semi-dry, *doux* = sweet). After recorking the champagne must be kept in the cellar for some considerable time before being put on sale.

Champagne cellars

The cellars used for the making and storage of champagne are artificial caves hewn from the local chalk. Altogether they have a total length of fully 200 km/125 miles. Some of the cellars (e.g. in Epernay) can be visited. A champagne market is held in Bar-sur-Aube on the second weekend in September.

Route du Champagne

The Route du Champagne runs through the famous Triangle Sacré du Champagne. With a total length of 120 km/75 miles, it covers the region between Epernay, Reims and Châlons-sur-Marne, the three great wine-growing areas of Champagne – the Montagne de Reims, the Côte des Blancs and the Vallée de la Marne, which together account for 80% of the total area of the Champagne vineyards, with some 120 champagne houses.

Sights in Champagne

Bar-le-Duc

Bar-le-Duc (pop. 20,000), the old capital of the duchy of Bar and now an industrial town, lies on the Rhine–Marne Canal and the river Ornain, with the upper town reaching on to the slopes above the valley. At the south-east end of the Boulevard de la Rochelle, in the lower town, is the handsome church of St-Jean, in neo-Romanesque/Byzantine style. The Pont Notre-Dame with its chapel leads to the church of Notre-Dame (13th–14th c., restored in 17th c.), which contains a wooden figure of Christ by Ligier Richier, a pupil of Michelangelo, and a beautiful 15th c. bas-relief. To the south-east, beyond the narrow Canal de l'Ornain, is the 14th c. church of St-Antoine, with frescoes of the same period. In the upper town is the 14th c. church of St-Etienne, with another masterwork by Ligier Richier, the tomb of Prince René de Châlon (d. 1544), known as the "Squelette" (Skeleton). The Rue du Bourg, Rue de Bar and Place St-Pierre are lined with handsome old houses. The Château Ducal contains a museum.

*Squelette

Brienne-le-Château

This little town (pop. 4000) has an 18th c. château. Napoleon spent five years at the military college here; there is a Musée Napoléon in the town.

Châlons-sur-Marne

*Notre-Dame-en-Vaux

Châlons-sur-Marne (pop. 55,000), chief town of the département of Marne and the see of a bishop, lies on the right bank of the Marne and is an important centre of the wine trade. Its most important building is the Early Gothic church of Notre-Dame-en-Vaux (12th–13th c.), with four towers, one of the most beautiful churches in Champagne, notable particularly for the splendid 16th c. stained glass (the "Troyes Windows") in the choir. The Musée du Cloître contains sculptured columns and capitals. The 13th c. Cathedral of St-Etienne, with a Romanesque tower over the choir, has fine stained glass (13th–16th c.) and a rich treasury. The Porte Ste-Croix, on the south side of the town, was built in 1770 in honour of Louis XVI and Marie-Antoinette.

*Cathedral

Charleville-Mézières

Charleville-Mézières (pop. 64,000), which straddles the Meuse, is a double town, consisting of Charleville, founded in the 17th c., with the Place Ducale, and the much younger Mézières. There are some remains of fortifications on the west side of the town.
Charleville was the birthplace of the poet Arthur Rimbaud (1854–1891), who is buried in the cemetery.

Rocroi

North-west of Charleville-Mézières is the little fortified town of Rocroi.

Cathedral of Notre-Dame in Laon

Rocroi

Epernay

Epernay (pop. 29,000) ranks along with Reims as a major centre of champagne production, with the headquarters of such well known firms as Moët et Chandon and Mercier and many miles of cellars hewn from the chalk. The Musée du Champagne displays old wine-presses and other items illustrating the history of champagne, together with archaeological material of the early historical period.

Hautvillers

At Hautvillers, 6 km/4 miles north-west of Epernay, is the abbey in which Dom Pérignon was cellarer. His tombstone is in the church. From the abbey garden there are very fine views.

Langres

This old fortified town (pop. 11,000), the see of a bishop, lies on the edge of a plateau. Its most notable features are its 4 km/2½ mile long circuit of walls, which incorporates a Gallo-Roman town gate, and its handsome Renaissance houses.

Laon

Laon (pop. 28,000), north-east of Soissons, the Roman Laudunum, is the chief town of the département of Aisne. In the Middle Ages it was the see of a bishop and the residence of the last Carolingian kings. It is attractively situated on a narrow hill ridge enclosing a deep depression, the Cuve de St-Vincent, to the west. The upper and lower towns are linked by a fully automatic monorail service (Poma).

**Cathedral

In the centre of the upper town is the Place de l'Hôtel-de-Ville, with the Town Hall (1838–1854). The Cathedral of Notre-Dame with its seven towers, built in the 12th–13th c. on the site of an earlier church, is one of the finest Early Gothic churches in France and provided the model for other large cathedrals. The west front with its three deeply recessed and richly decorated doorways and its beautiful rose window is flanked by twin towers.

*Interior

The interior is notable for its old stained glass, its 18th c. choir screen and its valuable treasury. There is a beautiful 13th c. cloister, accessible from the chapterhouse.
Beyond the choir is the former Bishop's Palace, now the Palais de Justice (Law Courts), with the remains of a Gothic cloister. North of the cathedral is the Maison des Arts et Loisirs, a cultural centre with a reading room, theatre, exhibition room and conference hall. A little way south of the cathedral is the Municipal Museum (art and archaeology), with a Templar chapel (Romanesque, with a Gothic dome) in the garden. Near the former abbey church of St-Martin (12th–13th c.) is the ruined Porte de Soissons (13th c.), with a leaning tower.

Reims

See entry

St-Amand-sur-Fion

St-Amand-sur-Fion, north of Vitry-le-François, is a typical Champagne village, with many half-timbered houses and an ochre-coloured Romanesque church (12th c.; nave and choir altered in Gothic style in 13th c.).

Sedan

This old fortified town (pop. 25,000), situated on the Meuse at the foot of the Ardennes, is now a busy industrial town. During the Franco-Prussian War a French army led by Napoleon III and Marshal Mac-Mahon capitulated here on September 2nd 1870. In the Place d'Armes is the 17th c. parish church. The large citadel, originally built in the 14th–15th c., is surrounded by numerous towers. Within the walls is a 17th c. château housing a museum which displays a large collection of material on the history of the town and the château.

Bazeilles

3.5 km/2 miles south-east is Bazeilles, with an imposing château of 1750.

Mouzon

18 km/11 miles south-east, on the Meuse, is the little town of Mouzon, which still preserves remains of its walls, notably the Porte de Bourgogne (15th c.). The church of Notre-Dame (consecrated in 1231) has a

Sedan

richly decorated west front and doorway; the north tower dates from the 15th c., the south tower from the 16th. The interior is of impressive size with the choir surrounded by a ring of chapels, and an organ dating from 1725.

Soissons

Soissons (pop. 33,000), situated on the Aisne to the north-east of Paris, has been the see of a bishop since the 3rd c. In antiquity it was the capital of a Celtic tribe, the Suessiones. In 486 Clovis defeated the Roman general Syagrius here, and in 752 Pépin the Short was elected king of the Franks in Soissons.

*Cathedral

In the Place Centrale is the Gothic Cathedral of St-Gervais-et-St-Protais (12th–13th c.; façade altered in 18th c.). Its most notable features are the beautiful rose window with 15th c. stained glass in the north transept, the fine south transept and an "Adoration of the Shepherds" by Rubens.

*St-Jean-des-Vignes

St-Léger

St-Médard

Soissons also has the remains of three abbeys. St-Jean-des-Vignes (13th–14th c.), to the south of the town, has preserved the magnificent Gothic façade of its church (15th c.), flanked by two towers. St-Léger has a 13th c. church with a 14th c. doorway; it now houses the Musée d'Archéologie et d'Art, with Gallo-Roman and medieval antiquities and a collection of pictures. St-Médard has a pre-Romanesque crypt.

Troyes

See entry

Chartres

I6

Region: Centre
Département: Eure-et-Loir
Altitude: 142 m/465 ft
Population: 41,000

Chartres Cathedral

Situation and characteristics

Chartres, situated on a hill above the river Eure 100 km/60 miles south-west of Paris, is the chief town of the département of Eure-et-Loir, the see of a bishop and the centre of the rich agricultural region of Beauce. Its magnificent cathedral is one of the great glories of French architecture. Apart from tourism the main contributions to its economy are made by the foodstuffs and animal feed industries, engineering and the manufacture of perfume.

History

Known in antiquity as Autricum, it was the capital of a Gallic tribe, the Carnutes, and became the see of a bishop in the 4th c. The Frankish county of Chartrain fell into the hands of the house of Blois in the 10th c. and in the late 13th c. passed to the French crown by purchase. In 1528 it was erected into a duchy.

Sights

**Cathedral

In an elevated position in the centre of the city stands the Cathedral of Notre-Dame, one of the finest and best preserved Gothic buildings in

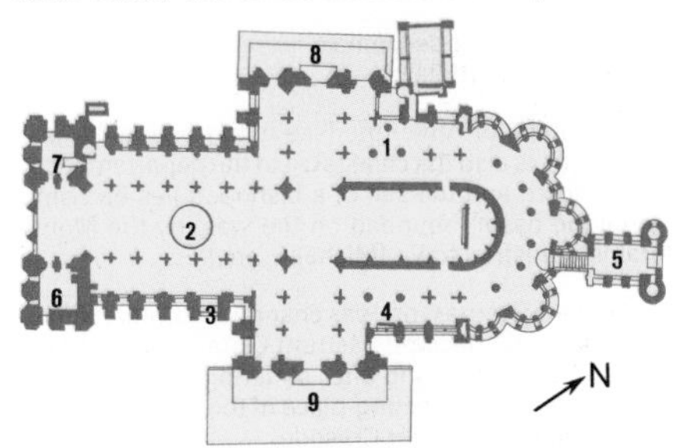

Chartres Cathedral

1 Vierge du Pilier
2 Labyrinthe
3 Chapelle Vendôme
4 Notre Dame de la Belle Verrière
5 Chapelle St-Piat
6 Clocher Vieux
7 Clocher-Neuf
8 N doorway
9 S doorway

France, with a three-aisled nave, transepts, a five-aisled choir and a ring of chapels round the ambulatory. After a series of devastating fires (743, 858, 1020, 1194), the original church, which is believed to have occupied the site of a Gallo-Roman temple, was almost completely rebuilt in its present form between 1195 and 1220 and consecrated in 1260. The west front, built about 1140–1160 in the severe style of Early Gothic, survived the 1194 fire, and is flanked by two fine towers of differing height and form. The south tower (Clocher Vieux), a superb example of the purest Gothic style, was completed in 1170; the north tower (Clocher Neuf) has a spire which was added in 1507–1513. Between the towers is the richly decorated Portail Royal (Royal Doorway), with statues which became models for the further development of Gothic sculpture. Above the three tall 12th c. windows is a 13th c. rose window 14 m/45 ft in diameter, and above this again is the Gallery of Kings, with 16 large statues of kings of Judah. The richly articulated doorways in the transepts (13th c.) also have magnificent sculptural decoration: on the south doorway the Last Judgment, on the north doorway the Virgin and Old Testament figures. Between two buttresses on the south side is the Chapel Vendôme, with Late Gothic stained glass (15th c.). Adjoining the apse is the Chapelle St-Piat (14th c.).

*Royal Doorway

**Stained glass

In the very impressive interior the windows, mostly dating from 1210–1260, form the most magnificent collection of medieval stained glass in existence, with a total area of more than 2000 sq. m/21,500 sq. ft. Particularly beautiful are the three rose windows, over 11.5 m/38 ft high.
Other notable features are the Late Gothic choir screens (1514–1529), already showing Renaissance forms, with scenes from the life of the Virgin and the Gospels, and the 41 groups of statues (16th–18th c.). On the north side of the choir is the Vierge du Pilier, a much revered figure of Notre-Dame de Chartres (*c.* 1510).
Below the choir and the lateral aisles are extensive crypts dating from Carolingian times and from 1024.
From the terrace to the east of the choir there is a fine view of the lower town. North of this is the former Bishop's Palace (17th–18th c.), now housing the Musée des Beaux-Arts (fine tapestries, pictures).

Museum

Enclos de Loëns

The Enclos de Loëns, which formerly belonged to the cathedral chapter, has a beautiful three-aisled crypt with Gothic vaulting (13th c.) and a handsome half-timbered façade. It is now an International Stained Glass Centre.

South-east of the cathedral are a number of fine old houses, among them the 15th c. Maison du Saumon. Lower down is the Escalier de la Reine Berthe, in a 16th c. turret, which leads down to the Gothic church of St-Pierre (12th–14th c.), with fine 14th c. stained glass.

Clermont-Ferrand L9

Region: Auvergne. Département: Puy-de-Dôme
Altitude: 410 m/1345 ft. Population: 152,000

Situation and characteristics

Clermont-Ferrand, the old capital of Auvergne (see entry) and its largest town by a considerable margin, is also the chief town of the département of Puy-de-Dôme, a university town and the see of a bishop. It lies on rising ground in the fertile Limagne basin, bounded on the west by the Monts Dômes. It is a considerable industrial town (Michelin, etc.).

History

The name of the town, originally Nemessos, was changed in Roman times to Augustonemetum, and later still became Castrum Claremunte or Clair-Mont. It was Christianised in the 3rd c., and after suffering devastation at the hands of various invaders was the meeting-place of the council in 1095 at which Pope Urban II proclaimed the First Crusade.

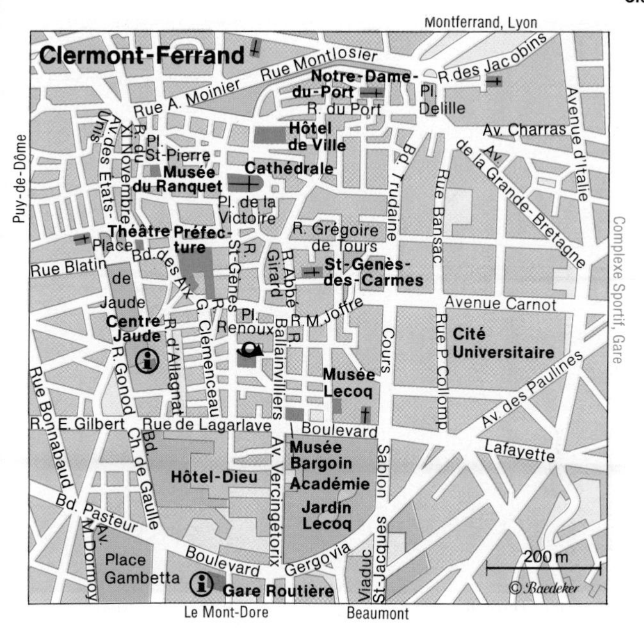

The philosopher and mathematician Blaise Pascal (1623–1662) was born in Clermont. In 1731 it was amalgamated with its neighbour and rival Montferrand to form the present town with its double-barrelled name.

Sights

Place de Jaude

The hub of the town's life is the busy Place de Jaude, with an equestrian statue of the Arvernian leader Vercingetorix (1903) by Bartholdi (who also created the Lion of Belfort and New York's statue of Liberty). The church of St-Pierre-des-Minimes (17th c.) has fine 18th c. carved woodwork in the choir. The Municipal Theatre was built in 1894 in a former textile warehouse.

From here Rue du 11-Novembre leads into Rue des Gras, which is lined by old houses, some of them with Romanesque reliefs on the façade and attractive courtyards. At No. 34 is the 16th c. Hôtel Fontfreyde, also known as the Maison des Architectes, with a beautiful courtyard, which now houses the Musée du Ranquet, with sculpture from medieval times to the 19th c., textiles, furniture and faience of the 18th c. The Pascal Room contains mementoes of Pascal, including two examples of his calculating machine.

Musée du Ranquet

Musée du Bargoin

On the south side of the town is the Musée du Bargoin (prehistoric and Gallo-Roman antiquities).

Cathedral

*Stained glass

The Cathedral of Notre-Dame de l'Assomption (13th–14th c.), built of dark-coloured volcanic stone, is one of the great Gothic cathedrals of central France. It is notable particularly for its beautiful stained glass (13th–14th c.), particularly in the choir chapels and the rose windows in the transepts. In the crypt, which belonged to an earlier 10th c. church, is a 4th c. sarcophagus.

Clermont-Ferrand

The Romanesque towers and west front were replaced by Viollet-le-Duc in neo-Gothic style in 1865.

Fontaine d'Amboise

In the Place de la Poterne, to the north of the cathedral, is the Fontaine d'Amboise, a beautiful Renaissance fountain of 1515.

Old town

In the picturesque old town around the cathedral are many houses of the 16th–18th centuries, for example in Rue des Chaussetiers (No. 3) the Maison de Savaron (1513), with a beautiful courtyard and staircase tower. Also worth seeing are the Musée Lecoq (mineralogical, botanical and zoological collections) and the Jardin Lecoq.

*Notre-Dame-du-Port

The church of Notre-Dame-du-Port (11th–12th c.) is a typical example of the Auvergnat Romanesque style. Particularly impressive is the view of the choir with its ambulatory and ring of chapels and the tower over the crossing. The doorway is richly decorated (Isaac, John the Baptist, the childhood of Christ).

Interior

Notable features of the interior are the capitals, carved with human and animal figures. In the crypt under the choir is a 17th c. Black Virgin, a copy of a Byzantine original which drew many pilgrims in the 13th c.

Montferrand

2 km/1½ miles north-east of the city centre is the suburban district of Montferrand, with the church of Notre-Dame-de-la-Prospérité and many Gothic and Renaissance houses, often with attractive courtyards. Particularly notable are 11, 18 and 28 rue Jules-Guesde, 1 rue des Cordeliers, 11 and 36 rue de la Rodade and 12 rue Kléber.

Surroundings of Clermont-Ferrand

Mozac

Mozac, north of Clermont-Ferrand, has a former abbey church with capitals which are among the finest achievements of Romanesque sculpture. Adjoining Mozac is the old town of Riom (see Auvergne).

Puy de Dôme

See Auvergne

Royat

Immediately west of Clermont-Ferrand is the much frequented spa of Royat.

Colmar

P6

Region: Alsace
Département: Haut-Rhin
Altitude: 190 m/625 ft
Population: 68,000

Situation and characteristics

Colmar, chief town of the département of Haut-Rhin in Upper Alsace and the third largest town in Alsace (after Strasbourg and Mulhouse), lies near the vine-covered foothills of the southern Vosges, in the climatically favoured Upper Rhine plain. Situated near the mouths of two major valleys in the Vosges, it is an excellent centre from which to explore the High Vosges; and with its picturesque old burghers' houses of the 16th and 17th centuries and its many treasures of art it is also one of the principal tourist attractions of Alsace in its own right.

Economy

Apart from the tourist trade, Colmar's economy depends on the textile industry, the production of foodstuffs and metal-working, together with market gardening (vegetables) and wine production, of which Colmar is Alsace's principal centre.
20 km/12½ miles south-east of the town is the Rhine port of Colmar–Neuf-Brisach.

History

The town, first recorded in 823 under the name of Columbarium ("Dove-cot"), was surrounded by walls in 1220. The Emperor Frederick II granted it the status of a free imperial city, which soon became the most important market town in Upper Alsace and a centre of art and learning. In 1354 Colmar joined the "Decapolis", the league of ten imperial cities in Alsace. The town was closely involved in the Reformation. During the Thirty Years War it was occupied by the Swedes and in 1673 by the French, and thereafter shared the destinies of Alsace.
Colmar was the birthplace of the painter and engraver Martin Schongauer (*c.*1445–1491), and the painter Matthias Grünewald (*c.*1470/83–1528), the last and greatest master of the Late Gothic period, also worked here.
Frédéric-Auguste Bartholdi (1834–1904), who created the Lion of Belfort and New York's statue of Liberty, was a native of Colmar.

Sights

Champ de Mars

On the west side of the old town, extending along the busy Avenue de la République, is the Champ de Mars, a long tree-planted open space which until 1804 was a military parade ground and then became a municipal park. On its west side is the Head Post Office, to the south is the Préfecture (1869), and 500 m/550 yds south-west is the railway station (1905). To the north of the Champ de Mars, in the Place du 18-Novembre, is the Municipal Theatre (1849).

** Musée d'Unterlinden

Immediately east of the theatre is the former Dominican convent of Unterlinden, founded in the early 13th c., which became a great centre of mystical thought in the 14th and 15th centuries. It has preserved a beautiful Early Gothic cloister with double arcades. The conventual buildings and the Early Gothic church (consecrated by Albertus Magnus in 1269) now house the Unterlinden Museum (Romanesque and Gothic sculpture, medieval painting, folk art and crafts, contemporary art, etc.).

Matthias Grünwald's Isenheim Altar in the Unterlinden Museum

Chapel

The chapel contains fine paintings by early German artists, including Passion scenes by Martin Schongauer and works by Isenmann, Lucas Cranach the Elder and other masters. Its chief treasure, however, is Matthias Grünewald's Isenheim Altar, one of the greatest and most moving masterpieces of German painting, a work of glowing colour and great imaginative power which was painted about 1515 for the convent of Isenheim or Issenheim near Guebwiller (statues by Nicholas of Haguenau). There is a good general view of the paintings from the gallery.

**Isenheim Altar

Cloister

Round the cloister are a lapidary museum and a room displaying works of religious art (Romanesque and Gothic sculpture, stained glass, goldsmith's work).

Cellar

The handsome 13th c. cellar of the convent contains prehistoric, early historical, Gallo-Roman and Merovingian antiquities and a collection of modern art, including works by Picasso, Léger, Rouault, Mathieu, Vasarely and Braque.

First floor

The first floor is devoted to Alsatian folk art (toys, furniture, weapons, pottery, porcelain, faience, stained glass, prints).

*Old town

In the old town with its narrow and winding streets are many burghers' houses of the 16th and 17th centuries. To the south of the Unterlinden Museum, at 19 rue des Têtes, is the Maison des Têtes ("House of the Heads"), a handsome Renaissance building (1609) decorated with numerous heads and figures; it is now occupied by a well-known restaurant. Farther south, in Rue des Boulangers and Rue des Serruriers (Bakers' Street and Locksmiths' Street), are other picturesque old half-timbered houses.

Dominican Church

In Rue des Serruriers is the Dominican Church (13th–15th c.), a fine example of the Early Gothic architecture of the Rhineland. The interior, its

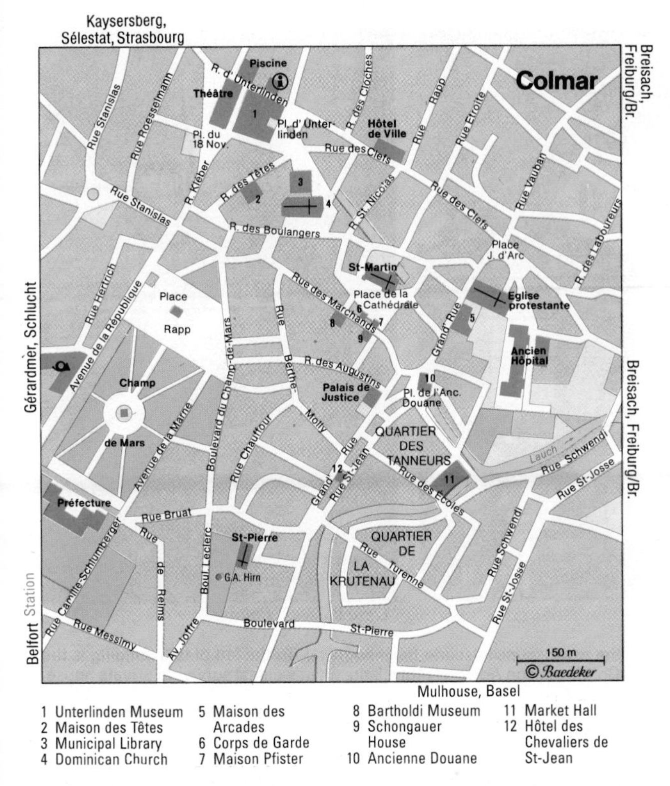

roof supported on extraordinarily slender pillars, contains fine stained glass (14th–15th c.) and altars from Marbach Abbey, near Eguisheim. In the choir is the famous "Virgin of the Rose-Garden", a masterpiece by Martin Schongauer (1473).
On the north side of the church is the former Dominican monastery, with a 14th c. cloister (serenade concerts). It now houses the Municipal Library (manuscripts of 8th–15th c., incunabula).

Rue des Clefs

North-east of the Dominican monastery, in Rue des Clefs (the main shopping street of the old town), is the 18th c. Town Hall.

Grand' Rue

South-east of the Town Hall, in the Grand' Rue, is a former Franciscan church (begun 1292), which has been a Protestant church since 1575, with a rood screen and a high choir. Opposite the church, to the south, is the Maison des Arcades, with arcades and oriel windows, which was built in 1606 to house the Protestant pastor.

St-Martin

In Place de la Cathédrale, in the centre of the old town, is the church of St-Martin, originally Gothic but largely rebuilt in the 18th c. It has preserved a High Gothic choir (1350–1366) and the richly decorated St Nicholas Doorway in the south transept; the choir contains 15th c. stained glass and fine carved woodwork.

Ancien Corps de Garde

Opposite St-Martin, to the south-west, is the former Guard-House (Ancien Corps de Garde, 1575), with an oriel window from which the decisions of

Maison Pfister

"Little Venice", Colmar

the town council used to be announced. To the left of this building is the Gothic Maison Adolph (14th c.), the town's oldest surviving private house.

Maison Pfister

At the corner of the picturesque rue Mercière and rue des Marchands is the Maison Pfister (1537), one of the finest old houses in Colmar, with wooden galleries.

Bartholdi Museum

Also in Rue des Marchands is the Bartholdi Museum, with mementoes of the famous sculptor (1834–1904), who was born here.

Ancienne Douane

A little way south-east of the Maison Pfister, in Place du Marché-aux-Fruits (Fruitmarket Square), is the Old Custom House (Ancienne Douane or Koifhus), built in 1480, with 16th and 18th c. additions. This was once the economic and political centre of the town: the ground floor was used as a warehouse for goods awaiting payment of duty, and on the first floor is the handsome council chamber of the league of imperial cities, with the coats of arms of the ten cities on the windows.
On the east side of the Custom House is the Place de l'Ancienne Douane, with the Schwendi Fountain (by Bartholdi), commemorating the Imperial General Lazarus von Schwendi (1552–1584), who is credited with having brought the Tokay vine from Hungary during the Turkish wars and introduced it into Alsace. (This claim is disputed, since the Ruländer grape which is known in Alsace as Tokay in fact came from France.)

Quartier des Tanneurs

To the south-east is the Quartier des Tanneurs (Tanners' Quarter), splendidly restored from 1968 onwards, with handsome half-timbered houses. At the west corner of the Market Hall is the Fontaine du Vigneron or Wine-Grower's Fountain (by Bartholdi, 1869).
Opposite the Ancienne Douane, to the south-west, is the 18th c. Palais de Justice (Law Courts). Farther south-west is the Venetian-style Hôtel des Chevaliers de St-Jean (1608), one of the most unusual Renaissance mansions in Alsace.

Quartier de la Krutenau

To the south-east is the picturesque Krutenau Quarter, traversed by the Rue Turenne.

*Petite Venise

From the bridges over the Lauch, beyond Rue St-Jean, there are attractive views of Colmar's "Little Venice", with picturesque old houses and willow-trees lining the river, and the tower of St Martin's church.

St-Pierre

Near the west end of the Boulevard St-Pierre is the church of St-Pierre, a handsome Baroque structure erected by the Jesuits in the mid 18th c. on the site of a Carolingian royal stronghold. In the gardens to the west of the church is a monument to the Colmar physicist G. A. Hirn (1815–1890), by Bartholdi.
South-west of this, in the Parc du Château d'Eau, is the Natural History Museum.

Surroundings of Colmar

See Alsace, Route du Vin

Les Corbières

K 11/12

Situation and characteristics

The Corbières are a range of hills in southern France, south-east of Carcassonne (see entry), which form a transition between the Massif Central and the Pyrenees, reaching a height of 1231 m/4039 ft in the Pic de Bugarach, to the east of Quillan. For centuries this was a region of strategic importance as a bulwark of the French kingdom against Spain, its natural strength being reinforced by a string of fortresses – Carcassonne, Puylaurens, Peyrepertuse, Quéribus, Termes and Aguilar.
The castles of the early medieval period in this area served as refuges for the Albigensians during the Albigensian war.
Since the region is only thinly populated, it is best explored in excursions from Carcassonne, Perpignan or Quillan.

Climate

The Mediterranean climate favours the growth of cedars and cypresses as well as firs and oaks. The lower parts of the region produce wines which were already esteemed in Roman times.

Sights

Carcassonne

See entry

***Fontfroide**

This Cistercian abbey, situated in a romantic upland valley south-west of Narbonne, has preserved a simple Romanesque church (13th c.), a fine cloister, the chapterhouse and the monks' refectories and dormitories.

Gorges de Galamus

These picturesque gorges, carved out of the hills by the river Agly, are up to 300 m/1000 ft deep.

Lagrasse

This little village (pop. 600) has remains of fortifications and the abbey of Ste-Marie d'Orbieu, founded in the 8th c., with a small cloister of the 11th–13th centuries and a larger one of the 18th c. which is now a hotel.

Lézignan-Corbières

Lézignan-Corbières has a large Wine Museum, installed in a house which belonged to an old wine-growing family. It offers an excellent introduction to all the various processes involved in making wine, with examples of old implements and equipment.

Quillan

This little town in the south-west of the region, with a ruined medieval castle and an 18th c. town hall, is a good base from which to explore the Corbières.

Coastal scenery, Bonifacio

A footpath in Corsica

Ruined castles

The impressive ruins of the five strongholds which reinforced the defences of Carcassonne, including the castles of St-Martin, Termes and Arques, lie close to N613, which runs through the Corbières region.
Along N117 (Quillan–Perpignan), perched on bare rocky crags, can be seen the Albigensian strongholds of Puylaurens (near Axat) and Quéribus (near the wine village of Maury). North of Maury, beyond Quéribus, is the strikingly impressive Albigensian citadel of Peyrepertuse (the "cleft rock").

*Montségur

North-west of Quillan, on a sheer crag between Bélesta and Lavelanet, are the massive ruins of Montségur, which was the scene of horrifying events during the Albigensian wars. After a siege of the castle in 1244 two hundred Albigensians were burned alive in a field at the foot of the hill which became known as the Prat dels Cremats (Meadow of the Burned). There are those who believe that Montségur is the fabled Montsalvat where the Holy Grail, the vessel containing Christ's blood, is hidden. It is now the symbolic centre of the movement which seeks independence for "Occitania", the old *langue d'oc*-speaking region.

Corsica

Q/R 11–13

**Situation and characteristics

The island of Corsica (French Corse), known to the ancient Greeks as Kalliste, the "Fair One", is a mountainous island in the Mediterranean, 180 km/112 miles from France and 84 km/52 miles from Italy. In the south it is separated from the Italian island of Sardinia only by the 11.5 km/7 mile wide Strait of Bonifacio.
Getting to Corsica: see Practical Information, Access.

The "Island of Light"

Thanks to its situation and topography Corsica, which has been christened the "Island of Light", offers scenery of great beauty and variety. The coastal areas are similar to the French Riviera, but less spoiled by tourism, with excellent facilities for bathing, water sports and diving. The mountains (highest point Monte Cinto, 2707 m/8882 ft), with their forests, wild gorges and peaks which are snow-capped right into summer, offer ample scope for walkers and climbers as well as for skiing.

Topography

With an area of 8722 sq. km/3368 sq. miles, a greatest length of 183 km/114 miles and a greatest breadth of 84 km/52 miles, Corsica is the fourth largest Mediterranean island (after Sicily, Sardinia and Cyprus). It has a population of 250,000, more than 40% of whom live in the two large towns of Ajaccio in the south-west and Bastia in the north-east, chief towns of the two Corsican départements of Haute-Corse and Corse-du-Sud.
Geologically Corsica belongs to an ancient land mass, later broken up, of which Sardinia, north-eastern Sicily and part of Calabria are also fragments. The island consists for the most part of a mountain massif slashed by deep valleys. In its western half, a region of granites and porphyries, are the jagged peaks of Monte Cinto (2707 m/8882 ft), Paglia d'Orba (2525 m/8285 ft) and the rounded summits of Monte Rotondo (2625 m/8613 ft), Monte d'Oro (2391 m/7845 ft) and Monte Renoso (2357 m/7733 ft). These mighty peaks, all within a relatively small area, combine with the rugged crest ridges, a number of beautiful mountain lakes (Lac de Rotondo, Lac de Nino) and the deep gorges to create a landscape of almost Alpine aspect. The lower reaches of the valleys, now sunk under the sea, form long inlets, flanked by steeply scarped hills, which cut far into the west coast.
In the eastern half of the island, where the hills consist of ancient schists, the highest peak, Monte San Pietro, reaches only 1766 m/5794 ft. Below this is a fertile plain, with a regular coastline edged by lagoons (Etang de Biguglia, Etang d'Urbino, Etang de Palo). In the almost rainless summers many rivers dry up altogether; the most important are the Gravone and the Golo.

Vegetation

Most of the land is uncultivated; some 45% is covered by macchia, 17% is under forest, 20% is pastureland and only 5.5% is arable. In spite of the fertility of the soil most of the island's food has to be imported from the mainland. The main crops are cereals, wine, fruit and tobacco, together with olives, figs, citrus fruits and sweet chestnuts. In the coastal regions peaches, almonds, olives, oranges, lemons, figs, cactuses, eucalyptus trees and palms grow up to 500 m/1640 ft, sweet chestnuts to 800 m/2600 ft, Corsican pines to 1200 m/3900 ft and beeches to 1800 m/5900 ft; above this the flora is Alpine. As a result of many forest fires the mountain forests (pines and beeches) are now confined to a few high valleys.

Population

Originally the Corsicans were probably a mixture of Iberians and Ligurians, with later infusions of Phoenician, Etruscan, Greek, Roman, Spanish, Moorish, Italian and French blood. The alien rule to which the island was subjected for so long (see History, below) gave rise to a feeling of dependence, and has also fuelled a striving towards independence and a separatist movement. The Corsican language, too – a Central Italian dialect – has become the expression of an independent Corsican culture (although the official language is French).
In political and economic matters a predominant role is played by large family groupings or clans, who choose their parliamentary representatives through a system of electoral lists.

Climate

The nature of its topography gives Corsica a wide range of climatic variations. Winter temperatures in the coastal regions, averaging 14°C/57°F, are distinctly higher than on the Côte d'Azur, the climate of which is comparable. In the height of summer, notwithstanding Corsica's insular situation, it can be very hot (average 25°C/77°F), so that the best time for a visit is in May, June or September. Spring comes to the south coast as early as the end of February or beginning of March. In the hills, however, the climate is considerably harsher, and the pattern of snowfall and snow-melt is similar to that of the Alps, so that many roads in the mountains may be impassable from October until May. In summer the cooler climate of the mountainous regions of the interior can be agreeable.

History

Archaeological evidence has shown that Corsica was settled from the Early Neolithic period. The original inhabitants, a mixture of Iberians and Ligurians, were followed by Phocaeans, who founded Alalia (later known as Aleria) on the east side of the island, and then by Etruscans and Carthaginians. In 259 B.C. the Roman conquest of Corsica began, but in face of the continuing resistance of the inhabitants took many years to complete. The mountainous and inhospitable island became a place of exile for distinguished Romans, among them the philosopher Seneca, who spent more than six years here. The fall of the Western Roman Empire was followed by the arrival successively of Vandals, Ostrogoths, Byzantines, Franks and Saracens. In 1070 Pisa gained control of the island, followed in 1284 by the Genoese, who, through their governors, pursued a deliberate policy of exploitation. In spite of several risings (revolt of the "Terre du Commun" in 1358, fight for liberation led by Sampiero Corso in 1564) the Corsicans managed to break free from the Genoese only in the 18th c., when a German adventurer, Theodor Freiherr von Neuhof, was appointed king; but although he carried out a number of reforms he was compelled by shortage of funds and disagreements with local leaders to leave the island after only eight months. In 1755 the Corsicans elected Pasquale Paoli as "General of the Nation". Paoli gave the island a popular constitution and an effective administration, suppressed the practice of the vendetta, established schools and a Corsican university, and promoted agriculture and trade. The Genoese were left in possession only of Bastia, and in 1768 ceded the island to France.

After overcoming initial resistance the French finally defeated the Corsican independence movement in the battle of Ponte Nuovo in 1769 – the year in which Napoleon was born in Ajaccio. After the outbreak of the French Revolution Paoli, who had fled to Britain, was elected by the National Assembly as President of Corsica. In 1793, however, suspected of aiming at secession from France, he was summoned to appear before the Convention in Paris and appealed to Britain for help. In the following year British forces drove out the French; but when the British authorities failed to grant the hoped-for independence and installed a British viceroy Paoli retired to Britain, where he died in 1807. Corsica was reconquered by Napoleon in 1796 and has since then remained part of France.

Present-day Corsica

The two world wars took a heavy toll, and the deterioration in the island's economy led to increased emigration. Compared with the island's present population of 250,000 (only 136,000 of whom are Corsicans, the rest being Frenchmen from the mainland or the former French colonies) there are now some 500,000 Corsicans in mainland France, 200,000 of them in Marseilles alone. Some emigrants have gone even farther afield, to such countries as Puerto Rico and Venezuela.

In 1974 the island was divided into the two départements of Haute-Corse and Corse-du-Sud, and in 1982 Corsica was given a special status, unique in the history of the French regions, which went a long way towards the ideal of an autonomous administration by establishing a Corsican regional assembly, consisting of 51 members, 28 right, 10 left and 13 nationalist.

Economy

The Corsicans draw their income from their traditional farming activities (cereals, fruit, wine, sheep and goat rearing) and from the tourist trade. In 1988 there were more than 1.5 million visitors to the island. The Corsican economy, however, is in a state of crisis, with a cost of living some 15% above the French average in spite of large subsidies from the French

Iles Sanguinaires

government. The millions of francs granted in subsidies seem to get lost on the way to their destination: thus premium petrol sent from France to Corsica is reduced by 30 centimes a litre, but the price to the Corsican consumer is higher than in France.

Circuit of the Island

A circuit of Corsica by car involves a journey, including side trips, of some 1200 km/750 miles; self-drive cars can be hired in the larger towns. The roads are good, but sometimes narrow, winding and hilly.
The route described below starts from Bastia, in the north-east of the island, runs round Cap Corse, follows the coast to Calvi and Porto, turns inland to Corte and continues via Zonza to Bonifacio, at the southern tip of the island, and then runs north-west to Corsica's capital, Ajaccio.

Principal sights

Even visitors whose time is limited should include in their programme the Bay of Ajaccio, the Col de Vizzavona, Castagniccia, Corte, the Scala di Santa Regina, the Bay of Porto, with the Calanche di Piana, Cap Corse and, if possible, the forests around Zonza and the Col de Bavella.

Round *Cap Corse

Bastia

The starting-point of this trip is Bastia (see entry).

*Cap Corse

The Cap Corse peninsula (40 km/25 miles long, 12–15 km/7½–9 miles across), the northernmost tip of Corsica and one of the most beautiful parts of the island, is occupied for its entire length by the Serra, a range of hills which reaches its highest point in Monte Stello (1305 m/4282 ft). On both sides of the hills are fertile valleys in which vines, fruit and olives are grown. The road runs via Ste-Lucie, from which there is a fine view of Bastia with its citadel and harbour, and San Martino di Lota (alt. 183 m/600 ft) to Miomo, with an imposing Genoese tower.

Erbalunga

At Erbalunga are the ruins of a castle and a watch-tower. Beyond this is the little port of Marine de Sisco. The chapel of St-Michel, on a crag 7 km/4½ miles inland (fine view), dates from the 11th c. The road then continues north past the church of Ste-Catherine (12th and 15th c.).

After passing the Tour de Losse, another old Genoese tower, the road comes to Marine de Porticciolo and Santa Severa, at the mouth of the Luri valley. From here a road (D180) cuts across the peninsula by way of Luri to the Col de Ste-Lucie (407 m/1335 ft), with a ruined medieval tower known as the Tower of Seneca, in which the philosopher is said to have been confined in A.D. 43–49. The road then runs on to Pino, which has the ruins of a Franciscan friary (1486).

Tower of Seneca

The road along the east coast continues from Santa Severa to Macinaggio, where Napoleon landed in 1793, and then turns inland into the hills.

**Col de la Serra

From the Col de la Serra (362 m/1188 ft), flanked on the left by two old watch-towers and on the right by a windmill, there is a fine view of the west coast. To the east is the island of Elba, to the north Cap Corse, with the little island of La Giraglia off the point. At Centuri the road returns to the coast.

Centuri

The village of Centuri (pop. 600) is beautifully situated between the road and the harbour.

Nonza

The road continues down the west coast of the peninsula to Nonza, picturesquely situated on a crag rearing steeply up from the sea, with a ruined tower. To the east is Monte Stello (1305 m/4282 ft).

At the Col de San Bernardino we join the road from St-Florent (D81), and turn left into it. It winds its way up through the villages of Patrimonio and Barbaggio, famed for their wine, to the Col de Teghime (548 m/1798 ft), from which there are superb views of the two seas and of inland Corsica to the south.

The direct road to Bastia, the starting-point of the trip round Cap Corse, runs down from the pass with many bends and magnificent views.

The circuit of the island continues to St-Florent.

St-Florent – Ile-Rousse – Calvi – Corte

St-Florent

This little town (pop. 1200), in the bay of the same name, originally grew up round a Genoese citadel (1440), and until the 18th c. was the seat of the bishop of Nebbio and of the Genoese governor. Nearby are the remains of medieval Nebbio, with the Cathedral of Santa Maria Assunta (12th c.), built of limestone in Lombard Romanesque style.

Ile-Rousse

A winding road runs over the Col de Lavezzo and through the lonely Désert des Agriates, a hilly region of pastureland and macchia, to Ile-Rousse (pop. 2630), a little port and seaside resort. It is not in fact an island, but takes its name from the red rocks of La Pietra. The town, which occupies the site of an old Roman settlement, was originally established by Paoli in 1758, during the war with the Genoese, under the name of Paolina, and was designed as a rival to Calvi. From here the coast road (N197) runs direct to Calvi.

*Recommended side trips

We recommend two rewarding side trips into the fertile upland region of Balagne.

Belgodere

The little town of Belgodere is picturesquely situated a little way inland, high up on the slopes of a hill on a crag crowned by a 13th c. castle. Farther inland is the Forêt de Tartagine, one of the finest forests in Corsica.

St-Antonio

The little walled town of St-Antonio, beautifully situated on a hill (views), is visible from a long way off. To the north of the town, on the road to Ile-Rousse, is the Dominican monastery of Corbara, founded in the 15th c. and rebuilt in the 19th.

Calvi

The lively little town of Calvi (pop. 3600), picturesquely situated on a projecting crag in the Bay of Calvi, has an unsheltered harbour which is the Corsican harbour closest to France. In the Middle Ages the town was a republic, and during the Genoese period it was the island's chief town. During the struggle for liberation in 1793–1794 it was laid in ruins by the British fleet. Near the harbour is the church of Santa Maria (17th c.), and in the upper town, which was fortified by the Genoese in the late 15th c., is the Cathedral of St-Jean-Baptiste, originally dating from the 13th c. and rebuilt in 1553 after its destruction; it contains a famous crucifix and other fine examples of woodcarving. The Maison Colomb in Rue Colombo, claimed to be the birthplace of Columbus, is unlikely to be authentic: there are several other alleged birthplaces in Italy and Spain. In the Bay of Calvi is a flat sandy beach 4 km/2½ miles long which makes Calvi with its numerous hotels a popular holiday resort.

*Col de la Croix

The road now runs over the hill of Bocca Serria (146 m/479 ft), with the Capo al Cavallo (296 m/971 ft; lighthouse) to the right, past the extensive ruins of the Argentella silver-mine, through the lonely Balagne Déserte and over the Bocca Bassa (122 m/400 ft) to Olmo; then into the level valley of the Fango and over the Col de Palmarella (374 m/1227 ft; wide views) and the Col de la Croix (272 m/892 ft), from which there are magnificent views of the Bay of Porto to the south and the Bay of Girolata to the west.

*Bay of Porto

**Calanche

The popular seaside resort of Porto lies in the beautiful Bay of Porto at the foot of a promontory which is crowned by an old Genoese watch-tower. The little harbour exports timber and granite among other products of the island. Farther south, between Porto and Piana, the road runs through the Calanche, a maze of fantastically fissured red granite rocks, with bizarrely shaped pinnacles towering up to 300 m/1000 ft above the Bay of Porto.
The route continues by way of Cargèse, founded in 1774 by immigrants from Greece, to Sagone, once the see of a bishop. It then runs up (D70) to the little town of Vico (alt. 400 m/1300 ft) and over the Col de St-Antoine (496 m/1627 ft) and the Col de Sevi (1272 m/4173 ft) to Evisa, a little holiday resort, beautifully situated above the Porto valley, which is a good base for exploring the surrounding area. From here there is a direct road to Porto through the Spelunca, a wild gorge in the Porto valley.

*Forêt de Valdo-Niello

*Monte Cinto

The road now runs through the beautiful forest of Aïtone, over the Col de Vergio (1464 m/4803 ft), the highest pass in Corsica, and through the Valdo-Niello Forest with its Corsican pines to Calacuccia, chief place in the Niolo basin, a good centre for excursions in the surrounding area and a good base from which to climb Corsica's highest mountain, Monte Cinto (2710 m/8891 ft; 7½ hrs with guide). From the summit there are magnificent panoramic views.
The route continues through the rocky valley, which narrows into the Scala di Santa Regina, a gorge enclosed by rock walls over 1000 m/3300 ft high, and then either on the direct road to Corte via the village of Castirla or on the slightly longer road via Francardo.

*Castagniccia

Those who prefer the Francardo road will find it well worth while to make a side trip into the upland region of Castagniccia with its forests of chestnut trees. The principal village, Piedicroce d'Orezza, is the base from which to climb Monte San Petrone (1766 m/5794 ft; 2½ hrs).

Corte

Corte (pop. 5446) lies in the centre of Corsica in a basin in the Tavignano valley, surrounded by high, bare granite hills. On a rocky ridge rising almost vertically above the river is its 15th c. citadel, formerly almost impregnable. Over the centuries Corte was an important and hotly con-

Citadel, Corte

tested stronghold. From 1755 to 1769 it was the capital of the island and the seat of the democratic government established by Pasquale Paoli, who also founded a university here. In the Palais National mementoes of Paoli are displayed. Adjoining the Eglise de l'Annonciation, which has a 17th c. façade and a notable interior, is a Baroque bell-tower.

*Gorges de la Restonica

From Corte an excursion (strongly recommended) can be made to the beautiful Gorges de la Restonica, below the imposing bulk of Monte Rotondo (2622 m/8602 ft).

Corte – Zonza – Bonifacio

*Side trip

From Corte a rewarding side trip can be made to the south-west, through the beautiful Vizzavona Forest to the Col de Vizzavona (1163 m/3816 ft), on the ridge formed by Monte Rotondo, Monte d'Oro and Monte Renoso, on which most of the island's rivers rise.

Vivario

From the beautifully situated little town of Vivario D69 runs south-east to Ghisoni. Here, however, a detour is recommended, going east from Vivario on D343 to Vezzani, situated high above the Tagnone valley, and then through two defiles flanked by tall rock pinnacles, the Défilé de l'Inzecca and the Défilé des Strettes, to Ghisoni.

Ghisoni

From Ghisoni D69 continues south over the Col de Verde (1283 m/4210 ft) to Zicavo, from which Mont l'Incudine (2136 m/7008 ft; 6 hrs) can be climbed. It then runs through beautiful mountain scenery over the Col de la Vaccia (1188 m/3898 ft) to Aullène. From here the direct road to Zonza is D420; but there is an attractive alternative route by way of the little town, noted for its wine, of Ste-Lucie-de-Tallano (alt. 450 m/1475 ft), picturesquely situated on a hill.

Ste-Lucie-de-Tallano

Zonza
**Col de Bavella

From Zonza a very rewarding excursion can be made to the Col de Bavella. The road runs north-east through fine scenery (remains of a Roman road) to the pass (1243 m/4078 ft), from which there are breathtaking views of the extensive forests and fertile plains, the sea to the east and the mountains to the north and west.

Porto-Vecchio

The route continues by way of L'Ospedale to Porto-Vecchio (pop. 9000), a port established by the Genoese and now a centre of the cork and wine trades, situated in the beautiful bay of the same name. It still preserves part of its circuit of walls and an 18th c. Genoese citadel. Round the town are beautiful sandy beaches.

*Bonifacio

From Porto-Vecchio the road runs down the east coast to Bonifacio (pop. 2300), a little fortified town said to have been founded in the 9th c. by Bonifazio, Marquis of Tuscany. It is picturesquely situated on a 1.5 km/1 mile long limestone promontory, 64 m/210 ft high, which is separated from the Italian island of Sardinia only by the 11.5 km/7 mile wide Strait of Bonifacio. Bonifacio is a town of medieval lanes flanked by old houses. The former cathedral of Ste-Marie-Majeure (12th–13th c., with later alterations), with a plain undecorated porch, contains a fine marble tabernacle (15th c.). The Gothic church of St-Dominique (13th–14th c.) has a 15th c. tower and contains interesting groups of carved wooden figures which are carried in processions.

Bonifacio – Sartène – Propriano – Ajaccio

*Sartène

From Bonifacio N196 runs north-west to Sartène. 32 km/20 miles from Bonifacio is the curious natural feature known as the Lion of Roccapina, a small rocky promontory which has been bizarrely carved by erosion into the form of a crouching lion. Sartène (pop. 3000), chief place in the fertile Sartenais district, is beautifully situated above the valley of the Rizzanèse. The medieval old town is entered through the arched gateway of the town hall.

Propriano

The route continues to Propriano, in the Bay of Valinco, with a fishing and commercial harbour and a beautiful bathing beach. From here the road runs north via Olmeto to Filitosa.

*Filitosa

The prehistoric settlement of Filitosa, on a projecting crag above the Taravo valley, is a sight not to be missed, with its remains of the 3500-year-old Torre culture (which displaced a megalithic pastoral culture around 3500 B.C.). The visible remains include groups of standing stones, the foundations of village houses and various tower-like cult buildings and fortifications.

Cauria
Fontanaccia

Other sites with remains of the earliest Corsican culture are Cauria and Fontanaccia, which lie between Bonifacio and Sartène, to the east of N196. The coast road now runs round the Gulf of Ajaccio to the town of Ajaccio.

Ajaccio

See entry

Sport and Recreation in Corsica

Sport

All the larger places have facilities for water sports and sailing, surfing and diving schools. For riders there are over 1000 km/600 miles of riding tracks and numerous riding clubs and stables. The shooting season is from the beginning of September to the beginning of January until the end of February, and there is fishing in the Corsican rivers with permits issued by local angling clubs. Other activities available are caving, flying and gliding. There are also facilities for tennis and minigolf.

Climbing

Corsica has more than 50 peaks over 2000 m/6500 ft. Climbs are organised by the Corsican climbing club, I Montagnoli Corsi, 11 Boulevard Sampiero, Ajaccio.

Hiking

A waymarked long-distance trail *(chemin de grande randonnée,* GR20), with a total length of 173 km/107 miles, runs through the centre of the island from Calenzana, near Calvi, in the north-west to Zonza in the south-east.

Rafting

It is now possible to sail down the Tavignano in rubber dinghies from Corte. For information apply to Base du Tavignano, Rafting Ernella, RN200 Giuncaggio, F-20251 Piedicorte di Caggio.

Winter sports

There are facilities for skiing (with lifts) at Haut-Asco, Ghisoni and the Col de Vergio, and for ski trekking (langlauf) at Evisa (hotels), Bastelica, Zicavo and Quenza.

Côte d'Argent

See Gascony

Côte d'Azur

N–P 11

** Situation and characteristics

The Côte d'Azur ("Azure Coast"), as the French Riviera is known in France, extends along the Ligurian Sea from Marseilles to the Italian frontier at Menton.

For a detailed description see the AA/Baedeker Pocket Guide **"Provence/Côte d'Azur"**

This beautiful region, whose attractions were discovered in the 19th c. by well-to-do British visitors, has now become a cosmopolitan holiday area, crowded with visitors during the main holiday season and ravaged by over-development, not only on the coast but also inland and in the hills.
Politically speaking, the Côte d'Azur and its hinterland lie within the Provence–Alps–Côte d'Azur. Nestling within this region, too, is the independent principality of Monaco on the coast. It is preferable to visit the Côte d'Azur at the less busy times of year, in spring or autumn or during the mild winter.

Topography

The varied topography of the Côte d'Azur reflects its varying geological structure. The Cretaceous limestone coast to the east of Marseilles, the Côte à Calanques, with its deeply indented inlets *(calanques,* from Provençal *calanco,* "steeply scarped"), gives place between Toulon and the mouth of the Argens to the Côte des Maures, formed by the Massif des Maures (alt. 779 m/2556 ft), with the offshore Iles d'Hyères. The Massif des Maures is an isolated range of ancient hills some 60 km/40 miles long by 30 km/20 miles wide, consisting of granites, gneisses and schists, pinkish or dark grey in colour with golden flecks of mica – the remains of a primeval continent which occupied the whole of the western Mediterranean.
From St-Raphaël, where the Côte d'Azur in the narrower sense begins, the Massif de l'Esterel (300–618 m/985–2028 ft) extends to just before Cannes. Geologically related to the Massif des Maures, it is partly Alpine in character, 20 km/12 miles long by 12 km/8 miles wide, and consists of a massif of gneiss enclosed by schists, interrupted in many places, particularly on the coast, by eruptive rocks, blue and red porphyry. The red porphyry of this much indented coast and the deep blue of the sea, here dotted with numerous islets, combine to produce charming effects of light and colour.
East of Cannes the coast rises in terraces from the shore. The Cap d'Antibes juts out into the sea, with the Iles de Lérins clustering picturesquely round it. Beyond this is the mouth of the Var.
Between Nice and the Italian frontier the foothills of the Alpes Maritimes, consisting of Cretaceous and Jurassic limestones, fall steeply down towards the coast, barely leaving room for the Principality of Monaco (see that entry), cramped into an area of 2 sq. km/¾ sq. mile on the narrow coastal strip.

Climate

Thanks to its sheltered situation at the foot of the hills which flank the coast and protect it from the cool north winds, the Côte d'Azur has an exceptionally equable climate – not too hot in summer (July average 25°C/77°F) and not too cold in winter, with day temperatures of 6°-15°C/43°-59°F, although it can become quite cool at night. Rainfall is not heavy, and occurs mainly in spring and autumn; the winter months are sunny. In the western part of the coast, between Hyères and Cannes, the mistral sometimes blows. In summer the sirocco will occasionally bring in hot air from the south.

Flora

With its Mediterranean climate, the Côte d'Azur has an extraordinarily rich flora. The original vegetation, including various species of pine (Aleppo pine, maritime pine, northern pitch pine) and deciduous trees (holm oak, cork oak, English oak, hornbeam, sweet chestnut), has suffered from human intervention and catastrophic forest fires and is much reduced from its former extent. The plants which are now characteristic of the landscape – the silver-green olive trees which cover the hills to a height of 500 m/1650 ft, the orange and lemon plantations, the palms, vines, cypresses, pines, agaves, aloes, cacti, etc. – have come from all over the world, some of them in Roman times.

Near the sea is found the maquis (macchia, garrigue) characteristic of the whole Mediterranean area – an impenetrable scrub of kermes oaks, lentisks, myrtles, strawberry trees, tree heaths, carob-trees, liana-like climbing plants and much else besides. Particularly prominent are strongly aromatic herbs and shrubs like lavender, thyme and rosemary.

Economy

The main contributor to the economy of the region is probably still the tourist trade (with 8 million visitors a year), but the economic structure of this classic holiday area is in process of change. The old-established trades of the region are still of considerable importance. Second to the tourist industry come the growing of flowers and the perfume industry which they supply. The main centre of these activities is Grasse with its surrounding area, where several million kilograms of flowers (oranges, roses, jasmine, thyme, rosemary, mignonette, violets, etc.) are processed every year. The distillation of lavender is mainly concentrated in the catchment area of the river Verdon.

The inland region, particularly round Brignoles, occupies the leading place in the extraction of bauxite, with some 70% of total French output.

In addition to agriculture and forestry the Côte d'Azur has another source of raw materials in the extraction of salt from seawater. There are productive salt-pans, for example, on the Etang de Berre and around Hyères and Giens.

Nowadays, however, "clean" industries like research establishments, computer manufacture and service industries are achieving turnovers which exceed the income from the tourist trade.

History

The Côte d'Azur first appears in history as the territory of the Ligurians, whose name is preserved in the Ligurian Sea and in the Golfe du Lion. The city of Massalia (Marseilles), founded by Greeks about 600 B.C., gained a monopoly of trade in southern France, with an eastern outpost in Nikaia (Nice). From the 3rd c. B.C. the Romans were involved in fiercely fought wars with the Ligurians for control of the military road which ran by way of Nice to Spain.

In 122 B.C. the Romans were victorious, and in 102 B.C. Marius halted the advance of the Teutons near Aix. After his conquest of Gaul Caesar founded the city of Forum Iulii (Fréjus) in 49 B.C.. In the early centuries A.D. there were further Roman foundations at Nice and Antibes. During the 4th and 5th centuries Christianity spread along the coast. Then in the first half of the 8th c. the Saracens reached the Mediterranean coast of France, settling in the Massif des Maures and harassing the whole coastal region in the 9th and early 10th centuries. The name of the range, however, does not come from the Moors but from the Provençal word *maouro* ("dark forest"). In later centuries the Côte d'Azur, like the rest of Provence, several times changed its political allegiance. In 1486 Provence finally became part of France, though from 1388 Nice was held by the Count of Savoy. In 1815 Nice was assigned to the kingdom of Sardinia, and finally in 1860 it was ceded to France.

Villages perchés

In addition to the endless variety of coastal scenery, the capes and bays and hills, the picturesque towns and villages, the interesting little harbour towns and the old local capitals farther inland, the Côte d'Azur offers another attraction in the numerous *villages perchés* (hilltop villages) or *nids d'aigle* (eagles' eyries), built on inaccessible sites on hills, crags or ridges of rock in order to escape the attentions of foreign raiders or conquerors. The limited space available on these sites made it necessary to build houses of small surface area but considerable height, huddled closely together. Although these villages are increasingly being abandoned because of the difficulty of access and often the shortage of water, they are popular places of resort for artists and modern practitioners of the *vie de bohème* (bohemian life). Typical examples of these villages are Castellar, Gorbio, Roquebrune, Peillon, Eze, Vence, Tourette-sur-Loup and Gourdon.

Along the Côte d'Azur

Art

Visitors interested in both classical and modern art will find a number of museums and galleries at various points along the Côte d'Azur, for example at Antibes, Biot, Cagnes-sur-Mer, Menton, Nice, St-Paul, St-Tropez, Vallauris, Vence and Villefranche.

Sights

The main places of interest on the Côte d'Azur are described below in geographical order, following the line of the road which runs east or north-east from Marseilles, with some side trips to places off the road.

Toulon

See entry

Hyères

Hyères (pop. 45,000), an important agricultural centre and the oldest winter resort on the Côte d'Azur, lies at the foot of Mt Castéou (204 m/670 ft).
The central feature of the picturesque old town is the Place Massillon (flower market), with the 12th c. Tour St-Blaise, all that remains of a Templar commandery.
In Rue Rabaton is the birthplace of the great preacher Massillon (1663-1742). In Place St-Paul is the church of St Paul (originally 12th c., restored in the 16th). In Rue Paradis is a lovingly restored 13th c. house.
In the modern part of the town is the interesting Musée Municipal (archaeology, local history, natural history).
South of the town centre are the Jardins Olbius-Riquier, beautifully laid out, with many exotic plants.

Costebelle

On a hill 3 km/2 miles south of the town is Costebelle, with a pilgrimage chapel on the summit, from which there are wide views. The chapel is the starting-point for the ascent of the Mont des Oiseaux (306 m/1004 ft; about 2 hours' climb).

Hyères-Plage

On the coast to the south of the Toulon-Hyères airport is the outlying district of Hyères-Plage, with a racecourse and the boating harbour of St-Pierre-de-la-Mer.

****Iles d'Hyères**

The Iles d'Hyères, also known as the Iles d'Or, belong geologically to the Massif des Maures. They are well wooded, with rugged cliffs and beautiful natural harbours.
The largest and most westerly of the islands is Porquerolles, to the east of which is the island of Port-Cros. Together with the neighbouring islets this was declared a nature reserve in 1963.

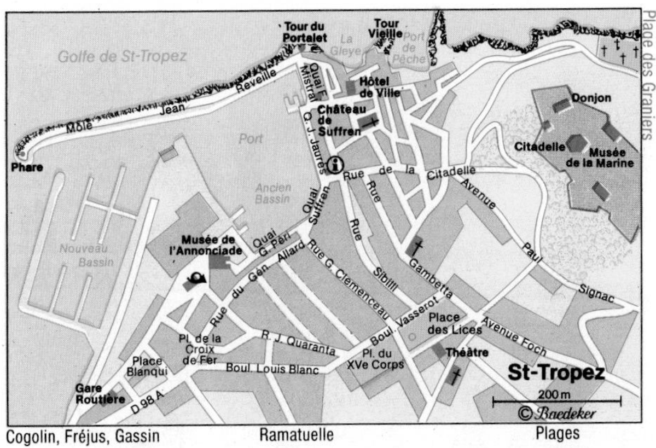

Immediately east of Port-Cros is the rocky Ile du Levant, in the western part of which is the naturist colony of Héliopolis, established as long ago as 1932.

Massif des Maures

This range of wooded hills extends for some 60 km/40 miles between Hyères in the west and Fréjus in the east, reaching its highest point in La Sauvette (779 m/2556 ft). The hills, once lonely and deserted, now attract increasing numbers of visitors.

* Corniche des Maures

The Corniche des Maures runs close to the coast from Hyères to St-Tropez. A beautiful trip through the Massif des Maures (rather more than 100 km/60 miles) is from Le Lavandou by way of the Col de Babaou (415 m/1362 ft; extensive views), the ruins of the Chartreuse de la Verne, Grimaud, the Col du Canadet and the rocky mass of the Pierre d'Avenon.

St-Tropez

St-Tropez (pop. 6000), once a small fishing port, lies on the south side of the Golfe de St-Tropez, under the east end of the Massif des Maures.
The place was known to the Greeks. It takes its name from the martyred St Tropez, who was said to have been beheaded by the Romans in A.D. 68 and whose relics were discovered here. Much harried by the Saracens, it became a republic in the 15th c. Since the Second World War St-Tropez has become a favourite haunt of artists, and with the increasing numbers of visitors has lost something of its original charm.

Citadel

In the citadel (1592), which looms over the town, affording wide views, is the Musée de la Marine et d'Histoire Locale (Museum of Seafaring and Local History).
Lower down, to the west, is the old town, with the harbour beyond it. In Rue du Portail-Neuf is the 18th c. church, in Italian Baroque style, with a bust of St Tropez and fine carved woodwork. At the south corner of the harbour is the former Chapel of the Annunciation, which now houses the Musée de l'Annonciade. with a collection of pictures ranging in date between 1890 and 1950, including works by many modern artists who lived in St Tropez. Among them were Signac (who "discovered" the little fishing village in 1892, settled there and brought many of his artist friends), Derain, van Dongen, Rouault, Matisse and Braque. There are also works of sculpture by Maillol and Despiau.

* Musée de l'Annonciade

Ramatuelle

South of St-Tropez is the old Saracen village of Ramatuelle, from which there are wide views.

Ste-Maxime

North of St-Tropez is the little port of Ste-Maxime. The church has a fine 18th c. marble altar. The Musée de la Photographie et de la Musique displays a large collection of cameras and musical instruments.

Port-Grimaud

Port-Grimaud

At the deepest point of the Golfe de St-Tropez, under the Massif des Maures, is Port-Grimaud, a modern holiday resort (1969) designed in imitation of a fishing village in the Venetian lagoon, with a maze of canals.

*Grimaud

5 km/3 miles west is the picturesque hilltop village of Grimaud, perched high above the plain of Cogolin. The site was occupied in Ligurian times. Notable features are the ruined 11th c. castle (views) and the 11th c. church of St-Michel.

Fréjus

The town of Fréjus (pop. 42,000), Caesar's foundation of Forum Iulii, lies on a rocky plateau in the plain between the Massif des Maures and the Esterel hills. It is not known whether there was a settlement here in pre-Roman times. In the reign of Augustus the place became a naval port, linked with the sea by a channel 500 m/550 yds long and 30 m/100 ft wide. In the 4th c. it became the see of a bishop, and in the 10th c. suffered from Saracen raids. In the 18th c. the harbour, by then silted up, was abandoned.

*Baptistery

The cathedral, which dates from the 11th and 12th centuries, has a tower with a square base and an octagonal upper part, topped by a spire. At the left-hand end of the narthex is the entrance to the Baptistery, an octagonal structure of the 4th–5th c., a prototype of later Romanesque forms. The cathedral itself, two-aisled, has a beautiful 15th c. altarpiece with sixteen panels (by Jacques Durandi of the Nice school).

The cloister (entered from the narthex by a flight of steps) has graceful columns and a coffered ceiling with scenes from the Apocalypse (14th–15th c.).

Other features of interest

The Musée Archéologique has an interesting collection of Greek and Roman material.

The Roman amphitheatre (Arènes), which dates from the 1st–2nd centuries A.D., measures 114 by 82 m (374 by 269 ft) and could accommodate 10,000 spectators.

North-east of the town, on N7, are remains of the Roman aqueduct which

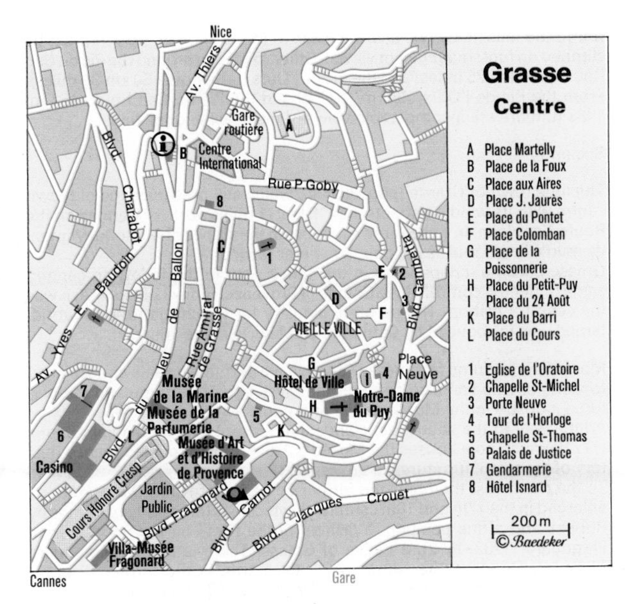

brought water to the town from the Massif de l'Esterel. A short distance west are some remains of a Roman theatre.
In the Zone Industrielle Capitou is a private museum, the Fondation Daniel Templon, containing works by contemporary artists.

Barrage de Malpasset

10 km/6 miles north of the town is the Barrage de Malpasset. Fréjus suffered a major disaster in 1959 when this dam burst, drowning more than 400 people.

Le Muy

The lively little town of Le Muy, 11 km/7 miles west of Fréjus, has an interesting 15th c. church and a round tower known as the Tour Charles-Quint. British and American parachutists landed here in 1944.

St-Raphaël

The port town of St-Raphaël (pop. 24,000) is attractively situated on the north side of the Golfe de Fréjus, at the foot of the Massif de l'Esterel. It was originally a residential suburb of Roman Fréjus. Napoleon landed here in 1799 on his return from his Egyptian campaign: an event commemorated by a pyramid in Avenue du Commandant-Guilbaud.
In the old part of the town is a fortified Templar church (12th c.). There is a museum containing archaeological finds from the sea, including many Greek amphoras of the 5th c. B.C.

Massif de l'Esterel
**Corniche d'Or

The Massif de l'Esterel, which rises above St-Raphaël, was opened up in 1903 by the construction of a coastal road, the Corniche d'Or. The dense stands of conifers, cork oaks and hard-leaved evergreens which once covered the hills were devastated by forest fires, and the process of replanting is slow and difficult.

*Mont Vinaigre

Mont Vinaigre (618 m/2028 ft) is the highest point in the range. From the little coastal town of Agay, on the Corniche de l'Esterel, a road runs up the Pic de l'Ours (496 m/1627 ft).

*Corniche de l'Esterel

The Corniche de l'Esterel runs from St-Raphaël to Cannes, passing through all the coastal resorts. A return route, making a circuit of 80 km/50 miles

* Pic du Cap Roux
* Pic de l'Ours

round the hills, is by N7, passing close to Mont Vinaigre (which must be climbed on foot: magnificent views). Other roads run around the Pic du Cap Roux (*c.* 40 km/25 miles) and the Pic de l'Ours (rather over 50 km/30 miles). From the Pic de l'Ours (496 m/1627 ft) and the Pic du Cap Roux (452 m/1483 ft) there are incomparable views of the coast and the hills.

Cannes

See entry

Grasse

The little town of Grasse (pop. 38,000), which still preserves the old town centre with its winding streets, lies 18 km/11 miles north of Cannes on the Route Napoléon, in a sheltered situation on the slopes of Mt Roquevignon. Its mild climate makes it a popular winter resort.
Grasse became independent in the 12th c., but in the following century came under the control of the Counts of Provence. From 1244 to 1790 it was the see of a bishop. The perfume industry for which the town is world-famed was introduced by Catherine de Médicis in the 16th c.

Musée de la Parfumerie

Most of the perfume factories in Grasse have perfume on sale and are open to visitors, who can also discover the mysteries of perfume and the perfume industry in the Musée de la Parfumerie.
A little way to the south-east stands the former Hôtel de Clapiers-Cabris (1771), which now houses the Musée d'Art et d'Histoire de Provence (history of the town, furniture, ceramics, etc.).
To the north-east thereof is the former Cathedral of Notre-Dame (12th c.; enlarged in the 17th and 18th centuries), which has three early paintings by Rubens and a fine painting "Washing of the Feet" by the Rococo artist Fragonard (1732–1802), a native of Grasse. There is a small Fragonard Museum. Opposite the cathedral, to the north, is the former Bishop's Palace (originally 13th c.), now the Hôtel de Ville (Town Hall).

Cours Honoré Cresp

There are fine views from the Cours Honoré Cresp, the town's principal promenade.

Cap d'Antibes

See Antibes

Biot

See Antibes, Surroundings

Cagnes-sur-Mer

This old-world little town (pop. 36,000), with its houses huddled within the old walls, is dominated by a 14th c. Grimaldi castle. The castle, which was rebuilt in the 17th c., has a beautiful Renaissance courtyard. It now houses a museum (art collection, with works by Chagall, Matisse and Renoir; ethnographic collection; olives and olive-growing).
The Chapelle Notre-Dame has fine 16th c. frescoes. Renoir (1841–1919) lived and died in the Maison des Colettes.
The old fishing port of Cros-de-Cagnes, at the mouth of the river Cagne, is now a well equipped seaside resort and boating harbour.

St-Paul

The little medieval town of St-Paul (alt. 182 m/597 ft; pop.1600) is picturesquely situated on a hill some 9 km/6 miles north of Cagnes. It has well preserved 16th c. walls with an imposing defensive tower. The 13th c. church has a valuable treasury. In the Place de la Fontaine is the Musée Provençal. St-Paul was "rediscovered" in the 1920s by painters like Signac, Modigliani and Bonnard.

* Fondation Maeght

On the Colline des Gardettes, a kilometre (¾ mile) from the town, is the Fondation Maeght, founded in 1960 by the art dealer Aimé Maeght and his wife. This museum of modern art, housed in a building (by José-Luis Sert) which fits harmoniously into its setting, displays works by Alexander Calder, Joan Miró, Giacometti, Bonnard, Braque, Chagall, Kandinsky and other modern artists. There are also periodic special exhibitions.

Vence

3 km/2 miles north of St-Paul is Vence (alt. 325 m/1066 ft; pop. 14,000). In the centre of the old town is the Cathedral of St-Véran (10th–15th centuries),

Eze village with its exotic gardens

with fine choir-stalls and an altar consisting of a Roman sarcophagus. The baptistery has a mosaic by Marc Chagall. The choir and the chapel under the tower have Carolingian interlace decoration.
In Place Godeau, to the east of the church, is an ancient column, a relic of the Roman town of Vintium. To the west, outside the town centre, is the 15th c. Chapelle des Pénitents-Blancs.
Marc Chagall lived in Vence until his death in 1985.

*Chapelle du Rosaire

On the northern outskirts of the town is the Chapelle du Rosaire (Rosary Chapel), which belongs to a Dominican convent (open Tues. and Thu. 10–11.30 a.m. and 2.30–5.30 p.m.). It was designed and decorated by Henri Matisse and built between 1947 and 1951. The altar vessels and vestments were also designed by Matisse; they are now in the Matisse Museum in Nice.

Nice

See entry

***Corniches**
*Petite Corniche
**Moyenne Corniche
**Grande Corniche

There are three corniche roads along the coast between Nice and Menton. The Corniche du Littoral or Petite Corniche keeps close to the coast and runs through many towns and villages. The Moyenne Corniche runs halfway up the slope, with many bridges (fine views) and rock-cut galleries. The Grande Corniche, built in the time of Napoleon I, reaches a height of 530 m/1740 ft and affords magnificent long-distance views of the much indented coast. The distance in each case is some 30 km/20 miles.

Beaulieu-sur-Mer

The hot climate of this little town (pop. 5000) has earned it the name of "Petite Afrique". The Villa Kerylos (open to the public) was built by an archaeologist in the style of a Roman villa.

Eze
**Situation

Eze (pop. 2100), charmingly situated near the Moyenne Corniche, consists of two parts. Eze-Village (alt. 427 m/1400 ft) is picturesquely situated on a crag crowned by a ruined castle (magnificent views) and is still surrounded

*Jardin Exotique

by its 17th c. walls. It has a Musée d'Histoire Locale et d'Art Religieux. The Chapelle des Pénitents-Blancs has modern frescoes by J.-M. Poulin. From the Jardin Exotique there are wide views.
On the coast is Eze-Bord-de-Mer, on a site occupied in Roman times, which is now a popular holiday resort.

Roquebrune-Cap-Martin

*Castle

Roquebrune-Cap-Martin (pop. 13,000), situated near the Italian frontier, also consists of two parts. Roquebrune, an old village of winding streets and arched lanes, lies inland on the slopes of a hill rising to 300 m/985 ft. It is dominated by its old castle, originally built in the 10th c. to provide protection from Saracen raids, a fine example of Carolingian military architecture which was enlarged in feudal times, two centuries later. From the keep there are wide views.

Cap Martin

Cap Martin, a long promontory reaching out to sea, offers pleasant walks. Along the west side runs the Promenade Le Corbusier (fine views), named after the famous architect, who was drowned here in 1965.

Monaco

See entry

Monte Carlo

See Monaco

Menton

At the eastern end of the Côte d'Azur is Menton (Italian Mentone; pop. 25,000), the last town before the Italian frontier.
Until 1848 Menton belonged to the Principality of Monaco, and after a period under the protection of the king of Sardinia was purchased by France in 1861.
The life of the resort centres on the Casino Municipal (1932). Opposite this is the Jardin Biovès. The Musée Jean Cocteau, housed in a 17th c. mansion, contains pictures, drawings and stage designs by Cocteau. The Salle des Mariages in the Hôtel de Ville (Town Hall) has wall paintings by Cocteau.

Musée Municipal

The Musée Municipal, in the Palais Carnoles, has a fine collection of pictures, including works by Chagall, Dufy, Modigliani, Picasso and Vlaminck, as well as embroidery from the 16th–18th c.
In the charming old town of Menton are 17th c. houses, the Old Cemetery (views) and the Jardin des Colombières.

Côte des Basques F11

Situation and characteristics

The Côte des Basques (Basque Coast), the continuation of the Côte d'Argent (see Gascony), runs south-west for some 35 km/22 miles from Biarritz (see entry) to Hendaye. Beyond the Spanish frontier it extends as far as San Sebastián. The two principal resorts on this stretch of coast are Biarritz and St-Jean-de-Luz, which, like the inland towns and villages though to a lesser degree, show distinctively Basque traditions, reflected both in place-names and in the local way of life.

The Basques

The Basques, who call themselves Euskaldunak in their own very distinctive language, live on both sides of the Pyrenees, some 200,000 of them in France and just under 2 million in Spain. Although the Spanish Basques have long fought stubbornly for self-government, it is only in the eighties that unrest has begun to make itself felt on the French side, though on a much smaller scale than in Spain.
All over the Basque territory there is now a rapidly increasing interest in Basque culture and cultural activities. Basque dramatic and musical groups, language schools and pelota schools are springing up all over the place, and the number of local festivals has increased: a great and growing concern with Basque traditions is evident everywhere.

Pelota

The Basque national sport is pelota or its variant, cesta punta. There are different ways of playing, but the essence of the game is to strike the ball against the pelota wall *(fronton)* with the bare hand or a special kind of curved bat and catch it on its return.

History

Euskadi is the land of the Euskaldunak (the Basque-speakers), and it is their language that binds the Basques together. There probably never was a separate Basque state. The origins of the Basques are the subject of controversy. It is supposed that the French Basques came from beyond the Pyrenees and that those who settled in the plain became assimilated with the local inhabitants, while the mountain Basques clung to their cultural heritage. The origin of the Basque language, which is non-Indo-European, is also uncertain.

Sights

Bayonne

The old town of Bayonne (pop. 42,000) lies near the Atlantic coast at the point where the river Nive flows into the broad Adour. Controlling access to the passes in the western Pyrenees, Bayonne was once strongly fortified, and is now surrounded by the attractive promenades which have replaced its walls. Here Basque and Gascon characteristics meet and mingle.
As its name indicates, the bayonet was invented by the armourers of Bayonne, and the town also claims credit for the introduction into France of chocolate, brought by Jews expelled from Spain.

The Pont St-Esprit leads from the outer district of that name (citadel built by Vauban, 1674–1679; 15th c. church) into the Place de la Liberté, the hub of the town's life. On its west side are the Theatre and the Hôtel de Ville (Town Hall).

*Cathedral

The Cathedral of Ste-Marie (1213–1544) is one of the handsomest churches in south-western France. The façade and the two towers date from the 19th c., the cloister from the 14th. Fine stained glass (1531).
To the north of the cathedral is the Château-Vieux, a medieval stronghold built on Roman foundations.
The Musée Bonnat displays the collection of pictures assembled by the painter Léon Bonnat, including works by Botticelli, Van Dyck, Rubens, Hals, El Greco and Turner and a rich collection of graphic art. The Musée Basque, housed in a 15th c. building, illustrates the history of the town and the Basque country.

Biarritz

See entry

St-Jean-de-Luz

From Biarritz the road runs by way of the little seaside resort of Bidart and the attractive little town of Guéthary, situated on rising ground above the Atlantic – a fashionable seaside and climatic resort which has preserved its original Basque character – to St-Jean-de-Luz (pop. 13,000). Since the Middle Ages this has been an important fishing port, from which ships were sailing to Newfoundland, Canada, Hudson Bay, Greenland and Spitzbergen in the 13th and 14th centuries. Since the Second World War the main activity of the port has been tunny-fishing. It is also a popular bathing and winter resort.
In Place Louis-XIV is the Maison Lohbiague, in which Louis XIV lived when he came here to marry Maria Teresa, daughter of Philip IV of Spain; it is now a museum, with period furniture. The church of St-Jean-Baptiste, originally built in the 13th c. but much altered in later centuries, still preserves a typically Basque interior; the three-storey oak gallery in the nave is a later addition.

Ciboure

Opposite St-Jean-de-Luz, on the left bank of the Nivelle, which flows into the sea here, is Ciboure, with old houses set along narrow streets and the

Collioure, on the Côte Vermeille

interesting church of St-Vincent. The composer Maurice Ravel (1875–1937) was born in a house at 12 Quai Ravel, on the harbour.

***Corniche Basque**

From St-Jean-de-Luz the Corniche Basque runs south-west to the resort of Hendaye and the Spanish frontier, affording impressive views, particularly at Socoa, of the wild and rugged coast.

Sare

This attractive little Basque town, still hardly affected by the tourist trade, lies a little way inland.

Côte Vermeille — K/L 12

Situation and characteristics

The Côte Vermeille ("Vermilion Coast") extends from Collioure (south-east of Perpignan) to the Spanish frontier at the Col des Balitres. The chief town is Perpignan. The stretch of coast to the north is in the Languedoc–Roussillon region (see entry).

Topography

The Côte Vermeille is rugged and much indented, with a few picturesque little towns, now popular seaside resorts, nestling in the inlets. On the hillsides, up to a height of around 300 m/1000 ft, are extensive vineyards. The name of the area comes from the reddish colour of the soil.
The road along the Côte Vermeille is an alternative to the inland road to Catalonia and the Costa Brava which crosses the frontier at the Col de Perthus.

Along the Côte Vermeille

Perpignan

See Languedoc–Roussillon

Elne

Elne (pop. 6000), once the see of a bishop, lies on a hill in the Roussillon coastal plain. In the 5th and 6th centuries it was capital of Roussillon, but it declined in importance after the bishop moved to Perpignan in 1602.

*Ste-Eulalie

The former cathedral of Ste-Eulalie is one of the most beautiful churches in France. Its right-hand tower dates from the 11th c.; the left-hand one is modern. The cloister was built in the 12th and 14th centuries; its cluster columns have richly carved capitals. The Museum displays archaeological finds from the area.

Argelès-sur-Mer

Argelès-sur-Mer, which lies a little way inland, shares with Argelès-Plage a beautiful sandy beach 6 km/4 miles long. The two places, set in a landscape of pinewoods and oleanders, are linked by a narrow-gauge railway, and offer attractive trips into the nearby hills. Argelès-sur-Mur has a small Catalan Museum. The Gothic church (14th c.) contains Late Renaissance panel paintings.

**Route des Pyrénées

The Route des Pyrénées (see Pyrenees) begins in Argelès-sur-Mer.

***Collioure**

In the Middle Ages the picturesque seaside resort of Collioure (pop. 2500) was the port of Perpignan (see Languedoc-Roussillon), and in even earlier times it was known to the Phoenicians. With its small harbour and its old castle (12th–17th c.) it attracted artists like Matisse, Derain, Braque, Picasso and Dufy. The Château des Templiers was once the summer residence of the kings of Majorca and the queen of Aragon. The fortified church dates from the 17th c.; its tower formerly served as a lighthouse. There are remains of the town's walls and ramparts.

St-Vincent

From the church a causeway runs out to the former islet of St-Vincent, crowned by a chapel, from which there are fine views of the coast.

Port-Vendres

In a sheltered inlet is Port-Vendres (the Roman Portus Veneris), a seaside resort as well as a fishing and commercial port with a harbour which is now also used by pleasure boats. In the 17th c. it was fortified by Vauban as a naval port, and still preserves the Fort du Fanal. To the east of the town Cap Béar reaches out to sea.

Banyuls-sur-Mer

Banyuls-sur-Mer, situated at the extreme southern end of the Côte Vermeille amid the last foothills of the Pyrenees, is the chief town of the wine-growing area of Banyuls, which extends from the coast into the Albères range of hills. A well-known seaside resort with a boating harbour, it is also noted for its institute of oceanographical research, which has an interesting aquarium.
Banyuls enjoys an exceptionally sheltered situation in which exotic plants flourish. On the Ile Grosse is a war memorial by the sculptor Aristide Maillol (1861–1944), who was born in Banyuls.

Cerbère

The last seaside resort before the Spanish frontier is Cerbère, with large railway marshalling yards – required because the Spanish railways have a broader gauge than the rest of Europe, so that it is necessary to change trains here. South-east of the town is Cap Cerbère, a rugged promontory of black rocks from which there is a fine view of the Spanish coast.

Col des Balitres

The French–Spanish frontier is on the Col des Balitres (173 m/568 ft).

Dauphiné

N/O 9/10

*Situation and characteristics

The French Alps, the most westerly and also the highest part of the great arc of the Alps, lie mainly within the regions of Savoy (see entry) and the Dauphiné, extending also into Provence in the south. The historical province of the Dauphiné borders Savoy on the south. With an area of some 20,000 sq. km/7700 sq. miles, it corresponds broadly to the present-day

départements of Isère (chief town Grenoble), Hautes-Alpes (Gap) and Drôme (Valence). Its capital is Grenoble.
The Dauphiné is bounded on the east by the French–Italian frontier and on the west by the Rhône. To the north it extends to the latitude of Grenoble, and to the south its boundaries are marked by the passes into Haute Provence and by such towns as Gap and Barcelonnette.
The landscape of the Dauphiné is dominated by the Pelvoux massif, one of the most magnificent parts of the Alps, which rises to 4100 m/13,450 ft to the south-east of its beautifully situated old capital of Grenoble. To the east is the high Alpine region of Upper Dauphiné, to the west the pre-Alpine region of Lower Dauphiné (see Vercors, Grande Chartreuse), an agricultural area in which plateaux alternate with valleys.
The French Alpine regions are made easily accessible by deeply indented river valleys running in different directions, and they also have most of the pass roads through the Alps, including the Route de la Bonette (2802 m/9193 ft), over the highest of the Alpine passes. The finest of the passes are linked by the Route des Grandes Alpes (Route d'Eté), while the Route Napoléon and the Route d'Hiver, which follows a similar course, run through the Alpine foreland.
An additional attraction is provided by a series of wild gorges lying close to the Routes des Alpes (Gorges de Daluis, Gorges du Cians, Gorges du Verdon, etc.).

History

The Dauphiné was inhabited by the Allobroges and other Gallic tribes when it was conquered by the Romans in 121 B.C.. Around A.D. 443 it was occupied by the Burgundians, coming from the east; then in 532 it was taken by the Franks. In 933, along with Lower Burgundy, it became part of the kingdom of Burgundy. In 1349 the territory was sold to the French crown. The name of the Dauphiné comes from the Counts of Albon, who took the forename Delfinus (French Dauphin) as their title and after conquering the County of Vienne in the 12th c. began to call themselves Dauphins du Viennois. Under an agreement reached when the territory was sold the Dauphiné became an apanage of the heir to the French throne, who then took the title of Dauphin and the heraldic emblem of a dolphin. During the religious wars of the 16th c. the Dauphiné was one of the strongholds of Protestantism.
The first stirrings of the French Revolution were felt in Grenoble and Vizille in 1788, and in 1791 the old province was divided into the départements of Isère, Drôme and Hautes-Alpes. Napoleon's return in 1815 and his passage through the Dauphiné aroused great enthusiasm for the Emperor: the troops stationed here came out in his support, and the people of Grenoble unbarred the town gates to let him in. Napoleon himself says in his memoirs: "Until I came to Grenoble I was an adventurer; in Grenoble I became a prince."

Sights

Grenoble

See entry

***Alpe d'Huez**

Alpe d'Huez, lying south-east of Grenoble at an altitude of 1860 m/6105 ft, is both a summer and a winter resort, with ample scope for walking and climbing, summer skiing and sunny ski-runs in winter. From the Dôme des Petites Rousses (2813 m/9229 ft) and the Pic du Lac Blanc there are superb panoramic views.

Bourg d'Oisans

This little climatic resort (alt. 720 m/2360 ft) in the valley of the Romanche is the chief place in the district of Oisans and an excellent base for excursions in the Dauphiné. It has interesting agricultural markets (butter, cheese, etc.). Near the town is the Cascade de la Sarennes.

Briançon

Briançon (pop. 11,800), chief town of the Briançonnais, is Europe's highest

The fortifications . . .

. . . of Briançon

town, picturesquely situated at an altitude of 1200–1326 m/3940–4350 ft above the junction of the Durance and the Guisane. It was fortified by Vauban in the 17th c. as a stronghold guarding the frontier with Italy on the Col de Montgenèvre. In 1815 it withstood a siege by Austrian forces twenty times superior in numbers, and in 1940 held out against Italian attacks.

*Old town

To the north-east of the newer district of Ste-Catherine, built on the slopes above the valley, is the old town or Ville Haute with its triple circuit of walls. The church of Notre-Dame (1718) was also designed by Vauban.

*Pont d'Asfeld

The Pont d'Asfeld, built in 1734, spans the Durance in a single arch 40 m/130 ft across and 56 m/185 ft high.
Near Briançon are the winter sports resorts of Serre-Chevalier and Montgenèvre.

Massif de Chamrousse

In the Massif de Chamrousse, to the east of Grenoble, are Chamrousse itself (alt. 1650–1750 m/5410–5740 ft), with its excellent facilities for winter sports, and Uriage-les-Bains, at the foot of the Belledonne range. The dominant feature of the landscape is the Croix de Chamrousse (2255 m/8383 ft; cableway), from which there are extensive panoramic views.

*View

Embrun

*Notre-Dame

Embrun (pop. 5800) lies at an altitude of 870 m/2855 ft on a crag 70 m/230 ft above the Durance. Once the residence of a Prince-Bishop, it is now a popular summer and winter resort. The Romanesque church of Notre-Dame, considered the most beautiful in the Dauphiné, dates from the end of the 12th c. and contains fine examples of Lombard sculpture, 15th c. stained glass, one of the oldest organs in France and a valuable church treasury.

****Col du Galibier**

*Col de l'Iseran

The Col du Galibier, in the northern Dauphiné, reaches a height (in the tunnel) of 2556 m/8386 ft and ranks with the Col de l'Iseran, 200 m/650 ft higher, as one of the highest passes in France, offering magnificent views

Gap, with the Alps as backdrop

on both the ascent and the descent. It may, however, be impassable on account of snow from October until the end of May. It is possible to climb, or take the chair-lift, to a height of 2704 m/8872 ft, the panoramic view from which is one of the most impressive in the French Alps. At the south entrance to the tunnel is a monument to Henri Desgranges, who initiated the Tour de France cycle race in 1903.

**View

Gap

Gap (pop. 31,000), chief town of the département of Hautes-Alpes, is finely situated under the chain of the Alps on the Route Napoléon, along which Napoleon travelled to Paris in March 1815.
The interesting Departmental Museum contains a 17th c. mausoleum of black marble, together with Alpine and historical collections.
Near the town, below Mont Charance (1902 m/6240 ft), is the Château de Charance, set in a beautiful park, once the residence of the bishop of Gap.

Barrage de Serre-Ponçon

20 km/12 miles east is the Barrage de Serre-Ponçon, a 120 m/395 ft high dam on the Durance, built in 1955–1961, which forms a lake with an area of some 3000 hectares/7500 acres.

La Grave
*Meije

La Grave, situated at an altitude of 1526 m/5005 ft in the upper valley of the Romanche, is a good centre for mountain walks and climbs, particularly in the Meije group, with its mighty glaciers, which rear above the village.

Hauterives

In this little town, north of Romans on N538, is the "Palais Idéal du Facteur Cheval", a fantasy building erected in the late 19th c. by the local postman, Ferdinand Cheval (b. 1836): an extraordinary structure 10 m/33 ft high, up to 26 m/85 ft long and 15 m/50 feet across, built with his own hands and inscribed with a variety of mottoes.

Route Napoléon
**Lacs de Laffrey

The four lakes of Laffrey, on the Route Napoléon, are the main features on the barren plateau of Matésine. Here, on March 7th 1815, Napoleon won over a battalion which had been sent to prevent him from advancing any farther.

Corps

Also on the Route Napoléon, between Gap and Grenoble, is the little township of Corps (pop. 1000).

*Notre-Dame de la Salette

From here a side trip can be made to the pilgrimage church of Notre-Dame de la Salette, situated at an altitude of 1170 m/3840 ft amid grand Alpine scenery. The church was built after an apparition of the Virgin to two children on September 19th 1851. Every summer something like 100,000 pilgrims make their way to Notre-Dame de la Salette.

***Pelvoux massif**

The Pelvoux massif is perhaps the most impressive group of mountains in the French Alps after Mont Blanc. It is now designated as a National Park, with glaciers, mountain valleys and breathtaking panoramic views.
The highest peaks are the Ecrins (4102 m/13,459 ft), the Meije (3983 m/13,068 ft), the Ailefroide (3953 m/12,970 ft) and Mont Pelvoux itself (3946 m/12,947 ft).

***Queyras**

The Queyras area, in the eastern Dauphiné near the Italian frontier, takes in some 45 km/28 miles of the valley of the Guil, a tributary of the Durance. The valley, dominated by the 3841 m/12,602 ft high Italian peak of Monte Viso, is one of the most unspoiled parts of the Dauphiné and has a number of resorts (Abriès, Aiguilles, Guillestre, etc.) which attract visitors in both summer and winter.

Château Queyras

Château Queyras, above the village of the same name, was built in the 13th c. and restored by Vauban. The original keep has been preserved.

Vallouise

Ailefroide

Vallouise, so named in the 15th c. in honour of Louis XI, lies in a side valley of the Durance, to the west of Briançon. In this expanse of lush green pastureland under a southern sky is the holiday resort of Ailefroide (alt. 1510 m/4955 ft), a good centre for walkers and climbers. The Cézanne Hut above the village is at the near end of the Pelvoux National Park (area 13,000 hectares/32,000 acres).

Vercors

See entry

Villard-de-Lans

The climatic and winter sports resort of Villard-de-Lans lies above Grenoble at an altitude of 1050 m/3445 ft.

Vizille

*Château

This little industrial town would be of no great importance were it not for the château of the Connétable de Lesdiguières. The nobleman who built this château was a leading Protestant who renounced his faith in 1662 in order to gain the title of Connétable. The château was begun in 1611 and completed in 1627 with the construction of a flight of steps leading down to the Renaissance-style park. At a meeting of the Estates of the Dauphiné held here in 1788 the foundation of the French Revolution was laid with a demand for the personal freedom of all Frenchmen.

Dijon

N7

Region: Bourgogne (Burgundy). Département: Côte-d'Or
Altitude: 250 m/820 ft. Population: 156,000

Situation and characteristics

Dijon, once capital of the duchy of Burgundy and now chief town of the département of Côte-d'Or, the see of a bishop and a university town, lies in hilly country at the junction of the rivers Ouche and Suzon. It preserves many buildings of the ducal period which are among the finest in France. Dijon is also an industrial town and a centre of the wine trade. Among its best known products are mustard and cassis (black currant liqueur).

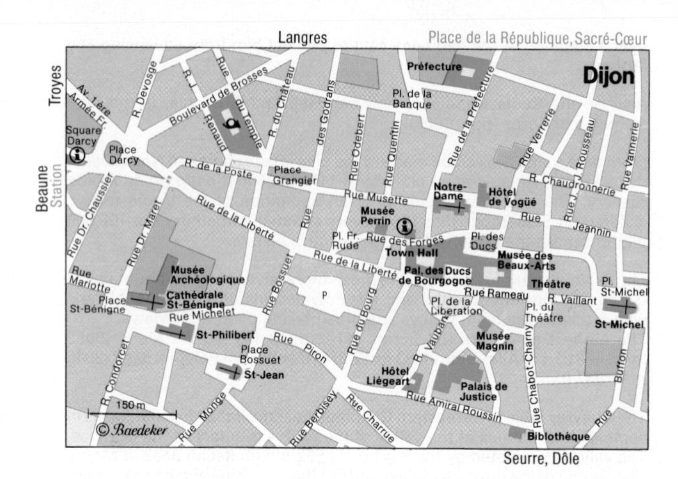

History

In Roman times Dijon (Dibio) was a fortified post on the road from Lyons to Mainz. After many centuries of vicissitudes it became part of the duchy of Burgundy in the 11th c. and was soon raised to the status of its capital. In the 14th and 15th centuries, under Dukes Philip the Bold (1364–1404), John the Fearless (1404–1419), Philip the Good (1419–1467) and Charles the Bold (1467–1477), Dijon enjoyed a first cultural growth.

At the end of the 18th c. the English traveller Arthur Young wrote: "Dijon, on the whole, is a handsome town; the streets, though old built, are wide and very well paved, with the addition, uncommon in France, of *trottoirs.*" At that time Dijon had no more than 20,000 inhabitants. It was only in the mid 19th c., with the increase in trade and traffic, that it began to develop into the large city that we see today.

Sights

Old town

The central feature of the old town is the semicircular colonnaded Place de la Libération, which was built between 1682 and 1701, along with the Ducal Palace, by Jules Hardouin-Mansart, the architect responsible for Versailles.

*Palais des Ducs

The Baroque Palais des Ducs de Bourgogne incorporates parts of the earlier medieval structure. To the rear of the palace is the 15th c. Tour de Philippe le Bon, from the platform of which (reached by climbing 316 steps) there are fine panoramic views.

**Musée des Beaux-Arts

The east wing of the Ducal Palace is occupied by the Musée des Beaux-Arts, one of France's leading art museums. On the ground floor are displays illustrating the history of the building and the museum and a collection of medieval and Renaissance Burgundian sculpture. In the old palace kitchen are six large fireplaces. The first floor is devoted to painting and sculpture: medieval Flemish, Swiss and German painting, Italian pictures of the 14th–18th centuries, Flemish and Dutch painting of the 16th and 17th centuries, French pictures of the 16th–20th centuries and sculpture of the 15th–20th centuries. In the Salle des Gardes are the tombs of two Dukes of Burgundy, Philip the Bold and John the Fearless, and altarpieces from the Chartreuse de Champmol, which was devastated in 1792.

Hôtel de Ville

In the west wing of the palace is the Hôtel de Ville (Town Hall), once the lodgings used by the kings of France when visiting Dijon, with a vaulted vestibule.

North of the Ducal Palace is the church of Notre-Dame (13th c.), a beautiful building in Burgundian Gothic style. The façade is articulated horizontally by two galleries, between which are gargoyles in the form of grotesque figures. The church has a clock-tower (1382) with mechanical figures; originally there was only a single male figure, but in the course of time (most recently in 1881) he has been joined by a woman and two children. Inside, in a chapel on the right, is an 11th c. "Black Virgin", one of the oldest pieces of wood sculpture in France. The church also contains a fine tapestry altar-cloth and a modern tapestry depicting the unsuccessful siege of 1513 and the liberation of 1944.

*Notre-Dame

There are charming old houses to the east of Notre-Dame, in Rue Verrerie, Rue Chaudronnerie and Rue Vannerie, and also in Rue des Forges, between the Ducal Palace and Notre-Dame.

*Rue des Forges

To the east of the Ducal Palace is the 16th c. church of St-Michel, in Flamboyant style, with three richly decorated doorways.
South of the Ducal Palace is the Palais de Justice (Law Courts; 16th and 17th c.).

*St-Michel

West of the Ducal Palace is the twin-towered Gothic Cathedral of St-Bénigne (1280–1314), originally the church of a Benedictine abbey. It incorporates a Romanesque doorway and a large crypt with the tomb of St Bénigne and pre-Romanesque capitals from an earlier church on the same site. The dormitory of the abbey now contains an archaeological museum (Roman and medieval antiquities).

*Cathedral

*Crypt

Also of interest is the Hôtel Lantin, a 17th c. mansion which was adapted by Auguste Perret to house the Musée Magnin, with a large collection of pictures, mainly French.

Musée Magnin

On the western edge of the town can be seen the remains of the Chartreuse de Champmol, with a church door and Moses fountain dating from 1404. Once the burial place of the Dukes of the House of Valois, it is now a psychiatric clinic.

Chartreuse de Champmol

Fontainebleau

See Ile de France

Gascony

G–I 10/11

The Pyrenean foreland, extending between the Atlantic and the Mediterranean, is essentially an area of passage, with a landscape pattern of Mediterranean type to the east, while the great forests in the west have something of a Central European character.
The southern part of the Garonne basin, most of which is in Gascony, is similar in many respects to the larger Paris basin, but is bordered on the south by the Pyrenees, rising out of the lower ground almost without transition.
Gascony takes its name from the Basques (Vascones), who were driven out of Spain by the Visigoths at the end of the 6th c. and settled in the Garonne lowlands.
Gascony takes in the present-day départements of Gers, Landes and Hautes-Pyrénées and parts of the Gironde, Lot-et-Garonne, Tarn-et-Garonne, Haute-Garonne and Ariège.

Situation and characteristics

Gascony is made up of a number of territories, some of them of considerable importance, which in earlier times had an independent existence. It lies in the western Pyrenean foreland, roughly between the Garonne in the north and east and the Atlantic (Gulf of Gascony or Bay of Biscay) in the

Topography

west. In the western part of Gascony, adjoining the beautiful Côte d'Argent (see below), are the extensive pine and cork-oak forests of the Landes *(lande* = "heath"). This was once a boggy area in which the herdsmen went about on stilts, but from the late 18th c. onwards the land was drained and planted with trees. Much of it is now also in agricultural use (maize). Along the flat coast of the Atlantic seaboard are chains of dunes over 100 m/330 ft high, the highest in Europe. On the landward side are large coastal lagoons *(étangs)*. To the south-west is the Basque country, extending far into Spanish territory. Farther east, round the town of Auch, is the old county of Armagnac.

Armagnac

The name of Armagnac has become well known thanks to the liqueur brandy which is produced here, principally in Haut-Armagnac, Ténarèze and Bas-Armagnac.

History

Gascony was part of the Roman province of Aquitania, into which the Basques, fleeing from the Visigoths in Spain, penetrated towards the end of the 6th c. During the period of Frankish rule, from 768, Vasconia was a separate duchy, and with the decline of Carolingian power it became increasingly independent. When the native dynasty died out in the middle of the 11th c. Gascony passed to the Aquitanian Duchy of Guyenne. Along with the County of Armagnac, and thanks to the valour of the Armagnacs, Gascony controlled almost the whole of France in the time of Count Bernard VII (1391–1418). Later the Armagnacs were employed by King Charles VII as mercenaries against the Swedes, who inflicted a crushing defeat on them in a battle near Basle in 1444. The remains of the mercenary army made their way into Alsace and south-western Germany, robbing and plundering, and then gradually dispersed.
Gascony's exposed situation meant that it was frequently ravaged by war, as its many ruined castles bear witness.
As part of the French kingdom from 1453, Gascony was one of its largest provinces, until the French Revolution replaced the old historical territories by the départements into which Gascony is now divided.

Sights in Gascony

Auch

In Roman times Auch (pop. 25,000), on the river Gers, was the chief town of the Ausci, which gave it its name. In the Middle Ages it became capital of the county of Armagnac and later of Gascony, and is now chief town of the département of Gers. Since the 9th c. Auch has been the see of an archbishop. In the old part of the town, beautifully situated on a hill above the river, is the Gothic Cathedral of Ste-Marie (1489–1662), with a beautiful porch.

*Choir-stalls

The cathedral is notable particularly for its 113 magnificent choir-stalls (1520–1551). The choir chapels have superb Renaissance stained glass by Arnaut de Moles; the organ is 17th c. From the square in front of the cathedral a monumental staircase (1864) of 232 steps leads down to the Gers. A former Jacobin chapel now houses a museum of art and archaeology.

Fleurance

Fleurance, 24 km/15 miles north of Auch, has an important 14th c. church in the Gothic style of southern France and a square surrounded by arcades. The layout of this little town still reflects the plan of the fortified settlement of 1280.

Lectoure

11 km/7 miles north of Fleurance, on a hill above the Gers valley, is Lectoure, once the see of a bishop. From the promenade laid out on a former bastion there are magnificent views extending to the Pyrenees. The town has a Gothic church and an archaeological museum with early medieval altars.

Condom (pop. 9000), on the river Baïse, was the see of a bishop until 1789. It is an attractive little town, with the former cathedral of St-Pierre (1506–1521) and a Town Hall housed in the former Bishop's Palace (16th c. cloister). The Musée de l'Armagnac has displays illustrating the manufacture of armagnac and the old trade routes along which it was transported.

Condom

Larresingle, west of Condom on D15, is a small fortified village of the 13th c.

Larresingle

Dax (pop. 20,000) was already noted for its thermal springs in Roman times, when it was known as Aquae Tarbellicae. The principal spring is the Fontaine Chaude (64°C/147°F). Other features of interest are the remains of the Roman town walls (4th c.) and the cathedral (17th–18th c.), which has a beautiful Gothic doorway (13th c.) from an earlier church.

Dax

Mirande (pop. 4000), north-east of Tarbes, has an arcaded square and a 15th c. church with an unusual tower. The Musée Delort has a series of charming paintings of Gascony.

Mirande

Mont-de-Marsan (pop. 31,000), chief town of the département of Landes, lies at the junction of two little rivers, the Midour and the Douze, which unite to form the Midouze. The Municipal Museum, housed in two 14th c. buildings, contains an archaeological collection and works by modern sculptors. The Fêtes de la Madeleine in July are a great annual occasion, with bullfights, horse races and other events.

Mont-de-Marsan

It is worth making a detour to see this little village (pop. 800), 8 km/5 miles south of Saramon on the Auch-Foix road. Its fortified church (14th–15th c.), restored by Viollet-le-Duc in the 19th c., has fine choir-stalls and stained glass.

Simorre

Vic-Fezensac is noted for a great annual event, the bullfights which take place at Whitsun.

Vic-Fezensac

Côte d'Argent

Situation and characteristics

The Côte d'Argent ("Silver Coast") extends from the Gironde estuary in the north to beyond Bayonne on the Spanish frontier in the south before joining the Côte des Basques (see entry) to the south-west.
The charm of this stretch of coast lies in its beautiful beaches of silvery sand, fringed by areas of woodland, a number of attractive lakes and dunes which reach a height of more than 100 m/330 ft at Pyla. Along the coasts are numbers of seaside resorts like Soulac-sur-Mer, Arcachon and Mimizan.

Topography

For many centuries the masses of sand deposited on the coast at an annual rate of around 15 cu. m per metre of coast (18 cu. yds per yard) were blown eastwards by the wind and formed travelling dunes which reached far inland, advancing at the rate of up to 25 m/80 ft a year. The land farther in from the coast became a mixture of sandy steppe and heathland, clogging up the rivers and forming expanses of infertile and unhealthy bog and marshland. Towards the end of the 18th c. efforts were made to consolidate the dunes by planting coniferous trees, and by 1867 3000 hectares/7500 acres of coastal dunes and 80,000 hectares/200,000 acres of inland dunes had been consolidated in this way, transforming the former barren landscape into a green belt of pines and oaks. Between 1943 and 1950, however, a third of the 900,000 hectares/2,250,000 acres in existence in 1939 was destroyed by devastating forest fires – a loss which has since been made good by reafforestation. The area is now increasingly being developed for agricultural use (maize).

Arcachon

The bathing and thermal resort of Arcachon (pop. 13,000) consists of the

Ville d'Eté ("Summer Town"), with many parks and gardens, which extends for 5 km/3 miles along the Bassin d'Arcachon, and the Ville d'Hiver ("Winter Town") to the south, in an area of wooded dunes. Round the Ile aux Oiseaux, in the middle of the Bassin d'Arcachon, are oyster-beds.
At Pyla, south-west of Arcachon, is a travelling dune 114 m/375 ft high, which can be climbed.

Mimizan
*Tower

In the Middle Ages Mimizan was a considerable port, but its harbour silted up in the 18th c. West of the town stands the tower of an old Benedictine church, and on the coast is the resort of Mimizan-Plage.

Hossegor

This fashionable resort, with numerous villas, lies on the coast north of Bayonne, round a brackish coastal lagoon.

Capbreton

Capbreton (pop. 4800) was once an important port, the home of seamen who had sailed as far afield as Newfoundland in 1392. It is now a popular seaside resort.

Gorges du Tarn L10

**Situation and characteristics
*Gorges de la Jonte

The canyon-like gorges of the Tarn, which are at their most impressive between Ste-Enimie and Les Vignes and are continued by the fine Gorges de la Jonte between Le Rozier and Meyrueis, are one of the most striking scenic features in France. They can be followed by road and also, in some stretches, by boat.

History

The Tarn, rising on Mont Lozère in the north-eastern and highest part of the Cévennes (see entry), follows a winding course hewn deep in the limestone of the Causses. The valley was carved out in a number of phases, the last of which extended over something like a million years, forming sheer cliffs which tower above the valley bottom to heights of up to 500 m/1650 ft.
After a course of some 375 km/235 miles the Tarn flows into the Garonne at Moissac, north-west of Toulouse.

Through the **Gorges du Tarn

Starting-point
*Ste-Enimie

Florac, at the foot of the Causse Méjean, to the east, is the best starting-point for a trip through the Gorges du Tarn, as well as a link with the exploration of the Cévennes. From here D907B runs parallel with the river to Ste-Enimie, an old-world little town situated above a bend in the Tarn. In the Vieux Logis, an old granary, is a small local museum. Encircling a former monastery with a Romanesque chapterhouse are remains of the old town walls. The church, originally 12th c., was much altered in later centuries. The Ermitage de Ste-Enimie, a chapel built in a cave, is said to have been occupied by the saint after whom the town is named.

Mende
**Aven Armand

From here it is possible either to go north to Mende or south on D986 to the Aven Armand, a magnificent stalactitic cave, with stalagmites up to 30 m/100 ft high, which was discovered in 1897 but opened to the public only in 1926.

La Malène
*Détroits
*Cirque des Baumes

The next place of any size in the Tarn valley is the finely situated village of La Malène, the starting-point of a boat trip of more than one hour through the narrow Détroits ("Straits"), which cannot be reached from the road, to the Cirque des Baumes. The road then runs past the Pas de Souci, where the river disappears under a tumble of rocks.

****Point Sublime**

From the little village of Les Vignes a side road winds steeply up to the most impressive viewpoint in the Gorges, the Point Sublime, 400 m/1300 ft above the bed of the river.

Le Rozier

From Les Vignes it is possible to take a boat trip to Le Rozier, at the junction

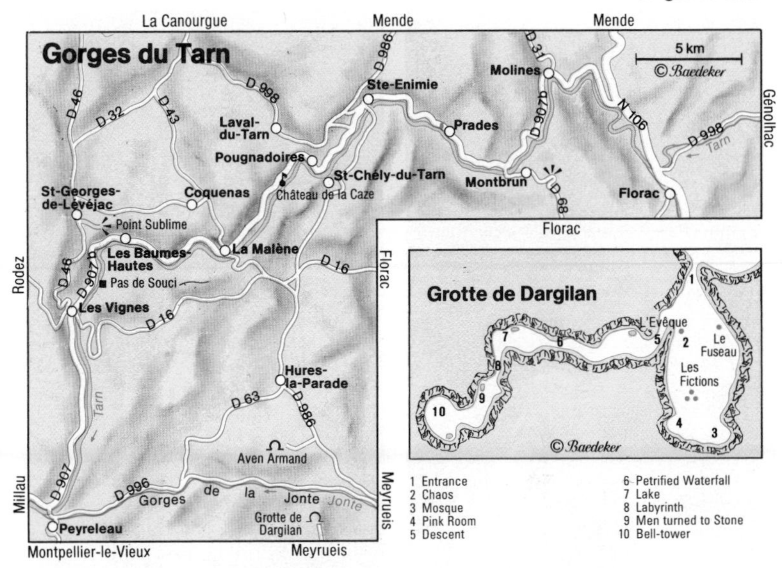

of the Tarn and the Jonte. Le Rozier gets its name from the roses grown here by monks in the 11th c. Above the village is the crag of Capluc, with a ruined castle and a view of the Causse Méjean.

***Gorges de la Jonte**

From Le Rozier it is possible to continue to Millau (pop. 22,000), situated in the Tarn basin at an altitude of 379 m/1245 ft, a glove-making town with old arcaded houses and a Gothic church. It is well worth while, however, to turn east through the Gorges de la Jonte, less imposing than the Tarn gorges but equally romantic. The gorges are particularly impressive between Le Rozier and Meyrueis; the best viewpoint is the Belvédère des Terrasses, just off the road.

***Montpellier-le-Vieux**

From Le Rozier or Millau there is a rewarding trip (12 km/7½ miles or 18 km/11 miles) to the rock labyrinth of Montpellier-le-Vieux, a series of bizarre rock formations which in places looks like a ruined town. A walk round the site (signposted) takes about 1½ hours. From the higher points there are fine views of the Causses.

Roquefort

20 km/12½ miles south-west of Millau is the little town of Roquefort, famous for its cheese; visitors can see round the cellars in which it is matured.

***Grotte de Dargilan**

Near Meyrueis, at an altitude of 850 m/2790 ft is an interesting stalactitic cave, the Grotte de Dargilan, 1600 m/1750 yds long, with magnificent stalactites and stalagmites. See plan above.

Excursion to Rodez

Rodez (pop. 27,000), chief town of the département of Aveyron, lies on a hill above the Aveyron, between Auvergne and Toulouse. On the east side of the Place d'Armes is the fortress-like Cathedral of Notre-Dame (13th–16th c.), its west front flanked by two unfinished towers. The upper part of the

*Cathedral

Gorges du Tarn

Bell-tower of Rodez Cathedral

bell-tower on its north side has delicate Flamboyant tracery. The interior is richly decorated. The third chapel on the right has a fine stone screen (15th c.) and a Holy Sepulchre (16th c.). In the transept are a magnificent 15th c. rood screen and a beautifully carved organ gallery (17th c.). The choir has Late Gothic stalls. On the north side of the cathedral are the Bishop's Palace (17th c.) and the Tour de Corbières (1443), a relic of the old town walls. Also of interest are the Romanesque church of St-Amans (12th c., rebuilt in 18th c.), with beautiful capitals and 16th c. tapestries, the Musée Fenaille (archaeological finds, medieval sculpture, applied art) and the Musée des Beaux-Arts (pictures and sculpture).

Belcastel

Farther upstream is the little town of Belcastel, dominated by the ruins of its castle.

Grasse

See Côte d'Azur

Grenoble

N9

Region: Rhône–Alpes
Département: Isère
Altitude: 210 m/690 ft
Population: 160,000

Situation and characteristics

Grenoble, the old capital of the Dauphiné, is beautifully situated in a basin in the Isère valley, surrounded by mountains rising to 3000 m/9900 ft. It is the chief town of the département of Isère, an important industrial centre

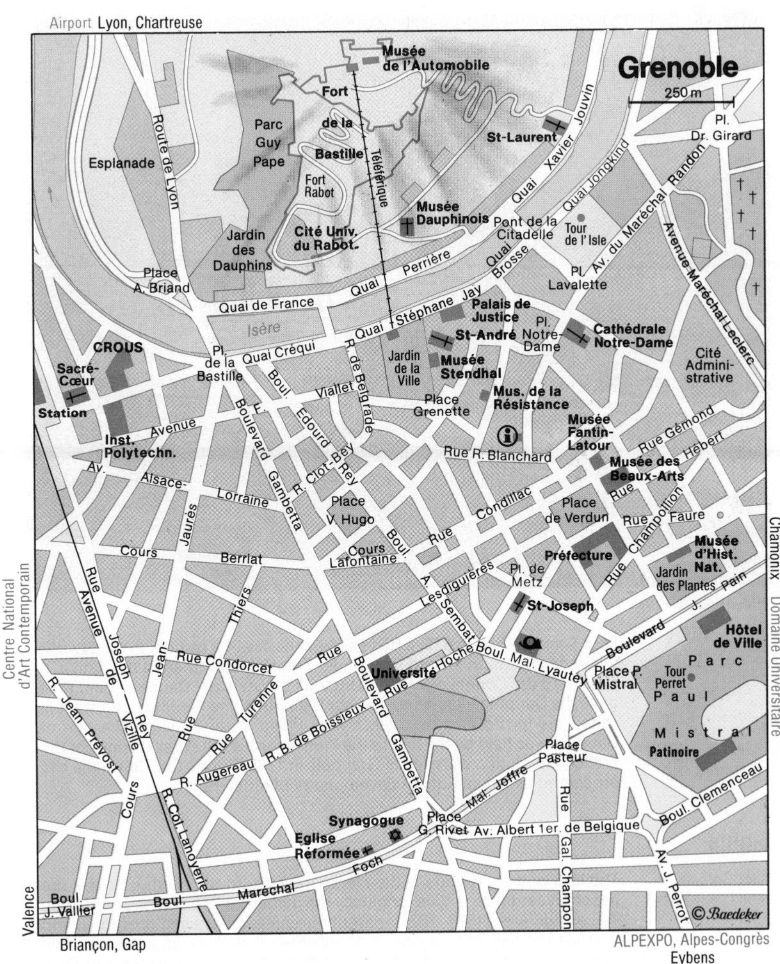

and a university town. The city attracted the eyes of the world when the Winter Olympics were held here in 1968, leading to a great increase in tourist traffic. Important contributions are made to the city's economy by glove manufacture and the walnuts which are grown in the lower Isère valley between Tullins and St-Marcellin.
The city is dominated on the north by Fort Rabot and, higher up, the Fort de la Bastille, both situated on foothills of the 5 km/3 mile long Mont Rachais range (1045 m/3429 ft).
Grenoble was the birthplace of the 19th c. novelist Stendhal (Henri Beyle, 1783–1842).

History

Originally a city of the Allobroges, under the name of Cularo, Grenoble was enlarged by the Emperor Gratian in A.D. 379 and renamed Gratianopolis.

Jardin de la Ville

Four years earlier, in 375, it had become the see of a bishop. In the 5th c. it fell under Burgundian and later under Frankish rule; then in the 12th c. it passed to the Counts of Albon, who took the style of "Dauphin" and thus gave the Dauphiné its name. The last Dauphin of the Viennois, Humbert II, ceded his territory to the French king Philip VI, after which the title of Dauphin was held by the heir to the French throne. The first stirrings of the French Revolution were felt in Grenoble in 1788. During the 19th c. the city prospered as a result of the development of industry.

Sights

Place Grenette
Jardin de la Ville

The hub of the city's life is the Place Grenette. To the north of this is the beautiful Jardin de la Ville, originally the gardens of the château of the Duc de Lesdiguières (1543–1626); part of the château has been preserved and

Musée Stendhal

the old town hall now houses the Musée Stendhal. The station for the cable railway (télérifique) leading to the Bastille is to the found on the Quai Stephane Jay.

St-André

On the east side of Place St-André is the church of St-André, built in 1220–1236 as the Dauphin's palace chapel, with a Gothic tower of 1298. In the north transept is a 17th c. monument to the Chevalier Bayard, the knight *sans peur et sans reproche*.

*Palais de Justice

On the north side of the square is the Palais de Justice (Law Courts; 15th–16th c.), originally the meeting-place of the Estates of the Dauphiné, with a beautiful Early Renaissance façade. The former Chambre de la Cour des Comptes has fine carved panelling (1521–1524).

Cathedral

In the Place Notre-Dame, to the east of Place St-André, is the Cathedral of Notre-Dame (11th–15th c.), with a beautiful interior. In the choir, on the right, is a tabernacle of 1455–1457, more than 14 m/45 ft high, robbed of its statues.

Parks and gardens

Grenoble is well supplied with parks and gardens. On the far side of the Isère, below the Fort de la Bastille, are the Jardin des Dauphins (orientation table) and the Parc Guy-Pape, both with views of Fort Rabot, built on a rocky crag. In the south-east of the city is the Parc Paul-Mistral, in which are a number of modern buildings including the Olympic Stadium, built in 1967, which seats 70,000 spectators. There is another park on the banks of the Isère opposite the church of St-Laurent.

Museums
*Musée des Beaux-Arts

The Musée des Beaux-Arts, in the Place de Verdun, is one of the most important museums in France. The old masters are well represented by Palmezzano, Le Pérugin, Veronese, Tintoretto, P. Brueghel, Cranach, Rubens, Velásquez, Murillo, Goya, Dürer, Zurbarán and many others; the moderns are not forgotten, either , with works by von Bonnard, Vuillard, Renoir, Monet, Sisley, Signac, Vlaminck, Matisse, Miró, Ernst, Tanguy, Mathieu, Soutine, Modigliani, Derain, Picasso, Delaunay, Braque, Léger, Fautrier and Giacometti. Contemporary artists include Morellet, Paolozzi, Cane, Sol Lewitt, Sam Francis and Wesselman. The museum also houses an important Egyptian collection.

*Musée Dauphinois
Musée Hébert

Also of interest are the Musée Dauphinois (history and culture of the Dauphiné), the Musée Hébert (works by the 19th c. painter of that name), a museum, in the house where Stendhal was born, which deals with the story of the French Resistance, and the Natural History Museum (fauna of the Alps, mineralogy).

Centre National d'Art Contemporain

In the west of the city, housed in an industrial building designed by Gustave Eiffel (1900), is the new Centre of Contemporary Art, opened in 1986. It puts on periodic special exhibitions, and also has facilities for the training of young artists.

*Fort de la Bastille

The best general view of the city is to be had by taking the cableway from Quai Stéphane-Jay up to the Fort de la Bastille. This fort high up on the hill was a prison; now old motor cars and motor cycles are on display.

St-Laurent

Under the east side of the hill crowned by the Fort de la Bastille is the church of St-Laurent (11th c., restored in 16th and 17th c.), which is built over a lower church, a Merovingian crypt of the 6th–7th c.

Tour Perret

There are also good views from the Tour Perret (86 m/282 ft high; lift) in the Parc Paul-Mistral. 2 km/1½ miles south of the park is the Olympic Stadium (1967), with seating for 70,000 spectators.

Other new buildings

Other interesting new buildings are the Town Hall (by Maurice Novarina, 1967), the Maison de la Culture (by André Vogenski, 1968, with three large halls and important modern works of art, and the Ice Stadium (by Junillon and Demartini).

Surroundings of Grenoble

Excursions

Possible excursions from Grenoble are to the Vercors (see entry) by way of the attractive winter sports resort of Villard-de-Lans (1043 m/3420 ft), to the Pelvoux massif and Chamrousse (see Dauphiné), and – an experience not to be missed – to the Grande Chartreuse (alt. 961 m/3153 ft), mother house of the Carthusian order, which was founded by St Bruno in 1084.

*Grande Chartreuse

Le Havre

H5

Region: Haute-Normandie. Département: Seine-Maritime
Altitude: 1–5 m/3–16 ft. Population: 200,000

Situation and characteristics

Le Havre, France's largest port after Marseilles, situated on the estuary of the Seine, here 9 km/6 miles wide, suffered heavy destruction during the Second World War and had to be almost completely rebuilt. The modern aspect of the city is due primarily to the architect Auguste Perret.
The Impressionist painter Claude Monet (1840–1926) lived and worked in

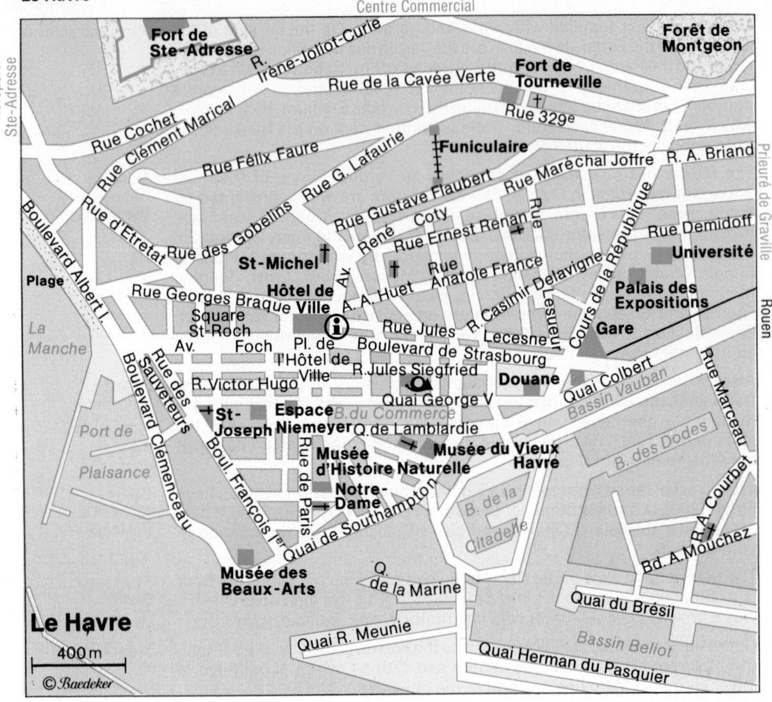

Le Havre, and the writer Raymond Queneau (1903–1976), author of "Zazie dans le Métro" and "Pierrot mon Ami", was born here.

History

The town was founded in 1517 and, on the orders of Francis I, was provided with a harbour which was ready to receive the first warship in the following year. Later Le Havre developed into an important commercial port, mainly involved in the North American traffic.
After the American War of Independence Le Havre became the main centre for the import of colonial products like coffee, tobacco, cotton, sugar and exotic woods.

Sights

City centre

The rebuilt city centre offers interesting examples of modern architecture, like the spacious Place de l'Hôtel-de-Ville with its functional tower blocks. From here the wide Avenue Foch runs west to the Porte Océane.
The modern church of St-Joseph, to the south of the Avenue Foch, is a steel and concrete structure with a 106 m/350 ft high tower from which there are magnificent views.
Another interesting feature is the 160 m/175 yd long escalator from Rue Aristide-Briand to the upper town (which can also be reached from the Cours de la République through the Jenner Tunnel).
From the west end of Avenue Foch the bathing beach runs north, flanked by the Boulevard Albert-1er, which continues for 4 km/2½ miles through the outlying district of Ste-Adresse with its numerous villas to the suburb of Nice Havrais (the "Nice of Le Havre").

Museums

Of the city's museums the Musée des Beaux-Arts is notable mainly for its collection of paintings from the 16th c. to the present day, while the Musée de l'Ancien Havre displays material on the history of the town and on seafaring.
The church of Ste-Honorine de Graville (11th–13th c.), which has a "Black Madonna", houses a museum of sculpture (works of the 12th–16th c.). In Place Gambetta, built partly underground, is the Oskar Niemeyer Cultural Centre, which bears the name of its architect.

Harbour tour

A trip round the modern port installations makes an interesting experience. Rouen–Le Havre is France's largest port after Fos–Marseilles and comes fourth in Europe, after Rotterdam and Antwerp as well as Fos–Marseilles.

Ile de France

I–L 5/6

Situation and characteristics

The Ile de France, the inner part of the Paris basin, is the heartland of France, surrounded by the plains of Normandy, Champagne and Beauce and the district of Caux. Altogether fourteen different historical territories form a girdle round Paris; and all the time the conurbation of Paris and its suburbs is reaching out ever farther into the open country which surrounds it.
The name of the Ile de France goes back to the 10th c., in the time of the Capetian kings, when the medieval counties in the region round Paris were united to form the duchy of Francia and later incorporated in the kingdom of France as the province of Ile de France. The province is now divided into the départements of Seine-et-Marne (chief town Melun), Yvelines (Versailles), Essonne (Evry), Hauts-de-Seine (Nanterre), Seine–St-Denis (Bobigny), Val-de-Marne (Créteil) and Val-d'Oise (Beauvais).
The Ile de France is the area in France where the French language and French art and culture had their origin. In this region round the capital are a series of splendid châteaux (Versailles, Fontainebleau and Compiègne being the best known) set in beautiful parks, great forests like those of Fontainebleau, Compiègne, Rambouillet and Chantilly, and such magnificent churches and cathedrals as those of Chartres (see entry), St-Denis and Senlis.
Although visitors will be mainly interested in sights such as these, they will discover that agriculture and industry are also important elements in the life of the Ile de France.

New towns

Since 1965 five new towns *(villes nouvelles)* – Cergy-Pontoise, Evry, St-Quentin-en-Yvelines, Marne-la-Vallée and Melun-Sénart – have been established to relieve the pressure on Paris. These futuristic examples of modern town planning have appeared on the map only since the 1970s. The best known of the architects responsible for these developments are Manolo Nuñes and Ricardo Bofill.

Sport and recreation in the Ile de France

The Valois district is traditionally the home of archery. The Forest of Fontainebleau offers scope for rock climbing among other activities. There are plenty of opportunities for riding in the forests, and there are horse shows and other events at Barbizon, Chantilly, Compiègne and Fontainebleau, and racecourses at Chantilly, Maisons-Laffitte and St-Cloud (flat racing), Vincennes (trotting), Enghien (steeplechasing), Compiègne, Fontainebleau and Rambouillet. The Seine and its tributaries offer facilities for water sports – rowing at Lagny, sailing at Draveil, Les Mureaux, Poissy, St-Fargeau, Ponthierry, Triel and Villennes-sur-Seine. Fishing is available in the rivers and lakes.
For information about golf and tennis, leisure parks, museums and gardens see the appropriate entries in the Practical Information section.

The principal sights in the Ile de France are listed below in alphabetical order.

Sights

Anet

Anet (pop. 2500), west of Paris, has a pretty Renaissance château (see Normandy).

Auvers-sur-Oise

This little town (pop. 5600), north of Paris, was the haunt of many painters in the 19th c. Among those who worked in Auvers-sur-Oise were Cézanne, Corot, Pissarro and Renoir. Vincent van Gogh committed suicide here in 1890, and he and his brother Théo are buried in the cemetery. The 18th c. château contains a museum devoted to the Impressionists and particularly to van Gogh.

Barbizon

Barbizon (pop. 1200), south of Paris on the edge of Fontainebleau Forest, gave its name to the Barbizon school of painters, a loosely knit group, including Corot, Millet and Daumier, who broke away from the classical academic school of studio painting and painted direct from nature. Visitors can see Millet's studio. The Musée de l'Ecole de Barbizon has works by Rousseau, Diaz, Troyon, Charles Jacques and other artists as well as various items illustrating the history of the town.

Beauvais

Beauvais (pop. 54,000), situated on the left bank of the Thérain in the northern part of the Ile de France, was once an important episcopal city with a famous tapestry manufactory (closed down during the Second World War). In the centre of the town is the spacious Place Jeanne-Hachette, named after the victorious defender of the city against Charles the Bold of Burgundy in 1472. On the south side of the square is the Hôtel de Ville (Town Hall), with an 18th c. façade. A little to the south is the church of St-Etienne (12th, 13th and 18th c.; rebuilt 1945), which has fine Renaissance stained glass (including a Tree of Jesse) and a Romanesque rose window in the north transept with an allegory of human life (the Wheel of Fortune).

* St-Etienne

** Cathedral

North-west of Place Jeanne-Hachette is the magnificent Gothic Cathedral of St-Pierre, the building of which began in 1227 and continued, with interruptions, until 1578, though only the choir and transept were completed. Faulty design led to the collapse of the vaulting in 1247 and again in 1284, but after rebuilding it is still the highest vaulted roof in the world. The crossing-tower, which was 153 m/502 ft high, collapsed in 1573 and was never rebuilt. The façades of the transepts (16th c.), in Flamboyant style, were the work of Jean le Pot. The 19th c. astronomical clock, which has over 90,000 individual parts, is a copy of the one in Strasbourg Cathedral. Other notable features are the stained glass (14th–16th c.), the rich treasury and the National Tapestry Museum behind the apse. The Gothic Bishop's Palace now houses an interesting museum (archaeology, painting and sculpture).

Bonneval

With its old houses and circuit of walls, this little town south-west of Paris has preserved something of its medieval character. The church is 12th c. The former abbey (12th–17th c.) is now a psychiatric hospital.

Le Bourget

Le Bourget, on the northern outskirts of Paris, is one of the city's three airports, established in 1914. Charles Lindbergh landed here in 1927 after his famous transatlantic flight. The Musée de l'Air et de l'Espace has a large collection of material illustrating the development of flying from 1884 to 1945.

Breteuil

6 km/4 miles south of Chevreuse is this sumptuously appointed 17th c. château, set in a park designed by the famous landscape architect André Le Nôtre (1613–1700).

Cergy-Pontoise

This new town north-west of Paris is planned to house an eventual population of 200,000. It has a leisure park, Mirapolis, offering 55 hectares/135 acres of entertainments for both adults and children.

Châalis

The remains of this Cistercian abbey, founded in 1136, still bear witness to

Château de Chantilly

its former greatness. One side of the 13th c. cloister, the chapel (also 13th c., with frescoes by Primaticcio) and the abbot's lodgings are all that have survived the devastation and plundering of the centuries. A sumptuous building of 1740 houses a museum (furniture, pictures, religious sculpture, mementoes of Jean-Jacques Rousseau).

Champeux

Champeux, south-east of Paris, has a beautiful church (1160–1315) with a fine interior (stalls of 1522).

Champlieu

Champlieu, north-east of Paris on the edge of Compiègne Forest, has Gallo-Roman remains (a theatre 70 m/230 ft in diameter with seating for 4000 spectators, baths and Christian catacombs).

*** Champs**

This early 18th c. château to the east of Paris, sumptuously decorated by Madame de Pompadour, was acquired by the State in 1935. The most notable feature of the interior is the Salon Chinois. The beautiful park was laid out by Claude Desgots, a nephew of Le Nôtre, and lovingly restored at the beginning of the 20th c.

Chantilly

Chantilly (pop. 10,000), north of Paris, was the residence of the Princes of Bourbon-Condé in the 17th and 18th centuries. On an island on the east side of the town is the château, which consists of the Petit Château, built about 1560 for Connétable Anne de Montmorency, and the modern Grand Château (1876–1881).

** Château

* Musée Condé

The interior of the Château, now owned by the Institut de France and open to the public as the Musée Condé, is a fine example of the magnificent residences of the *grands seigneurs* of the 19th c.
The Grand Château has a well stocked picture gallery. The principal treasure of the library in the Petit Château is a magnificently illuminated prayerbook, the "Très Riches Heures" of the Duc de Berry (1410–1416). The park, mainly laid out by Le Nôtre, the little 17th c. hunting lodge known as

the Maison de Silvie, the Jeu de Paume (Tennis Court) of 1757 and the Ecuries (Stables, designed by Jean Aubert), together with the Château itself and the surrounding forest, are the centre of a fashionable and popular holiday area. The Ecuries now house a Musée Vivant du Cheval et du Pony, which covers everything to do with horses. Important race meetings are held in the Hippodrome.

Chartres

See entry

Châteaudun
*Château

Châteaudun, south-west of Paris on the banks of the Loir, is dominated by its château (10th–16th c.). The most notable features of the interior are two staircases and the chapel (1464), which is richly decorated with wall paintings and sculpture. From the terrace there are fine views. Of interest in the old town are the church of the Madeleine and a number of old houses (mainly in Rue St-Lubin and Rue des Huiteries). The newer part of the town was laid out in 1723, after a fire, to the design of Jules Hardouin-Mansart. The principal features of interest are the Museum (prehistoric, Egyptian and medieval antiquities; ornithological collection) and the cemetery, with a fine doorway from the chapel of Notre-Dame-du-Champdé, destroyed at the end of the 19th c.

Château-Thierry

This little town to the east of Paris was the birthplace of La Fontaine (1621–1695), author of the famous "Fables". There is a small La Fontaine Museum. Other features of interest are the remains of a castle, old houses, an old town gate, a bell-tower of the 15th–16th c. and a hospital founded in 1304.

Châtenay-Malabry

Châtenay, south of Paris, was the birthplace in 1694 of Voltaire. The church of St-Germain-l'Auxerrois was built in the 11th c. and altered in the 13th. The Maison de Chateaubriand was the home of the writer René de Chateaubriand (1768–1848) for more than ten years.

Chevreuse

Above this little town on the river Yvette are the ruins of the Château de la Madeleine (towers of the 11th–12th c.). South of the church (12th–17th c., with a 12th c. tower) is the 12th c. doorway of the former priory of St-Saturnin.

Compiègne

*Château

Compiègne (pop. 44,000), north of Paris on the left bank of the Oise, was a favourite residence of the rulers of France from Merovingian times onwards, and with its great château and extensive forest is still a popular holiday destination. Here Joan of Arc was captured by the Burgundians in 1430 and handed over to the English.

*Forest of Compiègne

The armistice which ended the First World War was signed on November 11th 1918 in a railway carriage in the Forest of Compiègne, and a reproduction of the original carriage can still be seen there. The château, a plain classical-style building erected by Jacques-Ange Gabriel in 1751–1788 for Louis XV, now houses the National Museum of Antiquities and a Carriage Museum.
In the Hôtel de Ville (Town Hall, 1505–1511) is the Musée de la Figurine Historique. To the west of the Place de l'Hôtel-de-Ville is the 18th c. Hôtel de Songeons, now housing the Musée Vivenel (sculpture, pictures and drawings, ceramics, enamels, etc.). Also worth seeing are the church of St-Antoine (13th and 16th c.) and the Early Gothic church of St-Jacques (altered in 15th c.), with a 49 m/160 ft high tower.

Coucy-le-Château

Coucy-le-Château, north-east of Paris, was once France's largest and finest medieval castle, with a magnificent keep (now destroyed). The town is still well worth visiting, with its circuit of walls and 28 13th c. towers and the surviving round towers of the castle.

Courances

The Château de Courances, south of Paris, was created about 1630 by the reconstruction of an older castle. The park, designed by Le Nôtre, has a great variety of artificial lakes, fountains and cascades.

* Park

Crépy-en-Valois

The old town of Crépy-en-Valois (pop. 12,300), north-east of Paris, has a number of handsome medieval houses in Place Gambetta. The church of St-Denis dates from the 12th–16th centuries. The Château de Valois contains a Museum of Archery. There are impressive remains (façade, tower) of the church of St-Thomas (consecrated 1182).

Dampierre
* Château

The magnificent château of Dampierre was begun in 1550 by the Duc de Luynes and rebuilt between 1675 and 1683 by Jules Hardouin-Mansart.

Dreux

Dreux (pop. 34,000), situated west of Paris in the valley of the Blaise, has half-timbered houses from the 15th and 16th centuries and a tall watch-tower. The old chapel of the royal house of Orléans is now occupied by the Musée d'Art et d'Histoire Marcel-Dessal.

Ecouen
* Musée de la Renaissance

This charming little town (pop. 4500) has a 16th c. château (1541–1555) which now houses a museum of Renaissance art, the Musée National de la Renaissance. The church of St-Acceul has a Late Gothic choir and fine 16th c. windows.

Ermenonville

In this village north-east of Paris on the edge of the forest Jean-Jacques Rousseau died in 1778. 1.5 km/1 mile north is a zoo, and beyond this the Mer de Sable, a "sea of sand", with dunes, which is an unexpected sight in this forest region.

Etampes

This old town (pop. 19,500), south of Paris, has many handsome old churches, including Notre-Dame-du-Fort (12th–13th c.; fine sculpture on south doorway), St-Martin (12th and 16th c.), St-Basile (12th, 15th and 16th c.) and St-Gilles (12th, 13th and 16th c.). From the Tour Guinette, an old keep of 1140, there is a good general view of the town. There is a museum of local history.

La Ferté-Milon

La Ferté-Milon, situated to the north-east of Paris above the river Ourcq, was the birthplace of the dramatist Jean Racine (1639–1699). Above the town are the ruins of a 14th c. castle (impressive façade with a rectangular tower containing the living quarters and three round towers; monumental gateway with a relief of the Coronation of the Virgin).

Fontainebleau
** Château

The little town of Fontainebleau (pop. 20,000), south-east of Paris, is famed for its château, originally built by Francis I on the site of an earlier castle of Louis VII's (1137); the architects were Gilles le Breton, Pierre Chambiges and Philibert Delorme. Henry IV and Louis XIII added to the original building. Louis XIV, who came to Fontainebleau annually to hunt, signed the revocation of the Edict of Nantes here. Later kings paid little attention to the château, but it was a favourite residence of Napoleon's. Thereafter it was neglected until the reigns of Louis-Philippe and Napoleon III, who restored it.

* Cour des Adieux

The layout of the palace is rambling and irregular, with only one storey above the ground floor except in a few pavilions. The large forecourt, enclosed by railings, is known as the Cour du Cheval-Blanc or Cour des Adieux: it was here that Napoleon said farewell to his Guard after his abdication. A horseshoe-shaped double staircase (1634) leads up to the first floor of the main building. To the right is the Cour de la Fontaine, which opens on to the park with its carp pond; on the north side is the Galerie de François I (1528–1530).

Passing through the east wing and a corner pavilion, with the Porte Dorée (1528), one enters the Cour Ovale, an arcaded courtyard which is an outstanding example of French Renaissance architecture. The Porte du Baptistère is the second entrance to this courtyard; and opposite this, beyond a Baroque railing, is the Cour des Officiers.

Château de Fontainebleau, Cour des Adieux

*Interior

The interior of the château is splendidly decorated by Italian and French artists. (In the reigns of Francis I and Henry IV the first and second Fontainebleau schools strongly influenced French art and interior decoration.) To the left of the main entrance is the Chapelle de la Trinité (17th c.). On the first floor, looking on to the Jardin de Diane, are the Apartments of Napoleon I, with Empire furniture. Beyond these are the Salle du Conseil, which dates from the reign of Louis XV, and the Salle du Trône. The Queen's Apartments are splendidly furnished (Sèvres porcelain). In the Galerie de Diane is the library.
Opposite the apartments occupied by Marie-Antoinette, looking on to the Cour Ovale, are the King's Apartments, with ceiling paintings and stucco ornament by Primaticcio and fine tapestries. In the Escalier du Roi (King's Staircase) are scenes from the life of Alexander the Great.

Ballroom

On the south side of the Cour Ovale is the Ballroom (Salle de Bal), built by Francis I and splendidly decorated (paintings by Primaticcio) by Henry II for his mistress Diane de Poitiers.

*Galerie de François I

In the Galerie de François I, which has a terrace overlooking the Cour de la Fontaine, are 14 large paintings by Rosso de' Rossi.
In the adjoining wing, to the south, are the Apartments of the Queen Mother and the Apartments of Pope Pius VII, and at the far end is a pavilion containing the Musée Chinois, with a valuable collection of Chinese porcelain. In the restored west wing is the new Napoleonic Museum, which covers the period from 1804 to 1815.

Gardens

The gardens of Fontainebleau are very beautiful. To the west is the Jardin Anglais, laid out in the time of Napoleon I, to the east the Parterre, designed by Le Nôtre, with ornamental ponds and statues.
Beyond the canal constructed in the reign of Henry IV is the park, with the Labyrinthe (Maze) and the Treille du Roi (vine-covered trellises).

*Forêt de Fontainebleau

The Forest of Fontainebleau, which is bounded on the north-east by the meanders of the Seine and covers an area of some 25,000 hectares/62,000 acres, ranks as France's finest forest. The terrain is hilly, consisting mainly of sand and sandstone. The magnificent stands of tall trees and the wild gorges offer an impressive range of scenic beauty which has attracted many painters (the Barbizon school), and a network of paths open up the forest to walkers.

Gisors

Gisors, strategically situated north-west of Paris at the meeting of three valleys, has a ruined castle which in its day was one of the strongest fortresses in France. It was begun in 1097 and completed in the 12th and 13th centuries. There are remains of its twelve towers and keep.

Giverny

Giverny, west of Paris, was the home of the painter Claude Monet from 1883 until his death in 1926. Monet's house and his garden, which appears in so many of his pictures, are open to the public.

***L'Haÿ-les-Roses**

This little town to the south of Paris has a rose-garden, originally planted in 1892, containing thousands of roses. There is also a Rose Museum.

Jouarre

Jouarre Abbey, east of Paris, is one of France's oldest sacred buildings, founded in 630. It preserves a Merovingian crypt containing a number of sarcophagi and a tower of the Romanesque abbey church. The present conventual buildings, occupied by Benedictine nuns, date from the 18th c.

*Sarcophagi

Laon

See Champagne

Larchant

Larchant (pop. 550), south of Paris, is an old fortified town with a pilgrimage chapel of St-Mathurin (12th–13th c.). It contains fine 12th c. wall paintings and other Romanesque and Gothic works of art.
Nearby is the Massif de la Dame Jehanne, a range of sandstone crags which is popular with rock-climbers.

Longpont

Longpont, north-east of Paris, is a beautifully situated little town with considerable remains of a 12th c. Cistercian abbey (fortified gatehouse, magnificent ruined church).

Maintenon

Maintenon (pop. 3500), situated on the right bank of the Eure, has a handsome château which Louis XIV acquired for Madame d'Aubigné, later the Marquise de Maintenon. In the park, which was designed by Le Nôtre, are the ruins of an unfinished aqueduct designed by Vauban to convey water to the gardens of Versailles.

*Aqueduct

Maisons-Laffitte

Maisons-Laffitte, north-west of Paris, is noted not only for its racecourse but also for its château, built by François Mansart in 1642–1651, which ranks as one of the finest classical-style châteaux in France; it has a sumptuous interior.

Malmaison

See Paris, Surroundings

Mantes-la-Jolie

In Mantes-la-Jolie (pop. 43,000), situated on the left bank of the Seine to the west of Paris, Henry recanted his Protestant faith for the second time: "Paris is well worth a mass".

*Notre-Dame

The fine Gothic church of Notre-Dame (12th–14th c.), which shows similarities with Notre-Dame in Paris, has doorways with sculptural decoration and a beautiful interior. In the choir is the 14th c. Chapelle de Navarre.

Marais

The château of Marais, south-west of Paris, built in 1770 on the basis of an older castle, is a fine example of the architecture of Louis XVI's reign; it now houses a museum.

Marly-le-Roi

Of the château of Marly-le-Roi, west of Paris, the favourite residence of Louis XIV, nothing is left but the lines of the foundations, but the beautiful park has been preserved. Along the Musée-Promenade de Marly-le-Roi are reminders of the history of the château, including its original plan. This was a favourite resort of writers and artists (Dumas, Sardou, Sisley, Pissarro, Maillol). In the Château de Monte-Cristo, built for Alexandre Dumas in 1846, is a small museum devoted to the writer.

Meaux

The old town of Meaux (pop. 45,900), situated on the Marne to the north-east of Paris, has been the see of a bishop since 375, its most celebrated incumbent being the great preacher and historian Bossuet (1627–1704). In the old town is the Gothic cathedral (12th–16th c.), with a 76 m/250 ft high north tower and a fine five-aisled interior. In the old Bishop's Palace (17th c.) is a museum mainly devoted to Bossuet.

Meudon

See Paris, Surroundings

Montfort-L'Amaury

This old town (pop. 2700) lies west of Paris on the edge of Rambouillet Forest. The main features of interest are the old town walls, the church of St-Pierre (15th–17th c; fine Renaissance windows), a charnel-house (16th and 17th c.) with a finely carved doorway, the ruined castle (view) and the house (now a museum) occupied by the composer Maurice Ravel from 1920 until his death in 1937.

Montmorency

Montmorency, north of Paris on the edge of the forest, was the ancestral home of one of the great French noble families. Jean-Jacques Rousseau lived here from 1757 to 1762, writing three of his most important works, the "Nouvelle Héloise", "Emile" and the "Contrat Social"; there is a museum commemorating his stay. The church of St-Martin (16th c.), with beautiful Renaissance windows, was the burial chapel of the Montmorencys.

Morienval
*Notre-Dame

The three-towered Late Romanesque church of Notre-Dame, which belonged to an 11th c. Benedictine abbey, shows in the ambulatory (begun about 1125) one of the earliest examples of Gothic vaulting. The use of ribbed vaulting so reduced the load on the walls that large window openings, admitting increased light into the church, became possible.

Nemours

Nemours (pop. 11,000), situated south of Paris in the Loing valley, has a church dating from the 13th, 15th and 16th centuries. The castle (12th and 15th c.) houses the Musée de Préhistoire de l'Ile de France, which also has a number of tapestries.

Noyon

Noyon (pop. 14,000), north-east of Paris, was the birthplace of the Reformer Jean Calvin (1509–1564). The house in which he was born is now a Calvin Museum. Noyon, a town of brick-built houses, has been the see of a bishop since the 6th c. The former cathedral of Notre-Dame (12th–13th c.) is a good example of the transition between Romanesque and Gothic. It was completely restored for the 1000th anniversary of the establishment of the French kingdom. Features of particular interest are the beautiful 13th c. cloister, the chapterhouse, the library and the former Bishop's Palace, now the Municipal Museum.

*Notre-Dame

Ourscamp
*Abbey

North-east of Paris, on the edge of the forest, is the abbey of Ourscamp, founded in 1129 and enlarged in the 18th c., which is still occupied by monks. The church is now a ruin. The main surviving feature is the magnificent infirmary of 1260, now used as a chapel, with three vaulted aisles 30 m/100 ft long.

Pierrefonds
*Château

North-east of Paris is the château of Pierrefonds, with its picturesque battlements and massive round towers. Originally a fortified castle begun in 1390, it was slighted by Richelieu in the 17th c. but restored in its present form by Napoleon III.

Pont-Ste-Maxence

This convent of Poor Clares, north of Paris, was founded in 1309. It preserves a number of notable features (the entrance front, with two chimneys, the courtyard, the 16th c. cloister, the 14th c. dormitory).

Port-Royal-des-Champs

South-west of Paris are the remains of this important 13th c. Cistercian abbey, which has associations with Pascal and Racine. This centre of Jansenism (a Catholic reform movement directed against the Jesuits) was destroyed in 1710–1712 on the orders of Louis XIV. The building known as the Petites Ecoles now houses the Musée National des Granges (history of Jansenism).

Prémontré

The abbey of Prémontré, north-east of Paris in the Forêt de Coucy, was the mother house of the Premonstratensian order, founded in 1120. The abbey was rebuilt in the 18th c.

Provins

Provins (pop. 12,700), situated south-east of Paris on the rivers Voulzie and Durteint, is still partly surrounded by its old walls. In the Middle Ages it was an important commercial centre with a population of some 80,000, but it declined as a result of the wars with England and was even harder hit by the 16th c. wars of religion. The upper town has preserved a number of important medieval buildings, including the church of St-Quiriace (1160), with a beautiful Gothic choir and a modern dome, the Tour de César, a 12th c. watch-tower, the Porte St-Jean, and the Grange aux Dîmes, a 13th c. tithe barn which houses a small museum.

*Tour de César

In the lower town are several old churches, including the Romanesque/Gothic church of St-Ayoul (12th–16th c.), with fine 16th c. alabaster statues. To the north is the Tour Notre-Dame-du-Val (16th c.).

In the north of the town is the former Hôpital Général (now a hospice) housed in an old convent of Franciscan nuns (1246), which preserves two sides of the cloister.

Provins is a rose-growing centre, with fields of roses extending to Villecresnes, Brie-Comte-Robert, Grisly-Suisnes, Guignes-Rabutin and Nangis along N19 (the "Route des Roses").

Rambouillet

*Château

The Château de Rambouillet, south-west of Paris, is the summer residence of the President of the Republic, but is open to the public when he is not actually in residence. It was built in the early 18th c. on the site of an earlier manor-house and frequently enlarged and renovated thereafter. Louis XVI acquired the château in 1783 for use as a hunting lodge, and built the Laiterie de la Reine (Queen's Dairy), in the form of a Greek temple, for Marie-Antoinette. Also worth seeing are the English-style park and the Bergerie (sheep-farm), with merino sheep. The interior of the château is beautifully decorated.

*Park
*Bergerie

*Forest

There is good walking in Rambouillet Forest.

Rosny-sur-Seine

The château of Rosny, west of Paris, built by one of Henry IV's ministers, is worth a visit for its fine furniture and its large and beautiful park.

Royaumont

Royaumont Abbey, north of Paris, was founded in 1233 by Louis IX (St Louis). It was dissolved in 1791 and the church was destroyed, although it was later partly restored. The abbey is now a cultural centre. The most notable features are the ruins of the 13th c. church, originally more than 100 m/330 ft long, the Gothic cloister, the refectory, the sacristy, the kitchens and the lodging of the last abbot.

*Refectory

Rueil-Malmaison

See Malmaison

St-Cloud

See Paris, Surroundings

St-Denis

See Paris, Surroundings

St-Germain-en-Laye

See Paris, Surroundings

St-Sulpice-de-Favières

St-Sulpice-de-Favières, in a picturesque village setting, is a Gothic pilgrimage church of the 13th–14th c. The Chapelle des Miracles, all that remains of a 12th c. church, contains the relics of St Sulpice.

St-Vrain

This "African Nature Park", an open enclosure with many wild animals, lies south of Paris. Visitors can travel through the park either by car or by boat.

Sceaux

Sceaux, picturesquely situated on a hill south-west of Paris, has a château built in 1856 on the site of an earlier building, set in a large park (228 hectares/563 acres) designed by Le Nôtre which is one of the most beautiful in the surroundings of Paris.
The château now houses the Musée de l'Ile de France (history, art, literature, folk traditions).

Senlis

*Notre-Dame

The old-world little town of Senlis (pop. 15,300), north-east of Paris, was the see of a bishop from the 3rd c. until 1790. On the north-east side of the old town is the imposing former cathedral of Notre-Dame (1153–1184), with a richly carved main doorway and a beautiful interior. Near the church are remains of the town's Gallo-Roman walls and of a medieval castle (Hunting Museum). On the western outskirts of the town are the remains of a Roman amphitheatre.

Sèvres

See Paris, Surroundings

Soissons

See Champagne

Thoiry

*Réserve Africaine

Thoiry, west of Paris, has a beautifully proportioned 17th c. château with a charming interior and a vivarium. In the circular park are a zoo and the Réserve Africaine, in which large numbers of wild animals roam freely; visitors can drive through it in their cars.

Vaux-le-Vicomte
*Château

The château of Vaux-le-Vicomte, south-east of Paris, was built in the mid 17th c. for Fouquet, Louis XIV's finance minister. The young king was so delighted with it when he visited it in 1661 that he invited the artists responsible to work at Paris and Versailles and transported some of the works of art to Versailles. With its four corner pavilions, the château is a beautiful and impressive sight.

*Park

The park was Le Nôtre's first great masterpiece, surpassed only by Versailles.

Versailles

See entry

Villers-Cotterets

Villers-Cotterets, north-east of Paris, was the birthplace of Alexandre Dumas the Elder, who is commemorated by a museum. There is a fine Renaissance château (1520) with a park designed by Le Nôtre.

Vincennes

See Paris, Parks

Jura

N–P 7–9

*Situation and characteristics

The French Jura, roughly corresponding to the old province of Franche-Comté, lies in eastern France, bounded on the west by Burgundy and on the north by the Vosges, though compared with these areas it is relatively unknown to tourists.

Franche-Comté

Franche-Comté has a common frontier 250 km/155 miles long with Switzerland, and the French Jura, the range of mountains between the Saône and the lakes of western Switzerland, is continued beyond the frontier by the Swiss Jura. The region of Franche-Comté has an area of 16,202 sq.

km/6256 sq. miles (3% of the total area of France) and a population of 1.08 million. It takes in the départements of Doubs, Jura and Haute-Saône and the Territoire de Belfort. The administrative centre is Besançon.
Two great Frenchmen were born in the Jura – the biologist Louis Pasteur (1822–1895) and the painter Gustave Courbet (1819–1877).

Topography

Geographically the French Jura is the south-western section of the chain of mountains which extends for some 700 km/435 miles between the upper Rhône and the upper Main, bounded in the north by the Vosges, in the east by the Swiss Jura and in the west by the Tertiary uplands of the Saône basin and by the district of Bresse. The most north-westerly section, abutting on the Vosges, forms the tabular Jura, through whose horizontal strata numerous rivers have carved their courses. Beyond the Doubs is the plateau Jura, which falls down to the Saône depression in a steep and rocky scarp slashed by deep valleys *(reculées)* and to the east rises in a series of steps formed by erosion and gradually merges into the mountainous Jura, compressed during the Alpine folding movement into a number of parallel chains, with magnificent views of the High Alps, particularly from the most easterly and highest chain.
Characteristic of the Jura plateau, as of all areas of permeable limestone, are a variety of karstic phenomena like swallowholes (funnel-shaped cavities), caves and underground rivers, which emerge at the foot of the cliffs as abundantly flowing springs (e.g. the Loue and the Lison). The rivers, most of them flowing down the longitudinal valleys of the mountainous Jura, break through the ridges in transverse valleys known as *cluses* which facilitate communications within the region.

Climate

Apart from the climatically favoured south-western foreland area, where vines and fruit can be grown, the climate tends to have the rawness of a mountain region. The highest peaks in the Jura rise to over 1600 m/5250 ft (Crêt de la Neige, 1723 m/5653 ft, in the French Jura, Crêt Pela, 1495 m/4905 ft, and Mont d'Or, 1423 m/4669 ft, in Franche-Comté). In spite of the joking claim that it has eight months of snow and two months of wind, but the rest of the year is wonderful, Goethe, Ruskin and Lamartine all speak enthusiastically about the Jura, referring to one of its greatest attractions, the magnificent views of the snow-covered Alps to be had from so many places in the region.

Economy

But it is not only the distant views that appeal to the visitor in the Jura. The valleys have their old-established industries, with major centres like Besançon, Montbéliard, Belfort and Morez. In the foreland regions wine is produced (e.g. in Arbois) and fruit is grown. The valleys and plateaux support arable and pastoral farming, and the cheeses of the region (Gruyère, Morbier, Vacherin) are renowned. Timber from the extensive forests also makes a major contribution to the economy.

Tourism

Thanks to the Jura's romantic valleys, its seventy lakes, its forests, its footpaths, cycle tracks, bridle-paths and waterways and its well-equipped ski resorts (Les Rousses, Métabief), tourism is now making an increasing contribution to the economy of the region.

History

In Gallic times the Jura was the territory of the Sequani, whose chief town was Vesontio (Besançon). After Caesar drove back the advancing Germanic tribes in 58 B.C. and crushed a rising by the Sequani, who were allied with the Gauls, in 52 B.C. the region enjoyed a period of peace during which the towns of Besançon, Salins, Dole, Lons-le-Saunier and Portarlier flourished. Towards the end of the 2nd c. A.D. the Jura was Christianised. After being occupied by the Burgundians in 442 it shared the destinies of the Duchy of Burgundy, which became Frankish in 534, was divided into two independent kingdoms in 843, became the united kingdom of Burgundy in 934 and was incorporated into the German Empire as the free county of Burgundy in 1032. The weakness of central authority led to the establishment of local lordships, and numerous castles and fortresses were built. Soon the various counts and dukes appointed by the Burgundian rulers established hereditary authority over their territories. When Burgundy was divided the Jura formed the Comté de Bourgogne (County of Burgundy), or Comté for short, while the territories on the Saône became the Duchy of Burgundy. In 1322 the Franche-Comté returned to Burgundian control; in 1361 it passed to Flanders; and in 1384, along with the rest of Flanders, again became part of Burgundy. After many years of conflict with the king of France the region was incorporated in the German Empire in 1491. In 1674 it was conquered by Louis XIV, and in 1678, under the peace of Nijmegen, was finally assigned to France.

Sights in the Jura

Ambronay

This little town (pop. 1900) grew up around a Benedictine abbey, of which it preserves the church (mainly 13th and 15th c.), a cloister and the chapterhouse.

Arbois

Arbois (pop. 4100) is picturesquely situated amid vineyards. Louis Pasteur, a native of Dole, spent his early years in Arbois and frequently returned there. His parents' house has been preserved as it was and is open to the public. Other features of interest are the 18th c. houses in the Place de la Liberté, the Town Hall (formerly a monastic house), the church of St-Just (12th–13th c.), the Wine Museum and the Musée Sarret de Grozon (furniture, ceramics, pictures).
2 km/1½ miles south-east of the town is Pasteur's vineyard, grapes from which were used in his research into the fermentation of alcohol in 1878.

Grotte des Planches

Near Arbois, in a V-shaped valley, are the two sources of the Cuisance and the entrance to the Grotte des Planches. The D469 leads up to the Cirque de Fer à Cheval, from where there is a fine view.

Arc-et-Senans
*Saline Royale

Arc-et-Senans is noted for the former royal salt-works, with the imposing neo-classical buildings designed by Claude-Nicolas Ledoux (1736–1806), who was commissioned by Louis XV to create an ideal industrial town. His ambitious plan provided for a circular layout, only half of which was completed. Five pavilions and two large storage rooms are grouped around an administrative building. The salt-works closed down at the end of the 19th c., and the buildings are now occupied by an interesting Ledoux Museum of architectural plans and models, as well as a salt museum.

Audincourt

This industrial town (pop. 14,000) on the Doubs has an interesting modern church (by Novarina, 1951) with stained glass windows by Fernand Léger and mosaics by Bazaine.

Barrage du Génissiat
*Lake

The Génissiat Dam (1948) has formed an artificial lake on the Doubs which powers a hydro-electric station. The lake extends back for 23 km/14 miles to the Swiss frontier. The whole complex is a triumph of French hydraulic engineering.

Baume-les-Dames

Baume-les-Dames (pop. 5500), formerly called Baume-les-Nonnes, owes its name to a convent founded in the 7th c. for ladies of noble birth. The old abbey church has been restored. The church of St-Martin, in the Place de la République, was rebuilt in the 17th c.

Baume-les-Messieurs

The village of Baume-les-Messieurs, picturesquely situated at an altitude of 320 m/1050 ft under a chalk cliff, grew up round an abbey founded by the Irish monk Columban in the 6th c. The famous abbey of Cluny was founded by Benedictine monks from here in 910. The Romanesque-Gothic church (12th–15th c.) has a beautiful Flemish triptych (16th c.) as well as fine sculpture and a number of tombs.

*Cirque des Baumes

3 km/2 miles south of Baume-les-Messieurs is the Cirque des Baumes (see page 254), with an interesting cave.

Belfort

See entry

Besançon

See entry

***Cascades du Hérisson**

The river Hérisson, rising at an altitude of 805 m/2640 ft, forms a series of waterfalls on its way down the valley – though these can dry up completely after a long period of drought. The finest of the falls are the Grand Saut and, at the end of the gorge, the Cascade de l'Eventail. The best starting-point for a visit to the falls is Doucier, from which D326 leads to a car park; then on foot to the falls.

Col de la Faucille

The Col de la Faucille (1323 m/4341 ft), between Gex and La Cure, is the most important pass over the Jura, carrying the road into Switzerland (N5).

*Mont-Rond

From the pass there is a cabin cableway up Mont-Rond. From its two peaks (1534 m/5033 ft and 1614 m/4296 ft) there are magnificent panoramic views of the Jura.

***Colombey de Gex**

One of the finest viewpoints in the Jura is the Colombey de Gex (1689 m/5542 ft), near the Swiss frontier. It is reached on a road which runs south from the Col de la Faucille and a footpath which takes off from the road; the ascent takes about 2 hours. From the summit there are fine views of Lake Geneva and the Alps.
4 km/2½ miles north-east is Mont-Rond (see above).

***Crêt de Chalam**

The Crêt de Chalam (1548 m/5079 ft), which rears above the Valserine, is another fine viewpoint (to the east the Jura hills; to the south-east Mont Blanc, visible in clear weather).

Divonne-les-Bains

Divonne-les-Bains, situated between the Jura and Lake Geneva, is an important spa, with springs (6.5°C/43.7°F) which were once used by the Romans. Divonne has a racecourse, a golf-course and a casino.

Dole

Dole (pop. 28,000), situated just above the junction of the Doubs with the Rhine–Rhône Canal, was the birthplace of Louis Pasteur, who left the town at the age of five. The house in Rue Pasteur (formerly Rue des Tanneurs) in which he was born is now a museum, with mementoes of his parents and displays illustrating his scientific achievements. Other features of interest in the town are the church of Notre-Dame (16th c.; tower 75 m/245 ft high), 15th–18th c. houses in the old part of the town around the church, the Hôtel de Froissard (16th–17th c.), an old Carmelite convent and the former Jesuit Collège de l'Arc, now a school and museum of painting.

Ferney-Voltaire

Ferney-Voltaire (pop. 3050), lying close to the Swiss frontier and Geneva's airport of Cointrin, was from 1760 onwards the favourite residence of Voltaire, who enlarged and improved the château and the park. The château contains mementoes of the philosopher.

Gex

Gex (alt. 628 m/2060 ft; pop. 3200), 12 km/7½ miles below the Col de la Faucille, is a popular medium-altitude resort, conveniently close to the mountains and to Geneva. From Place Gambetta there is a fine view of Mont Blanc.

Nozeroy

This picturesquely situated little place (pop. 450) has preserved its old-world aspect, with two town gates, a 15th c. church, old houses in the Grande Rue and the Clock Gate, the last relic of the Château des Chalons.

Ornans

Ornans (pop. 4300), in the valley of the Loue, was the birthplace of the painter Gustave Courbet (1819–1877); the house in which he was born is now a museum. It is an attractive little town, with old houses and a 12th c. church, originally Romanesque, which was altered and enlarged in the 16th and 17th centuries and is richly furnished.

Poligny

Poligny (pop. 5000), lying in a rich agricultural region, is noted for its wine and its Gruyère cheese. The church of St-Hippolyte has fine 15th c. statues of the Burgundian school. Behind the church is a convent of Poor Clares founded in 1415. In the Grande Rue are handsome old houses with carved doors (17th c.). The church of Monthier-Vieillard, which dates in part from the 11th c., has an altar of 1534, a 14th c. Crucifixion group and sculpture of the 13th and 15th centuries.

Cheese Museum

There is a Cheese Museum illustrating the processes of cheese production.

Pontarlier

Pontarlier (pop. 19,000), close to the Swiss frontier, is of more interest as a centre from which to explore the surrounding area than for its own sights – a triumphal arch, the Porte St-Pierre, the church of St-Bénigne (originally 15th c., rebuilt in 17th c.) and a chapel.

Ronchamp
*Notre-Dame-du-Haut

Ronchamp (pop. 3000) is world-famed for Le Corbusier's chapel of Notre-Dame-du-Haut (1950–1954), on a hill above the town (illustration, page 337). It contains an ancient image of the Virgin (festival on September 8th). Ronchamp also has an interesting mining museum, the Maison de la Mine.

St-Claude

St-Claude (pop. 13,000), a town noted for the manufacture of pipes, with an interesting Pipe Museum, is one of the leading tourist centres of the Upper Jura. Its principal attraction is the Cathedral of St-Pierre (14th–15th c.), which was completed only in the 18th c. with a square tower and neo-classical west front. It has fine choir-stalls (mid 15th c.) and a notable altar. Originally belonging to an abbey which was destroyed during the French Revolution, it is one of the finest churches in the Jura. The Diamond Museum displays a collection of both rough and cut diamonds and precious stones and illustrates the process of cutting and the industrial use of diamonds.

*Choir-stalls

Salins-les-Bains

Salins-les-Bains, in the narrow valley of the Furieuse, is noted for its brine springs, which were already being exploited in Roman times and are still used for medicinal purposes. A tour of the workings, 250 m/820 ft underground, is an impressive experience. The town still preserves remains of its old walls. The church of St-Anatole (13th c.) is a fine example of Burgundian Gothic. In the 18th c. Town Hall is the 17th c. chapel of Notre-Dame-la-Libératrice.

Rivers and Valleys

One of the great attractions of the Jura is the impressive and constantly varying scenery of its valleys, the best known of which are the Ain, Doubs, Dessoubre, Loue and Valserine. Visitors to the Jura should make a point of exploring some of these valleys or the V-shaped transverse valleys known as *reculées* (see below, page 254).

***Ain**

The valley of the Ain traverses the Jura for a distance of 190 km/120 miles, with a succession of rapids, waterfalls and picturesque gorges. Possible routes are down the upper valley of the river from Nozeroy (near its source) to its junction with the Saine, or along the lakes formed by a series of dams between Pont-de-Poitte and Poncin, a distance of some 100 km/60 miles.

Dessoubre

*Cirque de Consolation

*Priest's Rock

The Dessoubre is a very attractive river, less well known than the other Jura rivers, which flows into the Doubs at St-Hippolyte. There is a pleasant drive of 30 km/19 miles from the Cirque de Consolation, in which the river rises, to the junction with the Doubs. In the cirque is the former monastery of Notre-Dame de Consolation. The best view of the cirque is to be had from the "Priest's Rock".

***Doubs**

The little Dessoubre is very different from the majestic valley of the Doubs,

◀ *Notre-Dame-du-Haut, Ronchamp*

which rises near Mouthe (alt. 937 m/3074 ft) and flows into the Saône after a winding course of 430 km/265 miles, though the distance as the crow flies is only 90 km/55 miles. The road runs down the upper valley from the source to Morteau, through the impressive Doubs gorges to Montbéliard, and from there to Besançon (see entry), after which the Doubs leaves the Jura near Dole. Among the principal attractions on this road are the gorge of Cluse-et-Mijoux (of which there is a fine view from Les Rosiers); the Lac de Chaillexon, with a 28 m/90 ft high waterfall; the Echelles de la Mort; the Corniche de Goumois, near the Swiss frontier, with magnificent views of the mountains; and the little town of L'Isle-sur-le-Doubs, divided by the river into three parts.

Lison

The name Source du Lison covers the actual source of the Lison, the Grotte Sarrazine and the Creux Billard: three interesting natural features which are all linked with one another, partly by underground channels.

***Loue**

*Source

The Loue was often painted by Courbet; and indeed, with its tree-lined banks, it is a very picturesque river, which is also attractive to canoeists. From its source at Ouhans it follows a winding course to its junction with the Doubs. Its main attractions are the source itself, in a large cave, which has been shown to be connected with the Doubs, its numerous viewpoints like the Moine de la Vallée and Mouthier, and the Nouailles gorges. The stretch between Cléron and the mouth of the Lison is particularly attractive.

Valserine

The Valserine is a high valley of great romantic charm, extending for some 60 km/37 miles from the Col de la Faucille to Bellegarde, where it flows into the Rhône. On either side of the valley rise the highest peaks in the Jura, with expanses of mountain pasture between them. A striking feature is the Pont des Pierres, which spans the river between Montanges and Mulaz in a single arch 80 m/260 ft wide. The finest viewpoint is at Mijoux, on the way up to the Col de la Faucille.

***Reculées*

*Cirque des Baumes

The *reculées* are the V-shaped transverse valleys which are found, for example on the Cuisance, the Seille and the Vallière. They extend from Arbois by way of the Cirque de Baume to Lons-le-Saunier and Pont-de-Poitte, a road distance of some 80 km/50 miles. These very attractive valleys cut their way through the hills to end in a cirque or corrie with sheer rock faces which often contain caves. The Reculée des Planches or Reculée d'Arbois, south-east of that town, contains the two sources of the river Cuisance and ends in the impressive Cirque du Fer à Cheval. Another striking cirque is the Cirque de Ladoye; but the finest of all is the Cirque de Baume, with fantastic views from its crags. From the top of the crags a steep path runs down to the caves at the foot, formed by a former source of the river Dard, which after heavy rain still emerges here in the form of a waterfall. The amphitheatre-like Creux de Revigny, between Lons-le-Saunier and Pont-de-Poitte, also contains many caves.

Languedoc–Roussillon

K–M 10/11

*Situation and characteristics

The region of Languedoc–Roussillon extends along the Mediterranean coast of France between the mouth of the Rhône and the Pyrenees for a distance of some 200 km/125 miles, bounded on the north and west by the river Aude, on the east by the Golfe du Lion and on the south by the Pyrenees.

Modern holiday centres

Originally the coast, with its fringe of marshy soil and numerous lagoons, offered little attraction to holidaymakers. In 1963, therefore, it was decided to change the whole coast of the Golfe du Lion, and under a plan developed

The Grande Motte holiday centre

by the government the marshland has been drained, beaches have been created, old towns like Sète, Agde and Perpignan have been expanded and a series of new holiday centres have been established, varying in style and layout and adapted with varying degrees of success to the natural setting. The first of these settlements, the Grande Motte (designed by Jean Balladur), was opened in 1974 and was followed by many others, including Port-Barcarès, Port-Leucate, Gruissan, Valras-Plage, Cap d'Agde, Carnon, Port-Camargue and Fleury d'Aude. Common to all these centres is a wide range of facilities for entertainment and sport.

Topography

The landscape of Languedoc–Roussillon offers a variety of attractions – wild rocky gorges, France's oldest vineyards, fertile orchards and market gardens (the much sought-after *primeurs,* early vegetables, come from Roussillon), old hill villages, the ruined castles of the Cathars on mountain crags and interesting old towns, as well as the seaside resorts along the coast. The mild climate is a further attraction which draws holidaymakers to this region.

Culture

The early settlement of this region led to a flowering of art. The earliest figural sculpture in the whole of western art, dating from 1020, is in the church of St-Genis-des-Fontaines, between Céret and Argelès-sur-Mer, to the south of Perpignan. And Languedoc–Roussillon has a whole series of towns with historic old buildings and works of art.

The region consists of the two provinces of Languedoc and Roussillon, which take in the five départements of Aude, Gard, Hérault, Lozère and Pyrénées-Orientales. It covers an area of 16,431 sq. km/6344 sq. miles and has a population of around 1.3 million, most of them living in the coastal areas.

The former county of Roussillon lies at the eastern end of the Pyrenees, between the Pyrenees and the Monts Corbières, and bears the imprint of

Catalan culture. To the north is Languedoc, which takes its name from the *langue d'oc,* the old Provençal language. The province was formed after the Albigensian wars out of the territories of the Duchy of Narbonne and the County of Toulouse. In terms of quantity Languedoc is France's principal wine-producing region, though for the most part the wine is of no more than average quality.

History

The coasts of the region were settled towards the end of the 6th c. B.C. by Phoenicians, who were followed later by Greeks and Romans. From the early 5th c. A.D. the Pagus Rossillionensis formed part of the Visigothic kingdom. In 720, however, the Arabs forced the Col de Perthus and overran the area. In 759 it was recovered by the Franks, who left the administration of the territory to the native counts. In 1172 the county of Roussillon passed to a collateral line of the Counts of Barcelona. Under the treaty of Corbei (1258) Louis the Pious made over Roussillon and the Spanish March to the kingdom of Aragon. This marked the beginning of a period of prosperity, particularly for Perpignan, the former residence of the Counts of Roussillon and now capital of the newly established kingdom of Majorca, which then included not only the Balearics but also territories on the mainland (Roussillon, Cerdagne and Montpellier).
In 1473 Perpignan came into conflict with the French crown, and in the following year was besieged and captured by Louis XI's forces, remaining under French rule until 1493. Later Charles VIII handed over Roussillon and Cerdagne, two areas which remained restless, to Ferdinand and Isabella of Aragon and Castile, who had just completed the Reconquista with the capture of the Moorish capital of Granada. The desire for independence, however, remained very much alive. In 1640 Roussillon rebelled against the central government in Madrid and was joined by the Catalans. Together they proclaimed Louis XIII of France Count of Barcelona, and in 1642 Louis entered Perpignan. The Peace of the Pyrenees (1659), however, did not satisfy the aspiration for a unified Catalonia, since the main ridge of the Pyrenees was declared to be the frontier between France and Spain.

Sights in Languedoc–Roussillon

Agde

Agde, situated at the mouth of the Hérault between Sète and Béziers, was originally a Phocaean settlement. The name comes from the Greek *agathos,* "good". It is a town of picturesque narrow streets, with three churches, including the 12th c. Cathedral of St-Etienne (originally 5th c.), a fortified church with thick walls of black volcanic stone. The Musée Agathois displays items recovered by underwater archaeology and examples of local folk art.

Cap d'Agde

4 km/2½ miles away is the modern holiday centre of Cap d'Agde, with all the amenities provided in these new developments.

Béziers

Béziers (pop. 78,000), originally a Roman military colony (Biterrae Septimanorum), is finely situated on a hill at the point where the Canal du Midi crosses the river Orb, 15 km/9 miles from the Golfe du Lion. During the Albigensian wars the town was almost completely destroyed. Its economy now centres on wine-production and the brandy trade.
In the centre of Béziers, running between the old and new towns, is the Allée Paul-Riquet. The church of the Madeleine, originally Romanesque but later altered in Gothic and then Baroque style, was the scene of one of the massacres of the Albigensians in 1209. Farther north is the church of St-Aphrodise (11th–15th c.), which contains a 3rd c. sarcophagus.
In the centre of the old town is the 18th c. Hôtel de Ville (Town Hall). The former cathedral of St-Nazaire, situated on higher ground, is a fortified church of the 12th–14th centuries with massive towers and a large rose window on the west front. The Gothic cloister now houses a Musée Lapidaire, with old tombstones and capitals.

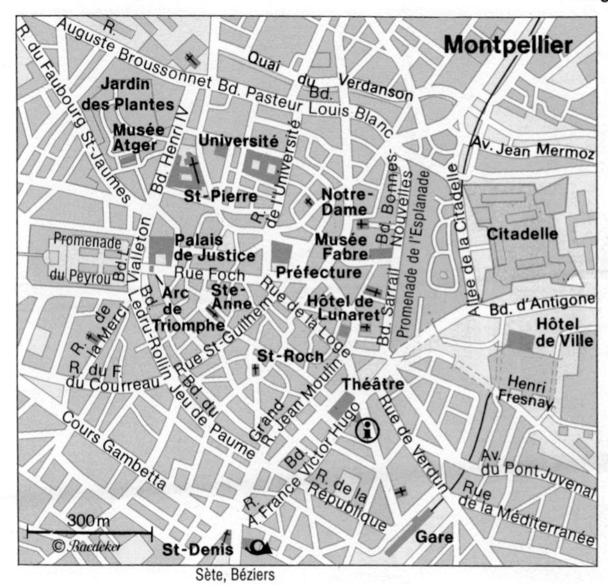

From the terrace in front of the church there are fine views.

Museums

A short distance away is the Musée des Beaux-Arts (pictures, Greek vases). To the south-east, housed in a former Dominican church, is the Musée du Vieux Biterrois et du Vin, a folk and wine museum.

St-Jacques

At the south end of the town is the church of St-Jacques, which dates in part from the 12th c. It has a richly decorated choir.

Oppidum d'Ensérune

14 km/9 miles west of the town is the Oppidum d'Ensérune, with the excavations of an Ibero-Greek settlement of the 4th and 3rd centuries B.C. There is a museum displaying finds from the site.

Elne

See Côte Vermeille

Montpellier

The old university town of Montpellier (alt. 50 m/165 ft; pop. 210,000), chief town of the region, its economic and cultural centre and the see of a bishop, lies near the Golfe du Lion, on the river Lez.

History

The town was established after the destruction of the nearby settlement of Maguelone by Charles Martel in 737. In the 13th c. it belonged to the kings of Aragon and then, until 1349, the kings of Majorca as vassals of the French crown. The university was founded in 1289, and among its students were Petrarch (1316–1319) and Rabelais (1530–1532 and 1537–1538). In the late 16th c. the town was a stronghold of the Huguenots. It was captured by Louis XIII in 1622.

Place de la Comédie

The centre of the town is the Place de la Comédie, with the Fountain of the Three Graces (by Etienne Antoine, 1776). On its south-west side is the Theatre (19th c.). In the old town, which extends to the banks of the Verdanson, a tributary of the Lez, numbers of finely decorated noble mansions and merchants' houses bear witness to the town's former wealth.

View of Narbonne

*Promenade du Peyrou

From the Place de la Comédie the Boulevard Victor-Hugo runs south-west to join the outer circle of boulevards leading north to the Promenade du Peyrou, a terraced park laid out in the 17th and 18th centuries from which there are fine views extending to the Cévennes and to the sea. The equestrian statue of Louis XIV was set up in 1838. At the west end of the Promenade is a water-tower, to which water is brought in a 14 km/9 mile long conduit constructed in 1753–1766, the last section being carried by an aqueduct 800 m/½ mile long and up to 21.5 m/70 ft high.

Arc de Triomphe

At the east end of the Promenade du Peyrou is a 15 m/50 ft high Triumphal Arch erected in 1691 in honour of Louis XIV which forms the entrance to the old town. On its north side is the Palais de Justice (Law Courts).

Jardin des Plantes
Musée Atger

To the north of the Arc de Triomphe is the Jardin des Plantes, France's first botanical garden, laid out in 1593. The Musée Atger (drawings by Italian and French artists) is housed in the former abbey of St-Benoît (14th and 16th c.), which is now occupied by the Faculty of Medicine (founded in 1221). North of this is the Tour des Pins, a relic of the town's medieval fortifications.

Cathedral

East of the Faculty of Medicine is the Gothic Cathedral of St-Pierre, founded in 1364, rebuilt after the wars of religion and renovated in 1867, with a severe west front flanked by towers.

*Musée Fabre

Bordering the old town on the east is the Esplanade, a simpler counterpart to the Promenade du Peyrou. On its west side is the Musée Fabre (old Italian and Dutch masters, modern French painters, fine 18th c. sculpture). At the northern end of the Esplanade stands the Corum Opera and Congress building designed by Claude Vasconi, and to the east is the old citadel built in 1624. The Antigone Quarter designed by Ricardo Bofill, a prime example of post-modern arthitecture, lies to the east of the Polygone shopping centre.

Maguelone

16 km/10 miles south is the old port of Maguelone, which was completely destroyed by Louis XIII in 1633, leaving only the 12th c. Cathedral of St-Pierre relatively unscathed. It has a beautiful west doorway and contains a 15th c. sarcophagus.

Narbonne

The old town of Narbonne (pop. 43,000), once an important port, now lies 16 km/10 miles inland as a result of the deposit of silt along the coast. The Canal de la Robine, which links the town with the river Aude and with the Mediterranean, was opened in 1789.

History

The Roman town of Narbo Martius, founded in 118 B.C., was an entrepôt in the trade between the Mediterranean and the Atlantic and until the fall of the Roman Empire was the seat of the Proconsul of the province of Gallia Narbonnensis. From 413 to 720 it was held by the Visigoths and thereafter by the Saracens, who were defeated by Pépin the Short in 759. In 817 it became the capital of the duchy of Septimania or Gothia; in 843 it passed to Charles the Bald; later it belonged to the Counts of Auvergne and then the Counts of Toulouse; and finally in 1507 it was united with France. Evidence of these vicissitudes is provided by numerous inscriptions, architectural elements and fragments of sculpture.

Place de l'Hôtel-de-Ville
* Archbishop's Palace

The central feature of the town is the rectangular Place de l'Hôtel-de-Ville, with the former Archbishop's Palace (13th–14th c.), between whose three massive towers Viollet-le-Duc inserted the neo-Gothic Hôtel de Ville (Town Hall) in 1845–1850. Within the Town Hall are the Musée d'Art et d'Histoire (paintings of the 19th and 20th c., enamels, furniture, ceramics) and the Musée Archéologique (prehistoric, classical and medieval antiquities).
The Passage de l'Ancre, a street running between the Tour St-Martial and the Tour de la Madeleine, links the Vieux Palais (12th c.) with the Palais Neuf (14th c.). The Cour de la Madeleine, in the Vieux Palais, is particularly fine.

* Cathedral

On the north side of the Town Hall is the imposing Cathedral of St-Just, with a magnificent choir (at 41 m/135 ft one of the highest and largest in France) built between 1272 and 1332 in a bold North French Gothic style; the rest of the building remained unfinished. It has beautiful stained glass (14th c.) and a rich treasury (tapestries, goldsmith's work).
In the south-west of the town is the Early Gothic church of St-Paul-Serge (12th–13th c.), with a fine choir and furnishings. In the Crypte Archéologique are the excavated remains of an Early Christian necropolis (4th c.).
A little way east is the Maison des Trois Nourrices (House of the Three Nurses), a 16th c. house in Renaissance style in which Cinq-Mars, one of the conspirators in a plot against Richelieu, was arrested.
Farther east is the old Eglise de Lamourgier (13th–14th c.), with a battlemented choir. It now contains a Musée Lapidaire with ancient and medieval remains.

Horreum

The Horreum is an underground Roman warehouse.

Narbonne-Plage

16 km/10 miles south-east is Narbonne-Plage, a modern seaside resort with a large sandy beach.

* Fontfroide

15 km/9 miles south-west is the Cistercian abbey of Fontfroide, with a Romanesque church (13th c.) and the finest cloister in southern France. Nearby, in Lézignan-Corbières, is a Wine Museum.

Perpignan

Perpignan (Catalan Perpinyà; alt. 24 m/80 ft; pop. 114,000), the old capital of Roussillon, from 1278 to 1344 capital of the kingdom of Majorca (which included the Balearics, Roussillon, Cerdagne and the coastal region extending east to Montpellier) and now the chief town of the département of Pyrénées-Orientales and the see of a bishop, lies near the Spanish frontier at the foot of the Pyrenees, at the junction of the rivers Têt and Basse, some 10 km/6 miles from the Mediterranean.

History

The history of Perpignan was closely bound up with that of the county of Roussillon. Like many other towns, it was surrounded by fortifications designed by Vauban which were pulled down around 1900 to allow the town to expand.

Old town

The central feature of the old town is the Place de la République, with the Theatre. On the north side of the old town is the Castillet, a fortified town gate (1367) built of red brick (fine view from tower) which is the town's principal landmark and emblem. It houses the Casa Pairal, a museum of Catalonian folk art and traditions.

Casa Pairal

*Cathedral

A little way east is the Cathedral of St-Jean, which dates mainly from the 14th–15th c. but also incorporates elements from the earlier Romanesque church of St-Jean-le-Vieux (the former entrance to the south aisle, the Portail du Christ and the chapel of Notre-Dame dels Correchs, the entrance to which is under the organ gallery). The interior of St-Jean is splendidly decorated: the most notable features are the 16th and 17th c. reredos, the 17th c. high altar of white marble (by Claude Perret) and the font, which is believed to be pre-Romanesque. Outside St-Jean, by the south doorway, is a chapel containing an expressive carved crucifix known as the "Dévot Christ".

*Loge de Mer

South of the Castillet, in the centre of the old town, is the Loge de Mer (14th–15th c.), which formerly housed the Exchange and the Maritime Court. It was given its present form in the 16th c., when extensive alterations were carried out.

Diagonally opposite the Loge de Mer is a bronze figure, "Venus", by Aristide Maillol.

Adjoining the Loge de Mer is the Hôtel de Ville (Town Hall, 13th–17th c.), with fine wrought-iron gates. In the courtyard is another piece of sculpture by Maillol, "La Méditerranée". The Palais de la Députation dates from the 15th century the Maison Julia, a small palace, from the 14th century.

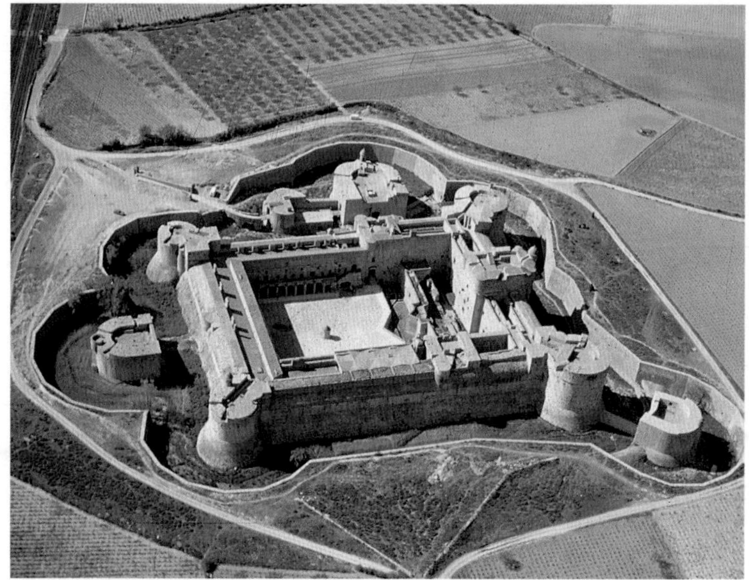
The fort of Salses

Museums

Farther south is the Musée Hyacinthe Rigaud, with works by the portrait-painter Hyacinthe Rigaud (1659–1743), paintings by Spanish and Catalan masters of the 14th–16th centuries and pictures by Ingres, Tintoretto and modern artists like Picasso, Maillol, Dufy and Calder.
The Musée d'Histoire Naturelle is devoted mainly to the flora and fauna of southern France.

Citadel

To the south of the old town is the massive citadel, built in the 17th and 18th centuries on a star-shaped plan. From the outer circuit of walls there is a good view of the town.

*Palais des Rois de Majorque

In the heart of the citadel is the Palace of the Kings of Majorca, a fine example of medieval architecture. Built in 1276 as the residence of King Jaime I, it is laid out round a courtyard with Gothic arcades. From the keep there are fine views.
The church of Ste-Marie-la-Réal, which dates from the 14th c., was the parish church of the kings of Majorca. In the first chapel on the right is a fine 15th c. entombment.

Côte des Perpignanais La Salanque

The stretch of coast between the Etang de Leucate in the north and the resort of Argelès-Plage (see Côte Vermeille) in the south, which is mostly flat, with beaches of fine sand, is known as the Côte des Perpignanais or La Salanque.

Port-Leucate Port-Barcarès

Port-Leucate and Port-Barcarès, the most northerly places on this stretch of coast, lie on the narrow spit of land which separates the Etang de Leucate (also known as the Etang de Salses) from the sea. These are two of the new and carefully planned holiday centres, laid out round boating marinas and equipped with every conceivable amenity and facility for entertainment and water sports.
Inland, at the west end of the Etang de Leucate, is the fort of Salses (see below).

Uzès

Côte Vermeille

South-east of Perpignan extends the Côte Vermeille (see entry), with a number of seaside resorts.

Canet-Plage

East of Perpignan is Canet-Plage, originally a seaside resort frequented by the Perpignanais but now a highly organised holiday and leisure centre. South of the town is the Etang de Canet et de St-Nazaire.

St-Cyprien-Plage

St-Cyprien-Plage too has undergone an intensive process of modernisation. It has an interesting museum with works by Matisse, Cézanne, Braque and Miró. A few kilometres inland is the attractive little town of Elne (see Côte Vermeille).

Argelès-Plage

See Côte Vermeille

Salses

15 km/9 miles north of Perpignan on the Etang de Leucate is Salses (alt. 12 m/40 ft; pop. 2000). The fort of Salses, built on the Via Domitia, the old Roman road from Narbonne to Spain, commands a narrow passage between the Mediterranean and the hilly hinterland, a route followed by Hannibal during his campaign against Rome. The fort was built by the Spaniards in the 15th c. and altered by Vauban in the late 17th c. From the five-storey tower there are fine views in all directions.

Rivesaltes

The road to Salses passes Rivesaltes, famed for its excellent wine. Other places noted for their wine are the neighbouring little town of Baixas and Thuir, to the south, where a well known aperitif is also made. Baixas has a 17th c. church with a magnificent altar.

Sète

Sète (pop. 42,000), situated at the foot of Mont St-Clair, is traversed by many canals. After Narbonne and Aigues-Mortes were cut off from the sea by the accumulation of sand it became the principal port for the North African trade. It is now an important fishing and commercial port. The Vieux Port dates from the time of Louis XIV. From the Môle St-Louis there are fine views of the town and Mont St-Clair (175 m/574 ft; views), on the slopes of which is the 18th c. citadel. In the "*cimetière marin*", the "cemetery by the sea" celebrated by Paul Valéry (1871–1945), a native of Sète, in a famous poem, Valéry himself is buried. Near the cemetery is the Musée Paul-Valéry, with mementoes of the poet and exhibits and documents on the history of the town. There is also a room devoted to the singer Georges Brassens (1921–1981), who lived as a boy in Sète and is also buried here.

*Mont St-Clair

Musée Paul-Valéry

Uzès

Uzès (pop. 8000) is picturesquely situated on a tree-planted hill above the valley of the Alzon. Its main square is the beautiful Place aux Herbes, surrounded by houses with vaulted arcades.

Château Ducal

North of the Place aux Herbes is the Château Ducal, residence of the Dukes of Uzès, which dates from the 11th–17th centuries. In the courtyard is a fine Renaissance façade of 1565. From the 11th c. Tour Bermonde, with a balustrade of 1839, there are fine panoramic views. Opposite the entrance to the Château is the Hôtel de Ville (Town Hall, 1773). North-east of the Château is the entrance to the Crypte, an Early Christian place of worship hewn from the rock.

Bishop's Palace

The former Bishop's Palace now houses a lawcourt, the municipal library and the Musée d'Art et de Tradition de l'Uzège (art and folk art; mementoes of the writer André Gide). The Hôtel du Baron de Castille opposite dates from the 18th c., and the Cathedral of St-Théodorit from the 17th–19th c. The Tour Fénestrelle, a round tower (12th c.) 42 m/140 ft high, is a bell-tower on the Lombard model.

The church of St-Etienne (on the southern edge of the old town) was built in 1765–1778, and the nearby tower in the 13th c. In Arpaillargues (4km/2½ miles west on the D982) there is a collection of vintage cars in the "Musée 1900".

Lille — L4

Region: Nord–Pas-de-Calais. Département: Nord
Altitude: 1–23 m/3–75 ft. Population: 174,000

Situation and characteristics

Lille, the largest city in French Flanders, chief town of the Nord département, the see of a bishop and a university town, lies near the Belgian frontier on the canalised river Deule. It is the centre of a large industrial area with a population of around a million, in which the textile, chemical and engineering industries predominate. Lille has few medieval buildings, and the pattern of the city centre is set by a number of imposing 19th c. buildings. General de Gaulle was born in Lille in 1890.

History

Lille, for long the capital of the County of Flanders, finally passed to France under the treaty of Utrecht in 1713. The earlier form of the name was L'Isle, reflecting its situation on an "island" between the Deule and the Lys.

Sights

Place du Théâtre

On the north side of this square are the New Theatre (1907–1914) and the New Exchange, a building in Flemish Renaissance style with a massive tower erected after the First World War.

Old Exchange

On the south side of the square is the Old Exchange (by Julien Destré, 1652), with 24 two-storey units surrounding an arcaded courtyard in an

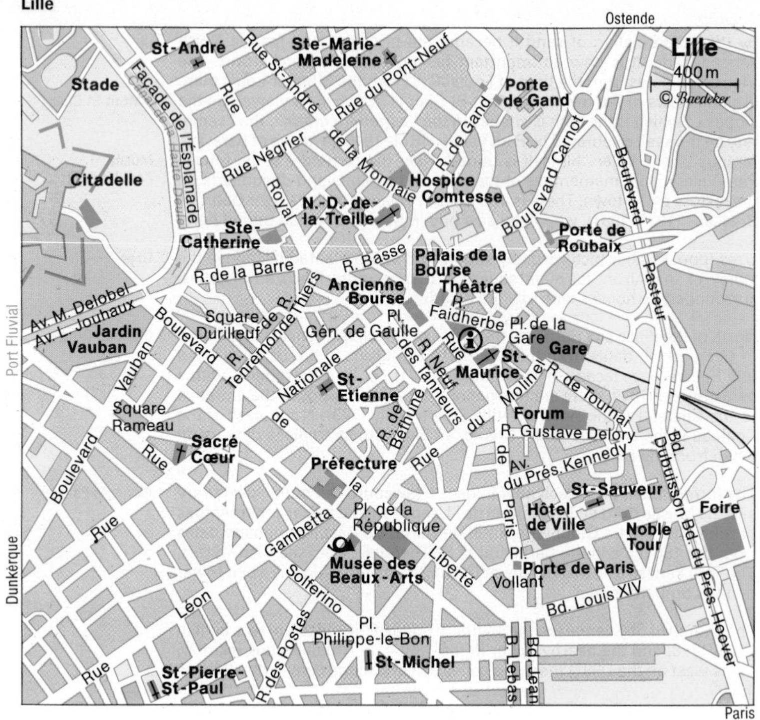

ornate Flemish Baroque style. In the courtyard is a monument to Napoleon I (1854). The west front looks on to the Place du Général-de-Gaulle.

Palais Rihour

A little to the south is Place Rihour, with a large war memorial and the Palais Rihour (15th c.), once the residence of the Dukes of Burgundy. Farther south-west is the Jesuit church of St-Etienne (18th c.; fine pulpit), with the former Jesuit college (1605), now the Military Hospital, to the left.

Churches
*St-Maurice

The Gothic church of St-Maurice (14th–19th c.) has five aisles of the same height and 36 tall columns; in one of its chapels is a 16th c. wood statue of the Scourging. North-west of St-Maurice, in Rue Royale, is the Gothic church of Ste-Catherine (15th c., enlarged in 1725), with a "Martyrdom of St Catherine" by Rubens (*c.* 1622) in the north aisle. At the other end of Rue Royale, which is lined by handsome buildings, is the 18th c. church of St-André. To the east of Ste-Catherine is the Cathedral of Notre-Dame-de-la-Treille (19th–20th c., unfinished).
To the north is the church of Ste-Marie-Madeleine (begun 1675), a handsome circular structure with a dome 50 m/165 ft high. The present façade dates from 1884.

Citadel

Beyond the Deule Canal is the imposing citadel, one of the finest of Vauban's fortifications, built for Louis XIV in 1668–1670 after the conquest of Lille. It is entered through the Porte Royale.

Porte de Paris

The Rue de Paris ends at the Porte de Paris, a large triumphal arch erected in honour of Louis XIV between 1682 and 1695 (architect Simon Vollant)

The Old Exchange in Place du Général-de-Gaulle

which originally formed part of the town walls. It is France's largest triumphal arch after the Arc de Triomphe in Paris. Immediately east is the Hôtel de Ville (Town Hall, 1925–1933).

Hospice Comtesse

The Hospice Comtesse, founded in 1237 and rebuilt in the 17th and 18th centuries, still preserves a 15th c. hospital ward with a handsome timber roof. It now houses the Musée d'Art et de Traditions Populaires (decorative art, folk art and traditions).

Vieux Lille

The old town of Lille, north of the Hospice, is now being carefully restored.

**Musée des Beaux-Arts

The Musée des Beaux-Arts, on the south side of the Place de la Liberté, is one of the richest museums in France. It has a celebrated collection of paintings by Flemish, Dutch, Italian, Spanish and French masters, including works by Goya, Rubens, Van Dyck, Delacroix, Courbet, Monet, Renoir and Toulouse-Lautrec, as well as sculpture, applied and decorative art, folk art and some 3000 Italian and French drawings.

Métro

Lille's most modern sight is the fully automatic underground railway, the Métro, which came into operation in 1983 and serves the main parts of the city.

Surroundings of Lille

*Villeneuve-d'Ascq

North-east of Lille is Villeneuve-d'Ascq, which has a fine Museum of Modern Art with over 200 exhibits, including works by Bauchant, Braque, Kandinsky, Klee, Laurens, Léger, Masson, Miró, Modigliani, Picasso, Rouault and Van Dongen. The founders of the museum were among the leading private collectors of Cubist art in France. There are periodic special exhibitions in a new annex.

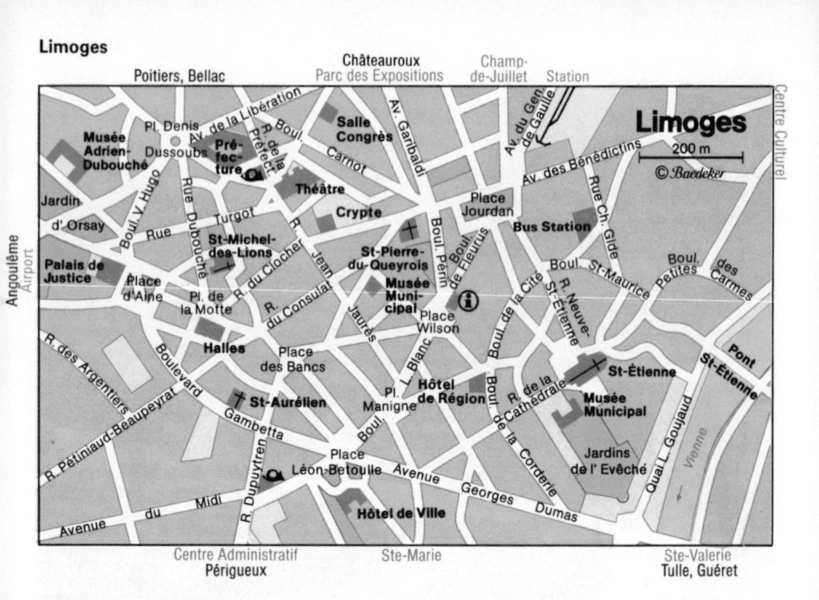

Limoges

I9

Region: Limousin
Département: Haute-Vienne
Altitude: 290 m/950 ft
Population: 145,000

Situation and characteristics

Limoges, originally the Gallo-Roman town of Civitas Lemoricum, the see of a bishop since the 3rd c. and now chief town of the département of Haute-Vienne, lies on the right bank of the Vienne in the hilly country of the Limousin (see entry). It is famous for Limoges enamel, which was made here from the 12th to the 17th c.; its greatest days were in the Middle Ages. Limoges is now a busy industrial town (principally porcelain and footwear).

Sights

*Cathedral

In the south-east of the town is its most important monument and only Gothic building, the Cathedral of St-Etienne, begun in 1273, continued in various later periods but not finally completed until the second half of the 19th c. In the north transept is the Portail de St-Jean, with carved doors (legends of St Martial and St Stephen) dating from the first half of the 16th c. The tower is 62 m/205 ft high, the three lower storeys being Romanesque and the four upper ones Gothic. Notable features of the interior are the monuments of three church dignitaries of the 14th and 16th centuries round the choir, the richly decorated rood screen in Italian Renaissance style and some old stained glass.

Musée Municipal

Adjoining the cathedral is the former Bishop's Palace, now the Municipal Museum (Limoges enamels, Egyptian antiquities, local history, pictures). Behind it are the Jardins de l'Evêché.

Other sights
*Pont St-Etienne

Below the cathedral, to the east, is the eight-arched Pont St-Etienne (13th c.). South of this is the 12th c. Pont St-Martial. To the west of the cathedral is the old-world Rue de la Boucherie, where the butchers had their shops in the Middle Ages. At its west end is the chapel of St-Aurélien (15th c.), with a 17th c. west front and tower and a richly decorated interior.

St-Pierre-du-Queyroix

A little way east of the Place de la République, the central feature of the town, is the church of St-Pierre-du-Queyroix (13th–14th c.), with choir-stalls of 1513, a 16th c. Pietà and a 14th c. figure of Christ. West of this is the church of St-Michel-des-Lions (13th, 14th and 16th c.), with Late Gothic stained glass, relics of St Martial and a 15th c. Pietà.

St-Michel-des-Lions

*Musée National Adrien-Dubouché

This museum, established in 1867, has an important ceramic collection, including items from the Limousin, China, Japan and Persia.
Visitors interested in Limoges enamel will want to see the Enamel Workshop at 31 rue des Tanneries, where the techniques of enamel-working are explained.

Surroundings of Limoges

Lakes

The Lac de St-Pardoux, 30 km/19 miles north, and the Lac de Vassivière, 50 km/31 miles east of Limoges, are two large lakes which offer scope for all kinds of water sports.

Limousin

H–K 8/9

*Situation and characteristics

The Limousin lies on the north-western edge of the Massif Central, in the geographical centre of France, taking in the départements of Creuse (chief town Guéret), Haute-Vienne (Limoges) and Corrèze (Tulle). It is the most thinly populated region in France apart from Corsica, with an area of 16,942 sq. km/6541 sq. miles and a population of 737,153. Its capital is Limoges.
The Limousin is frequently associated in visitors' minds with the neighbouring regions of Périgord to the south-west and Quercy to the south-east. Still rather off the beaten track of tourism, the Limousin has preserved much unspoiled natural beauty. Its ranges of hills, outliers of the Massif Central nowhere exceeding 1000 m/3300 ft in height, are broken up by plateaux and river valleys, the most important of which is the valley of the Vézère. It is well supplied with rivers, streams and lakes where fishermen and water sports enthusiasts will find plenty of scope.
The region's main sources of revenue are agriculture, the manufacture of porcelain and the production of carpets and tapestries. Uranium is worked in the départements of Haute-Vienne and Creuse.

History

The Limousin was one of the territories that developed out of the Roman province of Aquitania from the 5th c. onwards. After the centuries of Visigothic and Frankish rule there came into being within the French kingdom various counties, some of which were later raised to the status of duchies or became appanages of members of the royal family. After intermittent periods of English rule in the 12th, 13th and 14th centuries these territories returned to French allegiance between the 13th and 16th c., and in 1607 Henry IV brought the Limousin to the French crown. Then at the end of the 18th c. the provinces which had been formed from the old duchies and counties were divided into the present départements.
Like the neighbouring region of Périgord, the Limousin has many prehistoric remains like standing stones and megalithic chamber tombs.
There was a great emergence of Romanesque art between the 11th and 13th centuries, to such an extent that Gothic made relatively little headway. The 14th c. was a time of trial for the Limousin, with famine, plague, exploitation and plunder; and yet it was during this period, through the efforts of two French Popes, Clement VI (Pierre de Rosiers) and his nephew Gregory XI (Pierre-Roger de Beaufort), that the Limousin gave the Church a dozen patriarchs, forty cardinals and more than 300 bishops – thus fulfilling the prophecy by St Martial, who brought Christianity to this region about 250, that this "land of saints" would prove a fertile soil for the church.

Aubusson, on the Creuse

The manufacture of porcelain, which has won international fame for the Limousin, and for Limoges in particular, was brought to the region from Sèvres about 1770. It was little affected by the Revolution, and after the First Empire centred increasingly on Limoges, which thus in the course of time acquired a virtual monopoly. The great Impressionist Auguste Renoir (1841–1919) began his artistic career as a porcelain painter in Limoges.

Climate

The summer climate is relatively mild, but the winter is usually cold and rainy.

Sights in the Limousin

Ahun

Ahun (pop. 2000) was a place of some consequence in Gallo-Roman times. The church has a Romanesque choir and an 11th c. crypt containing a rare reliquary.

* Moutier d'Ahun

The former abbey of Moutier d'Ahun, with a square tower, has beautiful 17th c. carved woodwork by Simon Bauer.

Ambazac

The little town of Ambazac is surrounded by hills rising to 700 m/2300 ft. The church contains a valuable and unusual chest-shaped reliquary (1123).

Argentat

Argentat (pop. 3400), picturesquely situated in the Dordogne valley, is a good base for excursions in the surrounding area. The best view of the town is from the old stone bridge.

Aubazines

This Cistercian abbey was founded in the 12th c. by a local saint, Stephen of Obasine, whose tomb has fine carved decoration (13th c.). The church also contains a 12th c. oak press, remains of frescoes and a fine treasury.

Aubusson
* Tapestries

Aubusson (pop. 6000), in the Creuse valley, is a charming little town of narrow streets and lanes. It has been famed for its patterned carpets since

Château de la Treyne on the Dordogne

the 15th c., when Flemish Protestant incomers brought the craft with them. In the 18th c. Watteau, Boucher and other artists created the designs of Aubusson carpets. The town still has important carpet and tapestry manufactories (which visitors can see round). There is an exhibition of new works every summer in the Town Hall. An old tapestry-weaving workshop can be seen in the Maison du Vieux Tapissier. Aubusson is also a good base from which to explore the beautiful Creuse valley.

***Beaulieu-sur-Dordogne**

This little town (pop. 1600) on the right bank of the Dordogne grew up round the magnificent 12th c. abbey of St-Pierre. The south doorway is one of the great masterpieces of Romanesque sculpture, with a representation of the Last Judgment in the tympanum. The church has a rich treasury.

Bellac

Bellac (pop. 5400), picturesquely situated on the border with Poitou, was the birthplace of the dramatist Jean Giraudoux (1882–1944), and has a monument to him. He is commemorated by an annual festival of music and drama at the end of June and beginning of July. Giraudoux celebrated the beauty of the Limousin in his novel "Suzanne et le Pacifique".
The church of Notre-Dame has two parallel naves, one Romanesque and the other Gothic, and a 12th c. reliquary.

Bourganeuf

Bourganeuf lies on a hill at the meeting of three valleys. The Tour de Zimzim (so called because of a legend that the brother of a Turkish sultan was imprisoned here), a relic of an ancient castle, is notable for its three-storey structure of oak beams; there is a fine view from the top. The Town Hall contains late 18th c. Aubusson tapestries.

Brive-la-Gaillarde

Brive (pop. 54,000), situated on the Corrèze, near the border with Périgord, is called Brive-la-Gaillarde ("sturdy") in recognition of its stubborn resistance during numerous sieges. It has a number of handsome old houses like the Hôtel de Labenche and the 16th c. Tour des Echevins. The Musée

Ernest-Rupin, in an elegant building of the time of Louis XIII, displays works of art and documents of regional interest. The Musée Edmond-Michelet is devoted to the French Resistance of the Second World War.

Chambon-sur-Voueize

The beautifully situated little town of Chambon-sur-Voueize (pop. 1200) has one of the most important Romanesque sacred buildings in the Limousin, the church of Ste-Valérie (12th c.; restored 1850). The rectangular tower dates from the 13th c., and the interior has fine 17th c. panelling.

Evaux-les-Bains

2 km/1½ miles away is the little spa of Evaux-les-Bains, which was frequented in Roman times, with some 30 springs (14–60°C/57–140°F). The Romanesque church of St-Pierre-et-St-Paul has a fine tower.

Coussac-Bonneval

This little town (pop. 1600), in a beautiful setting, has a fine 14th c. castle (altered in the 18th and 19th c.). It contains a collection of exhibits telling the extraordinary story of Achmet Pasha, born in 1675 as the son of the seigneur of Bonneval, who went to Constantinople, became a pasha and died there.

Le Chalard

Le Chalard, near Coussac-Bonneval, has a massive Romanesque church.

Vallée de la Creuse

Crozant

The river Creuse, flowing down from the Massif Central, has carved out a picturesque valley, with impressive gorges and the 15 km/9 mile long artificial lake of Eguzon. At the south end of the lake is Crozant, with the ruins of an important medieval castle. The Creuse flows into the Vienne after a course of 250 km/155 miles.

* **Le Dorat**

The church of St-Pierre (12th c.) is one of the finest churches in the Limousin, with a three-storey tower on an octagonal plan.

* **Dordogne**

* Dams

The Dordogne, one of France's longest rivers, is also held to be its most beautiful. Between Bort-les-Orgues and Beaulieu-sur-Dordogne it flows through the Limousin and then on into Périgord, frequently dammed to produce hydroelectric power. There are large dams in the Limousin at Bort-les-Orgues and Marèges, as well as smaller ones like the Barrage de l'Aigle, Barrage du Chastang and Barrage du Sablier, near Argentat. These various dams, extending over a distance of more than 100 km/60 miles like a giant staircase, have transformed the landscape. Between Bort-les-Orgues and the Barrage du Sablier the river falls some 400 m/1300 ft, regulated by five dams.
The Dordogne is formed at the foot of the Puy de Sancy by the junction of the Dore and the Dogne, which also combine to give it its name. Leaving the volcanic region of Auvergne (see entry), it enters the granite hills of the Limousin, and after a course of almost 500 km/310 miles joins with the Garonne to form the Gironde, which flows into the Atlantic at Royan.

Limoges

See entry

* **Mont Gargan**

From the summit of Mont Gargan (731 m/2398 ft) there are marvellous panoramic views.

Plateau de Millevaches

* Lac de Vassivière

The Millevaches plateau, in the south-eastern Limousin between the valleys of the Vienne and the Vézère, reaches a height of just under 1000 m/3300 ft. The name has nothing to do with *vaches* (cows), but is derived from the Celtic word *batz,* "spring" – of which there are many in this region. The plateau, sparsely populated, has a number of picturesque artificial lakes formed by dams (Lac de Vassivière, Lac de Faux-la-Montagne, Lac de Viaman, Lac du Chamet), and is at its most beautiful in spring and autumn.

Felletin

Felletin lies south of Aubusson and, like Aubusson, is a carpet-making town. The Eglise du Moûtier (12th c., much rebuilt in 15th c.) has a tower with a finely carved keystone.

Meymac

Farther south is Meymac, with a 12th c. abbey church which has fine granite

Gimel Falls

In the Corrèze valley

capitals. Some of the abbey buildings have been restored. The highest of the beautiful surrounding hills is Mont Bessou, above Meymac. From the Signal d'Audouze (854 m/2802 ft), half way between Felletin and Meymac on D36, there are magnificent panoramic views, extending as far as the volcanic cones of Auvergne. This hill is the watershed between the Loire and the Dordogne. Adjoining the Millevaches plateau are the Monts des Monédières (911 m/2989 ft), from where there are also fantastic views.

Oradour-sur-Glane

This little town acquired tragic fame on June 10th 1944, when its 642 inhabitants were massacred by 160 SS men. The ruins of the village have been preserved as they were, along with the cemetery, which contains a memorial. A new village with the same name has been built nearby.

Pompadour

Pompadour is famous for the château which Louis XV presented to his mistress Madame de Pompadour. Louis also founded (1761) the stud farm which has made Pompadour a centre of horse-breeding (Anglo-Arab horses) and racing (annual horse shows). The National Stud (Haras National) can be visited.

St-Junien

St-Junien has a fine Romanesque church (11th–12th c.), typically Limousin in style. The richly carved tomb of St Junien is one of the masterworks of 12th c. Romanesque sculpture. There are still many 14th and 15th c. houses in the town.

St-Léonard-de-Noblat

St-Léonard-de-Noblat (pop. 5300) is a charming little town with picturesque old houses (13th–16th c.), the birthplace of the physicist Gay-Lussac (1778–1850), discoverer of the law of volumes. The town, situated on a hill, was a staging-point on the medieval pilgrims' route to Santiago de Compostela, and has a beautiful Romanesque church (11th c.) with 15th c. choir-stalls; the tower has fine capitals.

St-Yrieix-la-Perche

This little town (pop. 8000), situated in a fertile stock-farming region, had kaolin deposits which gave the first impulse to the manufacture of porcelain in Limoges. The collegiate church known as the Moûtier (12th–13th c.), with the austere aspect of a fortified church, occupies the site of an abbey founded in the 6th c. The Tour du Plo was once part of the town walls.

La Souterraine

La Souterraine (pop. 5850), on the site of a Gallo-Roman settlement, is another little town of medieval aspect. The Porte St-Jean, a town gate dating from the 14th–15th c., has two turrets. The church (12th–13th c.) is built over an early 11th c. crypt.

Tulle

Tulle (pop. 20,600), the industrial capital of the Lower Limousin (Bas-Limousin), chief town of the département of Corrèze and the see of a bishop since 1317, lies in the narrow valley of the Corrèze. Its main attractions are its many handsome Renaissance houses and the Cathedral of Notre-Dame (12th–14th c.), a former abbey church, the choir and transepts of which were destroyed in 1793. The 75 m/245 ft high tower dates from the 14th c. On the south side of the church is a small cloister, now housing a museum.

Corrèze valley
*Gimel Falls

A pleasant excursion from Tulle leads north-east up the valley of the Corrèze by way of the village of Gimel. Near the village, in the Parc Vuillier de Montane, are the magnificent Gimel Falls, which plunge down 143 m/470 ft in three stages. The return route is via Naves, which has a church with a large 17th c. carved altar.

Ussel

Ussel (alt. 631 m/2070 ft; pop. 12,250) has a number of 15th–17th c. buildings in the centre of the town and a Roman eagle found at the mill of Peuch, the original site of the town.

Uzerche
*Situation

Uzerche (pop. 3200) is one of the most attractive little towns in the Limousin, in virtue both of its situation and its buildings. There is a saying that if you have a house in Uzerche you can claim to possess a château in the Limousin. The town's main features of interest are the Romanesque church of St-Pierre and the Porte Bécharie, once part of the town's circuit of walls. There are fine views from the Esplanade de la Lunade.

Sport and Recreation in the Limousin

Water sports

There are numerous rivers and a number of lakes which offer scope for fishing and sailing. The rivers also offer the possibility of attractive canoe and kayak trips.

Riding

Information about riding holidays can be obtained from the Ligue Equestre du Limousin, La Jachère, F-19100 Brive.

Cycling and walking

For cyclists and walkers there are many quiet and sometimes lonely footpaths and tracks running through beautiful scenery. Several of France's waymarked long-distance trails (identified by the letters GR, for *grande randonnée,* and a number) run through the Limousin.

Other sports

Information about other facilities for sport and recreation (golf, cooking courses, craft activities, etc.) can be obtained from local tourist information offices.

Loire Valley

E–M 7–9

**Situation and characteristics

The beauty of the Loire valley, its mild climate and the former importance of the river as a navigable waterway led many French kings and noble families to build fortified castles and later magnificent châteaux in this area, particularly in the most beautiful middle section of the valley, and as a result the Loire valley is now one of the most popular tourist regions in France.

Castles and *châteaux

The fortified castles of the 13th and 14th centuries, like Sully, Langeais, Loches, Chinon and Angers, were followed by sumptuous Renaissance châteaux, the finest of which are Chambord, Blois (see entry), Chenonceaux and Amboise (see entry). Thus in the Loire valley it is possible to follow the development of French architecture over six centuries.

Parks

Many of the châteaux have beautiful gardens and parks in the French style, which in some cases, as at Villandry, are the château's principal attraction.

*Son et lumière

An additional attraction is provided in summer by the *son et lumière* shows at many of the châteaux.

Loire valley

The Loire valley in the narrower sense is thought of as extending from Giens to somewhere short of Nantes (perhaps around Ancenis), since the river's most westerly stretch is in Brittany. It passes successively through the four départements of Loiret, Loir-et-Cher, Indre-et-Loire and Maine-et-Loire, which have replaced the older territorial designations of the Orléanais, the Blésois (round Blois), Touraine and Anjou.

Course of the river

The Loire is France's longest river, with a course of 1020 km/635 miles, and along with its tributaries drains an area of 120,000 sq. km/46,000 sq. miles, or roughly 22% of France's total area.
The Loire rises on the Gerbier de Jonc (1551 m/5089 ft), in the northern Cévennes some 70 km/45 miles south of St-Etienne. From there it flows north through the hills of the Velay into the Le Puy basin and through the coalfields and industrial areas of St-Etienne and Roanne. It then pursues a winding course between the Bourbonnais and Nivernais districts to its most northerly point, which it reaches at Orléans, on the southern edge of the Paris basin. From there it flows west, flanked by wide river meadows, and through the Armorican massif to reach the Atlantic at the most southerly point of Brittany.

Navigability

The course of the Loire is interrupted in many places by sandbanks and low tree-clad islands. The level of the river varies considerably over the year, with a period of low water in summer and violent spates in spring and autumn. Efforts have been made since the 13th c., by the construction of dams and canals, to control the very serious flooding which has occurred on many occasions down the centuries (with particularly bad floods in 1846, 1856, 1866 and 1910). After the last great flood in 1980 there was much discussion of a controversial plan – claimed by its sponsors to be necessary not only to control flooding but also to improve the supply of cooling water for nuclear power stations and to meet the increased demand for water – to build a large new dam. This plan has now been abandoned in favour of making more subtle adjustments to the water flow in the upper reaches of the Loire.
Shipping traffic on the Loire, once considerable, finally declined when ships of greater draught came into use and there was increased competition from the railways. Now only the lowest part of the river, below Nantes, carries any commercial shipping.
The canals (Roanne–Dijon Canal, Loire Lateral Canal and other lateral canals) are increasingly being used by pleasure boats.

Tributaries

The Loire's most important tributaries are the Allier, the Cher, the Indre and the Vienne, all on the left bank. The two principal right-bank tributaries are the Maine and the Erdre.
They are well worth exploring, since they resemble the Loire in scenic beauty, and also in their possession of fine old buildings and places of historical interest.

Economy

The fertile alluvial plain formed by deposits from the Loire and its tributaries merges into a plateau ranging in height between 50 m/165 ft and 200 m/655 ft. Fruit, vines and vegetables flourish in this prosperous agricul-

tural region, with a climate which shows maritime influences. Woodland is found mainly on the less fertile soil.
The most important towns in the Loire valley – Orléans, Blois, Tours, Angers and Nantes, which is in Brittany – all lie near the river. Thanks to their industry (mainly engineering, motor vehicle construction, textiles, glass and ceramics) they have achieved an independent economic status. Tourism also plays an important part in the economy of the Loire valley.

History

Caesar conquered this territory, then occupied by Gauls, between 58 and 51 B.C., and the process of cultural and linguistic Romanisation began. At the end of the 5th c. Gaul was conquered by the Franks. Later the Carolingians extended their domains and divided the territory into counties. The Carolingian Renaissance of the 8th and 9th centuries brought a flowering of the arts and of learning in the spirit of late antiquity.
In subsequent centuries the Huns, the Saracens and the Normans pushed into the Loire valley, fighting and plundering. During the reigns of the weak later Carolingian kings wealthy nobles gained sovereign authority over their territories and fought among themselves. There was particularly bitter rivalry between the Counts of Anjou and Blois, and when the Plantagenet rulers of Anjou succeeded to the English throne in 1154 they controlled a territory extending from the borders of Scotland to the Pyrenees. From 1216 onwards the Capetian kings of France re-established their authority; but the English returned and the conflicts of the Hundred Years War began. The English advanced steadily until Joan of Arc, appearing before Charles VII in the castle of Chinon, was given supreme command of the French forces on March 9th 1429 and freed the English-held town of Orléans on May 8th of the same year. Although Joan of Arc later fell into the hands of the English and was burned at the stake, the Loire valley remained firmly in French hands and was frequently visited by the French kings. Louis XI built the little château of Plessis-lès-Tours and the more splendid Langeais; Charles VIII built the château of Amboise; Louis XII added a wing to the château of Blois; Francis I added another, and also built Chambord. The royal example stimulated the nobility to build their own mansions and châteaux, and important royal officials built themselves handsome town houses.
This period of splendour lasted little more than 150 years. The last king to reside in the Loire valley was Henry III, who died in 1589. The great days ended in the reign of Henry IV, and thereafter the region suffered from economic difficulties, which became worse in the 18th c., when many businesses in Orléans, Amboise, Tours and Saumur were forced to close down. During the French Revolution there was fighting in the territory of Anjou.

Sights in the Loire Valley

Amboise

See entry

Angers

See entry

Azay-le-Rideau
** Château

Azay-le-Rideau (pop. 3000) has a magnificent Renaissance château, partly surrounded by a moat. It is a building of great charm and elegance, erected between 1518 and 1529 by a financier who later had to flee the country and died in exile. It is now the property of the State.
The most notable features on the ground floor are the rib-vaulted kitchen and the dining room, which has a richly decorated chimneypiece and contains a number of tapestries.
The reception rooms, on the first floor, have fine Renaissance furniture and pictures.

St-Symphorien

The church of St-Symphorien is partly Romanesque and partly Gothic. On the façade of the south aisle are the remains of Carolingian reliefs.

Azay-le-Rideau

Ornamental chimneys, Château de Chambord

Saché

In the nearby château of Saché Honoré de Balzac (1799–1850) wrote some of his novels. The room in which he worked has been preserved as it was.

Beaugency

The old-world little town of Beaugency (pop. 7330) lies on the right bank of the Loire. The Château Dunois, built by the Comte de Dunois, the "Bastard of Orléans", in the 15th c. now houses the Regional Museum (folk art and traditions, agricultural history, toys). Adjoining is a massive keep 36 m/120 ft high, a relic of an earlier fortified castle. The church of Notre-Dame (12th c.) originally belonged to an abbey. The triangular Tour St-Firmin is all that remains of a church built in the 16th c. A drama festival is held here in July.

Old town

North-west of the Château Dunois is the old part of the town, with a number of handsome buildings – the Maison des Templiers, the 17th c. Hôtel de Ville (Town Hall) and the Tour de l'Horloge (Clock-Tower), once part of the town's circuit of walls.

Blois

See entry

Bourges

See entry

Brissac

See Angers, Surroundings

****Chambord**

The mighty château of Chambord, a forerunner of Versailles, lies on the Cosson, a left-bank tributary of the Loire. It measures 117 m/384 ft by 156 m/512 ft and has no fewer than 440 rooms. A particularly notable feature is its large double staircase. Construction began in 1519, in the reign of Francis I, who spared no expense, and even had the Loire diverted to enhance the effect of the château. The treaty of 1552 under which the German princes ceded the three bishoprics of Metz, Toul and Verdun to France was signed here. The château was also a favourite residence of later kings (except Henry III and IV). Louis XIV frequently stayed here, and Molière wrote several of his comedies in the château, including the "Bourgeois Gentilhomme" (1670). In the 17th c. the château was granted by Louis XV to Maurice of Saxony. It suffered no major damage during the French Revolution, though all the furniture was sold. Chambord became State property in 1930.

Park

The park, which has an area of 5500 hectares/13,600 acres, four-fifths of it under forest, is surrounded by a wall 32 km/20 miles long (the longest in France), with six gates giving access to six avenues which lead to the castle. The very beautiful terrace, constructed under Italian influence, was a central feature of court life when the king was in residence.

Châteaudun

See Ile de France

***Chaumont-sur-Loire**

The village of Chaumont (pop. 1000) lies above the Loire, with a fine view of the valley from its terrace. On higher ground stands the château with its four round towers, rebuilt in the 15th and 16th centuries on earlier foundations. On its south side extends the park with its tall old cedars.
The original fortress-like aspect of the château was relieved by the later insertion of windows. It contains fine tapestries and works of art of the 15th and 16th centuries. South-west of the château are the stables (1877).

****Chenonceaux**

The little village of Chenonceaux (pop. 500) lies on the north bank of the Cher. The Château de Chenonceau (without the x) was built from 1513 onwards on the site of an earlier building by Charles VII's treasurer, but was later surrendered to the crown. In 1547 Henry II presented it to his favourite Diane de Poitiers, who was later forced by Henry's widow Catherine de Médicis to exchange it for Chaumont. Thereafter it was the scene of splendid entertainments. In the 18th c. the château became the property of a tax-farmer named Dupin, and Jean-Jacques Rousseau lived here for some time as tutor to his son.
The château is still in private ownership, but it is open to the public. It is approached by a fine avenue of plane-trees, at the end of which a drawbridge leads on to a terrace in front of the entrance. The central structure of the château, the Corps de Logis, with four corner towers, is built over the Cher. Beyond this is a two-storey gallery built by Catherine de Médicis, also built over the river. The two lower floors, which are shown to visitors, contain pictures and tapestries. On both sides of the château are gardens laid out by Diane de Poitiers and Catherine de Médicis.

Château de Chambord, north-west front

*** Cheverny**

In the village of Cour-Cheverny (pop. 2000) is the château of Cheverny, in the classical style of the 17th c. which has preserved its original decoration and appointments. The château is in private ownership, but visitors can see the interior, which contains much period furniture and a Hunting Museum.

Forêt de Cheverny

South-east of Cheverny is the extensive Cheverny Forest, with many lakes.

Beauregard

West of Cheverny, in the Forêt de Russy, is the château of Beauregard, a hunting lodge built about 1550 and enlarged in the 18th c. It has a picture gallery containing 363 portraits.

Villesavin

10 km/6 miles north-east is the château of Villesavin, built in the 16th c. by Francis I's minister of finance.

*** Chinon**

Chinon (pop. 8000) lies on the right bank of the Vienne, with its ruined castle looming over it on a ridge of hill which was already fortified in Roman times. The most important event in the history of Chinon was the meeting between Charles VII and Joan of Arc on March 9th 1429 which marked the beginning of the reconquest of French territory from the English.
François Rabelais (1494–1553) was born near Chinon and spent his childhood here.
The castle ward contains three separate strongholds – from east to west Fort St-Georges, the Château du Milieu and the Château du Coudray – with moats between them. It is entered under a 35 m/115 ft high clock-tower which houses a Joan of Arc Museum.
The old part of the town lies between the castle and the river. Particularly worth seeing is Rue Voltaire with its 15th and 16th c. houses. In the main square, the Place du Grand Carroi, is the House of the States General. The church of St-Maurice is 12th c., St-Etienne 15th c. There is an interesting museum of local history, the Musée du Vieux Chinon.

Atomic Museum

In the atomic reactor of Avoine-Chinon (now closed down), 11 km/7 miles north-west of Chinon, is France's first Atomic Museum.

Cléry-St-André

Cléry-St-André (pop. 1850) has a 15th c. church containing the tombs of Louis XI (1423–1483) and his wife. The marble statue of the king dates from the 17th c., the original bronze statue having been removed and melted down by the Huguenots.

Chenonceau, Corps de Logis and Gallery

Château de Chaumont

***Cunault**

The former abbey church of Cunault (11th–13th c.) is a fine example of Romanesque architecture, with remains of Romanesque and Gothic frescoes in the apse domes. On the south side of the ambulatory is a reliquary of polychrome wood.

Fontevraud-l'Abbaye

See Anjou

Gien

Gien (pop. 16,800) is for many visitors the beginning of the real Loire valley. In spite of heavy destruction during the Second World War it is an attractive little town. The château, an unpretentious building of 1494–1500, now houses a Museum of Hunting and Falconry and displays a selection of the characteristic Gien earthenware. North-west of the château is the church of Ste-Jeanne-d'Arc (19th c., rebuilt after the Second World War), which has a 15th c. tower. In the north-west of the town, near the river, is a ceramic factory founded in 1821 which is open to visitors.

La Bussière

12 km/7½ miles north-east of Gien is the moated château of La Bussière (originally 13th c., later rebuilt). It contains a small Fishing Museum.

***Langeais**

Langeais (pop. 4100) has one of the fastest-built châteaux in the Loire valley: its construction took only four years. It has remained unchanged down the centuries; the medieval rooms with their original decoration and fine wall-hangings are particularly worth seeing. Within the castle ward is what is believed to be the oldest keep in France (10th c.). The present château was built by Louis XI in 1465–1469. Charles VIII was married here to Anne de Bretagne in 1491.

Loches

*Cité Médiévale

Loches (pop. 7000) is picturesquely situated above the Indre, a left-bank tributary of the Loire. On the hill above the town is the Cité Médiévale, surrounded by a circuit of walls 2 km/1½ miles long. This town within a town is entered through the Porte Royale (13th and 15th c.), a fortified gate which was once approached by a drawbridge.
Within the Cité is the church of St-Ours, originally founded in 962 but mostly dating in its present form from the 12th c. The château (15th–16th c.), once the residence of Charles VII, has a richly decorated interior. Its most notable features are the Salle Charles VII, the Salle Jeanne d'Arc (which contains a small collection of weapons and a number of tapestries), the Chapelle d'Anne de Bretagne and a room containing the alabaster tomb of Charles VII's mistress Agnès Sorel.
To the south, at the end of the upper town, is the 11th c. keep, from the top of which there are fine views.

Lower town

The main features of interest in the lower town are a number of gates, the 16th c. watch-tower of St-Antoine and the Town Hall, also 16th c.

Beaulieu

In the adjoining little town of Beaulieu are the ruins of an abbey founded about the year 1000, the Romanesque church of which has been preserved.

Le Mans

See entry

Nantes

See entry

Nevers

See Burgundy

Orléans

See entry

Paray-le-Monial

See Burgundy

St-Benoît-sur-Loire

*Church

St-Benoît-sur-Loire (pop. 2000) is famed for its great Benedictine abbey, the origins of which go back to the 7th c. The large Romanesque church, one of the finest in France, was built between 1067 and 1218. Originally the towers were higher than they now are. The outstanding feature of the church is the

Chinon, above the Vienne

porch tower (originally free-standing) with its richly carved capitals. The interior is light and beautifully proportioned. The crypt (12th c.), on the same ground-plan as the apse, contains the relics of St Benedict, brought here from the abbey of Monte Cassino in the late 7th c.

Saumur

See Anjou

St-Etienne

See entry

Suèvres

North-east of Blois, near the north bank of the Loire, is Suèvres (pop. 1200), an ancient little town with the two churches, originally Romanesque, of St-Lubin and St-Christophe.

Sully-sur-Loire

The busy little town of Sully (pop. 5800) is picturesquely situated on the Loire. The château, flanked by round towers with conical roofs and surrounded by a moat, was built in the 14th c. and enlarged in the 16th. The interior is worth seeing.
Sully several times provided a refuge for the young Voltaire, who wrote and produced his first plays in the château.

Tours

See entry

Ussé
*Château

The château of Ussé, the most romantic and fanciful of all the Loire châteaux, is said to have given Charles Perrault, the 17th c. writer of fairytales, the idea of the castle of the Sleeping Beauty. The château (which is in private ownership) was built in stages between the 15th and 17th centuries, and shows a mingling of Late Gothic and Renaissance features. The rooms open to the public contain old furniture, tapestries and weapons. In the park is a chapel in pure Renaissance style, built between 1520 and 1583.

Valençay

The château of Valençay, set in a large park, lies to the south-west of the

Ussé, the Sleeping Beauty's castle

little town of that name (pop. 3000). It was built in 1540 by Philibert Delorme, architect of the Palace of Fontainebleau. It was acquired by Talleyrand, Napoleon's foreign minister, in 1805. It shows a variety of styles: the main wing is influenced by the Italian Renaissance, while the two-storey side wing is Baroque. Only this wing is open to the public; it contains a gallery of portraits of Talleyrand's ancestors, Empire furniture, a small collection of porcelain and a Talleyrand Museum.
West of the château is an Automobile Museum.

Vendôme

Vendôme (pop. 20,000), the Gallo-Roman Vindocinum, lies 30 km/19 miles north-west of Blois on the Loir, here divided into several arms. The central feature of the town is the Place St-Martin, on the west side of which is the Tour St-Martin (15th–16th c.), a relic of a Renaissance church which was pulled down in 1857. At the north-east corner of the square is the Rue du Change, in which is the Chapelle du Lycée (1452). To the west, at the end of Rue St-Jacques, is the church of the Madeleine (1474).

*La Trinité

A little way east of Place St-Martin is the church of La Trinité (12th–15th c.), with a richly decorated façade. In front of it is a free-standing tower (12th c.). The church has fine stained glass and 15th–16th c. choir-stalls.
The buildings of the former abbey now house the Municipal Museum (religious art of the medieval and Renaissance periods).

Castle

Of the castle, originally founded in the 9th c., there survive a number of towers and extensive remains of walls (13th–15th c.).

Villandry
**Gardens

The village of Villandry (pop. 800) is noted not so much for its 16th c. château (which contains a museum with a collection of pictures) as for the beautiful Renaissance gardens. The French-style gardens as we see them today were first laid out in the 16th c.; in the 19th c. they were altered to the English style then fashionable; and in our own century they have been restored by a style-conscious owner to their original form.

The Château de Villandry

From the upper floor of the château a flight of steps leads down to the higher part of the gardens, which cover an area of some 5 hectares/12½ acres. To the left are the ornamental gardens, with the Garden of Love in the foreground, beyond which, on a lower level, are the vegetable gardens, also laid out in ornamental form.

Château

The state apartments of the château contain 18th c. furniture and tapestries, together with pictures by Italian and Spanish painters of the Renaissance and Baroque periods.
Particularly fine is the Hispano-Mauresque wooden ceiling, originally from a 13th c. mosque, which was bought by the owner of the château at an auction and then fitted together again in its new position – a task which took more than fifteen years.

Lorraine

N/O 5/6

*Situation and characteristics

The present-day region of Lorraine, with its capital Nancy (see entry), lies in eastern France in the valleys of the upper Meuse and the Moselle, bounded on the west by Champagne and on the east by the Vosges and extending northward to the Ardennes and southward to the Langres plateau. It consists of the départements of Meurthe-et-Moselle (chief town Nancy), Moselle (Metz), Meuse (Bar-le-Duc) and Vosges (Epinal) – though the eastern part of the Vosges département is in Alsace (see entry).
Outside the larger towns and industrial areas Lorraine has preserved its natural beauty almost unspoiled, with the steeply scarped forest-covered hills of the Vosges, its beautiful upland regions, its quiet mountain lakes and attractive holiday resorts.

Spas

The spas along the fringes of the Vosges have a long tradition behind them, and, particularly in the 18th and 19th centuries, such resorts as Bains-les-

Bains, Plombières, Vittel and Contrexéville were frequented by the fashionable world of Europe.

Population

The population of Lorraine goes back to Celtic and Frankish origins, mixed with Alemannic (Germanic) blood. The region preserves some remains of German language and culture.

History

The treaty of Verdun in 843 brought about a division of the Frankish empire between the sons of Louis the Pious. Under the treaty the western part of the empire fell to Charles the Bald, the middle section to Lothair and the eastern part to Louis (Ludwig) the German. In 855 the central part was again divided, when Lothair I handed over his domains to his sons, Louis, Charles and Lothair II. The last named called his territory "Lotharii Regnum", from which the name Lorraine is derived. In 870, however, Lorraine also passed to Ludwig. In 959 the duchies of Upper and Lower Lorraine (Lotharingia) were created, the latter, with its capital at Nancy, becoming known as Lorraine *tout court*. In 1552 France acquired the towns of Metz, Toul and Verdun, and in 1776 the Duchy of Lorraine also became French. After the Franco-Prussian War of 1870–1871 a large part of Lorraine, mainly German-speaking, including in particular Metz and the surrounding area, was incorporated in the newly established German Empire, becoming part of the province of Alsace-Lorraine. After the First World War it returned to France, and has since then remained French except for a brief interruption in 1940–1944.

Economy

In addition to its productive agriculture and forestry Lorraine possesses minerals (coal, iron ore) which are important to its industries.
A variety of causes (quality of raw materials, competition from cheaper and better foreign products) led to economic stagnation in the region, particularly in heavy industry, and since the early 1960s special efforts have been made to promote development in Lorraine.
Another important sector is the textile industry, which was brought into Lorraine from Alsace.

Sights in Lorraine

Bains-les-Bains

The much frequented spa of Bains-les-Bains (pop. 1800), with eleven springs which were already being used in Roman times, lies in the middle of the forest. It is recommended for the treatment of cardiac and nervous conditions and high blood pressure.

Bitche

Bitche (pop. 7700), a garrison town, lies amid extensive forests, dominated by a Vauban fortress (1680).

***Bliesbruck**

Bliesbruck, near the German frontier, was the site of a Gallo-Roman settlement which has been under excavation for many years. The remains of a large cult building and various workshops have been brought to light. It is planned to establish an open-air archaeological museum.

La Bresse

La Bresse (alt. 630–1366 m/2095–4480 ft; pop. 5600) lies on the Moselotte, a tributary of the Moselle. It is one of the leading winter sports resorts in the Vosges and is also a popular summer resort.

Colombey

At Colombey visitors can see General de Gaulle's residence, La Boisserie, in which he lived between 1946 and 1958 and to which he finally retired in 1969.

Dabo

The little town of Dabo (pop. 3200) lies in a beautiful setting. On the Rocher de Dabo (664 m/2179 ft) is the chapel of St-Léon (1890), on the site of a legendary castle of the Frankish king Dagobert. From the top of the lookout tower there are fine views of the surrounding country.

Gérardmer

Domrémy-la Pucelle

Domrémy (pop. 300) was the birthplace in 1412 of Joan of Arc, the Maid (Pucelle) of Orléans. The house in which she was born, near the church, is open to visitors; opposite it is a small museum.

Epinal

*Images d'Epinal

Epinal (pop. 40,950), chief town of the département of Vosges, lies on both banks of the Moselle amid extensive forests. Its most famous products are the coloured prints known as *images d'Epinal* which in the 19th c. enjoyed world-wide sales. A printer and publisher named Pellerin set up in business in the town in 1799 and began to produce prints which were not confined, as in the past, to religious subjects but also illustrated contemporary themes and, for children, fairytales. Examples of these prints can be seen in the former printing-house, the Vosges Departmental Museum (which also displays pictures and sculpture) and the International Museum of Folk Art.
The church of St-Maurice (13th c., with an 11th c. tower) contains in the transept a 14th c. Virgin and a 15th c. "Entombment". In the Parc du Château are the ruins of a castle destroyed in 1670.

***Gérardmer**

*Col de la Schlucht

The popular holiday resort of Gérardmer (alt. 666–1100 m/2185–3610 ft; pop. 10,000) lies below the Col de la Schlucht in a picturesque lake district in the High Vosges. In winter there is skiing in this area, and in summer the Lac de Gérardmer, with a perimeter of 5.5 km/3½ miles, offers facilities for a variety of water sports. Nearby are the lakes of Longemer and Retournemer.
There is excellent walking in the surrounding area.

Hagondange

At Hagondange, 15 km/9 miles north of Metz, is a recently opened leisure park, Le Nouveau Monde des Schtroumpfs.

Lunéville

Lunéville (pop. 25,000) was the residence of the Dukes of Lorraine between 1702 and 1737. The handsome 18th c. château was designed by Boffrand, a pupil of Mansart's. In the courtyard is an equestrian statue of General Lasalle. The château now houses a museum of art. The twin-towered

St-Nicolas, Neufchâteau

Baroque church of St-Jacques (1730–1747) has fine panelling in the interior.
There is a small Cycle and Motorcycle Museum, with over 200 pre-1939 models.

Metz

See entry

Nancy

See entry

Neufchâteau

Neufchâteau (pop. 9100), situated above the Meuse, was a place of some consequence in the Middle Ages, a free city within the Duchy of Lorraine. It has two notable churches, St-Nicolas (12th–15th c.), which has a 15th c. "Entombment", and St-Christophe (13th–14th c.), and a Renaissance Town Hall with a fine staircase.

Phalsbourg

Phalsbourg (pop. 4000) was built about 1570 as a fortified town and is still a garrison town. It fell to France in 1662, and its defences were considerably strengthened by Vauban in 1680. The Porte de France and Porte d'Allemagne, both richly decorated, are remains of the old fortifications. There is a museum on the history of the town in the Town Hall.

Plombières-les-Bains

Plombières (pop. 2300) is a spa, with 28 thermal springs (13–81°C/55–178°F) which were in use in Roman times, set in a beautiful park. The local museum displays works by the Plombières-born painter Louis Français and his artist friends (Corot, Courbet, Diaz, etc.).

Rambervillers

Rambervillers (pop. 7500), in the western Vosges, is a picturesque little town with a 16th c. Town Hall, old houses of the same period and remains of town walls.

Remiremont

Remiremont (pop. 10,800), beautifully situated at the foot of Mt Parmont (613 m/2011 ft), grew up around a famous convent founded on the Saint

Mont in the 11th c. for ladies of good family. The church of St-Pierre (13th–16th c.) contains the tombs of some of these noble ladies. Other buildings associated with the convent are the 18th c. Abbess's Palace and houses of the same period. The Grande Rue is lined by handsome 13th c. arcades. There are two regional museums illustrating the history and way of life of the area.

Notre-Dame

The former conventual church of Notre-Dame was much altered in the 18th c. Notable features of the interior are the marble cladding of the choir (17th c.) and an 11th c. figure of the Virgin. Under the choir is an 11th c. crypt.

St-Dié

The old episcopal city of St-Dié (pop. 24,800) was largely destroyed during the Second World War, and accordingly most of the town has a modern aspect. The first geographical work referring to the land discovered by Columbus as America was published in St-Dié in 1507. The Romanesque cathedral (12th–13th c.; rebuilt after suffering heavy damage in 1944) has a Gothic choir; the towers date only from 1711. There is a fine 14th c. cloister. The Romanesque church of Notre-Dame-de-Galilée is a fine example of 12th c. Rhineland architecture. The Municipal Museum displays archaeological finds from the area, a collection of birds and mementoes of Jules Ferry (1832–1893) and his family. In the north of the town is a hosiery factory designed by Le Corbusier.

St-Maurice-sur-Moselle
*Ballon d'Alsace

St-Maurice (pop. 2000), lying below the Ballon d'Alsace and the Rouge Gazon, is a popular summer resort which also offers facilities for winter sports in the surrounding hills.

St-Mihel

*Ligier Richier

St-Mihel or St-Michel grew up around a Benedictine abbey founded in 709, and in the 14th c. was one of the principal towns of the Barrois district. The sculptor Ligier Richier (*c.*1500–1567) was born in the town, and some of his works are to be seen in the local churches. One of his finest works, the "Pâmoison de la Vierge" (the Virgin fainting, supported by St John), is in a chapel in the church of St-Michel (12th c., much altered in the late 17th c.). Another, an "Entombment", is in the 16th c. church of St-Etienne.

Sarrebourg

The old town of Sarrebourg (pop. 15,000) lies on the fringe of the Vosges on the river Sarre (Saar). The Eglise des Cordeliers, a former Franciscan church (13th c., rebuilt in 17th c.) has a stained glass west window by Marc Chagall; it now houses a museum.
The Musée du Pays de Sarrebourg has a fine ceramic collection and also displays archaeological finds from the surrounding area.
On the outskirts of the town is a First World War military cemetery with 13,000 graves.

St-Ulrich

Outside the town, at St-Ulrich, is a large Gallo-Roman villa.

Sarreguemines

Sarreguemines (pop. 26,000) lies in eastern Lorraine. The former Town Hall, now a museum, displays a fine ceramic collection. There are fine views from the ruined castle on the Schlossberg.

Thillot
*Ballon d'Alsace

Thillot (pop. 5000), a popular holiday resort throughout the year, lies on the Moselle below the Ballon d'Alsace (1250 m/4101 ft), the most southerly peak in the Vosges.

Toul

*Cathedral

Toul (pop. 17,700), in the upper Moselle valley, was a place of considerable importance in the Middle Ages, the see of a bishop and (until 1648) a free imperial city. The town is still surrounded by its 17th c. walls, with four gates. The Porte de Metz was designed by Vauban. The Cathedral of St-Etienne (13th–14th c.) has a Late Gothic façade and two octagonal towers. The cloister, entered through a Renaissance doorway, dates from the 13th and 14th centuries. The Hôtel de Ville (Town Hall) occupies the former Bishop's Palace.

South-west of the cathedral is the church of St-Gengoult (13th–16th c.), a smaller and simpler version of the cathedral. The choir has some fine remains of 13th c. stained glass. On the south side of the church is a 16th c. cloister, in a light and elegant Flamboyant style. There are a number of old houses, particularly in Rue Général-Gengoult, some of them dating from the 14th c.

*Cloister

Verdun

See entry

***Vittel**

This attractively situated little town (pop. 6440) has been since the mid 19th c. one of the best known spas in Lorraine, with a reputation which goes back to Roman times. Its water, from four cold mineral springs, is used in the treatment of disorders of the stomach, liver and intestines, and enjoys a wide market in bottled form as table water. It has the Late Gothic church of St-Rémy. The leisure needs of visitors are catered for by beautiful parks, a golf-course, a racecourse and a casino. Vittel is also a good base from which to explore the beautiful surrounding area.

Sport and Recreation in Lorraine

Water sports

Lorraine's rivers and lakes offer facilities for a variety of water sports (diving, sailing, fishing, etc.).

Golf

There are golf-courses at Nancy, Combles (near Bar-le-Duc), Vittel and Metz.

Walking and cycling

There is plenty of scope for walkers and cyclists, as well as for nature-lovers, in the Vosges Regional Park (area 185,000 hectares/457,000 acres). There is also a considerable network of waymarked footpaths and trails.

Other sports

Information about facilities for other sports (tennis, riding, skiing, shooting) can be obtained from local tourist information offices. There are casinos at Contrexéville, Gérardmer, Plombières-les-Bains and Vittel.

Lot Valley

H–L 10

*Situation and characteristics

The river Lot is a river relatively little known outside France, though its valley has stretches of scenic beauty which fall little short of the grandeur of the Tarn valley.
The Lot rises at an altitude of 1400 m/4600 ft on Mont Goulet in the Cévennes, flows through the whole of the southern Massif Central and after traversing Quercy joins the Garonne in the Agenais (the region round Agen) after a total course of 480 km/300 miles. In earlier times it was an important navigable waterway, linking Auvergne and the wine-trading town of Cahors with Bordeaux. It is now popular with canoe and kayak enthusiasts, who find excitement in traversing the gorges between Espalion and Entraygues – though the less expert will do well to keep below Entraygues.

Topography

The scenery of the Lot valley alternates between the gently beautiful and the wild and rugged. The roads which run through the valley give visitors an excellent opportunity of enjoying the scenery of this most characteristic of French rivers and seeing its towns and villages.

*Gorges du Lot

The most striking section of the valley is in the Gorges du Lot, the succession of gorges which, particularly between Estaing and Pont de Coursavy, challenge comparison with the gorges of the Tarn. Here the valley is caught between walls of rock some 300 m/1000 ft high. At Entraygues-sur-Truyère the Lot is joined by the Truyère, with the impressive Gorges de la Truyère, which cut through the hills of Auvergne to the Viaduc de Garabit, interrupted by a number of imposing dams and beautiful artificial lakes; for

*Viaduc de Garabit

St-Cirq-Lapopie

Grotte de Pech-Merle, Salle Rouge

much of the way, however, the road runs at some distance from the river. There is also a dam in the Gorges du Lot, at Golinhac, near Estaing.

Sights in the Lot Valley

In this section the sights in the Lot valley are described in geographical order, going downstream from Mende to Villeneuve-sur-Lot.

Mende

**Gorges du Tarn

Mende (alt. 730 m/2395 ft; pop. 12,100), the Roman Mimate, in the upper valley of the Lot, is a good starting-point for an exploration of either the Lot valley or the Gorges du Tarn (see entry). Above the town rise the steeply scarped slopes of the Causse de Mende, more than 300 m/1000 ft high. The Cathedral of St-Pierre is mainly 14th c.; the towers were added 200 years later. The interior is richly decorated, with Aubusson tapestries of 1708. In the Middle Ages Mende possessed the largest bell in Christendom, weighing 25 tons, but this was destroyed in 1579 during the wars of religion and only the clapper, 2.15 m/7 ft long, survives.
The narrow Pont Notre-Dame over the Lot dates from the 14th c., having successfully withstood the river's spates for nearly 600 years. The Musée Ignon Fabre, a historical museum, is housed in a 17th c. building with a fine staircase.

Mont Mimat

From Mont Mimat there are fine views of Mende and the Lot valley.

Espalion

Espalion (pop. 4800) is a picturesque and attractive little town, with an old bridge spanning the Lot. The Vieux Palais is a masterpiece of Renaissance architecture. The church of St-Jean now houses the Musée du Rouergue et Joseph Vaylet (objets d'art, ethnography). The little Romanesque church of St-Hilarion has a fine tympanum.

Pont Valentré, Cahors ▶

Outside the town is the Château de Roquelaure, from which there is a marvellous view of the Lot valley. Below the château is a Romanesque chapel, with a 15th c. "Entombment" and a 16th c. "Pietà".

Estaing

This old-world little town (pop. 670) is charmingly situated at a point where the Lot valley opens out a little. The river is spanned by a 15th c. bridge. Above the town is an elegant 15th–16th c. château, from the terrace of which there are fine views. The 15th c. church contains the relics of St Fleuret.

Entraygues-sur-Truyère

Entraygues (pop. 1600) lies in a fertile hilly region at the junction of the Truyère and the Lot. It is a charming old town; particularly attractive is the Rue Basse, which has preserved its medieval aspect almost intact. The Truyère is spanned by a Gothic bridge.

Conques
*Ste-Foy

Conques (pop. 500) lies in the rocky Gorge de l'Ouche, its old houses huddled round the beautiful church of Ste-Foy (11th–12th c.), a well known place of pilgrimage in the Middle Ages and still one of the most visited churches in France. Over the west doorway is a Last Judgment which is one of the great masterpieces of Romanesque sculpture. The interior is also very fine. The church treasury, in an adjoining building, contains a rich collection of sacred art of the 9th–16th centuries, notably the gold reliquary of Ste Foy. The abbey to which the church belonged was, between the 11th and 13th centuries, an important staging-post on the "Way of St James", the pilgrim road to Santiago de Compostela. After the destruction of the abbey by Protestants in 1561 the church, partly destroyed by fire, was neglected and fell into disrepair, until it was discovered by the writer Prosper Mérimée in the mid 19th c. and restored after he had drawn attention to its plight.

Figeac

Figeac (pop. 10,500), situated on the river Celé a short distance from the Lot, was also on the old pilgrim road to Santiago. The town has preserved some charming old quarters. In the Hôtel de la Monnaie, a fine Gothic building, is a museum of local history. The oldest parts of the church of St-Sauveur date from the 11th c., but it was much altered in later centuries. Figeac was the birthplace of Jean-François Champollion (1790–1832), who first deciphered the Egyptian hieroglyphics.
Above the town is the church of Notre-Dame du Puy, originally built in the 14th c. but, like St-Sauveur, much altered in later periods.

Musée de Plein Air du Quercy

See Cahors, below

***St-Cirq-Lapopie**

St-Cirq-Lapopie (pop. 200), magnificently situated on a crag above the Lot, is a picturesque little village of lovingly restored old houses. In the Middle Ages it was a village of wood-turners.

***Grotte de Pech-Merle**

Near St-Cirq-Lapopie is the cave of Pech-Merle, a prehistoric cult site, discovered in 1922, with evidence of human occupation 20,000 years ago – painted or incised figures of bisons, mammoths (of the Aurignacian period) and horses.

Cahors

*Pont Valentré

Cahors (pop. 21,000), picturesquely situated in a bend on the Lot, was the old capital of Quercy and in medieval times an important commercial and university town. Its most important monument is the Pont Valentré (1308–1380), with three 40 m/130 ft high towers, an outstanding example of a medieval fortified bridge (restored in the 19th c.). Beyond the bridge, under a crag on the Lot some 400 m/440 yds south, is the Fontaine des Chartreux or Source de Divonne, which supplies Cahors with drinking water.

*Cathedral

A short distance north-east of Place Aristide-Briand (in which is a monument to Léon Gambetta, 1838–1882) is the Romanesque/Byzantine Cathedral of St-Etienne (11th–15th c.), with a fine Romanesque north doorway,

originally the main entrance, dating from the first building phase. The façade is 14th c. Fine paintings in the choir and on the dome. On the south side of the church is a Flamboyant-style cloister (16th c.). The Maison de Roaldès, in Place Henri-IV, dates from the late 15th c. (restored 1912). Henry IV is said to have lived in the house during the siege of Cahors in 1580. The former Bishop's Palace now houses the Municipal Museum (mementoes of the politician Léon Gambetta, a native of Cahors).
Just off Place de-Gaulle is the 34 m/112 ft high Tour Jean XXII, a relic of an old palace. Farther north, on a crag, is the Tour St-Jean, which, like the Barbacane, the old Guard-House (15th c.), was part of the town's defences. In the highest part of the old town is the church of St-Barthélemy (14th c.).

Musée de Plein Air du Quercy

At Cabrerets, between Figeac and Cahors, is the Domaine de Cuzals, with the Quercy Open-Air Museum. Here, on a site of 200 hectares/500 acres, farmhouses and farm buildings from all over Quercy have been re-erected. There are also a number of thematic collections (country life in the 19th c., folk art, local crafts).

Château de Bonaguil

Near Duravel, some distance from the Lot, is the massive castle of Bonaguil, a magnificent example of military architecture of the turn of the 15th–16th centuries, still impressive in spite of the damage it suffered during the French Revolution.

Villeneuve-sur-Lot

Villeneuve-sur-Lot (pop. 24,000), in the Middle Ages one of the most important towns in the region, has preserved two town gates dating from that period. The bridge over the Lot was built by the English in the 13th c.

Lourdes G11

Region: Midi–Pyrénées
Département: Hautes-Pyrénées
Altitude: 410 m/1345 ft
Population: 18,000

Situation and characteristics

Lourdes, beautifully situated on both banks of the Gave de Pau on the northern fringe of the Pyrenees, is the summer residence of the bishop of Tarbes and Lourdes and a famous place of pilgrimage. The impression which Lourdes makes on a visitor will inevitably depend on his attitude to the pilgrimages which bring millions of believers to Lourdes every year.
As a place of pilgrimage Lourdes owes its fame to the appearances of the Virgin to a shepherd girl named Bernadette Soubirous (1844–1879) in the nearby Grotte de Massabielle on the Gave de Pau, and to the spring found by Bernadette in the cave whose water is credited with healing qualities. Bernadette was beatified in 1925 and canonised in 1933.

Sights

Cité Religieuse

The Boulevard de la Grotte and the Pont St-Michel lead to the Cité Religieuse, to the west of the town in a bend in the Gave de Pau. Immediately beyond the bridge is the Esplanade des Processions, along which there is a candle-lit procession every evening to the Esplanade du Rosaire.
On the north side of the Esplanade des Processions is the Asile Notre-Dame-de-Lourdes, one of the town's two large hospitals. Below the south side of the Esplanade is the underground church of St-Pie X (St Pius X; by Pierre Vago, 1958), which can accommodate 20,000 pilgrims in its 12,000 sq. m/14,350 sq. yds.

St-Pie X

At the west end of the Esplanade des Processions is the Esplanade du Rosaire, where the daily procession ends and is followed by the blessing of the sick. On the west side of the square is the Romanesque/Byzantine Basilica of the Rosary (1885–1889), which can accommodate 5000 worshippers.

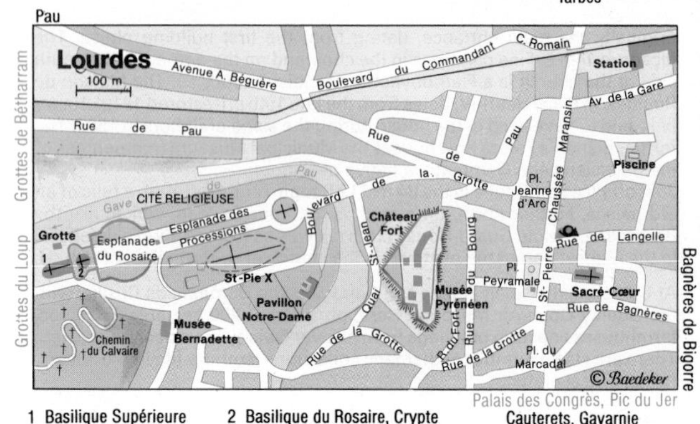

1 Basilique Supérieure 2 Basilique du Rosaire, Crypte

On each side of the Esplanade du Rosaire a ramp leads up to the neo-Gothic Upper Basilica (Basilique Supérieure), built in 1864–1871 (consecrated 1876) on the summit of the crag containing the cave of Massabielle. It has a 70 m/230 ft high tower. In the interior are innumerable ex-votos. Under the church is a large crypt.

Grotte de Massabielle

Under the Upper Basilica, to the north, is the Grotte de Massabielle, a cave measuring 12 m/40 ft by 10 m/33 ft. In the niche marking the spot where the Virgin appeared to Bernadette is a marble figure of the Virgin by the Lyons sculptor Fabisch (1863), based on Bernadette's description of her.

Lourdes

From the Basilica a Way of the Cross leads up to a Calvary, with 14 fine bronze figures.
In the Pavillon Notre-Dame are the Musée Bernadette and the Musée d'Art Sacré du Gemmail (stained glass).

Other sights

The central feature of the town proper is the Place Peyramale. A little to the east is the neo-Romanesque church of the Sacré-Cœur (1877–1903). South-west of the square is the Cachot, the former prison in which the Soubirous family lived. In Rue Bernadette-Soubirous is the Moulin de Boly, in which Bernadette was born. 80 m/260 ft above the town is the castle (13th–17th c.), which can be reached in a lift. From the terrace there are fine views. The castle now houses the Museum of the Pyrenees.

*Museum of the Pyrenees

Surroundings of Lourdes

Caves

Around Lourdes are a number of interesting caves – the Grotte des Sarrazins, the Grotte du Loup and the Grotte du Roy. 16 km/10 miles west of the town is the Grotte de Bétharram (open only in summer), with large rock chambers and an underground river (boat trips).

*Grotte de Bétharram

Mt Béout

2 km/1½ miles south of Lourdes is the lower station of a cableway up Mt Béout (792 m/2599 ft; fine views). In a 82 m/270 ft deep gully near the upper station prehistoric implements were found.

Pic de Jer

A little way east is the lower station of a cableway up the Pic de Jer (948 m/3110 ft), from which there are even wider views.

St-Savin

See Pyrenees, Argelès-Gazost

Lyons

M9

Region: Rhône–Alpes
Département: Rhône
Altitude: 170 m/560 ft
Population: 420,000 (conurbation 1.2 million)

Situation and characteristics

Lyons (in French spelling Lyon), France's second largest industrial and commercial city, is well situated at the junction of the navigable Rhône and Saône. It is the chief town of the département of Rhône and the see of an archbishop, with a university and a college of technology.
Lyons has long been the principal centre of the French textile industry, and in particular of silk production, but it also has a variety of other industries, notably the chemical and metalworking industries.
The Lyons Trade Fair, held annually in spring, provides a general survey of the city's industry and commerce.
Many notable figures were born in Lyons or lived and worked in the city, among them François Rabelais, who worked as a doctor in the Lyons hospital and wrote his principal works here, the physicist A.-M. Ampère, the writer Antoine de St-Exupéry, the inventor of the sewing machine, Barthélemy Thimonnier, the inventor of the jacquard loom, Joseph-Marie Jacquard, the Montgolfier brothers, who constructed the first hot-air balloon, and the inventors of the cinematograph, Louis and Auguste Lumière, who moved from Besançon to Lyons.

The city

The main part of the city, with the most important government offices and museums, lies on the Presqu'Ile, the peninsula 5 km/3 miles long and 600–800 m/660-880 yds across between the Rhône in the east and the narrower Saône in the west. On higher ground to the north is the suburb of La Croix-Rousse. On the right bank of the Saône are the hill of Fourvière, the site of the Roman town, and the former suburb of Valse; on the left bank are

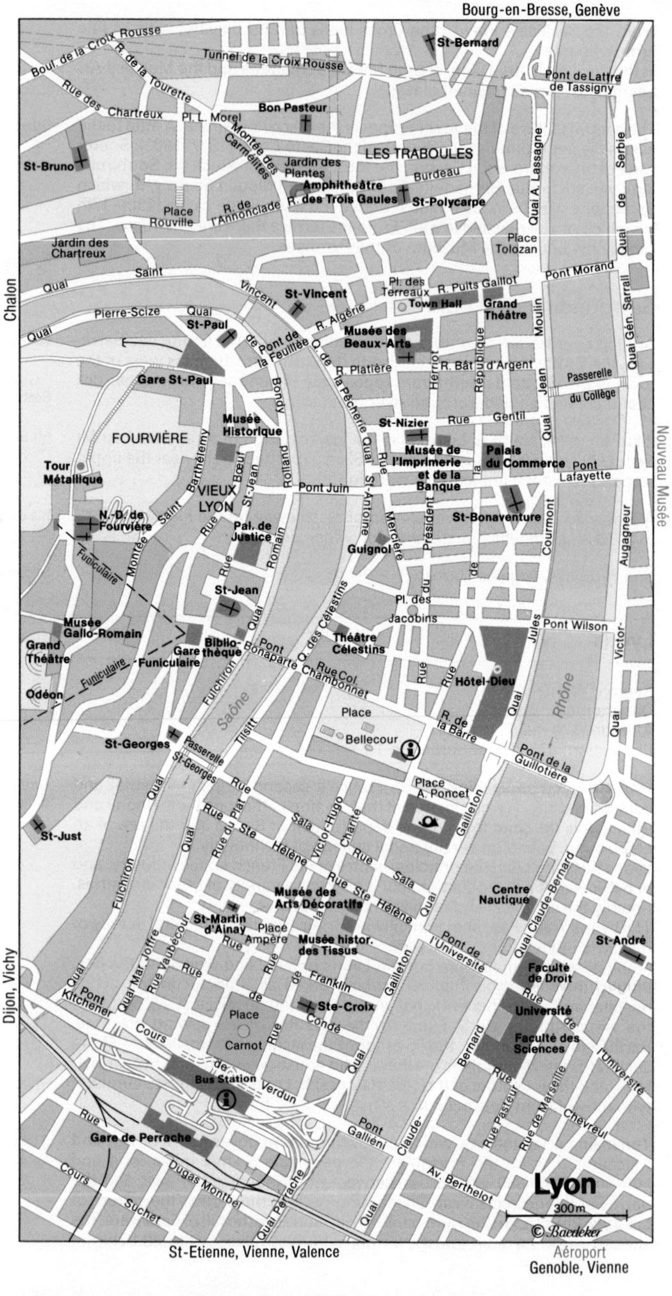

Bourg-en-Bresse, Genève

Boul. de la Croix Rousse
R. de la Tourette
Tunnel de la Croix Rousse
St-Bernard
Pont de Lattre de Tassigny
Rue des Chartreux
Pl. L. Morel
Bon Pasteur
Montée des Carmélites
St-Bruno
LES TRABOULES
Jardin des Plantes
Amphithéâtre des Trois Gaules
Burdeau
St-Polycarpe
Quai A. Lassagne
Serbie
Place Rouville
R. de l'Annonciade
Jardin des Chartreux
Place Tolozan
Quai de
Quai Saint Vincent
Pl. des Terreaux
R. Puits Gaillot
Pont Morand
Chalon
St-Vincent
Town Hall
Grand Théâtre
Quai Pierre-Scize
Quai St-Paul
R. Algérie
Musée des Beaux-Arts
Moulin
Quai Gén. Sarrail
Pont de la Feuillée
Q. de la Pêcherie
R. Platière
Herriot
République
R. Bât d'Argent
Jean
Passerelle du Collège
Gare St-Paul
Bondy
Musée Historique
St-Nizier
Rue Gentil
FOURVIÈRE
Rue Musée de l'Imprimerie et de la Banque
Palais du Commerce
Pont Lafayette
Nouveau Musée
Tour Métallique
Barthélemy
Boeuf
St-Jean
Rolland
Quai St-Antoine
VIEUX LYON
Pont Juin
N.-D. de Fourvière
Montée Saint
Rue
Pal. de Justice
Romain
Mercière
Président
St-Bonaventure
Courmont
Augagneur
Funiculaire
Guignol
du
de
St-Jean
Pl. des Jacobins
Musée Gallo-Romain
Quai
Q. des Célestins
Jules
Pont Wilson
Victor-
Grand Théâtre
Gare Funiculaire
Biblio-thèque
Pont Bonaparte
Théâtre Célestins
Rue Col. Chambonnet
Rue
Hôtel-Dieu
Rhône
Odéon
Fulchiron
Saône
Place Bellecour
R. de la Barre
Quai
St-Georges
Tilsitt
Passerelle St-Georges
Pont de la Guillotière
Place A. Poncet
Rue
Rue Ste Hélène
Rue du Plat
Sala
Victor-Hugo
Charité
Rue Sala
Gailleton
St-Just
Quai Fulchiron
Rue Ste Hélène
Musée des Arts Décoratifs
Centre Nautique
Quai Claude-Bernard
St-Martin d'Ainay
Place Ampère
Musée histor. des Tissus
Pont de l'Université
St-André
Quai Mar. Joffre
Rue Vaubecour
Rue
Rue de Franklin
Gailleton
Faculté de Droit
Dijon, Vichy
Quai Pont Kitchener
Ste-Croix
Rue de l'Université
Université
Place Carnot
Rue de Condé
Faculté des Sciences
Cours de Verdun
Bernard
Bus Station
Quai
Rue Pasteur
Rue de Marseille
Rue Chevreul
Rue
Gare de Perrache
Pont Gallieni
Claude-
Cours Suchet
Dugas Montbel
Quai Perrache
Quai
Av. Berthelot
Lyon
300 m
© Baedeker

St-Etienne, Vienne, Valence

Aéroport
Genoble, Vienne

the former suburb of La Guillotière and the district of Les Brotteaux, beyond which is the modern district of La Part-Dieu. The city is steadily expanding farther east. The rivers are lined with fine embankments and spanned by numerous bridges.

History

In the time of the Gauls Lyons (Lugdunum) was already a place of some importance. In 42 B.C. it became a Roman colony, and in the time of Augustus capital of the province of Gallia Lugdunensis. At the end of the 2nd c. A.D. there was a ruthless persecution of Christians in the town. In 1033 Lyons, along with the rest of Burgundy, became part of the German Empire; then in the early 14th c. the County of Lyonnais (now represented by the départements of Loire and Rhône) passed to France. During the French Revolution, in 1793, the Convention ordered the destruction of Lyons as a reprisal for the expulsion of the Jacobins after they had retaken the city – an operation in which 6000 citizens of Lyons perished.

Sights

*Place Bellecour

The city's finest square is Place Bellecour, situated between the Rhône and the Saône, with an equestrian statue of Louis XIV by the Lyons sculptor F. Lemot (1775–1827). The buildings on the east and west sides of the square were erected around 1800. To the south-east, near the Head Post Office, is a 17th c. tower. From the north side of the square there is a view of the hill of Fourvière (see page 297).
From the square Rue Victor-Hugo runs south by way of Place Ampère (monument) to the attractive Place Carnot, which has a large monument to the Republic erected in 1890.

St-Martin-d'Ainay

To the west of Place Ampère, on the site of a Roman temple, is the church of St-Martin-d'Ainay, which originally belonged to a Benedictine abbey founded in the 6th c. The present church, built in the 11th c., is the city's oldest. It contains four antique columns, a 12th c. mosaic pavement in the choir and paintings on a gold ground by the Lyons artist Hippolyte Flandrin (1809–1864) in the apses.

Musée des Arts Décoratifs
**Musée Historique des Tissus

East of Place Ampère, in a mansion built in 1739, is the Museum of Decorative Art (furniture, tapestries, coins, etc.). Adjoining, to the south, is the Musée Historique des Tissus (Museum of Woven Fabrics), with displays illustrating the development of weaving techniques and a very fine collection of Oriental (particularly Persian) carpets.

Hotel-Dieu

The city's two principal streets radiate from Place Bellecour, Rue de la République to the east and Rue du Président-Herriot to the west. To the east of Rue de la République, extending to the banks of the Rhône, is the Hôtel-Dieu, a hospital built in the 17th and 18th centuries. The main front looking on to the river, was begun in 1741 by Soufflot (architect of the Panthéon in Paris) but completed only in 1842. It now houses, among other things, the Musée des Hospices Civils (faience, furniture, etc.; medicine in Lyons).

Palais de la Bourse et du Commerce

Farther along Rue de la République, on the right, is the Renaissance-style Palais de la Bourse et du Commerce (by René Dardel, 1855–1860). To the south is the former Franciscan church of St-Bonaventure (14th–15th c.).
Rue du Président-Herriot leads to Place des Jacobins, with a monumental fountain. Rue Mercière, which leaves its north-west corner, is flanked by numerous houses of the Gothic and Renaissance periods.

St-Nizier

Farther up Rue du Président-Herriot, on the left, is the church of St-Nizier, once the city's cathedral, which was rebuilt in Gothic style in the 15th c. and has a handsome Renaissance doorway (16th c.) and a beautiful interior. Under the choir is a 6th c. crypt decorated with modern mosaics.

Place des Jacobins

Notre-Dame de Fourvière

Place des Terreaux
*Fountain

The Place des Terreaux is built over a Roman canal, and gets its name from the earth *(terre)* used to fill it up. In the square is a monumental fountain by F.-A. Bartholdi (1834–1904) representing the rivers flowing into the ocean. During the French Revolution the guillotine was set up in this square. On its east side is the Hôtel de Ville (Town Hall), built between 1646 and 1672 and rebuilt in Baroque style by Jules Hardouin-Mansart in 1700 after a fire. It has a main front richly decorated with sculpture, two courtyards separated by a graceful intermediate wing with three arches, and a 50 m/165 ft high tower. The rear of the building looks on to the Place de la Comédie, in which is the Grand Théâtre (19th c.).

*Musée des Beaux-Arts

On the south side of the Place des Terreaux is the Palais St-Pierre, a former Benedictine convent (1659–1685) which now houses the Musée des Beaux-Arts, with a rich collection of pictures, sculpture and decorative art; the modern period is particularly well represented.

*Cathedral

From the north-west corner of Place Bellecour Rue Chambonnet and the Pont Bonaparte lead west to the right bank of the Saône; from the embankment before the bridge there is a fine view, to the right, of the choir of the cathedral, the Palais de Justice and the hill of Fourvière. A little to the north is the Romanesque Cathedral of St-Jean (12th–15th c.), with a Late Gothic façade and a rose window of 1393. The most notable features of the interior are the 13th–14th c. stained glass and an astronomical clock by the Basle craftsman N. Lippius (1598) in the Romanesque transept.

Old town

To the north of the cathedral is the old town, which has been carefully restored and contains many fine old houses. In Rue St-Jean, on right, is the neo-classical Palais de Justice (Law Courts; by Baltard, 1832–1842). In the Quartier St-Georges is the well known Café du Soleil, originally a religious house and later used for performances of the Théâtre Guignol. In the same street are two interesting museums, the Musée Historique de Lyon (history of the city) and the Musée de la Marionnette (Puppet Museum), housed in the 15th c. Hôtel de Gadagne.

*Puppet Museum

Fourvière

Above the old town, to the west, is the hill of Fourvière (from Latin Forum Vetus, the "Old Forum"), rising to a height of 130 m/425 ft above the Saone, with two funiculars running up the hill. On the summit is the basilica of Notre-Dame de Fourvière (1872–1896), with an interior richly decorated with mosaics and paintings; under the church is a crypt, similarly decorated. From the north-east tower, there is a magnificent view of the city and surrounding area.

*View

Some 500 m/550 yds south, in a park, are two Roman theatres (excavated since 1933) and a Gallo-Roman Museum (vases, gravestones, coins and fine mosaic pavements).

New districts

Parc de la Tête d'Or

The newer parts of the city are on the left bank of the Rhône. On the Boulevard des Belges is the large and beautiful Parc de la Tête d'Or (area 105 hectares/260 acres), within which are a Zoo, a Botanical Garden, a rose-garden and a small lake.

The district of Les Brotteaux has many Art Nouveau houses. Adjoining this is the modern district of La Part-Dieu, with many administrative offices, a railway station, multi-storey car parks and a huge shopping centre, in which is the 142 m/465 ft high Crédit Lyonnais Tower.

East of the Gare des Brotteaux (railway station) is Villeurbanne, with a Media Library built in 1988 by the Swiss architect Mario Botta (b. 1943).

Surroundings of Lyons

L'Arbresle

25 km/15 miles west of Lyons is L'Arbresle (pop. 4900), with the Dominican convent of Ste-Marie-de-la-Tourette, built by Le Corbusier in 1957–1959.

Chazelles-sur-Lyon

South-west of Lyons is Chazelles-sur-Lyon (pop. 5000), once famous as a hat-manufacturing town. The Musée du Chapeau (Hat Museum) is a mine of information on the hat-maker's craft, its importance to the region and fashions in hats.

Rochetaillée

11 km/7 miles north of Lyons is the Château de Rochetaillée, which now houses the interesting Musée Automobile Henri-Malartre, with more than 130 old cars, motorcycles and bicycles.

Le Mans H6

Region: Pays de la Loire
Département: Sarthe
Altitude: 51 m/165 ft
Population: 151,000

Situation and characteristics

Le Mans, an important town in Roman times, the see of a bishop since the 4th c., capital of the medieval County of Maine and now chief town of the département of Sarthe, lies half way between Paris and Nantes on both banks of the Sarthe. A smaller river, the Huisne, flows into the Sarthe on the southern outskirts of the town. To the south of Le Mans is the car-racing circuit used in the famous 24-hour race, the "24 Heures du Mans".

Sights

Place de la République

The central feature of Le Mans is the large Place de la République, on the west side of which are the Palais de Justice (Law Courts), in an old monastic building, and the church of the Visitation (1730), with a Baroque interior.

Place de la République, Eglise de la Visitation

Notre-Dame-de-la-Couture

South-east of the Place de la République is the former abbey church of Notre-Dame-de-la-Couture, which was originally built in the 10th c. but was given its present aspect in the 13th and 14th centuries. The west front, which is preceded by a porch, has a richly carved doorway. The church contains tapestries and pictures, including (on right) "Elijah's Dream" by Philippe de Champaigne. Opposite the pulpit is a beautiful white marble Virgin by Germain Pilon (1571). The crypt dates from the 10th c.

*Doorway

To the south of the church, in the former abbey (18th c.), is the Prefecture, with a very fine staircase hall.

Old town

North-west of the Place de la République, on a hill above the Sarthe, is the old town, with many ancient houses. The main street is the Grande Rue, at No. 71 of which is the Maison d'Adam et d'Eve, a handsome Renaissance house of 1525.

North-east of this is the old-world Rue de la Reine Bérengère, at No. 13 of which (on right) is the Maison de la Reine Bérengère (1440–1515), now occupied by a museum of ethnography and regional history.

*Cathedral

At the north end of Rue de la Reine Bérengère is the Cathedral of St-Julien (named after a 3rd c. apostle). The Romanesque nave dates from the 11th–12th c., the Gothic choir from the 13th and the Late Gothic transepts from the 14th and 15th. On its south side is a 12th c. doorway decorated with statues, reminiscent of the Royal Doorway at Chartres, with a porch (Porche du Chevalier). The interior is impressive, with magnificent stained glass (13th–14th c.) in the choir, beautiful tapestries (15th–16th c.), two tombs (on left) and a 17th c. terracotta "Entombment" (on right). In the north transept are a fine 15th c. rose window and (on left) the tomb of Berengaria, wife of Richard Cœur-de-Lion (13th c.). In the Lady Chapel (Chapelle de la Vierge), in the apse, are beautiful 14th c. frescoes.

Other sights

Opposite the west end of the cathedral is the Hôtel du Grabatoire (1530). To the west, near Rues Denfert-Rochereau, St-Hilaire and de-la-Porte-Ste-

Anne, which run round the west side of the old town, are remains of the Gallo-Roman town walls, with towers.
Behind the choir of the cathedral is the spacious Place des Jacobins, on the east side of which, occupying the site of a Gallo-Roman amphitheatre, is the theatre, built in 1842 (with a modern extension). Beyond this is the pleasant Promenade des Jacobins.

**Musée de Tessé

Immediately north-east, in a park, is the former Bishop's Palace, now occupied by the Musée de Tessé, with a large collection of pictures. Among other items of interest is an enamel panel, made in Verdun between 1145 and 1150, from the tomb of Geoffrey Plantagenet.

To the west of the old town, on the right bank of the Sarthe, is the former abbey church of Notre-Dame-du-Pré, a fine Romanesque building (11th and 12th c., restored) with an impressive crypt.

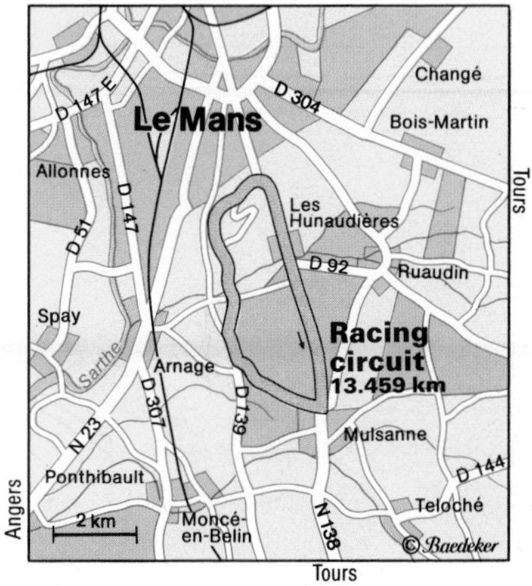

Surroundings of Le Mans

Just south of the town are the famous car-racing circuit, 13.5 km/8½ miles long, used in the Le Mans 24-hour race ("Les 24 Heures du Mans") and the Circuit Bugatti, a 4.25 km/2½ mile long training circuit.
There is an interesting Automobile Museum with 150 vehicles, including cars dating from 1914 and racing cars of 1920–1949.

Marseilles

N11

Region: Provence–Alpes–Côte-d'Azur
Département: Bouches-du-Rhône
Altitude: 0–160 m/0-525 ft
Population: 869,900 (conurbation 1,111,000)

Situation and characteristics

Marseilles (French spelling Marseille), France's oldest and third largest city (after Paris and Lyons) and its most important port, lies on the Mediterranean to the east of the Rhône delta. It is the chief town of the département of Bouches-du-Rhône, the see of an archbishop and a university town.
Beautifully situated on an inlet in the Golfe du Lion, the city extends up the slopes of an encircling range of bare limestone hills, dominated by the church of Notre-Dame-de-la-Garde. Though Marseilles is France's oldest city it has preserved few ancient remains or medieval buildings.

Economy

The importance of the port of Marseilles depends mainly on trade with North Africa and southern and eastern Asia. The Marseilles–Rhône Canal provides a link with inland France. The port has an annual turnover of more than 98 million tons (largely oil). The city's traditional industries, including shipbuilding, vegetable oil refineries and soap manufacture, are in a state of crisis, and even steel production and the petrochemical industries have declined, with the result that Marseilles has the highest rate of unemployment in France. The situation is aggravated by Marseilles' geographical position, which makes it one of the main points of entry for Arab and African immigrants. More than 100,000 Arabs live in Marseilles, and the Belsunce quarter north of Canebière is known as the "Marseilles Beirut".
Almost 5 million passengers pass through Marseilles airport, Marignane,

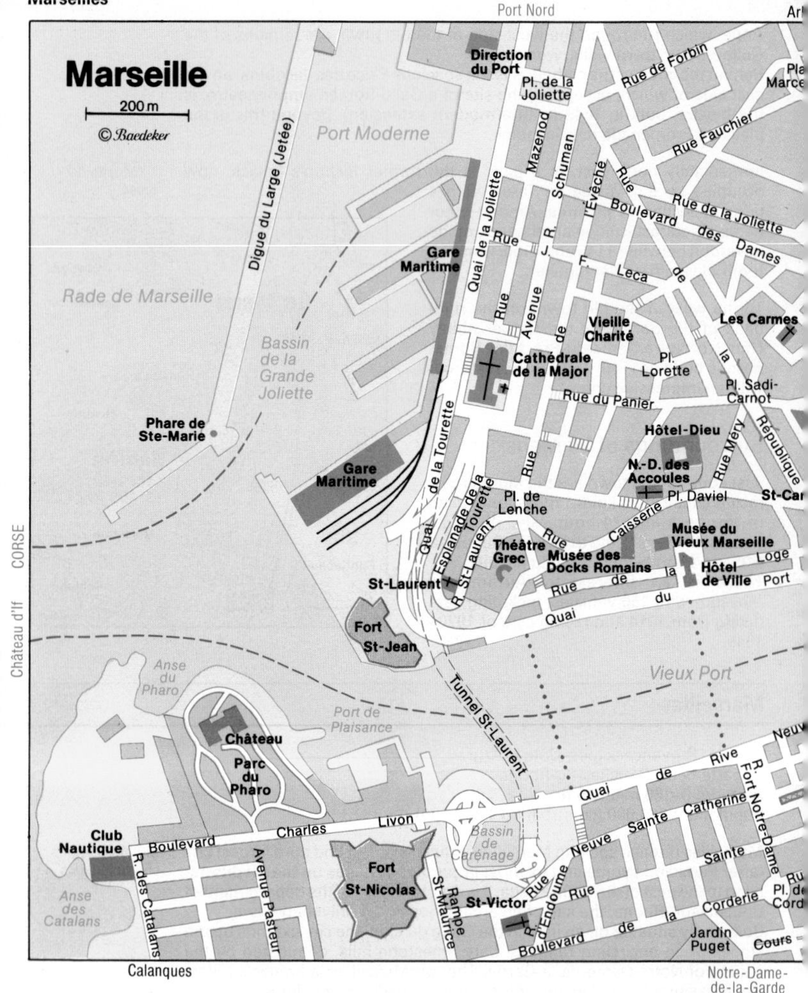

every year, making it the third largest in France after Paris and Nice. New high-tec industries have settled around Marseilles in recent years, probably an indication of the way its economy will move in the future.

History

The town was founded around 600 B.C. under the name of Massalia (Roman Massilia) by Greeks from Asia Minor, and until the Roman Imperial period was strongly marked by Hellenistic culture. A road link with Rome was provided by the construction of the Via Aurelia in A.D. 117. After the fall of the Roman Empire the town was held by the Visigoths and later by the Franks, subsequently becoming part of the kingdom of Arles. After being destroyed by the Saracens it was rebuilt in the 10th c. and became subject to the Vicomtes de Marseille. It gained its independence in 1218, but in 1250

-en-Provence
roport

Cité Radieuse, Cassis

Métro

was captured by Charles of Anjou and in 1481 was united with France. As a port of embarkation for the Crusades Marseilles grew in importance and prosperity, and in course of time acquired various defensive installations. In 1720–1721 it suffered a setback, when the town was devastated by an outbreak of plague. During the French Revolution a band of local revolutionaries marched from Marseilles to Paris, taking with them their marching song, the "Marseillaise", which became the national anthem.

With the growth of French influence in North Africa from 1830 onwards and the opening of the Suez Canal the city's importance as a port and commercial town increased still further, and the city expanded accordingly.

During the Second World War Marseilles suffered damage in air raids, and in 1943 almost the whole of the old town was demolished by the Germans.

The rebuilding of the city was carried out under the direction of the architect Auguste Perret (1874–1954). Le Corbusier's "Cité Radieuse", a huge block of flats built in 1947–1952, is an impressive example of modern architecture, though it now has its critics.

Sights

* La Canebière

The main traffic artery of central Marseilles is the famous Canebière (Provençal Canebiero), a wide street lined with shops, hotels and cafés and filled with a constant rush of traffic which runs north-east from the Vieux Port (Old Harbour) for something like a kilometre (¾ mile). Its name comes from *cannabis* (hemp), recalling the fields of hemp which once grew round the Vieux Port and provided the raw material for the local ropeworks.

Once a handsome avenue designed to challenge comparison with the Champs-Elysées in Paris, the Canebière now forms a social and cultural boundary between the poor Belsunce quarter to the north and the more prosperous districts to the south. Attempts are being made to mitigate the social problems by programmes of slum clearance and improvement.

At the end of the Canebière is the neo-Gothic church of St-Vincent-de-Paul.

Bourse

Near the harbour is the Bourse (Stock Exchange), an imposing building erected in 1852–1860 which now houses the Musée de la Marine (Maritime Museum), with the art collection of the Marseilles Chamber of Commerce, 17th c. plans of ships, ship models, etc.

Musée d'Histoire de Marseille

To the north of the Stock Exchange, in the Centre Bourse, excavation has brought to light remains of the ancient Greek ramparts and port installations (3rd–2nd c. B.C.), including fountains and water cisterns. The area is now open to the public as an open-air museum.

Musée Cantini

In Rue de Grignan, to the south of the Canebière, is the Musée Cantini (old porcelain; 20th c. art; special exhibitions).

* Palais Longchamp

At the east end of Boulevard Longchamp, which continues roughly on the line of the Canebière, is the Palais Longchamp, built by Espérandieu in 1862–1869 at the end of the canal from the Durance to Marseilles. It consists of two imposing museum buildings linked by a colonnade. To the left is the Musée des Beaux-Arts, with pictures, from the 16th/17th c. (Perugino, Rubens), works by Provençal masters, modern sculpture and works by Honoré Daumier, who was born in Marseilles in 1808, to the right the Musée d'Histoire Naturelle. Beyond the Palais is the Jardin Zoologique.

Musée Grobet-Labadie

In the Musée Grobet-Labadié, once the beautifully furnished house of a patrician family, are displayed musical instruments, medieval sculptures, 18th c. tapestries and furniture, and porcelain.

* Vieux Port

At the western end of the Canebière is the picturesque Old Harbour, which has been in use since the time of the first Greek settlers. With a depth of 4–7 m/13–23 ft, it can now handle only small vessels. From here there are boat trips to the Château d'If (see page 304) and the calanques round Cassis (see page 304). The quays are a constant bustle of activity. On the Quai du Port is the Hôtel de Ville (Town Hall, 1663–1683), in Genoese style. The harbour entrance is guarded by two forts, Fort St-Jean to the north and Fort St-Nicolas (17th c.) to the south. From the terrace of Fort St-Nicolas there is a fine view of the town.

* View

* St-Victor

Just to the east of Fort St-Nicolas is the fortress-like church of St-Victor, which originally belonged to an abbey founded in the 5th c. by St John Cassian. In its present form it dates from the 11th and 14th centuries (early Christian and Carolingian foundations). In the crypt the former catacomb chapel and the Grotto of St Victor have been preserved.

Parc du Pharo

On high ground on the south side of the harbour entrance (under which runs a road tunnel, the Tunnel St-Laurent) is the Parc du Pharo, with a château which once belonged to the Empress Eugénie (wife of Napoleon III). Open-air games are held here in summer. From the park there are fine views of the harbour and the city.

Notre-Dame-de-la-Garde

To the south of the city centre, on a limestone crag 160 m/525 ft high, is the church of Notre-Dame-de-la-Garde, the city's most conspicuous landmark. It was built by Espérandieu in 1853–1864 in light and dark natural stone in the neo-Byzantine style on the site of a medieval pilgrimage chapel. From the terrace there is a magnificent panoramic view; out to sea can be seen the islands of Pomègues and Ratonneau and the Château d'If. The crypt contains numerous ex-votos and aircraft models.

*View

Old town

To the north of the Vieux Port is what remains of the old town with its steep and winding lanes. On the north side of the harbour basin is the Quai du Port and the Town Hall (Hôtel de Ville) built in Genoese style in the second half of the 17th c.

Museums

North of the Old Harbour, in the Maison Diamantée (16th c.), is the Musée du Vieux Marseille (history of the town, Provençal furniture and costumes). West of this, in Rue Vivaux, is the interesting Musée des Docks Romains (Musée de Commerce Antique), with remains of the Roman port installations still in situ.

St Laurent

Near Fort St-Jean is the Romanesque church of St-Laurent (damaged during the Second World War), with side chapels of the 15th–16th c. and an octagonal tower (18th c.).

Cathedrals
La Major

On a terrace in the north-west of the old town is the massive neo-Byzantine Cathédrale de la Major (1852–1893), with two domed towers and a 16 m/50 ft high dome over the crossing. The interior is richly decorated with marble and mosaics. The choirs and transepts are from an earlier 11th c. church, as is a terracotta plaque by Luca della Robbia. Measuring 141 m/463 ft in length, it is the longest 19th c. cathedral (Cologne being 135.6 m/445 ft).

*St-Lazare

Immediately east, on a lower level, is the Old Cathedral of St-Lazare (4th–12th c.). It contains a Romanesque reliquary of 1122.

*Vielle Charité

North-east of the cathedrals is a 17th c. poorhouse, the Hospice de la Vieille Charité, built by Pierre Puget (1620–1694). It now houses a cultural and financial centre, as well as the Musée d'Archéologie Méditerranéenne (formerly in the Château Borély; an Egyptian collection, ceramics, bronzes and glass from the Etruscan, Greek, Celtic and Roman periods, drawings and paintings).

Musée
d'Archéologie

Other sights

South of this is the Cour des Accoules, with a 19th c. Calvary Chapel dominated by a tall bell-tower, the Clocher des Accoules. Nearby, in Place Daviel, is the Hôtel-Dieu, which is believed to have been founded in the late 12th c.; the present buildings date from the 17th c. In the forecourt is a monument to the painter and caricaturist Honoré Daumier, a native of Marseilles.
Also in Place Daviel is the handsome Vieux Palais de Justice (Old Law Courts, 1743–1747).

*Port Moderne

Below the Cathédrale de la Major, 1 km/¾ mile from the Vieux Port, is the Port Moderne, the new port, which has been developed since 1844 and now covers an area of over 200 hectares/500 acres, with some 25 km/15 miles of quays. Most passenger ships (to Corsica and other destinations) use the Bassin de la Grande Joliette. The Gare Maritime (Harbour Station) is opposite the end of the Boulevard des Dames. At weekends a fine view of the harbour can be had from the 5 km/3 mile long Jetée (breakwater); at other times it is not open to the public.
The Arc de Triomphe (1825–1832) in Place Jules-Guesde commemorated the taking of Fort Trocadero at Cádiz in 1823.

Parc Borély

South-west of this is the beautiful Parc Borély, with the 18th c. Château Borély.

Surroundings of Marseilles

Allauch

10 km/6 miles north-east, in beautiful upland country, is the climatic resort of Allauch. The church of St-Sébastien (17th c.) has a fine "Ascension" by Monticelli. Other features of interest are the restored 17th c. mills and the Musée du Vieil Allauch (local history). Above the little town, to the east, is the chapel of Notre-Dame-du-Château (12th c.), from which there are wide-ranging views.

Cassis

22 km/14 miles east, in a semicircular bay is the little port of Cassis, surrounded by high hills. South-west of Cassis are the beautiful calanques of Port Miou, En Vau and Port Pin – fjord-like inlets reaching far into the land which form natural boating harbours and also offer opportunities for rock-climbers.

Château d'If

A popular excursion from Marseilles is a boat trip (departure from the Quai des Belges) to the Château d'If, on a rocky offshore island, which is famous for its association with Dumas' "Count of Monte Cristo" (1844–1845). The castle was built by Francis I in 1529, and was later used as a state prison. There are fine views from the crag on which the castle stands.

Ratonneau
Pomègues

West of Château d'If lie the two largish islands of Ratonneau and Pomègues, linked by a causeway, as well as the small island of Le Planier (lighthouse) further out.

Château Gombert

On the northern outskirts of the city is Château Gombert, now housing the Musée de l'Art Provençal. a collection of Provençal art.

Grotte Loubière

1.5 km/1 mile beyond this, in the Massif de l'Etoile, is the Grotte Loubière, a cave system with impressive karstic formations.

La Ciotat

The port and industrial town of La Ciotat lies 30 km/20 miles south-east of Marseilles. It is dominated by the 155 m/508 ft high Bec de l'Aigle (Eagle's Beak). There are a number of 17th and 18th c. houses to be seen in the Old town. The best route to take when driving to La Ciotat from Cassis is the Corniches des Crêtes. This narrow and twisting road, which leads just below the Falaises, the highest steep cliffs in France, high above the sea to Cap Canaille (362 m/1190 ft above sea-level), offers a superb view of the coastline from the Calanques as far as Cap Croisette. The 15 km/9½ mile stretch leads via Grande Tête down to La Ciotat.

*Corniche des Crêtes

Metz

O5

Region: Lorraine. Département: Moselle
Altitude: 170 m/560 ft. Population: 119,000

Situation and characteristics

Metz, chief town of the département of Moselle and the region of Lorraine (see entry), the see of a bishop and since 1971 a university town, lies at the junction of the Seille and the Moselle, which at this point is divided into a number of arms. It is an industrial and commercial city.

History

Metz, under the name of Dividorum, was a place of some consequence in Roman times. In the 6th c. it was a residence of the Merovingian kings, and later became a free imperial city. It was incorporated in France in 1552. From 1870 to 1918 and during the Second World War it belonged to the German Reich and was capital of the province of Lorraine.

Sights

Place d'Armes

The central feature of the picturesque old town with its narrow streets and lanes and old houses is the Place d'Armes, in which are the cathedral and the 18th c. Hôtel de Ville (Town Hall).

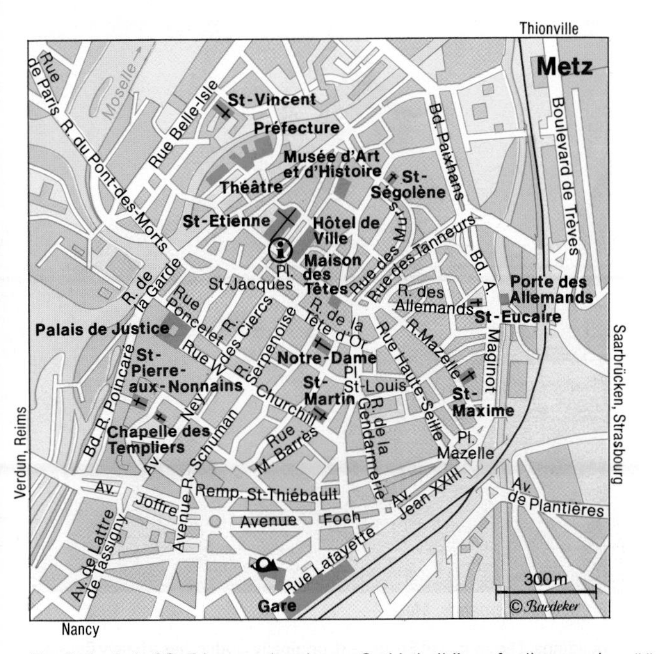

The Cathedral of St-Etienne, a handsome Gothic building of yellow sandstone flanked by two slender towers, was built between 1250 and 1380 on a unified plan, incorporating the earlier church of Notre-Dame-la-Ronde; the choir dates from the early 16th c. The porch and the doorway into the south aisle under the Tour de Mutte (with the famous Mutte, a large bell dating from 1605) are modern. On the Place d'Armes front, set at an angle to the façade, is the Portail de la Vierge (c. 1240), with old reliefs in the porch, in the tympanum and on the left-hand lintel (procession of the Apostles); the reliefs on the right-hand lintel are copies, based on the damaged originals by the Master of Naumburg (now in the cathedral workshops).

**Cathedral

The interior is of overwhelming effect, with its great height (42 m/140 ft) and width and its huge areas of beautiful stained glass (14th c. in the rose window on the west front, 16th c. in the choir and transepts). In the south aisle are the Chapelle Notre-Dame or du Mont-Carmel, once the choir of the older church of Notre-Dame-la-Ronde, and the Chapelle du St-Sacrement or des Evêques, with stained glass by Jacques Villon (1957). In the towers are abstract windows by R. Bissière (1959). In the aisles are the remains of wall-mounted tombs. In the north transept and the ambulatory (on left) are three windows by Marc Chagall (1960). In the choir (on left) is a marble bishop's throne of the Merovingian period. The church treasury contains some valuable items, but was originally much richer.

*Interior

North-east of the cathedral is the Musée d'Art et d'Histoire, which contains in the basement the excavated remains of Roman structures and also incorporates the old municipal granary (15th c.). The exhibits include Gallo-Roman finds and examples of medieval religious art and architecture. There is also an art gallery.

*Musée d'Art et d'Histoire

Below the cathedral, on the far side of the Moselle, is the wide Place de la Comédie, in which are the theatre and a number of handsome Baroque

St-Vincent

Porte des Allemands, Metz

buildings. The church of St-Vincent, originally Gothic, has a heavy Baroque façade and two elegant towers over the choir.

*Esplanade
Mont St-Quentin

On the south-west side of the inner city is the Esplanade, from the beautiful terrace of which there are views of the Moselle valley and Mont St-Quentin (350 m/1150 ft; view). On the north side of the Esplanade is the 18th c. Palais de Justice (Law Courts). To the south is the church of St-Pierre-aux-Nonnains, originally a Roman basilica or an early Christian church, which belonged to a Benedictine abbey founded in the 7th c. In the 16th c. the church was incorporated in the town's defences.

Cultural Centre

Templar chapel

The Cultural Centre, converted from an old 19th c. arsenal by the architect Ricardo Bofill, contains a large exhibition hall, two concert halls and rehearsal rooms. Nearby is a small octagonal Templar chapel which dates from the 12th c.

St-Martin

Beyond the Place de la République is the church of St-Martin (1202), with remains of old stained glass (15th, 16th and 19th c.), a charming funeral monument with a representation of the Virgin lying in (15th c.) and a Baroque organ gallery.

*Porte des
Allemands

From the centre of the old town Rue des Allemands runs east to the Porte des Allemands, a massive defence work projecting over the Seille, with two round towers (13th c.) on the inner side and two 15th c. bastions on the outer side. It is the last relic of the town's medieval fortifications.

Other sights

On the banks of the Seille, south of the Porte des Allemands, is the church of St-Maximin, which dates in part from the 12th c. and has stained glass by Jean Cocteau. Farther south is the modern church of Ste-Thérèse-l'Enfant (1954), with fine stained glass.

Hagondange

At Hagondange, 15 km/9 miles north, is the Nouveau Monde des Schtroumpfs, a leisure park opened in 1989.

Monte Carlo and Monaco

Monaco

P11

Principauté de Monaco
Area: 1.95 sq. km/¾ sq. mile
Population: 30,000 (of which 5000 are native Monégasques).
Vehicle registration letters: MC

Flag of Monaco

** Situation and characteristics

The old town of Monaco, at the east end of the Côte d'Azur near the Italian frontier, is capital of the little principality of that name which was established by the Genoese family of Grimaldi in 1338 and until 1848 also included Menton and Roquebrune. It is still ruled by princes of the house of Grimaldi (since 1949 by Prince Rainier III). Monaco, or more correctly the Principauté de Monaco, covers an area of only 1.95 sq. km/¾ sq. mile, making it the second smallest European state after the Vatican State.

Population

The population of the principality, which is predominantly Roman Catholic, consists of native Monégasques (as the people of Monaco are called), who account for around 17% of the population, French citizens (roughly 40%), Italians (about 20%) and other foreigners from all over the world. The Monégasques have their own language, Monegasco, a mixed Provençal/Ligurian dialect, though the official language of the principality is French.

Motor sport

Two famous events are associated with Monaco, the Grand Prix de Monaco, a Formula I race round the streets of the town, and the Rallye de Monte-Carlo, the course of which extends far into French territory.

History and Administration

History

Prehistoric finds on the territory of present-day Monaco-Ville show that the area was inhabited before the Stone Age. Around 900 B.C. Phoenicians

Vehicle registration letters

Arms of Monaco

dedicated a rock to the god Baal of Tyre (cult of Melkart). Later the place became a Greek trading station, and later still a Roman port under the name of Herculis Monoeci Portus. Its subsequent history was influenced by the great migrations and a period of Saracen rule. At the turn of the 12th and 13th centuries it fell into the hands of the Genoese, who in 1215 built a fortress of which some remains can still be seen. From 1297 it was ruled by the Grimaldi family, who assumed the title of prince in 1612. After a period under Spanish protection Monaco passed in 1731 to the French line of Goyon de Matignon-Grimaldi, and in 1793 it was united with France. In 1814 it was returned to Prince Honoré IV. From 1815 to 1860 the principality was under the protection of the kingdom of Sardinia. In 1860 it came under French protection, in return for which Prince Charles III was compelled to cede to France the towns of Mentone (Menton) and Roccabruna (Roquebrune). In 1866 the town of Monte Carlo was founded, with a Casino, an Opera House and a luxury hotel. In 1911 Albert I granted the principality a constitution. In 1918 relations with France were put on a new footing. In 1949 Rainier III succeeded Louis II, who had reigned since 1922, and in 1956 he married the American actress Grace Kelly (d. 1982).

Administration

Under the Constitution of 1962, thge political system is that of a constitutional monarchy. Formally, government authority resides in the Prince and is delegated by him to the Minister of State. The head of state has an absolute right of veto, except in relation to the budget. The government comprises a Minister of State (Ministre d'Etat) and three Government Ministers (Conseil de Gouvernement), for Internal Affairs, Finance and Economy and for Public Works and Social Services. In addition, there is a State Council and an Economic Council.

Popular representation

There are an 18-member National Council (Conseil National), elected for a five-year term, and a Communal Council (Conseil Communal) elected for

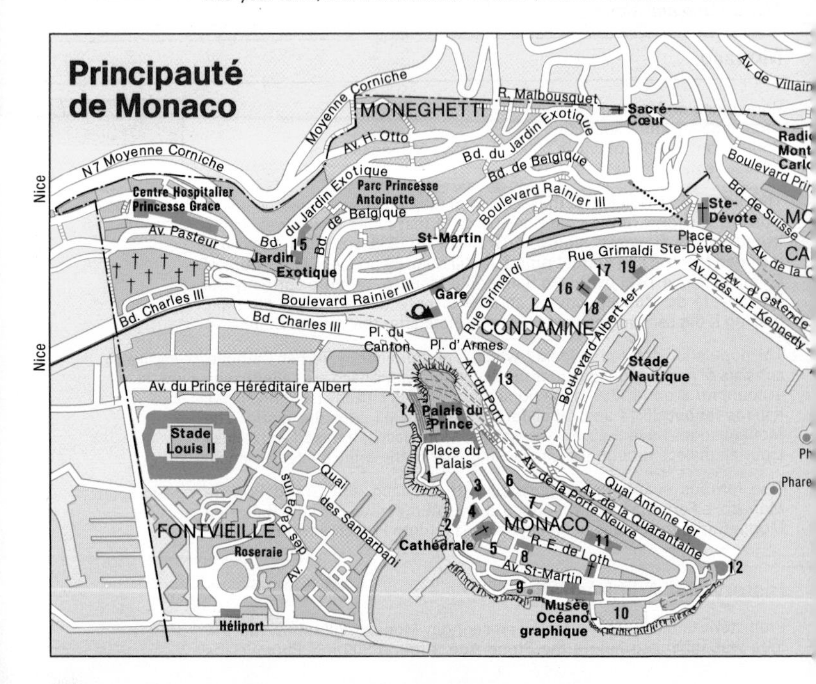

a four-year term. The real parliament of the principality is the Conseil National, which meets twice a year.

In both domestic and external affairs there are close links with France, for example in the customs union (from 1865), the currency union (from 1925) and the assimilation of tax law. Although the principality is within the French customs area it has issued its own postage stamps since 1985.

Economy

Income from the Casino now accounts for just under 4% of the principality's revenue, compared with almost 100% at the turn of the century; 55% comes from the high value-added tax (25–40%). Monaco's fame as a tax haven rests on the fact that the inhabitants pay no income tax, capital gains tax or property tax. The tourist and holiday trade makes the principal contribution to the economy, although the establishment of "environment-friendly" industrial installations (laboratories, electrical and electronic industries, foodstuffs) is now increasingly being promoted. Monaco is now also an important financial centre. In less than 15 years three new quarters of the town have been built on land reclaimed from the sea, increasing the total area of the principality by 20% to nearly 2 sq. km/¾ sq. mile.

Monaco City (Monaco-Ville)

Monaco-Ville, a town of narrow streets picturesquely situated on a rocky promontory 60 m/200 ft high projecting into the sea, with many remains of earlier fortifications, is the oldest part of the built-up area, the administrative centre of the principality and the see of a bishop.

*Place du Palais

At the west end of the peninsula is the commandingly situated Place du Palais, with the 13th c. Palais du Prince (changing of the guard at 11.55

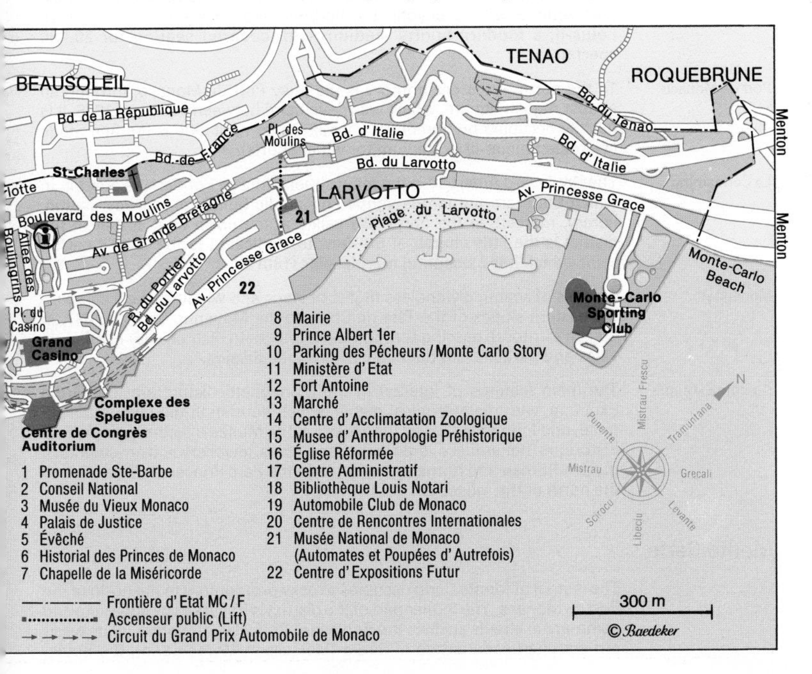

a.m.). The palace (open to the public only when the princely family is not in residence) has sumptuous state apartments (Throne Room in Empire style; Chambre d'York, 18th c., named after the Duke of York, George III's brother, who died here; beautiful 17th c. frescoes, Genoese work). There is a museum, the Musée Napoléonien et des Archives Monégasques, with many mementoes of Napoleon, a sample of rock from the moon and an exhibition of postage stamps.

Cathedral

From the Palace Rue du Tribunal leads to the cathedral. Built in 1884–1897 in the Romanesque-Byzantine style, it contains an altarpiece by Bréa (*c.* 1500), works of art of the Nice school and the tombs of princes of Monaco and bishops. Opposite the cathedral is the Palais de Justice (Law Courts). Nearby are the Historial des Princes (a historical museum) and the Chapelle de la Miséricorde (1639).

Musée Océanographique

At the end of the Jardins de St-Martin, which extend along the south side of the peninsula, is the Oceanographic Museum, established in 1910; the façade fronting the sea, almost 87 m/285 ft high, rests on massive substructures. The museum contains valuable scientific collections, objects brought back by Prince Albert I from his journeys of exploration, archaeological finds, submarines and diving equipment used by Jacques Cousteau, specimens of marine flora and fauna, a large aquarium, a laboratory and a library, as well as exhibitions of ship models and modern oceanographic apparatus. There are also shows of educational films. From the terrace of the museum, and from Fort Antoine at the eastern tip of the peninsula, there are superb views.
On the western slopes of the promontory is the Centre d'Acclimatation Zoologique, a form of zoo, with tropical and African fauna.

Fontvieille

To the west, at the foot of the rock of which the Old Town sits, is the new port Fontvieille, and beyond the harbour basin can be seen the Stade Louis-II, a modern sports stadium with covered seating for 20,000 spectators.

Port de Monaco

To the north of the promontory is the busy Port de Monaco, forming an almost regular square, which was developed between 1901 and 1926. It is usually occupied by numerous yachts. On its west side is the fine Stade Nautique Rainier-III (a stadium for water sports).

La Condamine

The Boulevard Albert-1er is the main street of the La Condamine quarter, in which there are numerous shops and public buildings (railway station, library, market). In the gorge-like valley at the north-west corner of the district is the little church of Ste-Dévote, dedicated to the town's patron saint, which has a beautiful marble altar (18th c.).

Moneghetti

A series of seemingly endless flights of steps and winding roads climb up the eastern slopes of the Tête de Chien to the Moyenne Corniche (N7, in French territory), passing through the Moneghetti district, with handsome villas and gardens laid out in terraces on the hillside.

*Jardin Exotique

The main features of interest in the Moneghetti district are the Jardin Exotique, with many tropical plants, which flourish in the favourable climate, and interesting caves (fine fossils); the Musée d'Anthropologie Préhistorique (bones discovered in the area, coins, jewellery and ornaments of the pre-Roman and Roman periods); and the Parc Princesse-Antoinette to the north of the museum.

Monte Carlo

The district of Monte Carlo occupies a rocky promontory to the north of the Port de Monaco. The higher part of the district is traversed by shopping and commercial streets such as the Boulevard Princesse-Charlotte (at its western end the headquarters of Radio-Telélévision Monte-Carlo), the Boulevard des Moulins (at its south-west end the Office de Tourisme, off its north side the church of St-Charles, 1883) and the Avenue de la Costa, with many luxury shops.

Casino

To the north of the harbour is the flamboyant Grand Casino, built in 1878 by Charles Garnier, the architect of the Opéra in Paris. It houses the legendary gaming rooms of the Société Anonyme des Bains de Mer (S.B.M.), founded in 1863.

Les Spélugues

Below the Casino is the congress centre of Les Spélugues, opened in 1978, a massive hexagonal complex traversed by the Boulevard Louis-II which includes a luxury hotel and about a hundred flats.
The topmost roof is covered with a mosaic of coloured tiles designed by Victor Vasarely (1979).

Larvotto
Musée des Automates

In the south-west of the Larvotto district is the Future Centre Culturel et des Expositions (due for completion in 1998). Nearby, in a villa of the *belle époque* in Avenue Princesse-Grace, is the Musée National des Automates et Poupées d'Autrefois, with a collection of several hundred dolls, more than 80 automata and over 2000 miniature objects of the 18th and 19th centuries. In the garden are sculptures by Zadkine, Maillol, Rodin and Bourdeille.

Surroundings of Monaco

La Turbie

8 km/5 miles north-east, commandingly situated on the mountain ridge between Tête de Chien and Mont de la Bataille, lies the little town of La Turbie, with a fine Baroque church. Conspicuously situated above the town is the Trophée des Alpes or Trophée d'Auguste, a monument erected by the Roman Senate in 6 B.C. to commemorate Augustus's conquest of the Alpine tribes. In the 14th c. it was converted into a fortress, which was blown up in 1705, during the War of the Spanish Succession. Restoration of the monument began about 1930. From the steeply sloping south and south-east sides of the site there are magnificent views.

Village Perché

Two excellent examples of Provençal "Nid d'Aigle" (Eagle's Nest) are Peillon (376 m/1234 ft, in the Monaco hinterland) and Peille (630 m/2068 ft), high above the Oeillon river, with its Romanesque church and ruins of the 13th c. château.

Montpellier

See Languedoc–Roussillon

Mont Saint-Michel F6

Region: Basse-Normandie. Département: Manche
Altitude: 3–80 m/10–260 ft. Population: 180

**Situation and characteristics

Mont St-Michel, rising out of the sea in the Baie de St-Michel on the coast of Normandy, is one of the most striking sights that France has to offer. Perched on its rocky islet and surrounded by walls and bastions, this old abbey has the appearance of a fortified castle. At this point in the English Channel the tides have a very considerable rise and fall (up to 14 m/45 ft): at low tide it is possible to walk round the island, while at high tide the waves surge up to its very walls and may even wash over the car park at the foot of the hill. It is a particularly impressive sight at the spring tides (three days after the new moon or full moon). There are pilgrimages across the sands following the tide at the end of July and in September, the Sunday nearest to the 29th (the feast of the Archangel Michael).

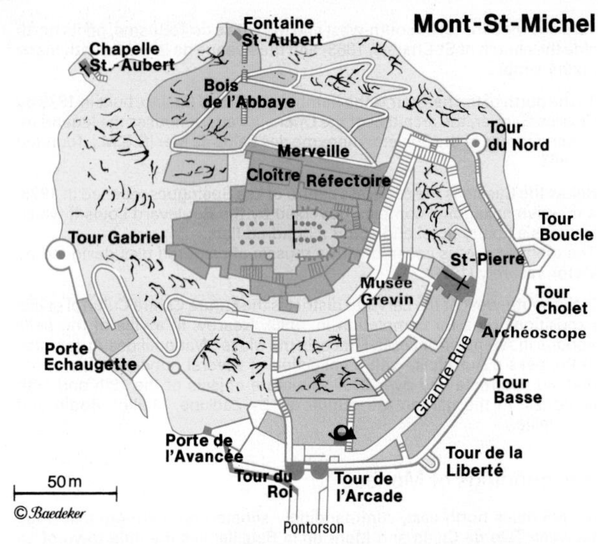

History

Legend has it that Archbishop Aubert of Avranches founded an abbey dedicated to St Michael on the island in the year 708 after the Archangel had appeared to him in a vision. This followed the example of Monte Gargano on the south-eastern coast of Italy, where the Archangel was said to have appeared in 492. Aubert obtained a relic from Monte Gargano, and Mont St-Michel then became a place of pilgrimage. From then until the 16th c. a succession of buildings in Romanesque and later in Gothic style were erected on the island, though the inaccessibility of the site must have created difficulties in the supply of materials for the buildings. Thanks to the strength of its defences the abbey, which became known as the "marvel of the West", was never taken by an enemy.

From the early medieval period onwards pilgrims flocked to the shrine, as they still do today. The monastery was dissolved in 1790, and in 1811 became a state prison. Finally in 1863 Napoleon III leased the abbey to the bishops of Coutances and Avranches, and thereafter it was gradually restored, making Mont St-Michel the major tourist attraction it is today.

Sights

Access

From the mainland a causeway 1.8 km/1 mile long, constructed in 1879, leads to the foot of the rock, where there is a car park (parking fee; beware of high tide!).

*Walls

From here we pass through the outer walls at the Porte du Roi and continue up the Grande Rue, the island's only street, running parallel to the Chemin des Remparts (the wall-walk). The street is lined by closely packed houses of the 15th and 16th centuries, now occupied by souvenir shops, snack bars, cafés, restaurants and hotels.

The parish church (15th–16th c.) contains 17th c. tomb slabs. The history of Mont St-Michel is related in the Musée Grevin (a wax museum) and the Archéoscope (a multi-media show). The street ends at the Grand Degré, a flight of steps leading to the entrance to the abbey.

**Abbey

The magnificent abbey of St-Michel on the highest point of the island was mainly built, in spite of great technical difficulties, between the 11th and 13th

Ancienne Aumônerie

Cloister

centuries. The neo-Gothic façade dates from 1780, and the 87.5 m/287 ft high spire of the church, crowned by a figure of the Archangel Michael (by Emmanuel Frémiet, late 19th c.), reaches a height of 155.5 m/510 ft above the sea.

**Interior

From the entrance another flight of steps leads up through the Salle des Gardes or Belle Chaise (13th c.) into the 13th c. north wing of the abbey, known as the Merveille (Marvel). On the lowest floor is the Aumônerie, a large columned hall which in the 13th c. was a dormitory for poor pilgrims, now the starting-point of the conducted tours, with a small exhibition hall. The conducted tour takes visitors through the Cellier (a cellar or storeroom) and up to the first floor, on which are the Salle des Hôtes, a reception room for distinguished guests situated over the Aumônerie, and the imposing Gothic Salle des Chevaliers (Knights' Hall, 1215–1220), later the working room of the Benedictine monks. Here too, below the choir of the church, is the Crypte des Gros Piliers (15th c.), with ten piers 5 m/16 ft in circumference. In another crypt is the pre-Romanesque church of Notre-Dame-sous-Terre, a 10th c. predecessor of the present church. On the second floor are the Refectory, later used as a dormitory (over the Salle des Hôtes), and the cloister built in 1225–1228 (over the Knights' Hall), with 220 graceful granite columns in double alternating rows. On the south side of the cloister is the abbey church, begun in 1020, its Romanesque nave forming a charming contrast to the 15th c. Gothic choir. From here the Escalier de Dentelle, a magnificent staircase supported on a buttress, leads up to an external gallery 120 m/395 ft above the sea from which there is an extensive view over the sea. There are also fine views from the terrace in front of the west façade of the church. Below the terrace, to the north, is the beautiful abbey garden.
At low tide it is possible to walk round the island, but before setting out visitors should enquire when the tide begins to come in. Walking is best done in bare feet. A boat trip round the island, however, is much more rewarding, particularly at the spring tide.

Mulhouse

See Alsace

Nancy

O6

Region: Lorraine
Département: Meurthe-et-Moselle
Altitude: 210 m/690 ft
Population: 99,400

Situation and characteristics

Nancy, the old capital of Lorraine and now chief town of the département of Meurthe-et-Moselle, the see of a bishop and a university town, lies on the left bank of the Meurthe and on the Rhine–Marne Canal. Its main glory is its magnificent 18th c. Baroque architecture.

History

In the 12th c. Nancy became capital of the Duchy of Lorraine. About 1475 Charles the Bold of Burgundy occupied the duchy and expelled Duke René; but two years later René reconquered Lorraine and Charles was killed outside the town while trying to escape. Under the peace of Vienna after the War of the Polish Succession (1733–1738) Lorraine was assigned to Stanislas Leszczyński, the deposed king of Poland and brother-in-law of Louis XV, who drew many artists to his court and gave the town its present splendid Rococo aspect. After his death in 1766 the duchy reverted to France.

Sights

Cathedral

The old town is centred on the Point Central, the intersection of the town's three main traffic arteries (Rue St-Dizier, Rue St-Georges and Rue St-Jean).

Place Stanislas

Art Nouveau window by Jacques Grüber

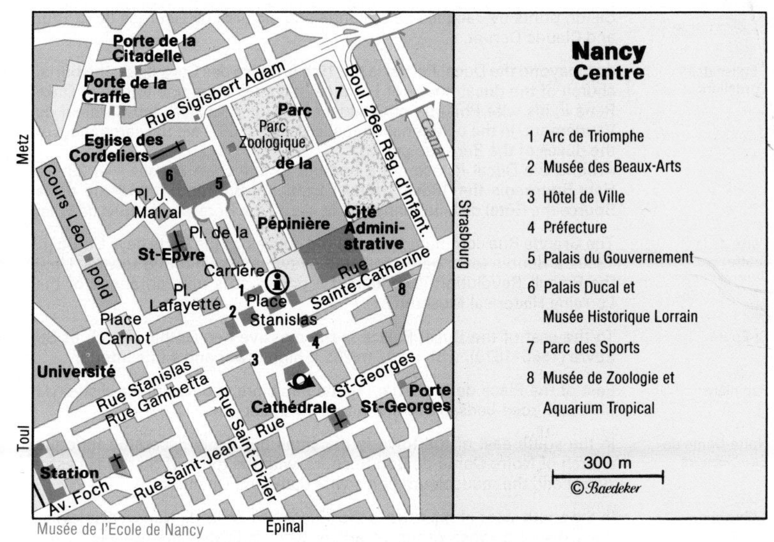

In Rue St-Georges is the twin-towered cathedral (1703–1742), with a Baroque interior (tombs, beautiful grilles, treasury). At the end of the street is the Porte St-Georges (1608).

**Place Stanislas

A little way north of the cathedral is Place Stanislas (originally the Place Royale), which along with the adjoining squares was mainly built by Emmanuel Héré between 1752 and 1760. Around the square are five imposing palaces, with balconies and balustrades. In the centre of the square is a statue of King Stanislas. Along its north side are single-storey galleried buildings, which continue along Rue Héré. The most characteristic feature of the square is the magnificent gilded wrought-iron railings (by Jean Lamour) at the ends of the streets entering the square and round the Fountains of Neptune and Amphitrite (both by Barthélemy Guibal). The largest of the palaces round the square is the Hôtel de Ville (Town Hall), with magnificent banisters by Lamour on the staircase.

*Musée des Beaux-Arts

On the west side of the square is the Musée des Beaux-Arts, with a representative collection of European paintings of the 16th–20th centuries and a fine collection of modern art, including works by Dufy, Utrillo, Modigliani and Zadkine.

Place de la Carrière

Adjoining the Musée des Beaux-Arts is a triumphal arch, erected in honour of Louis XV in 1757, which leads into the Place de la Carrière. At the near end of this square are two palaces of 1715 and 1753, followed by a series of town houses of uniform design. At the far end of the square are two richly decorated semicircular colonnades preceding the handsome Palais du Gouvernement (1760).

*Palais Ducal

To the left of the Palais du Gouvernement is the Grande Rue, in which is the former Ducal Palace (1502–1544, heavily restored in 1871), the most important secular building of the Late Gothic period in Lorraine, with a doorway and three balconies in richly decorated Flamboyant style.

*Musée Historique Lorrain

The Ducal Palace is now occupied by the Lorraine Historical Museum, with archaeological finds, medieval sculpture and rich collections of material on the history and folk traditions of Lorraine. On the first floor is the Galerie des Cerfs, with relics of the ducal period, tapestries, etchings by Jacques

Callot, prints by Jacques de Bellange and pictures by Georges de la Tour and Claude Deruet.

*Eglise des Cordeliers

Just beyond the Ducal Palace is the 15th c. Eglise des Cordeliers, the burial church of the ducal house of Lorraine. It contains the fine tombs of Duke René II, his wife Philippa of Guelders (by Ligier Richier) and Cardinal de Vaudémont. In the octagonal Chapelle Ducale (1607) are the sarcophagi of the dukes of the Baroque period.
Around the Ducal Palace are a number of fine town houses – at 29 rue Haut-Bourgeois the 18th c. Hôtel Ferrari (by Boffrand), at 12 rue de la Source the Hôtel de Lillebonne and at No. 10 the Hôtel du Marquis de Ville.

Porte de la Craffe

The Grande Rue continues, lined by old houses, to the Porte de la Craffe (*c.* 1360), a double town gate protected by two massive round towers. Until the French Revolution it contained a prison; it is now an annex of the Lorraine Historical Museum.

St-Epvre

To the east of the Ducal Palace is the massive neo-Gothic church of St-Epvre (1865–1870), with an 87 m/285 ft high tower and a fine interior.

Pépinière

East of the Place de la Carrière is the Pépinière, a beautiful English-style park with rose-beds, a zoo and a tropical aquarium.

Notre-Dame de Bon-Secours

In the south-east of the town is the small but richly decorated Baroque church of Notre-Dame de Bon-Secours, with the tomb of Stanislas Leszczyński and the mausoleum of his wife Catharina Opalinska.

*Musée de l'Ecole de Nancy

In the south-west of the town is the Musée de l'Ecole de Nancy, displaying the work of a loose group of artists who dedicated themselves to the establishment and development of Art Nouveau in Lorraine. The museum, appropriately housed in an Art Nouveau villa, contains glass, furniture and jewellery by Victor Prouvé, Emile Gallé, Antonin Daum, Louis Majorelle and Eugène Vallin.

Cristallerie

In the Cristallerie Daum, in Rue des Cristalleries, visitors can observe the process of manufacture of articles in crystal.

Nantes F7

Region: Pays de la Loire
Département: Loire-Atlantique
Altitude: 10 m/33 ft
Population: 239,000 (conurbation 500,000)

Situation and characteristics

The old Breton port of Nantes, chief town of the département of Loire-Atlantique, the see of a bishop and a university town, lies at the junction of the Erdre (flowing underground for the last part of its course) with the Loire, here divided into a number of arms and navigable, which 50 km/30 miles farther downstream flows into the Atlantic at St-Nazaire. The port of St-Nazaire, the first port in France to be entirely electronically controlled, has a turnover of 23 million tons.
Nantes was the birthplace of the writer Jules Verne (1828–1905).

History

Nantes, under the name of Condevincum, was the capital of a Gallic tribe, the Namnetae. Then and subsequently, down to the end of the 15th c., the town fought to maintain its independence against the Romans, the Normans, the English and the French. In the Middle Ages Nantes was for a time capital of the Duchy of Brittany, which fell to the French crown in 1532. In 1598 Henry IV signed here the famous Edict of Nantes, which granted freedom of religious belief to Protestants.
Thanks to its port Nantes developed into a flourishing commercial town by the 16th c. In the 19th c. its trade declined, since the larger vessels then coming into service could not sail up the Loire, so that it became necessary

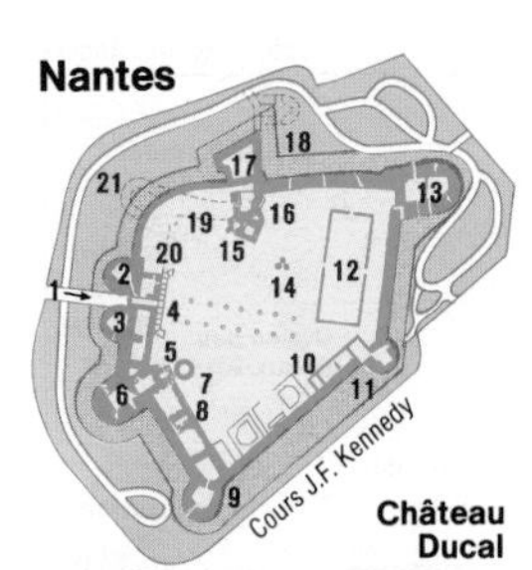

1 Entrance
2 Tour du Pied de Biche
3 Tour de la Boulangerie
4 Grand Gouvernement (Musée d'Art populaire régional/Musée de ferronnerie et céramique)
5 Tour de la Couronne d'Or
6 Tour des Jacobins
7 Puits (well)
8 Grand Logis
9 Tour du Port
10 Petit Gouvernement
11 Tour de la Rivière
12 Harnachement (Musée des Salorges)
13 Tour du Fer à Cheval
14 Remains of original castle
15 Loge du Concierge
16 Vieux Donjon
17 Bastion Mercœur
18 Tour au Duc
19 Vieux Logis
20 Chapelle
21 Tour des Espagnois

to build an outer harbour at St-Nazaire and develop new industries in Nantes.

Sights

Place Royale

In the centre of Nantes is the Place Royale, an elegant square laid out in 1790. North-east of the square is the neo-Gothic church of St-Nicolas (1844–1848), with an 85 m/280 ft high tower. Farther east is the church of Ste-Croix (1685), with a choir of 1840.

Old town

No visit to Nantes would be complete without a walk through the old 18th and 19th c. quarters. The Place Royale, Rue Crébillon, Place Graslin and Cours Cambronne will give the visitor a good impression of old Nantes.

*Château Ducal

Farther east is the imposing Château Ducal, surrounded by a moat, part of which is laid out as a park. The original castle was built in the 10th c., and after being rebuilt in 1466 was again enlarged in the 16th c. The Edict of Nantes was signed here.

Fortified castle entrance

Old doorway in the cathedral of St-Pierre

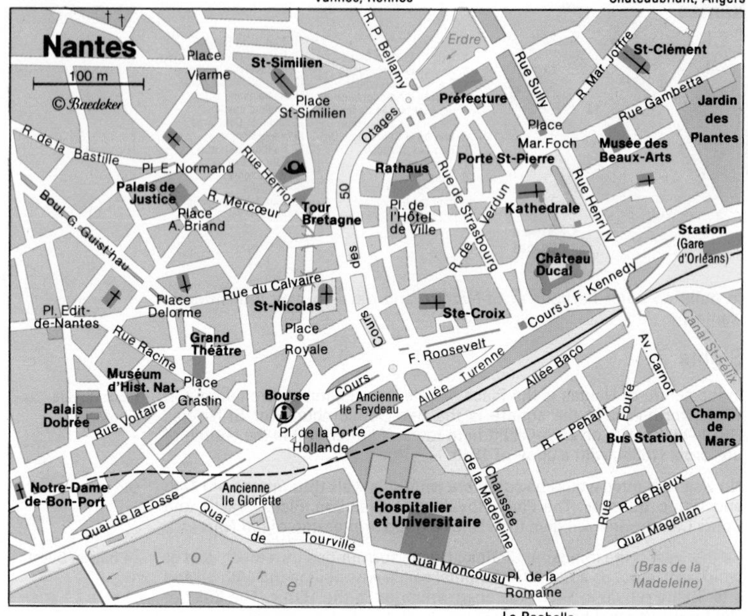

Near the gate leading into the inner courtyard is a beautiful Late Gothic well (12th c.).

From the south curtain wall, at the Petit Gouvernement, there is a fine view of the Château, with the cathedral beyond it.

Museums

Within the château are three museums. In the Tour du Fer à Cheval is the Musée des Arts Décoratifs (textiles); in the Grand Gouvernement is the Musée Régional des Arts Populaires (regional folk art); and in the Harnachement is the Musée des Salorges (history of seafaring, trade and industry of Nantes).

*St-Pierre-et-St-Paul

To the north of the château, in Place St-Pierre, is the cathedral, which occupies the site of two earlier churches (6th c. and 939). Building began in 1434 with the façade, continued in the 17th c. and was completed between 1840 and 1891. The three-aisled interior is very impressive. In the south transept is the tomb of the last Duke of Brittany, Francis II (d. 1488) and his wife Marguerite of Foix, a masterpiece of richly decorated Renaissance art (by Michel Colombe, 1502–1507, commissioned by Duchess Anne (Anne de Bretagne). The tomb is empty, as is the golden shrine which once contained Anne's heart. In the north transept is the tomb (also empty) of General Lamoricière (1805–1865), by Paul Dubois (1879).

*Musée des Beaux-Arts

North-east of the cathedral, in Rue Gambetta, is the Musée des Beaux-Arts, one of the finest provincial museums in France, with a collection of pictures ranging in date from the 13th c. to the present day.

Jardin des Plantes

Also in Rue Gambetta is the Jardin des Plantes, a beautiful botanical garden.

Grand Théâtre

South-west of the Place Royale is Place Graslin, on the north side of which is the Grand Théâtre, built in 1783–1788 but subsequently much altered.

Palais Dobrée

Farther south-west is the Palais Dobrée, built by a 19th c. collector of that name, which now houses the Archaeological Museum (finds from the surrounding area, history of the French Revolution, ethnography).
In the same building is the Musée Dobrée (illuminated manuscripts, incunabula and first editions; prints and pictures).

Musée d'Histoire Naturelle

A little way east is the Natural History Museum, with a large library.

Jules Verne Museum

In the south-west of the town is a museum devoted to the world-famous writer Jules Verne (1828–1905), a native of Nantes. It displays personal mementoes of the author and models and drawings illustrating his novels.

Planetarium

Close by is an excellently equipped Planetarium.

La Jonelière

North of the town, in La Jonelière, are a zoo and an Automobile Museum with more than 50 veteran and vintage cars.

Surroundings of Nantes

Boat trips on the Erdre

Excursion boats ply on the lower course of the river Erdre, to the north of the town; trips into the Erdre valley are particularly popular. Along the river are a number of elegant houses, like the 16th c. Château de la Gacherie on the west bank.

Champtoceaux

31 km/19 miles north-east of Nantes is the little town of Champtoceaux, on the left bank of the Loire, with a beautiful church and a ruined medieval castle. Oudon, on the right bank, has a keep dating from around 1400.

St-Nazaire

See Brittany

Narbonne

See Languedoc–Roussillon

Nice

P11

Region: Provence–Alpes–Côte-d'Azur. Département: Alpes-Maritimes
Altitude: 1–20 m/3–65 ft. Population: 400,000

Nice, chief town of the département of Alpes-Maritimes and the see of a bishop, is magnificently situated on the Baie des Anges, surrounded by the foothills of the Maritime Alps, some 30 km/19 miles from the Italian frontier. The old town is separated from the newer districts by the little river Paillon, most of it now covered over.
With its sheltered situation and mild climate, Nice is one of the oldest established winter resorts on the Côte d'Azur (see entry), and is also a very popular summer resort.

History

In 350 B.C. Phocaeans from Marseilles founded a settlement on what is now the Colline du Château, calling it Nikaia Polis in honour of Nike, goddess of victory. The Romans, who had a settlement on the hill of Cimiez, farther inland, showed little interest in the town, which later suffered from the attentions of the Saxons (6th c.) and the Saracens (9th c.). During the Middle Ages the town belonged to the County of Provence and from 1388 to the Duchy of Savoy, which was united with Sardinia. During this period the harbour and the castle were built. In 1792 Nice was incorporated in France, and in 1814 in Sardinia, before finally becoming French in 1860.

The harbour, Nice, with Mont Boron in the background

In the second half of the 19th c. Nice developed into one of the first great French tourist centres.
Giuseppe Garibaldi (1807–1882), the hero of Italian independence, was a native of Nice. The painters Dufy and Matisse are buried here. The University of Nice was founded in 1966.

Colline du Château

The oldest settlement on the site of Nice was on the Colline du Château (92 m/302 ft; lift). From the Terrasse Frédéric-Nietzsche there is an impressive view of the whole town and the old harbour. The citadel which once stood here was destroyed in 1706. Considerable remains of two churches, a 15th c. church overlying an earlier 11th c. one, have been excavated here.

Tour Bellanda

From the hill a flight of steps leads down to the seafront promenade, passing the Tour Bellanda, built in 1880 on the site of the St-Lambert bastion, which houses the Musée Naval.

Vieille Ville

The old town, a maze of narrow streets and lanes, lies under the west side of the Colline du Château, bounded on the north-west by spacious boulevards and gardens laid out over the Paillon (Jardin Albert-I, Place Masséna, Promenade du Paillon), in the south of the Ponchettes. A flower market is held every day on the adjoining Cours Saleya. At its eastern end is the Galerie de Malacologie, a branch of the Musée d'Histoire Naturelle (shell collection and aquarium).

Chapelle de la Miséricorde

A little way north of the flower market is the Chapelle de la Miséricorde (1736). It has an altar with an early 15th Vierge de la Miséricorde and a

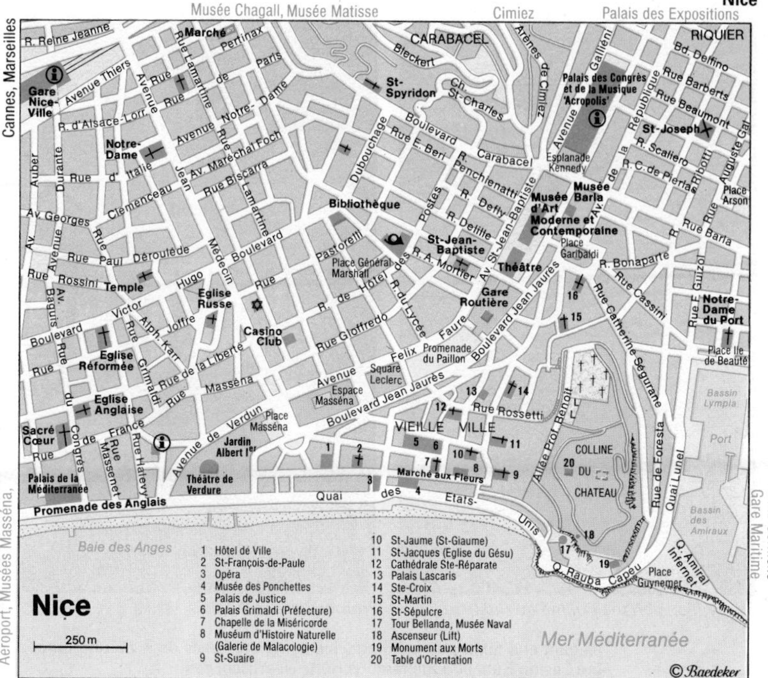

figure of the Virgin attributed to Bréa (however, the church is closed because of structural faults).

Palais Grimaldi

The Palais Grimaldi (1611–1613, renovated in 1907) is now the Préfecture. Adjoining it is the Palais de Justice (Law Courts, 1892).

St-Jacques

The former Jesuit church of St-Jacques (17th c.) has rich stucco decoration.

Cathedral

The Cathedral of Ste-Réparate (17th c.), also with rich stucco decoration, has fine choir-stalls and beautiful wood panelling in the sacristy.

Palais Lascaris

This magnificent Baroque building was once the palace of the Counts of Castellar. It has a handsome entrance hall, an 18th c. pharmacy, and rich stucco decoration and ceiling paintings in the state apartments.

* Galerie des Ponchettes

The former arsenal of the Sardinian navy, on the Quai des Etats-Unis, now contains an interesting collection of paintings by Raoul Dufy (1877–1953).

Musée Mossa

On the Quai des Etats-Unis lies the Musée Alexis et Gustav-Adolf Mossa. The latter was an artist and founder of the Nice Carnival.

Ville Moderne

Jardin Albert-1er

The Jardin Albert-1er runs north-east from the seafront to the busy Place Masséna, the hub of the city's traffic, in which are the Fontaine du Soleil and the Casino Municipal (1883). At the south end of the gardens is an open-air theatre, the Théâtre de Verdure.

* Promenade des Anglais

From the south end of the Jardin Albert-1er the magnificent Promenade des Anglais, laid out in 1822–1824, runs west along the seafront, lined by

Excavations on the Colline du Château

Promenade des Anglais

elegant and luxurious buildings, including the Palais de la Méditerranée, the Casino Ruhl and the famous Hôtel Negresco.

Musée d'Art et d'Histoire

The Musée d'Art et d'Histoire in the Palais Massena displays Roman finds, many works from the Nice School (Bréa, Durani, etc.), Italian and Provençal porcelain, a collection covering regional history and culture and 19th c. Nice water-colours, applied art and a collection of weapons.

Les Baumettes

Musée des Beaux-Arts

Farther west is the university quarter, in which is the Musée des Beaux-Arts Jules Chéret, with works by Charpeaux, Chéret, Fragonard, Braque, Chagall, Dufy, Raphael and other artists and ceramics by Picasso.

Musée d'Art Naïf

The Musée International d'Art Naïf gives a general overview of naïve art worldwide.

Cimiez

*Roman remains

On a plateau below Mont Gros are extensive remains of the Roman town of Cemenelum. The amphitheatre, with seating for over 5000 spectators, and the baths are well preserved. The Musée d'Archéologie displays finds from the site (coins, etc.).

*Musée Matisse

In a Genoese villa on this ancient site is the fine Matisse Museum, with works presented to the town of Nice by the Matisse family.

Notre-Dame-de-Cimiez

Above the excavation site is the monastery of Notre-Dame-de-Cimiez, a Benedictine foundation which was taken over by the Franciscans in the 16th c. and enlarged in the 17th; it was extensively restored and renovated in 1850. It contains a fine "Crucifixion" by Bréa.

Carabacel

*Musée Chagall

Farther in towards the town is the Musée National Message Biblique Marc Chagall, with the largest collection of work by the painter Marc Chagall (1887–1985), including paintings, etchings, lithographs, sculptures, mosaics.

Acropolis

Continuing on the Boulevard de Cimiez and then south-eastward on Boulevard Carabacel, we come back to the gardens laid out over the course of the Paillon. On the left is the Palais des Congrès et de la Musique, known as the Acropolis, a congress and function centre. To the south are the Musée Barla (a branch of the Natural History Museum with collections illustrating the development of species), the new Musée d'Art Moderne et Contemporain (modern and contemporary art) and the theatre.

Other Sights in Nice

Prieuré du Vieux Logis

In the northern district of St-Barthélemy, housed in a 16th c. building, is the rich collection of religious art of the Prieuré du Vieux Logis. The collection includes works of the Avignon and Paris schools and by Flemish, Burgundian and German masters of the 14th–16th centuries.

Harbour quarter

At the foot of Mont Boron (178 m/584 ft), which rises above the east side of the town, is the harbour quarter, with plain Italian-style houses.

Observatory

In the north-east of Nice, on the edge of Mont Gros (375 m/1230 ft) stands an observatory built by Charles Garnier, with a dome by Gustave Eiffel.

Villefranche

On the far side of Mont Boron is Villefranche, with a fine natural harbour which was developed by Charles II of Anjou in 1295. To the south of the picturesque old town is the citadel (1580). By the harbour are the fishermen's chapel of St-Pierre, the interior of which was decorated by Jean Cocteau, and the Palais de la Marine.

Phénix

South-west of the town, opposite the airport, is the new Arénas shopping centre. Between this and the Promenade des Anglais is a large park which offers a variety of attractions, including an artificial lake, aviaries and a hothouse in which tropical plants grow in seven different climatic zones.

Zygofolis

14 km/9 miles north-west of Nice is the large Zygofolis amusement park, with the motto "Round the water", which offers all the latest technical novelties.

Marineland

See Practical Information, Leisure Parks

Parc des Miniatures

Half-way between the city centre and the airport, on the Boulevard Impératrice-Eugénie, is the Parc des Miniatures, with reproductions on the scale of 1:25 of buildings and episodes which have featured in the history of Nice, from prehistoric times to the present day.

Nîmes

M11

Region: Languedoc–Roussillon. Département: Gard
Altitude: 39 m/130 ft. Population: 145,000

Situation and characteristics

Nîmes, the French city richest in Roman remains, is beautifully situated in the hilly foreland of the Cévennes, north-west of the Rhône delta, between Avignon and Montpellier. It is the chief town of the Gard département, the see of a bishop and a centre of the wine and spirit trade, with an important clothing industry (silk garments). It was the birthplace of the writer Alphonse Daudet (1840–1897).

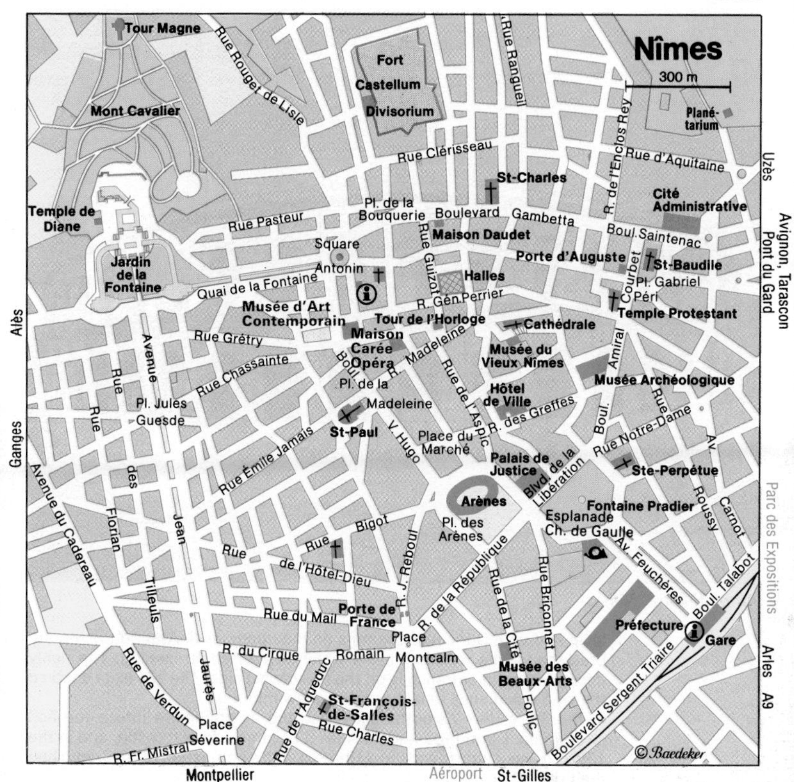

History

Ancient Nemausus was the capital of the Volcae Arecomici, who built their town round a sacred spring, the haunt of a spirit worshipped under the name of Nemausus. In 121 B.C. Nemausus submitted to the Romans, and thereafter rapidly developed into one of the most important towns in Gaul, situated on the main road from Italy to Spain. The remains of Roman structures and the extent of its walls bear witness to its splendour. During the Middle Ages Nîmes was ruled by its own Vicomtes until 1185, when it passed into the hands of the Counts of Toulouse. As a Protestant stronghold, with three-quarters of its population confessing the Reformed faith, Nîmes suffered greatly during the wars of religion and again in 1704 during the rising in the Cévennes.

Sights

**Arènes

The principal tourist attraction of Nîmes is the Roman amphitheatre (the "Arènes") in the centre of the town. Built in the 1st c. A.D., it is 133 m/435 ft long, 101 m/330 ft across and 21 m/70 ft high, with seating for 21,000 spectators. Although not the largest of the 70 known Roman amphitheatres, it is one of the best preserved, particularly in the upper parts. The 60 arches round the exterior are embellished with pilasters on ground floor

◀ *Maison Carrée*

Amphitheatre, Nîmes

level and with Doric half-columns on the upper level. Around the top are brackets for the wooden masts which supported an awning. The richly decorated main entrance is on the north-west side. The 124 exits enabled the whole audience to leave within a few minutes.
In the 5th c. the Visigoths converted the amphitheatre into a fortified stronghold. During the Middle Ages it became a feudal castle, and in the 13th c. it was a little township on its own with a population of 2000, who had their own chapel.
The amphitheatre is now covered by a huge air cushion which is supported on 30 metal pillars inserted into non-Roman parts of the structure. This enables theatrical performances and bullfights to be staged in the amphitheatre even in winter; the roof is removed in summer.

Esplanade

To the east of the amphitheatre is the busy Esplanade Charles de Gaulle, in which is the Fontaine Pradier (1848), a marble fountain with a personification of Nîmes.

*Maison Carrée

North-west of the Arènes, in the Place de la Comédie, is the Maison Carrée, an excellently preserved Roman temple of the time of Augustus (20–12 B.C.), with tall Corinthian columns bearing the richly ornamented entablature, which has a finely carved acanthus frieze. During the Middle Ages the temple was occupied for a time by a monastery. It was restored in the 18th c., and now houses the Musée des Antiques, with Roman statues, bronzes, mosaics and reliefs.
The Musée d'Art Contemporain (architect Norman Foster) is at present being built near the Maison Carrée.

*Jardin de la Fontaine

To the west of the Maison Carrée is the beautiful Jardin de la Fontaine, laid out around 1750, which incorporates the ruins of an ancient sanc-

Pont du Gard

tuary built at a sacred spring as well as a variety of other features – canals, grottoes, bridges, Baroque statues and urns. On the western edge of the park, under old trees, is the so-called Temple of Diana, a handsome building of dressed stone, partly collapsed, which was probably part of the Roman baths. Above the park rises Mont Cavalier (114 m/374 ft), with shady footpaths and a southern flora, topped by the Tour Magne, a 30 m/100 ft high Roman monument dating from 15 B.C., from the platform of which there is a wide view of the town and surrounding area.

Temple of Diana

Tour Magne

*View

Castellum Divisorium

South-east of the Tour Magne, under the walls of the Fort, are the remains (discovered in 1884) of a Roman water-tower, the Castellum Divisorium, which distributed the water brought in over the Pont du Gard (see below). The remains consist of a round collecting basin, from which ten pipes conveyed water to the different parts of the town.

Cathedral

In the centre of the old town, to the east of the 14th c. Clock-Tower, is the late 11th c. Cathedral of Notre-Dame et St-Castor. On the west front is a frieze of Romanesque reliefs depicting scenes from the story of the Creation.

Musée du Vieux Nîmes

To the south of the cathedral is the former Bishop's Palace, which now houses the Musée du Vieux Nîmes (municipal and regional history), with the associated Musée Taurin (Bullfighting Museum).

*Musée Archéologique

In Boulevard Amiral-Courbet, on the east side of the old town, is the Archaeological Museum, in a former Jesuit seminary. The exhibits include important Gallo-Roman remains and inscriptions, sculpture down to the medieval period and collections of coins, glass and pottery. In the former chapel is a fine mosaic.

Porte d'Arles

This Roman town gate, also known as the Porte d'Auguste, was the starting-point of the road to Rome.

Other sights

At 20 Boulevard Gambetta is the house in which Alphonse Daudet was born.

Musée des Beaux-Arts

The collection of the Musée des Beaux-Arts consists mainly of works by older masters (16th–18th c.).

Surroundings of Nîmes

**Pont du Gard

25 km/15 miles north-east of Nîmes is the Pont du Gard, a 275 m/300 yd long aqueduct 49 m/160 ft high spanning the deeply indented valley of the Gard or Gardon. This three-tier structure, probably built about 19 B.C. by Agrippa, Augustus's son-in-law and co-ruler, is one of the most massive and best preserved Roman structures that have come down to us. The 41 km/25 mile long water conduit to Nîmes was carried in a covered channel borne by the topmost tier of arches. It has been estimated that there was a daily flow of some 20,000 cu. m/440,000 gallons of water to the Castellum Divisorium in Nîmes (see page 327, above), from which it was distributed throughout the town. The road bridge carried by the first tier of arches was added in 1747.

Normandy

F–I 5/6

**Situation and characteristics

The region of Normandy in north-western France extends from the Ile de France, between Picardy (to the north) and Brittany (to the west), to the English Channel. Historically – as its name indicates – it is the territory conquered in the 9th c. by Norsemen from Denmark. Since then it has been constantly fought over, most recently after the Allied landings in 1944, and evidence of this is to be seen all over the region.
Apart from history, Normandy has much to offer the visitor: beautiful and varied scenery, ranging from the steep and rugged Channel coast to the charms of the "Norman Switzerland", as well as the architectural treasures of its old capital of Rouen (see entry), the extraordinary Mont St-Michel (see entry), castles and châteaux, churches and abbeys, and – not least – some of France's finest seaside resorts like Deauville, Trouville and Dieppe.
The old province of Normandy, with an area of 29,900 sq. km/11,550 sq. miles and a population of around 3 million, consists of the départements of Seine-Maritime (chief town Rouen) and Eure (Evreux) in Upper Normandy (Haute Normandie) and Calvados (Caen), Orne (Alençon) and Manche (St-Lô) in Lower Normandy (Basse Normandie).

Haute Normandie

Pays de Caux

Upper Normandy, which is traversed by the lower Seine, is the western part of an area of chalk tableland in the Paris basin rising to 250 m/820 ft and slashed by valleys, usually running parallel to one another. The most characteristic part of the area is the Pays de Caux (the "land of chalk"), which falls down to the Channel in steep cliffs *(falaises)* some 100 m/330 ft high.

Pays d'Auge

A transition to Lower Normandy is provided by the Pays d'Auge, the eastern part of the département of Calvados. Although it is part of the chalk tableland, this has been overlaid by layers of impermeable clay; it is much broken up by valleys and, like the Bocage (see below), is crisscrossed by hedges.

Basse Normandie

Bocage

Norman Switzerland

Lower Normandy consists of the Cotentin peninsula, part of a massif of ancient rocks, with a much indented coastline, particularly in the north-west, but elsewhere flat and sandy, and the Bocage Normand (also built up of ancient rocks), an area of woodland and meadowland with numerous springs and a great patchwork of hedges. In the south-east of this area, in the Orne valley, is the wildly romantic country known as the "Norman Switzerland" (Suisse Normande). In the wooded south Normandy rises to its highest point (417 m/1368 ft).

Calvados

Between the ancient massif and the chalk tableland, in Calvados, is an area of Jurassic rocks with much meadowland. In southern Normandy this

Vallée de la Seine

Perche

merges into the Perche uplands, consisting mostly of Cretaceous limestones.

Economy

Industry is concentrated mainly around Rouen and Le Havre (see entry). Otherwise Normandy is a region of intensive arable and stock farming, mainly cattle (hence Camembert cheese) and horses.

Tourism

Tourism also makes an important contribution to the economy. In addition to its scenery the attractions of Normandy include its seaside resorts and its beautiful beaches on the Côte d'Albâtre, the Côte Fleurie and the Côte de Nacre.

History

After Caesar's conquests Normandy became a Roman province. Raids by Germanic tribes in the 2nd and 5th centuries were followed in the 6th c. by incorporation in the Merovingian kingdom of Neustria. In 911 the Norsemen (Vikings) who had pushed into the lower Seine valley in the 9th c. founded a Norman duchy under their leader Hrolf or Rollo. This was soon expanded to take in the Côtentin peninsula and became a force to be reckoned with in the later history of France. After the Battle of Hastings in 1066 Duke William of Normandy (William the Conqueror) became king of England and Normandy became an English possession. In 1204 it was won back by the French king Philippe Auguste. During the Hundred Years' War, in 1417–1419, it was briefly held by England, and in 1431 Joan of Arc was tried by the English in Rouen. In 1450 it finally returned to France. During the Second World War Normandy was the scene of the Allied landings of 1944, and its numerous military cemeteries and memorials are a reminder of the many thousands who died in the fighting.

Calvados and cider

Cider has been made in Normandy since the 13th c., using pure apple juice from apples containing little acid. The juice matures, becomes cloudy and then clears, and finally ferments to produce a sparkling drink with the taste of apple wine which is a favourite thirst-quencher, drunk well cooled

(alcoholic content around 3–5%). Calvados is a spirit which frequently contains over 40% of alcohol, obtained by distillation from cider. For the best calvados the cider should be two or three years old. After being distilled either once or twice it is stored in oak casks, where it acquires its colour (ranging from light brown to ivory) and its bouquet.
Visitors can learn more about cider and calvados in one of the regional cider museums, for example at Valognes (Côtentin) or Barenton.

Sights in Normandy

Alençon

*Notre-Dame

Alençon (pop. 35,000), situated in southern Normandy at the entrance to the Normandie–Maine Regional Nature Park, has been noted since the 17th c. for its lace *(points d'Alençon)*, and it still has a lace-making school with exhibition and sale rooms. In the Grande Rue is the church of Notre-Dame (1444), in Flamboyant style, with an 18th c. tower and choir, an elegant porch and fine stained glass. The Musée des Beaux-Arts et de la Dentelle has interesting collections of pictures and of lace. Other features of interest are the Town Hall (1783) and the Maison d'Ozé (15th c.), now occupied by the tourist information office.

St-Cénérie-le-Gérei

14 km/9 miles west of Alençon, on the fringe of the Alpes Mancelles, is the village of St-Cénérie-le-Gérei, which has a Romanesque church (frescoes).

***Les Andelys**

*Château Gaillard

Les Andelys (pop. 10,000) lies in the Seine valley, here enclosed by high chalk cliffs, with the imposing ruins of Château Gaillard looming over the town. The castle was built by Richard Cœur-de-Lion in 1197 to bar the French king's access to Rouen. In spite of its strength, however, it was taken by the French in 1204. The outer walls have almost completely disappeared, but much of the keep with its surrounding walls has survived.

Notre-Dame

There are two churches in the town, the more notable of which is Notre-Dame, with a 13th c. nave, a façade of the 16th–17th c., a notable organ and fine stained glass. The Musée Nicolas Poussin displays pictures by Poussin (1594–1665), who was born in the neighbouring village of Villers. There is a fine view from the bridge over the Seine.

Anet

Anet (pop. 2400), in the valley of the Eure, is noted for the Renaissance château of Diane de Poitiers. Building began in 1548, and the greatest artists of the day contributed to its decoration, including Benvenuto Cellini and the tapestry-weavers of Fontainebleau, who together represent the style of Henry II's reign. The goddess Diana is a constantly recurring decorative theme, referring to the châtelaine, Henry's mistress Diane de Poitiers (of whom there is no actual portrait).

Argentan

Argentan (pop. 18,000), once an important lace-making town, was badly damaged in 1944. The church of St-Germain (15th–17th c.) was rebuilt after the war. There are remains of a 14th c. castle and the old town walls.

Arromanches-les-Bains

This little seaside resort (pop. 390) lies north-east of Bayeux. The Musée du Débarquement (Museum of the Landings) commemorates its role in the Second World War, when a huge artificial harbour, Mulberry B, was constructed to facilitate the British landings.

Avranches

Avranches (pop. 11,000) is prettily situated above the river Sée. At a council held here in 1172 Henry II of England, having done penance, received absolution for the murder of Thomas Becket. A tablet in the gardens of the Sous-Préfecture, in Place Daniel-Huet, marks the spot where Henry begged for forgiveness. The cathedral of Avranches was destroyed during the French Revolution. Avranches was in the thick of the fighting in 1944, and was the starting-point of General Patton's advance in July of that year. From the Jardin des Plantes (Botanical Garden) there are magnificent views of the estuary of the Sée and the Baie du Mont St-Michel. The town

Steep cliffs near Étretat ▶

hall possesses important manuscripts of the 8th–15th centuries concerning the Mont St-Michel (see entry).

***Bagnoles de l'Orne**

Bagnoles de l'Orne (pop. 780) ranks with Tessé-la-Madeleine as the best known spa in western France. Beautifully situated on a little lake in a gorge, it is a good base from which to visit some of the châteaux in the surrounding area and to explore the "Suisse Normande" ("Norman Switzerland"): see below.

Bayeux

*Cathedral

Crossing tower

Bayeux (pop. 15,300) lies in a fertile plain near the coast. In the centre of the old town, surrounded by many old houses (15th–16th c.), is the Cathedral of Notre-Dame, one of the finest examples of Norman Gothic (11th and 13th c.). The two west towers date from the 11th c., the 80 m/260 ft high tower over the crossing, in Flamboyant style, from the 15th. Notable features of the interior are the fine Baroque choir screen, the church treasury and an 11th c. crypt.

**Bayeux Tapestry

The great attraction which draws visitors to Bayeux, however, is the famous Bayeux Tapestry (known in French as the Tapisserie de la Reine Mathilde); it is to be found at the Centre Guillaume le Conquérant. This is actually not a tapestry at all, but a work of embroidery: a band of linen 70 m/230 ft long, which recounts the story of the conquest of England by Mathilde's husband William the Conqueror in 58 scenes with 623 figures, 759 animals and 37 buildings and ships, accompanied by a kind of running commentary in Latin, but with a headphone commentary in English. North of the cathedral is the former Bishop's Palace (12th–16th c.), which now houses the Musée Baron Gérard and the Palais de Justice (Law Courts). The chapel has a fine ceiling painting. The Hôtel de Ville (Town Hall) is 18th c.

Le Bec-Hellouin

North of Brionne, on the river Risle, is Le Bec-Hellouin, with an abbey of the 15th–18th centuries. There is a Musée Automobile, with 50 cars ranging in date from 1920 to the present day.

Cabourg

Cabourg (pop. 3000) is one of the most popular of Normandy's seaside resorts, which originally became fashionable during the Second Empire. Marcel Proust (1871–1922) often stayed here.

Caen

See entry

Cherbourg

Cherbourg (pop. 50,100), France's third largest naval base and an important port for the transatlantic traffic, lies on the north coast of the Cotentin peninsula. In 1853 a 3.6 km/2¼ mile long breakwater with two piers was built to protect the harbour, and later two other piers were built, separating the larger from the smaller harbour. In 1944 Cherbourg became the Allies' main landing point for heavy military equipment. The advantages of the harbour had been recognised three centuries earlier by Vauban.

*View

There is a fine view of the town and the harbour from the Montagne du Roule (112 m/367 ft), 3 km/2 miles south-east. On the hill are the Fort du Roule and the Musée de la Guerre et de la Libération. Notable features in the town itself are the Musée Thomas Henry (Italian and Dutch paintings), the church of La Trinité (1423–1504; fine interior) and the beautiful Parc Emmanuel Liais with its exotic plants and Natural History Museum. Foreigners are not admitted to the Arsenal and the naval harbour. There are regular car ferry services from Cherbourg to England and Ireland.

*Excursions

Cherbourg is a good base for excursions to the castles and châteaux of the northern Cotentin, for example Tocqueville, St-Pierre-Eglise and Belvédère.

***Cotentin**

*Cap de Carteret

The Cotentin peninsula in western Normandy reaches far out into the Channel, with the Cap de la Hague, the Baie d'Ecalgrain, the Nez de Jobourg and the port of Cherbourg. The lonely interior with its patchwork of hedges is less visited than the coasts. though it offers scenery of great beauty. On the west coast are the Cap de Carteret and the popular seaside resort of Carteret, from which there is a ferry service to Jersey and Guernsey in the Channel Islands.

Notre-Dame, Coutances

Impressive ruins in Jumièges

At the north-east corner of the peninsula is the Pointe de Barfleur, with a lighthouse from which there are panoramic views.

Coutances

* Cathedral

The old episcopal city of Coutances (pop. 13,400), which has given its name to the Cotentin peninsula, lies on a long hill above the surrounding plain. The central feature of the town is the Cathedral of Notre-Dame, built in 1251–1274 on the site of an earlier Romanesque church which was destroyed by fire. With its two towers flanking the west front it is one of the most magnificent churches in Normandy. Over the crossing is an octagonal tower from the top of which there are extensive views, extending to Jersey and St-Malo. Within the church the tower forms an impressive dome over the crossing. In the beautiful public park is the Musée Municipal (works by local artists). The massive Gothic church of St-Pierre (begun 1494) has a bell-tower of 1550 and a tower over the crossing, which, as in the cathedral, forms a dome in the interior.

***Deauville**

Deauville, like Trouville, is one of the largest and most popular resorts in Normandy, with a population of 4700 which becomes many times greater during the season. Its seafront promenade, boating marina, regattas, races and casinos attract visitors from many countries. From here the 30 km/20 mile long Côte Fleurie ("Coast of Flowers") extends south-west to Cabourg and the Corniche Normande runs north-east to Honfleur.

Dieppe

Dieppe (pop. 36,540), one of France's best known passenger harbours and a popular seaside resort, lies on the Channel coast some 60 km/37 miles north of Rouen. There was an abortive landing here by Allied forces in 1942. In the centre of the town is the little Place du Puits-Salé. To the west of this square is the large church of St-Rémy (16th–17th c.), with a fine interior. North-east of this is the magnificent Gothic church of St-Jacques (12th–16th c.), with beautiful doorways and a richly decorated interior. To the east of the church are the extensive port installations, with the passenger harbour to the north of the attractive fishing harbour. East of the

Harbours

passenger harbour is the district of Le Pollet, with the chapel of Notre-Dame-de-Bon-Secours perched high above the harbour and the sea (views). The 2 km/1½ mile long bathing beach extends westward to beyond the castle (1433), on a chalk crag above the town; it contains a museum (charts, ivories, pictures). From the Boulevard de la Mer, north-west of the castle, there are fine views.

*Museum

Domfront

Domfront (pop. 4500) is picturesquely situated on a narrow ridge of rock. An 11th c. watch-tower (views), in a beautiful public park, is all that remains of the town's medieval castle. The old part of the town, with 16th c. houses, is well preserved. Outside the town is the Romanesque church of Notre-Dame-sur-l'Eau (late 11th c., but much altered in later centuries), with 12th c. frescoes, tombstones and statues.

Étretat
**Cliffs

The popular little seaside resort of Étretat (pop. 1600) lies at the foot of 90 m/295 ft high chalk cliffs (illustration, page 331), from the top of which there are wide views. To the north of the town is the Falaise d'Amont, with a monument to Nungesser and Coli, who died in an attempt to fly the Atlantic in 1927. To the west is the Falaise d'Aval, with impressive natural rock bridges and an isolated stack 70 m/230 ft high, the Aiguille d'Étretat. Above the town to the east is the church of Notre-Dame (11th–13th c.).

Evreux

Evreux (pop. 48,600), chief town of the département of Eure, is an important commercial and market centre.

*Cathedral

The Cathedral of Notre-Dame (11th–18th c.) has fine 16th c. stained glass and delicately wrought Renaissance grilles in the chapels round the choir. The Bishop's Palace (1481) now houses the Municipal Museum. The Tour de l'Horloge (Clock-Tower) dates from 1490. The former abbey church of St-Taurin (11th–15th c.) contains the 13th c. reliquary of St Taurin (Taurinus), a masterpiece of French goldsmith's work.

*Reliquary

Evron

Evron (pop. 6700) is noted for its chapel of Notre-Dame-de-l'Epine (12th c.), with 13th c. wall paintings and Aubusson tapestries.
The nave and tower of the church of Notre-Dame date from the 11th c., the rest of the structure from the 18th.

Falaise

Falaise (pop. 8800), birthplace of William the Conqueror, is dominated by the magnificent ruins of the castle in which he was born in 1027. The main surviving remains are the keep and a massive 13th c. round tower 35 m/115 ft high. In the town are the churches of Ste-Trinité (13th–16th c.) and St-Gervais (11th–16th c.).

Fécamp

Fécamp (pop. 21,700) is an old-established seaside resort with a fishing and a commercial harbour. The writer Guy de Maupassant lived in Fécamp for some time, and some of his stories are set in the town. The main feature of interest in the town, apart from the harbours, is the former abbey church of Ste-Trinité, which was built in the 12th–13th c. and later partly rebuilt. The interior is remarkably spacious; notable features are the fine choir screen (1868), the choir-stalls (1748), a handsome Renaissance altar behind the high altar and a sculpture of the "Death of the Virgin" (1519) in the south transept. The first Benedictine liqueur, distilled from herbs growing on the rocky coast, was made in Fécamp in 1510. The Benedictine Distillery can be visited; the Musée de la Bénédictine contains a variety of works of art.
On a 114 m/374 ft high chalk cliff to the north of the town is the pilgrimage chapel of Notre-Dame-du-Salut (13th–14th c.).

*Ste-Trinité

Benedictine Distillery

Valmont

11 km/7 miles east of Fécamp is the village of Valmont, with a medieval castle and the ruins of an abbey founded in the 12th c.

***Fontaine-Henry**

This little place in the Mue valley (pop. 350) is noted for its château. Built in the 15th and 16th c. on the foundations of an 11th c. castle, this is a notable example of secular Renaissance architecture. It contains fine furniture and a collection of pictures, including works by Mignard, Rigaud and Robert. Also of interest is the 13th c. chapel (altered in 16th c.).

Granville

Granville (pop. 15,000), beautifully situated on a peninsula with a sheltered harbour, became a fashionable seaside resort in the 19th c. In the old walled town, on higher ground, are the beautiful Gothic church of Notre-Dame (15th–16th c.) and the Museum of Old Granville, housed in the Grande Porte. On the Pointe du Roc is a lighthouse from which there are fine views, and near this is an aquarium.

Iles Chausey

From Granville there are boat trips to the offshore Iles Chausey and to Jersey and Guernsey.

* **Hambye**

In the valley of the Sienne are the ruins of Hambye Abbey, founded in 1145. The surviving remains include parts of the church (12th–13th c.) and some of the conventual buildings.

Le Havre

See entry

Honfleur
* Vieux Bassin

The old seafaring town of Honfleur (pop. 8500), on the Seine estuary opposite Le Havre (to which it is to be connected by a bridge in 1994), is one of the most charming little towns in Normandy, with its picturesque Vieux Bassin (Old Harbour) and its many old houses. This was the home port of the seamen who made their celebrated voyages to Canada in the 16th c., making that country almost a Norman colony. On the north side of the harbour is the Lieutenance (16th c.), the old governor's house, built on the remains of the town walls, now housing the port office. The church of St-Etienne (14th–15th c.) and a neighbouring building now house the Musée de la Marine (the maritime history of Honfleur). The Late Gothic church of Ste-Catherine, with a free-standing belfry, is of wood, and was built by local shipwrights after the Hundred Years' War. It is now an annexe of the Musée Eugène Boudin; the main museum is in Place Erik Satie, with works by Boudin (who was Claude Monet's teacher) and other artists, mainly Impressionists.

Ste-Catherine

* Côte de Grâce

1 km/¾ mile north-west of the town centre, south of the road to Trouville, is the hill of Côte de Grâce (wide views), with the pilgrimage chapel of Notre-Dame-de-Grâce (1606). To the south-east is the Mont Joli, from which there is an even better view of the town.

Jumièges
** Abbey

In this little town (pop. 1500) are the imposing ruins of an abbey founded in 654 and destroyed in 1790, with the remains of two churches and the conventual buildings and a small museum. The church of St-Pierre dates in part from the Carolingian period and has clear traces of early Norman work (10th c.).

Lessay

Lessay (pop. 1300), between Carteret and Cherbourg, grew up round an abbey founded in the 11th c. The Romanesque church, destroyed in 1944, was lovingly rebuilt after the war.

* **Lisieux**

Lisieux (pop. 25,000), chief town of the Pays d'Auge and once the see of a bishop, lies some 30 km/20 miles south of the Seine estuary at the junction of the rivers Orbiquet and Touques. Most of the town was destroyed in 1944. The Cathedral of St-Pierre was begun about 1170 and completed in the 13th c., apart from the south tower, which dates from 1579. The most notable feature of the interior is the 15th c. Lady Chapel in the apse. The former Bishop's Palace now houses the local court and a collection of pictures.

Ste Thérèse

Lisieux is also the town of Ste Thérèse. Born in Alençon in 1873, Thérèse Martin grew up in Lisieux and in 1888 became a nun in the Carmelite convent in the south of the town. She died in 1897 and was canonised in 1925. There are great pilgrimages to the Basilica of Ste-Thérèse (1954) and the chapel in the convent where her remains lie, and there are many places associated with the saint in the town.

Mont St-Michel

See entry

Fishing harbour, Honfleur

Omaha Beach

Omaha Beach, north-west of Bayeux, was one of the landing points of the Allied forces on June 6th 1944. There are a memorial to the landings and an American military cemetery.

Rouen

See entry

** **Seine valley**

The Seine valley is the great scenic attraction of inland Normandy. The river flows through Normandy from Vernon by way of Rouen to Le Havre, with numerous windings which in spite of its gentle gradient (with a fall of only 16 m/50 ft from Vernon to its mouth, a distance of over 100 km/60 miles as the crow flies) almost double its length. Particularly attractive is the "Route des Abbayes" from Rouen to Le Havre, on the right bank of the river.

* **Norman Switzerland**

The name of Suisse Normande ("Norman Switzerland") is given to the beautiful stretch of country in the Orne valley extending between Thury-Harcourt (south of Caen) in the north, Flers-de-l'Orne in the south and Falaise in the east. The windings of the river, the rocky bluffs along its banks and the isolated hills standing farther back combine with the intricate pattern of hedges to give the landscape a particular charm. The most striking features are the Rocher d'Oëtre, in the hilliest part of the area, above the gorges of the Rouvre (fine views), the Vère and Noireau valleys and the 27 km/17 mile long stretch of the Orne between Thury-Harcourt and Pont-d'Ouilly.

* Rocher d'Oëtre

Tancarville
* Bridge

Tancarville (pop. 1140), at the mouth of the Seine, has a ruined 11th c. castle and a road suspension bridge which was opened for traffic in 1959, and which spans the Seine at a height of 51 m/167 ft above the water.

Le Tréport

This little port (pop. 6550), which is also a popular holiday resort, lies on the Channel coast at the mouth of the river Bresle, at the foot of the highest cliffs in France. Above the harbour is the church of St-Jacques, with a fine

Renaissance doorway. There is a cableway up to the Calvaire des Terrasses, from which there are fine views.

Trouville

Immediately north-east of Deauville, beyond the river Touques (bridge) is the popular resort of Trouville (pop. 6000), with a beautiful beach, a boating harbour and a handsome Casino. One excursion from Trouville which should not be omitted is a drive along the Corniche Normande, which skirts the coast, high above the sea, to Honfleur, with extensive views.

*Corniche Normande

Utah Beach

Utah Beach, north of Carentan, was another of the landing points used by Allied forces in 1944. The beach is a kind of open-air museum, with guns and landing craft left over from the landings. There is also a small museum.

Varengeville-sur-Mer

This attractively situated seaside resort lies on the cliff-fringed coast just to the west of Dieppe. Its main attractions, apart from the beach, are the Parc des Moustiers with its beautiful flowers and the Manoir d'Ango, a manor-house of 1533–1545. The church (11th, 13th and 15th c.) has fine stained glass; the painter Georges Braque (1882–1963) is buried in the churchyard. From the church there are fine views.
Outside the town is the Chapelle St-Dominique, which has stained glass by Braque and a picture by the painter Maurice Denis (1870–1943).

*View

Also outside the town is a modern lighthouse from which there is a magnificent view of the surrounding country and the rocky coast.

Villequier

Villequier (pop. 750) is prettily situated on the banks of the Seine under an old castle. Here in 1843 Victor Hugo's daughter and son-in-law were drowned – an event which inspired some of Hugo's finest poems. There is a small museum devoted to the poet and his family.

Vernon

The old town of Vernon (pop. 23,000) is beautifully situated on the left bank of the Seine, between the Forêt de Vernon and the Forêt de Bizy. The church of Notre-Dame dates from the 12th c., its west front, with a beautiful rose window, from the 15th. The interior is also very fine. Round the church are handsome old houses. Also of interest are the Musée A.-G. Poulain and the 12th c. Tour des Archives, a relic of a medieval castle.

Giverny

See Ile de France

Nature Parks
Normandie–Maine

The Normandie–Maine Nature Park in Lower Normandy, extending into the Loire valley, has an area of 234,000 hectares/578,000 acres. Of this area 45,000 hectares/111,000 acres are under forest, but there are also many rivers and lakes which offer plenty of opportunities for canoeing, kayaking and sailing.

Brotonne

Brotonne Nature Park, with an area of 50,000 hectares/124,000 acres, lies in the départements of Seine-Maritime and Eure, centred on the Brotonne Forest. There are many footpaths and trails in both parks.

Tourist routes
Route du Cidre

The tourist authorities have devised a number of specially signposted routes for visitors. The "Route du Cidre" runs through the apple-growing country round Cambremer, in the Pays d'Auge. Visitors can see round the cellars of the local cider-producers and sample and buy their cider and calvados. The "Route du Fromage" runs through such famous cheese-producing villages as Livarot, Pont-l'Evêque and Camembert. The "Route des Ducs de Normandie" guides visitors round a series of medieval and later churches and abbeys, castles, châteaux and manor-houses. The "Route of Ivory and Spices" follows the ancient route (centred on Dieppe) over which ivory and spices were conveyed, with visits to associated sites and monuments.

Route du Fromage
Route des Ducs de Normandie
Route de l'Ivorie et des Espices

Orange M10

Region: Provence–Alpes–Côte-d'Azur
Département: Vaucluse
Altitude: 46 m/150 ft
Population: 28,000

Situation and characteristics

Orange, situated in a fertile fruit- and vegetable-growing area in the lower Rhône valley, is famed for its well preserved Roman monuments.

History

The first encounter between Roman forces and two Germanic tribes, the Cimbri and the Teutons, took place at Orange (the ancient Arausio Secundanorum) in 105 B.C., when 100,000 Romans were killed. Three years later the defeat was avenged by Marius at Aix. During the "Roman peace" the population of Orange was four times as large as it is today. In the 16th c., surprisingly, the town – then capital of the little principality of Orange – passed to the Dutch house of Nassau. (The Queen of the Netherlands still bears the title of Princess of Orange-Nassau). In 1713, under the treaty of Utrecht, Orange was assigned to France.

Sights

*Arc de Triomphe

The road from Lyons passes the Triumphal Arch erected after Caesar's victory in 49 B.C., finest of its kind in France. It has three arched passages with coffered vaulting. Originally topped by a quadriga (four-horse chariot)

Roman theatre, Orange

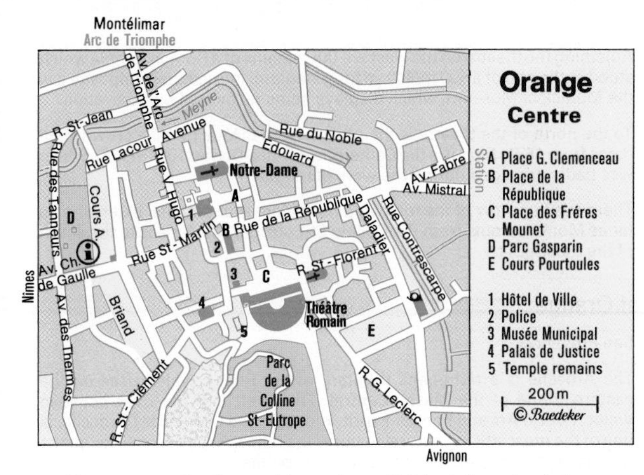

and four statues. On the entablature is a relief depicting a battle between Romans and Gauls, with Gallic ship trophies below it to left and right.

**Théâtre Romain

In the south of the town is the Roman Theatre, one of the finest and best preserved in the whole Roman world. It was built at the beginning of the Imperial period (1st c. A.D.), but was probably renovated in the 2nd c. The stage wall still preserves remains of its elaborate decoration. The theatre can accommodate 7000 spectators and has excellent acoustics. It is the only Roman theatre to have preserved a statue of the Emperor – in this case a figure of Augustus 3.55 m/11½ ft high.

Pont d'Arc . . .

and a bend in the Ardèche

Temple

Adjoining the theatre on the west are the remains of a Roman temple which stood at the end of a 400 m/440 yd long stadium. Immediately opposite it is the Municipal Museum, which displays items recovered by excavation.

Other sights

To the north of the theatre is the old town. The Hôtel de Ville (Town Hall) dates from 1671. Near it is the Cathedral of Notre-Dame (1083–1126), which was badly damaged during the wars of religion.

Colline St-Eutrope
*View

There is a fine view of the town and its ancient monuments, extending as far as Mont Ventoux, from the Colline St-Eutrope, which rises to the south of the theatre.

Surroundings of Orange

Châteauneuf-du-Pape

See Provence

**Gorges de l'Ardèche

The Ardèche is a right-bank tributary of the Rhône which rises on the eastern fringe of the Massif Central. The stretch of the river between Vallon-Pont-d'Arc and Pont St-Esprit, known as the Gorges de l'Ardèche, is one of the most striking natural features in France. A road runs through the gorges, and boats can be hired at various points.

**Aven d'Orgnac

Near the village of Orgnac is the Aven d'Orgnac, one of the most magnificent stalactitic caves in France, which was opened to the public in 1935.

Orléans

I7

Region: Centre. Département: Loiret
Altitude: 110 m/360 ft. Population: 110,000

Situation and characteristics

Orléans, the largest town in the middle Loire valley after Tours, chief town of the département of Loiret and the see of a bishop, with a university founded in 1309, lies in a fertile plain at the most northerly point in the course of the Loire. Its name is inseparably bound up with that of Joan of Arc, the Maid of Orléans. Orléans is a lively trading town (agricultural products and industry) and a good base for excursions to the châteaux in the Loire (see Loire Valley).

History

From the 3rd c. A.D. the Roman town of Aurelianum (from which the name of Orléans is derived) was a place of some consequence, situated at the junction of important roads. In 451 it was besieged by Attila, but was liberated by the valiant Bishop Aignan (later canonised). In 498 it was captured by the Frankish king Clovis. During the Hundred Years' War, in 1428–1429, it was the last French stronghold, then under siege by the English, but was relieved on May 8th 1429 by a French army led by Joan of Arc. This marked a turning-point in French fortunes. A festival in her memory is held annually on May 7th and 8th.
The town was badly damaged during the Wars of Religion and during the Second World War, but has since been rebuilt.

Sights

Place du Martroi

The central feature of the old town is the spacious Place du Martroi. In the 6th century there was a cemetery here, hence the name Martroi (originally Martyretum). The equestrian statue of Joan of Arc (Jeanne d'Arc), with reliefs of scenes from her life on the plinth, is by Foyatier (1855). The buildings on the west and south sides of the square were rebuilt after 1945. To the south lies Rue Royale, dating from 1752–1760, with a number of restored houses in the 19th c. style. 17th c. houses line Rue d'Escures to the north-east. At the end of this street, to the north-west of the cathedral,

Hôtel de Ville

stands the Hôtel de Ville (Town Hall), an attractive brick and stone building, formerly the Hôtel Groslot, where King Francis II died in 1530; the interior is modern, however. In the garden can be seen remains of the 15th c. Chapelle St-Jacques.

**Cathedral

To the east of the Place du Martroi is the massive Cathedral of Ste-Croix, on the site of an earlier 10th c. church, part of the foundations of which have been preserved. The building of the cathedral began in 1278 but was several times interrupted and continued into the 16th c. It was badly damaged during the 16th c. wars of religion but was rebuilt in the 17th and 18th centuries on the model of earlier Gothic churches. The west front, flanked by twin towers, has five doorways and much Baroque decoration. The towers themselves are over 81 m/266 ft high and are the work of the architect Trouard, although the original plans were drawn up by J. Gabriel. The central spire is 114 m/374 ft high and was built in 1858.

Interior

The sheer size of the interior (136 m/446 ft long) leaves a lasting impression. The nine chapels behind the high altar date from the late 13th c., and the outer walls of the two side aisles and those of the choir are 14th c. Other notable features are the fine 17th c. organ and the beautiful early 8th c. carved woodwork in the choir. In the crypt traces of three earlier churches can be seen, dating partly from the 4th c. and partly from the 10th/11th c.

*Treasury

Also of interest is the church treasure, which includes Byzantine fabrics and enamelwork, together with Limoges work.

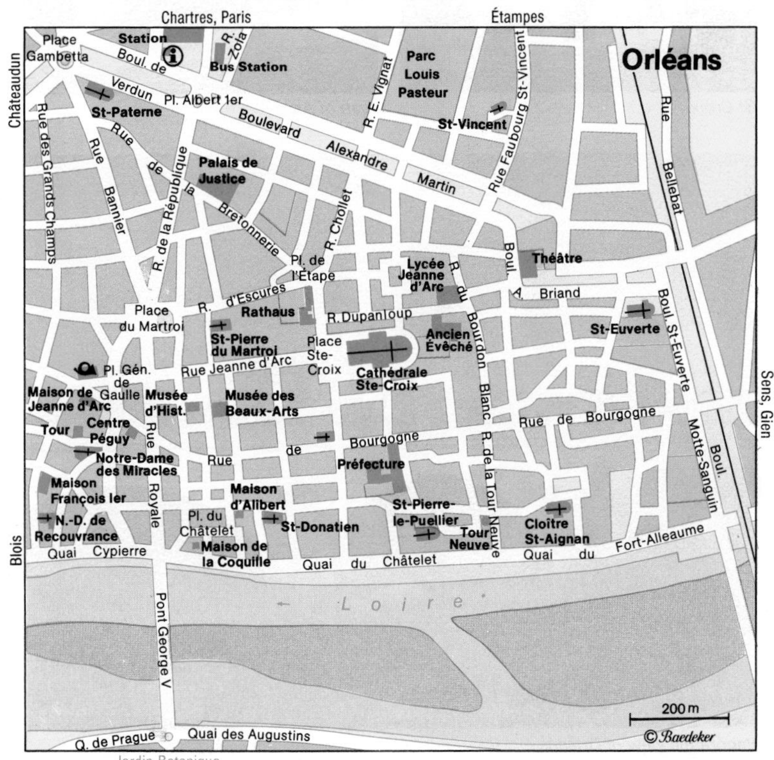

St-Croix

Joan of Arc

Panoramic view of Orléans

Musée des Beaux-Arts

This interesting art museum has an extensive collection of works from the 15th to the 19th c. by Gauguin, Sérusier, Rouault, Soutine, Kupka, Mathieu and Dufy, among others. Temporary exhibitions are also held.

Maison de Jeanne d'Arc

A small museum devoted to Joan of Arc is to be found in a faithfully restored 15th c. house.

*Musée Historique et Archéologique

This elegant Renaissance mansion, once the Hôtel Cabu, now houses the Musée Historique et Archéologique de l'Orléanais (Gallo-Roman and medieval antiquities).

Old town

To the south of the two museums is the charming old town of Orléans, with many Renaissance houses.

St-Paul

The 15th c. church of St-Paul, south of the Place du Martroi, was badly damaged during the Second World War. In the chapel of Notre-Dame-des-Miracles (rebuilt in the 17th c.) is a 16th c. Black Virgin.

Notre-Dame-de-Recouvrance

This 16th c. church, to the south of St-Paul, has Renaissance sculpture and fine stained glass in the 11th c. choir.

St-Aignan

The church of St-Aignan, dedicated to the warlike 5th c. bishop, was built in the 15th and 16th centuries and partly destroyed during the wars of religion. All that survives is the transept and the beautiful Late Gothic choir, under which is a crypt of 1029.

Surroundings of Orléans

La Source

In Orléans-La-Source (8 km/5 miles south-east, on the opposite bank of the Loire), are the attractive Botanical Gardens, with a fine assortment of native plants, together with waterfalls, animals and other attractions.

Forêt d'Orléans

To the north-east of Orléans lies a large forest of oak and pine.

Tigy

In Tigy (29 km/18 miles south-east) the Musée de l'Artisanat Rural Ancien displays examples of traditional handicrafts.

Bellegarde-du-Loiret

48 km/30 miles east of Orléans, in fertile agricultural country, is the little town of Bellegarde (pop. 1500), which has a castle with a 14th c. keep and a Romanesque church containing 17th c. pictures.

Paris

K6

Region: Ile de France
Départements: Ville-de-Paris, Yvelines, Essonne, Hauts-de-Seine, Seine-St-Denis, Val-de-Marne, Val-d'Oise
Altitude: 27–129 m/90–425 ft
Population: 2.1 million (city); 8.4 million (conurbation); 9.9 million (Région Parisienne)

N.B.

The description of Paris in this guide is deliberately abbreviated, since there is a detailed account in the AA/Baedeker guide **"Paris"**.

**Paris, Capital of France

Paris, France's national capital and an international metropolis, the seat of government, all the major government departments and many international organisations, the see of a cardinal archbishop and an ancient university town, lies in a wide basin on both banks of the Seine, which here receives its principal tributary, the Marne. Although Paris's free port (Port Autonome) has lost traffic to the roads and the railways it is still the largest French inland port, with facilities for handling individual consignments, container loads and oil.

The townscape of Paris, extending on both banks of the Seine with the hills of Montmartre (129 m/423 ft) and the Buttes Chaumont (101 m/331 ft) in the north and the Montagne de Ste-Geneviève (60 m/200 ft) in the south, has a charm all its own. The great ring of boulevards with their constant surge of traffic and their bright lights when darkness falls, contrasting with the peaceful parks and quiet side streets of the old residential quarters, the long lines of streets and the spacious squares, the legendary Champs-Elysées, the magnificent public buildings, palaces and churches, many of them floodlit at night, the profusion of historic buildings and the futuristic architecture of the present day, the fantastic views from the higher points of the city, the busy movement of shipping on the Seine, the little cafés and bistros with their varying personalities, the colour and bustle of the weekly markets, the sheer elegance or stylish nonsenses of the famous fashion houses, the unsurpassable gastronomy of France, the endless range of cultural offerings, from the great museums of international standing to the extreme manifestations of pop culture, the incomparable charm of Parisian *savoir vivre:* all these varied elements contribute to the irresistible attraction of Paris.
Paris, France's capital and largest city, is an economic and cultural metropolis of international importance and worldwide fame. In spite of the transfer of administrative authority from the central government to the regions in recent years Paris still remains the central reference point for the whole country. Although its population has fallen since the 1950s it is still one of the largest concentrations of people in the world.
The city is divided into twenty arrondissements (wards or districts), the numbering of which starts from the Louvre and continues in a double spiral, going clockwise. For the initiated the terms "Rive droite" and "Rive gauche" (right bank and left bank) not only have historical significance (the right bank was the middle-class district, the left bank the home of the nobility and aristocracy) but summon up associations with particular kinds of social status and quality of life.
The traditional names of the various *quartiers* ("neighbourhoods") of Paris, which often have very distinctive identities of their own, frequently do not correspond to the official designations but are derived from old place-names, important buildings or their particular character. The former *faubourgs* have long since been incorporated in the city, while the *banlieue* outside the city boundaries is the commuter belt of the modern city.

Population

The population of the historic centre of Paris is around 500,000 and of the city area (the Ville de Paris) more than 2,085,000, including many foreigners. At the beginning of the 12th c. the population of Paris was just under 100,000; by 1850, after the incorporation of the faubourgs, it had reached about 1.5 million within the then existing fortifications. With an area of 105 sq. km/41 sq. miles, of which 714 hectares/1764 acres are accounted for by the river, Paris is one of the most densely populated of the world's capitals. If the new départements (formed in 1965 in suburban areas which had coalesced with the city) of Hauts-de-Seine, Seine-St-Denis and Val-de-Marne are included, together with parts of the départements of Val-d'Oise, Yvelines, Essonne and Seine-et-Marne, the "Agglomération Parisienne" has a population approaching 10 million.

Arrondissements and quartiers

The département of Ville-de-Paris, the real city of Paris, is divided into twenty wards or administrative districts officially known as cantons but universally referred to as *arrondissements.*
Arrondissements I to VIII are centrally situated on both banks of the Seine, while Nos. IX to XX extend in a wide arc round the city centre. The arrondissements in turn are divided into *quartiers,* which are numbered from 1 to 80.

I. Louvre
1–4: St-Germain-l'Auxerrois, Les Halles, Palais-Royal, Place Vendôme

Eiffel Tower ▶

100 ans

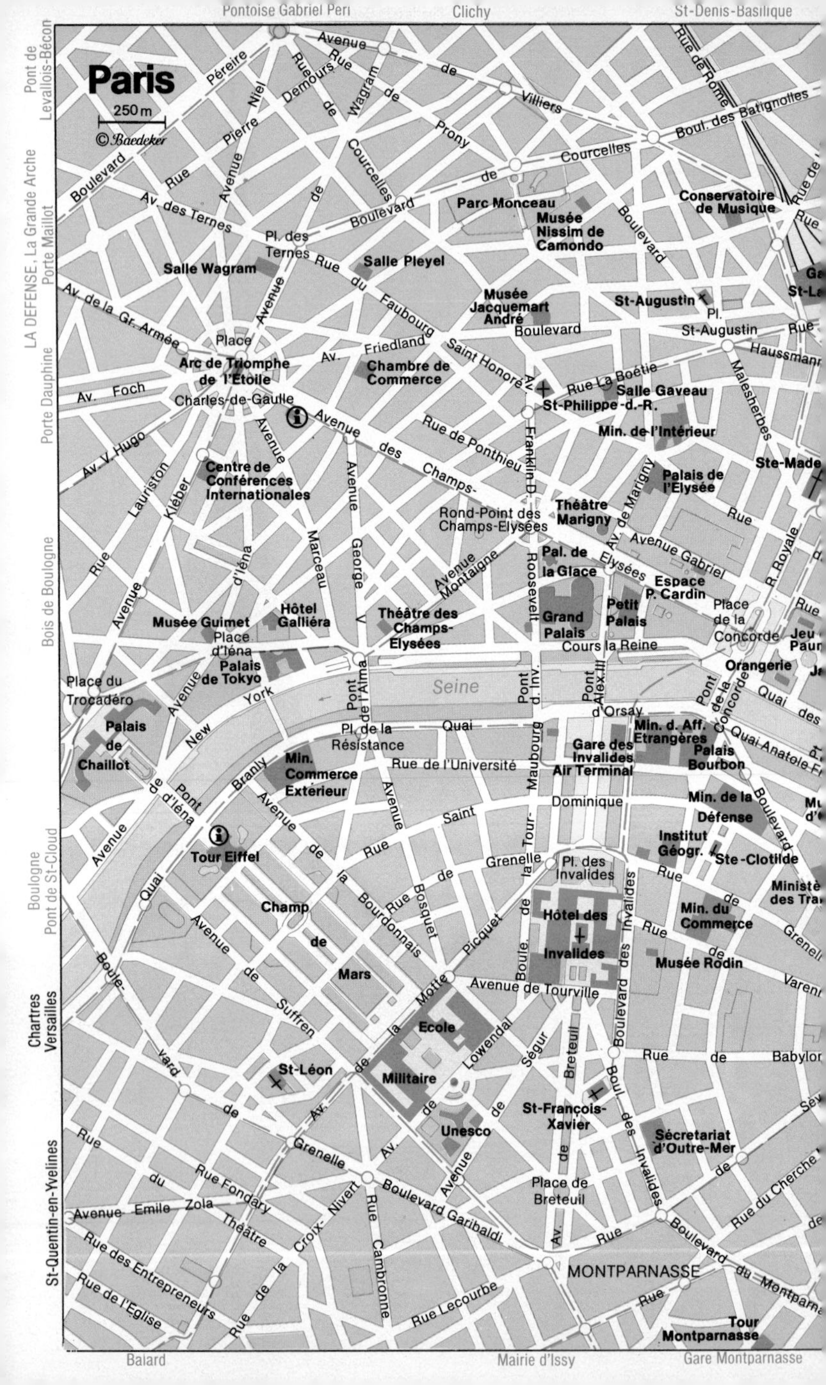

Paris
250 m
© Baedeker
Pontoise Gabriel Peri
Clichy
St-Denis-Basilique
Pont de Levallois-Bécon
LA DEFENSE, La Grande Arche
Porte Maillot
Porte Dauphine
Bois de Boulogne
Boulogne
Pont de St-Cloud
Chartres
Versailles
St-Quentin-en-Yvelines
Balard
Mairie d'Issy
Gare Montparnasse
Boulevard Péreire
Rue Pierre Niel
Avenue de Wagram
Rue Demours
Rue de Courcelles
Avenue de Villiers
Rue de Prony
Boulevard de Courcelles
Rue de Rome
Boul. des Batignolles
Av. des Ternes
Pl. des Ternes
Rue du Faubourg Saint Honoré
Parc Monceau
Musée Nissim de Camondo
Conservatoire de Musique
Salle Wagram
Salle Pleyel
Boulevard Malesherbes
Musée Jacquemart André
St-Augustin
Pl. St-Augustin
Boulevard Haussmann
Av. de la Gr. Armée
Place Charles-de-Gaulle
Arc de Triomphe de l'Etoile
Av. Friedland
Chambre de Commerce
Av. Foch
Avenue des Champs-Elysées
Rue La Boétie
Salle Gaveau
St-Philippe-d.-R.
Av. Franklin D. Roosevelt
Rue de Ponthieu
Min. de l'Intérieur
Av. V. Hugo
Avenue Kléber
Rue Lauriston
Avenue d'Iéna
Avenue Marceau
Avenue George V
Centre de Conférences Internationales
Ste-Made
Palais de l'Elysée
Rond-Point des Champs-Elysées
Théâtre Marigny
Av. de Marigny
Avenue Gabriel
R. Royale
Avenue Montaigne
Pal. de la Glace
Espace P. Cardin
Grand Palais
Petit Palais
Place de la Concorde
Jeu de Paum
Musée Guimet
Hôtel Galliéra
Théâtre des Champs-Elysées
Place d'Iéna
Cours la Reine
Palais de Tokyo
Orangerie
Place du Trocadéro
Avenue de New York
Seine
Pont de l'Alma
Pont d. Inv.
Pont Alex. III
Pont de la Concorde
Quai d'Orsay
Quai des
Quai Anatole F
Palais de Chaillot
Pl. de la Résistance
Min. d. Aff. Etrangères
Palais Bourbon
Quai Branly
Min. Commerce Extérieur
Rue de l'Université
Gare des Invalides
Air Terminal
Pont d'Iéna
Avenue Bosquet
Boulevard Maubourg de la Tour-
Rue Saint Dominique
Min. de la Défense
Institut Géogr.
Ste-Clotilde
Tour Eiffel
Rue de Grenelle
Pl. des Invalides
Quai
Avenue de la Bourdonnais
Rue Bosquet
Boulevard des Invalides
Ministè des Tra
Champ de Mars
Hôtel des Invalides
Min. du Commerce
Avenue Picquet
Boule. de la Tour-Maubourg
Musée Rodin
Rue de Varenne
Avenue de Suffren
Avenue de la Motte-Picquet
Avenue de Tourville
Ecole Militaire
Av. de Lowendal
Av. de Ségur
Av. de Breteuil
Rue de Babylone
Boulevard de Grenelle
St-Léon
St-François-Xavier
Unesco
Secrétariat d'Outre-Mer
Boul. des Invalides
Rue de Sèvres
Rue du Cherche-Midi
Rue du Théâtre
Rue Fondary
Avenue Emile Zola
Rue de la Croix-Nivert
Rue Cambronne
Boulevard Garibaldi
Avenue de Saxe
Place de Breteuil
Rue des Entrepreneurs
Rue de l'Eglise
Rue Lecourbe
MONTPARNASSE
Boulevard du Montparnasse
Tour Montparnasse

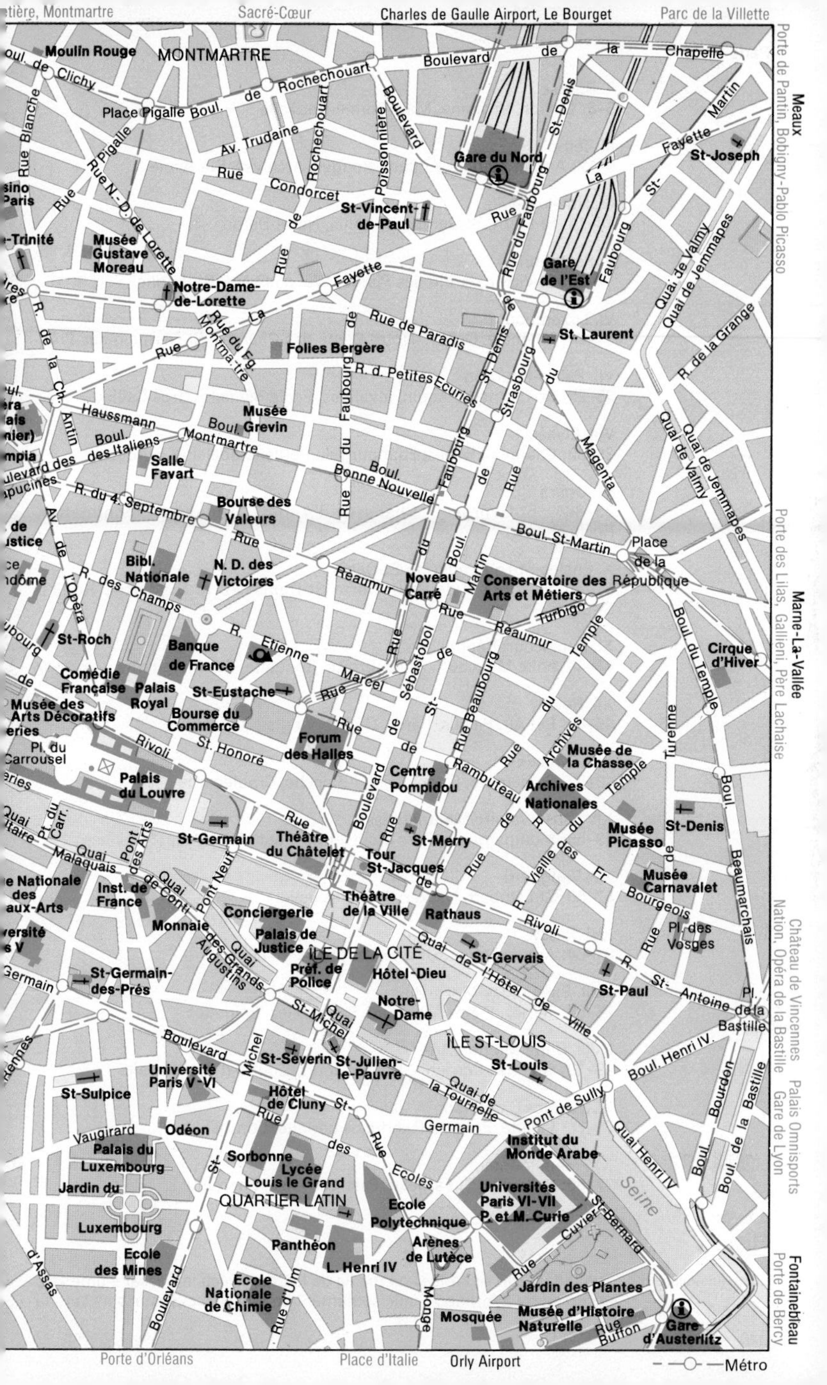
Sacré-Cœur
Charles de Gaulle Airport, Le Bourget
Parc de la Villette
Meaux
Porte de Pantin, Bobigny-Pablo Picasso
Marne-La-Vallée
Porte des Lilas, Gallieni, Père Lachaise
Château de Vincennes
Nation, Opéra de la Bastille
Palais Omnisports
Gare de Lyon
Fontainebleau
Porte de Bercy
Porte d'Orléans
Place d'Italie
Orly Airport
Métro
Moulin Rouge
MONTMARTRE
Place Pigalle
Gare du Nord
St-Joseph
St-Vincent-de-Paul
Musée Gustave Moreau
Gare de l'Est
Notre-Dame-de-Lorette
St. Laurent
Folies Bergère
Musée Grevin
Salle Favart
Bourse des Valeurs
Bibl. Nationale
N. D. des Victoires
Noveau Carré
Conservatoire des Arts et Métiers
Place de la République
St-Roch
Banque de France
Cirque d'Hiver
Comédie Française
Palais Royal
St-Eustache
Musée des Arts Décoratifs
Bourse du Commerce
Forum des Halles
Musée de la Chasse
Pl. du Carrousel
Palais du Louvre
Centre Pompidou
Archives Nationales
St-Germain
Théâtre du Châtelet
St-Merry
Musée Picasso
St-Denis
Tour St-Jacques
Musée Carnavalet
Inst. de France
Théâtre de la Ville
Conciergerie
Rathaus
Monnaie
Palais de Justice
ÎLE DE LA CITÉ
Pl. des Vosges
St-Gervais
St-Germain-des-Prés
Préf. de Police
Hôtel-Dieu
St-Paul
Notre-Dame
Pl. de la Bastille
ÎLE ST-LOUIS
St-Severin
St-Julien-le-Pauvre
Université Paris V-VI
St-Louis
St-Sulpice
Hôtel de Cluny
Odéon
Institut du Monde Arabe
Palais du Luxembourg
Sorbonne
Lycée Louis le Grand
Jardin du Luxembourg
QUARTIER LATIN
Universités Paris VI-VII P. et M. Curie
Ecole Polytechnique
Seine
Panthéon
Arènes de Lutèce
Ecole des Mines
L. Henri IV
Ecole Nationale de Chimie
Jardin des Plantes
Mosquée
Musée d'Histoire Naturelle
Gare d'Austerlitz
Boulevard de Rochechouart
Boulevard de la Chapelle
Av. Trudaine
Rue Condorcet
Rue La Fayette
Rue de Paradis
R. d. Petites Ecuries
Boul. Haussmann
Boul. Montmartre
Boul. Bonne Nouvelle
Boul. St-Martin
R. du 4. Septembre
Rue Réaumur
R. des Champs
R. Etienne Marcel
Rue de Rivoli
St. Honoré
Rue de Rambuteau
Rue Beaubourg
Boulevard de Sébastopol
Quai Malaquais
Quai de Conti
Pont Neuf
Pont des Arts
Quai des Grands Augustins
Quai de l'Hôtel de Ville
Boulevard St-Germain
Boul. St-Michel
Quai de la Tournelle
Pont de Sully
Boul. Henri IV
Quai Henri IV
Rue des Ecoles
Rue Cuvier
Rue Buffon
Rue Monge
Rue d'Ulm
Rue Vaugirard
Rue d'Assas
Boulevard du Temple
Boul. Beaumarchais
Boul. Bourdon
Boul. de la Bastille
Quai de Valmy
Quai de Jemmapes
R. de la Grange
Boul. de Magenta
Rue du Faubourg St-Denis
Rue du Faubourg Montmartre
Rue du Faubourg Poissonnière
Rue Blanche
Rue Pigalle
Rue N.-D. de Lorette
Av. de l'Opéra
Rue Turbigo
Rue du Temple
Rue Vieille du Temple
Rue des Francs Bourgeois
Rue de Turenne
Rue St-Antoine

II. Bourse
5–8: Gaillon, Vivienne, Mail, Bonne-Nouvelle

III. Temple
9–12: Arts-et-Métiers, Enfants-Rouges, Archives, Ste-Avoie

IV. Hôtel-de-Ville
13–16: St-Merri, St-Gervais, Arsenal, Notre-Dame

V. Panthéon
17–20: St-Victor, Jardin des Plantes, Val de Grâce, Sorbonne

VI. Luxembourg
21–24: Monnaie, Odéon, Notre-Dame-des-Champs, St-Germain-des-Prés

VII. Palais-Bourbon
25–28: St-Thomas-d'Aquin, Invalides, Ecole Militaire, Gros-Caillou

VIII. Elysée
29–32: Champs-Elysées, Faubourg du Roule, Madeleine, Europe

IX. Opéra
33–36: St-Georges, Chaussée-d'Antin, Faubourg Montmartre, Rochechouart

X. Enclos-St-Laurent/Porte-St-Denis
37–40: St-Vincent-de-Paul, Porte St-Denis, Porte St-Martin, Hôpital St-Louis

XI. Popincourt/République
41–44: Folie-Méricourt, St-Ambroise, Roquette, Ste-Marguerite

XII. Reuilly
45–48: Bel-Air, Picpus, Bercy, Quinze-Vingts

XIII. Gobelins
49–52: Salpêtrière, Gare, Maison-Blanche, Croulebarbe

XIV. Observatoire/Montparnasse
53–56: Montparnasse, Parc Montsouris, Petit Montrouge, Plaisance

XV. Vaugirard
57–60: St-Lambert, Necker, Grenelle, Javel

XVI. Passy
61–64: Auteuil, Muette, Porte Dauphine, Chaillot

XVII. Batignolles-Monceau
65–68: Ternes, Plaine Monceau, Batignolles, Epinettes

XVIII. Butte-Montmartre
69–72: Grandes-Carrières, Clignancourt, Goutte-d'Or, Chapelle

XIX. Buttes Chaumont
73–76: Villette, Pont-de-Flandre, Amérique, Combat

XX. Ménilmontant
77–80: Belleville, St-Fargeau, Père-Lachaise, Charonne

History

Lutetia Parisiorum

The oldest part of Paris is on the Ile de la Cité, which in Caesar's time was occupied by a fortified Gallic settlement known to the Romans as Lutetia

Parisiorum. Roman and Frankish Paris also included a small settlement on the left bank of the Seine, surrounded by forest and marshland, where in Frankish times the Church established its headquarters.

Middle Ages

In the later medieval period the town increasingly expanded on to the right bank. By the 12th c. Paris had become a great centre of Western culture, with a university to which students flocked from many countries to study under the leading international teachers of the day. The town's favourable situation and the royal protection it enjoyed promoted craft industry and trade, and this in turn led to much building activity.
The growth of the town can be measured by successive enlargements of its circuit of walls. The wall built in the reign of Philippe Auguste, about 1200, which extended from Rue Etienne-Marcel, near the Head Post Office, to the present Luxembourg Gardens, had become much too small by 1356, when Etienne Marcel began the building of a new wall on the right bank which ran northward from the Seine to the Porte St-Denis, on the line of the present-day Grands Boulevards.

15th–16th centuries

In the 15th c. the growth of Paris was hampered by the Hundred Years War. There was a fresh burst of building activity in the reign of Francis I (rebuilding of Louvre, Tuileries and Hôtel de Ville), but the real development of Paris began in the time of Henry IV, after the wars of religion.

17th–18th centuries

In the reign of Louis XII the extension of the town walls along the whole length of the Grand Boulevards west of the Porte St-Denis, which had been begun under the last Valois rulers, was carried through to completion (1633–1636). The Ile St-Louis was created and built up from 1614 onwards. In the reign of Louis XIV many new monumental buildings were erected (Louvre Colonnade, Hôtel des Invalides, numerous churches, Place Vendôme), and the outer districts of the town extended in all directions. It was not until shortly before the Revolution, however, that the new districts were enclosed within the Enceinte des Fermiers-Généraux (Wall of the Tax-Farmers), a wall designed to facilitate the collection of taxes on goods brought into the city, which extended along the line of the outer boulevards on both banks of the Seine from the Place de l'Etoile in the west to the Place de la Nation in the east.

French Revolution

During the French Revolution and its aftermath (1789–1804) the centralisation of France reached its peak, This period, too, saw the disappearance of most of Paris's many religious houses, which occupied large areas of land in very desirable situations.

First Empire

Under the First Empire (1804–1814) Paris was the centre of Europe. The treasures of art and learning which Napoleon brought back from his victorious campaigns went to embellish his capital. He began the construction of the north wing linking the Louvre and the Tuileries, the Rue de Rivoli, the Bourse, the Madeleine and much else besides; but most of this remained unfinished at the time of his fall, and the great landmark terminating the vista of the Champs-Elysées, the Arc de Triomphe de l'Etoile, was not completed until the reign of Louis-Philippe.

Restoration

Paris had a great upsurge of vigour during the Restoration (1814–1830), when French literature, art and learning began the great advance which led towards the recovery of their world supremacy, and French society reached a peak of elegance and refinement.

July Monarchy

Under the July Monarchy (1830–1848) this progress was continued. Louis-Philippe enthusiastically resumed the development of Paris which had been planned by Napoleon, spending more than 100 million gold francs on new streets, churches, government buildings, bridges, embankments and public gardens. Once again Paris was surrounded by a new circuit of walls, the Enceinte de Thiers, which took in 13 adjoining communes.

Second Empire

All previous building activity, however, was surpassed during the reign of Napoleon III. In 1853 he appointed Georges-Eugène Haussmann (1809–1891) Prefect of the Seine département, and Haussmann made Paris – which hitherto, apart from the old boulevards, had preserved its cramped medieval street pattern – into a modern city whose layout became a model for other towns both in France and abroad. The process began with the construction of a new north–south traffic artery formed by the Boulevards de Strasbourg and de Sébastopol on the right bank and the Boulevards du Palais and St-Michel on the Ile de la Cité and the left bank. Then came the Boulevard Haussmann and the Boulevard de Magenta on the right bank, the Boulevard St-Germain on the left bank, the extension of the Rue de Rivoli, the Avenue de l'Opéra and the district round the Champs-Elysées. Among public buildings erected during this period were the new wings of the Louvre and the Opéra.

Third Republic

Under the Third Republic work in progress was completed and new streets and squares were laid out. Sculpture purchased at the annual art shows (the Salons) was set up in public parks and gardens, making them open-air museums of modern sculpture. The city's public transport system was improved by the construction of an underground railway, the Métro. New residential areas surrounded by gardens and playgrounds were built on the site of the old fortifications, which had been purchased by the city. There, too, were laid out the Parc des Expositions (Exhibition Park) and the Cité Universitaire (students' residences). A succession of international exhibitions (in 1855, 1867, 1878, 1889, 1900 and 1937) led to the erection of many new buildings, among them the Eiffel Tower (1889) and the Palais de Chaillot and Musée d'Art Moderne (1937).

First and Second World Wars

During the First World War Paris was saved from German occupation by the "miracle of the Marne". During the Second World War it was occupied from 1940 to 1944, but fortunately came through the war almost completely unscathed.

Fourth and Fifth Republics

Since 1945, under the Fourth and Fifth Republics, many notable buildings have been erected in Paris – the UNESCO headquarters in 1958, the CNIT exhibition hall in the new district of La Défense in 1959, the Maison de la Radio (1963), the Tour Montparnasse and the Centre International de Paris (a congress centre) in 1974, the Centre Beaubourg (Centre Pompidou) in 1977. The famous Halles (Market Halls) were pulled down in 1971 and replaced in 1981 by the Forum des Halles, an ultra-modern shopping centre. The first part of a new Cultural Centre at La Villette was opened in 1983, to be followed by a Museum of Technology and other developments (1989). The Picasso Museum was opened in 1985, the Musée d'Orsay in 1986, the Institut du Monde Arabe in 1988. In March 1989 the glass pyramid in the Louvre's Cour Napoléon was completed – the first stage in the development of the "Grand Louvre", due for completion by 1993. The two hundredth anniversary of the French Revolution was marked in 1989 by the formal opening of the Opéra de la Bastille and the Grande Arche at La Défense.

The movement of Paris's steadily increasing traffic has been eased since the early seventies by the construction of through roads along the Seine and a ring motorway, the Boulevard Périphérique (1973). In 1970 the new express Métro (RER) came into operation, followed in 1974 by the opening of the Charles-de-Gaulle airport at Roissy-en-France, where a second air terminal was opened in 1989.

In 1977 the city acquired its first elected Mayor this century (Jacques Chirac), in place of the Prefect previously appointed by the government.

The Bicentenary of the French Revolution in 1989 was celebrated with great display in Paris, with a full programme of operatic, theatrical and other events and by the restoration of historic buildings and the erection of new prestige buildings (see above).

Port Alexandre III

Economy and Transport

Economic structure

Paris retains its predominant role in French culture and the French economy, in spite of the fact that since the seventies, and particularly since 1982, the regions have been given increased responsibility and authority. In the fields of learning and art, and in almost every branch of industry and commerce, it still occupies a leading position, and it is still the country's most influential financial market.
More than 4.5 million people work in the Paris region, and something like a million commuters flock into Paris every day from the suburbs. Some 71% are employed in the services sector, over 22% in industry, around 6% in the building trade and a bare 1% in agriculture.

Industries

Among traditional Paris industries are electronics, precision engineering, woodworking, textiles, pharmaceuticals, chemicals, aircraft construction and car manufacturing (e.g. Renault at Boulogne-Billancourt). The high cost of land in Paris, the need for expansion, environmental considerations and policies of decentralisation have led many industrial firms to move to new sites in the départements round Paris in the Ile de France. This applies mainly to the metalworking, engineering, woodworking, textile and chemical industries, though the firms concerned have usually kept their head offices in Paris. The industries left in the city are mainly small and medium-size establishments, which still largely determine the character of many *quartiers*.

For centuries Paris has ruled the world of European fashion. Its most famous couturiers, who present their latest models at shows held in the first week of February and the end of July or beginning of August, are to be found, along with world-renowned parfumiers, in the streets to north and south of the Champs-Elysées and round the Rue de la Paix and Place Vendôme. Most of the art galleries are round the Rue de Seine on the left bank and in the Faubourg St-Honoré and Rue La Boëtie on the right bank.

Bateau-mouche on the Seine

The best known antique dealers are also to be found in these areas. Most of the car firms have their showrooms on the Champs-Elysées. The furniture industry is established in the Faubourg St-Martin (east of the Place de la Bastille), with furniture shops jostling one another in Rue St-Martin, and to the south of the Gare de l'Est. The leatherworking industry is mainly to be found on the left bank of the Seine, along an old river, the Bièvre, which is now covered over. Most of the large newspapers and periodicals have their offices near the Bourse (Rue Réaumur, Rue des Italiens, etc.), while the book trade is centred on the left bank, round the Boulevard St-Germain. Along the quays on both banks of the Seine are the stalls of the *bouquinistes* who sell old books and prints. On the Quai de la Mégisserie and Quai de Gesvres, on the right bank, are shops selling seeds and birds. Opposite, on the Ile de la Cité, is the flower market. Since the demolition of the Halles and the redevelopment of the old market quarter from the late sixties onwards the Paris markets have moved to the southern suburb of Rungis.

The Foire Internationale de Paris, held at the end of April/early May in the Parc des Expositions at the Porte de Versailles on the south-western outskirts of the city, is one of Europe's leading trade fairs. Other exhibition centres are the Parc des Expositions Paris Nord at Villepinte, the CNIT building at La Défense and the Parc des Expositions at Le Bourget, where a great international air show is held in alternate (odd-numbered) years (1993, 1995, etc.).

Transport

In spite of its situation on the western edge of the European continent Paris is an important centre of international communications. Almost all the French motorways radiate from Paris, with access points on the Boulevard Périphérique Extérieur, the ring motorway with between six and ten lanes which encircles the city.

The siting of Paris's six railway termini, each handling traffic to and from a particular part of the country, and the underground railway system (Che-

min de Fer Métropolitain de Paris, or Métro for short) have spared Paris some of the problems of traffic congestion that afflict other large cities. The Métro/RER network, with its 19 lines, is the city's fastest form of public transport (one class on the Métro, first and second class on the RER network; tickets, valid also on buses, cheapest if bought in *carnets* of ten; reduced-price tourist tickets, "Formule 1" and "Paris-Visite"; first train about 5.30 a.m., last departure about half-past midnight; frequency 2–7 minutes). The stations (many of which are interestingly designed, like the Louvre station with its collection of sculpture) are on average 543 m/594 yds apart. Within city limits one ticket is sufficient for the Métro and RER and allows unlimited changes. The connections with other lines *(correspondances)* are shown, illuminated in yellow, on station platforms at the entrances to the connecting passages (which are sometimes very long). Passages with a blue sign, "Sortie", lead to the exit.
RER (Réseau Express Régional), the regional express Métro, has four lines (A, B, C and D), mainly designed to serve the outer districts of the city.
The municipal buses of the RATP run from 6.30 a.m., and the last bus leaves its terminus about 8.30 p.m.; some lines run until half an hour after midnight, and there is also a night service, look out for *Noctambus* (ten lines from Châtelet). One or two tickets will be required according to distance. Bus stops are marked by posts bearing red and yellow signs.
Car parking within the *Zone Bleue*, which covers the whole of central Paris, is permitted only with a parking disc (bought from police stations or obtainable free from tourist offices, motoring organisations or some commercial operations) or at parking meters. There are also numerous underground and multi-storey car parks. It is forbidden to park within a *Route Rouge*.
The cruise boats on the Seine *(bateaux-mouches)*, which cater exclusively for the needs of tourists, operate throughout the year.
A State-owned corporation, Aéroports de Paris, manages the city's three airports: Charles de Gaulle at Roissy (23 km/14 miles north-east; rail and bus connections), a third runway is to be added by 1997; Orly (14 km/9 miles south; rail and bus connections); and Le Bourget (13 km/8 miles north; bus connections) for business flights.

Culture

From the time of the Impressionists until the outbreak of the Second World War Paris was the world's "art capital", a city in which many different trends – Symbolism, Fauvism, Cubism, Futurism, Surrealism – came into being in the "Ecole de Paris" or were influenced by it. During this period world-famed European artists like Picasso, Miró, Dalí, Chagall, Modigliani and Max Ernst lived and worked in Paris. Although the centre of avantgarde art moved to New York after the war Paris remained a major art centre, attracting art-lovers from all over the world with its famous museums and galleries and its renowned art exhibitions. In recent years the city has acquired a number of important new museums and cultural centres, including the Centre Georges Pompidou in 1977, La Villette in 1984–1991, the Musée Picasso in 1985, the Musée d'Orsay in 1986, the Institut du Monde Arabe in 1987, the Opéra de la Bastille in 1989.
Paris has France's most important institutes of higher education (13 universities and the famous Grandes Ecoles), the most interesting museums and the largest libraries (in particular the Bibliothèque Nationale with its 12 million volumes and its associated research institutes, including the Centre National de la Recherche Scientifique, CNRS), the largest numbers of theatres and cinemas, all the large newspaper and book publishers and a great variety of smaller firms, and the national radio and television corporations. For the future a number of major new cultural developments are planned or already under way: the completion of the Grand Louvre by 1997; the building of a European House of Photography (planned for 1993; architect Kenze Tange) in the Place de l'Italie and a Centre of Ballet and Dance in Montmartre; the expansion of the city's art collections and the

Jean Tinguely and Niki de Saint-Phalle, Igor Stravinsky Fountain, Paris

The Théâtre Français, home of the Comédie Française

enlargement of the Petit Palais (the municipal art gallery); the development of a large European library, the Bibliothèque de France (planned for 1995; architect Dominique Perrault) in the Tolbiac area; and the restoration of many historic buildings.

Information

Information about theatre programmes, concerts, exhibitions and other events can be obtained from the Office du Tourisme (see Practical Information, Information), from their free monthly publication "Paris Selection", or from the weekly publications, "L'Officiel des Spectacles", "Pariscope" and "7 à Paris", which can be bought at news-stands. Two theatre ticket offices, they are situated at 15 Place de la Madeleine (open Tues.–Sun. 12.30–8 p.m.) and RER station Châtelet-Les-Halles (open Tues.–Sat. 12.30–8 p.m.), sell tickets at half price for the day's performances.

Theatres

Paris has 115 theatres, including many of international reputation, and a visit to one of them is part of the experience of Paris. Modern productions by such directors as A. Mnouchkine and P. Chéreau have enjoyed a European success, and leading European directors like C. Peymann, P. Stein and P. Book work in Paris. In addition to the classical houses there are experimental, boulevard and café theatres, as well as cabarets (which owe their origin to the Cabaret du Chat Noir established by Rodolphe Salis in 1884).
The most famous of the theatres are Garnier's Opera House (Théâtre de l'Opéra de Paris, but since 1990 only visiting companies and ballet), the Opéra de la Bastille (opened 1989) and the Comédie Française (classical French drama), together with the Opéra Comique (also called Opéra Studio or Salle Favart), the Théâtre National de Chaillot in the Palais de Chaillot (modern and classical plays), Odéon Théâtre de l'Europe in the Place de l'Odéon and the Théâtre Musical de Paris-Châtelet. Other leading theatres are the Théâtre des Ambassadeurs (1 Avenue Gabriel), the Théâtre de l'Atelier (Place Charles-Dullin), the Comédie des Champs-Elysées (15 Avenue Montaigne), the Théâtre Mogador (25 rue Mogador), the Théâtre de la Michodière (4 rue de la Michodière), the Théâtre du Palais Royal (38 rue Montpensier) and the Théâtre de la Ville, formerly the Théâtre Sarah-Bernarht (Place du Châtelet).
For popular revues and variety shows there are the great cabarets like the Crazy Horse Saloon (12 Avenue George V), the Folies Bergère (32 rue Richer), the Lido (116 Champs-Elysées) and the legendary Moulin Rouge (Place Blanche). There are many cabarets (champagne often compulsory: beware of rip-offs!) in Montmartre, round the Champs-Elysées and the Place de l'Etoile, the Madeleine and the Opéra, St-Germain-des-Prés and the old Odéon. Artists' dives are to be found in Montmartre, the Quartier Latin and Montparnasse.

Music

Paris is also one of the great musical metropolises of Europe, with numerous symphony orchestras, some of which rank among the best in Europe (Orchestre de Paris, Orchestre de l'Opéra Bastille, Orchestre National de France, Orchestre des Concerts Lamoureux, Orchestre des Concerts Colonne, Orchestre des Concerts Pasdeloup, Orchestre Symphonique Français), working with leading conductors and soloists from all over the world, as well as numbers of chamber music groups and choirs.
Concerts of classical music are given in the Salle Pleyel (252 rue du Faubourg St-Honoré; 3000 seats), the Salle Gaveau (45 rue La Boétie), the auditorium of Radio France (116 Avenue du Président-Kennedy), the Théâtre des Champs-Elysées (15 Avenue Montaigne; a large hall seating 2200), the Théâtre Musical de Paris-Châtelet (1 Place Châtelet), and the Conservatoire of La Villette (Cité de la Musique), and occasionally also in the Palais de Chaillot and the Palais des Congrès (Porte Maillot). For lovers of avantgarde music there are concerts organised by the IRCAM musical institute in the Centre Georges Pompidou (Beaubourg), with the Ensemble Intercontemporain.

Place de la Concorde

The Paris music halls like Bobino (Rue de la Gaîté) and Olympia (28 Boulevard des Capucines) are famous for their guest stars, both French and international.
French chansons can be heard in the Caveau des Oubliettes (52 Rue Galarde) and the Deux Anes (100 Boulevard de Clichy), while jazz-lovers will find what they want in one of the popular jazz cellars like the Caveau de la Huchette (5 rue de la Huchette) or Le Petit Journal (71 Boulevard St-Michel).

Museums

Paris has about 100 museums, including both internationally renowned institutions and a whole range of less famous museums which also have much of interest to offer. Even visitors with only a short time at their disposal should include the Louvre and the Musée d'Orsay in their programme. For those with a special interest in medieval art there is the Musée de Cluny, for lovers of modern art the Centre Georges Pompidou (Beaubourg) and the Musée Picasso. A selection of the most important museums are included in the descriptions in the following section. For a thorough visit to the larger museums the best plan is to use the catalogue which is usually available.
Visitors can buy a special ticket, the "carte musées et monuments", valid for one, three or five consecutive days, which gives admission to 65 museums and monuments in Paris. The tickets are available in museums, monuments, Métro stations and the Office de Tourisme (see Practical Information – Information).

Shopping

Paris is, of course, a shopper's paradise. It is not possible, in the space available in this guide, to give even a brief account of the opportunities and temptations that await the visitor. A useful book, which in addition to listing hotels and restaurants contains a mine of information about shops and shopping in Paris, is the "Nouveau Guide de Paris/Gault-Millau".

Sightseeing in Paris

The Tuileries and Place de la Concorde

**Place de la Concorde

Paris has a prestigious centre in the Place de la Concorde, one of the world's largest and finest squares. Lying on the magnificent long artery which extends from the Louvre to the Etoile, it offers a series of tremendous vistas – to the west, at the top of the Champs-Elysées, the Arc de Triomphe de l'Etoile; to the east the Tuileries Gardens, flanked by handsome buildings; to the north, at the end of Rue Royale, the Madeleine; and to the south, across the Seine, the Palais Bourbon. In this square, between 1793 and 1795, the guillotine claimed 2800 victims. The Place de la Concorde was given its present form between 1836 and 1854 by Jacob Ignaz Hittorff, an architect from Cologne. In the centre of the square is the Obelisk of Luxor, just under 23 m/75 ft high and weighing 22 tons, which originally came from a temple at Thebes in Upper Egypt (near the present town of Luxor) erected in the 13th c. B.C. by Ramesses II and was presented to King Louis-Philippe by Pasha Mohammed Ali in 1831. Flanking the obelisk are two fountains by Hittorff, symbolising "Agriculture and Industry" and "Seafaring and Fishing". The eight allegorical statues of women, symbolising the eight largest French towns, which stand round the square are also by Hittorff. Along the north side of the square are the Ministère de la Marine (Admiralty: on right), the French Automobile Club (ACF: Nos. 6–8) and the fashionable Hôtel de Crillon.

*Obelisk of Luxor

*Fountains

Pont de la Concorde

On the south side of the square is the Pont de la Concorde over the Seine, built 1787–1791 and reconstructed 1935–1939, from which there are magnificent views upstream to the towers of Notre-Dame and downstream to the Eiffel Tower.

***Jardin des Tuileries**

On the east side of the Place de la Concorde is a wide gateway, its pillars topped by handsome Baroque winged horses with figures of Mercury and Fama (by Coysevox) – the entrance to the Jardin des Tuileries (Tuileries Gardens), once the pleasure garden of the French kings, mainly laid out from 1664 onwards by the great landscape gardener André Le Nôtre, with numerous statues and octagonal formal ponds.

Galerie Nationale du Jeu de Paume

To the left of the entrance, on the Terrasse des Feuillants, is the old Jeu de Paume (Tennis Court), which until 1986 housed the Louvre's fine collection of Impressionists (now in the Musée d'Orsay). Since its reopening in June 1991, following reconstruction, the Jeu de Paume now boosts two exhibition floors dedicated to contemporary art, including painting, sculpture, photography, cinema and video (open Tue. noon–9.30 p.m., Wed.–Fri. noon–7 p.m., Sat. and Sun. 10 a.m.–7 p.m.).

Musée de l'Orangerie

To the right of the entrance to the Tuileries, on the Terrasse du Bord de l'Eau, is the Musée de l'Orangerie (open daily except Tue., 9.45 a.m.–5.15 p.m.), with the Walter-Guillaume collection of pictures (Cézanne, Renoir, Matisse, Picasso, Rousseau, Modigliani, etc.) and eight large mural paintings by Claude Monet, "Les Nymphéas" ("The Water-Lilies").
At the east end of the Tuileries, beyond the Avenue du Général-Lemonnier, is a terrace, recently reshaped, extending between the two wings of the New Louvre. This was the site of the Tuileries Palace, built in 1564 on land previously occupied by tile-works *(tuileries)*, which was the residence of French kings and emperors until its destruction in May 1871, during the Paris Commune.

Arc de Triomphe du Carrousel

Just off the Place du Carrousel is the Arc de Triomphe du Carrousel (14.60 m/48 ft high), once the main entrance to the courtyard of the Tuileries. A smaller version of the Arch of Severus in Rome, it was erected for Napoleon I in 1806–1808 to commemorate his victories over Austria. On top of the arch is a quadriga (four-horse chariot) by Bosio, set there in 1828 to symbol-

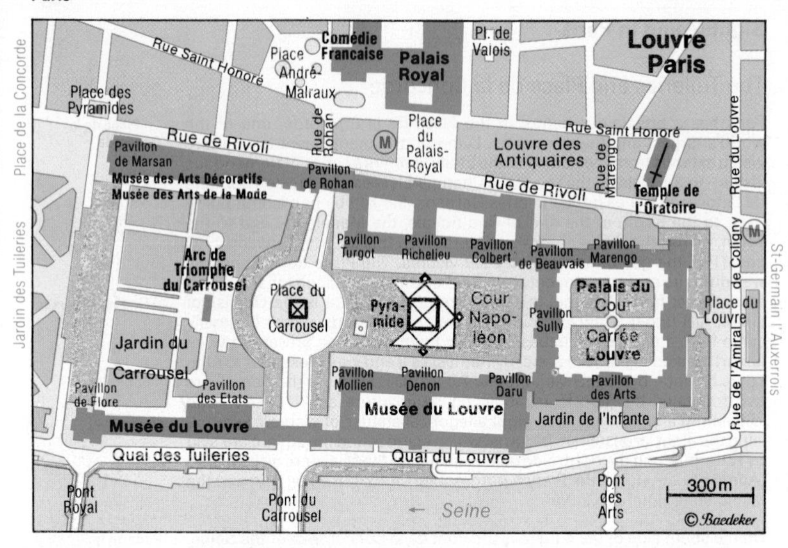

ise the triumph of the Restoration; until 1815 the arch was crowned by four ancient bronze horses removed from St Mark's Cathedral in Venice.

Until the mid 19th c. the area to the east, extending from the Place du Carrousel by way of the Square du Carrousel to the Old Louvre, was filled with a maze of narrow streets and old houses.

**The Louvre

**Grand Louvre

The eastern end of the Tuileries Gardens is closed off by the Louvre, Paris's most important public building, which houses one of the most famous art collections in the world. By 1996 the "Grand Louvre" is planned to have some 70,000 sq. m/84,000 sq. yds of exhibition space. The main entrance is the famous Glass Pyramid in the centre of the Cour Napoléon, designed by the American-Chinese architect Ieoh Ming Pei and opened in 1989. Standing just under 22 m/72 ft high, it contains 675 panes of glass. Steps and a lift lead down into the underground Hall Napoléon (open daily except Tue., 9 a.m.–10 p.m.), with information desks, the ticket office, souvenir shops, a bookshop, café and restaurant, lecture rooms and rooms for special exhibitions. From here corridors and escalators give access to three different sections of the museum.

*Glass Pyramid

Pavillon Richelieu

To the north, the Pavillon Richelieu (previously occupied by the Ministry of Finance) has since November 1993 housed the museum's Islamic art collections, plus a gallery of French sculpture and a museum of decorative arts.

Pavillon Sully

The Pavillon Sully, to the east, houses the new historical section of the Louvre: the excavations of the medieval crypt, art of the Ancient Orient, Egyptian antiquities (Pharaonic and Coptic art), Greek, Etruscan and Roman objets d'art, bronzes and terracottas, French painting (14th–17th c.), Italian pictures (17th–18th c.) and applied and decorative art from the Middle Ages to the 19th c.

Pavillon Denon

The Pavillon Denon, to the south, contains Greek, Etruscan and Roman sculpture, the French crown jewels (in the Galerie d'Apollon), sculpture

The Glass Pyramid of the Louvre

from France (Middle Ages to 19th c.), Italy (11th–18th c.), Germany and the Netherlands, paintings from France (18th–19th c.), Italy (13th–18th c.), Flanders and Holland (15th–17th c.), Germany (15th–16th c.), the northern European schools, Spain and Britain, the Beistegui, Lyon and De Croÿ collections, and displays illustrating the work of the Département des Peintures. Under the Cour Napoléon (reopened in 1988) and the Cour du Carrousel there is a car park for 800 cars and 80 coaches, other facilities are being developed – shopping arcades, restaurants, galleries, conference and exhibition centre, even a post office. It is also planned to provide a number of studios and, in the Aile de Flore, an art institute with a library, a painters' workshop and facilities for different fields of art. The Ecole du Louvre will also be housed here.

History of the Louvre

The earliest structure on the site was a fortified castle built in the reign of Philippe Auguste (1180–1223), which Charles V (1364–1380) extended and embellished. During the 15th c. the Louvre was neglected by the French kings, serving as an arsenal and a prison. In 1546 Francis I (1515–1547) resolved to build a new palace, and commissioned Pierre Lescot, the finest architect of the early Renaissance period in France, to build it. Lescot was responsible in particular for the south end of the courtyard front of the west wing, which, with sculpture by Jean Goujon and Paul Ponce, shows the full splendour of Renaissance architecture and ranks as the finest building of that period in France. Under later kings the building of the "Old Louvre" was continued by a number of different architects, including Claude Perrault, who between 1666 and 1674 completed most of the magnificent colonnade on the east front. Meanwhile the building of the Tuileries Palace which adjoined the Louvre on the west had been proceeding since 1564. In the reign of Louis XIV, who no longer lived in the Louvre after 1662 and was interested only in Versailles, the half completed buildings fell into disrepair. In 1793 a museum was opened in the Louvre, and from 1805 onwards a complete restoration was carried out on the orders of Napoleon. During his reign, too, and in that of Napoleon III two imposing wings crowned by

Venus de Milo

Victory of Samothrace

domes and sumptuously decorated were built along the north and south sides of the gardens to link the Louvre and the Tuileries Palace.

The whole complex of buildings, which cover an area of some 198,000 sq. m/237,000 sq. yds including the courtyards – three times the size of the Vatican including St Peter's – thus falls into two main parts: the Old Louvre, whose four wings enclose the large east courtyard, and the New Louvre, consisting of two palaces on the north and south sides of the Square du Carrousel, with wings extending westward to the Tuileries pavilions. The reconstruction of the palace on the north side (Pavillon Richelieu), until recently occupied by the Ministry of Finance, was completed in 1993, and now forms part of the museum. Also in 1993 the imperial apartments of the Palais Royal (Royal Palace), formerly reserved for visiting heads of state, were unveiled to the public. For the first time the sumptuous Salon Impérial is open to visitors to the Louvre. The project will be completed by 1996 with the re-landscaping of the Carrousel and Tuileries Gardens and a fully functioning underground city, as the Grand Louvre becomes a virtual pedestrianised city within a city.

**Musée du Louvre

The Louvre is open Thu.–Sun. 9 a.m.–6 p.m., Wed. 9 a.m.–10 p.m.; Mon. 9 a.m.–10 p.m. either the Pavillon Sully and Pavillon Denon (variations possible during reconstruction).
In view of the reconstruction which is still in progress it is not possible to include a layout plan of the museum in this guide. Visitors can, however, get a free plan showing the present layout of the Grand Louvre at the ticket office.
We can, therefore, give only a general summary of the collections:
1. Etruscan art (including a sarcophagus of the 6th c. from Cerveteri).
2. Oriental antiquities (art of Mesopotamia, Iran, Phoenicia and Assyria: stela of Naram-Sin, king of Akkad *c.* 2270 B.C.; Assyrian winged bulls of 8th c. B.C.; laws of Hammurabi, ruler of the first Babylonian empire).
3. Egyptian antiquities (Old, Middle and New Kingdom: stela of the snake

god Zet, *c.* 3000 B.C.; stela of Antef, a high official in the reign of Tuthmosis III; bust of Amenophis IV; sarcophagus of Imeneminet, 7th c. B.C.).
4. Greek sculpture (fragments of sculpture and friezes from the Parthenon, 447-438 B.C.; metopes from the temple of Zeus at Olympia, 5th c. B.C.; Venus de Milo, found in 1820 on the island of Melos, a work of the 2nd c. B.C. copied from a 4th c. statue; the "Lady of Auxerre"; the Victory of Samothrace, *c.* 200 B.C.; Apollo Sauroktonos and Aphrodite of Cnidos, 4th c. copies of Praxiteles).
5. Antique bronzes (Athlete of Beneventum, Ephebe of Agde).
6. Roman sarcophagi of the 2nd and 3rd c. A.D.; Greek and Roman frescoes and mosaics.
7. Greek pottery.
8. Sculpture of the 12th–19th c. (the famous statue of Amor by Edme Bouchardon; Michelangelo's "Chained Slaves"; Donatello's "John the Baptist" and "Virgin and Child"; Tilman Riemenschneider's "Virgin of the Annunciation"; tomb of Philippe Pot).
9. Spanish painting of the 14th–18th c. (El Greco, Zurbaran, Murillo, Ribera, Velázquez, Goya).
10. German and Dutch painting of the Late Gothic and Renaissance periods, 15th and 16th c. (self-portrait by Dürer; works by Hans Holbein the Younger and Lukas Cranach).
11. Flemish and Dutch painting of the 16th and 17th c. (Rubens, Jan van Eyck, Hieronymus Bosch, Brueghel the Elder, Frans Hals; Rembrandt's "Disciples at Emmaus"; van Dyck's "Portrait of Charles I").
12. Italian painting of the 13th–15th c. (Giotto, Filippo Lippi, Botticelli, Mantegna).
13. Italian painting of the 16th c. (Leonardo da Vinci's "Mona Lisa" or "Gioconda" and "Virgin of the Rocks"; Veronese's "Marriage at Cana"; Raphael's "Portrait of Baldassare Castiglione").

Mona Lisa

14. Italian painting of 17th c. ("Virgin" by Caravaggio, Tiepolo, Carracci).
15. French painting of the 16th c. (Jean Clouet, François Quesnel).
16. French painting of the 17th c. (Lebrun, Poussin, La Tour, Le Nain).
17. French painting of the 18th and 19th c. (Delacroix' "Liberty on the Barricades"; Millet's "The Gleaners"; Ingres' "Turkish Bath").
18. Applied arts and furniture.
19. Remains of the French crown jewels.

Musée des Arts Décoratifs

The western pavilion of the Louvre's north wing, the Pavillon de Marsan, houses the Museum of Decorative Art (open Wed.–Sun. 12.30–6 p.m., a rich collection of furniture and everyday objects from the Middle Ages to modern times. Since January 1986 it has also contained a Museum of Fashion (Musée des Arts de la Mode), with valuable dresses by Chanel, Dior, Worth, Cardin and other famous couturiers (temporary exhibitions only; open Wed.–Sat. 10 a.m.–6 p.m., Sun. 11 a.m.–6 p.m.).

Musée des Arts de la Mode

*Rue de Rivoli

Along the north side of the Tuileries Gardens and the Louvre runs the Rue de Rivoli, continuing east to the Hôtel de Ville. This is one of Paris's finest traffic arteries, built between 1811 and 1856, with a uniform façade along the whole of the western section (arcading on the ground floor, balconies on the upper floors). Here you will find an extraordinary range of shops of all kinds – elegant boutiques, way-out gift shops, friendly cafés, brash souvenir shops.

Quai des Tuileries

Along the south side of the Tuileries Gardens is the Quai des Tuileries, with three bridges across the Seine, all offering fine views of Paris – from west to east the Pont de Solférino, the Pont Royal (1685–1689) and the Pont du Carrousel (1831–1834).

Champs-Elysées and La Défense

**Champs-Elysées

Off the west side of the Place de la Concorde extends a magnificent avenue nearly two kilometres (just over a mile) long, the famous Champs-Elysées,

GEORGE V
PIZZA
VESUVIO
BATMAN
PIZZA VESUVIO
VESUVIO RISTORANTE
BISTRO ITALIEN GRILL BRASSERIE
PIZZA
EMPORTER

laid out at the end of the 17th c. and lined with famous restaurants, luxury shops, cafés, theatres and palatial cinemas. At the near end of the eastern section of the avenue, which runs through a park-like area 300–400 metres (330–440 yards) wide to the Rond-Point des Champs-Elysées, are two figures of "Horse-Tamers" by Guillaume Coustou (brought here in 1795 from the Château de Marly).

*Petit Palais, Musée du Petit Palais

Farther along, on the left, is the Petit Palais, built for the International Exhibition of 1900, with an imposing main entrance topped by a dome and rich sculptural decoration.
The Musée du Petit Palais now houses the city's art collection (open daily except Mon. 10 a.m.–5.40 p.m.), which has been built up since 1875, largely by purchase. There are periodic special exhibitions of 19th and 20th c. sculpture and painting. In the north wing is the Tuck Collection (pictures, tapestries, furniture, porcelain and drawings), in the south wing the Dutuit Collection of paintings, applied art, books and drawings (including works by Rembrandt and van Dyck).

Grand Palais

Opposite the Petit Palais, to the west, is the neo-Baroque Grand Palais, built 1897–1900, which is used for special exhibitions (open Thu.–Mon. 10 a.m.–8 p.m., Wed. 10 a.m.–10 p.m.). Linked with it, in Avenue Franklin-D.-Roosevelt, is the Palais de la Découverte, an interesting science museum which also incorporates a planetarium (open daily except Mon. 10 a.m.–6 p.m.).

Palais de la Découverte

*Pont Alexandre-III

Between the Grand Palais and the Petit Palais the Avenue Alexandre-III runs south to the Pont Alexandre-III, built in 1896–1900 for the International Exhibition and lavishly decorated with allegorical statues (regilded in 1989), which offers fine views, particularly of the dome of the Invalides.

Théâtre Marigny
Palais de l'Elysée

Opposite the Grand Palais, on the north side of the Champs-Elysées, is the Théâtre Marigny, and beyond this, set in extensive gardens, is the Palais de l'Elysée (1718), residence of the President of the Republic.

Rond-Point des Champs-Elysées

The park-like southern section of the Champs-Elysées ends at the Rond-Point des Champs-Elysées, a roundabout with six fountains at the junction with the Avenue Franklin-D.-Roosevelt and the Avenue Matignon-Montaigne. The section of the Champs-Elysées beyond the Rond-Point is lined by hotels, restaurants (with tables set out in the open air), cinemas, banks, newspaper offices, elegant boutiques and luxury shops, including many car showrooms.

Place Charles-de-Gaulle

The Avenue des Champs-Elysées ends in the Place Charles-de-Gaulle (until 1970 Place de l'Etoile), commandingly situated on high ground at the centre of the star *(étoile)* formed by twelve radiating avenues. In the centre of the square, a prominent landmark from every direction, is the Arc de Triomphe de l'Etoile (restored 1989; open Apr.–Sept. 10 a.m.–5.30 p.m., Oct.–Mar. 10 a.m.–5 p.m., closed on public holidays; access by subway from the north pavement of the Champs Elysées), one of the largest triumphal arches in the world and a French national monument (49 m/160 ft high, 45 m/148 ft wide and 22 m/72 ft deep). Designed by Chalgrin (d. 1811), it was intended, like its smaller counterpart in the Place du Carrousel, to proclaim the glory of Napoleon's victories; but in fact this massive structure – one of the finest achievements of the classical style of the Empire – was not completed until 1836, during the reign of Louis-Philippe.

*__Arc de Triomphe de l'Etoile__

The piers of the arch are decorated with colossal pieces of sculpture: on the east side, the rising of the people in 1792, known as "The Marseillaise", by Rude (right), and Napoleon crowned with laurel at the Peace of Vienna in 1810, by Cortot (left); on the west side, the resistance of the French people in 1814 (right), and the blessings of peace in 1815 (left), both by Etex. The scenes carved above these and on the ends of the arch depict battles of the Republic and Empire. Under the cornice is a frieze depicting the departure

◀ *Avenue des Champs-Elysées*

Arc de Triomphe de l'Etoile

The Grande Arche, Place de la Défense

and return of the army, and on the inner faces of the arch are inscribed the names of 172 battles and 386 generals (those who fell being underlined).

Unknown Soldier

Under the arch is the tomb of the Unknown Soldier, a nameless French soldier of the First World War who fell at Verdun and was buried here on November 11th 1920. At the head of the slab is an eternal flame, which is rekindled every evening at 6.30. From the platform on top of the arch (admission charge; lift; hours as above) there are magnificent panoramic views of Paris. Under the platform is a small museum (history of the construction of the arch; mementoes of Napoleon and the First World War). The most important of the twelve avenues radiating from the Place Charles-de-Gaulle are the Avenue Friedland to the north-east and its continuation the Boulevard Haussmann, in which (No. 158) is the Musée Jacquemart-André (open daily except Mon. and Tue. 1–5.30 p.m., closed Aug.; European furniture and tapestries of the 18th c., Venetian ceiling paintings, pictures by Rembrandt, Ruisdael, Carpaccio, Tiepolo and others, sculpture, faience and porcelain), beyond which is the Place St-Augustin; the Avenue Hoche, which leads to the Parc Monceau; the Avenue de Wagram; the Avenue Foch and the Avenue Victor-Hugo to the south-west, both leading to the Bois de Boulogne; the Avenue Kléber, leading to the Place du Trocadéro and the Palais de Chaillot; and the Avenue Marceau, which runs south-east to the Pont de l'Alma.

Musée Jacquemart-André

Porte Maillot

Palais des Congrès

From the Arc de Triomphe the Avenue de la Grande-Armée, continuing the line of the Champs-Elysées, runs north-west to the Porte Maillot, with the modern Palais des Congrès (exhibition halls, conference and function halls, auditorium, shops and restaurants) and the high-rise Hôtel Concorde–La Fayette.

***La Défense**

From the Porte Maillot the Avenue Charles-de-Gaulle (formerly Avenue de Neuilly) continues the line of the Avenue de la Grande-Armée to the Pont de Neuilly and the complex of futuristic office blocks, dating from the mid-sixties, of La Défense (see illustrations on page 71 and 364). Striking examples of the extravagant architectural creations of this new business district are the shell-shaped congress and function building of the Centre National des Industries et Techniques (CNIT) in the Place de la Défense and the triangular glass palace of the PFA in the Esplanade Général-de-Gaulle.

CNIT

*Grande Arche

Adjoining the CNIT building is the Grande Arche (open Mon.–Fri. 9 a.m.–6 p.m., Sat., Sun. and pub. hols. 9 a.m.–7 p.m.), a huge rectangular structure weighing 300,000 tons faced with Carrara marble (illustration, page 467), which was inaugurated in 1989 on the bicentenary of the French Revolution. Designed by the Danish architect Johan Otto von Spreckelsen, this "Triumphal Arch of Mankind" consists of two 35-storey blocks 110 m/360 ft high supporting a huge concrete slab with an area of a hectare (2½ acres), with a restaurant offering panoramic views.

Tour de la Folie

Another futuristically-designed building is the Tour de la Folie (architect–Jean-Marc Ibos), a 400 m/1300 ft high tower providing offices for service industries. Also, at present in the planning stage, the 412 m/1352 ft high "Tour sans Fin" ("Endless tower") is set to become Europe's highest tower. Latest plans are to extend the historical boulevards between La Défense and the Louvre by a further 3.3 km/2 miles and to enlarge the satellite town to some 160 hectares/⅔ sq. mile.

The Grands Boulevards

*Madeleine

From the Place de la Concorde the wide Rue Royale runs north to the Madeleine church, a classical-style building with a Corinthian colonnade. It was begun by P. Vignon in 1806 as a Temple of Fame, based on ancient models, but completed only in 1842 by Huvé. In the tympanum of the main

Opéra – now the home of ballet

front is a high-relief "Last Judgment" by Lemaire, and there is some fine sculpture in the interior. On the high altar is a marble group by Marochetti, the "Assumption of Mary Magdalene" (1837). In the apse is a mosaic by Gilbert-Martin, and over the altar a large fresco by J. Ziegler depicting famous personaities of the East and West (including Constantine the Great, Dante, Napoleon and Pope Pius VII). The church is famed for its organ recitals (particularly on Sundays at 11 a.m.) on the Cavaillé-Coll organ.

Grands Boulevards

The Madeleine is the starting-point of the Grands Boulevards, which run round the older part of the city for a distance of 4.3 km/2¾ miles to the Place de la Bastille. They date from the enlargement of the city in the reign of Louis XIV, when the old ramparts *(boulevards* = "bulwarks") were pulled down. The term was also applied to the "outer boulevards" which formed the city boundary until 1860 and also to the ring of boulevards which run on the line of the now demolished fortifications; and from 1852, when Haussmann gave Paris a series of fine new avenues, it was applied to streets which had no connection with the city's defences.
The Grands Boulevards, with their fashion shops, theatres, cinemas, discothèques, games arcades, restaurants and cafés, rank with the Champs-Elysées as the city's main traffic arteries, which are at their busiest in the late afternoon and are brilliantly illuminated with neon-lit advertisements after dark.

Boulevard des Capucines

From the Madeleine the Boulevard de la Madeleine and its continuation the Boulevard des Capucines run east to the Place de l'Opéra, one of Paris's busiest traffic intersections.
To the west of Place de l'Opéra is the Grand Hôtel Inter Continental, with the famous Café de la Paix, now a scheduled national monument.

Opéra

On the north side of the Place de l'Opéra is the Opera House (Théâtre de l'Opéra de Paris), built in 1860–1875 to the design of Charles Garnier (1825–1898). This is one of the most magnificent and largest theatres in the

world, covering an area of 11,237 sq. m/120,966 sq. ft, though in terms of the number of seats (just under 2000) it falls short of other theatres like the New York Metropolitan (3800), the La Scala in Milan (3600) and the Teatro San Carlo in Naples (2900). In the entrance hall with its profusion of statuary note particularly, to the left of the last arch on the right, Carpeaux's allegorical representation of "The Dance" (original in Louvre). The interior is open daily to the public between 11 a.m. and 4.30 p.m. except during rehearsals and in August. Beyond the vestibule with its statues is the splendid Grand Staircase (Escalier d'Honneur), a masterpiece of multi-coloured marble. No less magnificent are the richly gilded auditorium, with five tiers of boxes decorated in red and a ceiling painting by Marc Chagall (1964), and the Foyer du Public with its adjoining Loggia (fine views).
Since the completion of the new Opera House in the Place de la Bastille in 1989, Garnier's Opéra has been the home of ballet.

*Grand Staircase
*Auditorium

Musée de l'Opéra

In the Pavillon de l'Empereur, facing on to Rue Scribe, is the Musée de l'Opéra (open Mon.–Sat. 10 a.m.–5 p.m.), with an interesting collection of material on theatrical history and a large library.

Boulevard des Italiens

In the eastern section of the Boulevard des Capucines, beyond the Place de l'Opéra, and its continuation the Boulevard des Italiens are the most elegant shops in the whole of the Grands Boulevards.

Opéra Comique

On the right-hand side of the Boulevard des Italiens, with its main front on Place Boïeldieu, is the Opéra Comique or Salle Favart, rebuilt after a fire in 1887, with seating for 1500. Originally devoted mainly to Italian and French lyric and romantic operas, it is now also used for performances of experimental music and for the training of promising young performers (Opéra-Studio).

Boulevard Montmartre

Beyond the intersection with the Boulevard Haussmann, which comes in on the left, is the Boulevard Montmartre. Just beyond the intersection Rue Vivienne (on right) runs south to the Place de la Bourse (which can also be reached direct from the Place de l'Opéra along the busy Rue du 4-Septembre). In this square stands the Bourse (Exchange), an imitation of the Temple of Vespasian in Rome, with a Corinthian colonnade (by A.-T. Brongniart, 1808–1827). The hectic activity on the floor of the Exchange, which reaches its peak around midday, can be observed from the gallery in the vestibule to the left. (For conducted tours information, apply in gallery.)

Boulevard Poissonnière

Boulevard Bonne-Nouvelle

Beyond the Boulevard Montmartre are the Boulevard Poissonnière and the Boulevard Bonne-Nouvelle, both with more moderate traffic and more modest shops. At the far end of Rue d'Hauteville, which branches off the Boulevard Bonne-Nouvelle on the left, can be seen the church of St-Vincent-de-Paul (by J. I. Hittorff, 1844), which contains a fresco by Hippolyte Flandrin, "Procession of Saints" (1849–1853).
At the end of the Boulevard Bonne-Nouvelle, at the important intersection with Rue du Faubourg St-Denis on the left and Rue St-Denis (one of the oldest and for long one of the most important streets in Paris) on the right, stands the Porte St-Denis (by Blondel, 1673), a triumphal arch with allegorical figures and reliefs glorifying Louis XIV's victories in Holland.

Porte St-Denis

Boulevard St-Denis

Just beyond the Porte St-Denis the Boulevard St-Denis crosses another important traffic artery, the Boulevard de Sébastopol to the right and the Boulevard de Strasbourg to the left. Along the Boulevard de Sébastopol can be seen the dome of the Tribunal de Commerce, at the far end of the Boulevard de Strasbourg the Gare de l'Est.

Porte St-Martin

At the east end of the Boulevard St-Denis, where the Rue du Faubourg St-Martin goes off on the left and the Rue St-Martin on the right, is the Porte St-Martin, a triumphal arch (by Bullet, 1674–1675) in honour of Louis XIV, with allegorical reliefs referring to the taking of Besançon and Limburg and the French victories over the Germans, Spaniards and Dutch.

Place Vendôme

*Musée National des Techniques

To the south of the Porte St-Martin, at 292 rue St-Martin, is the Conservatoire National des Arts et Métiers, which has been housed since 1798 in the former priory of St-Martin-des-Champs and is now the National Museum of Technology (open Tue.–Sun. 10 a.m.–5.30 p.m.). Now one of the most important museums of technology in Europe, it originated in a collection of machinery and tools assembled by a mechanic named Vaucanson for the "instruction of the labouring classes". In its forty rooms, including the priory's Early Gothic church, are displayed a great range of scientific apparatus, models, inventions, etc., from the most varied fields of technology – mining, engineering, optics, building, general physics, the chemical industry, meteorology, geodesy, astronomy, photography and printing. In the handsome refectory of the priory, now a library, are modern paintings by Steinheil and Gérôme.

Boulevard St-Martin

Place de la République

The Boulevard St-Martin, beyond the Porte St-Martin, runs past three theatres – the Renaissance, the Porte St-Martin and the Ambigu – to end in the spacious Place de la République, laid out in 1880, at the intersection of many streets. In the centre of the square stands a statue representing the Republic (1883), in front of which is a bronze lion with an urn symbolising universal suffrage.

From the Place de la République the Boulevard du Temple, Boulevard des Filles-du-Calvaire and Boulevard Beaumarchais continue to the Place de la Bastille.

From the Place de l'Opéra to the Place de la Bastille

Avenue de l'Opéra

Rue de la Paix

From the Place de l'Opéra there are two routes to the Place du Théâtre-Français – either direct by the magnificent Avenue de l'Opéra, laid out between 1854 and 1879, with its elegant shops, or by going south-west down the wide Rue de la Paix, along one of Paris's most fashionable shopping streets, with famous fashion houses, jewellers, parfumiers and other luxury shops, to the Place Vendôme and then turning south-east along Rue St-Honoré.

*Place Vendome

The beautifully proportioned Place Vendôme, in classical style, was built between 1686 and 1708 to the design of Jules Hardouin-Mansart, the leading architect of the "Grand Siècle". In the centre of the square is the 43 m/143 ft high Colonne Vendôme, an imitation (by Gondouin and Lepère) of Trajan's Column in Rome, with a bronze relief running in a spiral up the column. Cast from the metal of 1200 Austrian and Russian cannons, it tells the story of the war with Austria and Russia in 1805. The column is topped by a statue (a copy) of Napoleon in the garb of a Roman emperor.
At No. 12 in the square, with a commemorative inscription, is the house in which the composer Frédéric Chopin died in 1849. At No. 15 is the legendary Ritz Hotel, whose regular guests included Ernest Hemingway, Scott Fitzgerald and Gertrude Stein. The shops round the square include such famous establishments as the jewellers Cartier, Van Cleef et Arpels and Boucheron.

Ritz Hotel

St-Roch

In Rue St-Honoré (on left) is the church of St-Roch (by Jacques Lemercier, 1653–1740), Paris's finest Baroque church. In the beautiful interior are numerous tombs, many of them from other churches now destroyed, and some fine sculpture, including a marble "Nativity" by Michel Anguier. The fourth chapel on the left commemorates Frenchmen deported to Germany during the Second World War. The church is noted for its fine music (recitals on Sundays at 10 a.m.).

Comédie Française

At the south end of Rue St-Honoré is the Place du Théâtre-Français, with two fountains. On its east side is the theatre Comédie Français, built in 1787–1790 and completely restored after a fire in 1900, with seating for 1500 (illustration, page 354). This has been the home since 1792 of the national company, the Comédie Française, whose classical repertoire extends from Corneille, Racine and Molière to Giraudoux and Anouilh. In the foyer is a seated figure of Voltaire as an old man (by J.-A. Houdon, 1781), a masterpiece of realistic portraiture.

Palais Royal

The north and east sides of the Comédie Français adjoin the Palais Royal, long a royal residence, from which an armed mob set off for the Bastille on July 14th 1789. All that remains of the original Palais Cardinal built for Richelieu by J. Lemercier in 1624–1639 is the Galerie des Proues (Gallery of Prows) on the east side of the courtyard, so called after its nautical decoration. The other parts of the building were erected or altered in the 19th c. The Palais Royal is now occupied by the Conseil d'Etat, the supreme administrative court, and the Ministry of Culture.
In the north courtyard of the Palais Royal is the attractive little Jardin du Palais-Royal, surrounded by colonnades (by Victor Louis, 1781–1786).
The Place du Palais Royal is now embellished by the controversial "Colonnes" erected in the mid 1980s by the modern sculptor Buren.

*Bibliothèque Nationale

Just north of the Palais Royal, beyond the Rue des Petits-Champs, is the Bibliothèque Nationale, France's National Library, housed in a mostly 19th c. building which occupies the site of a palace acquired by Cardinal Mazarin in 1649. The entrance is on the west side, at 58 rue de Richelieu. This is one of the richest libraries in the world, whose stock is constantly increasing, since copies of every book published in France must be deposited in the library. On the first floor is the Galerie Mazarine, part of the original Palais Mazarin, with a ceiling painting by Romanelli (1654). Here too is the Musée des Médailles et Antiques (open daily except Sun. and public holidays noon–6 p.m.), with a large collection of medals, cameos, jewellery, small objets d'art and other valuable items.
From 1995 the new Bibliothèque de France, at present under construction on a 7-hectare/17-acre site at Tolbiac (13th arrondissement), will house all new publications from January 1945 onwards.

Musée des Médailles et Antiques

Forum des Halles

The Pont Neuf, Paris's oldest bridge

A little way east of the Bibliothèque Nationale is the famous pilgrimage church of Notre-Dame-des-Victoires (1629–1740). South of this is the Banque de France, the French national bank (founded 1800) and one of the world's most important credit institutions.

Banque de France

From the north corner of the Banque de France it is a short distance east to the circular Place des Victoires, with an equestrian statue of Louis XIV (1822), and beyond this to the massive Hôtel des Postes et Télégraphes (Head Post Office), built in 1880–1884 (entrance at 52 rue du Louvre). This is the only post office in Paris which is open round the clock on Fridays, Saturdays and Sundays.

Place des Victoires

Head Post Office

South-east of the Post Office is St-Eustache, one of Paris's largest churches, which is internationally renowned for its music (recitals on public holidays at 11 a.m.). Begun in 1532 and completed only in 1637, it has a Gothic plan but Renaissance forms. The west front (1754–1788) is a masterpiece of French Baroque architecture, which always retained a classical restraint. In 1793 the "Festival of Reason" was celebrated here, and from 1795 to 1803 the church was a "Temple of Agriculture". Notable features of the spacious interior are a statue of the Virgin by Pigalle in the large Lady Chapel (built 1640) behind the high altar and the tomb (by Coysevox, to the design of Lebrun) of the great 17th c. statesman Colbert, Louis XIV's finance minister. Above the main entrance is a world-famed Ducroquet/Gonzalès organ, which has been several times restored.

*St-Eustache

From St-Eustache a large area of garden leads to the Forum des Halles, on the site of the old Halles (Market Halls), one of the largest cast-iron structures of their kind, built in 1854–1859 and demolished in the late 1960s. The markets – described by Zola in one of his novels as the "belly of Paris" – were then transferred to the southern suburb of Rungis, where the huge new market halls for fruit, vegetables, flowers and meat have an annual turnover of more than 45 billion francs.
The Halles area has now become one of the most important junction points in the Métro and RER system, with two stations, Les Halles and Châtelet–Les Halles, below the Forum des Halles. This is a multi-level underground shopping centre, with restaurants, cafés, cinemas, museums and theatres.

***Forum des Halles**

Within the Forum des Halles are the Musée de l'Holographie (open Sat.–Sat. 10 a.m.–7 p.m., Sun. and public holidays 1–7 p.m.) illustrates the history of three-dimensional photography. The Musée Grévin Forum (open Mon.–Sat. 10.30 a.m.–6.45 p.m.; Sun. 1–7.45 p.m.) is a wax museum depicting Paris life around the year 1900. The La Vidéothèque de Paris, opened in 1988, is an ultra-modern audiovisual archive with extensive collections of cinema, television and video films concerning Paris. The Parc Océanique Cousteau (Tue. and Thu. 10 a.m.–4 p.m.; Wed., Fri., Sat. and Sun. 10 a.m.–5.30 p.m.; closed Mon.), opened in 1989, offers a tour of the underwater world without a drop of water.

Musée de l'Holographie

Musée Grévin Forum

La Vidéothèque de Paris

Parc Océanique Cousteau

South-east of the Forum des Halles, in the Square des Innocents, is a Renaissance fountain from the workshop of P. Lescot, the Fontaine des Innocents (1547–49).

Fontaine des Innocents

Farther south-east, opposite the east front of the Louvre, is the church of St-Germain-l'Auxerrois, once the royal family's parish church. Built between the 13th and 16th centuries, the church has a Late Gothic façade, a porch of 1435–1439 with sculptured figures and a fine Flemish altar and triptych (both 16th c.) in the north aisle (organ recitals Sundays at 5 p.m.).

*St-Germain-l'Auxerrois

From St-Eustache it is only a few yards to the Quai du Louvre on the banks of the Seine. Along this to the west is the Pont des Arts (1804; pedestrians only) and to the east the Pont-Neuf (1578–1604). From this bridge, which in spite of its name is the oldest in Paris, there are fine views of the centre of the city.

Quai du Louvre

Pont Neuf

Bouquinistes

From here to the Pont Louis-Philippe, and on the opposite bank of the river, the quays are lined by the stalls of the bouquinistes, selling anything and everything from the works of the classical dramatists to modern comic books.

Place du Châtelet

The Quai de la Mégisserie continues the line of the Quai du Louvre eastwards to the busy Place du Châtelet, on the north side of which the Boulevard de Sébastopol comes in. In the centre of the square is the Fontaine de la Victoire (1808), commemorating the success of Napoleon's Egyptian expedition. On the west side of the square is the Théâtre Musical de Paris – Châtelet (3600 seats), on the east side the Théâtre de la Ville, formerly the Théâtre Sarah-Bernarht (1700 seats).

Pont-au-Change

From the south side of the square the Pont-au-Change crosses the northern arm of the Seine to the Ile de la Cité. Over this bridge rolled the tumbrils taking the victims of the French Revolution to their execution in the Place de la Concorde, where the guillotine had been set up.

Tour St-Jacques

In a public garden in the Rue de Rivoli, north-east of the Place du Châtelet, is the Tour St-Jacques, a Late Gothic tower which is all that remains of the church of St-Jacques-la-Boucherie, built in 1508–1522 on the site of an earlier Carolingian church and demolished in 1797. This was the starting-point of the old pilgrim road to Santiago de Compostela in Spain. The tower is now a meteorological station and is not open to the public.

A short distance north-east is the Late Gothic church of St-Merry (1515–1555), with fine stained glass and a 15th c. crypt.

***Centre Georges Pompidou/ Beaubourg**

Just north of this, on the Plateau Beaubourg, is the Centre National d'Art et de Culture Georges Pompidou, opened in 1977. This futuristic structure of glass and steel (open Mon. and Wed.–Fri. 12 noon–10 p.m.; Sat. and Sun. 10 a.m.–10 p.m.; admission free) was designed as a communications centre for artistic and cultural events.

Musée National d'Art Moderne

Within the Centre is the Musée National d'Art Moderne, with a collection of work by 20th c. artists, ranging from the Fauves (Matisse, Dufy, etc.) by way of the Cubists and the Expressionists, including works by Picasso and Kandinsky, to the modern sculpture of Calder and Moore (hours as above; admission charge except Sundays between 10 a.m. and 2 p.m.).

CCI, IRCAM

The Centre de Création Industrielle (CCI) organises exhibitions of industrial design. The Institut de Recherche et de Coordination Acoustique/Musique (IRCAM), extended in 1988, is involved in a variety of projects in the field of contemporary music.

Quai de Gesvres

From the Place du Châtelet the Quai de Gesvres (with many shops selling caged birds) runs east past the Pont Notre-Dame to the Place de l'Hôtel-de-Ville, from the south side of which the Pont d'Arcole crosses to the Ile de la Cité.

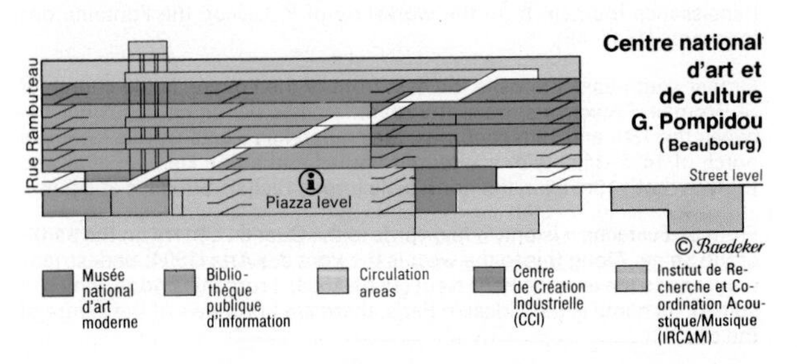

Hôtel de Ville

In the Place de l'Hôtel de Ville, formerly the much smaller Place de Grève, public executions were carried out from 1310 to 1832. On the east side of the square is the Hôtel de Ville (tours Mondays at 10.30 a.m.), built in 1874–1882 by Ballu and Deperthes to replace an earlier building of 1533 which was destroyed during the Paris Commune in 1871. It is an imposing building in French Renaissance style, with some 200 statues and groups of statuary. Since 1977 it has been the headquarters of the Mayor of Paris.

St-Gervais

Behind the Hôtel de Ville, at the far side of a small square, is the church of St-Gervais or St-Gervais-St-Protais, built in 1212 and rebuilt during the 16th c. in Late Gothic style, with some Renaissance features. Its west front, added in 1616–1621, was the first in France to use the classical orders in the normal sequence. The interior with its high vaulted nave is very impressive.

***Quartier du Marais**

North-east of the Hôtel de Ville is the Marais quarter, which until the 18th c. was a select and fashionable part of the city and still preserves some fine mansions *(hôtels)* of the 16th, 17th and 18th centuries, many of which were restored during the eighties. Particularly elegant are the Hôtel Amelot de Bisseuil or Hôtel des Ambassadeurs de Hollande (mid 17th c.) at 47 rue Vieille du Temple, the Hôtel d'Aumont (by Louis le Vau, 1630–1650; altered 1656 and recently restored) at 7 rue de Jouy, the Hôtel de Beauvais (17th c.) at 68 rue François-Miron and the Hôtel de Lamoignon (by Jean-Baptiste du Cerceau, 1594–1598) at 24 rue Pavée, which now houses the Bibliothèque Historique de la Ville de Paris (open Mon.–Sat. 9.30 a.m.–6 p.m.; reading room).

Hôtel Amelot de Bisseuil

Hôtel d'Aumont

Hôtel de Beauvais

Bibliothèque Historique

*Musée Picasso

The foundation of the Picasso Museum, housed in the Hôtel de Salé or Hôtel de Juigné (rich stucco decoration) at 5 rue de Thorigny, was due to the initiative of André Malraux, who when Minister of Culture introduced the practice of accepting works of art in lieu of inheritance tax. This enabled the state, after Picasso's death in 1973, to acquire a unique collection of his work, including pictures, sculpture and manuscripts from all his various periods, among them the famous "Demoiselles d'Avignon" (Pink period, 1904–1906). The museum is open Mon. and Thu.–Sun. 9.15 a.m.–5.15 p.m.; Wed. 9.15 a.m.–10 p.m.

Hôtel Guénégaud des Brosses, Musée de la Chasse et de la Nature

The Hôtel Guénégaud des Brosses, at 60 rue des Archives, was built in the mid 17th c. by François Mansart. It now houses a Hunting Museum, with old guns and hunting knives and pictures by 18th c. animal painters (open Mon. and Wed.–Sun. 10 a.m.–12.30 p.m. and 1.30–5.30 p.m.).

Hôtel Rohan-Soubise, Archives Nationales

Close by, with its main front on Rue des Francs-Bourgeois (No. 60), is the imposing Hôtel Rohan-Soubise, now occupied by the French National Archives. The house was built by Pierre-Alexis Delamaire in 1704–1712 and converted to its present use in 1808. It contains several million documents on the history of France from the 7th c. to the Second World War, forming the Musée de l'Histoire de France (open daily except Tue. 1.45–5.45 p.m.).

Musée de l'Histoire de France

*Musée Historique de la Ville de Paris

The Musée Historique de la Ville de Paris in Rue des Francs-Bourgeois (entrance at 23 rue de Sévigné) is housed in a Renaissance mansion (Hôtel Carnavalet) of 1544, probably designed by Pierre Lescot. It owes its name to a garbling of the name of a former owner, the widow of a Breton nobleman named Kernevenoy. In the late 17th c. it belonged to Madame de Sévigné, whose letters to her daughter give a fascinating picture of court life in her day. The Museum, now incorporating the adjoining Hôtel Le-Pelletier-de-St-Fargeau, was originally founded in 1880 and was restored and enlarged in 1988–1989. It presents a comprehensive account of the history of Paris from the 15th to the 20th c. (open Tue.–Sun. 10 a.m.–5.40 p.m.).

Musée Cognaq-Jay

Close by, in Rue Elzévir (no. 8), the Musèe Cognaq-Jay (recently transferred from the Boulevard des Capucines) contains French and English paintings, sculpture and drawings, and 18th c. furniture (open Tue.–Sun. 10 a.m.–5.40 p.m.).

Rue de Sévigné runs south to the former Jesuit church of St-Paul-St-Louis (1627–1641), with a fine Baroque doorway and an impressive interior.

***Place des Vosges**

At the east end of Rue des Francs-Bourgeois is the Place des Vosges (originally Place Royale), once the heart of the aristocratic quarter of the city. Laid out in 1607–1612 and extensively restored in 1987–1989, it has preserved its unified architecture and offers a characteristic example of early 17th c. French classical style. In the centre of the square is an equestrian statue of Louis XIII (1816–1819). At No. 6 is the Hôtel de Rohan-Guéménée, in which Victor Hugo lived from 1832 to 1848; it contains a small museum devoted to Hugo (open Tue.–Sun. 10 a.m.–5.40 p.m.).

Maison de Victor Hugo

***Place de la Bastille**

A short distance south-east of the Place des Vosges, at the end of the Grands Boulevards, is the Place de la Bastille (usually referred to simply as "la Bastille"), at the intersection of numerous streets. This was the site of the Bastille St-Antoine, built in 1370–1383, during the reign of Charles V, which was left standing when the old fortifications of Paris were pulled down and thereafter became a notorious state prison for persons (among them the Marquis de Sade) arbitrarily detained by royal authority. It earned its place in history when it was destroyed at the beginning of the French Revolution, on July 14th 1789. The Place de la Bastille also featured in the revolutions of 1830 and 1848 and in the Commune of 1871.
The Bastille Métro station has a huge mosaic by Pierre Guerchet-Jeannin (1988), a free interpretation of the Revolutionary flag, the *tricolore*.

Colonne de Juillet

In the centre of the square is the July Column, erected in 1831–1840 to commemorate those who fought on the barricades during the July Revolu-

Opéra de la Bastille

tion of 1830. It is topped by a statue of Freedom (regilded in 1989). In the circular substructure is a vault containing the remains of those who died in 1830 and 1848. From the platform on top of the column (reached by climbing 283 steps) there is a good view of the new Opéra de la Bastille opposite.

***Opéra de la Bastille**

The Opéra de la Bastille, designed by the Canadian architect Carols Ott and built on the site of the old fortress, was inaugurated on July 14th 1989 during the French Revolution bicentenary celebrations. This plain and functional glass complex, a combination of semicircular and rectangular elements, includes not only the large opera-house proper, which has seating for 2700 and a huge stage with five subsidiary stages to the sides and rear, but also an amphitheatre seating 500, a studio theatre (280 seats), other rehearsal rooms, a library, a café and a *vidéothèque*.
Immediately adjoining the Opera House is the Tour d'Argent restaurant, a replica of the original.
In the Boulevard Richard-Lenoir, which runs north-east from the Place de la Bastille, the famous Foire à la Ferraille (Scrap-Iron Fair) is held during Holy Week and in October. The Foire aux Jambons (Ham Fair) is also held here in October.

Gare de Lyon

From the Place de la Bastille the Rue de Lyon runs south to the Boulevard Diderot, in which the Gare de Lyon is situated (trains to central and southern France, Italy and Switzerland).

Palais Omnisports

Between the adjoining Rue de Bercy and the banks of the Seine is the Palais Omnisports de Bercy (by Pierre Parat, 1984), which has seating for up to 17,000 spectators and is used for cultural as well as sporting events.

*Ile de la Cité

Palais de Justice

From the Place du Châtelet the Pont-au-Change leads on to the Ile de la Cité, the oldest part of Paris. Immediately beyond the bridge, on the right, is the massive bulk of the Palais de Justice (Law Courts; the public are freely admitted Mon.–Fri. 9 a.m.–5 p.m.; illustration, page 376), on the Boulevard du Palais, the main street of the Ile de la Cité. The Palais de Justice occupies the site of an old royal stronghold of which, following fires in 1618 and 1776, nothing is left but the Sainte Chapelle, four towers and parts of the foundations. The Tour de l'Horloge (Clock-Tower) at the north-east corner, near the Pont-au-Change, dates from the early 14th c.; the clock has been repaired or restored on many occasions down the centuries. Along the north front, on the Quai de l'Horloge, are the Tour de César, the Tour d'Argent and the battlemented Tour St-Louis or Tour Bombec, all dating from the reign of Philippe le Bel (1285–1314). Most of the present building dates from the turn of the century, the south wing from 1911–1914.
From the Boulevard du Palais a wrought-iron gate (1785) gives access to the forecourt, the Cour de Mai – so called because the clerks attached to the courts used to set up here on May 1st a symbolic tree known as the *mai*. From here a flight of steps leads up to the Galerie Marchande, to the right of which is the Salle des Pieds Perdus ("Hall of the Wasted Footsteps", alluding to the unsuccessful litigants who waited here for their cases to be heard), the lobby of the civil courts of first instance, where barristers meet their clients during intermissions. This hall in neo-classical style, built in the 1870s, stands on the site of the Great Hall of the old royal palace. The courts, which sit from noon onwards, are entered from the lobby.

**Sainte-Chapelle

From the Cour de Mai a passage on the left, the Galerie de la Sainte-Chapelle, leads into the Cour de la Sainte-Chapelle, in which is the Sainte Chapelle itself. This jewel of Gothic architecture, which consists of two chapels, one over the other, was built as the palace chapel in 1246–1248, during the reign of Louis IX (St Louis), to house the Crown of Thorns and other relics brought to France in 1239 (now in Notre-Dame); the architect

Palais de Justice

Sainte-Chapelle, the upper chapel

was probably Pierre de Montereau. It was profaned during the French Revolution, in 1791, and is no longer used for worship (open daily Oct.–March 10 a.m.–4.30 p.m., Apr.–Sept. 10 a.m.–6 p.m.; admission charge).

Visitors first enter the lower chapel (Chapelle Basse), with a roof only 6.60 m/22 ft high, which was meant only for servants. From here a spiral staircase leads to the upper chapel (Chapelle Haute), which was reserved for the royal family. The wall surfaces of the chapel are almost entirely taken up by windows , with vivid stained glass, some of it dating from the time of St Louis, set in graceful tracery. The Late Gothic rose window, with scenes from the Apocalypse, dates from 1493–1498, in the reign of Charles VIII. On the buttresses of the nave are statues of the twelve Apostles.

Conciergerie

On the Quai de l'Horloge (No. 1) is the entrance to the Conciergerie, which has sinister associations from its use as a state prison during the French Revolution (open daily Apr., May and Sept. 9.30 a.m.–6 p.m., Jun.–Aug. 9.30 a.m.–6.30 a.m., Oct.–Mar. 10 a.m.–4.30 p.m.; admission charge).

Features of particular interest are the Salle des Gens-d'Armes, an imposing Gothic pillared hall under the Salle des Pas Perdus; the so-called Cuisines de St Louis, a square kitchen with four large Gothic fireplaces; the prisons in which famous prisoners like Marie-Antoinette (executed 1793) and Robespierre (executed 1794) awaited their fate; and the Salle des Girondins, a room converted into a chapel which now houses the Musée de la Conciergerie.

Tribunal de Commerce

Opposite the Palais de Justice, at the end of the Pont-au-Change, is the Renaissance-style Tribunal de Commerce (1860–1866) with a prominent dome.

To the east of this is the Marché-aux-Fleurs, a small square in which the Paris flower market is held Mon.–Sat. and a bird market (Marché aux Oiseaux) on Sundays.

Notre-Dame de Paris, south front

Préfecture de Police, Police Museum

On the south side of the Marché-aux-Fleurs is the Préfecture de Police, the police headquarters, with a Police Museum documenting the story of the criminal police (open Mon.–Fri. 9 a.m.–5 p.m., Sat. 10 a.m.–5 p.m.).

Hôtel-Dieu

On the east side of the square is the Hôtel-Dieu, one of the oldest hospitals in Europe, originally founded about 660 as a convent; the present buildings date from 1868–1878.

****Notre-Dame de Paris**

Crypte Archéologique

The south side of the Hôtel-Dieu looks on to the Place du Parvis-Notre-Dame, where remains of the Merovingian church of St-Etienne were discovered during the construction of an underground car park in 1960. The remains, along with various Roman structures, can be seen in the Crypte Archéologique under the square (open daily except pub. hols. 10 a.m.–5.30 p.m. in summer, 10 a.m.–5 p.m. in winter). On the east side of the square, which was much smaller before the construction of the present Hôtel-Dieu, stands Notre-Dame, the cathedral of the Archbishop of Paris, founded in 1163 on a site which had been occupied by two earlier churches. The choir and transepts were almost completed by 1177, but the rest of the building, including the chapel, was not finished until the 14th c. During the French Revolution the church was severely damaged, and in 1793–1794 it became a "Temple of Reason".

**West front

The monumental west front, the oldest of its kind and the model for many other churches in northern France, makes an unforgettable impression on the beholder. The sculpture on the doorways was destroyed during the Revolution, but was later restored on the basis of surviving fragments or on the model of other French cathedrals. The "Last Judgment" on the central doorway, with Christ in Majesty in the tympanum and the archangel separating the righteous from the sinners, is a masterpiece of 13th c. sculpture. The south doorway is dedicated to St Anne, the north doorway (1210–1220), through which the church is entered, to the Virgin. Over the doorways is a gallery containing 28 statues of the kings of Judah, set in niches,

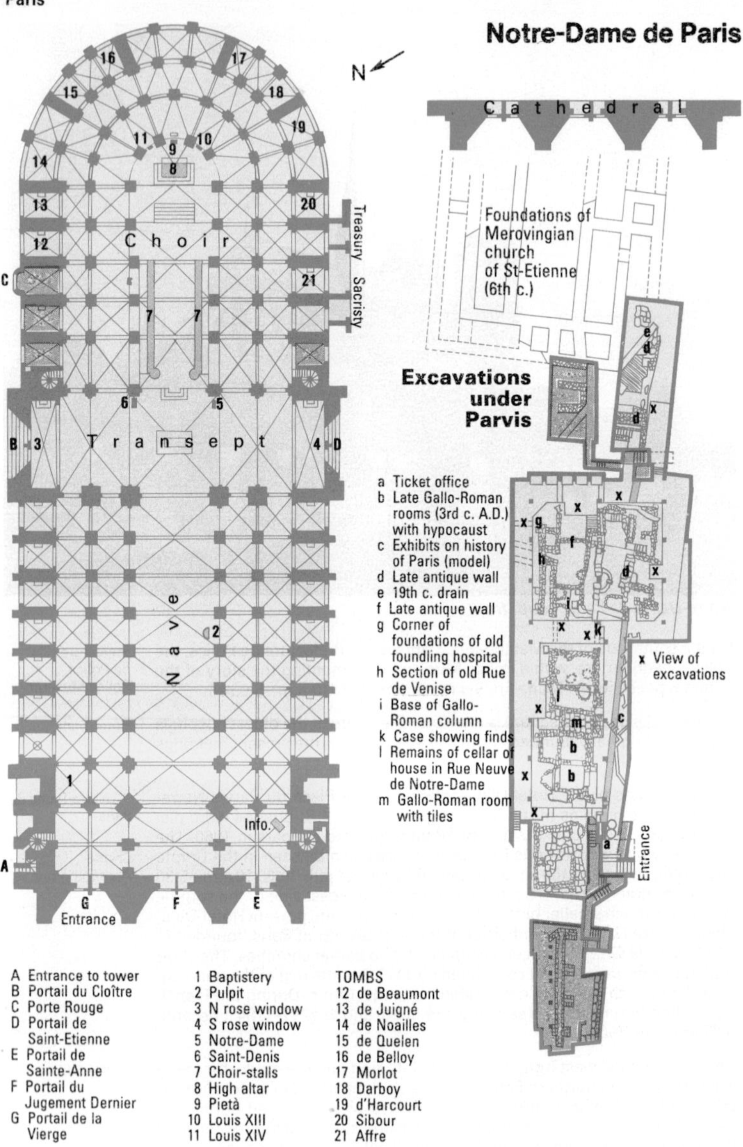
Notre-Dame de Paris
N
Cathedral
Foundations of Merovingian church of St-Etienne (6th c.)
Excavations under Parvis
Choir
Transept
Nave
Treasury
Sacristy
Entrance
Info.
a Ticket office
b Late Gallo-Roman rooms (3rd c. A.D.) with hypocaust
c Exhibits on history of Paris (model)
d Late antique wall
e 19th c. drain
f Late antique wall
g Corner of foundations of old foundling hospital
h Section of old Rue de Venise
i Base of Gallo-Roman column
k Case showing finds
l Remains of cellar of house in Rue Neuve de Notre-Dame
m Gallo-Roman room with tiles
x View of excavations
A Entrance to tower
B Portail du Cloître
C Porte Rouge
D Portail de Saint-Etienne
E Portail de Sainte-Anne
F Portail du Jugement Dernier
G Portail de la Vierge
1 Baptistery
2 Pulpit
3 N rose window
4 S rose window
5 Notre-Dame
6 Saint-Denis
7 Choir-stalls
8 High altar
9 Pietà
10 Louis XIII
11 Louis XIV
TOMBS
12 de Beaumont
13 de Juigné
14 de Noailles
15 de Quelen
16 de Belloy
17 Morlot
18 Darboy
19 d'Harcourt
20 Sibour
21 Affre

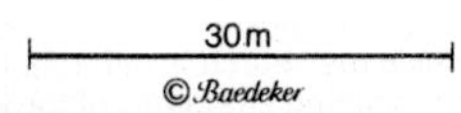
30 m

and above this again is a large rose window. The façade is flanked by two unfinished Gothic towers.

South tower
*View

Visitors can climb the south tower (open daily 9.30 a.m.–6.30 p.m. in summer, 9.30 a.m.–4.30 p.m. in winter; admission charge), 376 steps, for a bird's eye view of the heart of Paris. With its vista of the Seine and its bridges this is one of the finest views of Paris. In the south tower is the Bourdon de Notre-Dame, a large bell (cast in 1686) weighing 15 tons.
In the south transept is the Porte St-Etienne, with numerous statues, in the north transept the Porte du Cloître, with a late 13th c. figure of the Virgin. Particularly fine is the view of the choir, with its graceful windows and bold flying buttresses.

Interior

*Rose windows

*Figure of Notre-Dame de Paris

*Tomb of Comte d'Harcourt

The impressive effect of the interior (130 m/427 ft long, 48 m/157 ft wide, 35 m/115 ft high) is enhanced by the indirect lighting (open daily 8 a.m.–7 p.m.; High Mass daily at 10 a.m.; organ recitals on Sundays 5.45–6.15 p.m.). Of the numerous stained glass windows only the great rose window in the north transept (*c.* 1270) with 80 Old Testament scenes and the smaller one in the south transept (1257) are old. On the right-hand pier at the entrance to the choir is a 14th c. figure of the Virgin, Notre-Dame de Paris, who is revered as the patroness of the cathedral. On the choir screen are 23 carved scenes from the life of Christ, painted and in some cases gilded (by Jehan Ravy and his nephew Jehan le Bouteiller, 1319–1351). The most notable of the chapels round the choir is the second on the left of the entrance to the sacristy, which contains the tomb (by Pigalle) of the Comte d'Harcourt (d. 1718). The powerful Cavaillé-Coll organ is the largest in France, with 8500 pipes and 110 stops.

*Sacristy (Treasury)

In the Sacristy, built on to Notre-Dame in 1845–1850 on the site of the old Archbishop's Palace, which was demolished in 1831, is the Treasury (open daily 9.30 a.m.–5.30 p.m.; admission charge). Among other items it houses the reliquaries containing the "great relics" from the Sainte-Chapelle – the Crown of Thorns, a piece of the True Cross and a nail from the Cross.

Mémorial de la Déportation

At the south-eastern tip of the Ile de la Cité is the Mémorial de la Déportation (1962), an impressive monument (with crypt) commemorating the 200,000 French people who died in German concentration camps during the Second World War.

Ile St-Louis

Hôtel de Lauzun
Hôtel Lambert

Behind the choir of Notre-Dame de Paris is the Pont St-Louis (rebuilt 1969–1970; pedestrians only; cars must go round by the Pont Marie), which leads on to the Ile St-Louis, formed between 1614 and 1630, in the time of Cardinal Richelieu, from two smaller islands, the Ile Notre-Dame and the Ile aux Vaches. With its handsome aristocratic mansions, like the Hôtel de Lauzun (1657), now the guest-house of the city of Paris, and the Hôtel Lambert, the Ile St-Louis has preserved the unified effect of its 17th c. architecture. The island's residents, however, have included not only wealthy aristocrats but also famous writers and philosophers like Baudelaire, Voltaire and Rousseau. Behind the elegant 17th c. façades are now to be found some of the highest-rented flats in Paris, fine art galleries and famous antique-dealers.

St-Louis-en-l'Ile

In Rue St-Louis-en-l'Ile, the island's narrow main street, is the church of St-Louis-en-l'Ile (1664–1726), with a richly decorated interior.
A walk round the island along the quays offers attractive views of the river and central Paris.

The Northern Districts

Boulevard Malesherbes

From the Madeleine the Boulevard Malesherbes runs north-west to the Place St-Augustin, where it intersects with the Boulevard Haussmann and

Sacré-Cœur

St-Augustin

other important streets. On the north side of the square is the church of St-Augustin with its mighty dome (1860–1871), the finest achievement of the architect Victor Baltard, who made bold use of cast-iron in his imitation of early Renaissance forms.

Gare St-Lazare

La Trinité

From here the busy Rue de la Pépinière runs east to the Gare St-Lazare, built in 1886–1889 (trains to western and north-western France), from which Rue St-Lazare continues to the church of La Trinité (by Ballu, 1861–1867), in late Renaissance style, which is famed for its organ and its choir and contains many paintings.

Notre-Dame-de-Lorette

Farther east, in Rue de Châteaudun, is the church of Notre-Dame-de-Lorette (by Hippolyte Lebas, 1823–1836), in the form of an early Christian basilica, with a tall Corinthian portico and a beautiful interior.

Montmartre

North of this, on the Butte Montmartre, which extends from the outer boulevards to the city boundary, is the district of Montmartre, famous in the past for the *vie de bohème* of the artists who frequented it (Toulouse-Lautrec, Manet, Utrillo, Apollinaire, etc.) and still a great centre of night life. Under the south-west side of the hill, traversed by the Boulevard de Clichy, is Place Pigalle, in and around which are numbers of night spots, cabarets and bars. A few paces west, in Place Blanche, is the legendary Moulin Rouge.

From the Boulevard de Rochechouart, the eastward continuation of the Boulevard de Clichy, Rue de Steinkerque runs north to Place St-Pierre.

*Butte Montmartre

From here flights of steps, steep paths and a funicular continue north to Montmartre (the Butte Montmartre), a hill (127 m/417 ft) rising to 101 m/331 ft above the Seine, which commands views over the whole of Paris. On the summit is one of Paris's most conspicuous landmarks (most effective when

*Sacre-Cœur

seen from a distance), the church of the Sacré-Cœur (Sacred Heart), a huge basilica in Romanesque/Byzantine style with a dome 83 m/272 ft high. It was built in fulfilment of a vow taken by a group of Catholics after the

Franco-Prussian War of 1870–1871. Begun in 1875 to the design of Paul Abadie (d. 1884), it was completed in 1914 and consecrated in 1919. Behind the apse is a belfry (1905–1910) with the "Savoyarde", a bell 3 m/10 ft high weighing nearly 19 tons. From the terrace in front of the church or, better still, from the dome (entrance near north doorway; 350 steps; admission charge) there are magnificent views over Paris.
The interior is notable for its imposing spatial effect, and has some fine stained glass. In the choir vaulting is a large mosaic (by L.-O. Merson, 1923) depicting the glorification of the Sacred Heart, and on the marble high altar is a monstrance in which the Sacrament is permanently displayed. A spacious crypt (admission charge) extends under the whole church. The church is open daily 6 a.m.–9 p.m. (crypt, tombs and treasury 9 a.m.–6 p.m.).

*St-Pierre-de-Montmartre

To the west of the Sacré-Cœur is the church of St-Pierre-de-Montmartre, one of the earliest Gothic churches, built under the influence of St-Denis. It originally belonged to a Benedictine abbey founded in 1147 and dissolved during the Revolution. By the 19th c. it had fallen into disrepair, but was restored in 1900–1905. The groined vaulting of the choir is the oldest in Paris.

Place du Tertre

In the surrounding area there are many old streets and squares, among them the picturesque Place du Tertre; but the original character of the square, as of much of Montmartre, has been destroyed by the development of the tourist industry with its "auberges", cabarets, sex shops, games arcades, souvenir shops and so on. And by the extensive new building which is steadily displacing the old houses and reaching westward to beyond the famous old dance-hall, the Moulin de la Galette with its two old windmills.

Montmartre Cemetery

In the western part of Montmartre, a little way north of the Boulevard de Clichy, is the Montmartre Cemetery (Cimetière de Montmartre or Cimetière du Nord), which has fewer monuments and famous names than the cemetery of Père Lachaise but is still well worth a visit. Among notable people buried here are the German poet Heinrich Heine (1797–1856), in the Avenue de la Cloche (west side), the composer Hector Berlioz (1803–1869), in the Avenue des Carrières (east side), and the operetta composer Jacques Offenbach (1819–1880), in the Avenue des Anglais (west side), both the latter being near the northern tip of the cemetery.

Porte de Clignancourt
Marché aux Puces

1 km/¾ mile north of Montmartre is the Porte de Clignancourt, where the famous Marché aux Puces ("Flea-Market"), a treasure house of bric-à-brac, has been held on Saturday, Sunday and Monday since 1885. There are in fact seven separate markets, selling the most extraordinary range of goods; the best known is the Marché Biron (antiques), but perhaps the most impressive is the Marché Vernaison (period furniture and ornaments).

Gare du Nord

Gare de l'Est

The Boulevard de Magenta, which runs south-east from the east end of the Boulevard de Rochechouart to the Place de la République, passes close to Paris's two most important railway stations. Near the north end of the boulevard is the Gare du Nord (trains to Belgium, Germany and the Channel ports and the Channel Tunnel), built in 1864 by the Cologne architect J. I. Hittorff. Farther south-east is the Gare de l'Est or Gare de Strasbourg (trains to Luxembourg, Frankfurt, Strasbourg, Basle, etc.), which was considerably enlarged in 1928–1930.

*St-Vincent-de-Paul

A little way south-west of the Gare du Nord is the church of St-Vincent-de-Paul (1842–1844; begun by Lepère, completed by Hittorff), a church of basilican type with a porch. In the tympanum is a fine sculptured group showing St Vincent de Paul (1576–1660), "father of the poor", between Faith and Charity. The interior, with 86 columns, contains noble paintings

(1850–1854) by Hippolyte Flandrin, painted on a gold ground in the manner of the Ravenna mosaics, which can be appreciated only in full sunlight.

St-Laurent

South of the Gare de l'Est, near the north end of the Boulevard de Strasbourg, is the handsome church of St-Laurent, one of the oldest in Paris, which was completely rebuilt in 1862–1866.
1 km/¾ mile south-east of the church, at the end of the Boulevard de Magenta, is the Place de la République.

The Eiffel Tower and Invalides

Champ de Mars

In the western part of the large area of Paris that lies on the left bank of the Seine, between the Ecole Militaire and the river, is the Champ de Mars ("Field of Mars"), originally a military parade ground, later the scene of great national celebrations and international exhibitions.

**Eiffel Tower

Near the Seine is the Eiffel Tower (Tour Eiffel: illustration, page 447), Paris's best known landmark, erected in 1887–1889 for the International Exhibition of 1889 by the engineer Gustave Eiffel (1832–1923). When it was built it was the highest man-made structure in the world (300 m/984 ft), made up of some 16,500 metal parts; with the television aerial which was added in 1957 it is now 307 m/1007 ft high.
The tower is 129 m/424 ft square at the base. The first platform is 57 m/187 ft from the ground; the second 115 m/377 ft from the ground, and the third platform, 214 m/702 ft from the ground, has a glassed-in gallery which can accommodate 800 people. From the third platform a stair leads up to the lantern (24 m/79 ft high). The searchlight above this has a range of 70 km/45 miles.
The first and second platforms, which were thoroughly overhauled in 1981–1989 for the tower's hundredth birthday in 1989, can be reached either by lift or by stairs (350 and 730 steps respectively); the third platform can be reached only by lift. The view from the top platform extends for up to 90 km/55 miles in clear weather (which is rare): the best time is an hour before sunset. There are restaurants here and on the second platform (the Jules Verne luxury restaurant), together with a post office and a cinema with an audiovisual show on the history of the Eiffel Tower. When illuminated after dark the tower is a breathtaking sight. You can go up the tower from 9.30 a.m. to midnight in summer, 10 a.m. to 11 p.m. in winter.

Pont d'Iéna

*Palais de Chaillot

From the Eiffel Tower the Pont d'Iéna (built in 1806–1813 to commemorate Napoleon's victory over the Prussian army at Jena in 1806; widened 1935–1936) leads over the Seine to the Palais de Chaillot. beautifully situated above terraced gardens, this was built in 1937 on the site of the old Trocadéro, an exotic building erected for the International Exhibition of 1889. The two semicircular wings house four important museums. In the west wing is the Musée de la Marine (open Mon. and Wed.–Sun. 10 a.m.–6 p.m.; closed on pub. hols.), which illustrates the history of French commercial and naval shipping from the time of the galley to that of the steamship. The Musée de l'Homme (open Mon. and Wed.–Sun. 9.45 a.m.–5.15 p.m.; closed pub. hols.), in the east wing, has rich collections on the anthropology, prehistory and ethnology of cultures all over the world and a library of 180,000 volumes. Also in the east wing is the Musée des Monuments Français (open Mon. and Wed.–Sun. 9.30 a.m.–5.15 p.m.), with copies of the most important French monuments and frescoes. Finally there is the Musée du Cinéma (open daily except Tue.; conducted visits at 10 and 11 a.m. and 2, 3 and 4 p.m.), with interesting material on the history of the cinema. Here also is the Cinémathèque Française showing re-runs of internationally-acclaimed films. The terrace between the two wings, from which there are fine views of Paris, is the roof of the large Théâtre National de Chaillot (seating for 3000; entrance in east wing).

Musée de la Marine

Musée de l'Homme

Musée des Monuments Français

Musée du Cinéma

Jardins du Trocadéro

In the Jardins du Trocadéro (or du Palais de Chaillot), which descend in terraces to the Seine, is a large artificial pond. At the east end of the gardens

Palais de Chaillot

is an underground aquarium with a rich collection of French freshwater fishes (admission charge).

Place du Trocadéro

On the north-west side of the Palais du Chaillot, at the intersection of several streets, is the Place du Trocadéro. From here the broad Avenue Kléber runs north-east to the Arc de Triomphe de l'Etoile and the Avenue du Président-Wilson runs east to the Place d'Iéna, near which are a number of museums. The Musée Guimet (open Mon. and Wed.–Sun. 9.45 a.m.–5.15 p.m.) is devoted to the arts and ancient cultures of the countries of East Asia and the Far East. The Musée d'Art Moderne de la Ville de Paris (open Tue.–Sun. 10 a.m.–5.30 p.m., Wed. 10 a.m.–8.30 p.m.), in the west wing of the Palais d'Art Moderne, has a fine collection of modern art ranging from the Cubists, the Fauves and the Ecole de Paris to the latest Figurative artists. The east wing of the Palais d'Art Moderne, the Palais de Tokyo, is used for special photographic and cinematic exhibitions (open Mon. and Wed.–Sun. 10 a.m.–5 p.m.; closed pub. hols.).

Maison de Radio-France

In the Avenue du Président-Kennedy, the south-westward continuation of the Avenue de New-York, is the Maison de Radio-France (by H. Bernard, 1963), a massive circular structure with a central tower block 70 m/230 ft high (conducted tours daily except Sun. and pub. hols. at 10.30 and 11.30 a.m. and 2.30, 3.30 and 4.30 p.m.).

Musée Marmottan

From here it is well worth continuing west towards the Bois de Boulogne to see the Musée Marmottan (open Mon. and Wed.–Sun. 10 a.m.–5.30 p.m.), at the Jardin du Ranelagh, which has the largest collection of Impressionists after the Musée d'Orsay as well as fine collections of Empire furniture and medieval miniatures.

Ecole Militaire

On the south side of the Champ de Mars is the imposing bulk of the Ecole Militaire, built in 1752–1774 to the design of J.-A. Gabriel to house the

Dôme des Invalides

newly established Military (Cadet) Academy. In 1792 it became a barracks. Two wings were added in 1854–1859, and in 1880 it became the Ecole Supérieure de Guerre, in which staff officers are trained (not open to the public).

*UNESCO

Beyond the Ecole Militaire, in Place de Fontenoy, are the headquarters of UNESCO, a Y-shaped building designed by B. Zehrfuss (French), P. L. Nervi (Italian) and M. Breuer (American), which was opened in 1958. The interior was decorated by modern artists, including Picasso, Henry Moore and Alexander Calder (conducted tours by prior arrangement). The large Japanese garden was restored in 1988 under the direction of Toemon Sano.

Hôtel des Invalides

North-east of the Ecole Militaire is the Hôtel des Invalides (by Libéral Bruant, 1671), built on the orders of Louis XIV to house old soldiers. It originally had accommodation for 7000 veterans, but is now occupied only by a small number of war-disabled, mostly employed as museum attendants; the rest of the building is used as government offices.
In the gardens outside the north front is the 18-gun Batterie Triomphale, together with 20 bronze barrels from cannons captured in the 17th and 18th centuries and two Panther tanks from the Second World War.

*Musée de l'Armée

On the left-hand side of the Cour d'Honneur (Grand Courtyard; *son et lumière* in summer), which is surrounded by two-storey buildings, is the entrance to the Army Museum (open daily Apr.–Sept. 10 a.m.–6 p.m., Oct.–Mar. 10 a.m.–5 p.m.; closed pub. hols.), which occupies the wings on both sides of the courtyard. This world-famous collection includes arms and armour (40,000 items from Europe and the East), uniforms and historical relics and mementoes (e.g. in the Section Historique, devoted to the French army and its generals).

Musée des Plans-Reliefs

In the same building, the Musée des Plans-Reliefs houses a collection of scale models (1/6000) of French fortified towns from the 17th to 19th centuries (open daily 10 a.m.–5.45 p.m.).

Napoleon's tomb

St-Louis-des-Invalides

On the south side of the courtyard is the church of St-Louis-des-Invalides, built by Bruant at the same time as the main building. In the nave are two rows of flags captured in the wars of the 19th c. To the right of the choir is the Chapelle Napoléon, commemorating the Emperor's death and the transfer of his remains to Paris. The church is renowned for its fine organ recitals.

***Dôme des Invalides**

On the south side of the church (entrance from the south-east side of the Grand Courtyard by way of the Corridor de Metz) is the Dôme des Invalides, an imposing structure built by Jules Hardouin-Mansart in 1675–1706 as a fitting termination to the Hôtel des Invalides and an Eglise Royale in which the king could attend divine service in a setting of appropriate magnificence. The elegant dome (regilded in 1989) is 97 m/318 ft high (107 m/351 ft including the cross).

*Napoleon's tomb

The central feature of the Dôme des Invalides (open daily 10 a.m.–7 p.m.; admission charge) is the unroofed crypt under the dome containing Napoleon's tomb, which was designed by Visconti and built between 1843 and 1861. Also in the crypt is the bronze sarcophagus of Napoleon's only legitimate son (1811–1832) Napoleon II, known as the Roi de Rome and the "Aiglon".

In the two smaller chambers which open off the central rotunda are the tombs of Marshal Turenne (1611–1675; on left), who commanded French troops during the Thirty Years War and later in Alsace, and the famous military engineer Vauban (1633–1707; on right). In the four corner chapels, reached through narrow openings, are the tombs of Napoleon's eldest brother Joseph (1768–1844), who became king of Naples and later of Spain; his younger brother Jérôme (1784–1860), king of Westphalia, with the heart of his wife, Princess Katharina of Württemberg (d. 1835); and Marshal Foch (1851–1929).

Porte d'Enfer . . .

. . . in the Musée Rodin

From the Invalides to the Luxembourg

*Musée Rodin

To the east of the Invalides, at 77 rue de Varenne, is the Hôtel Biron, now housing the Musée Rodin (open daily except Tue. Oct.–Mar. 10 a.m.–5 p.m., Apr.–Sept. 10 a.m.–5.45 p.m.), with many of the great sculptor's works, including the "Gates of Hell", the "Kiss" and the "Burghers of Calais", as well as his personal art collection.

Ste-Clotilde

500 m/550 yds north-east is the large neo-Gothic church of Ste-Clotilde, begun in 1846 by an architect from Cologne, Gau, and completed in 1856 by Ballu.

Esplanade des Invalides/Aérogare Invalides

To the north of the Invalides is the spacious Esplanade des Invalides, leading to the Pont Alexandre-III. Just before the bridge, on the right, are the Invalides Métro station (RER line C5 to Versailles) and air terminal (buses to Orly airport).

Quai d'Orsay

From here the Quai d'Orsay runs along the Seine to the right. Immediately on the right is the imposing building erected in 1845–1853 for the Ministère des Affaires Etrangères (Foreign Ministry), on the east side of which is the residence of the President of the National Assembly (1722); visits by prior arrangement only (tel. 40 63 60 60).

*Palais Bourbon

Beyond this, opposite the Pont de la Concorde, is the Palais Bourbon, named after the Duchesse de Bourbon for whom the original palace was built in 1722 and which since 1795 has been the meeting-place of the National Assembly, the first chamber of the French Parliament. Notable features are the monumental figures of French ministers (Sully, L'Hospital, d'Aguesseau and Colbert) on the portico and five ceiling paintings (1838–1847) by Eugène Delacroix in the Library (seen only on written application to the Questure of the National Assembly).

Musée d'Orsay: the sculpture gallery in the central hall

Palais de la Légion d'Honneur

500 m/550 yds farther east, at the Pont de Solférino, is the Palais de la Légion d'Honneur (headquarters of the Légion d'Honneur since 1804), which was originally built for the Prince de Salm in 1782–1786.

**Musée d'Orsay

The Musée d'Orsay, housed in a former railway terminus, the Gare du Quai d'Orsay, was opened in 1986. The original structure of cast-iron and glass, built for the 1900 International Exhibition by Victor Laloux, was scheduled as a national monument in 1973 and was reconstructed for its present purpose by Gae Aulenti. The Museum, with 17,200 sq. m/185,000 sq. ft of exhibition space, presents a general picture of the development of art between 1848 and 1916, displaying paintings, sculpture and objets d'art from the national collections which were previously distributed between the Louvre, the Jeu de Paume and the Palais de Tokyo with the addition of new acquisitions. There are sections devoted to historical and portrait painting, Realism, Impressionism, the Second Empire, photography, the art and interior decoration of the Third Republic, Symbolism, Naturalism and Art Nouveau (open Tue., Wed., Fri. and Sat. 10 a.m.–6 p.m., Thu. 10 a.m.– 9.15 p.m., Sun. 9 a.m.–6 p.m.; opens at 9 a.m. in the summer).

*Impressionist paintings

Quai Voltaire

Beyond this Quai Voltaire, with its bouquinistes and antique-dealers, continues along the Seine, passing the Pont du Carrousel, and runs into Quai Malaquais, on which is the Ecole Nationale Supérieure des Beaux-Arts (National College of Art), which puts on periodic special exhibitions of modern art (building open Mon.–Fri. 8 a.m.–8 p.m.; closed Aug. and pub. hols.).

Institut de France

Farther along, at the Pont des Arts, is the Institut de France, an imposing building with a high dome which was erected to the design of Louis Le Vau in 1663–1672 at the expense of Cardinal Mazarin. Originally called the Collège Mazarin, and popularly known as the Collège des Quatre Nations, it was intended for the education of young people from the new French

St-Germain-des-Prés: Dupaty's figure of the Virgin

provinces of Roussillon, Pignerol, Flanders and Alsace. During the French Revolution it was used as a prison. Since 1805 it has been the home of various learned societies and the five French scholarly and scientific academies, including the Académie Française, founded by Cardinal Richelieu in 1635 to foster and cultivate the French language. The main feature of interest for visitors (tours Sat. and Sun. at 3 p.m.) is the Great Hall under the dome, in the vestibule of which is the tomb of Cardinal Mazarin (by Antoine Coysevox, 1689). The Bibliothèque Mazarine contains over 350,000 volumes. The three courtyards of the Institut provide an attractive means of access to Rue Mazarine.

Monnaie

Adjoining the Institut de France on the east is the Hôtel des Monnaies (1771–1775), or the Monnaie (Mint) for short. This was the first monumental building in Louis XVI style. The Musée de la Monnaie (open Tue. and Thu.–Sun. 1–6 p.m., Wed. 1–9 p.m.) has an interesting collection of French and foreign coins.

*St-Germain-des-Prés

From the Ecole National Supérieure des Beaux-Arts the Rue Bonaparte runs south to the 11th c. church of St-Germain-des-Prés (open daily 9 a.m.–8 p.m.), the oldest in Paris, built on the site of a still earlier church belonging to the famous abbey, founded in 543, of St-Germain "in the Fields" in which the Merovingian kings were buried. The present church, with interior painting (1850) in the style of the 11th c., contains a number of fine works of sculpture, including a figure of the Virgin (1822) by Dupaty, and tombs, among them that of the philosopher René Descartes (d. 1650).

Boulevard St-Germain

The south side of the church faces on to the Boulevard St-Germain, an avenue more than 3 km/2 miles long which was driven through older property in 1855–1856. Along the boulevard to the west are the Ministry of Public Works and the Ministry of Defence. The cafés round St-Germain-des-Prés have long been the haunt of Paris painters and intellectuals. The

"Deux Magots" was frequented by Jean-Paul Sartre and Simone de Beauvoir. The Café de Flore is the meeting-place of the younger generation of writers.

Rue Bonaparte, in which numerous art galleries rub shoulders with one another, runs into Place St-Sulpice, with the beautiful Fontaine des Orateurs Sacrés (1847), which is illuminated at night.

***St-Sulpice**

St-Sulpice (open daily 8 a.m.–7.30 p.m.), built between 1646 and 1745 on the site of an earlier church, was the work of no fewer than six architects. The façade, modelled on St Paul's in London, was built by Servandoni. During the Revolution, in 1792, the church became a "Temple of Victory". The spacious interior was the scene of a banquet in honour of the victorious General Bonaparte in 1799. The first chapel on the right has a number of frescoes by Eugène Delacroix (19th c.). The beautiful Rococo Lady Chapel behind the high altar contains a marble statue of the Virgin as Queen of Heaven by Jean-Baptiste Pigalle. The church has a very beautiful organ-loft of 1777; the organ itself was rebuilt in 1862 by Cavaillé-Coll.

*Lady Chapel

From Place St-Sulpice Rue Férou runs south into Paris's longest street, the Rue de Vaugirard, which extends south-west for almost 4.5 km/2¾ miles. A short distance along this street to the west is the Palais du Luxembourg (tours for groups only), built by Salomon de Brosse in 1620–1621 for Henry IV's widow Marie de Médicis. It is now the seat of the Senate, the second chamber of Parliament, which has 318 members elected to represent the French regions. Just beyond it is the old Théâtre de l'Odéon, built in 1779–1782, which was for long an annex of the Comédie Française (the Salle du Luxembourg) but is now the independent Théâtre de France.

Palais du Luxembourg

Théâtre de France

***Jardin du Luxembourg**

Behind the Palais du Luxembourg, to the south, extends the beautiful Jardin du Luxembourg, laid out in the 17th c. and replanned in the 19th. It is the finest and most popular park on the left bank of the Seine and the only surviving Renaissance garden in Paris, with numerous monuments and statues. The Fontaine de Médicis, picturesquely hidden under trees, recalls the former owner of the gardens, Marie de Médicis, mother of Louis XIII. Children are catered for by a play area and a very popular puppet theatre.

Fontaine de Médicis

The south gate of the Jardin du Luxembourg opens into the wide Avenue de l'Observatoire, which is laid out in gardens. At the south end of the gardens is the Fontaine des Quatre Parties du Monde (Fountain of the Four Parts of the World), an imposing bronze group by Carpeaux (1874), with the four parts of the world supporting an armillary sphere.

Fontaine des Quatre Parties du Monde

Farther south, beyond a statue of Marshal Ney (1853), who was shot here in 1815, is the Carrefour de l'Observatoire, the junction with the Boulevard du Montparnasse and Boulevard de Port-Royal. Beyond this is the Observatoire, built by Claude Perrault in 1667–1672, which stands on the Paris meridian (2°20'14" east of Greenwich). The shaft leading from the cellar 27 m/90 ft underground, with a constant temperature of 11.8°C/53.2°F, to the revolving dome 27 m/89 ft above the ground was used by the physicist Foucault for his experiments with the pendulum.

Montparnasse

From the Carrefour de l'Observatoire the Boulevard du Montparnasse runs north-east through the Montparnasse quarter, which in the 1920s and 1930s took over from Montmartre as the centre of Parisian artistic life. Matisse, Kandinsky and Chagall worked here, and it was the meeting-place of famous writers like Ernest Hemingway, Henry Miller, James Joyce, Jean-Paul Sartre and Simone de Beauvoir.

Between the Boulevard du Montparnasse and the Boulevard de Vaugirard is the Maine-Montparnasse complex developed during the 1970s, with huge blocks of offices and flats, including the gigantic 59-storey Tour Montparnasse (1974). From its open terrace at a height of 207 m/697 ft there are magnificent views over Paris (open 10 a.m.–10 p.m. in winter, 9 a.m.–11.30 p.m. in summer).

Tour Montparnasse

"Echelles du Baroque", by Ricardo Bofill

Gare Montparnasse

The Gare Montparnasse (trains to western and northern France), built in 1966–1969, replaced an older station on the Boulevard du Montparnasse. Further development is under way in preparation for the TGV, the French high-speed train; it includes a roofed-over garden which will provide a link between the Vaugirard and Plaisance districts.

Echelles du Baroque

The latest example of modern architecture in this part of Paris is the Echelles du Baroque complex (1986) in the Place de Séoul, designed by the Catalan architect Ricardo Bofill, whose reputation was established by his futuristic Palacio d'Abraxas in Marne-la-Vallée (1982) and the Belvédère de St-Christophe in Cergy-Pontoise (1985).

Cimetière du Montparnasse

A short distance south of the Boulevard du Montparnasse is the Montparnasse Cemetery (Cimetière du Montparnasse or Cimetière du Sud), the third of Paris's large cemeteries, established in 1824. Laid out on a regular plan, it has fewer notable graves than the Père-Lachaise and Montmartre cemeteries. Among those who are buried here are the poet Charles Baudelaire, the novelist Guy de Maupassant, the composer César Franck and the actress Jean Seberg. In the 20th section, to the right of the entrance, is the double tomb of Jean-Paul Sartre and Simone de Beauvoir.

Quartier Latin, Jardin des Plantes and Place d'Italie

***Quartier Latin**

To the east of the Palais du Luxembourg, between the Seine, the Gare d'Austerlitz and the Boulevard de Port-Royal, is the Quartier Latin (Latin Quarter), which ranks with the Ile de la Cité as one of the oldest parts of Paris and has since time immemorial been noted for its universities and learned institutions. The principal street of the Latin Quarter is the Boulevard St-Michel (familiarly known as the Boul' Mich'), one of Haussmann's great new avenues, running from the Carrefour de l'Observatoire to the Ile de la Cité. With its numerous shops, restaurants, brasseries, snack bars and souvenir shops, it is thronged with tourists all year round, and during the

The Boul' Mich': a popular meeting-place

university year (October–June) is a favourite meeting-place for students. In the little side streets there are numerous restaurants offering the cuisine of many different countries.

***Sorbonne**

Off the Boulevard St-Michel to the east is the main front, decorated with allegorical representations of the sciences, of the Sorbonne, now part of the University of Paris. Originally founded in 1253 by Robert de Sorbon, Louis IX's confessor, as a theological college, it later became the theological faculty of the University, which had been founded fifty years earlier, and played a leading part in French intellectual life. In 1470 the first printing press in France was established here. The present building dates from the time of Cardinal Richelieu (1624–1642), with extensive rebuilding and enlargement between 1885 and 1901. Since 1896 it has housed the faculty of philosophy and most of the faculty of mathematics and science, together with three state institutes not belonging to the University.
A notable feature of the interior is the Grand Amphithéâtre (which can seat 2700), with an allegorical painting by Puvis de Chavannes, "Le Bois Sacré" (the sacred grove of learning). On the first floor is the well-stocked Library.

Sorbonne

Eglise de la Sorbonne

In the centre of the complex of buildings is the Eglise de la Sorbonne (1636–1653), built by Jacques Lemercier for Cardinal Richelieu, with a dome which is a prominent Paris landmark. The north front, looking on to the Cour d'Honneur (Grand Courtyard), is particularly fine. The interior (for admission apply to the porter on the left of the main entrance) is bare and austere. In the south transept is the tomb of Cardinal Richelieu (1585–1642), the most important work (1694) of the sculptor F. Girardon.

Collège de France

To the east of the Sorbonne is the Collège de France, a college founded by Francis I in 1530 for the teaching of Latin, Greek and Hebrew which became a great centre of French humanism. The present building dates from 1610 but has been considerably enlarged over the centuries. Here public lectures are given in all fields of knowledge.

***Panthéon**

Just south of the Sorbonne is Rue Soufflot, which runs east to the Panthéon, situated on the Montagne de Ste-Geneviève, the highest point in the old part of the town on the left bank. The site was originally occupied by an earlier church built over the grave of St Genevieve (422–512). The present building, erected between 1764 and 1790 to the design of Jacques-Germain Soufflot in fulfilment of a vow made by Louis XV, was also dedicated to St Genevieve, but in 1791, by decision of the National Assembly, became a Pantheon for the burial of France's great men, and thereafter was used for worship only for brief periods between 1806 and 1830 and again between 1851 and 1885. On the pediment of the porch, which is borne by 22 Corinthian columns, is a famous bas-relief by David d'Angers (1831–1837), "France distributing garlands to her great sons".

*Frescoes

The interior of the Panthéon (open daily 10 a.m.–4.45 p.m. Oct.–Mar., 10 a.m.–6.15 p.m. Apr.–Sept.; admission charge) is decorated with frescoes on the life of St Genevieve. Notable among them are the "Childhood of St Genevieve" (1877) in the south aisle and "St Genevieve watching over the besieged city of Paris and bringing food to its people" (1898) on the north side of the choir, both by Puvis de Chavannes.

Dome

In the north transept are stairs leading up to the dome (425 steps to the lantern), from which there are extensive views. At the north-east corner of the choir is the entrance to the crypt (conducted visits), with the tombs of Mirabeau, Rousseau, Voltaire, the architect J.-G. Soufflot, the writers Victor Hugo and Emile Zola, the mathematician Gaspard Monge, the Resistance fighter Jean Moulin and other famous Frenchmen.
To the north of the Panthéon, at 10 Place du Panthéon, is the Bibliothèque Ste-Geneviève, founded in 1624 (open Mon.–Sat. 10 a.m.–10 p.m.).

***St-Etienne-du-Mont**

Behind the Panthéon, to the north-east, is the church of St-Etienne-du-Mont (15th–16th c.), which is Late Gothic in general plan but shows strong Renaissance influence. During the Revolution it became a "Temple of Filial Love". Notable features of the interior, in which Pascal and Racine are buried, are the rood screen (1525–1535; central section of marble), with rich Renaissance decoration, the pulpit (1640) and the fine 16th c. stained glass in the south aisle. In the second chapel on the right in the ambulatory is a richly ornamented modern reliquary containing part of St Genevieve's original sarcophagus. In the old charnel-house (reached from the choir) are twelve stained glass windows of 1612–1622 (open Mon.–Sat. 8 a.m.–noon and 2.30–5.30 p.m., Sun. 3–6 p.m.).

*Rood screen

Val-de-Grâce

In Rue St-Jacques, 1 km/¾ mile south of the Sorbonne, is the church of Val-de-Grâce, with a magnificent dome. It was originally built in 1645 by François Mansart for the adjoining Benedictine convent (which has been a military hospital since 1793); work was continued by Lemercier and completed by Le Duc in 1665.

****Musée des Thermes et de l'Hôtel de Cluny**

North of the Sorbonne, adjoining the imposing ruins of the Roman baths (thermes), is the Hôtel de Cluny, an elegant Late Gothic building erected in 1480–1510 on the site of a residence of the abbots of Cluny, which now houses one of Paris's finest museums, devoted to medieval art and culture. The museum (open Mon. and Wed.–Sun. 9.30 a.m.–5.15 p.m.) was founded in 1833 to house a collection of medieval and Renaissance objects assembled by the antiquary Alexandre du Sommerard, and its 24 rooms offer a magnificent survey of medieval European applied and decorative art. In addition to fine examples of wood and stone sculpture, valuable examples of goldsmith's work, bronzes, enamels, ivories, old textiles and embroidery and French, Italian and Hispano-Mauresque faience (mainly 15th–18th c.) it is particularly notable for its fine French and Brussels tapestries.

*Tapestries

*Tapisseries de la Dame à la Licorne

The famous Tapisseries de la Dame à la Licorne ("Lady with the Unicorn") of about 1500 from the château of Boussac in the département of Creuse

Roman baths in the Cluny Museum

(Room XI, on first floor) represent the five senses, alluding to the medieval legend of the unicorn that could be tamed only by a pure maiden. In the chapel are French tapestries from Auxerre (*c.* 1500) on the life of St Stephen and the finding of his relics.

*Altar frontal

*Chapel

On the rear wall of Room XIX (first floor) is a fine gold altar frontal from Basle Cathedral, probably Lombard work, presented by the German Emperor Henry II (d. 1024). The Late Gothic chapel on the first floor has richly ornamented altar canopies.

*Roman baths

Within and around the museum, facing on to the Boulevard St-Michel, are remains of Roman baths, including a vaulted frigidarium (cold bath).

*St-Sévérin

Farther north, at the end of Rue St-Jacques, is St-Sévérin, Paris's finest Late Gothic church, mostly dating from the 15th c., with delicate fan vaulting, 15th–16th c. stained glass and modern stained glass windows in the choir (by Jean Bazaine, 1966).

St-Julien-le-Pauvre

East of this is the Early Gothic church of St-Julien-le-Pauvre (altered in 1651), in which Rectors of the Sorbonne were elected until the 16th c. Since 1889 it has been a Greek Catholic (Uniate) church.

*Institut du Monde Arabe

St-Julien lies close to the banks of the Seine. From here Quai Montebello and Quai de la Tournelle run south-east to the junction with the Boulevard St-Germain, opposite the Pont de Sully. Here stands the Institut du Monde Arabe (by Jean Nouvel, 1987), an Arab cultural institute (open Tue.–Sun. 1–8 p.m.). This imposing glass structure with its filigree-pattern ornament consists of two parallel nine-storey blocks, with a book tower, a library, lecture rooms and a museum. A feature of the architecture is the square full-height windows on the south front, with ornamental openwork metal screens. From the restaurant terrace on the roof there is a magnificent view of the city centre.

St-Sévérin

Faculté des Sciences
*Jardin des Plantes

Immediately adjoining is the massive complex of the Faculty of Science (Universités Paris VI, Paris VII and P. et M. Curie), built in the 1960s on the site of the old Halle aux Vins. Just beyond this is the Jardin des Plantes (open daily 8 a.m.–5.30 p.m. in winter, 8 a.m.–6 p.m. in summer), originally laid out in 1635 as a "physic garden", which in 1793, with the addition of a zoological section, became the National Museum of Natural History. The gardens, with a total area of over 28 hectares/70 acres, consist of a botanical section (the Jardin Botanique; admission free) with over 10,000 species of plants and Paris's oldest tree, a false acacia (robinia), and a section for live animals, with a menagerie, an aquarium and a vivarium (open daily 9 a.m.–5 p.m. in winter, 9 a.m.–6 p.m. in summer; admission charge), together with a number of buildings housing large scientific collections (including mineralogy and palaeontology) which are internationally famed (library, laboratories and lecture rooms; open Mon. and Wed.–Sun. 1.30–5 p.m.).

Museum National d'Histoire Naturelle

Gare d'Austerlitz

Opposite the south-east corner of the Jardin des Plantes, on the Boulevard de l'Hôpital, which leads to the Place d'Italie, is the Gare d'Austerlitz (also called the Gare d'Orléans; trains to Orléans and south-western France).

Viaduc du Métro/ Pont d'Austerlitz

To the east of the station is the Viaduc du Métro, which crosses the Seine at a height of 30 m/100 ft; to the north the Pont d'Austerlitz, built in 1804–1806 and since widened.

*Pavillon de l'Arsenal

On the opposite side of the Seine, at 21 Boulevard Morland, is the Pavillon de l'Arsenal (opened in December 1988), a museum on the history of Paris (open Tue.–Sat. 10.30 a.m.–6.30 p.m., Sun. 11 a.m.–7 p.m.; documentation centre and photographic library Tue.–Sat. 3–6 p.m.). Among the exhibits is a large plan of the city (40 sq. m/430 sq. ft) on the scale of 1:2000.

Hôpital de la Salpêtrière

Immediately south of the Gare d'Austerlitz, on the Boulevard de l'Hôpital, is the extensive area occupied by the Hôpital de la Salpêtrière, built in 1657 on

Institut du Monde Arabe, south front

the site of an old arsenal *(salpêtrière)*, with a large domed church similar in structure to the Dôme des Invalides.

*Arènes de Lutèce

North-west of the Jardin des Plantes are the Arènes de Lutèce (open daily 10 a.m.–5.30 p.m. in winter, 10 a.m.–8.30 p.m. in summer; admission free), the remains of a Roman amphitheatre of the 2nd or 3rd c. A.D., which originally had seating for 17,000 spectators.

*Mosque

South of this, at the west end of the Jardin des Plantes (2 Place du Puits-de-l'Ermite), is a complex of buildings in Moorish style, including a mosque. The first mosque built in France (1922–1926), it is based on Moroccan models, with a 33 m/108 ft high minaret (conducted tours daily except Fri. and holy days 10 a.m.–12 noon and 2–6.30 p.m.).
Behind the mosque, in Rue Daubenton and Rue Geoffroy-St-Hilaire, are a Turkish bath (hammam), a Moorish café, an Arab restaurant and a bazaar selling North African and Oriental goods.

St-Médard

To the south-west, near the north end of the wide Avenue des Gobelins, is the Late Gothic church of St-Médard (15th–16th c.).

*Manufacture Nationale des Gobelins

In the Avenue des Goblins (No. 42) are the unpretentious premises of the famous Gobelins tapestry factory, founded by Henry IV in 1601 and later transferred to the workshops of a family of dyers named Gobelin. The factory, which was headed in the 17th c. by the painter Charles Lebrun (1619–1690), created a new form of court art, with such masterpieces as the four tapestries in the Queen's Antechamber in the Palace of Versailles and the "Lady with the Unicorn" now in the Musée des Thermes et de l' Hôtel de Cluny. A visit to the workshops (conducted tours Tue.–Thu. at 2 and 3 p.m.) and the museum is an interesting experience. The museum puts on periodic special exhibitions of French, Flemish, Italian and other tapestries from its rich resources.

Place d'Italie
*European Film Centre

At the south end of the Avenue des Gobelins is the circular Place d'Italie with a fountain. Here in January 1989 the foundation stone of a new European Film Centre (architect Kenzo Tange) was laid. Due for completion in 1993, the centre will have a cinema with seating for 800 and a huge screen measuring 20 m/66 ft by 10 m/33 ft, two smaller cinemas each seating 150 and other audiovisual facilities.

Parks in the Outer Districts

***Bois de Boulogne**

From the Place de-Gaulle the Avenue Foch runs south-west to the Porte Dauphine, the main entrance to the Bois de Boulogne, one of Europe's most beautiful public parks. The park, usually known simply as the Bois, has an area of over 845 hectares/2088 acres and is bounded on the east by the line of the old fortifications, on the west by the Seine and on the south and north by the suburbs of Boulogne and Neuilly. It is a relic of the old forest of Rouvray (from Latin *roveretum,* oak forest) which once covered the whole Seine peninsula. For long an area of waste land, it was acquired by the city in 1853 and laid out as a park in the English style. It is traversed by wide roads and a network of footpaths, and with its seven lakes, its waterfalls (particularly the Grande Cascade), an open-air theatre and two racecourses is one of Paris most popular recreation areas.

Near the eastern boundary of the Bois are two elongated artificial lakes, the Lac Inférieur (with two islands) and the Lac Supérieur, on which boats can be hired. The Auteuil racecourse (Hippodrome d'Auteuil), near the Lac Supérieur, is used only for steeplechasing. From the Butte Mortemart, an artificial mound at the west end of the racecourse, there are attractive views.

Hippodrome d'Auteuil

*Hippodrome de Longchamp

The Longchamp racecourse (Hippodrome de Longchamp: flat racing), on the south-western border of the Bois, is one of the most celebrated and fashionable racecourses in the world, which can accommodate 10,000 racegoers.

*Parc de Bagatelle

At the north-west corner of the Bois, set in 24 hectares/60 acres of English-style gardens, is the little château of Bagatelle, built in 1777 by the Comte d'Artois (later Charles X) in 66 days for a wager and acquired by the city of Paris in 1905. It has a famous rose-garden with 2650 varieties of rose (open daily 9 a.m.–6 p.m.; admission charge), in which an international rose show, Les Roseraies, is held annually in June.

Jardin d'Acclimatation

The north-west corner of the Bois is occupied by the Jardin d'Acclimatation (10 hectares/25 acres), established in 1854 to promote the introduction of foreign animals and plants. It is now a popular amusement park, with an open-air theatre, a miniature farm, a motorcycle track, roundabouts, mini-golf, a paddling pool, restaurants and a large childrens' play area (open daily 10 a.m.–6 p.m.).

Musée National des Arts et Traditions Populaires

At 6 Avenue du Mahatma-Gandhi is the National Folk Museum (open Mon. and Wed.–Sun. 9.45 a.m.–5.15 p.m.), devoted to French folk art, crafts and agriculture.

Parc de Montsouris
Meteorological Station

On the south side of the city, in Boulevard Jourdan, is the Parc de Montsouris (15 hectares/38 acres), opened in 1878. Situated on a hill, surrounded by a small lake, is the Meteorological Station of the City of Paris, housed in a copy of the Bey of Tunis's palace.

Cité Universitaire Internationale

To the south of the park, beyond the Boulevard Jourdan, is the Cité Universitaire Internationale, founded in 1922, with students' residences.

***Bois de Vincennes**

On the south-eastern outskirts of Paris, on both sides of the wide Avenue Daumesnil, is the Bois de Vincennes, laid out in its present form in 1860–1867. With an area of 995 hectares/2459 acres) it is Paris's largest park, vying with the Bois de Boulogne in the beauty of its scenery.

Musée des Arts d'Afrique et d'Océanie

At the main entrance (293 Avenue Daumesnil) is the Museum of African and Oceanian Art (open Mon. and Wed.–Fri. 10 a.m.–12 noon and 1.30–5.30 p.m., Sat. and Sun. 12.30–6 p.m.), housed in a building erected in 1931 for a colonial exhibition. It has a large collection of material from the Maghreb, Africa and Oceania, including weapons, jewellery, pottery and paintings. South of this is the romantic Lac Daumesnil or Lac de Charenton with two islands, and on the north-east side of the lake is the Zoological Garden, one of Europe's leading zoos, in which many species of wild animals, both native and foreign, live in open enclosures (open daily 9 a.m.–5.30 p.m.; to 6 p.m. in summer).
1 km/¾ mile east of the Zoo is the former Centre Universitaire, built in 1968, whose teaching activities were transferred to St-Denis in 1980.

*Château de Vincennes

On the northern edge of the park, at the end of the Avenue Daumesnil and on the southern fringe of the suburb of Vincennes (pop. 42,000), is the Château de Vincennes (or Fort de Vincennes; admission charge). It has a long history going back to the 14th c., when Philip VI and Charles V built a massive stronghold which until the 16th c. was a favourite residence of the French kings. Most of it is now a barracks. In the courtyard (entered from the north side of the castle), on the right, is the formidable Donjon (Keep), 52 m/170 ft high, frequently used in the past as a state prison and now occupied by a museum illustrating the history of the castle (open Mon. and Wed.–Sun. 10 a.m.–5 p.m. in winter, to 6 p.m. in summer; conducted tour, which includes the chapel). Also in the courtyard, to the left, is the Chapel (1387–1552), which was modelled on the Sainte Chapelle on the Ile de la Cité and has fine 16th c. stained glass. In the south-east and south-west corners of the courtyard are the Pavillon du Roi and Pavillon de la Reine, built by Le Vau in 1654–1659 and restored after a fire in 1944. Other features of interest are the apartments of the royal family, the treasury and the collection of arms and armour.

***Cimetière du Père-Lachaise**

In eastern Paris, on the Boulevard de Ménilmontant (main entrance), is the Cimetière du Père-Lachaise (Cimetière de l'Est), the largest and most celebrated of Paris's three principal cemeteries, established in 1804 and named after Louis XIV's confessor.

Monument aux Morts

*Famous tombs

At the end of the main avenue is the Monument aux Morts (by Albert Bartholomé, 1891–1899). Bartholomé himself is buried at the near end of the path leading to the monument. To the south of the monument are the tombs of the composers Luigi Cherubini (1760–1842) and Frédéric Chopin (1810–1839). A short distance to the north-east is the cemetery chapel, and on the right of this is a smaller chapel with the tomb of the statesman Adolphe Thiers (1797–1877). To the north is the novelist Honoré de Balzac (1799–1850), and 150 m north-west the composer Georges Bizet (1838–1875). South-east of the cemetery chapel are the empty tombs of La Fontaine (1621–1695) and Molière (1622–1673). Near the east side of the cemetery is the grave of Oscar Wilde (1856–1900). Among recent celebrities buried in Père-Lachaise are the singer Edith Piaf, the rock idol Jim Morrison and the actress Simone Signoret. At the south-east corner of the cemetery are four memorials to victims of Nazi concentration camps.

***La Villette**

In north-eastern Paris is the Parc de la Villette, a new leisure park with a cultural emphasis which was laid out in 1984–1991 to the design of Bernard Tschumi (illustration, page 398).

**Cité des Sciences et de l'Industrie

The Cité des Sciences et de l'Industrie, opened in 1986, is designed to make science and technology accessible to all and to illustrate the development of science in France and the results of the latest research. Among the most important elements in the Cité are the "Explora" permanent exhibition on technology and communication, the Médiathèque (a scientific documentation centre), the "Cité des Enfants", in which children are encouraged to become familiar with science and technology by observation and practical

Paris
Parc de la Villette

experiments, an aquarium and a very fine Planetarium (open daily except Tue. 10 a.m.–6 p.m.).

*Géode

The Géode is a spherical cinema of futuristic aspect, which shows specially produced documentary films (on the hour from 10 a.m.–8 p.m.) on a huge hemispherical screen with an area of 1000 sq. m/11,000 sq.ft.

"Argonaute"

Permanently moored alongside the Géode, after circling the globe ten times, is the fighter submarine "Argonaute" (conducted tours).

Grande Halle

The wrought-iron Grande Halle (1867), formerly the Halle aux Bœufs (Cattle Market), at the Avenue Jean-Jaurès entrance, is used for exhibitions, concerts and other cultural events.

Théâtre Paris-Villette

Next to this is the Théâtre Paris-Villette, with seating for 300, which specialises in plays by contemporary authors.

*Cité de la Musique

On the other side of the Grande Hall is the Cité de la Musique (architect Christian de Portzamparc), opened in 1989, which houses the Conservatoire. A new concert hall with seating for 1200 and additional function

Pavilion and the Géode spherical cinema in front of the Museum of Technology

rooms came into use in 1990. The Musée de la Musique (transferred here from Rue de Madrid) displays more than 4000 musical instruments of all periods.

Zénith

The Zénith concert hall on the east side of the park, designed by Philippe Chaix and Jean-Paul Morel, is mainly used for rock concerts and variety performances.

*Parc des Buttes-Chaumont

In the northern working-class district of Buttes-Chaumont (19th arrondissement) is the Parc des Buttes-Chaumont, laid out by Haussmann in 1864–1867 in an old quarry. In the centre of the park, on a crag (88 m/289 ft) surrounded by a lake and approached by two bridges, is a miniature temple, from which there are wide views of Montmartre and the St-Denis plain. There are even better views from another hill (101 m/331 ft) at the south end of the park, with a café and a restaurant.

*Parc Monceau

The Parc Monceau, on the Boulevard de Courcelles (17th arrondissement), was laid out in 1778 by Philippe, Duc d'Orléans, as a rendezvous for fashionable society, but was halved in size in 1861. With its palms and Asian conifers and its clumps of evergreen trees with silver or coloured foliage it has a very special charm of its own. Near the main entrance is a characteristic feature of 18th c. garden design – the "Naumachie", a lake surrounded by a ruined colonnade.

*Musée Nissim de Camondo

At 63 rue de Monceau is the Musée Nissim de Camondo (open Wed.–Sun. 10 a.m.–12 noon and 2–5 p.m.), a branch of the Museum of Decorative Art. The house, built by Comte Moïse de Camondo in 1911–1914, displays his very fine collection of 18th c. furniture, sculpture, pictures and tapestries.

Surroundings of Paris

The area round Paris offers so much scenic beauty and so much of artistic and historical interest that it is possible to refer here only to a few of the major features. For other possible excursions – e.g. to Beauvais or Soissons Cathedral, the Château de Chantilly with the Musée Condé, Maisons-Laffitte, the Château and Forest of Compiègne, the Tour de César in Provins or the Palace of Fontainebleau – see the entry for the Ile de France.

Meudon

Some 9 km/6 miles south-west of the city centre – an attractive trip on one of the Seine boats in good weather – is the suburb of Meudon (pop. 45,000), rising in terraces above the left bank of the Seine, once the residence of famous artists, politicians and musicians. Ronsard and Rabelais lived here, and in later centuries Balzac and Céline. Wagner composed his "Flying Dutchman" in 1841 at 27 Avenue du Château. Hans Arp lived in Meudon from 1926 to 1941.

*Terrasse de Meudon

Above the west side of the old town, which has a beautiful church of the 16th and 18th centuries, is the Terrasse de Meudon (open until dusk), which affords beautiful views of the Seine valley and Paris. At the south-west end of the terrace, in the Château de Meudon (which was destroyed in 1871 and later rebuilt), is an astrophysical laboratory. From the west end of the terrace a flight of iron steps leads up to the park of the château, in the Bois de Meudon, a favourite weekend resort of Parisians with its romantic little lakes (Etang de Villebon, Etang de Trivaux, etc.).

Bois de Meudon

*Villa des Brillants,

Musée Rodin

On the north-eastern outskirts of Meudon is the Villa des Brillants, in which the great sculptor Auguste Rodin spent the last twenty years of his life. He is buried in the park, along with his lifetime companion Rose Beuret. The Rodin Museum (open Wed.–Mon. 10 a.m.–5 p.m.) contains sketches, preliminary models and casts of his works, including his figures of Balzac (1891) and Victor Hugo (1890) and his "Gate of Hell" (1880).

Musée de Meudon

The Meudon Museum, in a house at 11 rue des Pierres which belonged to Molière's wife Armande Béjart, has exhibits illustrating the history of the Château de Meudon and interesting mementoes of prominent inhabitants of the town, including Wagner, Courbet and Rodin.

Bellevue

North-west of Meudon, on a terrace above the Seine, is the villa suburb of Bellevue. The sumptuous château built here in the mid 18th c. for Louis XV's favourite Madame de Pompadour, fell victim to the Revolution.

Sèvres

*Porcelain factory

Musée de Céramique

North of the Bois de Meudon, on the left bank of the Seine, is the suburb of Sèvres (pop. 22,000). On the north side of its Grande Rue, near the bridge over the Seine, is the famous porcelain factory, founded at Vincennes in 1723, moved to Sèvres in 1738 and installed in its present premises in 1876 (conducted tours on 1st and 3rd Thu. in month 2–3.30 p.m.; closed July and Aug.). On the ground and first floors is the Musée National de Céramique, founded by Alexandre Brongniart in 1824 (open Wed.–Mon. 10 a.m.–5.15 p.m.), with a rich collection which includes painted pottery, Oriental ceramics, faience and an extensive range of porcelain; one particularly notable item is the 3.15 m/10 ft high Neptune Vase (1867).

St-Cloud

Upstream from Sèvres, still on the left bank of the Seine, is the beautifully situated suburb of St-Cloud (pop. 28,500), with the headquarters of Interpol, established here in 1967. On a plateau between St-Cloud and Sèvres is the Parc de St-Cloud, laid out by André Le Notre in the 17th c. On a terrace at the east end is the "Lanterne de Diogène", from which there is a magnificent view of Paris and the Seine basin. A short distance north are the fountains and waterfalls of the Grande Cascade (1734) and a fountain called the Grand Jet, which on certain Sundays (alternating with Versailles) projects its water to a height of 42 m/140 ft. To the south-east, below the terrace, is the Pavillon de Breteuil, now housing the International Bureau of Weights and Measures, which keeps the standard measures (in platinum) of the metre and the kilogram (not open to the public).

Boulogne-Billancourt

From St-Cloud the Pont de St-Cloud crosses the Seine into the industrial suburb of Boulogne, which along with Billancourt has a population of 102,000. On the Quai du Quatre-Septembre beyond the bridge is the entrance to the Jardins Albert-Kahn (open 9.20–noon and 2–6 p.m.; closed in winter), laid out by the banker of that name at the beginning of the 20th c., with examples of different types of garden; the Japanese garden in the south-west part is particularly attractive.

Le Corbusier buildings

In this area are three houses designed by Le Corbusier: the privately owned Maison Lipchitz (9 Allée des Pins; 1924), the neighbouring Maison Miestchaninoff (also 1924) and the Maison Cook (6 rue Denfert-Rochereau; 1926).

Rueil-Malmaison
*Château de Malmaison

5 km/3 miles north-west of St-Cloud is the suburb of Rueil-Malmaison (pop. 66,500), with the Château de Malmaison, built in the early 17th c. and enlarged in 1799. The château, which now belongs to the State, was a favourite residence of Napoleon in 1803–1804, when he was First Consul, and from 1809 to 1814 was the home of Napoleon's divorced wife Joséphine. From 1861 it was also a favourite residence of the Empress Eugénie, wife of Napoleon III. The house is now a museum (open Wed.–Mon. 10 a.m.–12.30 p.m. and 1.30–5.30 p.m.; in winter only to 5 p.m.), decorated and furnished as it was in the time of Joséphine. Visitors are also shown Napoleon's library.

Château de Bois-Préau

The Château de Bois-Préau, which also belonged to Joséphine (open same hours as Malmaison), displays relics of Napoleon's period of exile on St Helena, documents on the Napoleonic legend and mementoes of Napoleon's son the King of Rome (including his cradle).

St-Germain-en-Laye

From Rueil-Malmaison the road from Paris runs south-west, passing close to the château, and soon comes to the Seine. 9 km/6 miles from Rueil is the beautifully situated suburb of St-Germain-en-Laye (pop. 40,000), which from the 12th c. onwards was a favourite summer residence of the French kings. On the east side of the town, near the railway station, is the Château de St-Germain-en-Laye, built in the mid 16th c. to the design of Pierre Chambiges (the Château Vieux) and Philibert Delorme (the Château Neuf). The Gothic chapel survives from the Château's medieval predecessor, a castle built in 1230–1238, during the reign of Louis IX (St Louis) and destroyed during the Hundred Years' War. The treaty of St-Germain between the Allied powers and Austria was signed in the Château on September 10th 1919.

*Musée des Antiquités Nationales

A Renaissance wing of the Château, renovated in the reign of Louis XIV and again in the 19th c., now houses the Musée des Antiquités Nationales (open Wed.–Mon. 9.45–12 noon and 1.30–5.15 p.m.), one of the largest collections of prehistoric and early historical antiquities from all parts of France, which gives a comprehensive survey of Gallic, Gallo-Roman and Frankish culture down to the time of Charlemagne.

*Terrace

A walk through the beautiful park leads to the famous Terrace laid out by Le Nôtre, which runs high above the Seine for 2.4 km/1½ miles along the edge of the magnificent Forest of St-Germain, offering outstanding views of the wide park-like plain below.

Musée Départemental du Prieuré

At 2 rue St.-Denis is the Musée du Prieuré (open Tue. and Wed. 10 a.m.–5 p.m., Sat. and Sun. 10 a.m.–6.30 p.m.), with a collection of works by the "Nabis", the group of painters and sculptors associated with Paul Gauguin.

*Mirapolis

A few kilometres west of the suburb of Cergy-Pontoise (A15 to Pontoise, then from exit 13 follow signposts) is the leisure park of Mirapolis, opened in 1987. Above the park towers a 35 m/115 ft high concrete figure of Rabelais' gluttonous giant Gargantua, his belly and limbs housing a restaurant and various boutiques. There are more than 36 attractions in the park, including a Time Machine, King Arthur's Round Table, an Enchanted Castle and Shooting the Rapids.

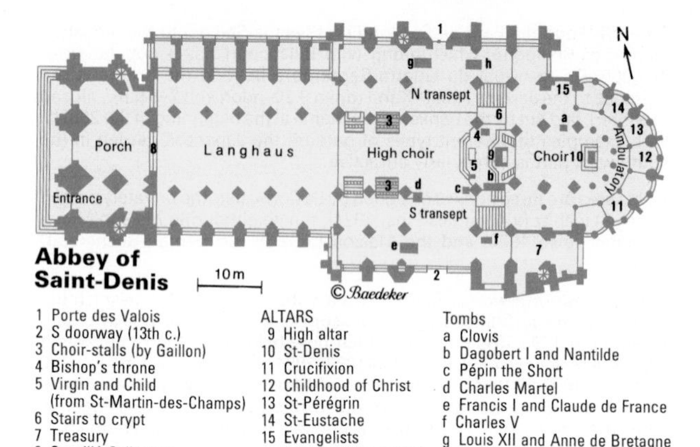

St-Denis

Some 10 km/6 miles north of central Paris, on the road to Chantilly and Compiègne, is the industrial town of St-Denis, with a population of 900,000.

* Cathedral

On the east side of the town is the Cathedral of St-Denis (open daily 10 a.m.–7 p.m.; in winter only to 5 p.m.), begun in 1137 and substantially completed by the end of the 13th c., on the site of a 5th c. church and abbey built over the grave of St Denis (Dionysius). This was the first monumental Gothic structure to be built in France, still showing some Romanesque features (e.g. on the west front). After Louis IX (St Louis) had built the first monumental royal tombs in the choir in honour of his ancestors the church became the burial place of all the French kings and of princes and other great persons. During the French Revolution, in 1793, the church and the tombs it contained were devastated, and attempts at restoration were ill-fated. Only when Viollet-le-Duc took over responsibility for the work in 1847 was the venerable old building restored to its former splendour. The interior is impressive with its tall columns and high windows (mostly modern).

* Tombs of Louis XII and Henry II

* Statue of Queen Nantilde

Of the numerous tombs (now empty) in the choir the most notable are the following: in the north transept the tomb (*c.* 1517–1531) of Louis XII (d. 1515) and his wife Anne de Bretagne (d. 1514) and the tomb (1573) of Henry II (d. 1559) and his wife Catherine de Médicis (d. 1589), with a smaller and simpler monument adjoining, and to the right of the high altar the 13th c. tomb of Dagobert I, with a statue of Queen Nantilde; nearby is a 12th c. painted Virgin.

The former abbey adjoining the church, a large complex built in the 18th c., has been since 1809 a girls' boarding school for daughters and other relatives of members of the Légion d'Honneur.

Musée d'Art et d'Histoire

This Museum, housed in a former Carmelite convent at 22 bis rue Gabriel-Péri (open Mon. and Wed.–Sat. 10 a.m.–5.30 p.m., Sun. 2–6.30 p.m.), displays mementoes of the Carmelite order, relics of the Paris Commune of 1871, archaeological finds and works of modern art.

* **Euro Disneyland**

Opened in 1992 and covering an area of nearly 2000 hectares/50,000 acres, Euro Disneyland – based on Disneyland in the USA – lies in Marne-la-Vallée, on the A4 32 km/20 miles east of Paris. It is divided in five main sections offering different kinds of amusements and space adventures, including Mainstreet USA, Frontierland, Adventureland, Fantasyland and Discoveryland. There are hotels of all categories, camp sites, restaurants and an 18-hole golf course.

Ecouen

See Ile de France.

*Parc Astérix

38 km/24 miles north of Paris the A1 motorway comes to the signpost to Parc Astérix (open April to October only), a leisure park opened in 1989, with five different magical worlds – the busy Via Antiqua, the Gallic village, with the houses of Astérix and his friend Obélix, the Roman town, with the "Ave Caesar" roundabout, the Dolphinarium and the Route de Paris, which covers a thousand years of history, down to the beginning of the cinema age, in a mere 200 m/220 yd.

**Versailles

See entry

Pau

See Pyrenees

Périgord

H/I 9/10

Situation and *characteristics

Périgord is a historical region in south-western France, on the western fringe of the Massif Central, which corresponds broadly to the present-day département of Dordogne, with an area of 9060 sq. km/3500 sq. miles and a population of around 390,000. Its chief town is Périgueux (see entry).

Périgord has a varied landscape with many forests and a generally mild climate. Numerous caves with prehistoric rock paintings bear witness to long-vanished cultures; fortified castles and towns are reminders of a warlike past, and picturesque country houses, churches and abbeys attract many visitors.

Quercy

To the east is the old historical region of Quercy, a less fertile limestone plateau with the extraordinary karstic terrain of the Causse de Gramat in the north.

In Périgord

Geographically there are four different Périgords – Périgord Blanc (White Périgord), the central plateau region through which the rivers Auvézère and Isle flow; Périgord Noir (Black Périgord) dominated by the valleys of the Vézère and Dordogne; Périgord Pourpre (Purple Périgord) the area around Bergerac to the south-east; and Périgord Vert (Green Périgord) the rolling hills to the north. Roughly a quarter of Périgord is covered with coniferous and deciduous woodland, the chestnut forests having a particular charm of their own.

Economy

Périgord is mainly an agricultural region. It is noted particularly for its truffles, which are found and dug out of the ground with the help of specially trained pigs. The truffle is an edible fungus of tuberous appearance, either light or dark in colour, which grows about 10 cm/4 in. under the ground in a kind of symbiotic relationship with the roots of oak-trees.

History

Few areas in France have such early traces of human occupation as Périgord. The Vézère valley in particular is rich in Palaeolithic sites. Much evidence of prehistoric settlement has been found, in the form of the ashes of fires, art objects, stone axes, human remains and realistic and symbolic cave paintings and engravings, dating from the time of Cro-Magnon Man, who lived in this area.
In historical times Périgord was occupied by a Celtic tribe, the Petrocorii, and the adjoining region of Quercy by the Cadurci; in the reign of Augustus both areas were part of the province of Aquitania. The Romans introduced walnut and chestnut trees and vines. For centuries this was a frontier territory fiercely contested between England and France, until it was finally united with France in 1607. The French Revolution left Périgord with its old boundaries almost intact in the new département of Dordogne.

Sights of Périgord

Bergerac

The busy little town of Bergerac (pop. 27,700), chief town of southern Périgord, lies on the Dordogne south-west of Périgueux and is a tobacco-manufacturing and winemaking town. Its most interesting features are the Musée du Tabac (Tobacco Museum) in the Maison Peyrarède and the Musée du Vin (Wine Museum) in the Cloître des Récollets (Cloister of Recollect Friars), but the old part of the town and the harbour quarter are also worth seeing.

Monbazillac

South of Bergerac is the 16th c. château of Monbazillac, surrounded by vineyards and containing a small museum.

Beynac-et-Cazenac

This little village (pop. 460) is picturesquely situated at the foot of a crag falling steeply down to the river which is topped by a 12th c. castle. In spite of its strength the castle was taken by Richard Cœur-de-Lion and Simon de Montfort. After being recovered by the French in the 14th and 15th centuries it was rebuilt and enlarged. From the wall-walk there are fine views of the valley. The church of Beynac, originally the castle chapel, dates from the 15th c., as does the church at Cazenac, 3 km/2 miles west.

Bonaguil

The castle of Bonaguil (1520), on a ridge of a hill, is a fine example of the medieval art of fortification.

Brantôme

Brantôme (pop. 2100), in the beautiful Dromme valley, has an abbey which was founded in 769, in the reign of Charlemagne, rebuilt in the 11th c. and altered in the 19th. In the nearby Château de Richemont (16th c.) Pierre de Bourdeille, Seigneur de Brantôme, wrote his "Vies des Dames Galantes". The oldest part of the abbey is the free-standing bell-tower of the church (11th c.), which stands on a rocky crag. The abbey now houses the Musée Fernand-Desmoulin, with works by the artist of that name (born in Périgord in 1835) and archaeological finds from the surrounding area.

Préhisto-Parc, Tursac

Cadouin

Cadouin Abbey was founded by Robert d'Arbrissel in 1115, and during the Middle Ages was a popular place of pilgrimage. The church was consecrated in 1154; the cloister was begun in the late 15th c. in Flamboyant style and completed, with some Renaissance features, in the mid 16th c.

Cahors

See Lot Valley

Domme

*View

Domme (pop. 900), beautifully situated on a hill which falls steeply down to the Dordogne, has preserved much of its old circuit of walls (13th c.); a walk round them affords magnificent views. In the Place de la Halle are a 17th c. market hall and the 16th c. Maison des Gouverneurs. Under the town is an interesting stalactitic cave (entrance in market hall) which provided shelter for the population during the wars of religion.

River Dordogne

See Limousin

Les Eyzies-de-Tayac

Les Eyzies (pop. 850), situated at the junction of the Beune with the Vézère, is a good base from which to visit the prehistoric sites of Périgord. In this area were found the first drawing of a mammoth and the 30,000-year-old skeleton of Cro-Magnon Man, named after the find-spot.
Within easy reach of Les Eyzies are the Grotte du Grand Roc, Cro-Magnon and several other caves and prehistoric sites.

*Musée National de Préhistoire

There are large collections of prehistoric material in the National Museum of Prehistory in the old castle of the Barons of Beynac and the Museum of Speleology in the Rocher de Tayac.

*Drawings of animals

Wonderfully preserved prehistoric drawings of animals (painted and engraved) can be seen in the Grottes des Eyzies, the Grotte des Combarelles, the Grotte de la Mouthe and above all in the Grotte de Font-de-Gaume.

Préhisto-Parc de Tursac

This open-air museum at Tursac, 6 km/4 miles from Les Eyzies, gives a vivid impression of the life of prehistoric man and his hunting activities.

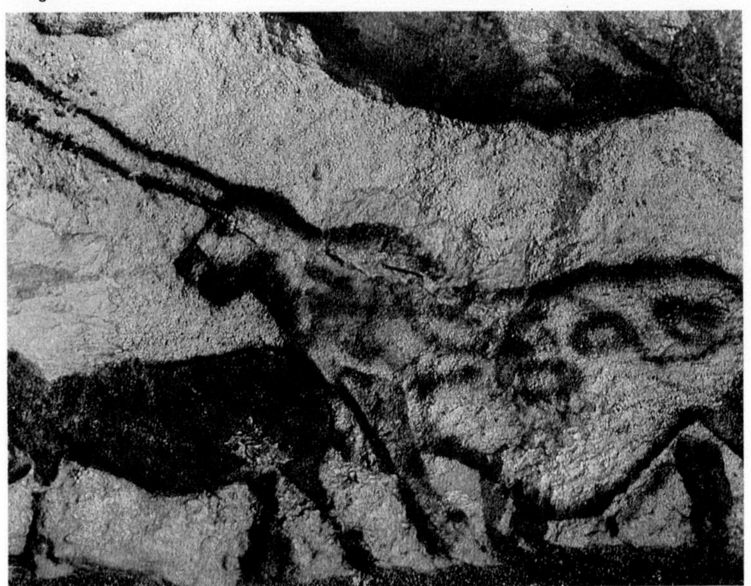

Cave paintings, Lascaux

Gourdon
Grottes de Cougnac

Gourdon (pop. 5000) lies on the borders of Périgord and Quercy. The nearby Grottes de Cougnac have cave drawings of the Magdalenian period (15,000–17,000 B.C.).

Lascaux
**Grotte de Lascaux

Near Montignac, which has a ruined castle, is one of the most remarkable prehistoric sites in Périgord, the famous Lascaux Cave, discovered in 1940, with its fine paintings of animals. The cave itself was closed in 1963 to prevent further damage to the paintings, which were suffering from damp and fungoid infection, but since 1983 visitors have been able to see Lascaux II, a faithful reproduction of the cave and its paintings. There is an information centre in which films of the interior of the cave are shown.

Périgueux

See entry

Rocamadour

This little town (pop. 780), one of France's most unusual places of pilgrimage, lies in an extremely picturesque situation, clinging to the rock face above a gorge on the Alzou (which is frequently dry) in the Causse de Gramat in Quercy. In the Middle Ages pilgrims flocked here to honour the Black Virgin of Roc-Amadour (12th c.). Above the town is its 12th c. castle, which is reached on a steep flight of steps with the Stations of the Cross. It is not known with certainty who St Amadour was – perhaps a hermit named Zacchaeus from Jericho. The great shrine of Rocamadour is the Chapelle Miraculeuse with the Black Virgin.

**Gouffre de Padirac

15 km/9 miles north-east of Rocamadour is the Gouffre de Padirac, a huge swallowhole and underground cave system which was first explored by the famous French speleologist A. Martel and is now the most visited cave in France (boat trip on an underground river).

***Sarlat**

Sarlat (pop. 10,600), a heart-shaped little town lying to the north of the river Dordogne, was once the chief town of Périgord Noir, and has preserved from that period numbers of elegant burghers' houses. In the south of the

Rocamadour

old town is the church of St-Sacerdos, rebuilt in its present form in the 16th c.; the tower on the west front is Romanesque. On its south side is the former Bishop's Palace, with a Renaissance façade. Behind the choir of the church is a *lanterne des morts* ("dead man's lantern"), a round tower with a conical roof of volcanic stone (12th c.). To the north of the church is the birthplace of the 16th c. writer Etienne de La Boëtie, a friend of Montaigne's. In Rue de la Liberté (on left) is the Hôtel de Maleville (16th c.). A little way east, in Rue Salamandre, is the Hôtel de Grezel (15th c.). In the north of the old town (Rue des Consuls) is the Hôtel Plamon (15th–17th c.), with a handsome façade.

Périgueux H9

Region: Aquitaine
Département: Dordogne
Altitude: 85 m/280 ft
Population: 35,000

Situation and characteristics

Périgueux, situated on the right bank of the river Isle, is chief town of the département of Dordogne and of the region of Périgord (see entry) and the see of a bishop. Its greatest attractions for visitors are the Roman remains and the medieval churches.

History

The Cité, in the west of the present town, lies on the site of Roman Vesona. The medieval settlement of Puy-St-Front grew up between the 5th and 11th c. around the abbey of St-Front. During the Hundred Years War the town withstood frequent attacks by English forces but was finally taken in 1356, to be restored to France four years later.

Périgueux Cathedral

Sights

*Cathedral

In the centre of Périgueux is the triangular Place Bugeaud, from which the picturesque old quarter of Puy-St-Front extends eastward to the Cathedral of St-Front. This, the youngest of the domed churches of Aquitaine, was built between 1125 and 1250 on the site of an earlier church and was restored in the 19th c. by the architect of the Sacré-Cœur in Paris, who gave the exterior of the church an unduly Eastern aspect. The almost completely undecorated interior, on a Greek cross plan, has five high domes (which can be seen at close quarters from the roof).

*Bell-tower

Over the porch is a Romanesque bell-tower, from which there are magnificent views. The 17 turrets round the roof are 19th c. additions. On the south side of the church is a Romanesque cloister, with some Gothic features; it contains a number of Merovingian sarcophagi.

*St-Etienne

The church of St-Etienne, west of the town centre, served as the cathedral until 1669. Built in the 12th c., it was partly destroyed in 1577, leaving only the west tower and two bays of the original building. It contains Baroque altars and a bishop's tomb.

*Musée du Périgord

In the Cours Tourny, which runs along the north side of the old town, is the Périgord Museum, with prehistoric and Gallo-Roman material from the surrounding area and a collection of pictures.

Roman remains

Although the Gallo-Roman town was used as a quarry of building stone, Périgueux has preserved a number of Roman remains. The most striking is the Tour de Vésone, a round tower 24 m/80 ft high with an internal diameter of 17 m/55 ft which was the cella of a Gallo-Roman temple. Near the church of St-Etienne are a few fragments of an amphitheatre which originally had seating for 20,000 spectators.

Château Barrière

Château Barrière, near the remains of the amphitheatre, is a ruined medieval tower house built on the line of the Roman walls.

Puy-St-Front, the old town of Périgueux, is now protected as an ancient monument. The Tour Mataguerre (late 15th c.) was part of the town's fortifications. Rue Limogeanne is lined with handsome Renaissance houses. From the Pont des Barris there is a fine view of St-Front and the riverbank with its old houses.

*Vieux Périgueux

Perpignan

See Languedoc–Roussillon

Picardie–Nord

I–L 4/5

Situation and characteristics

Northern France, between the Ile de France and the Belgian frontier, consists of the old provinces of Picardy, Artois and Flanders, now included within the two administrative regions of Picardy and Nord–Pas-de-Calais. In the centre of the area there are some of the finest French cathedrals, in the north there is France's largest industrial region, and in the west, along the shores of the Channel and the North Sea, there are stretches of beautiful coastal scenery and many attractive bathing resorts.

Picardy

The old province of Picardy, on the northern fringe of the Paris basin, with Amiens as its capital, corresponds broadly to the present-day département of Somme and parts of Pas-de-Calais, Oise and Aisne. It consists of a chalk plateau 100–200 m/325–650 ft above sea level covered by a fertile layer of loam and traversed in the west by the Somme and in the east by the Oise but otherwise little broken up by rivers. It is predominantly an agricultural region, growing wheat, sugar-beet and textile plants. The damp oceanic climate has favoured the development of pastoral farming (cheese production) over much of Picardy and the adjoining district of Thiérache to the east. Apart from agriculture, a major contribution to the economy is made by the textile industry.

Artois

Artois corresponds broadly to the département of Pas-de-Calais, with Arras as its chief town, and, with the exception of the marshland east of Calais, forms the northern part of the chalk plateau of northern France. In addition to wheat, oats, sugar-beet and textile plants the crops include hops and tobacco. Stock-farming is also of importance to the area. In north-eastern Artois, roughly between Douai and Béthune, is the northern French coalfield, which brought great prosperity to the area, particularly in the late 19th c. Since the mid 1960s, however, the mining industry has been in steady decline, and the output of coal is now little more than 10% of the output of the early sixties. Special support has, therefore, been given to the local textile industry.

Flanders

French Flanders, the southern part of the old province of Flanders, most of which is in Belgium, corresponds to the Nord département (chief town Lille). Most of it is completely flat and intensively cultivated. The real Flanders is the eastern part of the area with its Flemish-style towns and villages, in which the older inhabitants mostly still speak Flemish, while the eastern part has closer affinities to the predominantly Belgian district of Hainaut or Hainault. Central Flanders, south of Lille, includes part of the northern French coalfield, and is more industrialised than Artois. Flanders is famed for its linen and cotton. Here, as in Picardy and Artois, an extensive network of canals facilitates the transport of goods.

History

Artois, which from 863 belonged to the County of Flanders, was brought under the authority of the French crown by Philippe Auguste towards the end of the 12th c., together with Upper Picardy; Lower Picardy became part of France only in 1369. After a brief return to the County of Flanders the

Town Hall, Arras

County (from 1297 Duchy) of Artois passed to Burgundy in 1384, followed by Picardy (which had remained French) in 1435; after Charles the Bold's death in 1477, however, both territories reverted to France. In 1493, under the treaty of Senlis, Artois was ceded to Maximilian I of Habsburg. Most of it returned to France in 1659, under the treaty of the Pyrenees; the rest followed in 1678, under the treaty of Nijmegen.

Sights

Abbeville

Abbeville (pop. 26,000), the old capital of the district of Ponthieu, lies on the Somme, not far from the sea. It suffered heavy damage during the Second World War, and after the war was rebuilt in modern style. In the centre of the town is the unfinished and severely damaged church of St-Vulfran (15th–16th c.), with a magnificent Late Gothic façade. Outside the town is the château of Bagatelle (1752–1754), with period decoration and furniture. North of St-Vulfran is the Musée Boucher de Perthes (pictures, sculpture, prehistoric finds).

Amiens

See entry

Arras

Arras (pop. 45,400), once capital of the old County of Artois and now chief town of the département of Pas-de-Calais and the see of a bishop, lies between Amiens and Lille on the right bank of the Scarpe. With its spacious arcaded squares and high-gabled burghers' houses, it has preserved much of the character of an old Flemish commercial town. The town was famed for its tapestries (hence the English word "arras"). During the First World War the Arras area was the scene of heavy fighting, commemorated by many military cemeteries and memorials, particularly in the hilly country north of the town.

*Place des Héros

In the centre of the town is the arcaded Place des Héros, with the Hôtel de Ville (Town Hall; 15th–16th c., rebuilt after the First World War). The belfry, which also served as a watch-tower, displays the lion of Arras. The Grande Place to the north-east, which is also arcaded, has preserved its 17th c. aspect with its high-gabled houses.

*Belfry
*Grande Place

Cathedral

North-west of the Hôtel de Ville is the cathedral, originally the abbey church of St-Vaast, which was rebuilt in the 18th c. in neo-classical style. It contains a 15th c. head of Christ in wood and a 17th c. "Scourging". South of the church is the former abbey of St-Vaast (18th c.), now housing the Musée des Beaux-Arts (medieval sculpture, pictures of the 16th–18th c. and French 19th c. masters, including Corot and Delacroix). Farther south again is the birthplace of Maximilien Robespierre (1758–1794).

Bavay

Bavay (pop. 4400), east of Valenciennes, has remains of the Roman town of Bagacum (mid 2nd c. A.D.). The site was excavated from 1942 onwards and finds are displayed in the Musée Archéologique.

Bergues
*Town walls

Bergues (pop. 4760), surrounded by a deep moat and 17th c. walls, is a little town of very Flemish character. It has two town gates, the Porte de Cassel on the south side and the Couronne d'Hondschoote, dating from the 17th c. In the east of the town are the remains of the abbey of St-Winoc (a monumental gateway and two towers of the 18th c.). The 54 m/177 ft high watch-tower is a reconstruction of the original tower, destroyed in 1944, one of the finest in France. The Municipal Museum, housed in the old Mont-de-Piété (municipal pawnshop), contains paintings by Flemish and French masters and a fine collection of 16th and 17th c. drawings.

Museum

Hondschoote

13 km/8 miles east is Hondschoote, once a centre of the worsted industry, which has a Renaissance Town Hall and a mill (the Nordmolen) which is believed to date from the 12th c.

Boulogne-sur-Mer

Boulogne (pop. 50,000), situated on the river Liane, which here flows into the Channel (Straits of Dover), is France's largest fishing port and one of its most important commercial ports, as well as a popular seaside resort.

Lower town

From the Place Frédéric-Sauvage, on the right bank of the Liane Quai Gambetta runs to the harbour, formed in the estuary of the river. In the Grande Rue, to the east of Place Frédéric-Sauvage, is the church of St-Nicolas (13th–18th c.).

Upper town

At the east end of the Grande Rue is the upper town, a rectangle surrounded by massive walls with four gates. Near the south end are the Hôtel de Ville (Town Hall, 1734), with a keep (12th and 18th c.; views), the Palais de Justice (Law Courts) and the Library, housed in a former monastic building of the 13th c. Near the north end is the church of Notre-Dame (1827–1866), in Greco-Roman style, with a massive dome (11th c. crypt, treasury).
In the Castle is a museum with a geological collection, a collection of antiquities and works by 19th c. French painters.

Calais

Calais (pop. 77,000), situated at the narrowest point in the Channel (Straits of Dover; in French, Pas de Calais), is the largest town in the département of Pas-de-Calais and, with Boulogne, one of the two most important ports for the crossing to and from England (34 km/21 miles in 75 minutes, or about 40 minutes by hovercraft).

Channel Tunnel

The Channel Tunnel, from Sangatte, a suburb of Calais, to near Dover, is due to open in mid 1994. Three tunnels are at present being driven through

Rodin's "Burghers of Calais"

Windmill in Picardy

an impermeable stratum of chalk about 100 m/330 ft under the surface. The 50 km/30 mile journey is expected to take 30 minutes in high-speed trains. The first plans for a tunnel under the Channel were put to the future Emperor Napoleon by a Frenchman named Albert Mathieu in 1798, but were beyond the technological resources of the time. A further attempt in 1883 came up against British resistance, and a proposal put forward in 1975 foundered for lack of finance.
As well as an important port, Calais is also a popular seaside resort, with one of the finest beaches in northern France.
During the Second World War the old town of Calais (Calais-Nord) was almost completely destroyed, together with the port installations. After the war Calais was rebuilt, and the port regained its former importance.

Sights
Hôtel de Ville

In the centre of the town, between Calais-Nord and St-Pierre, is the Place du Soldat-Inconnu, with the Hôtel de Ville (Town Hall, 1910–1922), in Flemish Renaissance style, and Rodin's famous group, "The Burghers of Calais" (1895), commemorating the eleven-month siege of the town by the English in 1348 and its subsequent occupation by them until 1558.
In the rebuilt old town of Calais-Nord is the Tour Guet, a 13th c. watch-tower. South-east of this is the church of Notre-Dame (13th and 16th c.). On the north side of the town is a lighthouse (1848) from which there is a fine view of the harbour.

*Musée des Beaux-Arts

The Musée des Beaux-Arts et de la Dentelle (rebuilt) displays material on the history of the town, 19th and 20th c. sculpture, and a fine collection of pictures.

Cambrai

Cambrai (pop. 36,700), on the right bank of the canalised Escaut (Scheldt), was the home of the fine fabric known as cambric, first made here in the 15th c.
The central feature of the town is the spacious Place Aristide-Briand, with

the massive neo-classical Hôtel de Ville (Town Hall, 19th c.). A little to the west is the 18th c. church of St-Géry, with a 76 m/250 ft high tower, which has a Baroque rood screen (1632) and an "Entombment" by Rubens. Opposite the church is the former Archbishop's Palace, with a fine Renaissance doorway (1620).

Museum

South-east of this is the Beffroi (15th and 18th c.), the belfry of a church which has since been demolished. The Municipal Museum contains a variety of material, including archaeological finds from the area and an interesting collection of pictures from the 16th to 20th c.

* Maison Espagnole

Farther south is the Cathedral of Notre-Dame (18th c.; rennovated in 1859), with a fine Baroque interior. it contains the tomb of the theologian and writer Fénelon (1651–1715), with a monument by David d'Angers (1826), and other tombs, and also a number of pictures. Opposite it, to the west, is the fine Baroque façade of the Chapelle du Grand Séminaire (1692), which belonged to a Jesuit college. Other features of interest are a number of handsome old half-timbered houses like the Maison Espagnole, remains of earlier fortifications (Porte de Paris, 1390), two town gates and the 16th c. Citadel.

Cap Blanc-Nez,
Cap Blanc-Nez
* View

These two capes, the "White Nose" and the "Grey Nose", between Calais and Boulogne, afford wide views, extending in clear weather as far as the English coast, 35 km/22 miles away.

Cassel

This little town (pop. 2300), beautifully situated on a hill, has preserved many old burghers' houses (16th, 17th and 18th c.). In the Hôtel de la Noble Cour (16th–17th c.) is a historical museum. There are panoramic views from the Jardin Public. A walk up Mont Cassel, with its restored 18th c. wooden windmill and fine view, will be found rewarding.

Le Cateau

Le Cateau (pop. 8300) was the birthplace of the painter Henri Matisse (1869–1954). The Matisse Museum in the Town Hall has works by him and by contemporary artists. Also of interest are the church of St-Martin (1635) and the Archbishop's Palace.

Douai

Douai (pop. 44,500), an industrial town centred on coal, situated south of Lille on the river Scarpe, did not finally become French until 1713. From 1652 to 1889 it had a university, originally founded by the Spaniards. The central feature of the town is the Place d'Armes or Grand'Place. A short distance to the west is the 15th c. Hôtel de Ville (Town Hall), with a defensive tower (the interior of which is open to the public). To the east is the Porte de Valenciennes (15th c.), a relic of the old town walls, and to the south of this, in an area once occupied by defensive works, is the municipal park.

Hôtel de Ville
* Defensive tower

North of the Town Hall is the church of St-Pierre (18th c.) which contains numerous pictures and has a massive 16th c. tower. On the far side of the Scarpe, housed in a former Carthusian monastery (16th and 17th c.), is the Musée de la Chartreuse, with works by French and Dutch artists, including the beautiful Anchin Altar (by J. Bellegambe, 1509–1513), a fine collection of Italian Renaissance pictures and prehistoric and Gallo-Roman antiquities.

* Anchin Altar

Dunkirk

Dunkirk (French Dunkerque; pop. 73,700), France's most northerly town, lies on the North Sea coast near the end of the Straits of Dover, 14 km/9 miles from the Belgian frontier. It is a ferry port for the crossing to and from England and an important commercial port serving the industrial hinterland.

In the centre of the town is Place Jean-Bart, with a monument to Dunkirk's most famous seafarer (1651–1702). The Gothic church of St-Eloi (16th c.; badly damaged in 1940) has an 18th c. neo-classical façade and a free-standing defensive tower. At the north end of Rue Clemenceau is the Hôtel de Ville (Town Hall, 1896–1901), in Flemish Renaissance style. On the harbour is the massive Tour de Leughenaer, a relic of the old town walls which now serves as a lighthouse. West of this is the harbour, the third largest in France. From the lighthouse (59 m/194 ft tall) there is a fine view of the harbour, the town and out to sea. The Musée des Beaux-Arts, to the

* Harbour
* View

*Musée d'Art Contemporain

east of St-Eloi, has a rich collection of Dutch, French and Italian paintings. In the north of the town, set in a sculpture park, is the Musée d'Art Contemporain (designed by Jean Willerval), with over 600 works of the years 1950–1988.

Laon

See Champagne

Lille

See entry

Montreuil

Montreuil (pop. 2960), on a hill above the river Canche, is still surrounded by its 17th c. fortifications, designed by Vauban. The Citadel dates from the 16th c. (view). The former collegiate church of St-Saulve (11th and 12th c.) has some beautiful capitals and paintings (18th c.). The chapel of the Hôtel-Dieu, built in the Flamboyant style, is richly furnished. On the opposite bank of the Canche stands the former Carthusian priory of Notre-Dame-des-Prés (1314), restored by Viollet-le-Duc in 1870.

Noyon
*Notre-Dame

Noyon (pop. 14,000) is dominated by the former cathedral of Notre-Dame (12th–13th c.), one of the finest examples of the transition from Romanesque to Gothic (see Ile de France).

6 km/4 miles south, on the fringes of a forest, are the ruins of the Cistercian abbey of Ourscamp (see Ile de France).

Péronne

Péronne (pop. 9800), once a strongly fortified town, lies on the Somme, which here forms picturesque pools. In the 12th c. castle (destroyed during the war) Louis XI of France was held prisoner by Charles the Bold of Burgundy in 1468. The castle with its four round towers and the remains of the old town walls are still impressive. The Porte de Bretagne dates from 1602. In the Hôtel de Ville (Town Hall) is the Musée Danicourt, with a collection of coins and Greco-Roman and Merovingian jewellery.
The Historial de la Grande Guerre illustrates the horrors of the First World War.

Pierrefonds
*Castle

On the southern fringe of the Forest of Compiègne (see Ile de France) is the castle of Pierrefonds, heavily restored by Viollet-le-Duc in 1858–1867.

*Morienval

8 km/5 miles south-west is the former abbey church of Morienval (see Ile de France).

Le Quesnoy

Le Quesnoy (pop. 5000) has well preserved 17th c. fortifications designed by Vauban, now surrounded by public gardens.

Potelle

2 km/1½ miles east is the fortified castle of Potelle (15th c.).

Roubaix

North-east of Lille (see entry), near the Belgian frontier, is the large industrial city of Roubaix (pop. 101,900), the main centre of the textile industry in northern France. The Gothic church of St-Martin dates from the 16th c. A popular attraction for visitors is the large and beautiful Parc de Barbieux.

St-Omer

St-Omer (pop. 15,500), formerly belonging to the County of Flanders, lies in Artois, between Calais and Lille. The town grew up around a Benedictine monastery founded in the 7th c. In the west of the town, on Place du Maréchal-Foch, is the modern Hôtel de Ville (Town Hall), which also houses the Municipal Theatre. To the south are the Henri-Depuis Museum of Natural History and the former cathedral of Notre-Dame (13th–15th c.), with a 50 m/165 ft high tower, a fine south doorway and a richly decorated interior; in the church is the tomb of St Omer.

*Notre-Dame

North-east of Notre-Dame is the Musée des Beaux-Arts, with prehistoric and Roman remains, weapons, medieval objets d'art, faience, furniture, Flemish tapestries and a fine collection of pictures.

Musée des Beaux-Arts

On the east of the town are the ruins of the abbey of St-Bertin, founded in 1640. North-east of the Town Hall is the church of St-Sépulcre (13th–14th c.).

St-Quentin

The industrial town of St-Quentin (pop. 65,000) lies on the right bank of the canalised Somme. Originally the Roman settlement of Augusta Veromanduorum, it takes its present name from the 3rd c. Christian martyr St Quintinus or Quentin. The hub of the town's traffic is the Place de l'Hôtel-de-Ville, in which is a monument (1896) commemorating a Spanish victory over the French in 1557. Around the square are a number of elegant buildings – the Town Hall (begun in 1331, with a Gothic façade of 1509; carillon), the Theatre and, off to the north-east, the massive collegiate church of St-Quentin (12th–15th c.), with two high transepts and a beautiful apse decorated with reliefs. Under the choir is a 9th c. crypt containing the tombs of St Quentin and his companions. To the south of the Place de l'Hôtel-de-Ville is the Museum of Entomology, with a large collection of insects, including over 600,000 butterflies and moths. North of the square is the Musée Lécuyer, which has a famous collection of 80 pastels by Quentin de la Tour (1704–1788).

*St-Quentin

*Musée d'Entomology

*Musée Lécuyer

The Parc Ornithologique is a large bird reserve, with many species of birds flying freely or living in large enclosures.

St-Riquier

This little town (pop. 1200) grew up around a Benedictine abbey. The abbey church is a fine building in pure Flamboyant style with a richly decorated doorway, an unfinished tower and a beautiful interior.

Le Touquet

Le Touquet (pop. 5500) is one of the most fashionable resorts on the "Opal Coast", founded in the 19th c. Situated in a well-wooded area, it has a wide range of sports facilities and an attractive seafront promenade.

Tourcoing

Tourcoing (pop. 97,000) is a rapidly developing industrial town near the Belgian frontier. Along with Roubaix and other industrial towns it is part of a conurbation around Lille (see entry) with a population of around 300,000.

Valenciennes

The industrial town of Valenciennes (pop. 997,000), once famed as a lace-making centre, lies in the centre of a coalfield near the Belgian frontier. It was the birthplace of the painter Antoine Watteau (1684–1721). Its main features of interest are the Musée des Beaux-Arts, with a fine collection of Flemish, Dutch, Italian and French paintings, the neo-Romanesque pilgrimage church of Notre-Dame-du-St-Cordon (1852–1865) and the church of St-Géry, built in 1225 but altered in later centuries.

*Musée des Beaux-Arts

Condé-sur-l'Escaut

13 km/8 miles north of Valenciennes is the old fortified town of Condé-sur-l'Escaut, with a castle built in 1410.

Sport and Recreation in Picardy and the Nord

Sport

There are facilities for a great variety of sports, including riding, tennis and golf; a network of footpaths and tracks offers ample scope for walkers and cyclists; and boats can be hired at many places on the Somme, Marne, Oise and Aisne. All kinds of water sports can be practised on the rivers and on the coast. There are a number of nature and leisure parks, for example the "Domaine des Iles" leisure park at Ham and a country park at Ermenonville with a zoo and Wild West shows.

Caves

A popular attraction is the underground town (9th–14th c.) in the Grottes de Naours, between Amiens and Doullens.

Battlefields

The battlefields of the First World War on the Somme draw many visitors.

Poitiers

H8

Region: Poitou–Charentes
Département: Vienne
Altitude: 120 m/395 ft
Population: 85,000

Situation and characteristics

Poitiers, the old capital of Poitou (see entry) and now chief town of the département of Vienne, the see of a bishop and since 1432 a university town, is picturesquely situated on a rocky plateau, 50 m/165 ft high, above the valley of the rivers Clain and Boivre, which unite just north of the old town. The valley is spanned by high bridges offering wide views. The main attractions of Poitiers are its early Romanesque churches.

History

Poitiers was the Roman town of Limonum. The first Christians gathered here in the 3rd c., and the Baptistery is France's oldest Christian building. The city's first great bishop was St Hilarius (St Hilaire), St Martin's teacher. It was perhaps no accident, therefore, that the battle in which Charles Martel defeated the Arabs and halted the advance of Islam was fought near Poitiers in 732. During the 12th and 14th centuries Poitiers twice came under English rule. With the foundation of the University in 1432 the town became an important intellectual centre, with many churches. In 1569 it was besieged by Protestant forces, but ten years later it was the scene of the "grands jours de Poitiers", a meeting aimed at putting an end to religious strife.

Sights

Hôtel de Ville
Museums

In the centre of the town is the Place du Maréchal-Leclerc, with the Hôtel de Ville (Town Hall, 1869–1876), which houses the Musée des Beaux-Arts. A short distance west, in an 18th c. house (with the doorway of the former Augustinian church), is the Musée Chièvres (local history, drawings, prints, etc.).

* St-Hilaire-le-Grand

To the west of the square, reached by way of Rue Théophraste-Renaudot and Rue St-Hilaire, is the Romanesque church of St-Hilaire-le-Grand

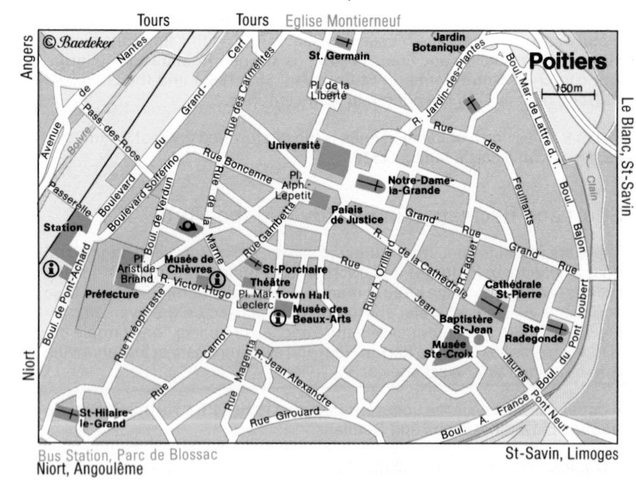

Notre-Dame-la-Grande

(11th–12th c.), the façade and seven domed aisles of which were severely damaged when the tower fell in 1590; the church was restored in the 19th c.

St-Porchaire
Palais de Justice

North of Place Leclerc is the church of St-Porchaire (16th c.), with a Romanesque tower. Beyond this is the Palais de Justice (Law Courts), which incorporates the keep (1386–1395) and parts of the former Ducal Palace. Particularly notable is the timber-roofed Grande Salle (12th–13th c., with further work about 1400).

*Notre-Dame-la-Grande
*West front

Just north-east of the Palais de Justice is the Romanesque/Byzantine church of Notre-Dame-la-Grande (11th–12th c.), one of the most richly decorated Romanesque churches in France. The west front (mid 12th c.), flanked by two towers, is a fine example of Poitevin Romanesque sculpture. Over the three doorways are representations of Biblical scenes.
The barrel-vaulted interior is notable for the beautiful capitals in the choir and a 12th c. fresco on the choir vaulting.

Cathedral

In the east of the town is the twin-towered Cathedral of St-Pierre, built between 1166 and 1271 (towers and upper part of façade 14th–15th c.). It has three richly decorated doorways, with a Last Judgment over the one in the centre, the Coronation and Death of the Virgin on the left-hand one and scenes from the life of St Thomas on the right-hand one. The most notable features of the interior are the beautiful 13th c. stained glass, the richly carved choir-stalls (also 13th c.) and the organ-loft (1778).

*St-Jean

A little way south of the Cathedral, in Rue Jean-Jaurès, is the Baptistery of St-Jean, probably the oldest surviving Christian building in France. Built in 356–368 on Roman foundations, it was enlarged in the 7th and 11th c. by the addition of an apse and a porch. It has frescoes of the 11th–14th c., and now houses an archaeological museum.

Musée Ste-Croix

To the south of the Baptistery is the Musée Ste-Croix (archaeological finds, Romanesque objects, folk art, pictures).

Futuristic architecture in the Futuroscope park

Ste-Radegonde

On the east side of the town is the little church of Ste-Radegonde, built in the 11th c. on the site of an earlier church (destroyed in 877) containing the tomb of the town's patron saint. The crypt, the choir and part of the west tower date from the 11th c., the nave and west doorway from the 13th–15th c. The ambulatory has beautiful capitals with human and animal figures. In the crypt is the sarcophagus of Ste Radegonde (d. 587), daughter of the pagan King Berthar of Thuringia and wife of the Frankish King Clotair I. In the north of the old town is the church of Montierneuf (11th c., rebuilt in 17th c.), originally belonging to a Benedictine monastery, which has a fine Renaissance doorway.

Futuroscope

6 km/4 miles north of Poitiers, at Jaunay-Clan, is the Futuroscope leisure and amusement park, which puts the emphasis on modern science and technology and has more than 70 other attractions for both young and old, including Europe's widest cinema screen, housed in a gigantic tomato.

Surroundings of Poitiers

Ligugé

See Poitou–Charentes–Vendée

Nouaillé-Maupertuis

See Poitou–Charentes–Vendée

Poitou–Charentes–Vendée

F–I 8/9

*Situation and characteristics

The regions of Poitou, Charentes and Vendée lie in western France, between the Atlantic on the west, the Loire on the north, the Gironde on the south and the Limousin on the east. They have a total population of around 2.05 million living in an area of 22,190 sq. km/8565 sq. miles with a coastline of 550 km/340 miles.

Topography

Poitou, lying between the Loire, the Massif Central and the Atlantic, is a fertile plateau at an average altitude of around 150 m/500 ft, across the middle of which runs a sill of ancient rocks, the Hauteurs de la Gâtine, rising to 285 m/935 ft. The western part of the plateau, near the coast, is the Vendée, which consists of the Bocage Vendéen, a gently undulating area of pastureland crisscrossed by hedges, and an extensive plain, on the northern and southern borders of which are expanses of former marshland (*marais*), now traversed by countless drainage canals, with large oyster-beds along the coast. The largest area of *marais* is the Marais Poitevin, a network of watercourses on both sides of the Sèvre Niortaise. Poitou now takes in the départements of Vienne (chief town Poitiers), Deux-Sèvres (Niort), Vendée (La Roche-sur-Yon) and the southern part of Maine-et-Loire (Angers).

South of Poitou, in the coastal area round La Rochelle, much of it still marshy, is Aunis, which was the smallest of the old French provinces and is now the north-western part of the département of Charente-Maritime (chief town La Rochelle).

South of this again, extending to the Gironde, the funnel-shaped estuary of the Garonne, is Saintonge, which has some areas of marshland but is mostly fertile agricultural land. It takes in most of the département of Charente-Maritime and the north-eastern part of Gironde (chief town Bordeaux).

Between Aunis and Saintonge and the Massif Central, around Angoulême, is the Angoumois, a former county which takes in the present-day département of Charente (chief town Angoulême) and parts of four neighbouring départements.

Tourism

The coastal regions of Vendée, extending from the borders of Brittany in the north to Royan in the south, offer a host of attractions for tourists and holidaymakers, with their beautiful beaches and well known resorts, their offshore islands, the wine-growing area round Cognac and a great range of sights of historical and artistic interest.

History

From the 5th c. onwards the area between the Loire and the Garonne, originally the Roman province of Aquitania (Aquitaine, Guyenne), broke up into a variety of more or less independent territories and lordships. After periods of Visigothic and Frankish rule there were established within the kingdom of France a series of counties, some of which were later raised to the status of duchies or became appanages of members of the royal family. In 732 Charles Martel defeated the Arabs at Tours and Poitiers. Later the region was harried by the Norsemen (Normans), and many keeps and defensive towers still bear witness to this troubled time. Then, with the foundation of numerous monasteries and other religious houses on the pilgrim road to Santiago de Compostela, prosperity began to return. The marriage of Eleanor of Aquitaine with Henry Plantagenet, later Henry II of England, was followed by centuries of conflict between England and France for possession of Poitou, during which, down to the 16th c., the various individual territories gradually returned to France. The region was ravaged by the 16th c. wars of religion and by the war in the Vendée between 1793 and 1795.

Sights in Poitou–Charentes–Vendée

Ile d'Aix

Off the Pointe de la Fumée lies the little island of Aix (pop. 180), which is closed to motor traffic. Parts of the 17th c. fortifications built by Vauban have been preserved. Napoleon stayed in the Maison de l'Empereur (9th–15th July 1815) before sailing into exile on St Helena; the house now

St-Pierre, Aulnay

contains a museum. A short distance away is an African Museum. The little church of St-Martin, originally belonging to a Benedictine abbey, has an 11th c. crypt.

Fort Boyard

Off to the west is Fort Boyard, built between 1804 and 1859 to defend the Charente estuary. In 1871 it was used as a prison for the defeated Communards. It is now being converted into television studios.

***Mont des Alouettes**

The Mont des Alouettes (231 m/758 ft) is the highest hill in the Vendée. In 1792 there were seven windmills on the hill, which served during the Vendée wars as signal stations, with different positions of the sails conveying the message "danger", "troops to assemble" or "all clear". From the top of the hill there are fine views of the surrounding country, Nantes and the sea.

Angoulême

Angoulême (pop. 52,000), once capital of the Angoumois and now chief town of the département of Charente and the see of a bishop, is beautifully situated on a hill above the Charente. Originally a Roman settlement (Encolisma), it suffered severely from fighting and plundering during the wars of religion. It was the birthplace (1492) of Marguerite de Valois, queen of Navarre.

In the Place de l'Hôtel-de-Ville, in the centre of the town, is the imposing Hôtel de Ville (Town Hall), built in 1858–1866 on the site of a castle of the Dukes of Angoulême, from which there survive the Tour Polygone (13th c.) and the Tour de Valois (15th c.). North of the Town Hall by way of Rue de la Cloche-Verte, passing the Hôtel St-Simon (1535–1540), is the Gothic church of St-André, which has fine stalls of 1692.

*Cathedral

The town's finest building is the Cathedral of St-Pierre (1105–1128, restored about 1650, altered by Abadie around 1875), which, like St-Front in Périgueux and Notre-Dame in Poitiers, shows a mingling of Romanesque and Byzantine styles. The west front has rich sculptural decoration, with more than 70 figures in representations of the Ascension and the Last Judgment. The cruciform interior has four domes.

Museums

The Musée des Beaux-Arts, housed in the former Bishop's Palace, has collections of prehistoric, Romanesque and overseas art. The Archaeological Museum displays finds from the surrounding area.

*Views

A walk (or a drive) around the old walls with their towers offers fine views of the surrounding countryside. The town preserves a number of 17th and 18th c. aristocratic mansions.

Aulnay
*St-Pierre

Aulnay (pop. 1500) lies on the old pilgrim road to Santiago de Compostela. The magnificent Romanesque church of St-Pierre has a handsome tower and steeple, a richly sculptured west doorway and fine capitals. In the churchyard is a 15th c. cross.

***Brouage**

The little town of Brouage (pop. 500), situated in an area of marshland, was built between 1630 and 1640. It is a fine example of a fortified town of the pre-Vauban period, with seven bastions and 13 m/40 ft high walls pierced by two gates.

River Charente

The river Charente winds its way for 360 km/225 miles through the old provinces of Angoumois and Saintonge before flowing into the Atlantic. Between Angoulême and Saintes it forms a valley just under 100 km/60 miles long, surrounded by the vineyards of Cognac and lined with interesting towns and churches like Bassac Abbey, the churches of Chaniers, Châteauneuf-sur-Charente and Châtres (all charming Romanesque buildings), the town of Cognac, the château and dolmen of Garde-Epée, Jarnac and the fine Romanesque church of Trois-Palis.

Chauvigny
*St-Pierre

East of Poitiers, on the Vienne, is Chauvigny (pop. 6500) dominated by its five castles. In the upper town is the Romanesque church of St-Pierre (11th–13th c.), with a magnificent series of capitals, mostly on New Testament themes. Nearby is an Archaeological Museum.

Cognac

120 km/75 miles north of Bordeaux is Cognac (pop. 21,000), in which Jean Martell, a native of Jersey, settled in 1715 and devoted himself to making brandy. He was followed by an Irish soldier named Hennessy, Baron Otard and others. Cognac is now the centre of some 70,000 hectares/175,000 acres of vineyards producing the wine from which cognac is distilled.

The main features of interest in Cognac itself are the picturesque old town, which preserves a number of 17th and 18th c. mansions, the Château des Valois (13th–14th and 16th c.) and the Romanesque/Gothic church of St-Léger. Visitors can see the wine-producers' establishments and learn all about the process of making cognac. Another attractive possibility is a drive around the vineyards, for example to Merpins, with remains of the Roman town of Condate, Châteauneuf-sur-Charente with its beautiful Romanesque church or the former river port of Port-Hublé.

*Round the vineyards

Cognac

There are altogether six areas producing grapes which can be used to make cognac. The two best vineyards, known as Grande Champagne, are round Segonzac, the others (Petite Champagne) round Jonzac, Barbezieux and Jarnac. The wine is distilled twice and the resultant brandy left to mature in oak casks, which give it its amber colour.

Confolens

Confolens (pop. 3300), famed for its annual folk festival, is picturesquely situated at the junction of the Vienne and the Goire. The Romanesque church of St-Barthélemy, on the left bank of the Vienne, dates from the 11th c., the old bridge over the Vienne from the 15th. The narrow streets are lined with high half-timbered houses of the 15th–18th c. The keep is all that remains of the town's old castle.

Cordouan

The Cordouan lighthouse, which can be reached from Royan at low tide, was built in stages between the 14th and the 18th c., and now stands 66 m/215 ft high. From the top there are magnificent views.

Fenioux

Fenioux, north of Saintes, has a small country church with walls dating from the Carolingian period; the richly ornamented façade and the octagonal tower are Romanesque. In the old churchyard is an interesting *lanterne des morts* ("dead man's lantern").

Lichères

The village of Lichères lies north of Angoulême. Its little Romanesque church, standing by itself in the fields, has a doorway with fine carved decoration and an apse surrounded by arcades.

Ligugé

8 km/5 miles south of Poitiers is the abbey of Ligugé, whose origins go back to the 4th c. It was reoccupied by Benedictine monks in 1853. Excavations round the abbey from 1953 onwards brought to light the remains of 6th c. buildings, and the present monastery also incorporates older work. The church of St-Martin was rebuilt in Flamboyant style in the 16th c.

Loudun

Loudun (pop. 8400) is a little town of charming old streets with an 11th c. Tour Carrée (Square Tower) from which there are fine views. The church of St-Hilaire dates from the 14th c., its beautiful doorway from the 16th. The church of Ste-Croix (11th c.) is now a market hall, and farther north stands the church of St-Pierre-du-Marché, built in 1215 and enlarged in the 15th c.

Luçon

Luçon (pop. 9500) is an old episcopal city of which Cardinal Richelieu was bishop. The Cathedral of Notre-Dame (1317) has a three-aisled nave of the 14th c. and a 17th c. façade, rebuilt by François Leduc after the devastations of the 16th c. wars of religion. The tower (1828–1829). The Bishop's Palace, with a fine Renaissance façade and a beautiful cloister, dates from the 16th c.

Jardin Dumaine

The beautiful Jardin Dumaine was laid out during the reign of Napoleon III.

St-Michel-en-l'Herm

15 km/9 miles south of Luçon is the abbey of St-Michel-en-l'Herm (11th and 15th c.; remodelled by François Leduc in 17th c.).

Lusignan

Lusignan (pop. 2780) is picturesquely situated on a hill. Legend has it that the castle, of which only ruins remain, was built by the fairy Mélusine in a single night. From the terrace there is a fine view of the Vonne valley. The Romanesque church (11th c.) has a 15th c. Gothic porch.

Jazeneuil

6 km/4 miles north-west is Jazeneuil, with a Romanesque church (11th–12th c.).

Maillezais

Maillezais, in the Marais Poitevin, has the remains (11th–15th c.) of an abbey founded at the end of the 10th c. and originally surrounded by walls. There is a small archaeological museum in the old kitchen.

Marais Poitevin

From the 11th c. onwards the sea withdrew from an area of some 15,000 hectares/37,500 acres, now covered by a patchwork of arable fields and pastureland, through which countless little streams and waterways wind their way, lined by trees (poplar, ash, alder) and meadows. The whole area is now a nature reserve. It can be visited by car, but to see it properly you must travel by boat – from Coulon (11th c. church), Arçais, La Garette, Magné or St-Hilaire-la-Palud. A distinction is made between the sparsely populated Marais Mouillé ("wet marsh"), known as Venise Verte ("Green Venice"), and the drained area near the coast. Also worth seeing are the villages on the Sèvre in the area round Niort and the Aquarium at Coulon.

Melle

*St-Hilaire

Melle, between Poitiers and La Rochelle, lay on the old pilgrim route to Santiago de Compostela. It has three fine Romanesque churches, St-Hilaire (dome over crossing, beautifully carved capitals), St-Savinien (music festival in summer) and St-Pierre.

Le Loubeau

1 km/¾ mile south, at Le Loubeau, are the old royal silver-mines.

Montmorillon

Montmorillon (pop. 7500) lies above the river Gartempe. The church of Notre-Dame is partly built over the crypt of Ste-Catherine, which has Romanesque wall paintings of the 12th and 13th centuries.
The old Maison-Dieu (a 12th c. hospital) now houses an archaeological museum. It has a 12th c. chapel of St-Laurent (with later alterations) and an octagonal bell-tower. In the courtyard is the Octogone, originally a funeral chapel.

Niort

Niort (pop. 60,000), chief town of the département of Deux-Sèvres, lies on the Sèvre Niortaise. All that remains of a castle built by Henry II of England and Richard Cœur-de-Lion is the keep, consisting of two massive square towers, which now houses a museum of folk art and traditions. Other features of interest are the old half-timbered houses in and around Rue St-Jean; the former Town Hall (16th c.), on a triangular plan, now containing the Musée du Pilori, an archaeological museum; the church of Notre-Dame, in the west of the town, with an elegant tower and Aubusson tapestries; the Natural History Museum; and the Musée des Beaux-Arts (tapestries, French, Italian, Flemish and Dutch paintings, etc.).

***Noirmoutier**

The island of Noirmoutier (pop. 8000), to the south of the Loire estuary, is 19 km/12 miles long and up to 7 km/4½ miles across. At low tide it can be reached by car on the Passage du Gois, a causeway which is under water at high tide; there is a ferry service from Pornic; and at the south end of the island there is a bridge connecting it with the mainland. An important contribution to the island's economy is made by its extensive salt-pans, in which salt is obtained from seawater by evaporation. There are also oyster-beds in its shallow coastal waters.
At the north end of the island is its chief town, Noirmoutier-en-l'Ile, which has a small harbour. There is a small well-preserved castle, part of which dates from the 12th c. It is possible to walk around the wall-walk, from which there are fine views of the harbour and the salt-pans. In the keep is a small museum (minerals, stuffed birds, naval history, English faience, etc.). The Romanesque and Gothic church of St-Philibert originally belonged to a Benedictine abbey; under the choir is a 12th c. crypt.
On the harbour is an aquarium, with fish and other marine fauna from local waters.
Popular with holidaymakers are the Bois de la Chaize, a 60 hectare/150 acre area of woodland, and the Plage des Dames, a beach of fine sand with the Promenade des Souzaux, from which there are views of the "Jade Coast". On the south-west coast there are other beaches of fine sand.

Nouaillé-Maupertuis

This Benedictine abbey lies in a wooded area near Poitiers. The Romanesque church (11th–12th c.; restored) contains a tomb of the 10th–11th c.

Oiron

At Oiron (pop. 800) is an elegant Renaissance château, once the residence of the Comte de Caravaz, who appears as the Marquis of Carabas in Charles Perrault's fairytale, "Puss in Boots". Its most notable features are the Salle des Gardes, with fourteen 16th c. frescoes of scenes from the "Aeneid", and a fine Renaissance church (16th c.).

***Oléron**
*Viaduct

The island of Oléron, which is connected with the mainland by France's longest viaduct (3027 m/3310 yds; 45 piers), is the largest French island after Corsica, with an area of 180 sq. km/70 sq. miles (30 km/19 miles long, 6 km/4 miles across) and a population of 15,000. In summer it is a very popular holiday resort, offering the attractions of its beautiful beaches and pleasant walking in its woods. The chief place on the island is the little port of Le Château- d'Oléron, with a 17th c. citadel.

Castle, Noirmoutier

View of St-Emilion

St-Pierre-d'Oléron

The economic centre of the island, however, is the little town of St-Pierre-d'Oléron, farther north. In Place Camille-Memain, on the site of the old churchyard, is a 30 m/100 ft high *lanterne des morts* ("dead man's lantern"), erected in the 13th c., when the island was in English hands.

Musée Oléronais

The Musée Oléronais is devoted to the history and folk art of the island.
Around the island, particularly on the east side, are extensive oyster-beds. At its north end stands the Phare de Chassiron, a lighthouse built in 1836 (fine views). On the west side of the island are long sandy beaches and the fishing port of La Cotinière.

Parthenay

Parthenay (pop. 11,000), west of Poitiers, lies on the old pilgrim route to Santiago de Compostela and is now an important market town. Legend has it that the town, with its double ring of walls, was built by the magic arts of the fairy Mélusine (see Lusignan, above). The Rue de la Vaux-St-Jacques has preserved its attractive old-world aspect, as have the Pont St-Jacques and Porte St-Jacques (13th c.) by which the town is entered from the north.

Citadel

Fascinating, too, is the 13th c. Citadel, with its massive walls and clock-tower of 1454.
Above the nearby Parthenay-le-Vieux is the Romanesque church of St-Pierre, with an octagonal tower (well restored) bearing a figure of the fairy Mélusine.

Poitiers

See entry

Pornic

This little fishing port (pop. 2300), situated at the end of an inlet (sandy beaches) on the "Jade Coast", is now a popular seaside resort. The old part of the town, with the harbour and a 13th–14th c. castle, is particularly attractive.
Along the Jade Coast remains of the "Atlantic Wall" built by the occupying German forces during the Second World War are still very visible.

Ile de Ré

The Ile de Ré, which lies off La Rochelle, can be reached either on a bridge from the mainland (much criticised on environmental grounds) or by boat from La Pallice, at the west end of La Rochelle. The island, surrounded by beaches of fine sand, is 28 km/17 miles long and 5–7 km/3–4½ miles across. Pretty villages bright with flowers and surrounded by vineyards lie near salt marshes, some of which are now being converted into oyster-beds. The principal resorts on the island, which is favoured by nature-lovers, lie on the south coast (Ars, La Couarde, Le Bois-Plage, Ste-Marie, etc.).

St-Martin-de-Ré

The chief place on the island is the pretty little town of St-Martin-de-Ré, with 15th c. fortifications which were remodelled by Vauban (1627 onwards) and are pierced by two massive gates. The fortified church of St-Martin dates from the 15th c. and there is also an interesting Seafaring Museum.
Ars is also an attractive little place with its narrow lanes and the church of St-Etienne, which has a slender spire, a beautiful Romanesque doorway and a Gothic choir.
In the north-west of the island is the Phare des Baleines ("Lighthouse of the Whales"), built in 1854 (view). On the north-east coast is a beautiful sandy beach.

La Rochecourbon

The 15th c. Château de la Rochecourbon, set in a beautiful park north-west of Saintes, was discovered by the writer Pierre Loti in a dilapidated condition, and as a result of his efforts was restored from 1920 onwards.

Rochefort-sur-Mer

Rochefort (pop. 32,700), 15 km/9 miles above the mouth of the Charente, was founded by Colbert in 1666 as a naval port and is now recognised as a spa town. The writer Pierre Loti (1850–1923), a former naval officer, was born in the town, and his birthplace is now a museum displaying the "splendours of foreign lands". The imposing Arsenal, built in 1690, has a monumental entrance, the Porte du Soleil, which dates only from 1830. In Place Colbert are a handsome fountain of 1750, the Town Hall and the church of St-Louis (1672). In the west of the town is the Musée d'Art et d'Histoire de la Ville, in the Hôtel des Cheusses the Musée de la Marine (17th and 18th c. ship models, charts, etc.).

La Rochefoucauld

La Rochefoucauld (pop. 3700), near Angoulême, has a fine château (12th–16th c.) reminiscent of the châteaux of the Loire. It was the ancestral home of François de la Rochefoucauld (1613–1680), author of the famous "Maxims". The keep of the château dates from the 11th c. The magnificent Cour d'Honneur (Grand Courtyard), which shows Italian influence, is one of the finest in France.

*Cour d'Honneur

La Rochelle

See entry

Royan

The seaside resort of Royan (pop. 18,000) was almost completely destroyed during the Second World War but was rebuilt in modern style. It is one of the many popular resorts with beautiful bathing beaches on the "Côte de Beauté", which extends from the Gironde estuary to the Avert peninsula; among the others are St-Georges-de-Didonne, Meschers, St-Palais, Vaux-sur-Mer, La Palmyre and Ronce-les-Bains.
The reinforced concrete Cathedral was designed by the architects Gilles and Hébrard and built in 1955–1958. Only the Pontaillac quarter in the west of the town preserves something of the tranquil atmosphere of old Royan.

Les Sables d'Olonne

*Beach

The resort of Les Sables d'Olonne (pop. 16,700), which also has an important fishing harbour, is one of the best known and most popular family resorts in France, with a beautiful beach over 2 km/1½ miles long. The great rendezvous for holidaymakers is the Promenade du Remblai, laid out in the 18th c. At its western end is the Casino de la Plage, at its east end the Zoological Gardens. The church of Notre-Dame-de-Bon-Port was built in 1646. In a former Benedictine abbey (17th c.) is the Musée de l'Abbaye Ste-Croix (regional history, modern and contemporary art). Round the Tour d'Arundel (12th c.) and Fort St-Nicolas (11th c., rebuilt in 1779) is the fishermen's quarter of La Chaume.

***St-Emilion**

The charming little town of St-Emilion (pop. 3400), famed for its red wines, lies on a hill to the east of Bordeaux, still partly surrounded by its old walls (13th–15th c.). It has a fine collegiate church in Romanesque/Byzantine style (12th–15th c.) with beautiful 16th c. stained glass and a 14th c. cloister. To the south, on the rim of a gorge, is a Romanesque/Gothic bell-tower (15th c.), below which, entirely hewn from the rock, is the "monolithic church" (12th–16th c.). Adjoining this is the Chapelle de la Trinité (13th c.), below which is the cave hermitage of St Emilion, with the saint's "bed" in a recess in the rock. The town has a picturesque market square and from here a street runs up to the Château du Roi, a castle built by Louis VIII in the 13th c.

St-Savin

**Wall paintings

The little town of St-Savin (pop. 1060), on the left bank of the Gartempe, has an 11th c. abbey church with what are surely the finest 12th c. Romanesque wall paintings in France. The most remarkable are those on the vaulting of the nave, covering an area of 412 sq. m/4435 sq. ft at a height of 15 m/50 ft above the ground and illustrating the Biblical story from the Creation onwards, and those in the crypt. There is a fine view of the church from the Pont-Vieux, the old bridge over the Gartempe.

Saintes

Saintes (pop. 28,800), in antiquity the capital (Mediolanum) of a Celtic tribe, the Santoni, and later chief town of the French province of Saintonge, is attractively situated on the left bank of the Charente. It was the birthplace of Dr J.-I. Guillotin (1738–1814), inventor of the guillotine.

In the old town is the former cathedral of St-Pierre, built between 1117 and the 15th c., which was destroyed by the Calvinists in 1568 and soon afterwards rebuilt. Its most notable features are the richly decorated Gothic doorway and the 72 m/236 ft high tower.

To the south-west is the church of St-Eutrope, consecrated in 1096, with a

Ste-Radegonde, Talmont

tower of 1496. In the crypt under the church is the tomb of St Eutrope (Eutropius), first bishop of Saintes.

*Abbaye Ste-Marie-aux-Dames

The Abbaye Ste-Marie-aux-Dames, founded in 1047, was for a time converted to other uses but was restored in 1938. The Romanesque doorways have rich sculptural decoration. The nearby church of St-Palais dates from the 12th–13th c.
The old part of the town has many 17th and 18th c. buildings.

*Roman remains

On the right bank of the Charente is the Arch of Germanicus, a triumphal arch erected in A.D. 19. Originally spanning the main bridge over the river, it was moved to its present site in 1842. There are also remains of an amphitheatre of the 1st c. A.D., one of the oldest structures of its kind. It was of medium size, with seating for 20,000 spectators.

Museums

Saintes has numerous museums. The Archaeological Museum, housed in an old faience works near the Arch of Germanicus, has a large Gallo-Roman collection. The Musée Dupuy-Mestreu is a folk museum (local costumes, headgear and jewellery). The collections of the Musée des Beaux-Arts are divided between the Ancien Echevinage (pictures, Sèvres porcelain) and a building north of the church of St-Pierre (works of the French, Flemish and Dutch schools).

Talmont

The little village of Talmont is picturesquely situated on a crag above the Gironde. The Romanesque church of Ste-Radegonde dates from the 12th c.

Ile d'Yeu

30 km/20 miles off the Vendée coast is the charming island of Yeu (10 km/6 miles long, 4 km/2½ miles across; pop. 4900), which is reached by boat from Fromentine. The Vieux Château, romantically situated on a crag on the west coast, dates from the 11th c. but was enlarged in the 16th. From the watch-tower there is a magnificent view of the Côte Sauvage. Farther down the coast, to the east, is the fishing harbour (crayfish, lobsters) of Port-de-la-Meule. In Port-Joinville, where the ferry from the mainland comes in, is a small museum devoted to Marshal Pétain, who was confined in a cell in Fort Pierre-Levée from 1945 to 1951. He died in 1951 at the age of 96 and was buried in the Port-Joinville cemetery.

Provence

M–O 10/11

For a more detailed version of Provence, see Baedeker Provence/Côte d'Azur.

**Situation and characteristics

Provence, in south-eastern France, is a region of varied natural beauty, with a wealth of history and art in its towns and picturesque villages, which is one of the most rewarding – and most visited – parts of France.

Topography

The name of Provence is derived from the Roman Provincia Gallia Narbonensis, established after the conquest of southern France from 125 B.C. onwards. Later there were frequent changes in the boundaries of Provence. Geographically, it consists of the coastal region between the lower Rhône (from about Montélimar) and the Var (at Nice), together with the slopes of the French Alps farther inland. It takes in the administrative region of Provence–Alpes–Côte d'Azur and the départements of Alpes-de-Haute-Provence (chief town Digne), Hautes-Alpes (Gap), Alpes-Maritimes (Nice), Bouches-du-Rhône (Marseilles), Var (Toulon) and Vaucluse (Avignon). Enclosed within its territory is the independent principality of Monaco (see entry).
Provence, although of distinctively southern character, is in geographical terms an upland region, with only the Plaine de la Crau (a barren plain formed of gravels deposited by the Durance) to the south-east. The land,

mostly stony and cultivable only with the aid of irrigation, serves in the hill regions mainly for sheep-farming and the rearing of goats; at lower levels vines, mulberries and olives are grown; and on the coast sweet chestnuts, almonds, figs, oranges and lemons flourish, as well as palms and an abundance of flowers.
Provence owes this subtropical vegetation, normally found in more southerly latitudes, to the protective rampart of the Alps to the north and its open southern exposure, which produces a warm, dry climate. On the coast the heat of summer is mitigated by the sea.

Mistral

The lower Rhône valley and Provence (particularly between Avignon and Marseilles), as well as the Côte d'Azur (see entry) as far east as Cannes, suffer frequently from the mistral, a cold, dry fall wind of considerable force which is drawn down the Rhône valley from the Cévennes and the Alps by a depression over the Golfe du Lion. To provide protection against the mistral many roads, fields and villages are given some degree of shelter by wind-breaks of closely planted cypresses or by stone walls, and early crops are surrounded by hedges or reed screens.

History

Provence made its appearance in history with the foundation of Massilia (Marseilles) by Greek settlers, though it had undoubtedly been inhabited long before that period. When threatened by Celtic invaders the Greeks sought help from the Romans, who in 122 B.C. established the province of Gallia Narbonensis, with Narbonne and Aix as their first bases. In the reign of Augustus the province flourished, and in the early centuries A.D. Nîmes and Arles became major centres of Roman culture. In the 5th and 6th c. the Vandals, Burgundians, Visigoths, Ostrogoths and Franks all successively pressed into Provence, and in 536 it became part of the Frankish kingdom. Between the 8th and 10th c. it suffered from the incursions of the Saracens. Under the treaty of Verdun in 843 Provence, together with Burgundy and Lorraine, passed to Lothair, who in 855 set up the kingdom of Provence for his son Charles. In the 10th c. Provence became part of the Holy Roman Empire. The Counts of Arles, however, had other ideas, and asserted their independence. Thereafter Provence passed from them to the Counts of Toulouse, and in 1125 to the Counts of Barcelona. In 1246 Charles of Anjou became Count of Provence by marriage, and for 200 years Provence was ruled by the House of Anjou. During this period, from 1309 to 1403, Avignon became the residence of Popes and Anti-Popes. In 1486 Provence was incorporated in France, and thereafter shared its destinies, including the 16th c. wars of religion. In 1720 Orange, then belonging to the house of Nassau, fell to France, followed in 1791 by Avignon. In 1792 Provence gave Revolutionary France its anthem, the "Marseillaise". Even after becoming part of France, however, Provence preserved its own characteristics, and in the 19th c. produced an outstanding representative of Provençal language and poetry (which had flourished many centuries earlier in the age of the troubadours) in Frédéric Mistral, who was awarded the Nobel Prize for literature in 1904. During the Second World War Provence was occupied by German forces in 1942. It was liberated by the Allies in 1944.

Sights in Provence

Aigues-Mortes See Camargue

Aix-en-Provence See entry

Antibes See entry

Ardèche See Orange, Surroundings

Arles See entry

Avignon See entry

Les Baux See Arles, Surroundings

A calanque, forming an excellent natural harbour

Beaucaire

See Arles, Surroundings

***Calanques**

The *calanques* are the deep, narrow inlets enclosed by sheer white limestone cliffs which cut into the land south-east of Marseilles. Some of them are used as natural boating harbours, and they offer endless scope for rock-climbers. They can be visited from the little port of Cassis (see Marseilles, Surroundings) either on foot or, in good weather, by boat.

Camargue

See entry

Carpentras

The little industrial town of Carpentras (pop. 26,000) lies between Mont Ventoux and the Vaucluse plateau in a plain opening on to the Rhône valley. The Auzon flows to the north of the old town centre. In the centre of the town is the Gothic church of St-Siffrein (1405–1509), formerly a cathedral. It is entered by a Flamboyant doorway (1470–1480) on the south side, the Porte Juive, and has a fine treasury and a number of panel paintings. On the north side of the church are remains of Romanesque work and a Roman triumphal arch of the 1st c. A.D. Other features of interest are the Palais de Justice (Law Courts, 1640), which has some sumptuously decorated rooms, a number of museums (folk art and traditions, pictures, archaeology) housed in a building complex in the west of the town, the Bibliothèque Inguimbertine (on the north side of the museums) and France's oldest surviving synagogue (15th c., rebuilt in 18th and 20th c.). In the south of the town is the Hôtel-Dieu, an elegant building of the mid 18th c. There is an old-fashioned chemist's shop on the ground floor.

Venasque

11 km/7 miles south-east is Venasque, which has a 13th c. church and a baptistery of the 6th and 12th c.

Castellane

Castellane (pop. 1500) lies in south-eastern Provence on the river Verdon, which to the west of the town flows through the famous Gorges du Verdon (see below). On the north side of the town are remains of its old walls, with the Tour Pentagonale, a five-sided tower. On the west side of the picturesque old town is the Tour de l'Horloge, a 14th c. clock-tower. The 12th c. church of St-Victor and the Fontaine des Lions are also of interest. Above the town rears a crag from which there are fine views of the town and the Verdon as it enters the gorges.

Châteauneuf-du-Pape

Châteauneuf-du-Pape is the name of a renowned wine and of the little town (pop. 2000) in the Rhône valley from which it comes. The impetus for the standardisation and classification of the quality of wine (see Practical Information, Wine) came from here. The Musée du Père Anselme is devoted to the history of wine-production.

Digne

Digne (pop. 17,000), in the Pre-Alpine region, a spa-town and the centre of the Hautes-Alpes nature reserve, has an attractive old town, with the Cathedral of St-Jérome (15th c.) and the former cathedral of Notre-Dame-du-Bourg (12th–13th c.), which has remains of 14th–16th c. wall paintings and a Merovingian altar.

Draguignan

The old part of Draguignan (pop. 28,000), chief town of the département of Var, is centred on a clock-tower built on a crag of rock. The Museum (ceramics, furniture, 17th c. French and Flemish painting) is housed in a former convent of Ursuline nuns.

Entrecasteaux

The little village of Entrecasteaux, 30 km/19 miles west of Draguignan, has a 17th c. château containing fine furniture and paintings, with a park designed by Le Nôtre.

***Fontaine-de-Vaucluse**

The little town of Fontaine-de-Vaucluse (pop. 600), named after its principal attraction, is picturesquely situated in a rocky cirque *(vallis clausa)*, with a ruined castle of the bishops of Cavaillon looming over it.
The Italian poet and humanist Petrarch (1304–1374) lived here for 16 years after his unrequited passion for Laura, who died of the plague in Avignon in

Pilgrimage chapel of Notre-Dame-du-Roc, high up on a hill in Castellane

Gordes, a typical hilltop town

1348. He is commemorated by a column in the Place de la Colonne and by a museum.
The Romanesque church of St-Véran (11th c.) has a crypt containing the tomb of St Véran (Veranus), bishop of Cavaillon in the 6th c.
At the foot of a high rock wall is the famous Fontaine de Vaucluse, the source of the river Sorgue. It is the resurgence of an underground river formed by water seeping through the limestone from the Vaucluse plateau, which after heavy rain can swell to many times its normal size.

Gap

See Dauphiné

***Gordes**

The hilltop town of Gordes (pop. 1600) is picturesquely situated on the edge of the Vaucluse plateau to the south of Mont Ventoux. Housed in its fortified Renaissance château is the Musée Vasarely, which displays works by the Hungarian-born French painter Victor Vasarely (b. 1908) one of the leading exponents of Constructivism and Op Art.

*Village des Bories

2 km/1½ miles south is the restored Village des Bories. The *bories* are primitive windowless beehive-shaped houses of drystone construction – a type of structure which had precedents in the Neolithic period and was used in Provence until the early 20th c. 5 km/3 miles to the north lies Sénanque, with its interesting Cistercian abbey (see below).

Grignan

The little town of Grignan (pop. 1200), in the hilly country to the east of the Rhône valley, huddles round the handsome 17th c. château (fine view from terrace) in which Madame de Sévigné, the famous letter-writer, died in 1696. She is buried in the 16th c. church of St-Sauveur.

Montagne du Lubéron

The Montagne du Lubéron is a long range of hills in inland Provence which rises to a height of 1125 m/3691 ft in the Mourre Nègre. Most of it lies within the Parc Régional du Lubéron, a nature park established in 1977.
The Lubéron offers visitors not only beautiful scenery but also many attractive little towns and villages such as Apt (noted for its candied fruit),

The bare summit of Mont Ventoux

Bonnieux, Lourmarin (with the grave of Albert Camus in the churchyard and a 15th/16th c. château) Cucuron, Lacoste (under the château of the Marquis de Sade) and Rustrel (steep ochre hills known as the "Colorado de Rustrel")

Marseilles

See entry

Mercantour

*Gorges de la Vésubie

The Massif du Mercantour, with peaks rising to 3045 m/9991 ft, lies 50 km/30 miles north of Nice, in the southern reaches of the Alpine chain. The French–Italian frontier runs along the crest of its main ridge. Much of it is now in the Parc National du Mercantour. A drive through this area can also take in the magnificent Gorges de la Vésubie.

Montélimar

Montélimar (pop. 30,000), famous for its white nougat, lies just to the east of the Rhône, which at this point is pounded by a dam. Above the old town is the 12th–14th c. castle, with extensive views from its terrace and tower.

Montmajour

See Arles, Surroundings

***Mont Ventoux**

Mont Ventoux (Provençal Ventour, the "Windy Hill") is a long limestone ridge rising to a height of 1912 m/6273 ft. On the completely bare summit, often snow-covered in winter (skiing), are an observatory and a television transmitter, with a radar station lower down. From the top there is a magnificent view to the north over the valley of the Toulourenc and the hills beyond.

Moulin de Daudet

See Arles, Surroundings

Nîmes

See entry

Orange

See entry

Pont du Gard

See Nîmes, Surroundings

Route Napoléon

Pont St-Esprit

Pont St-Esprit takes its name from the bridge built over the Rhône between 1265 and 1309. 1000 m/1100 yds long, it has 25 arches, 19 of which date from the 13th c. There is a fine view of the bridge from the terrace in front of the church of St-Pierre (17th c.).

Roussillon

The village of Roussillon (not to be confused with the old province of Roussillon at the foot of the Pyrenees) is strikingly situated on a hill between the Coulon valley and the Vaucluse plateau, in an area long famed for the working of ochre (once used in the making of paint but now superseded by synthetic pigments). From the "Castrum" there are fine views of the ochre-coloured rocks of the surrounding area. Near the village is the "Val des Fées", with the rock formations known as "Fairies' Needles".

***Route Napoléon**

The 325 km/200 mile long Route Napoléon, opened to traffic in 1932, runs north-west from Cannes by way of Grasse and Digne to Gap, reaching its highest point at the Col Bayard (1240 m/4068 ft) and linking the Mediterranean with the Alps. It follows the route taken by Napoleon on the way to Grenoble in March 1815 after his return from Elba and his landing at Golfe-Juan, and is signposted by small figures of eagles. The road, which runs through breathtaking scenery, is normally open throughout the year.

*Scenery

St-Gilles

See Arles, Surroundings

St-Rémy-de-Provence

See Arles, Surroundings

Ste-Maries-de-la-Mer

See Camargue

Salon-de-Provence

This attractive little Provençal town (pop. 36,000) lies on the edge of the Plaine de la Crau, north of the Etang de Berre. The town grew up round the hill of Valdemech, once occupied by the Roman settlement of Castrum Salonense. The present town was laid out in the reign of Charlemagne,

Sénanque Abbey

*Château de l'Empéri

after the local salt marshes had been drained. The Château de l'Empéri (10th–15th c.) which dominates the town is one of the largest and best preserved castles in Provence; it now houses a museum. The chapel of Ste-Catherine dates from the 12th c. To the east of the castle is the 13th c. church of St-Michel, with a Romanesque doorway and a sculptured tympanum. Adjoining the church are the 17th c. Town Hall and the Porte Bourg-Neuf, part of the old fortifications. The house once occupied by the astrologer Nostradamus (Michel de Nostre-Dame, 1503–1566) is now an interesting museum. To the north of the town centre is the church of St-Laurent (14th–15th c.), a fine example of Provençal Gothic.

*St-Laurent

La Barben

8 km/5 miles east is the village of La Barben, charmingly situated in the valley of the Touloubre. To the east of the village is the Château La Barben.

***Sénanque**

The Cistercian abbey of Sénanque lies under the south side of the Vaucluse plateau, to the north of Gordes (see above), surrounded by fields of lavender. It was originally founded in 1148 and has been occupied up to the present day, with some interruptions due to the vicissitudes of history. Visitors can see the dormitory, cloister, chapterhouse, refectory and three-aisled church (12th c.). The restored abbey now houses temporary exhibitions, cultural events and seminars.

Silvacane

The former Cistercian abbey of Silvacane, on the plain south of the Montagne du Lubéron, was founded in 1144, but began to decline during the Middle Ages. The three-aisled church dates from the 12th–13th c. and, like the one at Sénanque, has an unusually broad transept, with a principal choir and two subsidiary choirs. The cloister dates from the end of the 13th c. Some of the monastic buildings have been restored.

Sisteron

*Citadelle

Sisteron (pop. 7000) lies on the Route Napoléon in northern Provence. Above the town is a citadel (12th, 16th and 19th c.), a magnificent viewpoint. In the lower town is the former cathedral of Notre-Dame-des-

Vaison-la-Romaine: remains of basilica

An idyllic spot in the upper town

Pommiers (1160–1220). The old town is attractive, with a number of fine 16th and 17th c. houses.

***Le Thoronet**

Thoronet abbey, together with those at Sénanque and Silvacane, is one of the oldest and most beautiful Cistercian abbeys in Provence. It is 12th c. and lies 26 km/16 miles south-west of Draguignan.

Vaison-la-Romaine
*Roman excavations

The site of Vaison-la-Romaine (pop. 6000), under the north side of Mont Ventoux, was already occupied in the 4th c. B.C. The excavation of its extensive Roman remains began in 1907.
In the Quartier de Puymin the foundations of many important buildings have been uncovered, including the House of the Messii, the Portico of Pompey and a nymphaeum. The museum in the centre of the excavations displays many finds from the site and reconstructions of the Theatre and a dwelling-house. Above the museum is the entrance to the much restored Theatre (1st c. A.D.), which is rather smaller than those of Arles and Orange.

Cathedral

On the west side of the Quartier de la Villasse is the former cathedral of Notre-Dame, built in the 11th–13th c. on the site of an earlier Merovingian church, which has a pre-Romanesque high altar and a beautiful cloister. North-west of the excavation site is the chapel of St-Quentin (late 12th c.), with a Romanesque choir on a triangular plan.
A Roman bridge with a 17 m/56 ft high arch leads over the Ouvèze into the upper town, which grew up from the 14th c. onwards under the protection of the 12th c. castle.

Gigondas

The region's best wine, with its own Appellations Controlée, is grown in Gigondas, 15 km/9 miles to the south-west.

****Grand Canyon du Verdon**

The Verdon, 175 km/110 miles long, is the most important tributary of the Durance. Between Castellane (see above) and the artificial Lac de Ste-Croix it flows through the tremendous wild gorges known as the Grand Canyon du Verdon, where, over a distance of 21 km/13 miles, with a fall of 153 m/

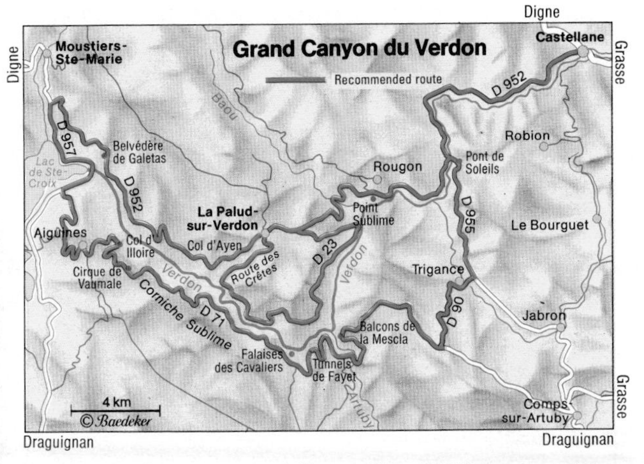

500 ft, the river has cut a narrow defile up to 700 m/2300 ft deep through the fossiliferous limestone of the hills.

Round trip

A round trip through the gorges involves a journey of 120–140 km/75–90 miles, for which at least six hours, or anything up to a full day, should be allowed. The best starting-point is Castellane, on the Route Napoléon.
At the road junction at Pont de Soleils take the road to the left, signposted "Rive gauche". This leads to the Balcons de la Mescla (*mescla* = "mingling", a reference to the nearby junction of the Artuby with the Verdon), with magnificent views into the gorge, here 250 m/720 ft deep. At the Falaises des Cavaliers there are a restaurant and a viewpoint. Then comes a fine stretch of road reaching heights of up to 400 m/1300 ft above the river. After passing round the Cirque de Vaumale and going over the Col d'Illoire (965 m/3166 ft) the road winds its way down to the turquoise-green Lac de Ste-Croix formed by a dam on the Verdon. The route then continues on D952 along the right (north) bank of the Verdon. The road passes the Belvédère de Galetas, goes over the Col d'Ayen (1032 m/3386 ft) and runs down to La-Palud-sur-Verdon. From here there are two possibilities – either the direct road (D952) or the longer but more rewarding alternative, turning right onto D23, which runs close to the river. This "Route des Crêtes" (23 km/14 miles) approaches the rim of the Grand Canyon and passes through the Belvédère de Trescaïre and Belvédère du Tilleul, des Glacières and L'Imbut, returning to La Palud. It then rejoins D952, which continues to the finest viewpoint on the whole route, the Point Sublime. From the car park it is a 10 minutes' walk to the lookout terrace, 180 m/590 ft above the junction of the Baou with the Verdon. 5 km/3 miles beyond the Point Sublime is the Pont de Soleils road junction, from which it is only a few kilometres back to Castellane.

*Point Sublime

Viviers

This old episcopal city has a history back to the 5th c. There are a number of notable buildings in the old town, including a tower from the original fortifications, the Maison des Chevaliers (Renaissance façade) and the Cathedral of St-Vincent (partly Romanesque), with fine tapestries. There are other attractive old buildings between Place Riquet and the Grande Rue.

Le Puy

L9

Region: Auvergne. Département: Haute-Loire
Altitude: 630 m/2065 ft. Population: 30,000

◀ *The classic view of the Verdan from the Point Sublime*

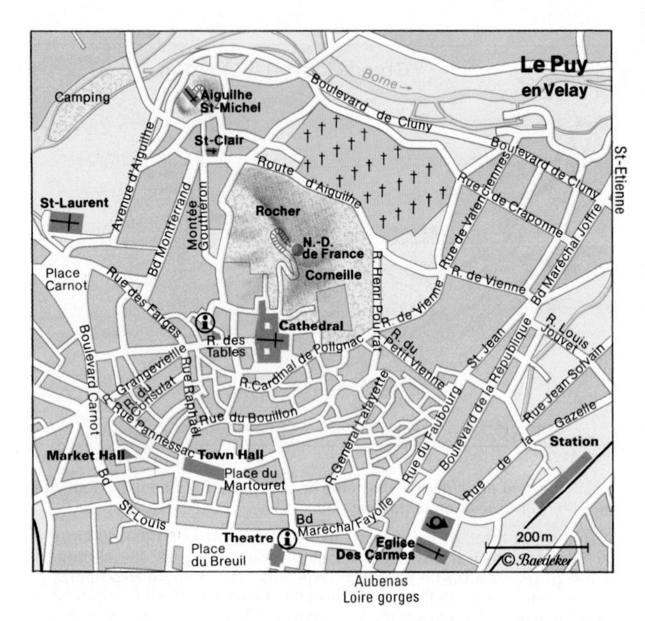

Situation and characteristics

Le Puy, chief town of the département of Haute-Loire, lies on the right bank of the river Borne, on a rolling plateau on the eastern border of Auvergne (see entry). The town is dominated by its Cathedral and by two extraordinary natural features, the Rocher Corneille (755 m/2477 ft) and the rock pinnacle known as the Aiguilhe St-Michel (both volcanic chimneys shaped by erosion and weathering).

Le Puy has a long tradition in the manufacture of pillow lace.

History

Le Puy was founded in the 6th c. as the see of the bishop of the Velay, and since the 10th c. has been a great pilgrimage centre with a much revered Black Virgin (pilgrimage on Aug. 15th). It was also the starting-point of one of the pilgrim routes to Santiago de Compostela, and among the earliest pilgrims was a 10th c. bishop of Le Puy, who after his safe return built the chapel of St-Michel on the Aiguilhe.

Sights

Place du Breuil

The hub of the town's life is the busy Place du Breuil, in which are the Theatre and the Prefecture. Behind the Prefecture is the Jardin Vinay, at the south end of which is the Musée Crozatier (archaeology, local history, lace, enamels, faience, pictures, etc.).

The Cathedral, to the north of the Place du Breuil, is reached by way of the Place du Plot (18th c. fountain), Rue Raphaël and the Place des Tables, from which the steep Rue des Tables climbs up in a flight of broad steps to the porch of the Cathedral, with the fine Gothic façade of the Hotel-Dieu to the left.

Panoramic view of Le Puy

Cathedral cloister

A richly sculptured capital

**Cathedral

The famous pilgrimage church and Cathedral of Notre-Dame du Puy stands at the foot of the Rocher Corneille, above the old town. Built towards the end of the 12th c., it shows a mingling of Auvergnat Romanesque and the style of south-western France, with clear Byzantine influence. A broad flight of steps (19th c.) leads up to the Cathedral façade, in multi-coloured volcanic stone, and into the three-arched porch, which has 13th c. paintings showing Byzantine influence on the vaulting. The steps end at the former main entrance to the Cathedral, which was walled up in 1780.

Interior

The solemn effect of the interior is enhanced by the dark colouring of the stone, the dim light, the heavy vaulting and the high cupolas. On the Baroque high altar is the Black Virgin which is the object of so many pilgrimages. To the left is the large Chapelle des Reliques, with a wall painting depicting the Seven Liberal Arts (15th c.). On the east wall of the south transept is the Porche du For; from the Place du For there is a fine view of the town. The valuable church treasury is housed in the sacristy. In the north transept is the Porche St-Jean, which leads out of the Cathedral. Opposite is the Baptistery of St-Jean (11th–12th c.). In the adjoining Maison du Prieur is a small folk museum.

*Cloister

On the south side of the Cathedral is the cloister, with richly sculptured capitals. In the Chapelle des Morts, on the east side of the cloister, is a large 13th c. wall painting.

Trésor d'Art Religieux

In the former Salle des Etats, above the cloister, is a collection of religious art.

*Rocher Corneille

Above the Cathedral to the north rises the Rocher Corneille (755 m/2477 ft), a volcanic chimney left isolated by the erosion of the softer rock surrounding it, from the top of which there are extensive views. It is crowned by a statue of the Virgin erected in 1860 (which can be climbed on a spiral staircase inside the figure).

*Aiguilhe St-Michel

To the north of the town is the Aiguilhe St-Michel, an 85 m/280 ft high rock pinnacle, also a remnant of a former volcano. At the foot stands the chapel of St-Clair (12th c.), and daringly perched on the tip of the rock is the chapel of St-Michel d'Aiguilhe, built in the 10th–11th c., probably on the site of a Roman temple of Mercury. It contains well preserved frescoes. From the path round the chapel there are fine views of the Rocher Corneille and the surrounding country.

St-Laurent

To the south of the Aiguilhe St-Michel, on the north-west side of the old town, is the Gothic church of St-Laurent (14th c.), originally belonging to a Dominican monastery.

Lace Museum

Near St-Laurent is the Atelier Conservatoire National de la Dentelle à la Main, where visitors can watch the making of pillow lace and can see a collection of lace from the 17th c. onwards.

Rocher St-Joseph

1 km/¾ mile west is the Rocher St-Joseph, topped by a statue of St Joseph (fine panoramic views).

Surroundings of Le Puy

Château de Polignac

5 km/3 miles west are the ruins of the Château de Polignac (13th–14th c.).

Lac du Bouchet

5 km/3 miles south by way of the Pépinière de Taulhac (view of a bend on the Loire) is the Lac du Bouchet, a crater lake at an altitude of 1208 m/3963 ft.

Pyrenees

F–L 11/12

**Situation and characteristics

The Pyrenees, which separate France from Spain, extend for a distance of some 450 km/280 miles between the Atlantic and the Mediterranean. Roughly a third of their area lies within France, with the French–Spanish frontier generally following the crest of the range. With peaks rising to over 3000 m/9800 ft, the Pyrenees fall little short of the Alps in grandeur.

Origins

Geologically the Pyrenees, extending over an area 450 km/280 miles long by about 100 km/60 miles across, are a relatively young range of folded mountains consisting of schists (interrupted by gneiss and granite) and limestones, with a summit ridge of fairly uniform height and high-altitude passes. The summit regions show the effects of glacier action in their trough-shaped valleys and cirques, the best known of which is the Cirque de Gavarnie, and still have areas of névé and small glaciers, since the snow line on the north side is only just under 3000 m/9800 ft. In contrast to the dry and therefore relatively bare slopes on the Spanish side, the French slopes support extensive forests (beech, oak and chestnut), increasing towards the west.

Topography

Geographically the range is divided by two deeper passes into the Western, Central and Eastern Pyrenees. The Western Pyrenees are hills of medium height with great expanses of fine deciduous forest and mountain pastures and wide valleys suitable for agriculture. From the Atlantic they rise through the Basque country, with the pass of Roncesvalles (1207 m/3960 ft), to the Col de Somport (1631 m/5351 ft) and reach a height of 2504 m/8216 ft in the Pic d'Anie. From the Col de Somport to the Col de Puymorens (1915 m/6283 ft) extend the Central Pyrenees, which on the Spanish side rise to 3404 m/11,169 ft in the Maledetta group (Pico de Aneto). The Eastern Pyrenees descend gradually from the Col de Puymorens and Col de Perche (1610 m/5282 ft) towards the Mediterranean coast, divided by the longitudinal valley of the Tech into a northern range reaching its highest point in Le Canigou (2785 m/9138 ft) and a southern range with Puigmal (2912 m/9554 ft), in Spanish territory, as its highest peak.

Climate

The Pyrenees extends over a number of different climatic zones. In the west is the lush green Basque country, in the east the pinewoods and scrub forests of the Mediterranean with its generally drier climate, in the north is a region of mixed forest, hills and plains, and in the middle are the rugged high peaks. Characteristic of the Pyrenees are its numerous lakes, waterfalls, gorges and hot and mineral springs. In the high-altitude National Park of the Pyrenees rare plants grow and endangered species of animals live in peace.

Tourism

Though still attracting relatively few foreign tourists, the Pyrenees have much to offer the visitor – the magnificence of their mountains and valleys, the beautiful footpaths and long-distance trails, the hills to be climbed and the rock faces to be scaled, the endless scope for water sports of all kinds on the Atlantic and Mediterranean coasts and the numerous rivers and lakes, the many holiday resorts with their facilities for sport (golf, tennis, etc.) and entertainment and, in season, for winter sports.

**Route des Pyrénées

An ideal way of discovering the attractions of the Pyrenees is to follow the Route des Pyrénées, which runs for over 700 km/435 miles from Argelès-sur-Mer on the Mediterranean coast to St-Jean-de-Luz on the Atlantic, with plenty of opportunities for side trips.
The best time of year for a visit to the Pyrenees is from about the middle of May, since earlier in the year, depending on snow conditions, the highest passes, in particular the Col d'Aubisque (1710 m/5611 ft) and the Col du Tourmalet (2115 m/6939 ft), may be closed.
Although there are no large cities in the Pyrenees, there are a number of considerable towns like Pau, Lourdes (see entry) and the industrial town of

Tarbes. There are also numerous holiday resorts, a variety of spas and a number of winter sports resorts

History

Evidence of prehistoric settlement in the Pyrenees was provided by the caves at Aurignac (22 km/14 miles from St-Gaudens), which gave its name to the Aurignacian culture. In historical times the region was occupied by Ligurians and later (6th c. onwards) by Iberians. Between 60 and 50 B.C. it was conquered by the Romans. An Iberian tribe advanced through the Pyrenees and settled in Gascony, but the Basques remained in the western Pyrenees and have preserved to this day their cultural independence and their language, on both the French and the Spanish sides of the mountains. The French Basque country lies in the western part of the département of Pyrénées-Atlantiques, with Bayonne as the principal town (see Côte des Basques). The eastern part of the département, also predominantly occupied by Basques, was the old Merovingian County of Béarn, which came under the control of Gascony in the 7th c., was united with Foix and Navarre (now Spanish) in 1290 and was incorporated in France in 1589.
To the east of the Basque country, in Gascony, is the territory of the old County of Bigorre, occupied in antiquity by a Celtic tribe, the Bigerriones, whose chief town was Bigorra or Turba (Tarbes). Bigorre remained independent from the 9th to the end of the 13th c., when it passed to the Counts of Foix. In 1607, along with the rest of Foix, it became French. It now forms the département of Hautes-Pyrénées (chief town Tarbes).
Farther east again is the former County of Foix, originally a fief of the Counts of Toulouse, which passed by inheritance to Henry IV of France in the 16th c. and now forms the département of Ariège (chief town Foix).
At the eastern end of the Pyrenees, between them and the Monts Corbières, is the former County of Roussillon, which belonged to Spain from the 12th to the 17th c. and still has Catalan as its language in addition to French. It is now the département of Pyrénées-Orientales, with Perpignan (see Languedoc–Roussillon) as its chief town.

Sights in the Pyrenees

Albi

See entry

Amélie-les-Bains

Amélie-les-Bains (alt. 243 m/797 ft; pop. 3780), in the valley of the Tech, is a popular spa, named after Louis-Philippe's queen. Its mineral springs were already being used in Roman times, and remains of Roman baths are to be seen in the modern spa establishment. The local festivals – the traditional masquerade on Shrove Tuesday and the blessing of the mules on June 25th – attract many visitors. Above Amélie lies the little Catalan town of Palalda. Parts of its church date from the 10th c.

Palalda

Mondony valley

Amélie-les-Bains is also a good base for a trip into the Mondony valley (8 km/5 miles south-east). The Roc de France near Montalba will prove a rewarding climb; it is 1450 m/4760 ft high and the climb takes about three hours.

Andorra

See entry

Argelès-sur-Mer

See Côte Vermeille

Argelès-Gazost

Argelès-Gazost (pop. 3500) lies at an altitude of 457 m/1500 ft in the High Pyrenees, between Lourdes and Cauterets. It is a popular spa (sulphurous springs) with beautiful spa gardens. From the Tour Mendaigne (17th c.) in the upper town there are fine views (orientation table).

St-Savin

South of the town is the church of the former Benedictine abbey of St-Savin (11th–12th and 14th c.), once the religious centre of Bigorre, with a Romanesque doorway and a fine church treasury.

Arles-sur-Tech

Arles-sur-Tech lies 3 km/2 miles south-west of Amélie-les-Bains, with the Puig de l'Estelle (1778 m/5834 ft) rearing above the little town.
In the centre of the town are the remains of an abbey founded around 900. To the left of the main entrance to the well preserved church are two ancient sarcophagi, one of which dates from the 4th c. A.D. The Late Romanesque/Early Gothic cloister is entered from the north aisle of the church.
Near the abbey is the little aisleless church of St-Sauveur (Early Gothic), with a massive tower.

*Gorges de la Fou

Upstream are the Gorges de la Fou, first completely explored in 1926. A stretch 1400 m/1500 yds long is open to visitors. At some points the gorge is no more than a metre wide.

Aulus-les-Bains

This little spa (alt. 762 m/2500 ft), also a winter sports resort, lies below the Col de Latrape (1336 m/4383 ft). It has four springs of water containing sulphur, calcium and iron salts. There are a number of waterfalls in the area, including the Cascade d'Arse.

Ax-les-Thermes

Ax-les-Thermes (alt. 720 m/2360 ft; pop. 1500), in the valley of the Ariège 15 km/9 miles from the Spanish frontier, is an old-established spa, with springs which were frequented in Roman times. The "Bassin des Ladres" was used in the Middle Ages for the treatment of Crusaders suffering from leprosy. There are altogether 60 springs, serving three spa establishments.
Ax is a good centre for mountain walking and climbing in summer. Near the town are the skiing areas of Ax 1400 and Ax 2300, both reached by cableways.

Bagnères-de-Bigorre

This spa in the Adour valley (alt. 550 m/1805 ft; pop. 9850) has a picturesque old town, with the 15th c. Tour des Jacobins and remains of the cloister of St-Jean and the church of St-Vincent (15th–16th c.). In and around the extensive spa gardens are the Casino, the thermal springs and the Musée Salies (natural history, Flemish and French paintings, drawings, ceramics). The old village windmill now houses the Musée du Vieux Moulin, a museum of folk-art. South-west of the town is the Mont du Bédat (881 m/2891 ft with information boards), which commands wide views.

*Grotte de Médous

About 2 km/1¼ miles from the town is the Grotte de Médous, discovered in 1948, with beautiful stalactites and stalagmites. It is 760 m/836 yds long, 160 m/175 yds being navigable.

Bagnères-de-Luchon

This fashionable spa (alt. 630 m/2065 ft; pop. 3600) is beautifully situated at the junction of the rivers Pique and One, under the highest Pyrenean peaks, with the winter sports resort of Superbagnères (1800 m/5900 ft) 19 km/12 miles away. The springs were frequented in Roman times, and three Roman baths have been excavated. In the 17th c. the spa was made fashionable by Cardinal Richelieu, the springs having one of the highest sulphur contents and one of the highest degrees of radioactivity in the world. The Musée du Pays de Luchon is informative on local history.
Near the town is the important Romanesque church of St-Aventin (11th c.), with two square towers and a doorway with figured capitals.
Luchon is a good base for an excursion to the Vallée du Lys.

Cambo-les-Bains

The climatic resort of Cambo-les-Bains (alt. 65 m/215 ft; pop. 5000) lies above the valley of the Nive, in the Basque country. The lower part of the town, Bas-Cambo, has preserved its typically Basque character. The Villa Arnaga, 1.5 km/1 mile west, was the home of the playwright Edmond Rostand (1868–1918); it now contains a small museum. There is a monument to Rostand in the centre of the town.

Villa Arnaga

***Cauterets**

This spa, climatic resort and winter sports centre (alt. 932 m/3060 ft), surrounded by the peaks of the High Pyrenees, has 24 springs of sulphurous water. The skiing area on the Lys plateau (1850–2300 m/6070–7550 ft) can be reached by cableway.

*Lac de Gaube

Cauterets is also a good base for a trip to the Lac de Gaube (10 km/6 miles) by way of the Pont d'Espagne (waterfall) and for mountain walks and climbs.

Le Canigou

Le Canigou (2785 m/9138 ft) is one of the highest peaks in the Eastern Pyrenees, commanding extensive views.

*St-Martin-du-Canigou

Near the little village of Casteil, picturesquely situated on a crag at an altitude of 1094 m/3590 ft, is the abbey of St-Martin-du-Canigou (11th c.; restored), with a beautiful cloister.

Céret

Céret (alt. 171 m/560 ft; pop. 7000) lies at the point where the Tech valley enters Roussillon. The Catalonian sculptor Manolo (1872–1945) and the composer Déodat de Sévérac drew numbers of artists to this little town, which now possesses many works of modern art.

*Musée d'Art Moderne

The war memorial was designed by Maillol, and the Musée d'Art Moderne has works by Matisse, Chagall, Maillol, Dalí, Manolo, Picasso and Tapiès. The Casa Catalane de la Culture has rooms devoted to mineralogy and ethnology. The Vieux Pont or Pont du Diable, which spans the Tech in a single arch 22 m/72 ft high, dates from the 14th c. It affords fine views of Le Canigou and the Monts des Albères.

Collioure

See Côte Vermeille

Les Corbières

See entry

Cordes

See Albi, Surroundings

Foix

Foix (alt. 400 m/1300 ft; pop. 10,000), once capital of the old County of Foix, was independent from 1001 to 1290, when it passed under the control of Béarn. Of its formidable castle, on a crag above the town, there remain three imposing towers; the free-standing round tower now houses the Musée de l'Ariège. The former monastic church of St-Volusien (12th and 15th c.) has a beautiful choir, fine choir-stalls (15th c.) and an unfinished square tower. Nearby are a number of old half-timbered houses and the curious Goose Fountain.
There are many Romanesque churches of the 11th and 12th centuries in the surrounding area, including Bénac, Loubens, Mercus, St-Jean-de-Verges, Serres-sur-Arget and Vernajoul.

*Caves

Around the town are a number of caves with prehistoric rock drawings, notably the Grotte de Niaux and the Grotte du Portel. 6 km/4 miles from Foix is the underground river of Labouiche (boat trips).

***Font-Romeu**

This climatic and winter sports resort (alt. 1800 m/5900 ft), renowned for its sunny situation, was established in 1920, and now has a population of 3200. The skiing area offers a varied range of terrain, and the resort is surrounded by extensive forests, making it a good centre for walkers and climbers. Between the neighbouring villages of Odeillo and Via is a solar power station run by the Conseil National de la Recherche Scientifique which came into operation in 1969. In the Ermitage is a miracle-working figure of the Virgin, the Vierge de l'Invention (pilgrimages on third Sunday after Whitsun, Aug. 15th and Sept. 8th). Near the Ermitage is a beautiful Calvary from the top of which there is a magnificent view of the surrounding mountains.

Belvédère

From Belvédère 2000, a viewpoint 6 km/4 miles from Font-Romeu, there are (in clear weather) breathtaking views.

Gavarnie

**Cirque de Gavarnie

This little mountain village (alt. 1357 m/4452 ft; pop. 190), a good base for walks and climbs in the mountains, is popular with visitors in summer who are attracted particularly by the imposing Cirque de Gavarnie. This is

Cirque de Gavarnie

reached by taking the path which runs past the Hôtel du Cirque and follows the stream to the head of the valley; the walk takes about an hour. The Cirque is surrounded by sheer rock walls rising to over 3000 m/9800 ft and by numerous waterfalls. The Grande Cascade, which has its source in Spanish territory, is the highest waterfall in Europe, with a drop of 422 m/1385 ft. Nearby, at a height of 2804 m/9200 ft, is the Brèche de Roland, a 100 m/330 ft deep gash in the rocks which legend claims was hewn by Roland with his sword Durandal.
The village church dates from the 14th c.

La Mongie

La Mongie (alt. 1800 m/5900 ft), 4 km/2½ miles below the Col du Tourmalet and 25 km/15 miles from Bagnères-de-Bigorre, is one of the leading Pyrenean winter sports resorts, well equipped with lifts and cableways.

**Pic du Midi

North-west of La Mongie is the Pic du Midi de Bigorre (2865 m/9400 ft), which commands magnificent views.

Les Eaux-Bonnes

This little spa lies in a forest setting at an altitude of 750 m/2460 ft. 8 km/5 miles east is Gourette (1385 m/4545 ft), the oldest winter sports resort in the Pyrenees.

Les Eaux-Chaudes

The spa of Les Eaux-Chaudes (alt. 656 m/2150 ft) lies in a steep-sided wooded gorge 4 km/2½ miles south of Laruns. From here there is an attractive excursion to the Lac d'Artouste.

Lourdes

See entry

Lux-St-Sauveur

This climatically favoured spa and holiday resort lies on the Gave de Pau at an altitude of 685 m/2245 ft. The fortified church (12th and 14th c.) has a beautiful Romanesque doorway. In the chapel of Notre-Dame-de-la-Pitié is a small museum of religious art. The resort became fashionable in the 19th c., when it was frequented by the imperial court. South of the town is the Pont Napoléon, built in 1860, with a span of 47 m/155 ft.

*** Mas d'Azil**

The little river Arize and the road run through this cave, 410 m/450 yds long and up to 50 m/165 ft wide, situated at an altitude of 310 m/1015 ft. Visitors can see prehistoric rock drawings and various objects discovered in the cave. The Musée de la Préhistoire is informative on the history of the area.

*** Moissac**

Moissac (pop. 11,900) lies on a lateral canal of the Garonne and on the Tarn, which flows into the Garonne 4 km/2½ miles below the town. In the north of the town is the church of St-Pierre (12th and 15th c.), which belonged to a Benedictine abbey founded in the 7th c. and dissolved in 1790. On its south side is a magnificent Romanesque doorway (12th c.), with rich sculptural decoration – the finest in southern France. On the north side of the church is a cloister (11th–13th c.), which also ranks as one of the finest in France. The former Abbot's Lodging now houses the Musée Moissagais (folk art). From the tower there are fine views of the picturesque old town and the surrounding area.

Montauban

Montauban (pop. 54,000), chief town of the département of Tarn-et-Garonne, is beautifully situated on the river Tarn. It was a Protestant stronghold during the 16th c. wars of religion. From the fortified bridge (1304–1348) there is a good view of the town.

* Musée Ingres

At the east end of the bridge, in the former Bishop's Palace (17th c.), is the Ingres Museum, with an important collection of pictures, including in particular over 4000 drawings by Jean-Auguste-Dominique Ingres (1780–1867), and sculpture by Antoine Bourdelle (1861–1921).
Other features of interest are the arcaded Place Nationale (18th c.), the church of St-Jacques (14th–15th c.), with a fine Gothic tower, and the Cathedral of Notre-Dame (1732), which contains a painting by Ingres, "Louis XIII's Vow".

Mont-Louis

Mont-Louis (alt. 1600 m/5250 ft), now a summer holiday resort and winter sports centre, has a Citadel built by Vauban in 1681 and remains of its town walls. The church (1736) contains a 16th c. crucifix.

Montségur

See Les Corbières

Oloron-Ste-Marie

The busy little town of Oloron-Ste-Marie (alt. 250 m/820 ft; pop. 12,300) lies at the junction of the Aspe and the Ossau. In the south-west of the town is the former cathedral of Ste-Marie (11th–14th c.), with a beautiful richly sculptured Romanesque doorway. On the arch is depicted the taking of Jerusalem by the Count of Béarn.
On the hill between the Gave d'Aspe and the Gave d'Ossau, once occupied by the Roman settlement of Iluro, is the church of Ste-Croix (c. 1080), with a Moorish-style dome of the 13th c. From the terrace at the west end of the church there are fine views. In the old town are a number of handsome old houses of the 15th and 17th centuries.

Orthez

Orthez (alt. 62 m/205 ft; pop. 10,600), beautifully situated on the Gave de Pau, was capital of the County of Béarn from 1194 to 1460, and later became a Protestant stronghold with a Calvinist university. The Pont Vieux with its imposing tower dates from the 13th c. Other old buildings are the Tour Moncade (13th–14th c.), a relic of the castle of the Counts of Béarn, the Maison de Jeanne d'Albret (1500), the 14th c. Hôtel de la Lune, once the guest-house of the Counts of Foix, and many burghers' houses. The medieval church of St-Pierre, which was incorporated in the town's defences, was restored after the wars of religion.

*** Pau**

Pau (alt. 207 m/680 ft; pop. 85,800), chief town of the département of Pyrénées-Atlantiques, is magnificently situated on a plateau above the valley of the Gave de Pau. It is a climatic resort popular in both summer and winter as well as an important economic centre.
Originally a village which grew up round a hunting lodge of the Counts of Béarn, it developed into a town which became the capital of Béarn in 1464.

The Château, Pau

It was the residence of Jeanne d'Albret, queen of Navarre and a convert to Protestantism, whose son became king of France as Henry IV. The town, which had barely 8000 inhabitants at the end of the 18th c., was "discovered" by British visitors in the 1820s and thereafter developed rapidly.

Boulevard des Pyrénées

Between the Château and the Parc Beaumont runs the Boulevard des Pyrénées, just under 2 km/1½ miles long, which was laid out on the orders of Napoleon and affords magnificent views of the Pyrenees.

Château

The Château, originally a fortified castle of the 14th c., was rebuilt in the 16th c. as a Renaissance palace. There have been many subsequent additions; the entrance hall is modern.

Musée du Château

The main features of the Château are its fine tapestries and the apartments of Jeanne d'Albret and Henry IV. It contains two museums, the Musée National du Château (interior decoration, tapestries, works of art of the time of Henry IV) and the Musée Béarnais (crafts, history, folk art).

*Musée des Beaux-Arts

The Musée des Beaux-Arts is of more than regional importance, with pictures by Tintoretto, El Greco, Rubens and Degas.

Musée Bernadotte

The Bernadotte Museum is devoted to Marshal Jean-Baptiste Bernadotte, later king of Sweden, who was a native of Pau.

Parc Beaumont

The Parc Beaumont contains the remnants of the gardens which surrounded the Château in the 16th c.

Lescar

8 km/5 miles north is the little town of Lescar, situated above the Gave de Pau valley. The former cathedral of Notre-Dame (12th c., with much later alteration) has a beautiful interior.

Prades

At the foot of Le Canigou, in the valley of the Têt, is the little town of Prades (alt. 350 m/1150 ft; pop. 6900), where the famous cellist Pablo Casals

(1876–1973) lived in exile. The Gothic church of St-Pierre has a Romanesque tower and contains a fine 17th c. reredos by a Catalan artist.

Molitg-les-Bains

7 km/4½ miles away, in the Gorge de Castillane, is the spa of Molitg-les-Bains, which is recommended for the treatment of skin diseases and metabolic disorders.

St-Michel-de-Cuxa

3 km/2 miles south is the abbey of St-Michel-de-Cuxa, once the religious centre of Roussillon. Its decline began with the French Revolution, and a hundred years later, in 1889, one of its two towers collapsed. The Metropolitan Museum of New York acquired numerous fragments of the building, which were incorporated in a reproduction now to be seen in New York's Cloisters Museum. Since then half of the cloister has been rebuilt from the surviving remains and fragments found in the area. The beautiful four-storey tower is Romanesque, and pre-Romanesque work and 11th c. features can be detected in the church. The Pablo Casals Musical Festival is held here every year.

***St-Bertrand-de-Comminges**

On a hill above the Garonne lies St-Bertrand-de-Comminges (alt. 446 m/1465 ft; pop. 250). a half deserted village with an interesting past. It was the site of the Roman town of Lugdunum Convenarum, which at one time had a population of 60,000 and was the place of banishment of Herod Antipas and his wife Herodias, who feature in the story of Christ's Passion.

Excavations

Excavations have brought to light the forum, a temple, baths, a theatre, an amphitheatre and many other buildings. The Galerie du Trophée, housed in a former Benedictine abbey, displays statues of the 1st and 2nd c. A.D.. The Romanesque church of Notre-Dame, begun in 1120, was completed in Gothic style in 1350; it has 16th c. choir-stalls and a fine organ (restored). In the little Romanesque cloister (on right) is a famous pillar with figures of the four Evangelists.
The Musée de Comminges contains Gallo-Roman antiquities.

*St-Just-et-St-Pasteur

In the neighbouring village of Valcabrère is the little church of St-Just-et-St-Pasteur (11th–12th c.).

*Grottes de Gargas

Nearby are the Grottes de Gargas, with prehistoric rock paintings and hand impressions.

St-Jean-Pied-de-Port

The picturesque little town of St-Jean-Pied-de-Port (alt. 160 m/525 ft; pop. 1900), once a staging-point on the pilgrim road to Santiago de Compostela, lies on the river Nive under a 17th c. citadel. In the old upper town, still surrounded by 15th c. walls and entered through a gate under the tower of the church of Notre-Dame-du-Pont, are many 16th and 17th c. houses. From the Citadel, which was rebuilt by Vauban in 1688, there are wide views.

*Caves of Oxocelhaya and Isturits

The nearby caves of Oxocelhaya and Isturits have prehistoric rock drawings as well as fine stalactites.
The Forêt d'Iraty is one of the finest in the Basque country.

St-Lizier

St-Lizier (alt. 380 m/1245 ft; pop. 1900), the Gallo-Roman town of Lugdunum Consoranorum, now partly ruined, is picturesquely situated on a hill above the river Salat and still preserves remains of its Roman walls. Its other main features of interest are the former cathedral (11th–14th c.), which has Romanesque frescoes, a beautiful cloister and a valuable treasury, and the old Bishop's Palace (17th c.).

Tarascon-sur-Ariège

This little town (alt. 480 m/1575 ft; pop. 3900) lies on the Ariège. The Tour St-Michel dates from the 14th c., and the Gothic church has a fine 14th c. doorway.

*Grotte de Niaux

4 km/2½ miles south-west is the Grotte de Niaux, with rock paintings of the Magdalenian period (14,000–10,000 B.C.). The village of Niaux has an interesting Country Museum.

Other caves in the area include the Grotte de Bédeilhac, the Grotte de Lombrives and the Grotte de la Vache.

Tarbes

Tarbes (alt. 320 m/1050 ft; pop. 57,800), originally a Roman town, later the capital of the County of Bigorre and now chief town of the département of Hautes-Pyrénées and a busy industrial and commercial centre, lies on the Adour in a fertile plain. In the west of the town is the Cathedral of Notre-Dame-de-la-Sède (12th–14th c.), with a massive dome. In the north of the town is the beautiful Jardin Massey, with a layout designed by a director of the gardens of Versailles and a 40 m/130 ft high lookout tower. In the gardens are a cloister from the abbey of St-Sever-de-Rustan (15th–16th c.) and a museum (pictures, folk art and traditions, history of horse-breeding in Tarbes).

Jardin Massey

Tarbes was the birthplace of Marshal Foch, and the house in which he was born is now a small museum.

Villefranche-de-Conflent

The old fortified town of Villefranche (alt. 435 m/1425 ft; pop. 600), once an important staging-point on the pilgrim road to Santiago de Compostela, lies at the junction of the rivers Cady and Têt. Above the town is a massive citadel which could be reached on an underground staircase. The fortifications were rebuilt by Vauban in the 17th c. Other features of interest are the church of St-Jacques (12th–13th c.), with a richly decorated interior, and some elegant old houses of the 15th, 16th and 17th centuries.

Corneilla

South of Villefranche, at the foot of Le Canigou, is Corneilla, with the church of Notre-Dame, which is thought to have been built in the early 11th c., and was later incorporated in a monastery. Over the doorway is a finely carved tympanum; the interior is richly decorated.

*Cerdagne

Villefranche is a good centre from which to visit the district of Cerdagne, a high valley with beautiful and varied scenery.

Reims M5

Region: Champagne–Ardenne
Département: Marne
Altitude: 83 m/270 ft
Population: 182,000

Situation and characteristics

The historic city of Reims (in the English traditional spelling Rheims), the place of coronation of the French kings, the see of a bishop from the 4th c. (and now of an archbishop), lies in northern Champagne (see entry), some 150 km/95 miles north-east of Paris on the right bank of the little river Vesle. It owes its fame to its Cathedral, one of the supreme achievements of Gothic architecture, and to its champagne.

History

The city takes its name from a Celtic tribe, the Remi, whose capital it was. Later it became the Roman Durocortorum, one of the most flourishing cities in Gaul and originally more important than Paris. The high standing of the bishops of Reims, enhanced by their role in the conversion of the Franks, earned them in Carolingian times the right to anoint the king, and from 988 to 1825 almost all the kings of France were crowned in Reims. On July 17th 1429 Joan of Arc conducted Charles VII into the Cathedral for his anointing.

During the First World War much of Reims, including the Cathedral, was destroyed or badly damaged. The city suffered further damage, though on a lesser scale, during the Second World War, which ended with the German surrender in Reims on May 8th 1945.

Sights

**Cathedral

The Cathedral of Notre-Dame stands in Place du Cardinal-Luçon, in the centre of the city. On the north side of the square is the Palais de Justice (Law Courts), with a small bronze equestrian statue of Joan of Arc (by

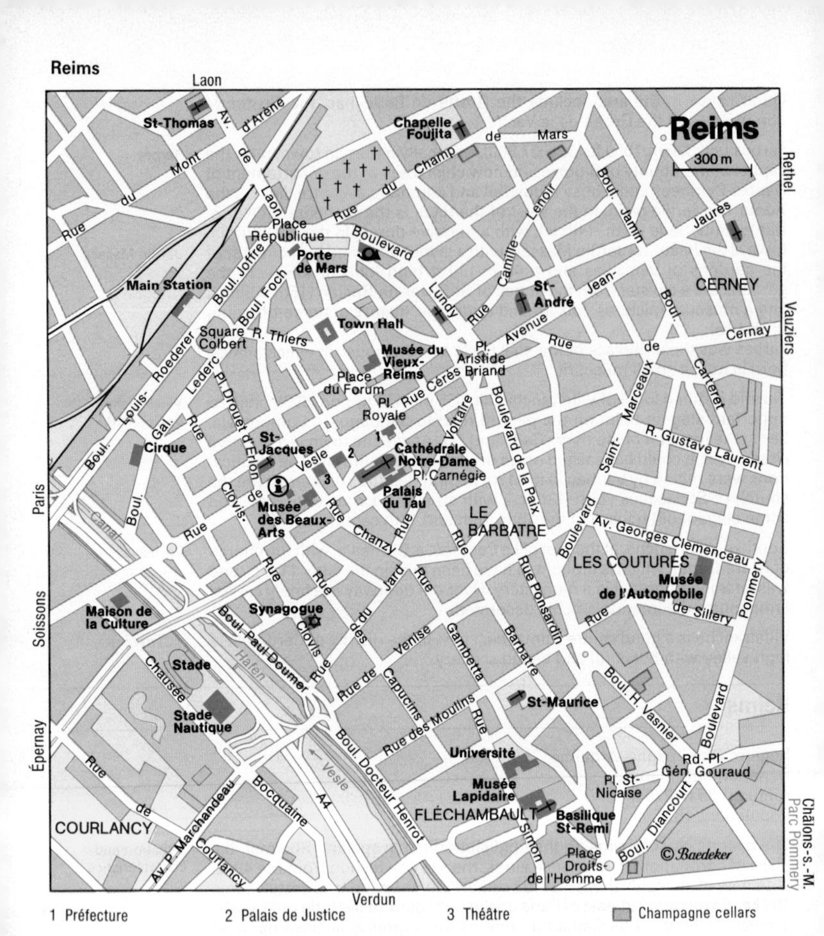

P. Dubois, 1896) in front of it. With its unity of form, harmonious proportions and rich sculptural decoration, the Cathedral is a master-work of High Gothic architecture, one of the great cathedrals of Europe. The damage it suffered during the 1914–1918 war has been repaired, but much of the sculpture is badly weathered, and restoration work is constantly in progress.

Built on the site of the 5th c. church in which the Frankish king Clovis was baptised by Bishop Rémi (Remigius) and used for more than eight centuries for the coronation of French kings, Reims Cathedral enjoys a very special position in French history. The present building was begun by Jean d'Orbais in 1211, following the destruction of an earlier church by fire, and was practically complete by 1294 (the upper parts of the towers being completed only in 1428). The tower over the crossing which was added in 1485 was destroyed by fire in 1914 and was not rebuilt.

*Façade

The richly patterned west front has three magnificent doorways, with a beautiful rose window over the central doorway. Above this is the Gallery

Reims Cathedral ▸

Reims Cathedral

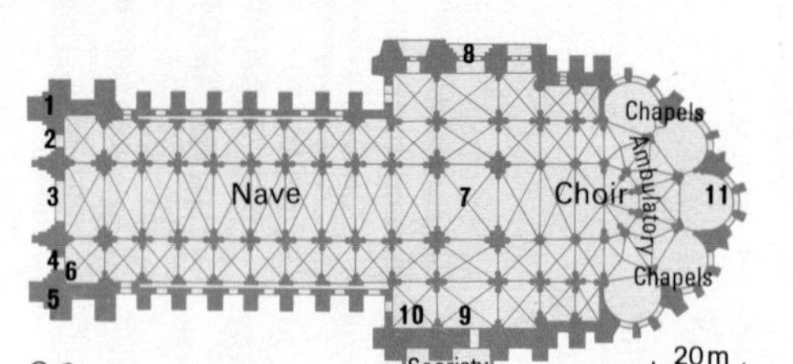

1 N tower
2 N doorway
3 Main doorway; rose window
4 S doorway (entrance)
5 S tower
6 Entrance to tower
7 Crossing
8 N transept
9 S transept
10 Window of the Wine-makers
11 Window of the Baptism
12 Chagall windows

of Kings, a long row of statues set in niches, and above this again are the two squat towers. The large statues and reliefs with which the whole building is covered, almost to excess, are among the greatest achievements of medieval sculpture. The sculpture on the central doorway depicts the life of the Virgin (right, the Visitation and Annunciation; left, Joachim and Anne, Mary and a magnificent figure of Solomon). On the left-hand doorway (left side, next to door) is the smiling angel known as the "Sourire de Reims" (restored).
The façade of the north transept is also very fine. On the central doorway are statues of bishops and other figures; on the left-hand doorway is a large figure of Christ in the attitude of benediction, and below this a Last Judgment, the finest achievement of the stone-masons of Reims (13th c.).

Interior

The interior of the Cathedral is freer from later additions than most other cathedrals, giving it an atmosphere of solemnity, almost of severity. Unfortunately most of the old stained glass has been lost; a few windows have been restored, and there are six new ones by Marc Chagall (1974).
On the west wall, in architectural niches, are 120 figures which illustrate the development of French relief sculpture in the 13th c.; particularly fine is the communion scene in the lowest row, to the right of the doorway.
In the sacristy is the valuable cathedral treasury.

*Palais du Tau

Adjoining the Cathedral is the former Bishop's Palace, now occupied by the Cathedral Museum, with the originals of many statues from the Cathedral, 15th c. Arras tapestries and other items from the cathedral treasury. Here too are the royal apartments, in which the king lived during the coronation ceremonies.

*Musée des Beaux-Arts

To the west of Place du Cardinal-Luçon, in the former Abbaye de St-Denis (18th c.), is the Musée des Beaux-Arts, a large municipal collection of paintings, sculpture, antiquities and applied art. Particularly notable are ten 16th c. tapestries depicting the story of St Rémi, a number of portraits (mostly of Saxon Electors and their wives) by the elder and the younger Cranach, and the so-called *toiles peintres* (15th and 16th c. paintings).

Other sights

The elongated Place Drouet-d-Erlon forms the busy town centre. At its southern end stands the 12th–16th c. church of St-Jacques; inside can be seen modern windows by Vieira da Silva.
On its northern side Place Drouet-d'Erlon opens into Square Colbert. A bronze statue (1860) is in memory of the Reims-born statesman Jean Baptiste Colbert (1619–83).
The Chapelle Notre-Dame-de-la-Paix, in Rue Champs-du-Mars, was consecrated in 1966, and was decorated by the Japanese artist Léonard Foujita (1886–1968).

Salle de Guerre

In the Collège Technique, in Rue Franklin Roosevelt behind the railway station, visitors can see the Salle de Guerre, where the Germans surrendered on May 7th 1945.

Sculptural decoration on the Cathedral façade

Hôtel de Ville

South of the Place de la République is the Town Hall (Hôtel de Ville), built in 1627–1630 (restored). Rue Colbert leads to the Place du Forum, where part of the Roman forum has been excavated.

Musée du Vieux Reims

At the north-east corner of the square stands the Hôtel le Vergeur (1522, extended in the 17th and 18th c.), with the municipal museum. To the south lies Place Royale, surrounded by buildings in the classical style, with a bronze statue of Louis XV by Pigalle, restored by Catellier in 1818. Further westwards along Rue Carnot are the Palais de Justice (1846) and the Theatre (1875).

*Porte de Mars

On the large Place de la République is the imposing Porte de Mars, a Roman triumphal arch (3rd c. A.D.), which served as a town gate until 1544. It was fully exposed to view by the removal of adjoining buildings in 1817.

Centre Historique de l'Automobile

This Automobile Museum, in the district of Les Coutures, displays 130 vehicles, together with an unusual collection of toy cars.

*St-Rémi

On the south side of the town is the former abbey church of St-Rémi, the oldest church in Reims and one of the finest Early Romanesque churches in northern France. It was built between 1005 and 1049 on the site of an earlier Carolingian church and was given a Gothic vaulted roof in 1162–1182. The choir and the west front are Early Gothic, the south transept Late Gothic (*c.* 1506). The church, which was badly damaged during the First World War, contains the tomb of St Rémi (Remigius).

Musée St-Rémi

This historical museum, in the old conventual buildings adjoining the church (13th, 17th and 18th c.), also includes a collection of material on the military history of the region down to 1870.

Champagne

A visit should be made to one or more of the famous champagne firms like Pommery, Mumm, Taittinger or Ruinart, with their huge underground cellars hewn from the local chalk. (On the production of champagne, see under Champagne).

Surroundings of Reims

Laon See Champagne

Rennes F6

Region: Bretagne (Brittany). Département: Ille-et-Vilaine
Altitude: 30 m/100 ft. Population: 192,000

Situation and characteristics

Rennes, situated at the junction of the canalised Ille and the Vilaine, is the chief town of the département of Ille-et-Vilaine, the see of an archbishop and a university town. The old capital of Brittany (see entry), Rennes is still its economic and cultural centre. Important elements in its economy are the foodstuff industries and car-manufacturing, and it also has a large research centre (computer, video and communications technology).
Rennes is a modern town, with its streets laid out at right angles to one another. In 1720, after a great fire which burned for a week, much of the town had to be rebuilt and further reconstruction was necessary as a result of severe damage during the Second World War.

History

In the 3rd c. A.D. Rennes was surrounded by a massive brick wall, and in the early Middle Ages it became one of the principal Frankish frontier strongholds against the Bretons. With the Duke of Brittany's victory over Charles

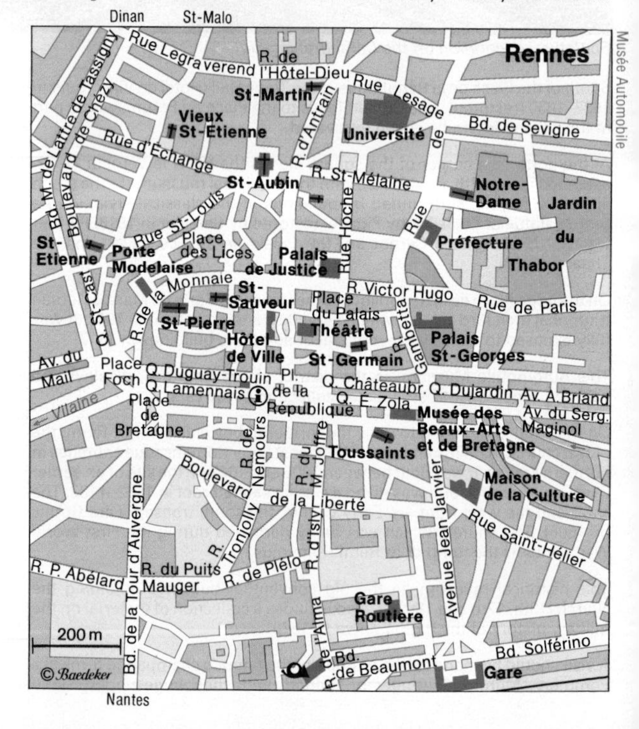

Place de la Mairie, with Theatre

the Bald in the 11th c., however, Rennes fell into Breton hands, and until the union of Brittany with France in 1532 was the capital of a Grand Duchy. Under the Ancien Régime it was an administrative centre and the seat of the Breton Parlement. After the great fire in 1720 it was rebuilt to the plans of the royal architect Jacques Gabriel.

Sights

Hôtel de Ville

In the centre of the older part of the town is the Place de la Mairie, with the handsome Hôtel de Ville (Town Hall) built by Gabriel in 1734 and the Theatre (1831–1835). To the east of the Theatre is the Place du Palais, surrounded by fine 18th c. houses.

*Palais de Justice

On the north side of the square is the Palais de Justice (Law Courts), built between 1618 and 1654 by Salomon de Brosse, the architect of the Palais du Luxembourg in Paris, which was originally the meeting-place of the Breton Parlement. It has a richly decorated interior; particularly notable is the Grand' Chambre, with a beautiful wooden ceiling and fine tapestries.

Notre-Dame

North-east of the Palais de Justice is the old abbey church of Notre-Dame (St-Melaine, 11th–13th c.), with a richly sculptured façade. To the left of the church are the old monastic buildings, now housing the City Planning Department, with a beautiful cloister. Behind the church, to the east, extends the Jardin du Thabor, the old abbey gardens and now the city's finest park, adjoining which is the Botanical Garden.

St-Sauveur
Cathedral

West of the Place de la Mairie is the handsome church of St-Sauveur (17th–18th c.), with a fine pulpit. Beyond this is the Cathedral of St-Pierre, a very old foundation which was completely rebuilt in the 19th c. It has a west front in classical style, with two towers built between 1541 and 1703. The most notable feature of the spacious interior is a very beautiful altar (German school) in the last chapel in the south aisle.

Other sights

In the narrow streets south of the Cathedral many old houses have been preserved, like the 18th c. Hôtel de Blossac at 6 rue du Chapitre. A short distance west of the Cathedral is the Porte Mordelaise, a relic of the town's 15th c. defences.
To the south of the Place de la Mairie and the Cathedral the canalised river Vilaine flows from east to west, flanked on either side by busy streets with many new blocks of flats. These streets cut across the animated Place de la République, on the south side of which, in the newer part of the town on the left bank of the Vilaine, is the massive Palais du Commerce (Chamber of Commerce, 19th–20th c.), also housing the Head Post Office.

*Palais des Musées

To the east, on Quai Emile-Zola, is the Palais des Musées. The Musée des Beaux-Arts has fine French, Italian and Dutch paintings, sculpture and ceramics. The Musée de Bretagne (history, archaeology, ethnography) has a wide range of exhibits, including much excavated material from Brittany and the Mediterranean area, applied and decorative art, furniture, traditional costumes and pictures, mainly from Brittany.
Opposite the Palais des Musées, to the south-west, is a former Jesuit church, the Eglise de Toussaints (1624–1657), with a richly decorated interior.

Old town

Visitors who have enough time will find it rewarding to walk around some of the little streets that escaped the 1720 fire. They are mostly to be found to the south of the Cathedral, e.g. in Rue des Dames and Rue du Chapitre.

La Rochelle

F8

Region: Poitou–Charentes. Département: Charente-Maritime
Altitude: sea level. Population: 80,000

Situation and characteristics

The interesting old port town of La Rochelle, once capital of the district of Aunis and now chief town of the département of Charente-Maritime and the see of a bishop, lies between Nantes and Bordeaux in a bay on the Atlantic which is sheltered on the seaward side by the islands of Ré and Oléron. To the south of the old town is the picturesque Vieux Port (Old Harbour). Since this is too small for modern requirements, however, large seagoing ships and La Rochelle's fishing fleet (the fifth largest in France) now use the new harbour beyond the Pointe des Minimes.

History

Between the 14th and the 18th c. La Rochelle was one of France's leading maritime towns, carrying on an independent trade with North America from an early period. During the 16th c. wars of religion, as a Huguenot stronghold, it was the scene of much fighting. In 1628 it was besieged by Richelieu's forces and starved into surrender. The revocation of the Edict of Nantes in 1685 and the loss of Canada in 1763 ended La Rochelle's great days; but with its old harbour defences and its arcaded houses the town has preserved much of the character of the Huguenot period.
The famous physicist René-Antoine de Réaumur (1683–1757), inventor of the Réaumur temperature scale, was born in La Rochelle.

Sights

*Hôtel de Ville

In the centre of La Rochelle is the Place de l'Hôtel-de-Ville, with the Hôtel de Ville (Town Hall), a richly decorated Renaissance building mainly dating from 1595–1606, surrounded by an older defensive wall (1498). In Rue des Merciers, an arcaded street which runs from the north-east corner of the Town Hall to the market square, are many picturesque old houses (particularly Nos. 3, 5, 8, 17 and 23).

Cathedral

From the Town Hall Rue Dupaty runs west into the town's main north–south axis: to the left Rue du Palais, lined by arcades of the 16th–18th c., to

La Rochelle harbour with its massive defensive towers

the right Rue Chaudrier, which runs north into the Place de Verdun. At the end of Rue Chaudrier, on the left, is the Cathedral of St-Louis, a building in classical style designed by Jacques Gabriel (1742–1762), with a 15th c. tower.

Musée d'Orbigny

A short distance south-west of the Cathedral is the Musée d'Orbigny (local history, ceramics, East Asian art). To the south of the museum is Rue de l'Escale, lined with handsome Baroque houses.

Musée des Beaux-Arts

A little way west of the Place de Verdun, in Rue Gargoulleau, is the former Bishop's Palace (18th c.), now housing the Musée de Peinture (the municipal art gallery) and the Municipal Library. Notable among the pictures in the Museum are a landscape by Corot and an "Adoration of the Shepherds" by E. Le Sueur.

Jardin des Plantes

In Rue Albert-1er, the northward continuation of Rue Chaudrier, is the Jardin des Plantes (Botanical Garden), with the Fleuriau Museum (natural history) and the Lafaille Museum (oceanography and ethnography).

Palais de Justice
Bourse

In Rue du Palais, on right, are the Palais de Justice (Law Courts, 1789) and the Bourse (Exchange, 1785), with a handsome courtyard; both buildings have fine façades.
In a side street, Rue des Augustins, is the Maison de Henri II, a town house of 1555.

Porte de la Grosse-Horloge

At the end of Rue du Palais is the Porte de la Grosse-Horloge (14th–15th c.), the only surviving town gate; the top portion dates from 1746.

Vieux Port

Beyond the Porte de la Grosse-Horloge, flanked by Quai Duperré and the Cours Wilson, is the Vieux Port, a busy and picturesque scene with its crowded fishing boats (boat trips round the harbour). The entrance is guarded by the massive Tour St-Nicolas (1384; view) on the east side and the Tour de la Chaîne on the west. The Tour de la Chaîne (which contains an interesting relief model of the medieval town) gets its name from the chain which was drawn across the mouth of the harbour at night during the Middle Ages. From the south side of the outer harbour there is a magnificent view of the harbour and the towers of the town.

*View

The fishermen's quarter lies round the Bassin à Flot, to the south of the Vieux Port.

Tour de la Lanterne *View

The Rue sur les Murs, to the north of the Tour de la Chaîne, runs west to the Tour de la Lanterne, built in 1445–1476 as a lighthouse, with an octagonal top (view).

Mail

From the Cours Wilson Rue St-Jean-du-Pérot runs south-west to the beautiful Parc Charruyer, which extends along the old fortifications. From the south end of the gardens the Mail continues west along the seafront. On this popular promenade flanking the beach is the Casino.

Aquarium

In the Port des Minimes district is France's largest aquarium.

Surroundings of La Rochelle

Esnandes

12 km/7½ miles north is Esnandes, with a Romanesque church which was altered in the 14th and 15th centuries but still preserves its original façade, incorporated in a defensive wall.

La Pallice

7 km/4½ miles north is the little town of La Pallice, with La Rochelle's New Harbour (1883–1890). This steadily developing commercial port can handle large seagoing vessels.

Ile de Ré

Just off La Rochelle, on the north side of a wide bay, the Pertuis d'Antioche, is the Ile de Ré with its extensive vineyards, salt-pans and oyster-beds (see Poitou–Charentes–Vendée).

Ile d'Aix
Ile d'Oléron

South of La Rochelle lie the two islands of Aix and Oléron (see Poitou – Charentes – Vendée).

Rouen

I5

Region: Haute-Normandie. Département: Seine-Maritime
Altitude: 10 m/33 ft. Population: 118,000

Situation and characteristics

Rouen lies north-west of Paris on the lower Seine, some 130 km/80 miles above its mouth. The ancient capital of Normandy (see entry), it is now chief town of the Haute-Normandie region, the see of an archbishop, France's largest river port and one of its largest seaports, situated at the highest point on the river navigable by seagoing vessels. It is also a major centre of the cotton industry.

In spite of the heavy destruction it suffered during the Second World War Rouen is still one of the great tourist centres of northern France, with magnificent Gothic churches and richly stocked museums which fully justify its style of "museum city" *(ville musée).*

The dramatist Pierre Corneille (1606–1684) and the novelist Gustave Flaubert (1821–1880) were born in Rouen.

History

The Gallic town known to the Romans as Rotomagus, capital of the Veliocasses, flourished under Roman rule and became the see of a bishop in 260. In the 9th c. it was devastated several times by Norsemen from Denmark, whose leader Rollo became the first Duke of Normandy as Robert I in 911. After Duke William of Normandy became king of England in 1066 Rouen, along with the rest of Normandy, became an English possession, and remained under English rule until 1204. During the Hundred Years' War, in 1419, it was taken by Henry V after a six months' siege. Here in 1431 Joan of Arc was tried and burned at the stake. The town was recaptured by Charles VII of France in 1449, and thereafter it prospered until the outbreak of the wars of religion. The bitter fighting between Catholics and Calvinists in the

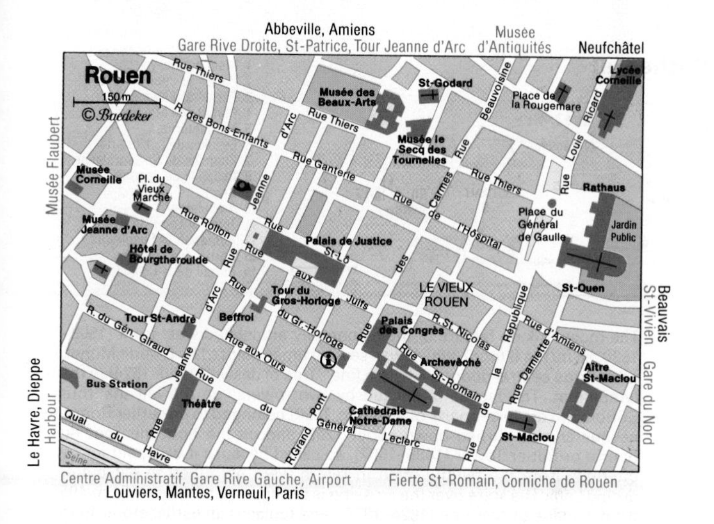

16th and 17th centuries hampered the development of the town stimulated by the rise of the textile industry, and after the revocation of the Edict of Nantes in 1685 it lost more than half its population. Prosperity began to return only in the 18th c. with the revival of the textile industry.

Sights

*Place du Vieux Marché

The old market-place and centre of Rouen is the Place du Vieux Marché, surrounded by handsome old houses. In 1979 new buildings were erected to the east and north, which include the Market (Les Halles), the Galerie du Souvenir (with an exhibition portraying the square's history) and a church. The church of Ste-Jeanne-d'Arc (inside which can be seen a 16th c. window from the church of St-Vincent which was destroyed during the last war) and a large cross bear memory to Jeanne d'Arc, who was burned at the stake here on 30th May 1431. Excavations have revealed fragments of the church of St-Sauveur, which was destroyed during the French Revolution.
On the south side of the square stands the Musée Jeanne d'Arc, with wax figures portraying her life and work.

Hotêl de Bourgtheroulde

To the south of the Place du Marché stands the Hotêl de Bourgtheroulde, a splendid mansion built between 1486 and 1531 for Guillaume Le Roux, with a beautiiful courtyard and fine relief ornament.

Rue du Gros-Horloge

From the south-east corner of the Place du Vieux Marché Rue du Gros Horloge leads to the Cathedral. Half way along it passes through the Tour du Gros-Horloge, a defensive tower built in 1389–98 (clock dates from 1889), adjoining which is a Renaissance pavilion.

*Palais de Justice

The Palais de Justice (at the end of the pedestrian zone, a little to the north of the Gros Horloge) is a masterpiece of Gothic architecture. Once the meeting-place of the Parlement (Exhiquier) of Normandie, it was built by Roulland Le Roux in 1508–1509, badly damaged in 1944 and subsequently restored.

*Cathedral

In the Place de la Cathédrale, in the centre of the old town on the right bank of the Seine, stands the Gothic Cathedral of Notre-Dame, one of the largest and most magnificent in France. The main structure was completed between 1202 and 1220 and the transept was built in 1280, but the building was not completed until the 16th c.

Rouen Cathedral

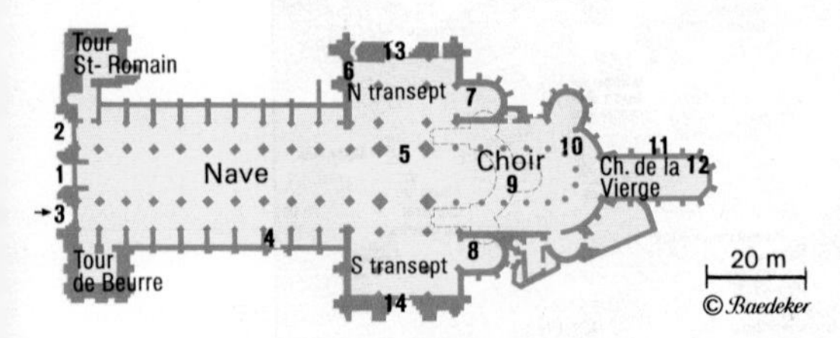

1 Main doorway
2 Portail St-Jean
3 Portail St-Etienne
4 Portail des Maçons
5 Tourlanterne
6 Escalier de la Librairie
7 Chapelle du St-Sacrament
8 Chapelle de Jeanne d'Arc
9 Crypt
10 Ambulatory
11 Tomb of Louis de Brézé
12 Adoration of Shepherds
13 Portail des Libraires
14 Portail de la Calende

*West front

The most striking feature of the elaborately articulated west front (1509–1530, 56 m/184 ft long), which was several times painted by Claude Monet, is the large central doorway, with a fine "Tree of Jesse" (1520–1524) in the tympanum. The façade is flanked by two towers: on the left the Tour St-Romain, the lower parts of which (*c.* 1150) belonged to an earlier Romanesque church burned down about 1200, and on the right the Tour du Beurre or Butter Tower (1485–1507), so called because it was paid for by offerings from the faithful, who in return were permitted to eat butter during Lent. The spire over the crossing is the highest in France (151 m/495 ft); it is made of cast-iron (1824–1876), and replaces an earlier stone spire destroyed by lightning in 1822. The side doorways are also very beautiful, particularly the one on the north side, the richly sculptured Portail des Libraires, named after the booksellers' shops once numerous in this quarter. Also of interest is the fine south doorway, the Portail de la Calende.

Interior

The interior of the Cathedral, restored after the severe damage it suffered during the Second World War, still preserves some old stained glass. Behind the high altar is the Chapelle de la Vierge (Lady Chapel, 1302–1320), on the left-hand wall of which is the tomb of Pierre II de Brézé (d. 1465) and his wife, and next to it the white marble tomb of his grandson Louis de Brézé (d. 1531), by Jean Cousin and Jean Goujon (1535–1544). Opposite, on the right-hand wall, is the tomb of Cardinals Georges I and II of Amboise (d. 1510 and 1541), both archbishops of Rouen, by Roulland Le Roux, a master builder who worked on the Cathedral and the Palais de Justice (1522–1525). In the crypt, which belonged to the earlier 11th c. church, is preserved the heart of Charles V. Opposite the Cathedral stands a pretty Renaissance building (1510), formerly the Bureau des Finances, now the Rouen Tourist Office.

Archbishop's Palace

Adjoining the Cathedral on the east is the Archbishop's Palace (Archevêché), parts of which date from the 15th c.

*Eglise St-Maclou

Farther east stands the Late Gothic church of St-Maclou (1437–1521), with a high tower over the crossing added in 1868. On the twin-towered west front with its magnificent porch are two doors with fine wood carvings of Biblical scenes, probably by Jean Goujon.

*Aître St-Maclou

Just north of the church, at 184–186 Rue Martainville, is the Aître St-Maclou, a medieval charnel-house, with fine wooden galleried buildings (16th–17th c.) round the courtyard.

*St-Ouen

Rue Damiette leads north to the church of St-Ouen, an outstanding example of Late Gothic architecture. The main structure was built between 1318 and 1339; the west doorway and the two towers date from 1846–1851. Over the crossing is a magnificent tower, the pinnacled topmost section of which (1490–1515) is known as the "Crown of Normandy". In the south transept can be seen the Portail des Marmouses, with representations of the Death and Assumption of the Virgin.
In the harmoniously proportioned interior (134 m/440 ft long, 26 m/85 ft wide – 42 m/138 ft wide in the transept – and 32.5 m/107 ft high) are 135

View of Rouen

windows, some with 15th and 16th c. stained glass, a beautiful choir screen (1738–1747) and a famous organ in an organ-loft of 1630.
On the Place du Général du Gaulle, with an equestrian statue of Napoleon I (1865) stands the Hôtel de Ville (Town Hall), and behind it are the old abbey gardens, now a municipal park.

* Musée des Beaux-Arts

On the east side of the tree-planted Square Verdrel is the Musée des Beaux-Arts, one of the finest provincial museums in France, with a notable collection of 16th to 20th c. pictures, including works by David, Rubens, Veronese, Caravaggio, Ribera, Velázquez, Clouet, Poussin, Fragonard, Ingres, Géricault, Delacroix, Monet, Sisley, Renoir, Dufy, Duchamp, Soulage and Dubuffet. The museum is being extended and work is expected to take until 1995, but it should remain open to visitors.

* Musée de la Céramique

This museum, housed in the former Hôtel d'Hocqueville (1657), has one Europe's richest collections of ceramics.

* Musée Le Secq des Tournelles

In the old Gothic church of St-Laurent is the Musée Le Secq de Tournelles, with a unique collection of wrought-iron work, including grilles, signs, doors, locks and clocks. Nearby stands the Gothic church of St-Godard (15th c.), with magnificent stained glass, including a "Tree of Jesus" in the Lady Chapel.

Other museums

In a former monastery is the Musée des Antiquités, with a collection of religious sculpture, architectural elements, tombstones, goldsmith's work and ancient mosaics, displayed in the Gothic cloister and adjoining rooms.
The Musée d'Histoire Naturelle, de Préhistoire et d'Ethnographie displays interesting zoological, mineralogical, palaeontological, ethnographic and prehistoric collections.

Fierte St-Romain

To the south of the Cathedral, extending to the banks of the Seine, is a district of modern flats. The only remnant of the old town here is the Fierte St-Roman (near the old market halls), a unique Renaissance building of 1542.

Bridges

There are fine views of the riverside quays and the towers and spires of the city from the Seine bridges, rebuilt after the last war, e.g. from the Pont Corneille, which cuts across the tip of the Ile Lacroix, and particularly from the Pont Boïeldieu at the end of Rue Grand-Pont. There are also excellent views from the left bank of the river.

St-Romain

The richly decorated church of St-Romain (17th–18th c.) lies to the east of the Gare Rive Droite (railway station). West of the station stands the neo-Romanesque church of St-Gervais (1868–1876), with a 4th c. crypt, a relic of an earlier church, under the choir. The site was formerly occupied by a priory in which William the Conqueror died in 1087.

Tour Jeanne d'Arc

Rue Jeanne-d'Arc was driven through the old town in 1860, and today provides the main link road between the north and south of the city. In Rue du Donjon, a small side road, stands the the Tour Jeanne d'Arc, all that remains of a castle built by Philippe Auguste in 1207. In this tower Joan of Arc was brought before her judges and tortured in 1431.
To the west of Rue Jeanne-d'Arc is the 16th c. church of St-Patrice, with fine stained glass (1538–1625). Gustave Flaubert was born in the Hôtel-Dieu, in the west of the city, which now houses the Musée Flaubert and also a Museum of Medical History.

*Côte Ste-Catherine

From the hill in the east of the city known as Côte Ste-Catherine there is a fine view of Rouen and the Seine.

Surroundings of Rouen

Croisset

6 km/4 miles west of Rouen is Gustave Flaubert's house at Croisset, now a museum.

*Route des Abbayes

The well-signposted "Route des Abbayes" leads between Rouen and Le Havre, running parallel to the Seine for much of the way. The ever-changing landscape and the many interesting old buildings such as the abbeys of Jumièges and St-Wandrille make this journey well worthwhile.

Saint-Etienne M9

Region: Rhône–Alpes. Département: Loire
Altitude: 517 m/1695 ft. Population: 222,000

Situation and characteristics

St-Etienne, chief town of the département of Loire, lies south-west of Lyons on the little river Furan, a few kilometres east of the upper Loire. Its importance as a busy industrial centre dates only from the 19th c. As the principal centre in the Loire coalfield, it has developed a variety of industry – most importantly metal-working, but also the manufacture of arms and glass. It has been noted since the 16th c. for the manufacture of ribbons.
The people of St-Etienne are called Stéphanois (Etienne = Stephen).

Sights

Hôtel de Ville

In the centre of St-Etienne is the Place de l'Hôtel-de-Ville, in which stands the Town Hall (1882).

St-Etienne

South-west of the Place de l'Hôtel-de-Ville, in Place Boivin, is the 15th c. church of St-Etienne, which was damaged during the wars of religion. Around the square are a number of 16th c. houses, and in the adjoining Place du Peuple is a fine half-timbered house, also 16th c.
A little way south is the Comédie de St-Etienne, a theatre founded by Jean Dasté in 1947, which has had, and continues to have, a great influence on the theatre in France.

Musée d'Art et d'Industrie

The Museum of Art and Industry, to the south of the city centre, has four sections devoted to mining, arms technology, textile manufacture and two-wheeled vehicles – all subjects of economic importance to St-Etienne.

In the Museum of Modern Art

*Musée d'Art Moderne

In the northern district of La Terrasse is the new Museum of Modern Art, a long tile-faced building designed by Didier Guichard (1987), with a large collection which ranks it among the leading French museums. It displays works by the "classic" modern painters such as Picasso, Léger, Miró, Picabia and Schwitters, but concentrates particularly on the art of the post-war period including the German Neo-Expressionists.

Surroundings of St-Etienne

Chazelles-sur-Lyon

25 km/15 miles north-east of St-Etienne is the little town of Chazelles-sur-Lyon. The Musée du Chapeau (Hat Museum) illustrates the history and explains the techniques of hat-making. See Lyons, Surroundings.

Grangent

West of St-Etienne is one of the few dams on the Loire, forming the long narrow Lac de Grangent, which is almost completely surrounded by forest. On what was formerly a hill but is now an island in the lake is the ruined castle of Grangent.

Montbrison

36 km/22 miles north-west is the ancient little town of Montbrison, huddled around a hill between the Loire plain and the Monts du Forez. In the south of the town, near the river Vizézy, is the Gothic church of Notre-Dame-d'Espérance (early 13th c.), with a 15th c. doorway in Flamboyant style. Behind the apse is the former chapterhouse (known as the Diana), now used as a library, with a fine wooden ceiling of 1728. On the boulevard which runs around the town, to the west, is the Musée d'Allard, with an interesting collection of dolls and puppets and a cabinet of minerals. Beyond the museum is the Parc d'Allard.

Montrond-les-Bains

23 km/14 miles north of St-Etienne, on the right bank of the Loire, is the little spa of Montrond-les-Bains, with a ruined castle (14th–16th c.) from which there are fine views of the hills of Forez and the Parc du Pilat.

Parc Régional du Pilat

This nature park, established in 1974, lies 3 km/2 miles south-east of St-Etienne and extends for a further 27 km/17 miles. It is centred on the Mont Pilat massif, which separates the Loire from the Rhône and reaches heights of 1370 m/4495 ft in the Crêt de l'Œillon, to the north-east, and 1432 m/4698 ft in the Crêt de la Perdrix. On the northern slopes of the range are a number of artificial lakes formed by dams.

St-Galmier

16 km/10 miles north of St-Etienne, on the little river Coise, is St-Galmier, with mineral springs which yield a well known table water. The church (15th–17th c.), in Flamboyant style, has a beautiful figure of the Virgin (the Vierge du Pilier) and a Flemish triptych.

Saint-Malo

E/F 6

Region: Bretagne (Brittany)
Département: Ille-et-Vilaine
Altitude: sea level
Population: 47,000

Situation and characteristics

The Breton port of St-Malo has a magnificent situation on a former island now joined to the mainland at the mouth of the broad river Rance, facing the town of Dinard (see Brittany) across the river to the west. Still surrounded by its old walls, it preserves the aspect of a fortified coastal town of the Middle Ages.

*Old town

During the Second World War the old town was largely destroyed, with the exception of the walls, but was rebuilt after the war in its original style, with narrow little streets and tall granite houses.

History

The town takes its name from a Gallic monk named Maclow who became bishop of Aleth in the 6th c., Aleth was the predecessor of the present town of St-Malo, which was founded about 1150 on a nearby rocky island. St Malo's heyday was in the 16th–18th centuries, when Jacques Cartier (1491–1557), a native of the town, discovered Canada (1534) and established some of his fellow-citizens as its first settlers, and when other daring seamen from St-Malo were sailing the seas in all directions. The writer and statesman François-René de Chateaubriand (1768–1848) was born in St-Malo.

Sights

Place Chateaubriand

Inside the walls at the north-east corner of the old town, near the handsome Porte St-Vincent, is Place Chateaubriand. The Hôtel France et Chateaubriand occupies the site of the house in which Chateaubriand was born.

Castle

On the east side of the square is the massive bulk of the castle (14th and 15th c.), with four towers. In one of the towers, the Tour Quic-en-Groigne at the north-west corner, is the Galerie Quic-en-Groigne, which has interesting displays, with wax figures, illustrating events in the history of the town. In the south-west wing of the castle is the Municipal Museum, also mainly devoted to the history of the town. From here visitors can gain access to the towers, from which there are fine views.

Other sights

Immediately west of the castle, in Place Vauban, is an interesting Aquarium, built into the town walls, opposite which is an "Exotarium". South-west of the castle is the parish church of St-Vincent, formerly a cathedral (14th and 15th c., with a façade of 1713).

*Ramparts

From the Porte St-Thomas, immediately north of Place Chateaubriand, and from the other town gates, steps lead up to the ramparts, which in some

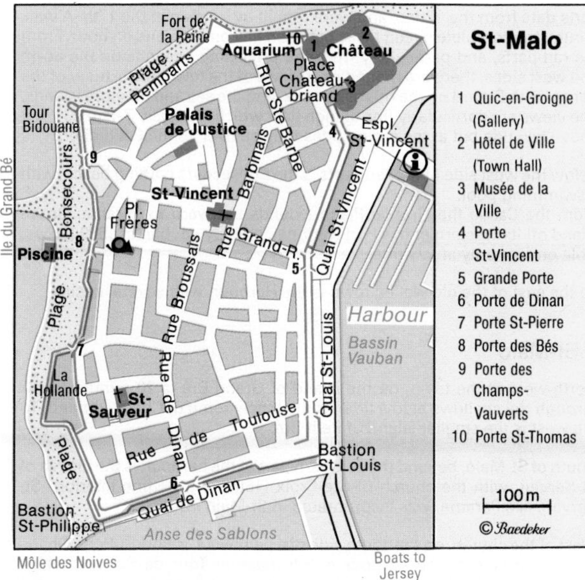

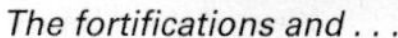
The fortifications and . . .

. . . harbour of St-Malo

parts date from the 12th c. and were rebuilt by Vauban in the 17th. A walk around the complete circuit takes between half an hour and an hour. From the ramparts, and particularly from the projecting bastions on the north and west sides, there are magnificent views of the town, the estuary of the Rance, with Dinard on the opposite bank, and the sea and offshore islands. The views are particularly fine at high tide, which is usually 7–8 m/23–26 ft above low tide but at the spring tides may be over 15 m/50 ft higher.

Bathing beaches

Below the west side of the ramparts is the Bonsecours bathing beach, with a swimming pool.
From the Castle the Grande Plage extends eastward to Paramé. On an island off its western end is Fort National, built by Vauban in 1689 (accessible on foot only at low tide).

Harbour

To the east of the old walled town is the Harbour, with several basins.

Surroundings of St-Malo

Grand Bré

North-west of the town, on the island of Grand Bré (a 20 minutes' walk through the shallows at low tide), is the lonely tomb of Chateaubriand. To the west is the smaller island of Petit Bré.

St-Servan
Ste-Croix

South of St-Malo, beyond the southern part of the harbour, is the district of St-Servan, with the church of Ste-Croix (18th–19th c.; fine interior). St-Servan, like Paramé, was incorporated in St-Malo in 1967.

Port St-Père

West of the church, on the south side of a peninsula, is Port St-Père. On the south-east side of the harbour is the massive Tour de Solidor, which actually consists of three towers; long used as a prison, it now houses the Musée International du Long-Cours-Cap-Hornier, with exhibits illustrating the history of the voyages of discovery and seafaring on the high seas.

*Corniche d'Aleth

From the north side of the harbour a magnificent promenade, the Corniche d'Aleth, encircles the Aleth peninsula, offering wide-ranging views. On the west side of the peninsula, on the site of the Gallo-Roman town of Aleth, is the Fort de la Cité, which was strengthened and stubbornly defended by German forces during the Second World War.

*River cruise
Tidal power station

A cruise up the river Rance, passing Dinard and the tidal power station, to Dinan and back is strongly to be recommended. The return trip, without disembarking, takes about 4 hours.

Saint-Tropez

See Côte d'Azur

Savoy

N/O 8/9

*Situation and characteristics

The French Alps, the most westerly and the highest part of the great arc of the Alps, occupy the old provinces of Savoy and Dauphiné (see entry) and extend also into Provence (see entry).
The historical region of Savoy (French Savoie, Italian Savoia), corresponding broadly to the present-day départements of Haute-Savoie (chief town Annecy) to the north and Savoie (Chambéry) to the south, extends from the southern shores of Lake Geneva (Lac Léman) to a line running from Les Echelles (between Chambéry and Grenoble) by way of the Col de la Croix

View of Val-d'Isère ▶

de Fer to the Col du Galibier, and is bounded on the west by the middle Rhône valley and on the east by the Italian region of Piedmont.
Most of this area is occupied by the magnificent Savoy Alps, extending between Lake Geneva and the Isère valley and rising to a height of 4807 m/15,772 ft in Mont Blanc, the highest peak in the Alps. To the west is a beautiful pre-Alpine lake district, with the Lac d'Annecy and the Lac du Bourget, surrounded by mountains rising to 1800 m/5900 ft.

History

The history of Savoy, the ancestral territory of the Italian royal house, has followed a different course from that of the Dauphiné. Early traces of human settlement have been found on the shores of the Lac du Bourget and Lac d'Annecy. The region, originally inhabited by a Celtic tribe, the Allobroges, was occupied by the Romans in the 2nd c. B.C. and became part of the province of Gallia Cisalpina. From the 5th c. the Burgundians began to settle here, founding the kingdom of Burgundy which (including Savoy) was incorporated in the German Empire (the Holy Roman Empire) in 1033. Nevertheless the Counts of Savoy retained their independence and, secure in their possession of the Alpine passes, sought to extend their domains into Italy and France and consequently became involved in bitter warfare. In 1101 the Counts of Savoy gained the status of Counts of the Empire and in 1416 became Dukes of Savoy. In 1418 they transferred their residence to Turin in the northern Italian principality of Piedmont but continued to call themselves Dukes of Savoy. After the wars of religion, in 1564, Savoy was compelled to cede Geneva, Vaud and the Valais to the Swiss Confederation. It saw further fighting during its wars with Louis XIV of France, Following a victory by Prince Eugene of Savoy at Turin, the treaty of Utrecht (1713) brought Savoy additional territory in the form of the kingdom of Sicily, which it exchanged soon afterwards for Sardinia. After the unification of Italy the House of Savoy ceded Savoy and Nice to France in recognition of French military assistance, and this transfer was confirmed by a plebiscite in 1860.
The 19th c. saw the development of the railway (which reached Fréjus in 1872) and the road system.

Tourism

Climbers and winter sports enthusiasts have long recognised the attractions of Savoy.
Winter sports resorts like Chamonix (see entry), Megève, Morzine and Val d'Isère have an international reputation, as have spas like Aix-les-Bains, Thonon and Evian.

Mont Blanc Tunnel

The Mont Blanc Tunnel, a road tunnel 11.6 km/7¼ miles long, gives Savoy (and Europe north of the Alps) a direct link with Italy.

Agriculture – cattle-rearing, dairy farming, wine-making, fruit-growing – still plays an important part in the economy.

Sights

Aix-les-Bains
* Lac du Bourget

Aix-les-Bains (pop. 23,500) lies under Mont Revard on the east side of the Lac du Bourget (18 km/11 miles long, 2–3 km/1½–2 miles across, 60–100 m/200–330 ft deep). It has an international reputation as a spa with an equable climate. Its springs were already being used for curative purposes in Roman times, and up to 45,000 people now come here every year to take the waters.
The Thermes Nationaux (two spa establishments, the older one dating from 1864, the other from 1934, with an extension in 1972; remains of Roman baths) are open to visitors. Other Roman remains are the 9 m/30 ft high Arch of Campanus and the Temple of Diana. The Town Hall occupies the 16th c. château of the Marquis d'Aix; the elegant Renaissance staircase is built of stone from Roman structures.
The Musée du Docteur-Faure has a collection of pictures, mainly by Impressionists, and faience.

Château de Menthon

Lac d'Annecy

Aix-les-Bains is a good centre for drives around the lake and cruises on the lake, for example to the abbey of Hautecombe, with the tombs of the Dukes of Savoy. The elaborately decorated church, restored in the 19th c., has a 16th c. doorway.

*Hautecombe Abbey

Albertville

This lively town (pop. 17,500), situated at the junction of the Arly and the Isère, was founded by King Charles-Albert of Savoy in the 19th c., and is laid out on a regular plan. A good base from which to explore the Trois Vallées district, it is also a much frequented winter sports resort, with excellent facilities for skiing in the surrounding area. It is due to stage the Winter Olympics in 1992.

*Conflans

Conflans, the oldest part of Albertville, lies on a spur of hill above the town. It is an attractive relic of the past with its Gothic town gates, massive walls, old houses and Baroque church.
From the Col de la Tamié (cableway) there are breathtaking views.

Annecy

The attractive little town of Annecy (alt. 448 m/1470 ft; pop. 55,000), beautifully situated on its lake, has a considerable amount of industry, including the bell-foundry which made the famous "Savoyarde" bell for the Sacré-Cœur in Paris.

*Old town

The old town, traversed by innumerable little water channels, lies round the river Thiou (here canalised), which flows out of the lake. It has a number of churches, including the 15th c. church of St-Maurice and the Cathedral of St-Pierre (16th c.), to the west of which is the Bishop's Palace (1784). Other fine buildings are the modern Palais de Justice (Law Courts, 1978) and the Conservatoire d'Art et d'Histoire, with the Payot collection. Rue Ste-Claire is an attractive arcaded street with houses of the 16th–18th centuries.
On an island in the Thiou is the 15th c. Palais de l'Isle, which contains a small museum (stones with inscriptions). Along the beautiful shores of the lake runs the Avenue d'Albigny, shaded by plane-trees, which offers fine

Landscape near Evian

views over the lake. The château, once the residence of the Counts of Geneva, was given its present form in the 15th and 16th centuries; it too contains a museum.

*Mont Veyrier

A drive round the lake is one of the great attractions of Annecy. From Mont Veyrier (1691 m/5548 ft) there are magnificent views.

Menthon

The Château de Menthon, picturesquely situated on the east side of the lake, dates from the 13th–15th centuries.

Chambéry

Chambéry (alt. 270 m/885 ft; pop. 55,000), capital of the independent state of Savoy from the 13th to the 16th c., lies on the fast-flowing river Leysse in a fertile basin surrounded by hills and mountains. It is dominated by the old castle of the Dukes of Savoy (14th–15th c.). At the end of the castle's north wing is the Gothic Ste-Chapelle (1408), with fine stained glass and paintings in the apse by Vicario (1831). Other features of interest are the Treasury Tower (Tour Trésorerie), the state apartments and the Portail St-Dominique, a doorway in Flamboyant style which belonged to an earlier Dominican house.

Elephant Fountain

*Musée Savoisien

The best known monument in the town is the Elephant Fountain commemorating General Comte de Boigne (1751–1830). In close proximity to one another are the cathedral, with an unfinished west front (15th c.), an old monastic chapel with a beautiful Flamboyant doorway and the former Bishop's Palace, now housing the Musée Savoisien (prehistoric material, folk art and traditions, mementoes of the House of Savoy). The Musée des Beaux-Arts, in a former granary, has works by Uccello, Titian, Guérin and Watteau. The town's finest old mansions are in Rue Croix-d'Or.

Les Charmettes

2 km/1½ miles south is the little country house of Les Charmettes, where Jean-Jacques Rousseau stayed with Mme de Warens from 1736 to 1742. His impressions of the place are recorded in his "Confessions".

Chamonix

See entry

Evian-les-Bains
Lake Geneva

Evian-les-Bains (alt. 375–500 m/1230–1650 ft; pop. 6200; casino) is beautifully situated on the south side of Lake Geneva (Lac Léman), which has an area of 582 sq. km/225 sq. miles (72 km/45 miles long, up to 14 km/9 miles across) and a maximum depth of 310 m/1015 ft. Evian is popular both as a spa and as a holiday resort, and its annual musical festival attracts many visitors.

Grenoble

See entry

Megève
*Excursions

Megève (alt. 1113 m/3650 ft; pop. 5300) is one of France's leading winter sports resorts, and is also a popular summer holiday resort. There are a number of cableways, e.g. up the Croix de Rochebrune (1750 m/5742 ft), Croix des Salles (1704 m/5591 ft) and Mont d'Arbois (1829 m/6001 ft).

Mont Blanc

See Chamonix

Morzine-Avoriaz

Morzine-Avoriaz (alt. 1000–1800 m/3300–5900 ft; pop. 3000) lies at the meeting of six valleys and offers endless scope for mountain walking and climbing in summer and skiing in winter. Nearby, at an altitude of 1049 m/3442 ft, are the Lac de Montriond and the Ardent Falls, which are particularly impressive when the thaw sets in.

St-Gervais-les-Bains

St-Gervais (alt. 900 m/2950 ft; pop. 4800) has been for more than a century one of the best known spas in Savoy. It is a good base for the ascent of Mont Blanc, either on foot or by cableway, and is also a popular winter sports resort, connected by a network of cableways with the skiing areas of Megève and Chamonix.

Thonon-les-Bains

Thonon (alt. 425 m/1395 ft; pop. 28,200), situated on a terrace above Lake Geneva (magnificent views), is a popular holiday place, both in summer and in winter, as well as a spa. The Place du Château occupies the site of a stronghold of the Dukes of Savoy which was destroyed in 1589. The 17th c. Château de Sonnaz houses a museum devoted to the folk art and traditions of the Chablais district round Thonon.
A few kilometres west are the attractive lakeside resorts of Excenevex, with a beautiful natural beach, and Yvoire, which still preserves its old 14th c. walls (with two gates) on the landward side as well as a number of medieval houses.

Tignes

Tignes (alt. 1810 m/5940 ft; pop. 1000) is notable both for the Lac de Tignes (alt. 2100 m/6890 ft), a popular summer and winter resort and one of the highest and most modern skiing centres in France, and for the huge dam built to supply a hydroelectric power station, the largest on the upper Isère, producing over a billion kilowatts.
From the Lac de Tignes there are cableways to a height of more than 3000 m/9840 ft, e.g. to the Grande Motte (3459 m/11,349 ft), so that skiing is possible even in summer.

Val d'Isère
*Excursions

Val d'Isère (alt. 1850 m/6070 ft; pop. 1300) has long been a favourite skiing area with numerous lifts and cableways, for example up the Rocher de Bellevarde (2826 m/9272 ft) and the Tête de Solaise (2551 m/8370 ft).

Valloire

Valloire (alt. 1430 m/4690 ft; pop. 1000) is a popular resort both in summer and in winter. It has a richly decorated 17th c. church.

Sport and Recreation in Savoy

Walking and climbing in summer and all kinds of winter sports are the main attractions, but there are many other possibilities, for example fishing in the mountain streams and lakes. Many resorts have tennis courts and facilities for riding and bathing, as well as a number of golf-courses (see Practical Information, Sport).

Strasbourg **P6**

Region: Alsace
Département: Bas-Rhin
Altitude: 136 m/445 ft
Population: 252,000

Situation and characteristics

Strasbourg – capital of Alsace (see entry), a university town, the see of a bishop, seat of the Council of Europe, the European Commission of Human Rights and the European Science Foundation, and as the meeting-place of the European Parliament the germ of a future united Europe – lies at the intersection of important traffic routes on the left bank of the Rhine, which at this point is joined by the river Ill, the Rhine–Marne Canal and the Rhine–Rhône Canal.
With its soaring cathedral and many burghers' houses of the 16th and 17th centuries, Strasbourg still retains something of the character of an old free city of the Holy Roman Empire, but is also typically French with its elegant buildings in Louis XV style, dating from the time of the French Cardinal-Bishops of the 18th c., and its numerous mansard roofs.

Economy

The city's principal industries are metal-working, the manufacture of building materials and the production of foodstuffs (brewing, pâté de foie gras), followed by papermaking, textiles and tanning. The port of Strasbourg is the largest on the Upper Rhine, and is particularly active in the export trade. Tourism has now also become an important element in the economy of the city, which attracts increasing numbers of visitors as the principal tourist centre of Alsace and the venue of numerous congresses and conferences.

History

About A.D. 16 the Romans established a fortified post which they called Argentoratum beside an earlier Celtic settlement situated on important trade routes. In the 4th c. the Alemanni built a new settlement on its ruins, and this appears in the records in the 6th c. under the name of Strataburgum ("the fortified town on the roads"). In 842 Louis (Ludwig) the German and Charles the Bald confirmed their alliance against Lothair I in the "Serments de Strasbourg" ("Strasbourg Oaths"), one of the earliest specimens of Old French. Strasbourg became the see of a bishop in 1003 and rose to considerable prosperity through its shipping and its trade. In 1262, after a conflict with the bishop and the nobility, it achieved independence as a free imperial city, which for a time was the wealthiest and most brilliant in the Holy Roman Empire, a city in which art and learning flourished. In the 14th c. the Dominican preachers and mystics Meister Eckhart and Johannes Tauler lived in Strasbourg, and between 1434 and 1444 Gutenberg developed the art of printing here. After the coming of the Reformation in 1520 Strasbourg numbered among its citizens the Protestant writer and satirist Johannes Fischart (1546–1590) and the educationalist Johannes Sturm (1507–1589), rector of the Protestant grammar school and founder of a theological academy which was the forerunner of the University.
In 1681, taking advantage of the weakness of the Holy Roman Empire, Louis XIV occupied Strasbourg and soon afterwards had it fortified by Vauban. Until 1793, however, the town retained a degree of autonomy, and French cultural influence did not assert itself until the time of Napoleon.
After the Franco-Prussian War of 1870–1871 Strasbourg, along with the rest of Alsace (apart from Belfort) and part of Lorraine, returned to German sovereignty, and remained German until the end of the First World War.

View of Strasbourg Cathedral from Rue Mercière ▶

TABAC
SOUVENIRS

Strasbourg

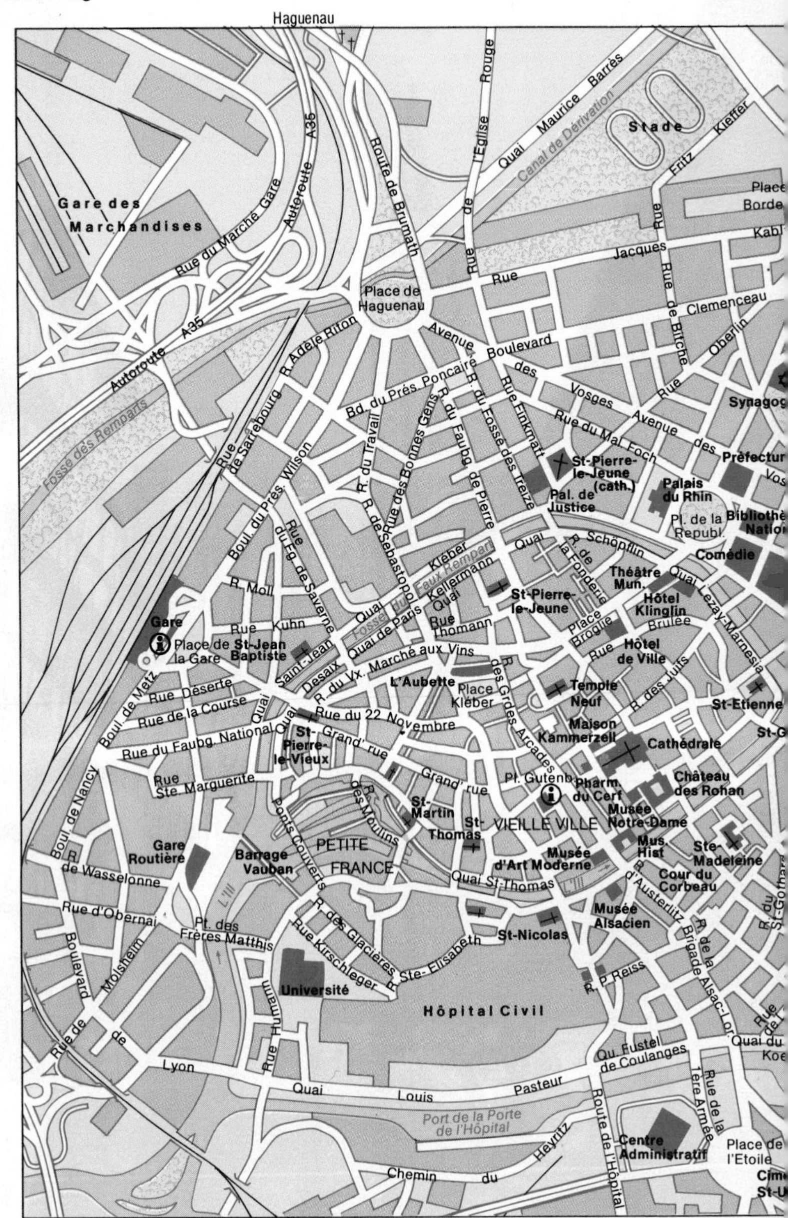

Haguenau
Gare des Marchandises
Rue du Marché Gare
Autoroute A35
Route de Brumath
Rue de l'Eglise Rouge
Quai Maurice Barrès
Canal de Dérivation
Stade
Fritz Kieffer
Place Bordeaux
Rue Jacques
Rue de Bitche
Place de Haguenau
Clemenceau
Oberlin
R. Adèle Riton
Avenue des Vosges
Boulevard des Vosges
Bd. du Prés. Poincaré
Rue du Mal. Foch
Synagogue
Préfecture
Fossé des Remparts
Rue de Sarrebourg
Boul. du Prés. Wilson
R. du Travail
R. de Sébastopol
Rue des Bonnes Gens
R. du Faubg. de Pierre
R. du Fossé des Treize
Rue Finkmatt
St-Pierre-le-Jeune (cath.)
Pal. de Justice
Palais du Rhin
Pl. de la Républ.
Bibliothèque Nationale
Quai Schöpflin
Comédie
Théâtre Mun.
Hôtel Klinglin
Quai Lezay-Marnésia
R. de la Fonderie
Rue du Fg. de Saverne
Quai Kleber
Fossé du Faux Rempart
Quai Kellermann
St-Pierre-le-Jeune
R. Moll
Gare
Place de la Gare
Rue Kuhn
St-Jean Baptiste
Quai Saint-Jean
Quai de Paris
Rue Thomann
Place Broglie
Rue Brulée
Hôtel de Ville
Quai Desaix
R. du Vx. Marché aux Vins
L'Aubette
Place Kléber
R. des Grdes Arcades
Temple Neuf
R. des Juifs
St-Etienne
Boul. de Metz
Rue Déserte
Rue de la Course
Quai
Rue du 22 Novembre
Maison Kammerzell
Cathédrale
Rue du Faubg. National
St-Pierre-le-Vieux
Grand' rue
Rue Ste. Marguerite
Pl. Gutenb.
Pharm. du Cerf
Château des Rohan
Boul. de Nancy
St-Martin
R. des Moulins
St-Thomas
VIEILLE VILLE
Musée Notre-Dame
Ponts Couverts
PETITE FRANCE
Mus. Hist
Ste-Madeleine
Gare Routière
Barrage Vauban
Musée d'Art Moderne
R. de Wasselonne
Quai St-Thomas
Cour du Corbeau
L'Ill
R. d'Austerlitz
Rue d'Obernai
Pt. des Frères Matthis
R. des Glacières
Musée Alsacien
Rue Kirschleger
St-Nicolas
Brigade Alsac-Lor.
Boulevard de Lyon
Rue de Molsheim
Rue Ste-Elisabeth
R. de la
R. P. Reiss
Université
Hôpital Civil
Rue Humann
Qu. Fustel de Coulanges
Quai du
Rue de Lyon
Quai Louis Pasteur
Rue de la 1ère Armée
Port de la Porte de l'Hôpital
Route de l'Hôpital
Rue du Heyritz
Centre Administratif
Place de l'Etoile
Chemin du
Colmar, Mulhouse, Basle
Airport
Illhaeursern, Obernal, Neuf-Brisach, C

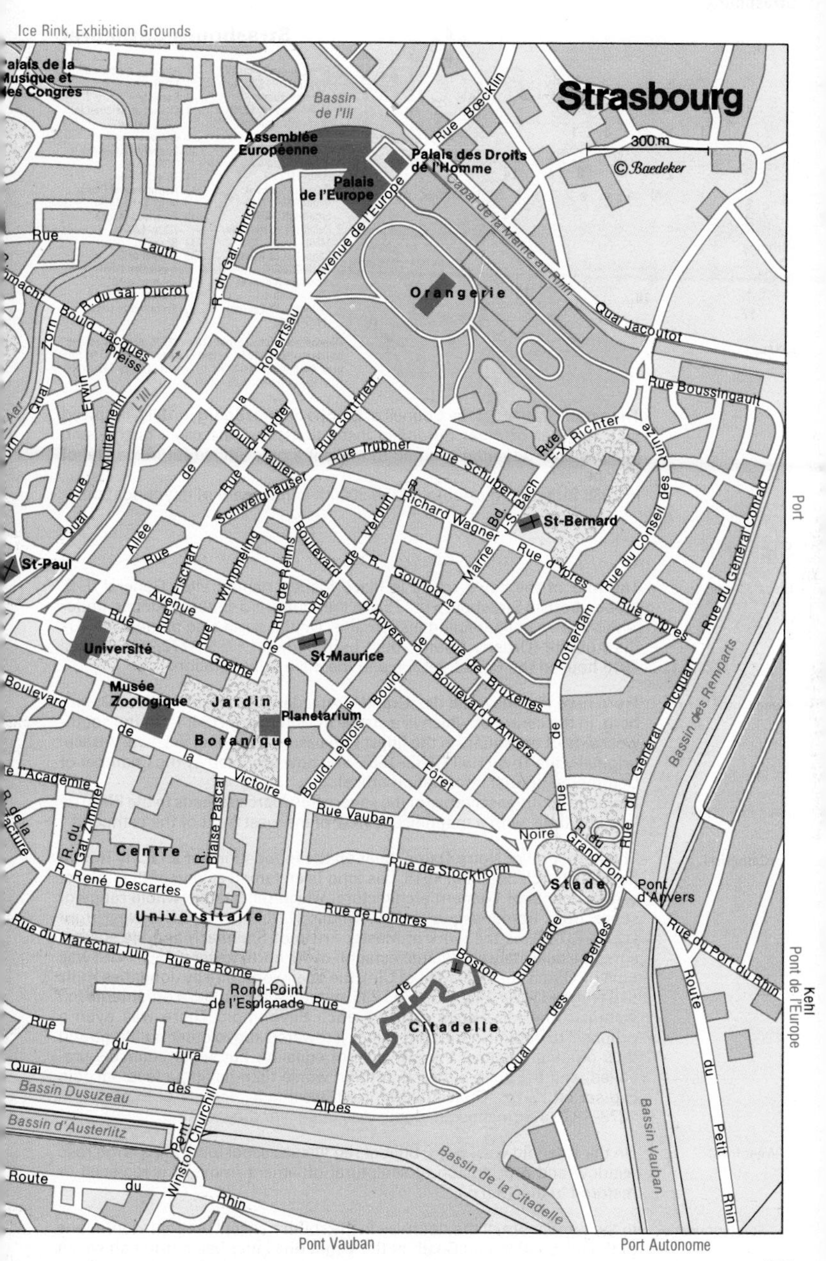
Ice Rink, Exhibition Grounds
Strasbourg
300 m
© Baedeker
Palais de la Musique et des Congrès
Assemblée Européenne
Palais de l'Europe
Palais des Droits de l'Homme
Bassin de l'Ill
Orangerie
St-Bernard
St-Paul
Université
St-Maurice
Musée Zoologique
Jardin Botanique
Planetarium
Centre Universitaire
Citadelle
Stade
Rond-Point de l'Esplanade
Pont d'Anvers
Bassin Dusuzeau
Bassin d'Austerlitz
Bassin de la Citadelle
Bassin Vauban
Bassin des Remparts
Port
Kehl
Pont de l'Europe
Pont Vauban
Port Autonome

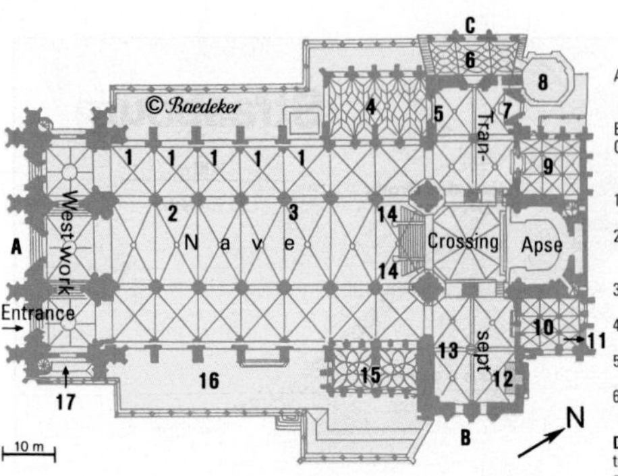

Strasbourg Cathedral

A Main doorway on W front (1270–1330); rose window above
B S doorway (c. 1230)
C Portail St-Laurent (1495–1505)

1 'Royal windows' (12th–14th c.)
2 Organ (orig. by A. Silbermann, 1714–1716; organ-loft 1489)
3 Pulpit (by J. Hammer, 1486)
4 Chapel of St-Martin (1515–1520)
5 Jesus on Mount of Olives (15th c.)
6 Chapel of St-Laurent (1495–1505)
7 Font (by J. Dotzinger, 1453)
8 Sacristy
9 Chapel of St-Jean (c. 1240; below chapterhouse)
10 Chapel of St-André (12th c.)
11 To exhibition
12 Astronomical Clock (orig. 1570–1574)
13 Pilier des Anges (1230–1240)
14 Stairs to crypt
15 Chapel of Ste-Catherine (1331; vaulting 1563)
16 Gallery
17 Entrance to tower

Dimensions: Total length 118 m/387 ft; breadth across transepts 58 m/190 ft; height of nave 31.5 m/103 ft; total area 4087 sq. m/44,000 sq. ft; height of spire 142 m/466 ft. to tower platform 66 m/217 ft.

The establishment of the Council of Europe in Strasbourg in 1949, followed by a number of other European institutions, and the city's history and geographical situation seemed to make it a predestined future capital of Europe.
In 1988 Strasbourg celebrated the 2000th anniversary of its foundation.

Sights

Place Kléber

The hub of the city's traffic is Place Kléber, named after General J.-B. Kléber, born in Strasbourg in 1753. In the square is a statue of Kléber, under which is a vault containing his remains. On the north side of the square is the Aubette (Orderly Room), built by Blondel in 1765–1772, which until 1918 housed the Conservatoire and the main police station.

Place Gutenberg

From here the busy Rue des Grandes-Arcades runs south to Place Gutenberg, in the centre of which is a statue of Gutenberg (1840). On the south-west side of the square is the finest Renaissance building in Lower Alsace, originally the Town Hall (1582–1585) and now occupied by the Chamber of Commerce (tourist information office).
From the south-east corner of the square Rue Mercière leads to the Place de la Cathédrale, with a magnificent view of the west front of the cathedral.

**Cathedral

The Cathedral of Notre-Dame, built on the foundations of an Early Romanesque church begun in 1015, has long been famed as one of the noblest achievements of Western architecture, which reflects the whole range of styles from Romanesque to Late Gothic (12th–15th c.). The west front (1277–1318) was the work of Master Erwin of Steinbach and his successors; the delicately articulated octagon of the north tower (1399–1419) was built by Ulrich von Ensingen of Ulm, the openwork spire by Johannes Hültz of Cologne (1420–1439). In 1793 235 statues and countless ornaments fell victim to the fanaticism of the French Revolution. There was even a proposal to demolish the spire, since it towered above other buildings and thus offended against the principle of equality; but saner counsels prevailed, and the spire suffered nothing worse than having a lead Jacobin cap set on its tip. The cathedral itself became a "Temple of Reason". In 1878–1879 a Romanesque dome was built over the crossing.

*West front

On the splendid west front, built of red Vosges sandstone, are a large rose window and a profusion of sculptural ornament (most of it replaced or restored in the 19th c.).

**South doorway

In the tympanum of the doorway in the south transept are representations of the Coronation and Death of the Virgin (the latter being original) which

Maison Kammerzell

Petite France

The picturesque Quartier des Tanneurs

rank among the highest achievements of medieval art. On either side are two other masterpieces, the famous allegorical figures of the Church and the Synagogue (by a German sculptor, *c.* 1230). Built on to the end of the north transept is the chapel of St-Laurent (1495–1505), with a magnificent Late Gothic façade.

*Interior

The interior has beautiful stained glass, including representations of 21 German emperors and kings in the north aisle, a Late Gothic pulpit (1484–1485) and an organ (1714–1716) by Andreas Silbermann (d. in Strasbourg 1734). In the south transept are the "Angels' Pillar" (Pilier des Anges, 1230–1240) and the famous Astronomical Clock (by Tobias Stimmer, 1539–1584; mechanism 1834–1842). Other notable features are the chapel of Ste-Catherine (1331 and 1563) in the south aisle and, in the north transept, the font (1453) and a sculptured group, "Christ on the Mount of Olives" (15th c.). Entered from the north transept (but not always open) is the chapel of St-Jean-Baptiste (*c.* 1240), with the tomb of Bishop Konrad von Lichtenberg (d. 1299).

*Tower

From the top of the tower there is a magnificent view of the city, the Rhine plain, the Black Forest and the Vosges.

*Maison Kammerzell

On the north side of the Place de la Cathédrale is the Maison Kammerzell (restaurant), the finest old burgher's house in the city, with a stone-built ground floor (1467), half-timbered upper floors (1589), leaded windows and rich carved ornament. At the corner of the Place de la Cathédrale and Rue Mercière is the half-timbered Pharmacie du Cerf (1567), on a site which has been continuously occupied by a pharmacy since 1268. Nearby, in Rue des Juifs, are the excavations of the Roman fort, begun in 1986.

Château des Rohan

On the south side of the cathedral is the Place du Château, with the Château des Rohan (1728–1742), which until the French Revolution was the residence of the Cardinal Bishops of the great Rohan family. On the ground and first floors are the bishop's apartments, with a library, a print room and a chapel. The château also houses the Archaeological Museum and the Municipal Art Gallery, with pictures by Italian, Spanish, Flemish, Dutch and French masters from the Middle Ages to modern times. In the right-hand wing is the Musée des Arts Décoratifs (ceramics, porcelain).

Maison de l'Œuvre Notre-Dame

At the south-west corner of the Place du Château is the Maison de l'Œuvre Notre-Dame, which has housed the Œuvre Notre-Dame (the authority responsible for the maintenance of the cathedral) since 1349. The east wing dates from 1347 (renovated in the 16th c.), the west wing from 1579–1585. It contains the Musée de l'Œuvre Notre-Dame, with the originals of sculpture from the cathedral and a number of pictures, mainly by artists from the Upper Rhine region.

Other sights

To the south-west, behind the Maison de l'Œuvre Notre-Dame, is the picturesque Place du Marché-aux-Cochons-de-Lait (Sucking Pig Market). Farther west is the Grande Boucherie, built in 1586–1588 as a meat market, which now houses the Municipal Historical Museum. Across the street to the west is the Ancienne Douane (Old Custom House), the oldest part of which dates from 1358. It is now occupied by the Museum of Modern Art, with a collection of 19th and 20th c. painting and culture, including works by Hans Arp, Braque, Klee, Max Ernst, Rodin, Renoir and Degas.
From the Ancienne Douane the Pont du Corbeau leads over the Ill to the Place du Corbeau, with an old inn, the Hôtellerie du Corbeau (14th c.; picturesque courtyard), once a posting station, where many notable people stayed between the 16th and 18th centuries, including Frederick the Great in 1740.

Musée Alsacien

West of the Place du Corbeau, in a patrician house of 1620, is the Musée Alsacien (folk art, furniture, costumes, domestic equipment, etc.).

The European Parliament

From Place Gutenberg the Rue des Serruriers (Locksmiths' Street) runs south-west to the church of St-Thomas, the only hall-church in Alsace, which has a Romanesque west end (1230–1250), a Gothic nave (*c.* 1330) and an octagonal tower over the crossing (1348), with a clock which for 400 years has struck the hours four minutes too soon, in order to make itself heard before the cathedral clock strikes. In the apse is the tomb of the French marshal Maurice de Saxe (d. 1750), an allegorical marble group by J.-B. Pigalle (1777). The church has a Silbermann organ (1737–1740), on which Albert Schweitzer frequently played.

*Quartier des Tanneurs
Petite France

North-west of St-Thomas is the old Quartier des Tanneurs (Tanners' Quarter), with picturesque half-timbered buildings lining its narrow streets, an area known as "Little France" (Petite France). In Rue du Bain-aux-Plantes is the old Gerwerstub or Maison des Tanneurs (restaurant). Farther south-west are the Ponts Couverts (Covered Bridges), four bridges, formerly roofed, over the Ill, which is here divided into four arms. Four of the town's medieval defence towers are also preserved here. The best view (and also a fine view of the town) is to be had from the Grande Ecluse, a dam built by Vauban.
North of the Ponts Couverts, on the western edge of the old town, is the church of St-Pierre-le-Vieux (14th–15th c.). From the south side of the church the old-world Grand' Rue leads back to Place Gutenberg.

Place Broglie

To the east of Place Kléber is the elongated rectangle of Place Broglie, laid out in 1742 on the site of the old horse market. Along the south side of this square are a number of imposing 18th c. buildings, with their main fronts on Rue Brûlée. The Old Town Hall, built in 1730–1736 as the residence of the Landgrave of Hesse, was the seat of municipal administration from 1805 to 1976. To the east, set in gardens, is the Hôtel du Gouvernement Militaire (*c.* 1760). At the east end of the square is the Opéra du Rhin, the Municipal Theatre (1804–1822), and on the north side (No. 5) is the Banque de France,

on the spot where Rouget de Lisle sang the "Marseillaise" for the first time on April 26th 1792.
Beyond the theatre, on the far side of the old town moat, is the Place de la République, surrounded by public buildings, with a monument commemorating the dead of the First World War. On the north-west side of the square is the Palais du Rhin (1883–1889), formerly a German imperial palace. On the south-east side is the National and University Library (1889–1894; *c.* 3 million volumes), with the Conservatoire de Musique (1889–1894) to the right. A little way north-west is the Roman Catholic church of St-Pierre-le-Jeune (1889–1893), with an imposing dome.

University

To the east of the old town, beyond the Ill, is the University (1879–1885), with various institutes added later, the Observatory and the Botanical Garden. Farther south, beyond the Boulevard de la Victoire, is the new university quarter, the Centre Universitaire, with the Ecole National Supérieure des Ingénieurs (College of Engineering), the 15-storey Institute of Chemistry and the Faculty of Letters.
To the south and east of the new university buildings, extending to the river port, is the Esplanade district, which has been developed since 1962, with tall blocks of flats.

Citadel

Farther east, towards the river port, is the old citadel, built in 1682–1684 as the central element in Vauban's system of fortifications. It is now an attractive park, laid out in 1967.

Other sights

1 km/¾ mile west of the University is the large complex of buildings occupied by the Hôpital Civil, one of France's largest teaching hospitals.
1 km/¾ mile north of the Place de la République, on the east side of the Place de Bordeaux, is the Maison de la Radio, the Strasbourg headquarters of the French radio and television service, and farther north, in a large park, is the hexagonal Palais de la Musique et des Congrès, an international congress centre built in 1973–1975. North-east of this is the Terrain d'Exposition (Exhibition Grounds), with an exhibition hall and ice rink, flanked by sports and recreation grounds.
To the south-east, beyond the Ill, is the new Palais de l'Europe (1972–1977), near the older Maison de l'Europe. This is a fortress-like structure of nine storeys with an interior courtyard containing the tent-like chamber in which the parliamentary assembly of the Council of Europe and the 434 members of the European Parliament meet.
North-east of the Palais de l'Europe is the Palais des Droits de l'Homme, the headquarters of the Commission of Human Rights.
To the south-east of the Palais de l'Europe extends the beautiful Parc de l'Orangerie, laid out in the early 19th c., with the Orangery built for the Empress Joséphine now used for exhibitions and receptions.

River Port

To the east and south of the city are the extensive installations of the River Port (sightseeing boat trips), with 12 basins, making it the largest port on the Rhine after Duisburg and France's largest river port after Paris. 90% of its turnover is concerned with exports (mainly mineral ore, petroleum products and grain). The old port was considerably enlarged from 1882 onwards, and the Port Autonome de Strasbourg, including all subsidiary installations, now extends for more than 100 km/60 miles along the French bank of the Rhine from Marckolsheim to Lauterbourg.

Surroundings of Strasbourg

See Alsace, Lorraine and Vosges

Toulon **N11**

Region: Provence–Alpes–Côte d'Azur
Département: Var
Altitude: 1–10 m/3–33 ft
Population: 182,000

Situation and characteristics

The southern French port of Toulon, some 70 km/45 miles south-east of Marseilles, lies under the south side of Mont Faron. The harbour, consisting of the inner Petite Rade and the outer Grande Rade, is protected by the St-Mandrier peninsula. Toulon is France's principal naval port.

History

The town, which was called Telonion by the Greeks and Telo Martius by the Romans, was noted in antiquity for the production of purple dye from

Toulon

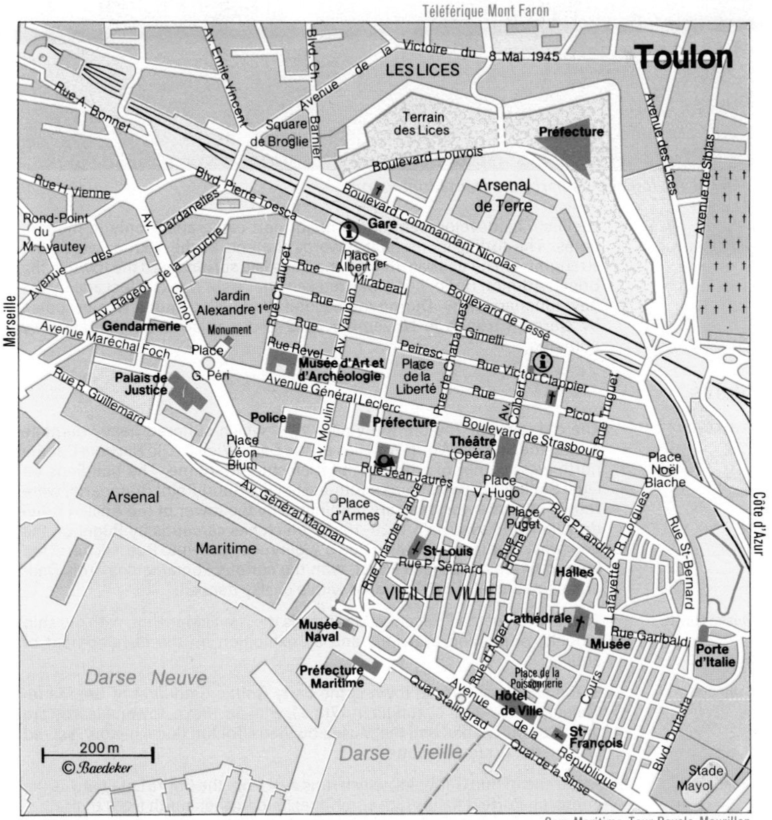

View of Toulon and its harbours from Mont Faron

shellfish. Its development into a major port came about only in modern times. The fortifications built towards the end of the 16th c. were later strengthened by Vauban. In 1793 the Royalists surrendered the town to the British Admiral Hood, but it was retaken after a six weeks' blockade by the Revolutionary army. During the Second World War Toulon was occupied by German troops in November 1942 and was severely damaged by bombing.

Sights

Old town

The old town of Toulon, the Vieille Ville, which suffered heavy damage during the Second World War, lies on the Darse Vieille (Old Harbour), at the north-west corner of which is the Préfecture Maritime. The buildings on Quai Stalingrad, which runs south-east to the Rond-Point Bonaparte, were rebuilt after the war; they are dominated by the tower of the Ancien Hôtel de Ville (Old Town Hall, 1620–1694), which has caryatids by Puget on the doorway. From here the busy Rue d'Alger runs north into Rue Hoche, at the far end of which is Place Puget, with the curious Fontaine des Trois Dauphins (by Castel, 1782), covered with a chalky deposit.

Musée Naval

To the north of the Préfecture Maritime is the Naval Museum, with old ship models, prints and drawings and an exhibition on the development of artillery.

Cathedral

In the centre of the old town is the Early Gothic Cathedral of Ste-Marie-Majeure (11th–12th c., rebuilt in 17th c.), with an 18th c. tower. Nearby are the colourful Market and the Musée du Vieux Toulon (local history, sacred art), on the Cours Lafayette.

Other sights

At the end of Rue Garibaldi, which runs east from the Cours Lafayette, is the imposing Porte d'Italie (18th c.; bridge), and further south from the cathedral is the Place de la Poissonnerie, with the fish-market.

From Place Puget Rue Muraire leads to the Opera House (1862–1864). To the north-west is the Place de la Liberté, with the Monument de la Fédération (by Allard) and further west is the Musée d'Art et d'Archéologie (paintings of the 13th–20th c., prehistoric and classical antiquities), with the Musée d'Histoire Naturelle (geological and palaeontological collections) in the same building. Adjoining is the beautiful Jardin Alexandre-1er, with the Palais de Justice (Law Courts) to the south.

Harbours

At the west end of Quai Stalingrad, on the Darse Neuve (New Harbour), are the workshops, docks and magazines of the Arsenal Maritime, which is entered through the fine Porte de l'Arsenal (1738).

Le Mourillon

The south-eastern district of Le Mourillon is reached by way of the Rond-Point Bonaparte. From the Tour Royale, a massive round tower built in 1514–1524 at the southern end of the bay, there are fine panoramic views. To the north-east is Fort St-Louis (1707), protecting a small harbour.

*Corniche Mistral

The beautiful Corniche Mistral runs along the Grande Rade de Vignettes from Le Mourillon, passing the Jardin d'Acclimatation (Botanical Garden) to the attractive residential district of Cap Brun (alt. 103 m/340 ft), with an old fort (views). Below the coast road runs the Sentier des Douaniers (the Excisemen's Path).

*Mont Faron

A cabin cableway from the Super-Toulon district will take visitors up to the Mémorial du Faron an the Tour Beaumont (493 m/1618 ft) on Mont Faron (542 m/1778 ft) which dominates the town in the north. There is also a steep and narrow road up to the summit. There is a museum commemorating the Allied landings of August 1944 and from the roof of the fort there are magnificent all-round views.

Surroundings of Toulon

Cuers

Cuers, 22 km/14 miles north, is a well known wine town and cork-processing centre with a picturesque old quarter and a castle which dominates the town.

Ollioules

Ollioules, 8 km/5 miles west on the slopes of the Gorges d'Ollioules, is a noted flower-growing town which also has a ruined castle.

*Gorges d'Ollioules

Just north of the town are the beautiful Gorges d'Ollioules, with bizarre rock formations. Above the gorges, on a rugged volcanic crag, is the village of Evenos.

Toulouse

I11

Region: Midi–Pyrénées. Département: Haute-Garonne
Altitude: 146 m/480 ft. Population: 383,000

Situation and characteristics

Toulouse, France's fourth largest city, the cultural and economic centre of southern France, the see of an archbishop, a university town since 1230 and chief town of Languedoc (see Languedoc–Roussillon) and the département of Haute-Garonne, lies on the right bank of the Garonne and on the Canal du Midi, which since 1681 has provided a link between the Mediterranean and the Atlantic by way of the Garonne. Known as the "red city" because of its numerous brick buildings, it is rich in art and architecture, and is also the centre of the French aircraft and space industry.

History

Around 200 B.C. the Volcae Tectosages, a Celtic people driven from their homeland in south-eastern Germany, established a settlement here. This was succeeded by the Roman fortified town of Tolosa, on the road from

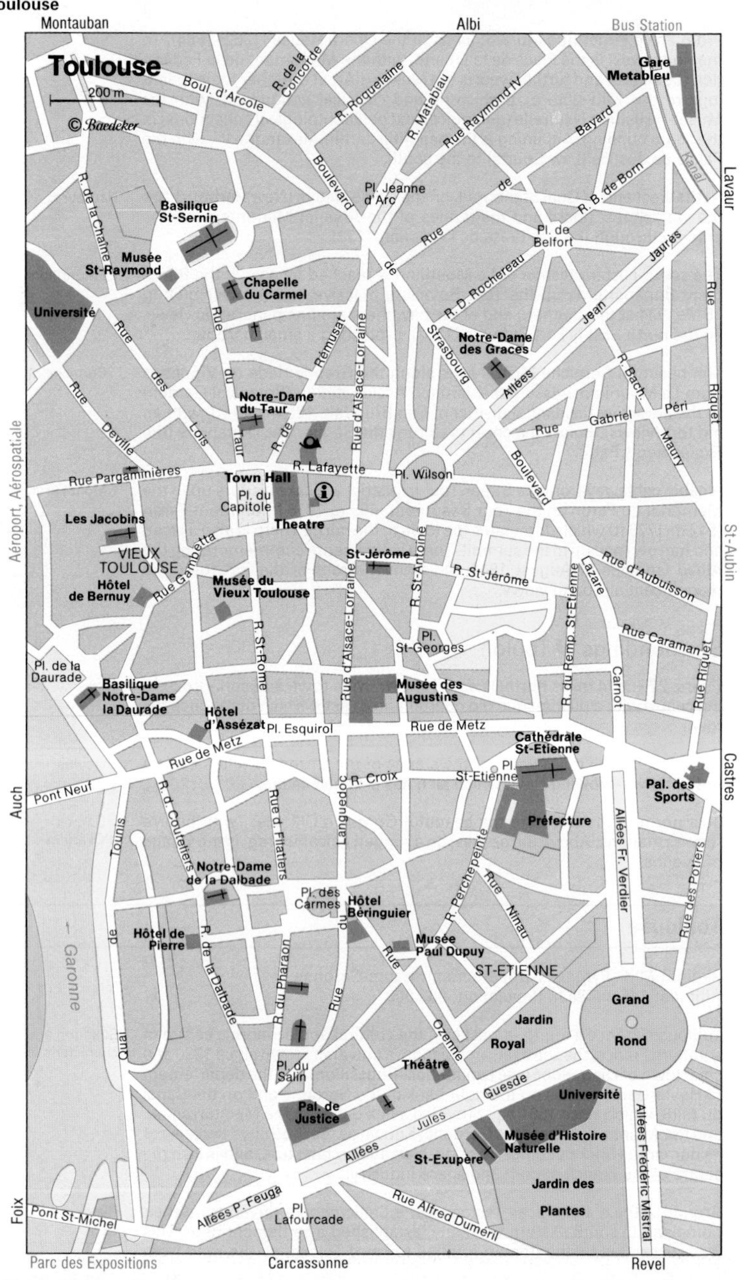

Montauban
Albi
Bus Station
Toulouse
200 m
© Baedeker
Boul. d'Arcole
R. de la Concorde
R. Roquelaine
R. Matabiau
Rue Raymond IV
Bayard
Gare Metableu
Kanal
Lavaur
Boulevard
Pl. Jeanne d'Arc
Rue de Bayard
R. B. de Born
Pl. de Belfort
Basilique St-Sernin
R. de la Chaîne
Musée St-Raymond
Chapelle du Carmel
Université
R. D. Rochereau
Allées Jean Jaurès
Rue Riquet
Rue du Taur
Rue des Lois
Rémusat
Rue d'Alsace-Lorraine
Boulevard de Strasbourg
Notre-Dame des Graces
R. Bach.
Rue Deville
Notre-Dame du Taur
R. de Rémusat
Rue Gabriel Péri
Maury
Aéroport, Aérospatiale
Rue Pargaminières
R. Lafayette
Town Hall
Pl. Wilson
Pl. du Capitole
Les Jacobins
Theatre
VIEUX TOULOUSE
Rue Gambetta
St-Jérôme
R. St-Antoine
R. St-Jérôme
Rue d'Aubuisson
St-Aubin
Hôtel de Bernuy
Musée du Vieux Toulouse
Lazare
R. St-Rome
Rue Caraman
Pl. St-Georges
Pl. de la Daurade
Basilique Notre-Dame la Daurade
Musée des Augustins
R. du Remp. St-Etienne
Carnot
Rue Riquet
Hôtel d'Assézat
Pl. Esquirol
Rue de Metz
Cathédrale St-Etienne
Castres
Pl. St-Etienne
Pal. des Sports
Auch
Pont Neuf
R. Croix
R. d. Couteliers
Rue d. Filatiers
Languedoc
Préfecture
Tounis
Allées Fr. Verdier
R. Perchepeinte
Rue Ninau
Rue des Potiers
Notre-Dame de la Dalbade
Pl. des Carmes
Hôtel Béringuier
Garonne
Hôtel de Pierre
R. de la Dalbade
Musée Paul Dupuy
Quai de Tounis
ST-ETIENNE
R. du Pharaon
Rue du Languedoc
Rue Ozenne
Grand Rond
Jardin Royal
Théâtre
Pl. du Salin
Université
Allées Jules Guesde
Pal. de Justice
Musée d'Histoire Naturelle
St-Exupère
Allées Frédéric Mistral
Jardin des Plantes
Foix
Pont St-Michel
Allées P. Feuga
Pl. Lafourcade
Rue Alfred Duméril
Parc des Expositions
Carcassonne
Revel

Bird's eye view of Toulouse

Narbonne to Bordeaux. The town was Christianised by St Saturninus in the 3rd c. After the end of the Roman period Toulouse was from 419 to 506 capital of the Visigothic kingdom, and later became the principal place in Aquitaine. From 845 to 1249 it was ruled by the Counts of Toulouse. Under the treaty of Paris in 1229 Toulouse passed to the French crown along with the rest of Languedoc. The University was founded by Pope Gregory IX in 1230, after the Albigensian wars. The Académie des Jeux Floraux was founded by Louis XIV.

Sights

Capitole

The hub of the city's life is the busy Place du Capitole, the west side of which is lined with beautiful arcades. On the east side of the square is the Capitole, named after the old chapter *(capitulum)* of magistrates *(capitouls)* who ruled the city. In the right-hand wing of the Hôtel de Ville (Town Hall) is the Municipal Theatre. To the rear is the Donjon, a defensive tower of 1529; in the courtyard are numerous works of modern sculpture.
From the Place du Capitole Rue du Taur runs north, passing the 14th c. church of Notre-Dame-du-Taur, with a fortified façade, to the church of St-Sernin.

**St-Sernin

The basilica of St-Sernin, a wide brick-built church with a five-aisled nave and three-aisled transepts, is one of the most magnificent pilgrimage churches on the pilgrim road to Santiago de Compostela and one of the finest of all Romanesque churches. The choir was built between 1075 and 1080 and consecrated in 1096, and the church was completed during the 13th c. It was restored by Viollet-le-Duc in the 19th c. It stands on the site of an earlier church in which St Saturninus (Sernin) was buried. Particularly fine are the choir with its ring of nine chapels and the six-storey tower over the crossing which was much imitated in Languedoc and Gascony. It has imposing doorways, particularly the Porte Miégeville in the south aisle,

Doorways

St-Sernin

Eglise des Jacobins

with 12th c. Romanesque sculpture (on left King David, on the lintel the Apostles, in the tympanum the Ascension). In the south transept is the Porte des Comtes, with capitals depicting Lazarus and the rich man and the torments of the damned; to the left of the doorway is a recess containing four sarcophagi of Counts of Toulouse.

Interior

The cruciform interior has some notable features including seven 11th c. marble reliefs in the ambulatory, the 16th and 17th c. choir screens and the choir-stalls of 1670. In the apse is the tomb of St Sernin and in the north transept a large carved Romanesque crucifix. In the crypt is the church treasury, with numerous relics and six large polychrome wood statues of Apostles (14th c.).

Musée St-Raymond

Opposite St-Sernin is the Musée St-Raymond, with prehistoric and Roman antiquities and a rich collection of medieval and Renaissance decorative art.

*Eglise des Jacobins

West of the Place du Capitole is the brick-built Gothic church of the Jacobins (1260–1292), with a cloister of 1307. On one side is a handsome tower, built in 1301–1304 on the model of St-Sernin. The two-aisled nave has dark-veined groined vaulting, which radiates in fan form from the last of the seven central piers in the choir. The remains of St Thomas Aquinas (1225–1274) were deposited in this church in 1974.

Hôtel de Bernuy

To the south is the Hôtel de Bernuy, built in 1509–1534 by a Spanish merchant of that name, with a beautiful courtyard in early Renaissance style.

Notre-Dame-de-la-Daurade

From here Rue J.-Suau runs south-west to the Place de la Daurade, with views of the Garonne, the Pont-Neuf (1543–1614) and the St-Cyprien district across the river. On the banks of the Garonne is the Baroque church of Notre-Dame-de-la-Daurade, built in 1773–1790 on the site of an earlier 12th

c. church. South-east is the church of Notre-Dame-de-la-Dalbade (1503–1545), with a large Renaissance doorway of 1537. Farther south is the Hôtel de Pierre (16th and 17th c.), and to the east of this the Hôtel Béringuier-Maynier (1517–1527), the earliest example of the so-called "Toulouse Renaissance" style. Around this church and in all this quarter of the town are many handsome old houses.

Hôtel d'Assézat

A little way east of the Pont-Neuf, in Rue de Metz, is the Hôtel d'Assézat, the most elegant of the city's burghers' houses, built by Nicolas Bachelier in 1555–1557 for the Capitoul d'Assézat, with a beautiful courtyard.

*Musée des Augustins

This museum, housed in a former Augustinian monastery, including the chapterhouse and the cloisters (14th and 17th c.), has a large collection of sculpture, with fine examples of Early Christian sarcophagi and medieval sculpture, and of pictures.

Cathedral

Near the east end of the Rue de Metz, in a spacious square, is the Cathedral of St-Etienne, dominated by its massive tower. Its irregular plan is the result of the long period over which it was constructed (11th–17th c.). The 13th c. rose window in the west front is similar to the one in Notre-Dame in Paris. When it was built at the end of the 12th c. the three-aisled nave, in northern French Gothic style, was the widest vaulted structure of the kind in Europe, with a span of 19 m/62 ft. The windows date from the 14th–17th centuries, the choir-stalls from 1611, the numerous tapestries from the 16th–18th centuries.

Other museums

The Musée d'Histoire Naturelle is in the Jardin des Plantes, and the Musée du Vieux Toulouse (history of the town) is housed in a handsome 16th–17th c. mansion to the south of the Place du Capitole.

Toulouse-le-Mirail

3 km/2 miles west is the new district of Toulouse-le-Mirail (pop. 100,000), designed by G. Candilis.

Tours H7

Region: Centre
Département: Indre-et-Loire
Altitude: 55 m/180 ft
Population: 145,000

Tours, the busy capital of Touraine (the much lauded "Garden of France"), chief town of the département of Indre-et-Loire, the see of an archbishop and a university town, lies on both banks of the Loire. In addition to considerable industry the town has an extensive trade in agricultural produce and wine.

History

In Roman times Tours was known as Caesarodunum and later as Urbs Turones (the city of a Gallic tribe, the Turones). In the 3rd c. St Gatien brought Christianity to the region, and in the 4th c. the preaching of St Martin made Tours an important religious centre. Round the church in which he was buried there grew up the little town of Martinopolis (later known as Châteauneuf), which subsequently joined up with the Roman settlement to form the town of Tours. In 732 Charles Martel defeated the Arabs advancing into France from Spain in the battle of Tours and Poitiers. During the Carolingian Renaissance there was a famous school of painters here.

Tours was ravaged by Norman raids, during which the basilica of St Martin, the abbey and 28 churches were burned down, and by conflicts between the Counts of Blois and Anjou. In the 15th and 16th centuries silk-weaving brought the town prosperity: at one time no fewer than 8000 looms were at work in the town, employing 20,000 weavers and 40,000 assistants – altogether three-quarters of the population of 80,000. Tours became a stronghold of Protestantism, and as a result was the scene of a horrifying massacre ten years before the St Bartholomew's Day massacre in Paris.

Sights

Place Jaurès

The town's principal streets intersect in Place Jean-Jaurès, in which are the imposing Hôtel de Ville (Town Hall, 1905) and the Palais de Justice (Law Courts, 1840). From here Rue Nationale, laid out in 1763 on a uniform plan, runs north to the Loire.

Archbishop's Palace

* Musée des Beaux-Arts

Halfway between Place Jean-Jaurès and the Loire Rue Emile-Zola runs east to the Archbishop's Palace (Archevêché), parts of which date from the 11th and 14th centuries; it was rebuilt in its present form in the 17th and 18th centuries and now houses the Musée des Beaux-Arts, with a large collection of pictures, sculpture and furniture. Particularly notable are the paintings of the Dutch and Italian schools (Rembrandt, Mantegna).

* Cathedral

Opposite the Archbishop's Palace, to the north, is the twin-towered Gothic Cathedral of St-Gatien, dedicated to the first bishop of Tours, which was begun in the 12th c. but not completed until the 16th.
The west front, flanked by twin towers, with three doorways, is richly decorated in Flamboyant style, while the towers show the first signs of Renaissance influence. To the left is the Cloître de la Psalette (15th–16th c.).

* Cloister

Interior

The walls of the nave consist almost entirely of windows. The choir and the chapels round the ambulatory have beautiful 13th c. stained glass. The rose windows in the north and south transepts are 14th c. In the ambulatory, adjoining the south transept, is the beautiful marble Renaissance tomb of two of Charles VIII's children.

* Château Royal Museums

To the north of the cathedral, in the Château Royal (13th–15th c.), once the residence of the Valois kings, are three museums: the Historial de Touraine or Musée Grévin (history of Touraine), the Aquarium (many tropical sea and freshwater fishes) and the Atelier Histoire de Tours (history of the town).

St-Julien

Wine Museum

Farther along Rue Colbert, near Rue Nationale, is the former abbey church of St-Julien (10th and 13th c.; rebuilt after destruction in Second World War), with the remains of a Romanesque tower. In the abbey's wine-cellar is the Musée des Vins de Touraine, while the dormitory houses the Musée du Compagnonnage (history of the craftsmen's guilds and their customs).

* Hôtel Gouin

A little way west is the Hôtel Gouin, an Italian-style mansion built about 1510 which now houses the collections of the Archaeological Society of

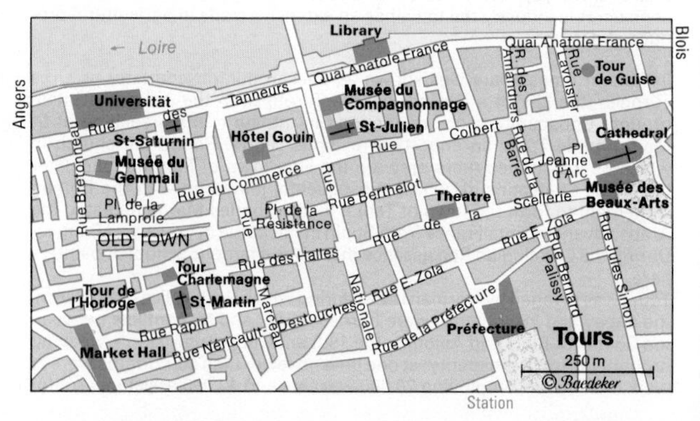

Stained glass in Tours

Place Plumereau

A shop in the old town

Touraine (prehistoric, Gallo-Roman and medieval antiquities, art from the Middle Ages to the 18th c.).

Old town

To the west of the Hôtel Gouin is the old part of the town, centred on Place Plumereau, with numerous half-timbered houses. A walk through the streets between the Loire, Place Plumereau and the Place du Grand-Marché will give an impression of the character of the old town. The Tour Charlemagne in Place de Châteauneuf and the Tour de l'Horloge in Rue des Halles are all that remains of the great abbey church of St-Martin, built in the 11th–13th centuries and destroyed in 1562 and 1802. The new basilica, with the tomb of St Martin, was built between 1887 and 1924 in neo-Romanesque/Byzantine style.

Surroundings of Tours

Marmoutier

4 km/2½ miles east of Tours, on the right bank of the Loire, are the ruins of the old abbey of Marmoutier founded by St Martin. Here too are the priory of St-Côme, in which the poet Ronsard, who was titular prior, died in 1585; the house of La Béchellerie, the residence of Anatole France (1844–1924), which is open to the public as he left it; La Grenadière, which was occupied by Balzac (1799–1850); and La Gaudinière, which belonged to the philosopher Henri Bergson (1859–1941).

Troyes — M6

Region: Champagne–Ardenne
Département: Aube
Altitude: 113 m/370 ft
Population: 75,000

Situation and characteristics

Troyes, the old capital of Champagne (see entry), now chief town of the département of Aube and the see of a bishop, lies on the Seine, here divided into a number of arms. Its main industry is hosiery.

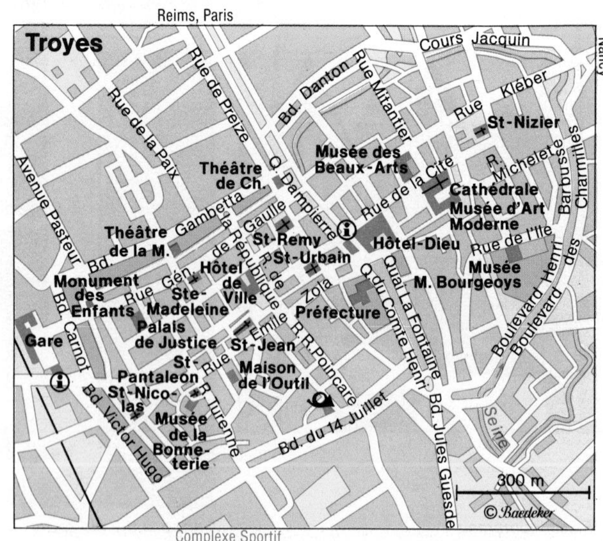

St-Urbain, in Place de la Libération

The town's tourist attractions include many churches and old buildings which bear witness to its one-time cultural importance.

History

Troyes, the Roman Augustobona, was originally the chief town of a Gallic tribe, the Tricasses, from whom it took its later name of Trecae. It was the see of a bishop from the 4th c. During the battle of the Catalaunian Fields in 451 Troyes successfully held out against the Huns. In the 10th c. the town passed to the Counts of Champagne, who, along with the bishops, fostered its development, building churches and hospitals and founding the fair which is still held annually. In 1304 the County was united with France.

Sights

Hôtel de Ville
Ste-Madeleine

The central feature of Troyes is the Place du Maréchal-Foch, with the Hôtel de Ville (Town Hall; built 1624–1670, extended in 1935). North-west of this is the church of Ste-Madeleine (13th c., rebuilt in 16th c.), with a fine Renaissance tower of 1560 and a Flamboyant doorway on the charnel-house. The interior is Gothic, with a beautiful stone rood screen, richly decorated in Flamboyant style (by Jean Gailde, 1508–1517). In the south aisle are a 16th c. figure of St Martha in peasant costume and beautiful 16th c. stained glass windows.

*Rood screen

Rue des Chats

From here Rue des Chats, lined with fine medieval half-timbered houses packed closely together, runs south-east towards the church of St-Jean.

St-Jean

In the church of St-Jean (14th and 16th c.) Henry V of England married Princess Catherine of France in 1620. The nave is Gothic; the choir, which is considerably higher than the nave, dates from the 16th c. Notable features are the sumptuous 17th c. high altar and a 16th c. stone "Visitation" in the south aisle.

Other sights

To the north-west, in Rue Champeaux and Rue Brunneval, are numbers of old half-timbered houses. Beyond Rue Emile-Zola (the main traffic artery of the old town), at 2–7 rue de la Trinité, are a number of 16th c. houses which were converted into an orphanage in the 18th c., a fine example of Renaissance civic architecture.

St-Pantaléon

Near Rue Emile-Zola is the Late Gothic church of St-Pantaléon (16th–17th c.), with a fine Baroque façade, numerous statues and 16th c. stained glass.

Museums

Opposite St-Pantaléon is the Hôtel de Vauluisant (16th c.), housing the Musée de la Bonneterie (development of the hosiery industry in Troyes). The Musée Historique (13th and 14th c. sculpture, coins, prints, costumes) is in the same building.

St-Nicolas

Farther west is the church of St-Nicolas (16th c.), with a 17th c. porch, fine 16th c. stained glass and 17th c. choir-stalls.

*St-Urbain

North-east of the Town Hall, in Place de la Libération, is the church of St-Urbain, one of the finest Gothic buildings in Champagne, built between 1262 and 1286 by Pope Urban IV, a native of Troyes. The façade, which was completed only in the 19th c., has a 13th c. doorway with a Last Judgment in the tympanum. The great area of glass (13th and 14th c.) in the walls makes the interior very light. To the right of the choir is a charming figure of the Virgin, the Vierge au Raisin (Virgin of the Grapes), a masterpiece of Renaissance sculpture (16th c.).

St-Rémy

North-west of this is the church of St-Rémy (14th–16th c.), which has a fine Cross by Girardon (1638–1715).

*Cathedral

Beyond the canalised arm of the Seine Rue de la Cité runs north-east to the Cathedral of St-Pierre-et-St-Paul, one of the master-works of Gothic architecture in Champagne (1208–1638), with unfinished towers. The north transept with its richly decorated doorway, the "Beau Portail", and its 15th c. rose window is a particularly fine example of medieval sculpture.
The nave is flanked by double aisles and has fine 13th and 14th c. stained glass (in the 4th chapel on the left the "Mystic Wine-Press", 1625) and a rich treasury (numerous psalters, enamel-work, embroidery).

St-Loup
*Library

Opposite the cathedral is the former abbey of St-Loup, now housing the Municipal Library, one of France's richest libraries, with over 200,000 volumes, 3000 manuscripts and 700 incunabula.

Musée des Beaux-Arts

In the same building is the Musée des Beaux-Arts (antiquities, pictures).

*Musée d'Art Moderne

The former Bishop's Palace (16th, 17th and 19th c.) now houses the Museum of Modern Art. The nucleus of the museum is the Levy Collection of art between 1850 and 1950, with works by Bonnard, Cézanne, Derain, Degas, Gauguin, Matisse, Modigliani, Picasso, Rouault, Soutine and Vuillard. There is also a collection of African art and a collection of sculpture which is displayed in the garden.

St-Nizier

At the end of Rue de la Cité is the Late Gothic church of St-Nizier (1528–1573), with a west front in pure Renaissance style and fine 16th c. stained glass in the interior.

Vendée

See Poitou–Charentes–Vendée

Vercors

N 9/10

**Situation and characteristics

The Vercors, in the Dauphiné (see entry), is a range of forest-covered hills between the Rhône valley and the Route d'Hiver des Alpes rising to 2346

Landscape in the Vercors

m/7697 ft in the Grand Veymont and broken up by deeply indented valleys and gorges. Since 1970 it has been part of a Regional Nature Park which also takes in the surrounding districts of Royans, Diois and Trièves.
Between 1942 and 1944 the Vercors was a stronghold of the French Resistance, and during the fighting the villages of St-Nizier, Vassieux and La Chapelle were destroyed.
In 1968 some events in the Winter Olympics were staged in the Vercors (Autrans, St-Nizier, Villard-de-Lans).
There are numerous paths and trails allowing visitors to explore the Vercors either on foot or on horseback. In winter there are excellent facilities for winter sports.

Circuit of the Vercors

It is well worth while making a special trip around the Vercors, the itinerary of which must certainly include the Combe Laval road and the Gorges de la Bourne (west of Villard-de-Lans), which are very typical of the unusual scenery of the region.

****Combe Laval**

Through the Combe Laval runs a mountain road constructed in 1897, originally for the transport of timber from the Forêt de Lente to St-Jean-en-Royans. The finest stretch of the road begins at the wooded Col de la Machine on the way down to St-Jean, affording magnificent aerial views of the country below.

***Gorges de la Bourne**

Beyond Villard-de-Lans D531 runs down into the Bourne valley, which narrows into the Gorges de la Bourne, a tremendous rocky defile in which the road is carried through tunnels and over bridges. Between Choranche and Pont-en-Royans two interesting caves can be reached from the road, the Grotte du Bournillon and the Grottes de la Choranche (in which is an underground lake).

**** Grands Goulets**

From Pont-en-Royans, a little town situated at the junction of the Vernaison with the Bourne, the road crosses the two rivers and continues south-east up the Vernaison valley to enter the picturesque Vernaison gorges. After passing through the Petits Goulets it climbs, with many bends, to the grandiose Grands Goulets, in which the road is caught between high rock walls above the foaming river. After passing through a series of tunnels and galleries it emerges suddenly into the green Vercors valley.

Grenoble

See entry

Léoncel

Léoncel has a Romanesque church, all that remains of a Cistercian abbey founded in 1137, which contains a wooden figure of Christ carved by a local sculptor in 1860.

St-Jean-en-Royans

St-Jean-en-Royans is one of the best places – the other good centre being Villard-de-Lans – from which to explore the Vercors.

St-Nizier-du-Moucherotte
* Le Moucherotte

This little place (pop. 600), a popular resort all the year round, lies under Le Moucherotte (1901 m/6237 ft; lift). From the village there are fine views of the mountains and Grenoble, and even more magnificent views are obtained from the summit. The church dates from the 12th c., and the cemetery contains the graves of those who fell in the Resistance.

Vassieux-en-Vercors

Vassieux-en-Vercors was completely destroyed in 1944 but was rebuilt after the war. Those who fell during the Second World War are commemorated by a memorial, the National Cemetery of the Vercors and a museum.

Villard-de-Lans

Villard-de-Lans (alt. 1043 m/3422 ft.; pop. 3500), 30 km/20 miles from Grenoble in a wide expanse of Alpine meadows, is both a summer holiday resort and a winter sports centre. There is a cabin cableway to Côte 2000 (i.e. an altitude of 2000 m/6560 ft), where there are magnificent views and good skiing.

Valchevrière

8 km/5 miles south-west of Villard-de-Lans, approached by a modern Way of the Cross, is the Calvary of Valchevrière, a memorial to the fallen and to the destruction of this village in July 1944.

Verdun N5

Region: Lorraine
Département: Meuse
Altitude: 199 m/655 ft
Population: 25,000

Situation and characteristics

The old and much fought-over fortified town of Verdun lies at what is strategically the most important crossing of the Meuse, on the road between the Rhine and Paris. Surrounded by fortified hills, Verdun was one of France's strongest fortresses in the First World War.

History

The Roman town on this site was called Virodunum, and became the see of a bishop in the 3rd c. When, under the treaty of Verdun in 843, Charlemagne's Frankish empire was split up into the three territories of France, Germany and Lorraine Verdun was at first included in Lorraine, but in 870 passed to the East Frankish kingdom, and then, under the name of Virten, became a free imperial city in the Holy Roman Empire. In 1552 Henry II of France occupied the town, and in 1648 it was permanently incorporated in France. Thereafter its defences were built up, particularly by Vauban (1633–1707).

During the First World War Verdun was the pivot of the French front line, and between February 21st and July 12th 1916 withstood all German attempts to take it. The number of dead on both sides is estimated at

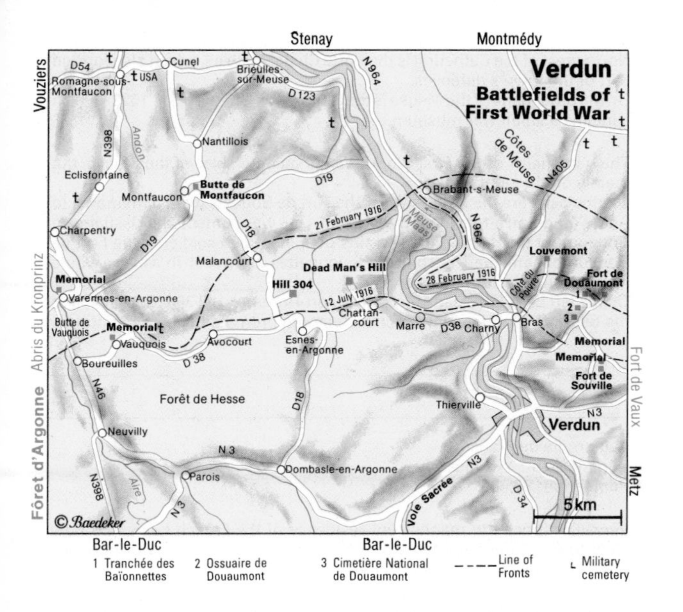

between 500,000 and 800,000, and the name of Verdun has become a synonym for senseless slaughter. After the war the town was completely rebuilt.

Sights

Victory Memorial

In Rue Mazel, in the centre of the town, is the massive Victory Monument (Monument à la Victoire et aux Soldats de Verdun, 1929), in the crypt of which is a book containing the names of all those who took part in the fighting.

Cathedral

To the south of the Victory Monument, on the site of an earlier church burned down in 1047, is the Cathedral of Notre-Dame, in the Romanesque style of the Rhineland, with two transepts and two apses. Consecrated in 1147, it was much altered in the 14th c. and again in 1755. It has a fine 12th c. crypt and a Late Gothic cloister (16th c.). On the north side of the church is the beautiful Lion Doorway (12th c.), with a sumptuously decorated tympanum.

Immediately adjoining the cathedral is the Bishop's Palace (16th c.), with a cloister; the Palace now houses the Municipal Library.

Citadel

West of the cathedral is the citadel built by Vauban on the site of the abbey of St-Vanne, of which only the Tour de St-Vanne (12th c.) is left. Under the citadel is a system of subterranean passages.

Hôtel de la Princerie

North of the cathedral is the Hôtel de la Princerie, a handsome Renaissance mansion (16th c.) which now houses the Municipal Museum (local history and folk art).

In the north of the town, in front of the Porte St-Paul, is a fine bronze by Rodin symbolising the defence of Verdun.

On the Quai de la République is a war memorial, and on the opposite bank of the Meuse is the Porte Chaussée, with two round towers (14th c.).

North-west of the Cathedral is the Porte Châtel (15th c.), which also formed part of the town's defences.
On the other bank of the Meuse is the Hôtel de Ville (Town Hall, 1623), which contains a small war museum.

Battlefields

The battlefields of the First World War lie on both sides of the Meuse, but mainly on the right bank.
On this bank are the Fort de Vaux, the Fort de Souville (with a memorial to André Maginot, after whom the Maginot Line was named), the Ossuaire de Douaumont (containing the remains of unidentified soldiers), the Fort de Douaumont and the Tranchée des Baïonnettes (the trench in which a whole infantry unit was buried alive).
On the left bank are Dead Man's Hill (Mort-Homme), Hill 304 (Cote 304) and the Butte de Montfaucon, which all featured prominently in the fighting.

Versailles **K6**

Region: Ile de France
Département: Yvelines
Population: 97,000

Situation and characteristics

Versailles, once the magnificent residence of the French kings and now chief town of the département of Yvelines and the see of a bishop, lies 20 km/12½ miles south-west of Paris.

The Palace of Versailles, with its park and gardens, is one of the great monuments of European culture and one of Europe's major tourist attractions. Its architecture and decoration, its park and the whole pattern of French court life in the 17th and 18th centuries were a model which kings and princes all over Europe sought to imitate.

History

A small hunting lodge built for Louis XIII by Philibert Le Roy in 1631–1634 was developed by Louis XIV between 1661–1710 into the present magnificent palace. First Louis Le Vau (d. 1670) added two east wings to the original

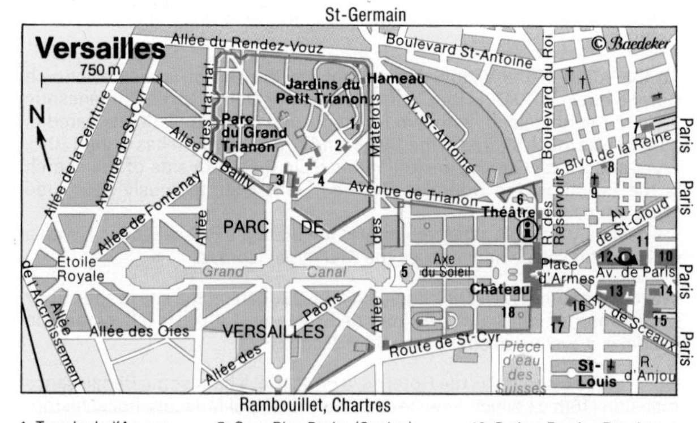

1 Temple de l'Amour
2 Petit Trianon
3 Grand Trianon
4 Musée des Voitures
5 Bassin d'Apollon
6 Bassin de Neptune
7 Gare Rive Droite (Station)
8 Musée Lambinet
9 Notre-Dame
10 Préfecture
11 Palais de Justice
12 Grandes Ecuries Royales
13 Petites Ecuries Royales
14 Mairie (Town Hall)
15 Gare Rive Gauche (Station)
16 Palais des Congrès
17 Bibliothéque
18 Orangerie

Château de Versailles

hunting lodge around the Cour de Marbre. Then in 1676 he was succeeded by Jules Hardouin-Mansart, who added another storey to Le Vau's wings and built the Hall of Mirrors and the long north and south wings on the garden front of the palace. Last of all came the two pavilions in classical style on the Cour Royale, built by Jacques-Ange Gabriel (18th c.) and Dufour (1820).

The whole gigantic structure, which could house a population of 10,000, is said to have cost 500 million gold francs, not counting the forced labour of the peasants, and to have involved the employment of anything up to 36,000 men and 6000 horses at any one time.

The interior decoration was the work of Charles Le Brun, and the park and gardens were designed by André Le Nôtre. Louis XIV's successors changed little and added little, apart from the Rococo apartments and the Petit Trianon, which date from the reign of Louis XV.

For just over a hundred years (1682–1789) Versailles was the residence of the French kings. The system of absolutism required the great nobles to live permanently at court, and Versailles bcame the setting in which the absolute power of the monarchy was displayed.

In 1789 the States General were summoned to meet at Versailles. The three estates (the nobility, the clergy and the ordinary people) resolved to deliberate together and constituted themselves into a National Assembly. It was the first step towards the Revolution.

On October 5th–6th 1789 Louis XVI was compelled by the Paris mob to leave Versailles and move to the Tuileries in Paris, and thereafter Versailles lost its importance.

During the Franco-Prussian War Versailles was occupied by German troops on September 19th 1870, and remained the German headquarters until March 6th 1871. On January 18th 1871 the new German Empire was proclaimed in the Hall of Mirrors.

After the First World War, on June 28th 1919, the treaty of Versailles was signed in the Hall of Mirrors.

Sights

Versailles

The town's main traffic artery is the wide Avenue de Paris, which meets the Avenue de St-Cloud and Avenue de Sceaux in the Place d'Armes in front of the Palace.
A little way south of the Place d'Armes is the Salle du Jeu de Paume (Tennis Court), built for the king and court in 1686, in which the National Assembly met in 1789.
Farther south is the Cathedral of St-Louis (18th c.).
In Rue de l'Indépendance-Américaine, west of the Place d'Armes, are the Grand Commun, built by Mansart in 1682 to accommodate persons attached to the court (now a military hospital), and the Municipal Library, with a beautifully decorated interior.
In the north of the town are the church of Notre-Dame (by Mansart, 1684–1686) and the Lambinet Museum (18th c.), with furniture, paintings, prints, weapons, etc.
On the east side of the spacious Place d'Armes are the Ecuries Royales (Royal Stables; by Mansart, 1679–1685), now used as barracks, which could accommodate 2500 horses and 200 carriages.

**The Palace

Exterior

A gate in the wrought-iron railings gives access to the Avant-Cour (Forecourt), which is flanked by two wings, separate from the main palace, intended for the king's ministers. Beyond this is the Cour Royale, with an equestrian statue of Louis XIV (1835), and beyond this again the narrower Cour de Marbre, which until 1830 was paved with marble.
The buildings around the Cour de Marbre, Louis XIII's original hunting lodge, are the oldest part of the Palace. They contain the king's private apartments (first floor). Around the two side wings of the hunting lodge Le Vau built an outer ring of rooms, the state apartments and the apartments of the royal princes and princesses. Mansart linked these two complexes by building the Hall of Mirrors on the garden front and added the north and south wings. With the further additions of the Chapel (by Mansart and Robert de Cotte) and the Opera House (by Jacques-Ange Gabriel) the Palace was completed in its present form.

**Interior

The Palace (entrance on right-hand side of Cour Royale; closed Mondays), which ranks as a National Museum, contains the state apartments and residential apartments of Louis XIV and his successors (themselves a unique museum of decorative art), the Musée de l'Histoire de France (paintings and sculpture from the 15th c. to the present day) and the Opera House. Of the Palace's innumerable rooms – only a selection of which are open to the public – the following are of particular interest.
In the Galerie des Batailles, a series of huge pictures illustrate fourteen centuries of French history.
The Salle du Sacre (Coronation Room) became a chapel in the reign of Louis XVI.
The Queen's Staircase (1679–1681) leads up to the queen's state and private apartments.

Queen's Apartments

The Salle des Gardes de la Reine leads into the Antichambre de la Reine, beyond which is the Salon de la Reine. This was altered by Marie-Antoinette in 1785, and only the ceiling painting (by Michel Corneille, 1671) survives from the time of Louis XIV. The large portrait is of Louis XV.
Beyond the Salon de la Reine is the queen's bedroom, the Chambre de la Reine, from which the queen's private apartments, the Petits Appartements de la Reine, decorated in the style of Marie-Antoinette's time (1770–1781), can be visited.

Salon de la Paix

The Salon de la Paix (Hall of Peace) is at the south end of the Hall of Mirrors, with the Salon de la Guerre (Hall of War) as its counterpart at the north end –

Hall of Mirrors

English Garden

an example of the classical symmetry of the design of the Palace. The ceiling painting is by Lebrun, the portrait of Louis XIV over the fireplace by Lemoyne.

Hall of Mirrors

The world-famed Galerie des Glaces or Hall of Mirrors (73 m/240 ft long, 10 m/33 ft wide, 12 m/40 ft high) was designed by Jules Hardouin-Mansart, the interior decoration by Charles Le Brun, director of the royal tapestry factory. It served as a means of passage between the king's and the queen's apartments, in which the courtiers paid their court. The 17 arched mirrors on the inner wall, each with 18 panes (making a total of 306), are matched by the 17 round-arched windows on the garden front. The furniture is an exact reproduction of furniture of the period. The paintings on the barrel-vaulted ceiling relate the history of Louis XIV's reign.
Off the Hall of Mirrors is the Salon de l'Œil-de-Bœuf, named after the oval window known as the "Ox-Eye", which dates from 1701 and contains pictures by Veronese. Notable also is the 53 m/175 ft long stucco frieze of children's games.

King's Apartments

The king's bedroom, the Chambre du Roi, in which Louis XIV died in 1715, dates from 1701. It has been carefully restored to its original appearance. In the Cabinet du Conseil (Council Chamber) all important government decisions were taken during the reigns of Louis XV and XVI. The decoration, by Jacques-Ange Gabriel, is a masterpiece of French Rococo.
From here the king's private apartments, the Petits Appartements du Roi (also decorated by Gabriel), can be visited.

Salon de la Guerre

From the Salon de la Guerre (Hall of War) there are impressive vistas along the Hall of Mirrors to the Salon de la Paix at the other end and through the Grands Appartements (State Apartments) towards the rear of the Palace. The Grands Appartements are a series of seven splendid rooms – the Salon d'Apollon (with a ceiling painting by Charles de la Fosse, "Apollo on the Chariot of the Sun, accompanied by the Seasons"), the Salon de Mercure, the Salon de Mars, the Salon de Diane, the Salon de Vénus, the Salon d'Abondance and the Salon d'Hercule. All seven rooms have large mythological ceiling paintings, reflecting Louis XIV's desire to use the great legends of antiquity to support his own glorification.

Chapel

The Chapel (1699–1710) was begun by Jules Hardouin-Mansart and completed by Robert de Cotte.

Musée de l'Histoire

The Musée de l'Histoire de France illustrates the history of France in a long series of rooms filled with paintings and sculpture.

Opera House

The Opera House, built in 1768–1770, was designed by Jacques-Ange Gabriel for Louis XV.

**The Park

The park and gardens of Versailles are the supreme achievement of 17th c. French landscape gardening and the finest example of the work of Louis XIV's great landscape architect André Le Nôtre (1613–1700), the son of a gardener who worked at the Tuileries Palace in Paris.
The essential characteristics of French gardens, in which nature was forced into symmetry and geometric forms, corresponded to the ideal of French classicism, which saw in such creations an expression of man's command over nature.
In contrast to Le Nôtre's French gardens were the 18th c. English-style gardens laid out round the Petit Trianon in the reign of Louis XVI. These were a man-made landscape of unspoiled nature, where the royal family could play at leading a simple country life.

As far as the Allée d'Apollon the gardens have been preserved in their original state, with their regularly planned shrubberies, paths and orna-

Versailles: the Bassin d'Apollon, Allée Royale, Tapis Vert and Château

mental ponds and their hundreds of statues and vases. They are seen at their finest from the topmost terrace when the fountains are playing.
From the Parterres du Midi two flights of marble steps lead down to the Orangery (by Mansart, 1684–1686). The central avenue, the Tapis Vert, leads to the Bassin d'Apollon and beyond this the Grand Canal, 1588 m/1737 yds long and 62 m/68 yds across, with arms extending to left and right in the shape of a cross.

The Avenue de Trianon leads to the Petit Trianon and Grand Trianon, two charming smaller châteaux set in gardens on the north side of the park.

Petit Trianon

The Petit Trianon with its beautiful English-style gardens was built by Louis XV in 1766 for Madame du Barry; the architect was Gabriel. It was a favourite resort of Marie-Antoinette. The interior decoration is simple compared with Versailles.

Hameau

In the garden, planted with rare trees, is the Hameau (Hamlet), a group of cottages with a farmhouse, a dairy, a mill and a dovecot where the ladies of the court liked to dress up as country girls and lead a make-believe simple life.

Grand Trianon

At the end of the Avenue de Trianon is the Grand Trianon, built for Louis XIV by Mansart and Cotte (1678–1688), with one wing for the king and another for his favourite Madame de Maintenon. The interior is tastefully decorated in the style of the period, with paintings by Mignard, Lebrun, Boucher and other artists.
The park was laid out by Le Nôtre.

Musée des Voitures

In the Musée des Voitures (Carriage Museum), is a collection of state coaches, sleighs, sedan chairs and harness of the Baroque period.

Vichy L8

Region: Auvergne
Département: Allier
Altitude: 260 m/855 ft
Population: 31,000

Situation and *characteristics

Vichy, France's leading spa, lies on the Allier on the northern borders of Auvergne (see entry). Its alkaline water, at temperatures of 16–43°C/61–109°F, which was already used by the Romans for curative purposes, is recommended for the treatment of diseases of the liver, stomach, intestines and kidneys, and is also widely sold as table water. Between 1940 and 1944 the town was the seat of Marshal Pétain's government.

Sights

Parc des Sources

The life of Vichy centres on the Parc des Sources, a triangular area of gardens surrounded by covered promenades. At the south end is the Grand Casino (originally built in 1864 but much extended since then), with the Theatre. At the north end is the Hall des Sources, with three of the four principal springs, the Grande Grille (42°C/108°F), Chomel (43°C/109°F) and Lucas (27°C/81°F). The fourth, the Source de l'Hopital (34.4°C/93.9°F), is in a pavilion behind the Casino. The water of two other, colder, springs is drunk for curative purposes (the Parc, 22°C/72°F, and the Célestins, 21°C/70°F). Beyond this is the Grand Etablissement Thermal (opened in 1903 and enlarged in 1933 and 1977), the largest spa establishment in Europe.

Old town

Maison du Bailliage

In the old part of the town are a number of old buildings, including the Tour de l'Horloge (15th c.), the last relic of a castle built by Louis II of Bourbon. East of the Tour de l'Horloge is the church of St-Blaise, an old church rebuilt in 1935. The Maison du Bailliage or Chastel Franc (16th c.) contains a small

Source des Célestins, Vichy

Roman mosaic, Vienne

museum (Gallo-Roman antiquities, local history, folk art and traditions). To the west and south of the town are the beautiful Parcs de l'Allier. On the other side of the river is the Parc Omnisports Pierre-Coulon, with facilities for all kinds of sport.

Parcs de l'Allier

Vienne

M9

Region: Rhône–Alpes
Département: Isère
Altitude: 158 m/520 ft
Population: 30,000

Situation and characteristics

Vienne lies 30 km/20 miles south of Lyons on the left bank of the Rhône, which is joined here by its tributary the Gève, on the important traffic route between Burgundy and the Mediterranean.

History

Originally the chief town of a Gallic tribe, the Allobroges, the Roman town of Vienna became in the Imperial period the second capital of southern Gaul. In the 3rd c. it became the see of a bishop, and thereafter enjoyed a period of prosperity under episcopal rule. In 879 Boso, Count of Vienne, became king of Lower Burgundy, and in the 12th c. the town was capital of the Dauphiné. It was united with France in 1450–1451.
Vienne has many well preserved buildings of the Gallo-Roman, Romanesque and Gothic periods.

Sights

Place de l'Hôtel-de-Ville

In the centre of the town is the Place de l'Hôtel-de-Ville, with the Hôtel de Ville (Town Hall). South-east of the square are the Portiques des Thermes Romains, part of the colonnade round the Roman forum, and the remains of a temple of the Oriental goddess Cybele.

Temple d'Auguste et de Livie

To the north-west, in the Place du Palais, is the Temple of Augustus and Livia (25 B.C.), which in the Middle Ages became a church, during the

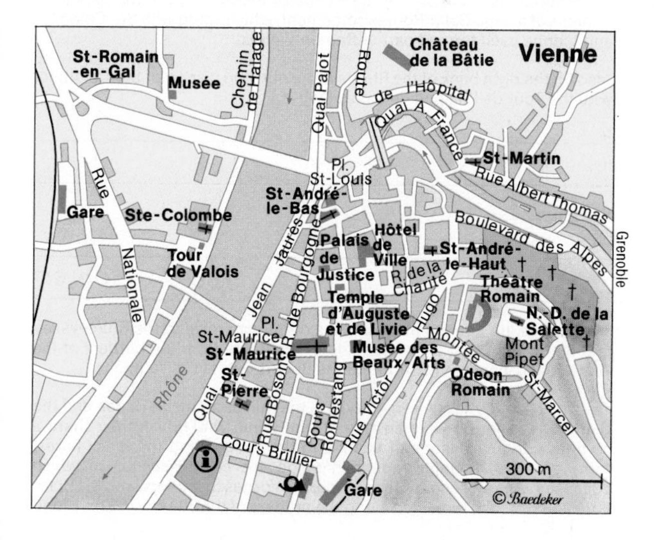

Revolution a "Temple of Reason", later a courthouse and until the mid 19th c. a museum.

St-Maurice

South of this is the former cathedral of St-Maurice (12th–16th c.), with a Late Gothic façade (14th–15th c.) which is a fine example of the Flamboyant style, containing Romanesque sculpture, Flemish tapestries (16th c.) and beautiful stained glass.

Musée des Beaux-Arts et d'Archéologie

Just east of the church is the Musée des Beaux-Arts et d'Archéologie (Gallo-Roman antiquities, faience, pictures of the 16th–19th c., fine old furniture).

*St-Pierre Musée Lapidaire

To the south-west, near the Rhône, is the church of St-Pierre, one of France's oldest medieval churches (6th–10th c.), which now houses the Musée Lapidaire, with a large collection including mosaics, sarcophagi, fragments of sculpture and architectural elements.

Other sights

In the Jardin Public, to the south of the town, is a short section of a Roman road of the 4th c. A.D..
Farther south is the Pyramid, a 26 m/85 ft high obelisk which stood at one end of the Roman circus.

Roman Theatre

South-east of the Place de l'Hôtel-de-Ville, at the foot of Mont Pipet, is a large Roman theatre of the 1st c. A.D., which originally had seating for 13,500 spectators.

Mont Pipet

From the summit of Mont Pipet, on which are a statue of the Virgin, a modern chapel, the ruins of the Château de la Bâtie and remains of defensive walls, there is a fine view of the town and the church of St-Maurice.

St-André-le-Bas

In the north of the town, on the banks of the Rhône, is the former monastic church of St-André-le-Bas, which is mainly Romanesque but preserves substructures and an apse from an earlier 9th c. church; the cloister is 12th c. The church, which has fine capitals, now houses the Musée d'Art Chrétien (Museum of Christian Art).

St-Romain-en-Gal

At St-Romain-en-Gal, on the right bank of the Rhône, are the extensive remains of a large Gallo-Roman settlement, which along with Ste-Colombe and Vienne itself formed part of Roman Vienna.

Ste-Colombe

Also on the right bank of the Rhône is the outlying district of Ste-Colombe, with the Tour de Philippe de Valois (14th c.).

Vittel

See Lorraine

Vosges

O/P 6/7

*Situation and characteristics

The Vosges are a range of mountains running parallel to the Rhine valley and the Black Forest on the far side of the Rhine from the borders of the German Palatinate in the north to the Belfort Gap in the south.

Origins

The Vosges and Alsace (see entry) are the mirror image of Baden and the Black Forest on the German side of the Rhine, with which they share a common origin. Millions of years ago the Vosges and the Black Forest formed part of a single mountain range, the central section of which collapsed. Only the edges of the range, the Vosges to the west and the Black Forest to the east, remained along the borders of the 300 km/185 mile long

View of the Vosges from the Col du Kreuzweg

rift valley of the Upper Rhine, which was gradually filled with deposits from the Rhine and its tributaries.

Topography

The Vosges extend for a distance of some 170 km/105 miles from north to south and up to 20 km/12½ miles from east to west, rising to their greatest height in the Grand Ballon (1423 m/4669 ft) and the Ballon d'Alsace (1250 m/4100 ft), to the south. To the north they fall away gradually, rising to only 581 m/1906 ft in the Grand Wintersberg. They fall steeply into the Rhine valley, but on the west slope gently down into the Lorraine uplands.

Passes

The main passes in the Southern Vosges are the Col de la Schlucht (1139 m/3737 ft), the Col du Bonhomme (949 m/3113 ft) and the Col de Ste-Marie (763 m/2503 ft).
In the higher Southern Vosges ancient rocks like granite and gneiss form sharply defined ridges, while the lower Northern Vosges consist mainly of variegated sandstones, frequently forming rugged crags, many of them crowned by medieval castles. There are a number of lakes formed by glacial action, and numerous cross valleys which provided good sites for the building of castles, monasteries and churches.

History

See Alsace

Economy

The abundance of timber in the Vosges has promoted the development of woodworking and papermaking industries, while the plateaux, known as *chaumes,* provide pasture for large numbers of dairy cows, whose milk is used to produce a well known cheese (Munster Géromé).

Sport and recreation in the Vosges

Although in recent years the Vosges have attracted increasing numbers of visitors, there is still plenty of lonely, unspoiled country for walkers and nature-lovers.

Long-distance trails

There are three main long-distance trails through the Vosges: No. 1 (way-marked by a red rectangle) runs from Wissembourg to Masevaux (388 km/241 miles), No. 2 (blue rectangle) from Lembach to Masevaux (282 km/175 miles), No. 3 (yellow rectangle) from Obersteinbach to Masevaux (324 km/201 miles). There are also linking paths (red rectangle with white stripe) from railway stations and villages to route No. 1.

Winter sports

The Vosges are increasingly being discovered by winter sports enthusiasts.

Water sports

The numerous lakes provide opportunities for all kinds of water sports.

Other sports

There are also tennis courts and facilities for riding.

Folk events

There are a variety of folk events and traditional pilgrimages.

Sights in the Vosges

***Ballon d'Alsace**

The Ballon d'Alsace (1250 m/4101 ft) is the most southerly of the high peaks of the Vosges. The plateau-like summit is treeless and affords wide views. On the top are a statue of the Virgin, a monument to Joan of Arc and the Monument des Démineurs (mine-clearance and bomb-disposal experts).

Bruyères

This little town (alt. 500 m/1640 ft), in a wooded region in the western Vosges, is a good base for walkers and skiers. The church of Champ-le-Duc dates from the 11th c.

Bussang

Bussang (alt. 500 m/1640 ft) is a popular summer and winter resort in the upper Moselle valley, on the road to the Col de Bussang (731 m/2398 ft) in the High Vosges. Near the town is the source of the Moselle (monument).

***Champ du Feu**

The Champ du Feu (1110 m/3642 ft) is a plateau in the central Vosges which is popular with winter sports enthusiasts. From the lookout tower there are fine views extending, in good weather, to the Alps.

***Le Donon**

Le Donon (1009 m/3311 ft), a hill in the central Vosges, attracts many visitors. It was an ancient Celtic religious centre, succeeded in Roman times by a temple of Mercury. There is a museum, opened in 1869, containing Roman objects found here, and in a hollow below the summit are a number of Roman stelae set in a semicircle.
On the Col du Donon (727 m/2385 ft), in a clearing in the forest, is a copy of a Roman Jupiter column.

Ferrette

Ferrette (alt. 470 m/1540 ft) is beautifully situated on the fringes of the Alsatian Jura below a hill (613 m/2011 ft) crowned by the ruins of the Château de la Ferrette (1125), which was destroyed in 1633, during the Thirty Years War. In the little town are a number of half-timbered houses of medieval aspect and the 11th c. church of St-Bernard-d'Aoste.

Gérardmer

See Lorraine

***Grand Ballon**

The Grand Ballon (1423 m/4669 ft), above the town of Guebwiller, is the highest peak in the Vosges, with views extending in clear weather as far as the Alps (Säntis to Ste-Odile-Blanc). In early historical times there was a shrine here to a Celtic sun god named Bel or Belen, from which the name of the hill seems to be derived. There is a monument commemorating the defence of the hill by French Chasseurs Alpins during the First World War.

Lac du Ballon

400 m/1300 ft below the summit, surrounded by forest, is the Lac du Ballon, which was dammed by Vauban in 1699 and now serves industrial purposes. The area is popular with winter sports enthusiasts.

Hartmanns-willerkopf

Hartmannswillerkopf, also known as the Vieil Armand, is a hill (956 m/3137 ft) falling steeply down on one side to the Rhine plain which was the scene

Haut-Kœnigsbourg

of bitter fighting during the First World War. On the summit are a cross, a military cemetery with 60,000 graves and a crypt with the remains of 12,000 unknown soldiers, with a French war memorial and a museum commemorating the dead. Some of the old German positions can still be recognised in the surrounding area.

***Haut-Kœnigsbourg**

The Haut-Kœnigsbourg (755 m/2475 ft) is the largest castle in Alsace, with massive walls and towers of red sandstone rearing 500 m/1640 ft above the Rhine plain. Originally held (*c.* 1147) by the Hohenstaufens, it was destroyed by the cities of the Upper Rhineland in 1462 and rebuilt in 1479 by the Count of Thierstein, who was granted it as a fief by the German Emperor. In 1633, during the Thirty Years War, it was besieged and destroyed by the Swedes. In 1865 the ruin was acquired by the town of Sélestat, which presented it in 1899 to the Emperor Wilhelm II, who had it restored (by Bodo Ebhard, 1901–1908), as near as possible, to its appearance in 1479.

Hohneck

Hohneck (1362 m/4469 ft) ranks along with the Grand Ballon and the Ballon d'Alsace as one of the highest peaks in the Vosges. Between 1870 and 1918 the Franco-German frontier ran over its summit. In winter the bare rounded slopes offer excellent skiing,

*Col de la Schlucht

with the Col de la Schlucht (1159 m/3803 ft) only 4 km/2½ miles away. In clear weather there are magnificent views of the Vosges, the Alsatian plain and the Black Forest.

Le Hohwald

This popular climatic and winter sports resort (alt. 643 m/2110 ft) lies in the high valley of the Andlau, with expanses of Alpine meadow surrounded by coniferous forests.

Markstein

The Markstein (1176 m/3858 ft), on the Route des Crêtes (see below), a saddle affording extensive views, is a good base for walkers and skiers.

The pilgrimage church Ste-Odile

Below it is the Lac de la Lauch, an artificial lake in a forest-fringed cirque, formed by a dam built in 1889–1894.

Masevaux

Masevaux (alt. 405 m/1330 ft; pop. 3500) is a finely situated little industrial and commercial town in the Doller valley which is also a popular climatic resort. It originally grew up around a Benedictine abbey founded in 728 and dissolved during the French Revolution. It is a town of elegant old burghers' houses of the 16th and 17th centuries and squares decorated with fountains.
Masevaux is the starting-point for the ascent of the Rossberg (1191 m/3908 ft) by a number of different routes. From here there is also an attractive trip up the Doller valley, with the artificial Lac d'Alfeld, to the Ballon d'Alsace.

La Petite-Pierre

See Alsace.

Plombières-les-Bains

See Lorraine

St-Amarin

The little industrial town of St-Amarin (alt. 420 m/1380 ft) lies at the mouth of the St-Amarin valley, one of the most beautiful in the Vosges, at the head of which is the Rainkopf. The town was founded in the 7th c. In the parish church is a reliquary containing the remains of St Amarin, after whom the valley and the town are named.

Ste-Marie-aux-Mines

Ste-Marie-aux-Mines (alt. 360 m/1180 ft) is an old mining town, around which silver and other minerals were worked from the Middle Ages, and probably earlier; it now has textile industries. It is a good centre for excursions into the surrounding area.
The Old Town Hall (1634) contains a small museum. The 16th c. St-Barthélemy silver mine is open to visitors in summer (conducted tours). On the

Sunday after Ash Wednesday the traditional Carneval des Paysans, with a cavalcade, is held.

*Mont Ste-Odile

Mont Ste-Odile (763 m/2503 ft) is one of the high spots of a visit to the Vosges. This wooded ridge is surrounded by a prehistoric defensive wall some 10 km/6 miles in extent known as the Mur Païen (Heathens' Wall). In places the wall, 2 m/6½ ft thick, still stands to a height of 2–3 m/6½–10 ft; the stones were originally bonded together with oak dowels. On the summit of the hill, once occupied by a Roman fort, is the famous convent of Ste-Odile, originally founded towards the end of the 7th c. on the site of a castle belonging to Attich, Duke of Alsace, by his daughter Odilia (Odile). The original convent was destroyed by the Huns.

Mur Païen

The heyday of the convent was in the 12th and 13th centuries. In 1546 it was destroyed by fire and abandoned by the nuns, but was later reoccupied and rebuilt by Premonstratensian canons. In the mid 19th c. the bishop of Strasbourg revived the pilgrimage to the shrine of St Odile, which is now visited by countless pilgrims. In the church (rebuilt in the 17th c.) is the tomb of the foundress (d. 720), who according to her legend was born blind and gained her sight when she was baptised.

From the terrace there is a magnificent view, and there are even wider views from the Männelstein (823 m/2700 ft), to the south-east, the highest point on Mont Ste-Odile. Near the convent are the Chemin de Croix (Stations of the Cross), the Fontaine Ste-Odile (to the south, on the road to St-Nabor) and the ruins of the convent church consecrated in 1180 (to the east, at the foot of the steep hillside).

Schirmeck

Schirmeck (alt. 317 m/1040 ft), in a wooded setting in the Bruche valley, at the foot of Le Donon, is a popular holiday resort with an old-established textile industry. On the Côte du Château (416 m/1365 ft) are the ruins of a castle which belonged to the bishops of Strasbourg; it now contains a museum.

Le Struthof

5 km/3 miles south-east of Schirmeck is Le Struthof, a former concentration camp preserved as a memorial to the 40,000 people who were imprisoned here between 1941 and 1944.

Les Trois-Epis

See Alsace

Tourist Routes in the Vosges

*Route des Crêtes

Of the various tourist routes which pass through the Vosges or run close to them the most important are the Route des Crêtes and the Route des Vosges. The Route des Crêtes (75 km/47 miles), constructed during the First World War by the French army to facilitate the supply of ammunition, runs from the Col du Bonhomme by way of the Col de la Schlucht, the Markstein, the Grand Ballon and Hartmannswillerkopf to Mulhouse. The Route des Vosges runs from to Mont Ste-Odile and then continues by way of Le Hohwald and Andlau to Sélestat. The Route Joffre runs between the Thur and Doller valleys, at the south end of the Vosges, while the Route Verte runs through the central Vosges.

*Route des Vosges

Practical Information

Warning

In the larger towns and tourist centres there has been a considerable increase in property thefts. It is advisable, therefore, to carry money, cheques, etc., on your person and not to leave valuable articles on view in your car. If you have a motor or trailer caravan you should not spend the night in isolated locations away from organised camping sites.
During the long dry period in summer, particularly in southern France, there is increased danger of forest fires. It is therefore strictly forbidden to light fires within a safety zone of 200 m/220 yds, to smoke in forests and to drop glowing cigarette ends or other inflammable objects. Camping is permitted only on sites designated for the purpose.

Telephone numbers

The local dialling codes of the French telephone system have recently been incorporated in subscribers' numbers, and are therefore not shown separately in the lists of addresses in this section. The numbers given are used both for local calls and trunk calls. The only exception is Paris. To phone from Paris to anywhere else in France the caller must dial a preliminary 16; from the provinces to Paris precede the number by 16 1.

Accommodation

See Camping, Country Holidays, Holiday Villages and Clubs, Hotels, Youth Hostels.

Air Lines

Domestic services

In addition to its international services (see Getting to France) Air France flies the main domestic routes, and also represents the two smaller French airlines, Air Inter and TAT. Air Inter has the largest number of services within France (see map). Air Inter and TAT (Transport Aérien Transrégional) offer cheap off-season tariffs. There are also a dozen or so small airlines serving airports of merely regional importance. TAT flies to Figari airport in southern Corsica (opened 1987), with services throughout the year from Paris, Marseilles and Nice and seasonal services from Lyons, Montpellier, Toulon and Toulouse.

Airline addresses

Air France
119 Avenue des Champs-Elysées, F-75384 Paris, tel. (1) 42 99 21 24
Colet House, 100 Hammersmith Road, London W6 7JP, tel. (081) 742 6600
Air Inter, 1 avenue du Maréchal-Devaux, F-91550 Paray-Vielle-Poste, tel. (1) 46 75 12 12
TAT, 47 rue Christiaan-Huygens, F-37002 Tours Cédex, tel. 47 42 30 00
220 Ashdown House, Gatwick Airport, West Sussex, RH6 0EW, tel. (0293) 568888
Map Travel, 45 rue de Babylone, F-75007 Paris, tel. (1) 47 53 74 74
British Airways, 91 Avenue des Champs-Elysées, F-75008 Paris, tel. (1) 47 78 14 14
156 Regent Street, London W1R 5TA, tel. (081) 897 4000
Delta Airlines, 4 Place des Vosges, Immeuble Lavoisier, F-92052 Paris, tel. (1) 47 68 92 92
TWA, 101 Avenue des Champs-Elysées, F-75008 Paris, tel. (1) 47 20 62 11

Fly-drive

It is also possible to book a fly-drive package through an airline or a travel agency.

Hire of private aircraft

At most airports it is possible to hire a plane for private use. Map Travel (see above) also arranges helicopter trips.

◀ *Edible decoration at the Menton Festival of Lemons*

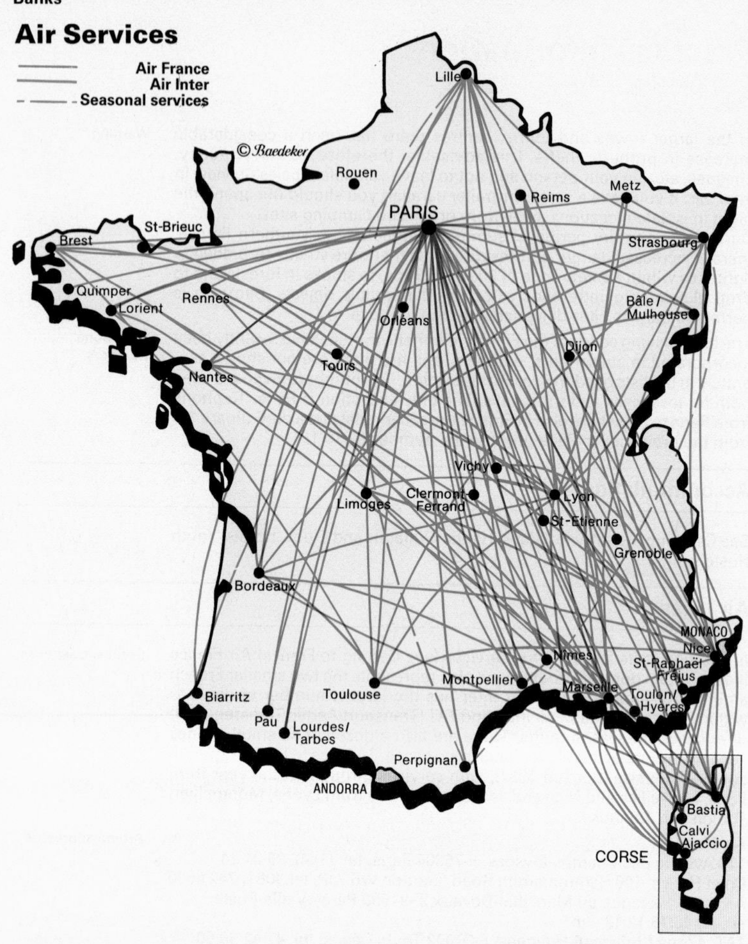

Banks

See Business Hours, Currency

Breakdown assistance

See Motoring

Business Hours

France has no general legislation on shop hours, and museums and châteaux will often close half an hour before their official closing time. The

Aircraft of Air France

information given below, therefore, can only be a general guide; and to be on the safe side it is as well, when proposing to go somewhere, to allow a margin of an hour or so. On the other hand visitors may sometimes be pleasantly surprised to find that if they show themselves to be genuinely interested in a particular sight and ask tactfully they may be admitted outside the stated hours and may even get a specially conducted tour.

Shops

Ordinary shops are usually open from 9/10 a.m. to 6.30/7.30 p.m. Food shops are often open earlier, usually 7 a.m.; small shops usually close at lunch-time, anywhere between noon and 4.30 p.m., and stay open later in the evening. Shops are normally closed on Sunday, but bakers, butchers, wine shops and flower shops are open until noon or 1 p.m.
Many shops close all day or a half-day on Monday.

Department stores

Department stores (and often other large shops) are open on weekdays from 9.30 a.m. to 6.30 p.m., but normally have one or two late opening nights anytime up to 10 p.m.

Shopping centres/hypermarkets

Shopping centres and hypermarkets (*centres commerciaux, hypermarchés*) on the outskirts of large towns are usually open from 9/10 a.m. to 9 (and sometimes 10) p.m., including Saturday, but are closed on Monday morning.

Banks

In large towns banks are open on weekdays from 9.30 a.m. to noon and 2.30 to 4 p.m.; in the provinces Tuesday to Saturday, same hours. On the day before a public holiday they close at noon.

Post offices

Post offices open weekdays from 8 a.m. to 7 p.m. (sometimes with a break for lunch), on Saturday from 8 a.m to noon. Times may vary for small offices in rural areas.

Museums

See Opening Times

Camping

Camping sites

Camping is more popular in France than in other European countries, and practically every place of tourist interest has a camping site (*terrain de camping*), and often several. The sites are officially classified, according to the facilities and amenities offered, with one to four stars.
During the main holiday season sites along the main tourist routes are usually full (*complet*), but it is almost always possible to find a place on a site off the main road.

Information

Fédération Française de Camping et de Caravaning
78 rue de Rivoli
F-75004 Paris
tel. (1) 42 72 84 08

Camping Club International de France
14 rue des Bourdonnais
F-75001 Paris
tel. (1) 42 36 12 40

Camping Club de France
218 Boulevard St-Germain
F-75007 Paris
tel. (1) 45 48 30 03

Castel Camping

The Castel Camping organisation lists camping sites in the grounds of châteaux and country houses. Information from:
Castel Camping
Château des Ormes
F-35120 Epiniac
tel. 99 48 10 19

Camping à la Ferme

See Country Holidays

Camping carnet

It is advisable to have an International Camping Carnet, which can be obtained from national camping clubs and motoring organisations.

Camping guide

A useful list of camping sites in France, with full information about facilities and amenities, is the green Michelin guide, "Camping/Caravanning France", of which there is a new edition every year.

Canal and River Cruising

Cruising holidays on France's rivers and canals are becoming more popular every year. House boats in particular are much in demand.

Boat hire

Many firms have boats for hire and organise cruises. For information apply to local tourist offices (Offices de Tourisme/Syndicats d'Initiative) or to a travel agency.

Types of boat

The hire firms offer cabin cruisers with two to twelve berths, ranging in length from 5.50 to 11 m (18 to 36 feet), for which normally no "driving licence" is required. They are frequently equipped with refrigerator, cooking facilities, heating and toilet.
The latest innovation is the "carabarge", an unsinkable pontoon complete with motor and steering, on to which a trailer caravan can be loaded, producing a kind of house boat.
Bicycles can often be hired with the boat – a convenient way of doing your sightseeing and shopping while moored at some attractive spot.

Syndicat National des Loueurs de Bateau
à Passagers/Navig France
172 Boulevard Berthier
F-75017 Paris
tel. (1) 46 22 10 86

Motorboats

The person in charge of a motorboat on waterways or in coastal waters in France must possess the licence required in his own country for operating a motorboat in similar waters.

Information

Fédération Française Motonautique
49 rue de Boulainvilliers
F-75016 Paris
tel. (1) 45 25 61 76

Car Rental

There are numerous car rental firms in France, including the well-known international names. Cars can be rented in advance through travel agencies or the local offices of international firms. Within France many rental firms have offices at airports and major railway stations as well as in towns. The following is only a brief selection of car rental offices in France:

Avis

Bordeaux: 59 rue Peyronnet, tel. 56 92 69 38
Nice: 2 Avenue des Phocéens, tel. 93 80 63 52
Paris: 5 rue Bixio, tel. (1) 45 50 32 31

Budget

Bordeaux: Aéroport de Mérignac, tel. 56 47 84 22
Nice: Aéroport Nice/Côte d'Azur, tel. 93 21 36 50
Paris: tel. (1) 43 87 55 55. The firm has offices in six Paris railway stations.

Citer

Paris: 11 rue Erard, tel. (1) 43 41 45 45

Europcar (France)

Bordeaux: 79 rue de Tanzia, tel. 56 91 83 83
Nice: 6 Avenue de Suède, tel. 93 88 64 04
Paris: 50 Avenue du Maine, tel. (1) 43 21 28 37

Hertz

Bordeaux: 7–8 rue Charles-Domercq, tel. 56 91 01 71
Nice: 12 Avenue de Suède, tel. 93 87 11 87
Paris: 120 Boulevard Magenta, tel. (1) 42 85 32 03

Serval

Paris: 39 rue St-Didier, tel. (1) 45 04 22 13

Service Prestige

Paris: 43 rue des Acacias, tel. (1) 46 22 62 20

TT Car Transit

Paris: 2 Avenue de la Porte-de-St-Cloud, tel. (1) 46 51 70 50

Caves

Speleology

France can claim pioneering achievements in the exploration and study of caves. There are many caves open to the public, and many more, particularly in the karstic terrain of Périgord, that have not been fully explored and made accessible to visitors. There are caving societies in many areas.

Information

Ecole Française de Spéléologie
23 rue de Nuits
F-69004 Lyon
tel. 78 39 43 30

Fédération Française de Spéléologie
130 rue St-Maur
F-75011 Paris
tel. (1) 43 57 56 54

Caves open to the public

1 Grottes d'Arcy, nr Arcy-sur-Cure (Yonne) Sinter formations

2 Grotte d'Osselle, nr Roset-Fluans (Doubs) Underground river, sinter formations

Aven d'Orgnac: Stalactitic cavern

3 Grotte de Baume, nr Baume-des-Messieurs (Jura) Spring, sinter formations

4 Grotte du Cerdon, nr Nantua (Ain) Sinter formations

5 Grotte de la Balme, nr Balme-les-Grottes (Isère) Sinter formations

6 Cuves de Sassenage, nr Sassenage (Isère) Erosional features

7 Grotte de Choranche, nr Choranche (Isère) Erosional features, stalactites

8 Grotte de la Luire, nr La Chapelle-en-Vercors (Drôme) Erosional features

9 Grottes de l'Observatoire Principality of Monaco Stalactites, sinter formations

10 Grotte de St-Cézaire, nr Grasse (Alpes-Maritimes) Sinter formations

11 Aven de Marzal, nr Bourg-St-Andéol (Ardèche) Stalactites, sinter formations

12 Aven d'Orgnac, nr Aven-l'Orgnac (Ardèche) Stalactites

13 Grotte de Clamouse, nr Gignac (Hérault) Stalactites, sinter formations

14 Grotte des Demoiselles, nr Ganges (Hérault) Stalactites, sinter formations

15 Abîme de Bramabiau, nr Camprieu (Gard) Underground river, erosional features

16 Grotte de Dargilan, nr Dargilan (Lozère) Sinter formations, stalactites

17 Aven Armand, nr Meyrueis (Lozère) Stalactites

18 Grotte de Presque, nr St-Céré (Lot) Stalactites

19 Gouffre de Padirac, nr Padirac (Lot) Underground river

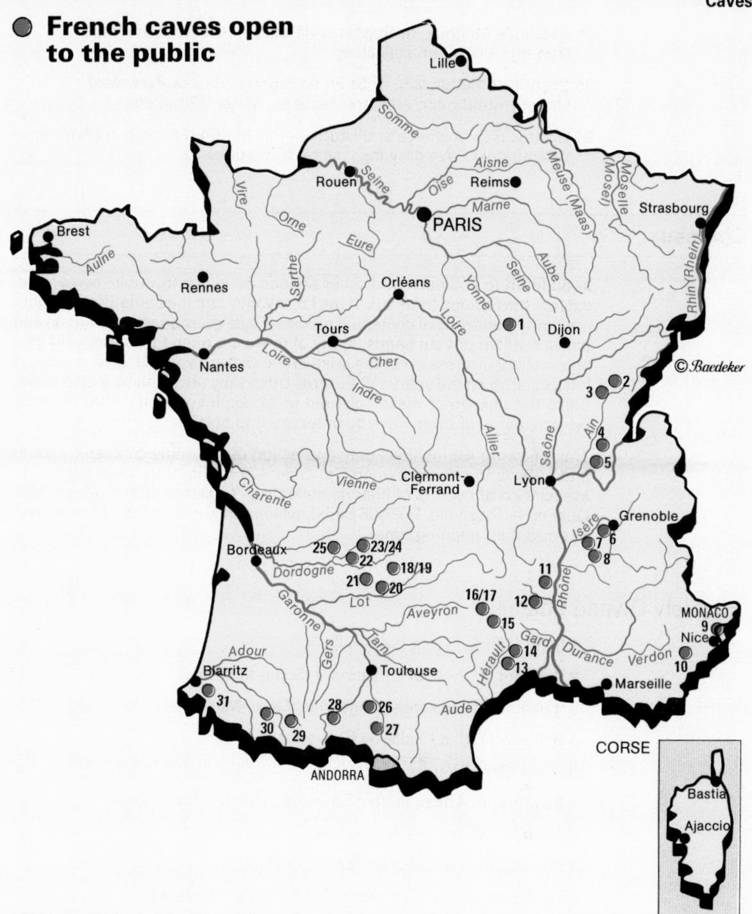

20 Grotte de Pech-Merle, nr Cabrerets (Lot) Cave drawings, sinter formations, stalactites

21 Grottes de Cougnac, nr Gourdon (Lot) Cave drawings, sinter formations, stalactites

22 Gouffre de Proumeyssac, nr Le Bugue (Dordogne) Sinter formations

23 Grotte de Lascaux, nr Montignac (Dordogne) Cave paintings. Closed to public since 1963; replica near site; film shows in information centre

24 Grotte de Rouffignac, nr Rouffignac (Dordogne) Cave drawings

25 Caverne de Bara-Bahau, nr Le Bugue (Dordogne) Cave drawings

26 Grotte du Mas-d'Azil, nr Le Mas-d'Azil (Ariège) Cave drawings, remains of skeletons

27 Grotte de Niaux, nr Niaux (Ariège) Cave drawings, sinter formations

28 Grottes de Gargas, nr Aventignan (Hautes-Pyrénées) Cave drawings

29 Grotte de Médoux, nr Bagnères-de-Bigorre (Hautes-Pyrénées) Underground river, stalactites

30 Grottes de Bétharram, nr St-Pé-de-Bigorre (Hautes-Pyrénées) Underground river, erosional features, sinter formations

31 Grottes d'Oxocelhaya et d'Isturits, nr St-Martin-d'Arberoue (Pyrénées-Atlantiques) Cave drawings, sinter formations

Châteaux

In addition to châteaux and other historic buildings in public ownership, such as the famous châteaux of the Loire valley and the Ile-de-France, there are many hundreds of châteaux, medieval castles, monastic buildings and palaces still in private hands. Many of these are open to visitors, and give an excellent impression of the aristocratic society which created them and left its stamp on the culture of Europe. Often they are set in beautiful parks. Since the upkeep of these splendid buildings involves a heavy financial burden, some of them have been turned into hotels.

The following list includes only a selection of the many châteaux, castles and abbeys in private ownership. Over 400 of them are members of an association of owners of historic buildings, "La Demeure Historique" (57, Quai de la Tournelle, F-75005 Paris), which can supply a list of the properties and their opening times.

Privately Owned Châteaux

1 Long (18th c.) Long (Somme)

2 Valmont (11th–15th c.) Valmont (Seine-Maritime)

3 Bailleuil (Renaissance) Angerville (Seine-Maritime)

4 Balleroy (17th c.) Balleroy (Calvados)

5 Bizy (18th c.) Vernon (Eure)

6 Royaumont Abbey (13th c.) Asnières-sur-Oise (Val-d'Oise)

7 Thoiry (16th c.) Thoiry (Yvelines)

8 Dampierre (17th c.) Dampierre (Yvelines)

9 Gros-Bois (Louis XIII) Boissy-St-Léger (Val-de-Marne)

10 Guermantes (17th–18th c.) Guermantes (Seine-et-Marne)

11 Maintenon (12th–17th c.) Maintenon (Eure-et-Loir)

12 Jeurre (18th c.) Morigny (Essonne)

13 Vaux-le-Vicomte (17th c.) Maincy (Seine-et-Marne)

14 Kintzheim (14th c.) Kintzheim (Bas-Rhin)

15 Rosanbo (12th–17th c.) Lanvellec (Côtes-du-Nord)

16 Malesherbes (14th–17th c.) Malesherbes (Loiret)

17 Fleurigny (14th–15th c.) Fleurigny (Yonne)

18 Josselin (Renaissance) Josselin (Morbihan)

19 Martigny-le-Gannelon (12th–19th c.) Cloyes (Sarthe)

20 Tanlay (16th–17th c.) Tanlay (Yonne)

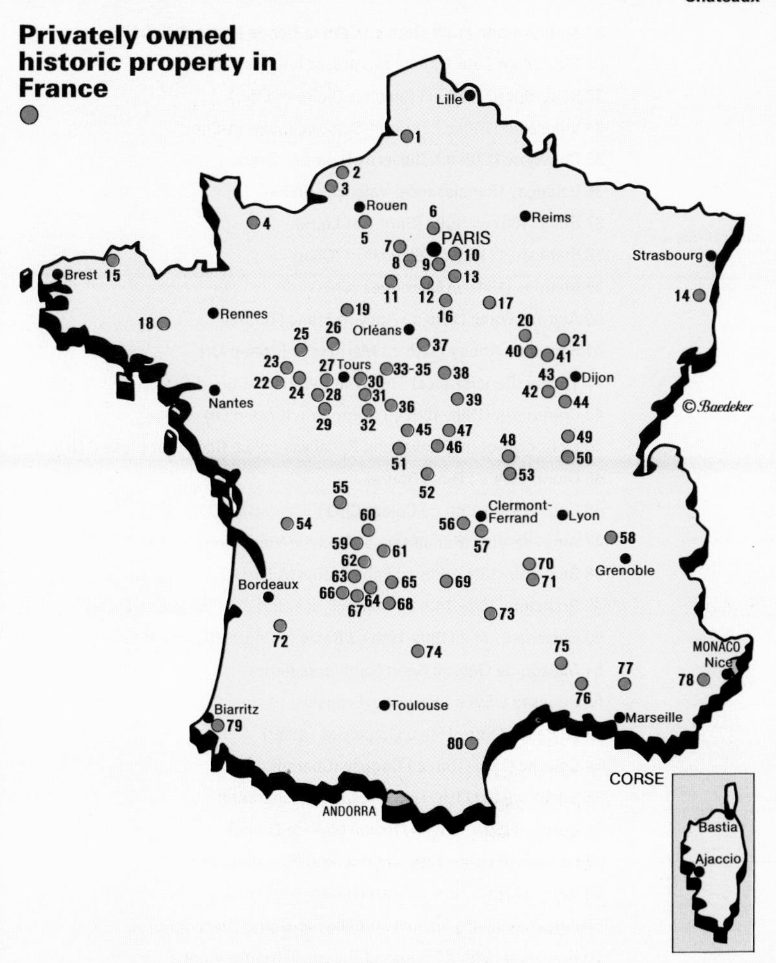

21 Montigny-sur-Aube (12th–19th c.) Montigny-sur-Aube (Côte-d'Or)
22 Brissac (15th–17th c.) Brissac (Maine-et-Loire)
23 Montgeoffroy (18th c.) Maze (Maine-et-Loire)
24 Boumois (15th–17th c.) St-Martin-de-la-Place (Maine-et-Loire)
25 Le Lude (15th–18th c.) Le Lude (Sarthe)
26 Poncé (16th c.) Poncé-sur-le-Loir (Sarthe)
27 Cinq-Mars (12th–13th c.) Cinq-Mars (Indre-et-Loire)
28 Ussé (15th–18th c.) Ussé (Indre-et-Loire)
29 Le Rivau (18th c.) Lémeré (Indre-et-Loire)
30 Le Clos-Lucé (15th c.) Amboise (Indre-et-Loire)

Châteaux

31 Montpoupon (13th–16th c.) Céré-la-Ronde (Indre-et-Loire)

32 Montrésor (late 15th c.) Montrésor (Indre-et-Loire)

33 Beauregard (16th c.) Cellettes (Loire-et-Cher)

34 Villesavin (16th c.) Tour-en-Sologne (Loire-et-Cher)

35 Cheverny (17th c.) Cheverny (Loire-et-Cher)

36 Valençay (Renaissance) Valençay (Indre)

37 Sully (16th c.) Sully (Saône-et-Loire)

38 Blancafort (15th c.) Blancafort (Cher)

39 Maupas (13th c.) Morogues (Cher)

40 Ancy-le-Franc (16th c.) Ancy-le-Franc (Yonne)

41 Fontenay Abbey (12th c.) Marmagne (Côte-d'Or)

42 Thoisy (Renaissance) Thoisy-la-Berchère (Côte-d'Or)

43 Commarin (15th–18th c.) Commarin (Côte-d'Or)

44 La Rochepot (medieval and Renaissance) La Rochepot (Côte-d'Or)

45 Diors (16th c.) Diors (Indre)

46 Culan (12th–15th c.) Culan (Cher)

47 Ainay-le-Vieil (Renaissance) Ainay-le-Vieil (Cher)

48 Beauvoir (13th–18th c.) Echassières (Allier)

49 Brancion (10th–14th c.) Martailly-lès-Brancion (Saône-et-Loire)

50 Berzé-le-Châtel (18th–19th c.) Berzé-le-Châtel (Saône-et-Loire)

51 Maison de George Sand Gargilesse (Indre)

52 Boussac (15th c.) Boussac (Creuse)

53 La Palice (13th–16th c.) Lapalisse (Allier)

54 Cognac (13th–16th c.) Cognac (Charente)

55 Rochebrune (11th–12th c.) Etagnac (Charente)

56 Cordès (15th–16th c.) Orcival (Puy-de-Dôme)

57 La Batisse (10th–18th c.) Chanonat (Puy-de-Dôme)

58 Virieu (11th–17th c.) Virieu (Isère)

59 Jumilhac (13th–17th c.) Jumilhac-le-Grand (Dordogne)

60 Bonneval (14th c.) Coussac-Bonneval (Haute-Vienne)

61 Ségur (15th c.) Ségur-le-Château (Corrèze)

62 Hautefort (14th–17th c.) Hautefort (Dordogne)

63 Coulonges (13th–15th c.) Montignac-sur-Vézère (Dordogne)

64 Richemont (16th c.) St-Crépin-de-Richemont (Dordogne)

65 Turenne (12th–13th c.) Turenne (Corrèze)

66 Fages (medieval and Renaissance) St-Cyprien (Dordogne)

67 Beynac (13th c.) Beynac-et-Cassenac (Dordogne)

68 La Treyne (14th–17th c.) Lacave (Lot)

69 Anjony (15th–18th c.) Tournemire (Cantal)

Langeais: courtyard of the château

70 Voûte-Polignac (10th–18th c.) La Voûte-sur-Loire (Haute-Loire)
71 Volhac (11th c.) Coubon (Haute-Loire)
72 Roquetaillade (12th–14th c.) Mazères (Gironde)
73 La Baume (17th–18th c.) Prinsuéjols (Lozère)
74 Najac (13th c.) Najac (Aveyron)
75 Le Duché Uzès (Gard)
76 Roussan (18th c.) St-Rémy-de-Provence (Bouches-du-Rhône)
77 Ansouis (11th–15th c.) Ansouis (Vaucluse)
78 Gourdon (9th–17th c.) Gourdon (Alpes-Maritimes)
79 Maison de Louis XIV (Louis XIII) St-Jean-de-Luz (Pyrénées-Atlantiques)
80 Fontfroide Abbey (11th c.) Narbonne (Aude)

Son et Lumière

See entry

Consulates

See Diplomatic and Consular Services

Country Holidays

Visitors who want to get to know the French countryside and French country people will find what they are looking for in Brittany and Normandy, Charente, Poitou, Limousin and Périgord, the Massif Central, the Cévennes and the Alps.

Tourisme vert

This term covers a wide range of facilities for enjoying the French countryside. Places designated as *stations vertes* offer not only attractive surroundings but also reasonably priced accommodation in hotels, *chambres d'hôte* (bed and breakfast accommodation) and camping sites and a variety of sporting activities and events. The standard of the facilities provided is vouched for by the "ears of corn" symbol (with a range from one to four).

Information

Association Française des Stations Vertes de Vacances
Hôtel du Département B.P. 21×
F-72040 Le Mans
tel. 43 81 72 72.

Camping à la ferme

"Camping à la ferme" covers not only camping sites on farms but also *chambres d'hôte* (bed and breakfast accommodation) in farmhouses. It is also possible to get overnight accommodation with an evening meal at *tables d'hôte*, and the meal will often include local dishes prepared according to traditional recipes.

Information

Centre de Documentation et d'Information Rurale
92 rue de Dessous-des-Berges
F-75013 Paris
tel. (1) 45 83 04 92.

Gîtes ruraux

The *gîtes ruraux* which are now so popular with visitors to France offer reasonably priced self-catering accommodation in houses (often old houses which have been restored and equipped with modern amenities) in rural – often truly rural – areas in France. The houses are usually privately owned, and the local people are always ready to be helpful.

Information

La Maison des Gîtes de France
35 rue Godot-de-Mauroy
F-75439 Paris
tel. (1) 47 42 20 20.

Gîtes de France
178 Piccadilly
London W1V 9DB
tel. (071) 493 3480.

Currency

The unit of currency is the French franc (F), which is made up of 100 centimes. There are banknotes for 20, 50, 100, 200 and 500 francs and coins in denominations of 5, 10 and 20 centimes and ½, 1, 2, 5 and 10 francs.

Exchange rates

These fluctuate; the current rates are published in national newspapers and they can also be obtained from banks and tourist offices.

Import and export

There are no restrictions on the import or export of French or foreign currency. In order to avoid difficulties when leaving the country, however, it is advisable to declare amounts over 50,000 francs when entering France.

Travellers' cheques

It is advisable to take money in the form of travellers' cheques, Eurocheques or Postcheques of the British Girobank. Postcheques can be cashed at a post office up to the equivalent of £120 per cheque.

French currency

Eurocheques

Eurocheques can be drawn for amounts up to 1400 francs.
If you lose your Eurocheque card you should at once inform your bank by telephone so that a stop can be put on it.

Credit cards

Most international credit cards (American Express, Diners Club, Eurocard, Visa, etc.) are accepted by banks, hotels, restaurants and many shops. Motorway tolls can be paid by credit card.
The loss of a credit card should be notified by telephone to the issuing organisation.

Changing money

Money can be changed in official exchange offices (*bureaux de change*) and in banks, but not in savings banks (*caisses d'épargne*). Banks are usually closed on Mondays.

Customs Regulations

Entry to France

Personal effects and such things as camping and sports equipment (including two sporting guns and 100 cartridges each) are admitted without formality. For a television set, other than a portable set, a returnable deposit must be paid; for an outboard motor over 92 cc a *triptyque* or *carnet de passage* is required. Videos must be declared on entry. Regulations on taking in citizen's band radios and car telephones are still under consideration; apply to your motoring organisation for the latest information.

Customs allowances in European Community countries

From 1 January 1993 new regulations came into operation. In theory there are no limits to the amounts of goods imported from one EC country to another, *provided they have been purchased tax paid in an EC country, are for personal use and are not intended for resale.* However the customs authorities have issued a list of maximum amounts considered reasonable for persons over 17 years of age of alcoholic drinks and tobacco goods. These are: spirits or strong liqueurs over 22% volume – 10 litres; fortified wines (port, sherry, etc.) – 20 litres; table wine – 90 litres (of which not more than 60 litres may be sparkling wine); beer – 110 litres; cigarettes – 800 or cigarillos 400 or cigars 200 or pipe tobacco 1 kg. There is no limit on perfume, toilet water, coffee, tea or other goods. Personal use includes gifts, but if a passenger is receiving any payment in return for buying alcohol and tobacco (such as help with travelling expenses) the transaction will be dutiable and the duty must be paid to the Customs authorities.

For those coming direct from a country outside the EC or who have arrived from another EC country without having passed through customs control with all their baggage, the allowances for goods obtained anywhere outside the EC are (for persons over 17 years of age): spirits – 1 litre or fortified wine – 2 litres or table wine – 3 litres plus a further 2 litres of table wine. Perfume – 60 cc; toilet water – 250 cc, 200 cigarettes or 100 cigarillos or 50 cigars or 250 g of tobacco; (for those over 15 years of age) coffee – 500 g, coffee extract – 200 g, tea – 100 g, tea extract – 40 g. All other goods, including gifts, 150 francs worth. "Duty-free" goods are still available at major airports, on aircraft and ferries; amounts are the same as those above and are controlled by the carriers concerned. The duty-free allowances are scheduled to be phased out by 1996.

Return to the U.S.A.

U.S. citizens can take in 200 cigarettes, 100 cigars, a reasonable quantity of tobacco, one litre of alcohol (for persons over 21 years of age), a bottle of perfume, plus $400 worth of other purchases (with a 10% tax on the next $1000 worth).

Cycling

Cycle tracks

In addition to France's fine network of roads cyclists are catered for by some 3000 km/1900 miles of special cycle tracks.

Hire of bicycles

At almost 200 railway stations bicycles can be hired from SNCF (French Railways); they can be picked up at one station and returned at another. The same system applies on the RER in the Paris area.

Information can be obtained from:

Bicyclub S.A.
8 place de la Porte-Champerret
F-75017 Paris
tel. (1) 47 66 55 92.

Fédération Française de Cyclotourisme
8 rue Jean-Marie-Jégo
F-75013 Paris.
tel. (1) 49 35 69 00

Organised cycle tours

A number of French tour operators now run cycle tours in many of the most popular French holiday areas. Information about the possibilities can be obtained from the French Government Tourist Office (see Information) or from the two cycling organisations mentioned above.

Diplomatic and Consular Services

United Kingdom

Embassy:
35 rue du Faubourg St-Honoré
F-75383 Paris
tel. (1) 42 66 91 42

Consulates-General:
353 Boulevard du Prés.-Wilson
F-33073 Bordeaux
tel. 56 42 34 13

11 Square Dutilleul
F-59800 Lille
tel. 20 57 87 90

24 rue Childebert
F-69288 Lyon
tel. 78 37 59 67

24 Avenue du Prado
F-13006 Marseille
tel. 91 53 43 32

9 avenue Hoche
F-75008 Paris
tel. (1) 42 66 38 10

There are also consulates at Biarritz, Boulogne, Calais, Cherbourg, Dunkirk, Le Havre, Nantes, Nice, St Malo/Dinard and Toulouse.

United States

Embassy:
2 Avenue Gabriel
F-75008 Paris
tel. (1) 42 96 12 02 and 42 61 80 75

Consulates-General:
22 Cours du Maréchal-Foch
F-33080 Bordeaux
tel. 56 52 65 95

7 Quai Général-Sarrail
F-69454 Lyon
tel. 78 24 68 49

12 Boulevard Paul-Peytral
F-13286 Marseille
tel. 91 54 92 00

2 rue Saint-Florentin
F-75001 Paris
tel. (1) 42 96 14 88

15 Avenue d'Alsace
F-67082 Strasbourg
tel. 88 35 31 04

Canada

Embassy (Consular Section):
35 avenue Montaigne
F-75008 Paris
tel. (1) 47 23 01 01

Consulates:
74 rue de Bonnel (3rd floor)
F-69003 Lyon
tel. 72 61 15 25

Polysar France
Rue du Ried
F-67610 La Wantzenau
Strasbourg
tel. 88 96 25 00

Electricity

France is committed to introducing the international norm (adopted in 1983) of 230 volts AC by the year 2003. In the meantime there is no problem about using 220-volt appliances.
There are still a few areas where the supply may be 110 volts. In case of doubt, enquire.
An adapter is necessary for British-type plugs and for American appliances (bought from home) a voltage transformer-type plugs.

Emergencies

Emergency telephones giving direct communication with the police are stationed at 2 km (1¼ mile) intervals along all motorways and some *routes nationales.*
In Paris and the larger towns *Police Secours* can be called by dialling 17. In country areas the local *gendarmerie* should be called.

Events (a selection)

January — Paris: start of Paris-Dakar Rally
Burgundy: Wine Festival (in a different village each year)

January–March — Paris: Film Festival

February — Riviera, Côte-d'Azur (Alpes-Maritimes): Carnival in many places (particularly Nice)

February–March — Menton (Alpes-Maritimes): Lemon Festival (with parade)

March — Ajaccio (Corsica): Festival of Notre-Dame de la Miséricorde
Bastia (Corsica): St Joseph's Procession
Chalon-sur-Saône (Saône-et-Loire): Carnival
Epinal (Vosges): Spring Festival
Hyères (Var): Flower Parade, horse-racing
Montagney (Haute-Saône): Daffodil Festival
Nancy (Meurthe-et-Moselle): Spring Carnival
Paris: Scrap-Iron and Ham Fairs, Book, Domestic and Agricultural Fairs
Paris: Tourism and Travel Fair
Paris–Nice: Cycle race
Strasbourg (Bas-Rhin): Film Festival
Toulon (Var): Spring Festival

April — Burzet (Ardèche): Passion Play
Caen (Calvados): Easter Market
Champagne (Sarthe): Festival of Lances
Marseilles (Bouches-du-Rhône): International Boating Week
Nyons (Drôme): Spring Festival, Flower Parade
Paris: Musical Spring, Model Fair, Paris Marathon (second half of month)
Paris–Roubaix: Cycle race
St-Tropez (Var): Water Sports Day
Toulon (Var): Flower Parade

Cannes (Alpes-Maritimes): International Film Festival Strasbourg (Bas-Rhin): Spring Fair	April–May
Angoulême (Charente): Puppet plays, International Comic Fair, Jazz Festival Antibes (Alpes-Maritimes): Veteran Car Rally Bordeaux (Gironde): Music Weeks Cavaillon (Vaucluse): Great parade Cerisi-Belle-Etoile (Orne): Rhododendron Festival Chaville (Hauts-de-Seine): Lily of the Valley Festival Clermont-Ferrand (Puy-de-Dôme): Festival of Notre-Dame-du-Port Compiègne (Oise): Lily of the Valley Festival Fontainebleau (Seine-et-Marne): "Concours Complet" (dressage) Fontfroide (Aude): Music Weeks in the Abbey Gignac (Hérault): "Donkeys' Dance", procession Grande-Synthe (Nord): Cavalcade (May 13th) Grasse (Alpes-Maritimes): Rose Festival Guebwiller (Haut-Rhin): Wine Market Ile d'Yeu (Vendée): Festival of the Sea La Garde-Freinet (Var): Film and Book Festival La Rochelle (Charente-Maritime): Sailing Week (Whitsun) Mâcon (Saône-et-Loire): Wine Market Magnac-Laval (Haute-Vienne): "Nine-League Procession" (54 km/34 miles) Magny-Cours (Nièvre): International Car Race Mazères (Ariège): Flower and Veteran Car Parade Nice (Alpes-Maritimes): May Fair Orcival (Puy-de-Dôme): Pilgrimage to Notre-Dame d'Orcival (May 24th) Paris: Spring Fair Rambouillet (Yvelines): Lily of the Valley Festival St-Cloud (Hauts-de-Seine): French Open (golf tournament) Stes-Maries-de-la-Mer (Bouches-du-Rhône): Gipsies' pilgrimage (May 24th–25th) St-Tropez (Var): Second-Hand Fair Sancerre (Cher): Wine Market Toulon (Var): Cartoon Film Festival, Veteran Car Rally	May
Monaco: Formula I World Championship Paris: International Telecommunications Fair, French Open Tennis Championships Seine-Maritime: Summer Festival from Le Havre to Rouen Toulon (Var): Musical Festival Versailles (Yvelines): Palace of Versailles Festival	May–June
Domrémy (Vosges): Festival of the Maid of Orléans Versailles (Yvelines): "Grandes Eaux" (fountains playing in park)	May–September
St-Germain-en-Laye, Vincennes, St-Cloud, Sèvres, Rambouillet, Fontainebleau: Promenade and other concerts in châteaux	May–October
Ajaccio (Corsica): Festival of St Erasmus, procession Albertville (Savoie): Festival of Military Music Alpes-Maritimes: Village Festival (Fêtes du Haut-Pays) Antibes (Alpes-Maritimes): Flower Festival Aubusson (Creuse): Film Festival Basque country (Pyrénées-Atlantiques): Corpus Christi processions in many places Beauvais (Oise): Summer Festival Bernay (Eure): Pilgrimage of Caritas confraternity Biarritz (Pyrénées-Atlantiques): Festival of Industrial Films Bordeaux (Gironde): World Wine Week (trade only) Bourges (Cher): Festival of Experimental Music Cavalaire (Var): Festival of St Peter	June

	Chambéry (Savoie): Cartoon Film Festival Coaraze (Alpes-Maritimes): Festival of St John Conflans-Ste-Honorine (Yvelines): Pilgrimage of river boatmen Coravillers (Haute-Saône): Broom Festival Dijon (Côte-d'Or): French Grand Prix Epinal (Vosges): Festival of Popular Prints (mid-month) Gerberoy (Oise): Rose Festival Givet (Ardennes): Rose and Children's Festival Gruissan (Aude): Fishermen's Festival Honfleur (Calvados): Seamen's pilgrimage La Ciotat-Martigues (Bouches-du-Rhône): Midsummer Bonfire La Louvesc (Ardèche): Broom Festival Le Mans (Sarthe): "24 Heures du Mans" (car race) Le Russey (Doubs): Gentian Festival Levier (Doubs): Fir-tree Festival Lyon-la-Forêt (Eure): Midsummer Bonfire Marcoussis-Bièvre (Essonne): Strawberry Festival Menton (Alpes-Maritimes): Festival parade Nice (Alpes-Maritimes): Fishermen's Festival, St Peter's Fair Nîmes (Gard): Féria, bullfights, folk events Paris: Air Show (alternate years) Pyrénées Orientales: Festival of St John in many places Préaux-en-Auge (Calvados): Pilgrimage of Caritas confraternity Propriano (Corsica): Fishermen's Festival St-Jean-de-Luz (Pyrénées-Atlantiques): Festival of St John St-Maurice-sous-les-Côtes (Meuse): Côtes-de-Meuse Festival St-Quentin (Aisne): Rose Festival Sanary-sur-Mer (Var): Fishermen's Festival Sète (Hérault): Georges Brassens Festival Strasbourg (Bas-Rhin): International Musical Festival Tarascon (Bouches-du-Rhône): Festival of the Tarasque Toulon (Var): Festival of the Sea Wissembourg (Bas-Rhin): Costume Festival
June–July	Angers (Maine-et-Loire): Festival of Anjou Divonne-les-Bains (Ain): International Chamber Music Festival Le Havre (Seine-Maritime): Festival of the Sea
June–September	Chartres (Eure-et-Loir): Organ recitals in Cathedral Guebwiller (Haut-Rhin): Musical Festival in Dominican church (first Saturday of month) Corsica: Musical Festivals in Ajaccio, Bastia, St-Florent and Calenzana
July	Annecy (Haute-Savoie): Festival of Old Annecy Antibes (Alpes-Maritimes): Golden Rose Song Festival Arbois (Jura): Wine Market Bayonne (Pyrénées-Atlantiques): Folk Festival Besse-en-Chandesse (Puy-de-Dôme): Pilgrimage to Notre-Dame de Vassivière Bourgneuf-en-Retz (Loire-Atlantique): Costume Festival Bourg-St-Maurice (Savoie): Edelweiss Festival Bricquebec (Manche): Festival of St Anne, with cavalcade Buis-les-Baronnies (Drôme): Lime, Olive and Lavender Festival Doué-la-Fontaine (Maine-et-Loire): Rose Festival Fécamp (Seine-Maritime): Festival of the Sea Font-Romeu (Pyrénées-Orientales): Sardana Festival Fougerolles (Haute-Saône): Cherry Festival Fumay (Ardennes): Boatmen's Tournament Granville (Manche): Pilgrimage of seamen's guilds Hersin-Coupigny (Pas-de-Calais): Pageant of French Revolution Hyères (Var): Festival of Mary Magdalene, Gardeners' Festival La Ménitré (Maine-et-Loire): Festival of Traditional Headdresses La Rochelle (Charente-Maritime): Festival of French Song

Les Mazures (Ardennes): Bilberry Festival
Martigues (Bouches-du-Rhône): Folk Festival
Menton (Alpes-Maritimes): Torchlight procession
Mont-de-Marsan (Landes): Festival of Mary Magdalene
Munster (Haut-Rhin): Albert Schweitzer Musical Festival
Nîmes (Gard): Jazz Festival
Nyons (Drôme): Olive Festival
Palavas (Hérault): Festival of the Sea
Réalmont (Tarn): International Mineral and Fossil Market
Ribeauvillé (Haut-Rhin): Wine Market
St-Christophe-de-Jajolet (Orne): Motorists' pilgrimage
St-Jean-de-Luz (Pyrénées-Atlantiques): Tunny Festival
St-Mandrier (Var): Fishermen's Festival, Santon Fair
St-Malo–Paramé (Ille-et-Vilaine): Carnation Festival
St-Tropez (Var): Fishermen's Festival
Ste-Eulalie (Ardèche): Violet Fair
Saumur (Maine-et-Loire): Cavalry School Tournament
Souillac (Lot): Jazz Festival
Toulon (Var): Santon Fair
Val-d'Isère (Savoie): Valley Festival
Vézelay (Yonne): Pilgrimage

July–August

Aix-en-Provence (Bouches-du-Rhône): International Musical Festival
Avignon (Vaucluse): Festival (drama, music)
Biarritz (Pyrénées-Atlantiques): Regatta
Cannes (Alpes-Maritimes): Festival of Music and Drama
Cherves (Vienne): Village Festival
Collioure (Pyrénées-Orientales): Festival in château
Colmar (Haut-Rhin): Music in Dominican cloister (Thursdays)
Hagetmau (Landes): Flower Festival
Nice (Alpes-Maritimes): International Summer Academy
Orange (Vaucluse): Performances in Roman theatre
Prades (Pyrénées-Orientales): Casals Festival in Abbey of St-Michel-de-Cuxa
Saintes (Charente-Maritime): Musical Festival
Sarlat (Dordogne): Drama Festival
Sénanque (Vaucluse): Medieval music
Sénones (Vosges): Changing of the Guard and Trooping of the Colour

July–September

Burgundy: In many places tours of illuminated vineyards
Dax (Landes): Stilt races
Paris: Summer Festival
St-Jean-de-Luz (Pyrénées-Atlantiques): Folk Festival, bullfights, pelota tournament
Sceaux (Hauts-de-Seine): Orangery Festival (classical music)
Vichy (Allier): Folk Festival

August

Aix-les-Bains (Savoie): Flower Festival
Ajaccio (Corsica): Commemoration of Napoleon's Birthday (Aug. 15th)
Annecy (Haute-Savoie): Lake Festival
Antibes (Alpes-Maritimes): Concerts in château
Arcachon (Gironde): Parade of veteran cars
Ardèche: Festivals of folk art in many places
Aurillac (Cantal): Festival of Street Theatre
Auxerre (Yonne): Fireworks
Bandol (Var): Fishermen's Festival
Basque country (Pyrénées-Atlantiques): Basque sporting contests in many places
Bayonne (Pyrénées-Atlantiques): Traditional Folk Festival
Beaulieu (Alpes-Maritimes): Torchlight procession
Beuzec–Cap-Sizun (Finistére): Bilberry Festival
Béziers (Hérault): Féria, bullfights, folk events

	Biarritz (Pyrénées-Atlantiques): "Night of Magic", with fireworks Bordeaux (Drôme): Historical pageant Chamonix (Haute-Savoie): Mountain Guides' Festival Chaon (Doubs): Lake Festival Cher district: Wine festivals Cheverny (Loir-et-Cher): Illuminations of château Clermont-Ferrand (Puy-de-Dôme): Country Dance Festival Colmar (Haut-Rhin): Alsatian Wine Fair Confolens (Charente): International Folk Festival Coulanges-sur-Yonne (Yonne): Fishermen's Tournament Dax (Landes): Traditional Folk Festival Dieppe (Seine-Maritime): Folk Festival Digne (Alpes-de-Haute-Provence): Lavender Festival Fréjus (Var): Féria, Vintage Festival, bullfights, encierro Gap (Hautes-Alpes): Summer Festival, Flower Parade Gençay (Vienne): Country Festival Gérardmer (Vosges): Festival of Light on lake (Aug. 14th) Grasse (Alpes-Maritimes): Jasmine Festival Guingamp (Côtes-du-Nord): Festival of St Loup (Breton folk dances) La Baule (Loire-Atlantique): Concours d'Elégance (cars) La Font-Sainte (Cantal): Pilgrimage and Shepherds' Festival Le Havre (Seine-Maritime): Flower Parade Le Mayet-de-Montagne (Allier): Puppet Festival Lesches-en-Diois (Drôme): Lavender Festival Lorient (Morbihan): Celtic Bagpipe Festival Lorraine: Mirabelle festivals in many places Maiche (Doubs): Horsemen's Festival Maraye-en-Othe (Aude): Cider Festival Marlenheim (Bas-Rhin): "Ami Fritz" Folk Festival Menton (Alpes-Maritimes): Lantern Parade Metz (Moselle): Mirabelle Festival Mèze (Hérault): Traditional Folk Festival Moncrabeau (Lot-et-Garonne): "Funny Faces" competition Peisey-Nancroix (Savoie): Costume and Mountain Festival Peyrebrune (Aveyron): Knights' Festival Pont-Aven (Finistère): Broom Festival Pont-d'Ouilly (Calvados): Pilgrimage of St Roch Puilly-sur-Loire (Nièvre): Wine Market Rignac (Aveyron): Horsemen's Festival Roquebrune-Cap-Martin (Alpes-Maritimes): Votive procession Ste-Baume (Var): Festival of Provençal Song St-Jean–Cap-Ferrat (Alpes-Maritimes): Venetian Festival St-Palais (Pyrénées-Atlantiques): Basque Sports Festival St-Raphaël (Var): Sea Procession St-Rémy-de-Provence (Bouches-du-Rhône): Provençal Costume Festival Séguret (Vaucluse): Provençal Festival Sélestat (Bas-Rhin): Flower Parade Sète (Hérault): Fishermen's Tournament, Festival of the Sea Southern Atlantic coast (Gironde, Landes, (Pyrénées-Atlantiques): oyster and sea festivals in many places. Tende (Alpes-Maritimes): Traditional Folk Festival Thiézac (Cantal): Pilgrimage to Notre-Dame de Consolation, torchlight procession Wasselonne (Bas-Rhin): Parade of drum-majorettes (mid-month)
August–September	Besançon (Doubs): International Musical Festival Digne (Alpes-de-Haute-Provence): Lavender Market Dijon (Côte-d'Or): International Folk and Wine Festival Haguenau (Bas-Rhin): Hop Festival
September	Bar-sur-Aube (Aube): Champagne Market Besse-en-Chandesse (Puy-de-Dôme): Procession from Notre-Dame de Vassivière

Bordeaux and district (Gironde): Vintage festivals in many places
Cannes (Alpes-Maritimes): International Festival of Amateur Films, "Grand Prix des Nations" cycle race

September–October

Chartres (Eure-et-Loir): "Musical Saturdays of Chartres"
La Ciotat (Bouches-du-Rhône): Michaelmas Market, Fishermen's Festival
Lyons (Rhone): International Puppet Festival, International Dance Festival (Biennale)
Mont-St-Michel (Manche): Autumn pilgrimage
Nîmes (Gard): Vintage Festival, bullfights
Paris: International Photographic, Video and Sound Fair
Ribeauvillé (Haut-Rhin): Pfifferdag (Strolling Musicians' Festival)
St-Jean-de-Luz, Ciboure, Ascain, Bayonne, Biarritz and Anglet (Pyrénées-Atlantiques): "Musical September"

October

Espelette (Pyrénées-Atlantiques): Spice Festival
Montigny-en-Ostrevent (Nord): Chrysanthemum Festival
Montpellier (Hérault): International Wine Fair
Nogentel (Aisne): Flower Festival
Paris: Scrap-Iron and Ham Fairs (beginning of month), Montmartre Vintage Festival (beginning of month), International Dance Festival, Motor Show (alternate years), Winter Sports Fair

November

Corsica: Rally des Mille Virages (international car race)
Nuits-St-Georges, Beaune, Meursault (Côte-d'Or): "Les Trois Glorieuses" (wine festival)
St-Bris-le-Vineux (Yonne): Sauvignon Wine Fair
Sauzé-Vaussais (Deux-Sèvres): Chestnut Market
Strasbourg (Bas-Rhin): International Mime and Clown Festival
Toulon–Solliès-Ville (Var): Santon Fair

November–December

Marseilles (Bouches-du-Rhône): Santon Fair

December

Epinal (Vosges): Festival of St Nicholas
Lyons (Rhône): Pontifical high mass (Dec. 25th)
Metz-Thionville (Moselle): St Nicholas Procession (Dec. 6th)
Nancy (Meurthe-et-Moselle): St Nicholas Procession (Dec. 3rd)
Paris: International Boat Show
St-Bauzille-de-Putois (Hérault): Midnight mass in Grotte des Demoiselles (Dec. 24th)
Strasbourg (Bas-Rhin): Christmas Fair

Other events

The Tour de France, the famous cycle race round France, takes place in July. In summer and autumn there are wine and food fairs, regattas and water sports tournaments, etc., in many places all over regattas and water sports tournaments, etc., in many places all over France.
On Easter Monday, Whit Monday, July 14th (the French national day, commemorating the taking of the Bastille) and Aug. 15th (Assumption) there are celebrations of various kinds all over France, with processions, flower parades, fireworks, etc.

Information

Further information can be obtained from the French Government Tourist Office in a brochure "Festive France" and from local Offices de Tourisme or Syndicats d'Initiative (see Information)

Festivals

A great variety of festivals – large and small, of local, regional or international importance, mostly concerned with classical or modern music, singing, drama, dance and cinema – are held in many parts of France. Most of them are held during the summer months, but there are also some festivals at other times of year.

Festivals

Information

The French Government Tourist Office (see Information), issues a brochure ("Festive France") every year listing the most important festivals in chronological order. Information can also be obtained from local Offices de Tourisme and Syndicats d'Initiative.

The following is merely a small selection:

1 Paris: music, drama, dance, cinema
2 Lille: cinema
3 Deauville, cinema
4 Jersey (Channel Islands): music
5 Coutances: music
6 Reims: music, cinema
7 Metz: music
8 Ile-de-France: music
9 Mont-St-Michel: music
10 Dinard: cinema
11 Sceaux: music
12 Nancy: drama
13 Strasbourg: music
14 Quimper: music, drama, dance
15 Lassay: drama
16 Chartres: music
17 Ancy-le-Franc: music, drama
18 Le Mans: music
19 Lorient: music
20 Amboise: music
21 Angers: music
22 Sully: dance, music
23 Divonne-les-Bains: music
24 Tours: music
25 Dijon: music, drama, dance
26 Bourges: music
27 Besançon: music
28 Poitiers: music
29 Nohant: music
30 Autun: music
31 Divonne-les-Bains: music
32 Evian: music
33 La Rochelle: music, drama, dance, cinema
34 Bellac: music, drama
35 Gannat: music, dance
36 Clermont-Ferrand: dance
37 Avoriaz: cinema
38 Saintes: music
39 La Chaise-Dieu: music
40 Lyons: music

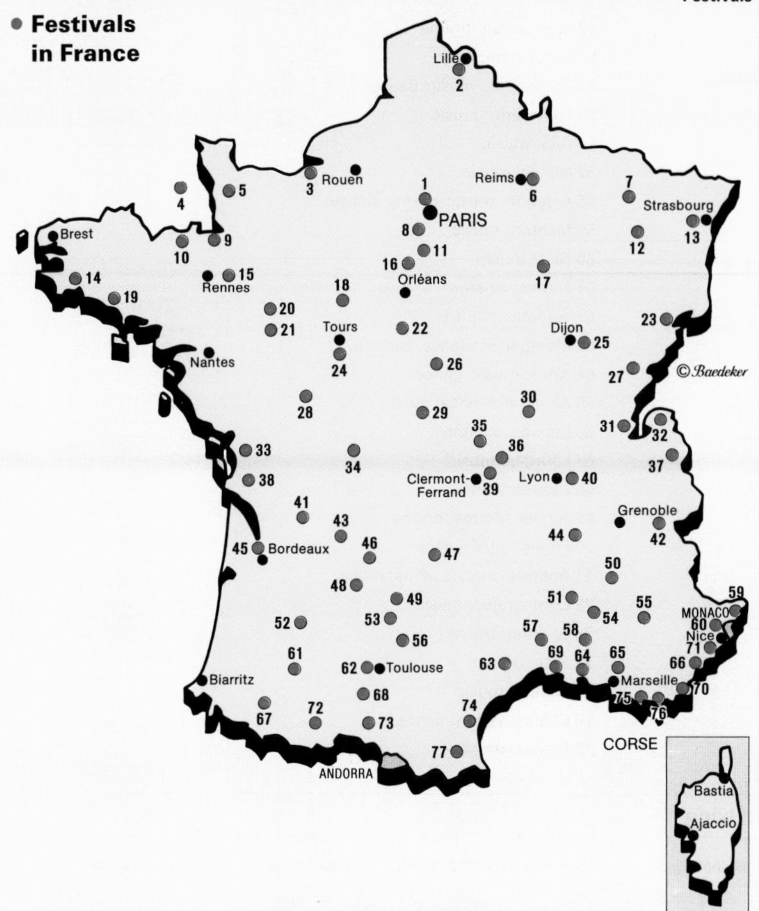

41 Cognac: cinema
42 Les Arcs: music
43 St-Céré: music
44 Romans: music
45 Bordeaux: music, drama, dance
46 Sarlat: drama
47 Aurillac: drama
48 Gourdon: music, drama
49 Sylvanès: music
50 Vaison-la-Romaine: music, dance
51 Orange: music

52 Montauban: drama

53 Cordes: music

54 Carpentras: music, dance

55 Lourmarin: music

56 Albi: music

57 Nîmes: music

58 Avignon: music, drama, dance

59 Menton: music

60 Nice: music

61 Tarbes: cinema

62 Toulouse: music

63 Montpellier: dance, cinema

64 Arles: music, dance

65 Aix-en-Provence: music

66 Cannes: cinema

67 Lourdes: music

68 Castres: dance

69 Aigues-Mortes: drama

70 Fréjus: music, dance

71 Antibes–Juan-les-Pins: music

72 Comminges: music

73 St-Lizier: music

74 Sète: drama

75 Toulon: music

76 Châteauvallon: dance

77 Prades: music

Flying

Ballooning

Visitors interested in ballooning can obtain a list of events from:

Fédération Française d'Aérostation (FFA)
6 rue de Galilée
F-75016 Paris
tel. (1) 46 33 56 82.

Gliding

There are excellent conditions for gliding in the upland regions of France. For information about gliding clubs and organised training courses, apply to:

Fédération Française de Vol à Voile (FFVV)
29 rue de Sèvres
F-75006 Paris
tel. (1) 45 44 04 78.

Hang gliding

The most popular areas for hang gliding, with the right thermal conditions, are Aquitaine, Auvergne, Savoy and the Pyrenees. A number of regional clubs run hang gliding schools with a programme of training courses. Information from:

Fédération Française de Vol Libre (Deltaplan)
54 bis rue de la Buffa
F-06000 Nice
tel. 93 88 62 89.

Light aircraft

Information from:

Aéro Club de France
6 rue de Galilée
F-75762 Paris
tel. (1) 47 23 72 52.

Parachute jumping

Information about parachute-jumping centres, training courses and events can be obtained from:

Fédération Française de Parachutisme
35 rue St-Georges
F-75009 Paris
tel. (1) 48 78 45 00.

Ultra-light aircraft

To practise this relatively new type of flying, now becoming increasingly popular in France, it is necessary to have a licence (minimum age 15). Information from:

Fédération Française de Planeurs et Ultra-Légers-Motorisées
489 Chemin de la Sacristie
F-84140 Montfavet (nr Avignon)
tel. 90 32 56 75.

Food and Drink

General

French cuisine

French cuisine is famed both for its quality and its variety. Since the average Frenchman attaches importance to a well-chosen menu and sets aside between one and two hours for his meals, eating plays an important part in daily life and cooking has developed into an essential component of French culture.
A concern with the quality and variety of meals is believed to have been brought to the French court by Henry II's wife Catherine de Médicis, and like all courtly fashions, to have spread from there to the ordinary French household. Henry IV declared that he wanted every peasant to have a chicken for his Sunday dinner. The French Revolution brought with it not only civil liberties but also a higher standard of cuisine for ordinary people. In 1825 Anthelme Brillat-Savarin wrote his "Physiologie du goût" ("Physiology of Taste"), which still provides a philosophical basis for the enjoyment of good food, and in 1986 a university of cooking was established in the Château du Vivier (Ecully, department of Rhône), where France's most celebrated chefs introduce students to the high art of French cuisine.

Haute cuisine

Typical features of the highest standard of French cooking – *haute cuisine* – are elaborate preparation and the use of fresh ingredients (anything canned or preserved is anathema!), delicacies like truffles, mushrooms and cognac, and plenty of butter and cream (*crème fraîche*). Herbs and spices are used on a large scale and in a variety of combinations. French sauces are famous.

Nouvelle cuisine

In recent years there has been much talk of *nouvelle cuisine,* which avoids over-elaboration and seeks to bring out the natural taste of the finest fresh ingredients.

Cuisine régionale

There are also various regional cuisines which are much esteemed by discriminating gourmets.
Visitors to France should not ignore this side of French culture, even though it may sometimes occupy a good deal of valuable sightseeing time. Some experience of this essential element in the famous French *savoir vivre* is necessary for anyone who really wants to get to know France.

Restaurants

Even quite modest-looking restaurants can offer a choice of excellent dishes. In such places it is often usual (and advisable) to discuss the menu with the host or hostess before deciding what to have. If there is no menu it is as well to enquire about prices, since the abundance and quality of the fare offered is likely to be reflected in the cost of the meal. In general, however, restaurant prices (which usually include service: (*service compris*) are not unduly high when measured against the quality of the meal.
It is cheaper to take the fixed-price (*prix-fix*) menus (sometimes including wine) which most restaurants offer than to eat à la carte. The "dish of the day" (*plat du jour*) is usually good value.

Tipping

See entry

Snacks

Visitors who want a cheap snack will not usually get it in a restaurant: they will find what they require in more modest establishments calling themselves *rotisseries, bistros* or *brasseries.* In Paris there are numerous self-service restaurants where excellent cheap meals can be had. In holiday resorts there are likely to be stalls and kiosks selling *pommes frites,* hot dogs, *merguez* (highly spiced sausages), *crêpes* (pancakes), *chi-chis* (a kind of doughnut) and sandwiches.

Cafés

French cafés are not confined to selling coffee but offer a choice of alcoholic and non-alcoholic drinks and ices as well, remaining open all day and sometimes late at night. In the larger towns there are *salons de thé* (tearooms), which may offer a variety of cakes and pastries. These can also be obtained in *pâtisseries,* though usually not for consumption on the premises.

Meals (repas)

Breakfast (petit déjeuner)

The simple French *petit déjeuner* (breakfast), with white or black coffee, tea or chocolate and croissants or rolls, is often taken in a café.

Lunch (déjeuner)

Lunch (*déjeuner*) is served in restaurants between 12 and 2.30, and may be either a set meal (*menu*) consisting of an hors d'oeuvre, main course and cheese and/or dessert, followed by coffee, or an *à la carte* meal selected from the full menu (*carte*).

Evening meal (díner, souper)

The evening meal (*dîner* or *souper*) is similar to lunch, except that the hors d'oeuvre is usually replaced by soup.
White bread is the regular accompaniment to a meal, cut either from the long crisp *baguettes* or the shorter *flûtes.*

Wine

The meal is accompanied by wine almost as a matter of course. (See the entry Wine on p. 623.) For everyday drinking the ordinary local wine (*un petit blanc, un petit rouge*) is recommended, in a *carafe* (about half a litre) or *carafon* (quarter litre). It may be diluted with water if desired. When ordering wine in bottle – either a full bottle (*bouteille entière*) or half bottle (*demi-bouteille*) – it is a good idea to ask the waiter's advice.

Beer

The beers of Alsace (Pêcheur, Kronenbourg, Kanterbräu, Mutzig) and Lorraine (Champigneulles, Vézélise) are excellent and are becoming increasingly popular. Beer is either bottled (*canette*) or draught (*pression*). A small glass of draught beer is called a *demi,* a half litre usually a *véritable,* a litre a *formidable.*

Mineral waters

Mineral water may be either still *(eau minérale)* or carbonated *(gazeuse)*. The best known brands are Perrier, Vichy, Evian, Vittel and Contrexéville.

Reading a French Menu (la carte)

The table-setting

Couvert, the place-setting (knife, fork, spoon, etc.); *cuillère,* spoon; *couteau,* knife; *fourchette,* fork; *assiette,* plate; *verre,* glass; *tasse,* cup; *serviette,* napkin; *tire-bouchon,* corkscrew.

Hors d'oeuvres

Artichauts, artichokes; *huîtres,* oysters (the best being Belons, Fines de Claires and Portugaises); *bouchées,* pasties; *canapés;* cornichons, gherkins; *foie gras,* goose liver; *crudités,* a selection of salad vegetables; *jambon cru,* raw ham; *saumon fumé,* smoked salmon.

Soups (soupes, potages)

Bouillon, clear meat soup; *consommé,* clear soup; *potage,* soup containing a variety of ingredients.

Egg dishes

Œufs au plat, fried eggs; *œufs pochés,* poached eggs; *œufs brouillés,* scrambled eggs; *œufs à la coque,* soft-boiled eggs; *omelette aux champignons,* mushroom omelette; *omelette aux fines herbes,* omelette with mixed herbs; *omelette au fromage,* cheese omelette; *omelette au jambon,* ham omelette.

Fish (poisson)

Aiglefin, haddock; *anchois,* anchovy; *anguille,* eel; *barbeau,* barbel; *barbue,* brill; *bondelle,* whitefish; *brochet,* pike; *cabillaud,* cod; *carpe,* carp; *carrelet,* plaice; *colin,* hake; *congre,* conger-eel; *féra,* dace; *flétan,* halibut; *glamis,* catfish; *hareng,* herring; *limande,* dab; *maquereau,* mackerel; *merlan,* whiting; *meuille,* grey mullet; *ombre,* grayling; *ombre chevalier,* char; *perche,* perch; *plie,* plaice; *raie,* ray; *sardine,* sardine; *saumon,* salmon; *sole,* sole; *tanche,* tench; *thon,* tunny; *truite,* trout; *turbot,* turbot.
Crevettes, shrimps; *écrevisses,* crayfish; *homard,* lobster; *huîtres,* oysters; *langouste,* spiny lobster; *moules,* mussels; *palourde,* pullet-shell; *clam,* clam; *clovisse,* carpet-shell; *oursin,* sea-urchin.
Cuisses de grenouilles, frogs' thighs; *escargot,* snail; *tortue,* turtle.

Meat (viande)

Agneau, lamb; *bœuf,* beef; *cochon de lait,* sucking pig; *mouton,* mutton *(pré-salé,* from the salt meadows of Brittany); *porc,* pork; *veau,* veal.

Cuts of meat

Ballottine, meat roll; *cervelle,* brain; *côte,* rib; *entrecôte,* steak cut from the ribs; *escalope,* fillet (of veal); *filet,* fillet (of beef); *foie,* liver; *gigot,* leg of mutton; *jambon,* ham; *langue,* tongue; *pieds,* feet, trotters; *poitrine,* breast; *ris,* sweetbreads; *rognons,* kidneys; *selle,* saddle (of mutton); *tête,* head; *tournedos,* fillet steak; *tripes,* tripe.

Methods of cooking

Carbonade, meat grilled on charcoal; *cassoulet,* stew made in an earthenware dish; *chaudfroid,* in aspic; *civet,* stew (of venison, etc.); *civet de lièvre,* jugged hare; *émincé,* thinly sliced meat served in sauce; *pâté,* pâté; *rôti,* roast; *soufflé,* soufflé; *terrine,* potted meat, pâté.

Poultry (volaille)

Domestic poultry from Brittany and the Lyonnais, wildfowl from Gascony: *bécasse,* snipe; *caille,* quail; *canard,* duck; *caneton,* duckling; *coq,* cock; *dindonneau,* turkey; *faisan,* pheasant; *oie,* goose; *perdreau,* partridge; *pigeon,* pigeon; *pintade,* guineafowl; *poulet,* chicken; *poularde,* fattened pullet.

Game (gibier)

Cerf, venison (red deer); *chevreuil,* roe-deer; *lièvre,* hare; *sanglier,* wild boar.

Vegetables (légumes)

Ail, garlic; *artichauts,* artichokes; *asperges,* asparagus; *betterave,* beetroot; *cardon,* cardoon; *carotte,* carrot; *céleri,* celery; *céleri-rave,* celeriac; *chicorée,* endive; *chou (blanc),* cabbage; *chou rouge,* red cabbage; *chou-fleur,* cauliflower; *chou-rave,* kohlrabi; *choux de Bruxelles,* Brussels

Riesling

sprouts; *concombre,* cucumber; *endive,* chicory; *épinards,* spinach; *fenouil,* fennel; *haricots verts,* French beans; *laitue,* lettuce; *lentilles,* lentils; *oignon,* onion; *petits pois,* peas; *poireau,* leek; *salade verte,* green salad; *salsifis,* salsify; *tomate,* tomato.

Mushrooms

Cèpes, boletus mushrooms; *champignons de Paris,* mushrooms from the Loire valley; *chanterelles, girolles* chanterelles; *helvelles,* turban-top mushrooms; *morilles,* morels; *truffes,* truffles (particularly from Périgord).

Potatoes and rice

Pommes de terre, potatoes; *pommes frites,* chips; *pommes allumettes,* thin ("match-stick") fried potatoes; *pommes paille,* potato straws; *purée de pommes,* potato purée, mashed potatoes; *pommes croquettes,* potato croquettes; *pommes dauphines,* dauphine potatoes.
Riz, rice.

Methods of cooking

Braisé, braised; *farci,* stuffed; *frit,* fried; *glacé,* glacé; *gratiné,* au gratin; *grillé,* grilled; *(à la) meunière,* fried in butter; *poché* (fish), poached; *sauté,* sauté.

Sweets (desserts)

Biscuits, biscuits; *coupe glacé,* ice-cream sundae; *crème,* cream; *crème Chantilly,* whipped cream; *crêpes,* pancakes; *crêpes Suzette,* dessert pancakes; *flan,* custard; *gâteau,* cake; *gaufrettes,* waffles; *glace,* ice; *mousse,* mousse; *petits fours,* petits fours; *sorbet,* water ice, sorbet; *tarte,* tart; *vermicelles à la Chantilly,* chestnut mousse with whipped cream.

Fruit (fruits)

Abricots, apricots (particularly from Roussillon); *amandes,* almonds; *avelines,* hazelnuts; *cerises,* cherries (grown round Yonne in Burgundy); *citron,* lemon; *fraises,* strawberries; *framboises,* raspberries; *marrons,* chestnuts (from the Lyonnais, Provence and Alsace); *melon,* melon (from Cavaillon); *noisettes,* hazelnuts; *noix,* walnuts (from Périgord); *orange,* orange; *pastèque,* water-melon; *pêche,* peach; *poire,* pear; *pomme,* apple; *prune,* plum; *pruneau,* prune (from Agen); *raisin,* grapes.

Cheese (fromage)

Only a selection from the enormous range of French cheeses can be given here: *Roquefort,* a ewe's-milk cheese from Roquefort (Aveyron), matured in natural caves (conducted tours); *Camembert,* a famous soft cheese from Normandy; *Brie,* a delicate soft cheese from the Ile de France; *Munster, Géromé,* a strong-smelling soft cheese made in Alsace and Lorraine; *Pyrenean cheeses,* ewe's-milk cheeses with a light-coloured rind and cow's-milk cheeses with a dark rind; *Bleu de Bresse,* a mild creamy blue cheese from the Lyonnais; *nut cheese,* a soft cheese containing walnuts or almonds produced in various areas, particularly Savoy, which has recently become very popular.

Butter

From Normandy and Brittany come very good salt butter and *crême fraîche,* a sourish-tasting cream with a fat content of 40%.

Milk products

Yaourt, yoghurt; *fromage blanc,* cream cheese.

Regional Specialities

Cassoulet, a rich stew containing beans, knuckle of pork, preserved goose, bacon and sausage (Toulouse region); *potée auvergnate,* vegetable stew (Auvergne); *soupe à l'oignon,* onion soup with bread and cheese gratiné (Paris); *potage St-Germain,* pea soup (Paris); *crême de cèpes,* mushroom soup (Poitou).
Andouilles, chitterling sausages (Brittany, Loire valley); *confit d'oie,* goose preserve (Périgord); *foie gras d'oie,* goose-liver pâté (Alsace, Périgord); *saucissons de Lyon,* large meat sausages (Lyonnais); *rillettes,* pork pâté (Brittany, Loire valley).

◀ *Alsace Specialities*

Chou au lard, cabbage with bacon (Alsace); *fabonade,* fat beans, ham and garlic in egg sauce (Languedoc); *cousinat,* stew with mixed vegetables (Béarn); *porrosalda,* a stew with garlic and potatoes (Aquitaine); *gratin dauphinois,* potatoes gratiné with cream and garlic (Dauphiné); *lentilles du Puy,* lentils Auvergnat-style (Auvergne); *truffiat,* potato cake (Berry); *choucroute garnie,* sauerkraut with sausages, etc. (Alsace, Lorraine); *choucroute au riesling, choucroute au champagne,* choucroute with wine or champagne (highly recommended); *escargots,* snails (Alsace, Burgundy); *flamiche aux poireaux,* garlic tart (Picardy); *tarte à l'oignon,* garlic cake (Alsace); *matafam,* a substantial pancake (Franche-Comté); *corniottes,* cheese-cakes (Burgundy); *gougère,* a kind of cheese-cake (Burgundy); *fondue savoyarde,* cheese fondue (Savoy); *salade fécampoise,* salad of potatoes, smoked herring and eggs (Normandy); *fondue bourgignonne,* meat fondue with sauces (Burgundy); *quiche lorraine,* bacon quiche (Lorraine); *anguilles au vert,* eels with herbs (Picardy); *cotriade,* fish and potato stew (Brittany); *brandade de morue,* salt cod with garlic, oil and cream; *coquilles St-Jacques à la landaise,* scallops with pine kernels (Landes); *coq au vin,* chicken in red wine (Burgundy); *canard à la Montmorency,* duck with cherries (Paris); *bonhomme normand,* duck in a cider and cream sauce (Normandy); *civet de lièvre,* jugged hare (Savoy); *lapin à l'ail,* rabbit with twenty cloves of garlic (Cévennes); *cailles à la vignerolle,* quails with vine-leaves (Touraine); *salmis de bécasse,* snipe stew (Franche-Comté); *caghuse,* pork with onions (Artois); *miroton lyonnais,* beef with onions (Lyonnais); *carbonnades flamandes,* ribs of beef Flemish-style (Flanders); *pot-au-feu,* meat and vegetable stew; *alouettes sans têtes,* beef olives (Corsica); *pistache de mouton,* lamb stew (Roussillon); *hochepot,* meat and vegetable stew (Flanders); *baeckoffe,* meat stew (Alsace); *beuchelle tourangelle,* kidneys and veal sweetbreads with mushrooms (Touraine); *tripes à la mode de Caen,* a highly spiced tripe stew (Normandy); *tripoux,* lamb's tripe with herbs (Limousin).

Bêtises de Cambrai, a peppermint sweet (Cambrai); *dragées de Verdun,* glacé almonds and hazelnuts (a local speciality since the 13th century); *gugelhupf* (Alsace); *clafoutis,* cherry mousse (Auvergne); *mousse au chocolat,* chocolate mousse (Charente); *pescajoun aux fruits,* egg pancake with fruit (Périgord); *vacherin,* strawberry meringue tart (Lyonnais); *douillons,* apple dumplings (Normandy); *Pithiviers,* almond puff pastry (Orléanais); *Paris-Brest,* stuffed choux pastry ring (Paris); *madeleines de Commercy,* butter cakes (Burgundy); *marrons,* chestnuts, candied, roasted, purée'd or boiled as a vegetable garnishing or a dessert (Lyonnais); *nonnettes de Dijon,* gingerbread (Dijon).

Moutarde, mustard: from Meaux (large-grained, mild) or Dijon (sharp).

Provençal cooking

Provençal cooking stands on its own. Unlike French cuisine, it makes much use of olive oil and tomatoes. The herbs mainly used are garlic and onions, rosemary, thyme, basil, sage and saffron.

Bouillabaisse, fish soup with garlic, rosemary and saffron; *aigoboulido,* herb soup with cheese; *aigo-saou,* fish soup; *soupe au pistou,* pumpkin soup with basil; *sea-urchin soup; aïoli,* garlic mayonnaise; *anchoiade,* a slice of white bread spread with anchovy and garlic pâté; *bagna caudo,* a sharp anchovy sauce; *pan-bagnat,* a huge roll sandwich; *pissaladière,* an onion tart with olives and anchovies; *sardines farcies au vert,* sardines stuffed with spinach; *loup au fenouil,* sea perch grilled with fennel; *caillettes,* mince cakes (Nice); *mouton gardienne,* lamb cutlets; *bohémienne,* purée of aubergines and tomatoes; *tian de légumes,* spinach au gratin (Nice); *ratatouille,* a stew of mixed vegetables; *salade niçoise,* a substantial salad of raw vegetables, tunny, egg and olives.

Calissons, honey and almond biscuits; *candied fruit,* sometimes in a *fougasse* (girdle cake); *nougat* from Montélimar.

Drinks

There are also regional differences in the preparation of drinks. Some are found all over France, others only in particular areas.
Café, coffee; *café crême,* coffee with cream; *café au lait,* coffee with milk; *café noir,* black coffee; *thé,* tea; *thé au citron,* lemon tea; *lait,* milk; *chocolat,* chocolate; *bière,* beer; *cidre,* cider (Brittany and Normandy); *eau minérale,* mineral water; *sirop de menthe,* a sweet peppermint drink; *vin blanc,* white wine; *vin rouge,* red wine.

Spirits

Cognac, brandy from the Charentes, matured for many years in oak casks, in various grades; *Armagnac,* a brandy made in Gascony; *Calvados,* an apple brandy from Normandy, commonly drunk during a meal to stimulate the appetite (a practice known as the *trou normand,* the Norman hole or gap); *Quetsch* (made from plums), *Kirsch* (cherries) and *Mirabelle* (mirabelle plums), fruit brandies made in Alsace, Lorraine and Franche-Comté; *Chartreuse,* a herb liqueur made by monks in the Dauphiné (green Chartreuse made since 1735, using 130 herbs; the lighter yellow Chartreuse since the mid 19th century); *Cointreau,* an orange liqueur from Anjou; *cassis,* a blackcurrant liqueur from Burgundy; *Bénédictine,* from Fécamp, famous since the 16th century; *pastis* or *anisette,* an aniseed brandy drunk in a large glass of iced water, a favourite aperitif (Provence); *brou, ratafia* and *eau de noix,* walnut liqueurs from Périgord; *Grand Marnier,* a mandarine liqueur based on cognac; *kir,* an aperitif of white wine and cassis; *Mauresque,* an aperitif of pastis and orgeat (almond milk).

Wine

See entry

Gardens

France is now in process of rediscovering its gardens, which are of interest for their layout, their history and – not least – the variety and abundance of the flora. Many gardens throughout France, varying from region to region, are now open to visitors. The Association pour l'Art des Paysages et des Jardins, 85 Boulevard Pasteur, F-75015 Paris, publishes a leaflet, "Jardin Français", listing over 120 selected parks and gardens, with addresses and opening times.

Getting to France

Paris plays a central role in the French system of communications as in other aspects of French life. Most of the main motorways and trunk roads start from Paris, and it is also the centre of France's rail and air networks. This section, therefore, is mainly concerned with the best ways of getting to Paris and from there to other parts of the country. Apart from Paris the most important focal points for traffic are Lyons and Marseilles in the south, Toulouse in the south-west, Bordeaux and Rennes in the west, Lille and Reims in the north and Strasbourg in the east.

By Car

Car ferries

There is a wide choice of car ferry services from Britain to France: which one you choose will depend on where you come from and where you want to go.

Ferries between England and France

Dover–Calais	Stena Sealink (ship) P&O (ship) Hoverspeed (hovercraft) and "Seacat")
Folkestone–Boulogne	Hoverspeed ("Seacat")
Newhaven–Dieppe	Stena Sealink (ship)
Poole–Cherbourg	Brittany Ferries "Truckline" (ship)
Portsmouth–Caen	Brittany Ferries (ship)
Portsmouth–Cherbourg	P & O (ship)
Portsmouth–Le Havre	P & O (ship)
Portsmouth–St Malo	Brittany Ferries (ship)
Ramsgate–Dunkirk	Sally Line (ship)
Southampton–Cherbourg	Stena Sealink (ship)
Plymouth–Roscoff	Brittany Ferries (ship)

Addresses

Brittany Ferries
The Brittany Centre
Wharf Road, Portsmouth PO2 8RU
tel. (0705) 827701

Brittany Ferries
Millbay Docks, Plymouth PL1 3EW
tel. (0752) 221321

Hoverspeed Ltd
The International Hoverport
Marine Parade, Dover CT17 9TG
tel. (0304) 240241

P & O European Ferries
Channel House
Channel View Road, Dover CT17 9TJ
tel. (0304) 203388
and
The Continental Ferry Port
Mile End, Portsmouth PO2 8QW
tel. (0705) 827677 (reservations); (0705) 772244 (port office)

Sally Line
Argyle Centre
York Street, Ramsgate CT11 9DS
tel. (0843) 595522

Stena Sealink Ltd.
Charter House, Park Street, Ashford, Kent TN24 8EX
London NW1 1BG
tel. (reservations) (0233) 647047 (latest information) (0304) 240028

Truckline Ferries
New Harbour Road, Poole BH15 4AJ
tel. (0202) 666466

Motorail

The journey to a particular holiday area in France can be shortened by using one of the French Railways' Motorail services from Calais or Dieppe. There are services from Calais to Avignon, Biarritz, Bordeaux, Brive, Fréjus/St-Raphaël, Moûtiers (Savoie), Narbonne, Nice and Toulouse, and from Dieppe to Avignon and Fréjus/St Raphaël. There are also services from Paris and Lille.

Information

French Railways
179 Piccadilly, London W1V 0BA
tel. (071) 409 3518

From Calais and other Channel ports the French motorway system offers the best way of making a quick start on your journey. From the ports in Normandy and Brittany the ordinary French roads are perfectly adequate. Tolls are payable on French motorways except on limited stretches near cities. The Paris ring road (Boulevard Périphérique) provides a link between the motorway from the Channel and the motorways and main roads to the south; drivers who prefer to avoid this rather testing motoring experience can take a slightly wider line round the east of Paris, perhaps branching off the motorway at Senlis.

By Bus

A number of companies run bus services from Britain to France. Eurolines has services to Paris (about 9 hours); Chamonix via Péronne, Auxerre, Grenoble, Chambéry, Annecy, Annemasse and Geneva (46 hours); Marseilles via Grenoble, Sisteron, Manosque and Aix-en-Provence (26½ hours); Nice via Grenoble, Digne, Grasse, Cannes, Juan-les-Pins and Antibes (29 hours); Lyons via Paris (16 hours); Bordeaux via Tours and Poitiers (17½ hours); and Lourdes via Paris, Bordeaux, St-Jean-de-Luz, Pau and Tarbes (24 hours).

Address

Eurolines UK
52 Grosvenor Gardens, Victoria, London SW1W 0AU
tel. (071) 730 0202

By Train

There are rail services from London to the Channel ports.
For rail services within France, see Rail Services (p. 601).

By Air

There are numerous flights daily by British Airways and Air France from London to Paris; direct flights to Paris from other airports in Britain, including Birmingham, Bristol, Dublin, Edinburgh, Glasgow, Manchester and Southampton; and flights from London to Bordeaux, Lyons, Marseilles, Montpellier, Nantes, Nice, Perpignan, Strasbourg, Tarbes/Lourdes and Toulouse. Other routes are offered by fifteen more airlines. From the United States there are flights by TWA, American Airlines and Delta to Paris. For addresses of international airlines and details of French domestic airlines, see Air Services (p. 511).

To Corsica by Car Ferry

The Société Nationale Maritime Corse Méditerranée (SNCM) runs ferries from Marseilles, Toulon and Nice to Ajaccio, Bastia, Calvi, L'Ile-Rousse, Porto-Vecchio and Propriano in Corsica. The crossing takes between 5 and 12 hours.

Information

Continental Shipping and Travel Ltd
179 Piccadilly, London W1V 9DB
tel. (071) 491 4968

Help for the Handicapped

Information

Comité National Français de Liaison pour la Réadaptation des Handicapés (CNFLRH)
38 boulevard Raspail, F-75007 Paris
tel. (1) 45 48 98 90

This organisation publishes a booklet, "Touristes quand même! Promenades en France pour les voyageurs handicapés", which gives descriptions of places of interest in some 90 French towns which are accessible to the handicapped, as well as a detailed list of accommodation, transport facilities and public institutions.
In its brochure "Guide pratique voyageur: Supplement a l'intention des personnes à mobilité réduite" the SNCF (French railways; see Railways) gives details of the facilities it offers for the handicapped.

Holiday Villages and Clubs

Villages de gîtes

A number of French companies run *villages de gîtes* (holiday villages), which are now becoming increasingly popular. The houses or chalets are grouped round a leisure centre with a restaurant, offering visitors something of the atmosphere of a club but leaving them free to spend their time as they wish.

Information

Further information, and the addresses of holiday villages and clubs, can be obtained from the French Government Tourist Office (see Information).

Hotels

French hotels are usually good, and well up to the standards laid down for their particular category. Outside the larger towns the rooms almost invariably have a *grand lit,* the large French double bed, and the charge for two people is only slightly higher than for one. Most recommended hotels are approved and classified by the Direction de l'Industrie Touristique as *hôtels de tourisme* and display a sign showing their classification.
Many hotels mainly in the one- and two-star category, especially in areas where tourism is being promoted, have been modernised with assistance from the Fédération Nationale des Logis de France, and these *Logis de France* offer modern standards of comfort and amenity at reasonable prices. There are also *chambres d'hôte* (bed and breakfast accommodation) and *tables d'hôte* which offer a family atmosphere and traditional country cooking at even more moderate rates. These types of establishment are listed in a booklet published annually and for sale through French Government Tourist Offices. Some hotels, especially roadside hotels in the country, are known as *relais* (the old word for a posting station where travellers changed horses). They are usually excellent establishments, often with a distinct character of their own.

Full board, half board

Many hotels, particularly on the coast and in winter sports areas, offer accommodation with either full board (*pension complète*, or simply *pension*) or half board (*demi-pension*). Prior reservation is advisable. When booking accommodation a distinction is made between a payment to account (*acompte*) and a deposit (*arrhes*), which can be retained by the hotel in the event of cancellation or non-arrival; if the hotel fails to honour the booking, twice the sum deposited will be reimbursed.

Reservations

It is advisable to book in advance. If staying at a hotel belonging to a chain, most have a centralised booking office, otherwise many *départements* offer an officially-recognised booking service under the name "Loisirs Accueil", usually charging no fee (a list is available from the French Government Tourist Office, see Information). Once in France reservations can be made through the nationwide "Accueil de France" organisation with offices in major French cities; the service is available, for a small fee, to *personal callers only* for same-day bookings or for up to eight days in advance.

Hotel categories

French hotels are officially classified in five categories, ranging from luxury (shown as L plus four stars) through four, three and two stars to one star.

Tariffs

Hotel rates vary considerably according to season. The following table shows rates in the various categories for a double room with bath. Single rooms are rarely available. A third bed can usually be provided at an additional charge of about 30%. Many hotel chains offer free accommodation to children sharing their parents' room. Rates in Paris are considerably higher.

Category	Double room
L****	600–2300 F
****	400–2000 F
***	350– 700 F
**	200– 500 F
*	150– 300 F

The following list of hotels gives the official category, the address and telephone number and number of rooms (r). "SP" indicates that the hotel has a swimming pool.

Abbeville

**France, 19 Place Pilori, tel. 22 24 00 42, 69 r.
**Ibis, Route d'Amiens, tel. 22 24 80 80, 45 r.
**Relais Vauban, 4 Boul. Vauban, tel. 22 31 30 35, 22 r.

Agde

***La Tamarissière, 21 Quai Théophile-Cornu, tel. 67 94 20 87, 27 r., SP
**Le Donjon, Place Jean-Jaurès, tel. 67 94 12 32, 22 r.

Aigues-Mortes

***St-Louis, 10 rue Amiral-Courbet, tel. 66 53 72 68, 22 r.
**Le Victoria, Place Anatole-France, tel. 66 53 64 55, 15 r.

Aix-en-Provence

***Augustins, 3 rue Masse, tel. 42 27 28 59, 32 r.
***Caravelle, 29 Boul. du Roi-René, tel. 42 21 53 05, 30 r.
***Grand Hôtel Nègre Coste, 33 Cours Mirabeau, tel. 42 27 74 22, 37 r.
***Paul Cézanne, 40 Avenue Victor-Hugo, tel. 42 26 34 73, 44 r.
***Le Pigonnet, 5 Avenue Pigonnet, tel. 42 59 02 90, 50 r., SP
**Cardinal, 24 rue Cardinal, tel. 42 38 32 30, 23 r.
**Casino, 38 rue Leydet, tel. 42 26 06 88, 24 r.
**Le Moulin, 1 Avenue R.-Schumann, tel. 42 59 41 68, 37 r.
**Le Mozart, 49 Cours Gambetta, tel. 42 21 62 86, 48 r.
**St-Christophe, 2 Avenue Victor-Hugo, tel. 42 26 01 24, 56 r.

Aix-les-Bains

***Ariana, Avenue de Marlioz à Marlioz, tel. 79 88 08 00, 60 r., SP
***Cloche, 9 Boul. Wilson, tel. 79 35 01 06, 54 r.
**Beaulieu, 29 Avenue Charles-de-Gaulle, tel. 79 35 01 02, 31 r.
**Paix, 11 rue Lamartine, tel. 79 35 02 10, 70 r.

Ajaccio

L****Campo dell'Oro, Place Ricanto, tel. 95 22 32 41, 130 r.
***Albion, 15 Avenue Général-Leclerc, tel. 95 21 66 70, 63 r.
***Costa, 2 Boul. Colomba, tel. 95 21 43 02, 53 r.
**San Carlu, 8 Boul. Casanova, tel. 95 21 13 84, 44 r.
**Spunta di Mare, Quartier St-Joseph, tel. 95 22 41 42, 64 r.

Albertville

***La Berjann, 33 Route Tours, tel. 79 32 47 88, 11 r.
**Roma, Route Nationale 90, tel. 70 37 15 34, 85 r.

Albi

****La Réserve, Route Cordes, tel. 63 60 79 79, 24 r., SP
***Chiffre, 50 rue Séré-de-Rivières, tel. 63 54 04 60, 40 r.
**Grand Hôtel Orléans, Place de la Gare, tel. 63 54 16 56, 62 r.

Alençon

***Grand Cerf, 21 rue St-Blaise, tel. 33 26 00 51, 33 r.
**France, 3 rue St-Blaise, tel. 33 26 26 36, 31 r.

Alpe d'Huez

***Le Christina, Rue Maurice-Pajon, tel. 76 80 33 32, 27 r.
***Le Dôme, Place Cognet, tel. 76 80 32 11, 20 r.
**Bel Alpe, Chaussée des Bergers, tel. 76 80 32 33, 16 r.
**Les Bruyères, Place Jean-Moulin, tel. 76 80 32 74, 20 r.

Amboise

****Le Choiseul, 36 Quai Ch.-Guinot, tel. 47 30 45 45, 23 r., SP
***Belle Vue, 12 Quai Ch.-Guinot, tel. 47 57 02 26, 34 r.
**Le Brèche, 26 rue J.-Ferry, tel. 47 57 00 79, 14 r.

Hotels

Amélie-les-Bains	***Grand Hôtel Reine Amélie, 30 Boul. Petite-Provence, tel. 68 39 04 38, 69 r. **Castel Emeraude, Route Corniche, tel. 68 39 02 83, 59 r.
Amiens	***Charlton-Belfort, 42 rue Noyon, tel. 22 92 26 44, 36 r. ***Univers, 2 rue Noyon, tel. 22 91 52 51, 41 r. **Ibis, 4 rue Mar.-de-Lattre-de-Tassigny, tel. 22 92 57 33, 94 r. **Nord-Sud, 11 rue Gresset, tel. 22 91 59 03, 26 r. **Paix, 8 rue de la République, tel. 22 91 39 21, 26 r.
Anduze	**Porte des Cévennes, Rte de St-Jean-du-Gard, tel. 66 61 99 44, 18 r.
Angers	***Anjou, 1 Boul. Maréchal-Foch, tel. 41 88 24 82, 51 r. ***Concorde, 18 Boul. Maréchal-Foch, tel. 41 87 37 20, 72 r. **Champagne, 34 rue D.-Papin, tel. 41 88 78 06, 30 r. **Europe, 3 rue Château-Gontier, tel. 41 88 67 45, 29 r. **Fimotel, 23 bis Route P.-Bert, tel. 41 88 10 10, 52 r.
Angoulême	***Grand Hôtel de France, 1 Place des Halles, tel. 45 95 47 95, 61 r. **Epi d'Or, 66 Boul. René-Chabasse, tel. 45 95 67 64, 33 r.
Annecy	***Charlton, 6 rue Glières, tel. 50 45 47 75, 55 r. ***Splendid, 4 Quai E.-Chappuis, tel. 50 45 20 00, 51 r. **D'Aléry, 5 Avenue d'Aléry, tel. 50 45 24 75, 20 r. **Allobroges, 11 rue Sommeiller, tel. 50 40 03 11, 54 r.
Antibes	***Josse, 8 Boul. James-Wyllie, tel. 93 61 47 24, 22 r. **Etoile, 2 Avenue Gambetta, tel. 93 34 26 30, 26 r.
Arbois	**Messagerie, Rue Courcelles, tel. 84 66 15 45, 26 r.
Arcachon	****Arc Hôtel, 89 Boul. de la Plage, tel. 56 83 06 85, 30 r., SP ***Grand Hôtel Richelieu, 185 Boul. de la Plage, tel. 56 83 16 50, 43 r. ***Les Ormes, 1 rue Hovy, tel. 56 83 09 27, 28 r. **Marinette, 15 Allées J.-M.-de-Hérédia, 56 83 06 67, 24 r. **Le Nautic, 20 Boul. de la Plage, tel. 56 83 01 48, 36 r.
Argelès-sur-Mer	***Lido, 50 Boul. de la Mer, tel. 68 81 10 32, 73 r., SP **Mouettes, Route de Collioure, tel. 68 81 21 69, 25 r. **France, 8 Boul. Carnot, tel. 33 67 03 65, 13 r. **Renaissance, 20 Avenue 2e-Division-Blindée, tel. 33 36 14 20, 15 r.
Argentat	Gilbert, Rue Vachal, tel. 55 28 01 62, 28 r.
Arles	****Jules César, Boul. des Lices, tel. 90 93 43 20, 55 r. ***D'Arlatan, 26 rue Sauvage, tel. 90 93 56 66, 42 r. ***L'Atrium, 1 rue E.-Fassin, tel. 90 49 92 92, 91 r. **Calendal, 22 Place Pomme, tel. 90 96 11 89, 27 r. **Constantin, 59 Boul. Craponne, tel. 90 96 04 05, 15 r.
Arras	***Univers, 3 Place Croix-Rouge, tel. 21 71 34 01, 36 r. **Astoria, 12 Place Foch, tel. 21 71 08 14, 31 r.
Aubusson	**France, 6 rue des Déportés, tel. 56 66 10 22, 21 r.
Aurillac	***La Thomasse, 48 rue Dr-Mallet, tel. 71 48 26 47, 22 r. **La Ferraudie, 15 rue Bel-Air, tel. 71 48 72 42, 22 r.
Autun	***Hostellerie du Vieux Moulin, Porte d'Arroux, tel. 85 52 10 90, 16 r. **Arcades, 22 Avenue République, tel. 85 52 30 03, 40 r.
Auxerre	**Cygne, 14 rue 24-Août, tel. 86 52 26 51, 24 r. **Les Clairions, Avenue Worms, tel. 86 46 85 64, 60 r.
Avignon	****Europe, 12 Place Crillon, tel. 90 82 66 92, 43 r. ***Cité des Papes, 1 rue J.-Vilar, tel. 90 86 22 45, 63 r.

***Mercure, 2 rue M.-de-Médicis, tel. 90 88 91 10, 102 r., SP
**Angleterre, 20 Boul. Raspail, tel. 90 86 34 31, 40 r.
**Fimotel, 4 Boul. St-Dominique, tel. 90 82 08 08, 95 r.

Ax-les-Thermes

***Royal Thermal, Esplanade du Couloubret, tel. 61 64 22 51, 54 r.
**Chalet, Avenue Turrel, tel. 61 64 24 31, 10 r.

Azay-le-Rideau

**Grand Monarque, Place de la République, tel. 47 45 40 08, 28 r.

Bagnères-de-Bigorre

***La Résidence, Parc Thermal de Salut, tel. 62 95 03 97, 30 r., SP
**Grand Hôtel Angleterre, 32 Allées des Coustous, tel. 62 95 22 24, 30 r.

Bagnères-de-Luchon

See Luchon

Banyuls-sur-Mer

***Le Catalan, Route de Cerbère, tel. 68 88 02 80, 36 r.
**Les Elmes, Plage des Elmes, tel. 68 88 03 12, 25 r.

Bar-le-Duc

**Grand Hôtel Metz et Commerce, 17 Boul. La Rochelle, tel. 29 72 02 56, 50 r.

Barr

**Château d'Andlau, 113 Vallée St-Ulrich, tel. 88 08 98 54, 25 r.

Bastia

***Ostella, Montesoro, tel. 95 33 51 05, 30 r.
**Bonaparte, 45 Boul. Gén.-Graziani, tel. 95 34 07 10, 24 r.

La Baule

L****Castel Marie-Louise, 1 Avenue Andrieu, tel. 40 60 20 60, 29 r.
***Alcyon, 19 Avenue Pétrels, tel. 40 60 19 37, 32 r.
**Concorde, 1 Avenue Concorde, tel. 40 60 23 09, 47 r.

Bayeux

***Lion d'Or, 71 rue St-Jean, tel. 31 92 06 90, 30 r.
**Argouges, 21 rue St-Patrice, tel. 31 92 88 86, 25 r.

Bayonne

***Aux Deux Rivières, 21 rue Thiers, tel. 59 59 14 61, 66 r.
**Loustau, 1 Place de la République, tel. 59 55 16 74, 45 r.

Beaugency

**Ecu de Bretagne, 5 rue du Mail, tel. 38 44 67 60, 23 r.

Beaune

****Le Cep, 27 rue Maufoux, tel. 80 22 35 48, 49 r.
***La Cloche, 42 Faubourg Madeleine, tel. 80 24 66 33, 15 r.
**Le Home, 138 Route de Dijon, tel. 80 22 16 43, 22 r.

Beauvais

***Chenal, 63 Boul. Gén.-de-Gaulle, tel. 44 45 03 55, 29 r.
**La Résidence, 24 rue L.-Borel, tel. 44 48 30 98, 23 r.

Belfort

***Altéa Hôtel du Lion, 2 rue G.-Clemenceau, tel. 84 21 17 00, 82 r.
**Capucins, 20 Faubourg Montbéliard, tel. 84 28 04 60, 35 r.
**Climat de France, Rue Gideferre, tel. 84 22 09 84, 46 r.
**Modern, 9 Avenue Wilson, tel. 84 21 59 45, 45 r.

Bergerac

***Europ Hôtel, 20 rue Petit-Sol, tel. 53 57 06 54, 21 r.
**Bordeaux, 38 Place Gambetta, tel. 53 57 12 83, 41 r., SP

Besançon

***Altéa Parc Micaud, 3 Avenue E.-Droz, tel. 81 80 14 44, 95 r.
***Epicure, 159 rue Dôle, tel. 81 52 04 00, 59 r., SP
***Novotel, 22B rue Trey, tel. 81 50 14 66, 107 r., SP
**Florel, 6 rue Viotte, tel. 81 80 41 08, 24 r.
**Foch, Avenue Foch, tel. 81 80 30 41, 28 r.
**Franc-Comtois, 24 rue Proud'hon, tel. 81 83 24 35, 22 r.
**Gambetta, 13 rue Gambetta, tel. 81 82 02 33, 26 r.
**Ibis, 4 Avenue Carnot, tel. 81 80 33 11, 66 r.
**Nord, 8 rue Moncey, tel. 81 81 34 56, 44 r.
**Urbis, 5 Avenue Foch, tel. 81 88 27 26, 96 r.

Béziers

***Nord, 15 Place Jean-Jaurès, tel. 67 28 34 09, 43 r.
**Lux, 3 rue Petits-Champs, tel. 67 28 48 05, 22 r.

Hotels

Biarritz	L****Miramar, Avenue Impératrice. tel. 59 41 30 00, 109 r., SP L****Palais, 1 Avenue Impératrice, tel. 59 24 09 40, 116 r. ***Florida, 3 Place Ste-Eugénie, tel. 59 24 01 76, 45 r. ***Marbella, 11 rue Port-Vieux, tel. 59 24 04 06, 28 r. ***Plaza, Avenue Edouard-VII, tel. 59 24 74 00, 60 r. **Argi-Eder, 13 rue Peyroloubilh, tel. 59 24 22 53, 17 r. **Central, 8 rue Maison-Suisse, tel. 59 22 02 06, 16 r.
Blois	***L'Horset La Vallière, 26 Avenue Maunoury, tel. 54 74 19 00, 78 r. **Anne de Bretagne, 31 Avenue J.-Laigret, tel. 54 78 05 38, 29 r. **Savoie, 6 rue Ducoux, tel. 54 74 32 21, 27 r. **Urbis, 3 rue Porte Côte, tel. 54 74 01 17, 55 r.
Bonifacio	***Solemare, Nouvelle Marine, tel. 95 73 01 06, 60 r.
Bordeaux	L****Sofitel Aquitania, Boul. Domergue, tel. 56 50 83 80, 212 r., SP ****Pullman Mériadeck, 5 rue R.-Lateulade, tel. 56 90 92 37, 196 r. ***Français, 12 rue Temple, tel. 56 48 10 35, 35 r. ***Grand Hôtel, 2 Place Comédie, tel. 56 90 93 44, 98 r. ***Majestic, 2 rue Condé, tel. 56 52 60 44, 50 r. ***Normandie, 7 Cours 30-Juillet, tel. 56 52 16 80, 100 r. **Atlantic, 69 rue E.-Leroy, tel. 56 92 92 22, 36 r. **Centre, 8 rue Temple, tel. 56 48 13 29, 15 r. **Gambetta, 66 rue Porte Dijeaux, tel. 56 51 21 83, 33 r. **Notre Dame, 30 rue Notre-Dame, tel. 56 52 88 24, 21 r.
Boulogne-sur-Mer	**Londres, 22 Place France, tel. 21 31 35 63, 20 r.
Bourganeuf	**Commerce, Rue Verdun, tel. 55 64 14 55, 16 r.
Bourg-en-Bresse	***Le Logis de Brou, 132 Boul. Brou, tel. 74 22 11 55, 30 r. **Ariane, 18 rue Dîmes, tel. 74 22 50 88, 40 r.
Bourges	***Angleterre, 1 Place Quatre-Piliers, tel. 46 24 68 51, 31 r. **Christina, 5 rue Halle, tel. 48 70 56 50, 76 r. **Hostellerie Grand Argentier, 9 rue Parerie, tel. 48 70 84 31, 14 r. **Tilleuls, 7 Place Pyrotechnie, tel. 48 20 49 04, 30 r.
Brest	***Continental, Square La-Tour-d'Auvergne, tel. 98 80 50 40, 75 r. ***Voyageurs, 15 Avenue Clemenceau, tel. 98 80 25 73, 40 r. **Bellevue, 53 rue Victor-Hugo, tel. 98 80 51 78, 26 r. **Bretagne, 25 rue Harteloire, tel. 98 80 41 18, 21 r. **Colbert, 12 rue Lyon, tel. 98 80 47 21, 27 r.
Briançon	***Vauban, 13 Avenue Gén.-de-Gaulle, tel. 92 21 12 11, 44 r. **Mont-Brison, 3 Avenue Gén.-de-Gaulle, tel. 92 21 14 55, 45 r.
Brioude	**Le Brivas, Avenue Velay, tel. 71 50 10 49, 30 r.
Caen	****Le Relais des Gourmets, 15 rue Geôle, tel. 31 86 06 01, 26 r. ***Malherbe, Place Foch, tel. 31 84 40 06, 44 r. ***Mapotel Moderne, 116 Boul. Mar.-Leclerc, tel. 31 86 04 23, 56 r. ***Mercure, 1 rue Courtonne, tel. 31 93 07 62, 101 r. **Astrid, 39 rue Bernières, tel. 31 85 48 67, 13 r. **Bristol, 31 rue 11-Novembre, tel. 31 84 59 76, 25 r. **France, 10 rue de la Gare, tel. 31 52 16 99, 47 r. **Métropole, 16 Place de la Gare, tel. 31 82 26 76, 71 r. **Quatrans, 17 rue Gemare, tel. 31 86 25 57, 36 r. **Royal, Place de la République, tel. 31 86 55 33, 45 r.
Cahors	***La Chartreuse, Quartier St Georges, tel. 65 35 17 37, 34 r. **Le Melchior, Place de la Gare, tel. 65 35 03 38, 30 r.

Calais
**Bellevue, 23 Place d'Armes, tel. 21 34 53 75, 54 r.
**Climat de France, Boul. de la Plage, tel. 21 34 64 64, 44 r.
**George V, 36 rue Royale, tel. 21 97 68 00, 45 r.
**Ibis, Rue Greuze, tel. 21 96 69 69, 55 r.

Calvi
***Balanea, 6 rue Clemenceau, tel. 95 65 00 45, 40 r.
**Caravelle, on beach, tel. 95 65 01 21, 20 r.

Cambrai
***Château de la Motte-Fénelon, Square du Château, tel. 27 83 61 38, 28r., SP
**Mouton Blanc, 33 rue Alsace-Lorraine, tel. 21 81 30 16, 31 r.

Cannes
L****Carlton International, 58 Boul. Croisette, tel. 93 68 91 68, 325 r.
L****Martinez, 73 Boul. Croisette, tel. 93 94 30 30, 421 r., SP
L****Majestic, Boul. Croisette, tel. 93 68 91 00, 248 r., SP
***Abrial, 24 Boul. Lorraine, tel. 93 38 78 82, 48 r.
***Novotel, 25 Avenue Beauséjour, tel. 93 68 91 50, 181 r., SP
***Paris, 34 Boul. Alsace, tel. 93 38 30 89, 48 r.
**Cheval Blanc, 3 rue Maupassant, tel. 93 39 88 60, 16 r.
**Festival, 3 rue Molière, tel. 93 38 69 45, 17 r.

Carcassonne
****Domaine d'Auriac, Route St-Hilaire, tel. 68 25 72 22, 23 r., SP
***Montséjour, 27 Allée Léna, tel. 68 25 31 41, 21 r.
**Pont Vieux, 32 rue Trivalle, tel. 68 25 24 99, 15 r.

Carnac
****Diana, 21 Boul. de la Plage, tel. 97 52 05 38, 32 r.
***Novotel, Avenue Atlantique, tel. 97 52 53 54, 110 r.
**Armoric, 53 Avenue de la Poste, tel. 97 52 13 47, 25 r.

Carpentras
***Safari, Avenue J.-H.-Fabre, tel. 90 63 35 35, 56 r.

Cauterets
***Bordeaux, 23 rue Richelieu, tel. 62 92 52 50, 15 r.
**Le Sacca, Boul. Latapie-Flurin, tel. 62 92 50 02, 28 r.

Cerbère
**Dorade, Avenue Gén.-de-Gaulle, tel. 68 88 41 93, 25 r.

Céret
***La Terrasse du Soleil, Route Fontfrède, tel. 68 87 01 94, 18 r., SP
**La Châtaignerie, Route Fontfrède, tel. 68 87 03 19, 8 r., SP

Châlons-sur-Marne
***Angleterre, 19 Place Mgr-Tissier, tel. 26 68 21 51, 18 r.
**Bristol, 77 Avenue P.-Sémard, tel. 26 68 24 63, 24 r.

Chambéry
****Grand Hotel Ducs de Savoie, 6 Place de la Gare, tel. 79 69 54 54, 50 r.
***Le France, 22 Faubourg Reclus, tel. 79 33 51 18, 48 r.
**City, 9 Avenue Denfert-Rochereau, tel. 79 85 76 79, 40 r.

Chamonix
L****Mont-Blanc, Place de l'Eglise, tel. 50 53 05 64, 49 r., SP
***Albert 1er, 119 Impasse du Montenvers, tel. 50 53 05 09, 23 r., SP
***Alpina, 79 Avenue Mont-Blanc, tel. 50 53 47 77, 136 r.
**International, 255 Avenue M.-Croz, tel. 50 53 00 60, 32 r.
**Vallée Blanche, 36 rue Lyret, tel. 50 53 04 50, 20 r.

Chantilly
**Campanile, Les Huit Curés, on N16, tel. 44 57 39 24, 50 r.

Chartres
Grand Monarque, 22 Place Epars, tel. 37 21 00 72, 54 r.
**Ibis, 14 Place Drouaise, tel. 37 36 06 36, 79 r.

Châteaudun
**Beauce, 50 rue Jallans, tel. 37 45 14 75, 24 r.

Chenonceaux
***Bon Laboureur et Château, 6 rue Dr-Bretonneau, tel. 47 23 90 02, 26 r., SP
**Hostel Roy, 9 rue Dr-Bretonneau, tel. 47 23 90 17, 40 r.

Cherbourg	***Mercure, Gare Maritime, tel. 33 44 01 11, 83 r. **Louvre, 2 rue H.-Dunant, tel. 33 53 02 28, 42 r.
Chinon	**Chris' Hôtel, 12 Place Jeanne-d'Arc, tel. 47 93 36 92, 40 r.
Clermont-Ferrand	***Altéa Gergovie, 82 Boul. Gergovia, tel. 73 93 05 73, 122 r. ***Gallieni, 51 rue Bonnabaud, tel. 73 93 59 69, 80 r. ***Lafayette, 53 Avenue Union-Soviétique, tel. 73 91 82 27, 50 r. ***Lyon, 16 Place Jaude, tel. 73 93 32 55, 34 r. ***Mercure Arverne, 16 Place Delille, tel. 73 91 92 06, 57 r. **Bordeaux, 36 Avenue Roosevelt, tel. 73 37 32 32, 32 r. **Le Damier, 47 Boul. J.-B.-Dumas, tel. 73 91 87 52, 22 r. **Floride II, 30 Cours R.-Poincaré, tel. 73 35 00 20, 29 r. **Grand Hôtel Midi, 39 Avenue Union-Soviétique, tel. 73 92 44 98, 39 r. **Régina, 14 rue Bonnabaud, tel. 73 93 44 76, 27 r.
Cluny	Bourgogne, Place de l'Abbaye, tel. 85 59 00 58, 14 r.
Cognac	***Mapotel Le Valois, 35 rue 14-Juillet, tel. 45 82 76 00, 44 r. **L'Auberge, 13 rue Plumejeau, tel. 45 32 08 70, 22 r.
Collioure	***Ambeille, Route Porte d'Avail, tel. 68 82 08 74, 21 r. **Triton, 1 rue Jean-Bart, tel. 68 82 06 52, 18 r.
Colmar	***Altéa Champ-de-Mars, 2 Avenue Marne, tel. 89 41 54 54, 74 r. ***Terminus-Bristol, 7 Place de la Gare, tel. 89 23 59 59, 70 r. **Colbert, 2 rue Trois-Epis, tel. 89 41 31 05, 50 r. **Turenne, 10 Route de Bâle, tel. 89 41 12 26, 85 r.
Compiègne	***Harlay, 3 rue Harlay, tel. 44 23 01 50, 20 r. **Arcade, 1 rue Pierre-Sauvage, tel. 44 86 00 66, 48 r.
Condom	**Logis des Cordeliers, 1 rue des Cordeliers, tel. 62 28 03 68, 21 r.
Conques	***Sainte-Foy, tel. 65 69 84 03, 20 r.
Cordes	***Grand Ecuyer, Rue Voltaire, tel. 63 56 01 03, 12 r. **Cité, Grand'Rue, tel. 63 56 03 53, 8 r.
Corsica	See Ajaccio
Coussac-Bonneval	**Voyageurs, tel. 55 75 20 24, 9 r.
Coutances	**Cositel, Route Coutainville, tel. 33 07 51 64, 40 r.
Dax	***Splendid, Cours Verdun, tel. 58 74 59 30, 174 r. **Dax-Thermal, 1 Boul. Carnot, tel. 58 90 19 40, 128 r.
Deauville	L****Normandy, 38 rue J.-Mermoz, tel. 31 88 09 21, 295 r., SP L****Royal, Boul. Cornuché, tel. 31 88 16 41, 320 r., SP ***Marie-Anne, 142 Avenue République, tel. 31 88 35 32, 24 r. **Continental, 1 rue Désiré-Le-Hoc, tel. 31 88 21 06, 49 r.
Dieppe	***La Présidence, 1 Boul. Verdun, tel. 35 84 31 31, 88 r. **Windsor, 18 Boul. Verdun, tel. 35 84 15 23, 46 r.
Digne	***Grand Paris, 19 Boul. Thiers, tel. 92 31 11 15, 27 r. **Coin Fleuri, 9 Boul. Victor-Hugo, tel. 92 31 04 51, 15 r.
Dijon	***Altéa Château Bourgogne, 22 Boul. Marne, tel. 80 72 31 13, 117 r., SP ***Chapeau Rouge, 5 rue Michelet, tel. 80 30 28 10, 30 r. ***La Cloche, 14 Place Darcy, tel. 80 30 12 32, 76 r.

***Ducs, 5 rue Lamonnoye, tel. 80 67 31 31, 31 r.
***Grésill' Hôtel, 16 Avenue R.-Poincaré, tel. 80 71 10 56, 47 r.
**Allées, 27 Cours Gén.-de-Gaulle, tel. 80 66 57 50, 37 r.
**Central Ibis, 3 Place Grangier, tel. 80 30 44 00, 90 r.
**Nord, Place Darcy, tel. 80 30 58 58, 29 r.
**Relais Arcade, 15 Avenue Albert-1er, tel. 80 43 01 12, 128 r.
**Les Rosiers, 22 bis rue Montchapet, tel. 80 55 33 11, 10 r.

Dinan

***D'Avaugour, 1 Place Champ-Clos, tel. 96 39 07 49, 27 r.
**Bretagne, 1 Place Duclos, tel. 96 39 46 15, 46 r.

Dinard

L****Reine Hortense, 19 rue Malouine, tel. 99 46 54 31, 10 r.
****Grand Hotel Dinard, 48 Avenue George-V, tel. 99 46 10 28, 100 r.
***Crystal, 15 rue Malouine, tel. 99 46 66 71, 25 r.
**Emeraude-Plage, 1 Boul. Albert-1er, tel. 99 46 15 79, 54 r.

Divonne-les-Bains

****Le Château de Divonne, tel. 50 20 00 32, 28 r.
****Les Grands Hôtels, tel. 50 20 06 63, 135 r., SP
**Coccinelles, Route de Lausanne, tel. 50 20 06 96, 18 r.

Douai

**Grand Cerf, 46 rue St-Jacques, tel. 27 88 79 60, 39 r.

Dunkirk

***Europ' Hôtel, 13 rue Leughenaer, tel. 28 66 29 07, 125 r.
**Hirondelle, 46 Avenue Faidherbe, tel. 28 63 17 65, 33 r.

Epernay

***Berceaux, 13 rue Berceaux, tel. 26 55 28 84, 29 r.
**Climat de France, Rue Lorraine, tel. 26 54 17 39, 33 r.

Epinal

***Ducs de Lorraine, 16 Quai Cl.-Sorot, tel. 29 34 35 20, 10 r.
**Mercure, 13 Place E.-Stein, tel. 29 35 18 68, 40 r.

Espalion

**Moderne, 27 Boul. Guizard, tel. 65 44 05 11, 28 r.

Etretat

**Falaises, 1 Boul. R.-Coty, tel. 35 27 02 77, 24 r.

Evian-les-Bains

****Royal, in park, tel. 50 75 14 00, 129 r., SP
***Le Bourgogne, Place Charles Cottet, tel. 50 75 01 05, 24 r.
**Continental, 65 rue Nationale, tel. 50 75 37 54, 32 r.

Evreux

***Normandy, 37 rue E.-Feray, tel. 32 33 14 40, 26 r.
**L'Orme, 13 rue des Lombards, tel. 32 39 34 12, 42 r.

Les Eyzies-de-Tayac

***Centenaire, tel. 53 06 97 18, 28 r., SP
**Centre, tel. 53 06 97 13, 18 r.

Fécamp

**Poste, 4 Avenue Gambetta, tel. 35 29 55 11, 36 r.

Figeac

***Des Carmes, Enclos des Carmes, tel. 65 34 20 78, 40 r., SP
**Hostellerie Champollion, 51 Allées Victor-Hugo, tel. 65 34 10 16, 30 r.

Foix

***Pyrène, Le Vignoble, tel. 61 65 48 66, 21 r., SP
**Audoye-Lons, 6 Place G.-Dutilh, tel. 61 65 52 44, 37 r.

Fontainebleau

**** L'Aigle Noir, 27 Place Napoléon Bonaparte, tel. 64 22 32 65, 57 r., SP
***Legris et Parc, 36 rue du Parc, tel. 64 22 24 24, 30 r.
**Londres, 1 Place Gén.-de-Gaulle, tel. 64 22 20 21, 22 r.

Font-Romeu

***Cimes, Rue des Ecureuils, tel. 68 30 17 77, 23 r., SP
**Carlit Hotel, Avenue Egat, tel. 68 30 07 45, 58 r., SP

Fréjus

***Catalogne, Avenue La Corniche, tel. 94 81 01 44, 32 r., SP
**Oasis, Impasse J.-B.-Charcot, tel. 94 51 50 44, 27 r.

Hotels

Gap	***La Grille, 2 Place F.-Euzière, tel. 92 53 84 84, 30 r. **Mokotel, Route de Marseille, tel. 92 51 57 82, 27 r.
Gérardmer	****Beau-Rivage, Esplanade du Lac, tel. 29 63 22 28, 48 r. ***Grand Hotel Bragard, Place Tilleul, tel. 29 63 06 31, 58 r., SP **Paix, 6 Avenue Ville-de-Vichy, tel. 29 63 38 78, 25 r.
Gien	**Sanotel, 21 Quai Sully, tel. 38 67 61 46, 58 r.
La Grande-Motte	***Altéa, 140 rue du Port, tel. 67 56 90 81, 135 r., SP **Azur, Terre-Plein de la Capitainerie, tel. 67 56 56 00, 20 r., SP
Grasse	****Le Régent, Route de Nice, tel. 93 36 40 10, 40 r., SP ***Des Parfums, 1 Terrasse Tressemannes, tel. 95 36 03 15, 71 r., SP **Panorama, 2 Place Cours, tel. 93 36 80 80, 36 r.
Grenoble	****Park Hôtel, 10 Place Paul-Mistral, tel. 76 87 29 11, 56 r. ***Alpotel, 12 Boul. Mar.-Joffre, tel. 76 87 88 41, 88 r. ***Angleterre, 5 Place Victor-Hugo, tel. 76 87 37 21, 70 r. ***Lesdiguières, 122 Cours Libération, tel. 76 96 55 36, 36 r. ***Patrick, 116 Cours Libération, tel. 76 21 26 63, 59 r. **Alpazur, 59 Avenue Alsace-Lorraine, tel. 76 46 42 80, 30 r. **Bristol, 11 Avenue F.-Viallet, tel. 76 46 11 18, 46 r. **Institut, 10 rue Barbillon, tel. 76 46 36 44, 51 r. **Patinoires, 12 rue M.-Chamoux, tel. 76 44 43 65, 35 r. **Rive Droite, 20 Quai France, tel. 76 87 61 11, 56 r.
Guebwiller	**Alsace, 140 rue de la République, tel. 89 76 83 02, 28 r.
Haguenau	**Europe, 15 Avenue Prof.-R.-Leriche, tel. 88 93 58 11, 83 r., SP
Le Havre	***Astoria, 12 Cours République, tel. 35 25 00 03, 37 r. ***Bordeaux, 147 rue L.-Brindeau, tel. 35 22 69 44, 31 r. ***France Bourgogne, 19–21 Cours République, tel. 35 25 40 34, 31 r. ***Le Marly, 121 rue de Paris, tel. 35 41 72 48, 37 r. ***Mercure, Chaussée d'Angoulême, tel. 35 21 23 45, 96 r. **Angleterre, 1 & 3 rue Louis-Philippe, tel. 35 42 48 42, 30 r. **Bauza, 15 rue G.-Braque, tel. 35 42 27 27, 26 r. **Celtic, 106 rue Voltaire, tel. 35 42 39 77, 14 r. **Petit Vatel, 86 rue L.-Brindeau, tel. 35 41 72 07, 29 r. **Richelieu, 132 rue de Paris, tel. 35 42 38 71, 19 r.
Le Hohwald	***Grand Hôtel Hohwald, tel. 88 08 31 03, 72 r.
Honfleur	****Ferme St-Siméon, Rue A.-Marais, tel. 31 89 23 61, 28 r. ***L'Ecrin, 19 rue E.-Boudin, tel. 31 89 32 39, 16 r. **La Tour, 3 Quai de la Tour, tel. 31 89 21 22, 48 r.
Ile-Rousse	***Napoléon Bonaparte, 3 Place Paoli, tel. 95 60 06 09, 100 r., SP **Cala di Loru, Boul. Fogata, tel. 95 60 14 75, 24 r.
Juan-les-Pins	L****Juana, Avenue G.-Gallice, tel. 93 61 08 70, 45 r., SP ***Mimosas, Rue Pauline, tel. 93 61 04 16, 35 r., SP **Astor, 30 Boul. R.-Poincaré, tel. 93 61 07 38, 41 r., SP
Kaysersberg	***Les Remparts, 4 rue Flieh, tel. 89 47 12 12, 30 r.
Laon	**Commerce, 13 Place de la Gare, tel. 23 79 10 38, 23 r.
Leucate	**Loisirôtel, tel. 68 40 90 22, 57 r., SP
Lille	***Grand Hôtel Bellevue, 5 rue J.-Roisin, tel. 20 57 45 64, 80 r. ***Mapotel Charlton, 3 rue de Paris, tel. 20 55 24 11, 61 r.

***Royal, 2 Boul. Carnot, tel. 20 51 05 11, 102 r.
**Flandre Angleterre, 15 Place de la Gare, tel. 20 06 04 12, 48 r.
**France, 10 rue Béthune, tel. 20 57 14 78, 32 r.
**Grand Hôtel de l'Univers, 19 Place Reignaux, tel. 20 06 99 69, 56 r.
**Minerva, 28 rue Anatole-France, tel. 20 55 25 11, 42 r.
**Nord-Motel, 46 rue Faubourg d'Arras, tel. 20 53 53 40, 80 r.
**Paix, 46 bis rue de Paris, tel. 20 54 63 93, 36 r.

Limoges

***Caravelle, 21 rue A.-Barbès, tel. 56 77 75 29, 39 r.
***Jeanne d'Arc, 17 Avenue Gén.-de-Gaulle, tel. 55 77 67 77,55 r.
***Luk Hôtel, 29 Place Jourdan, tel. 55 33 44 00, 54 r.
***Richelieu, 40 Avenue Baudin, tel. 55 34 22 82, 34 r.
**Antoine, 35 & 37 rue des Combes, tel. 55 77 16 94, 37 r.
**Orléans Lion d'Or, 9–11 Cours Jourdan, tel. 55 77 49 71, 42 r.
**Petit Paris, 48 bis Avenue Garibaldi, tel. 55 77 39 82, 24 r.
**Résidence, Route de Paris, tel. 55 39 90 47, 20 r.

Lisieux

***Mapotel Plage, tel. 31 31 17 44, 36 r.
**Grand Hôtel Normandie, 11 bis rue au Char, tel. 31 62 16 05, 70 r.

Loches

**Luccotel, Rue Lézards, tel. 47 91 50 50, 42 r., SP

Lons-le-Saunier

***Grand Hôtel Genève, 39 rue J.-Moulin, tel. 84 24 19 11, 42 r.
**Nouvel Hôtel, 50 rue Lecourbe, tel. 84 47 20 67, 26 r.

Lourdes

****Gallia et Londres, 26 Avenue B.-Soubirous, tel. 62 94 35 44, 90 r.
***Ambassadeurs, 66 Boulevard Grotte, tel. 62 94 32 85, 50 r.
***Jeanne d'Arc, 1 rue Alsace-Lorraine, tel. 62 94 35 42, 154 r.
**Miramont, 40 Avenue Peyramale, tel. 62 94 70 00, 94 r.
**Roissy, 16 Avenue Mgr-Schoepfer, tel. 62 94 13 04, 157 r.

Luchon

***Corneille, 5 Avenue A.-Dumas, tel. 61 79 36 22, 52 r.
**Bains, 75 Allées d'Etigny, tel. 61 79 00 58, 52 r.

Lunéville

***Des Pages, 8 rue Chanzy, tel. 83 74 11 42, 41 r.
**Europe, 56 rue d'Alsace, tel. 83 74 12 34, 30 r.

Luz-St-Sauveur

**Touristic, at Esquièze, tel. 62 92 82 09, 25 r.

Lyons

L****Sofitel, 20 Quai Gailleton, tel. 78 42 72 50, 191 r.
****Grand Hôtel Concorde, 11 rue Grolée, tel. 78 42 56 21, 140 r.
***Beaux Arts, 75 rue E.-Herriot, tel. 78 38 09 50, 79 r.
***Bristol, 28 Cours Verdun, tel. 78 37 56 55, 131 r.
***Mapotel Carlton, 4 rue Jussieu, tel. 78 42 56 51, 87 r.
***Résidence, 18 rue Victor-Hugo, tel. 78 42 63 28, 65 r.
***Royal, 20 Place Bellecour, tel. 78 37 57 31, 90 r.
**Axotel, 12 rue M.-A.-Petit, tel. 78 42 17 18, 128 r.
**Berlioz, 12 Cours Charlemagne, tel. 78 42 30 31, 38 r.
**Paris, 16 rue Platière, tel. 78 28 00 95, 30 r.
**Savoies, 80 rue Charité, tel. 78 37 66 94, 46 r.

Le Mans

***Chantecler, 50 rue Pelouse, tel. 43 24 58 53, 32 r.
***Concorde, 16 Avenue Gén.-Leclerc, tel. 43 24 12 30, 68 r.
***Moderne, 14 rue Bourg-Belé, tel. 43 24 79 20, 32 r.
***Novotel Le Mans, Boul. R.-Schumann, tel. 43 85 26 80, 94 r., SP
**Anjou, 27 Boul. de la Gare, tel. 43 24 90 45, 30 r.
**Central, 5 Boul. R.-Levasseur, tel. 43 24 08 93, 37 r.
**L'Escale, 72 rue Chanzy, tel. 43 84 55 92, 49 r.
**Fimotel, 17 Route Pointe-Rocade Sud, tel. 43 72 27 20, 42 r.

Marseilles

L****Le Petit Nice, 16 rue Bravese, tel. 91 59 25 92, 13 r., SP
L****Sofitel Vieux-Port, 36 Boul. Ch.-Livon, tel. 91 52 90 19, 127 r.

****Pullman Beauvau, 4 rue Beauvau, tel. 91 54 91 00, 71 r.
***Altéa Bourse, rue Neuve St-Martin, tel. 91 91 91 29, 200 r.
***Castellane, 31 rue Rouet, tel. 91 79 27 54, 55 r.
***Genève, 3 bis rue Reine-Elisabeth, tel. 91 90 51 42, 45 r.
***Novotel Marseille Est CD, 2 rue St-Menet, tel. 91 43 90 60, 131 r., SP
***Petit Louvre, 19 Canebière, tel. 91 90 16 27, 33 r.
***Rome et St Pierre, 7 Cours St-Louis, tel. 91 54 19 52, 63 r.
**Ibis Prado, 6 rue Cassis, tel. 91 25 73 73, 118 r.
**Martini, 5 Boul. G.-Desplaces, tel. 91 64 11 17, 40 r.
**Paris, 11–15 rue Colbert, tel. 91 90 06 45, 90 r.
**Sainte Anne, 23 rue Breteuil, tel. 91 33 13 21, 28 r.

Megève
L****Mont-Blanc, Place de l'Eglise, tel. 50 21 20 02, 38 r., SP
***Fer à Cheval, Route Crêt, tel. 50 21 30 39, 39 r.
**Alpina, Place Casino, tel. 50 21 54 77, 14 r.

Mende
***Mapotel Lion d'Or, 12-14 Boul. Britexte, tel. 66 49 16 46, 40 r., SP
**Urbain, 9 Boul. Th.-Roussel, tel. 66 49 14 49, 60 r.

Menton
***Chambord, 6 Avenue Boyer, tel. 93 35 94 19, 40 r.
**Moderne, 1 Cours George-V, tel. 93 57 20 02, 31 r.

Metz
***Altéa Saint-Thiébault, 29 Place St-Thiébault, tel. 87 36 17 69, 112 r.
***Novotel Metz Centre, Place Paraiges, tel. 87 37 38 39, 98 r., SP
***Royal-Concorde, 23 Avenue Foch, tel. 87 66 81 11, 74 r.
**Bristol, 7 rue Lafayette, tel. 87 66 74 22, 67 r.
**Cécil, 14 rue Pasteur, tel. 87 66 66 13, 39 r.
**Foch, 8 Place R.-Mondon, tel. 87 75 40 75, 42 r.
**Gare, 20 rue Gambetta, tel. 87 66 74 03, 40 r.
**Ibis, 47 rue Chambière, tel. 87 31 01 73, 79 r.
**Métropole, 5 Place Gén.-de-Gaulle, tel. 87 66 26 22, 80 r.

Moissac
***Mapotel Moulin de Moissac, Place Moulin, tel. 63 04 03 55, 57 r.
**Chapon Fin, Place Récollets, tel. 63 04 04 22, 32 r.

Molsheim
***Diana, Pont Bruche, tel. 88 38 51 59, 60 r.
**Centre, 21 Place Hôtel-de-Ville, tel. 88 38 54 50, 29 r.

Monaco
L****Hermitage, Square Beaumarchais, tel. 92 16 40 00, 236 r., SP
L****Loews, 12 Avenue Spélugues, tel. 93 50 65 00, 639 r., SP
L****Paris, Place du Casino, tel. 92 16 30 00, 198 r., SP
***Balmoral, 12 Avenue Costa, tel. 93 50 62 37, 77 r.
***Louvre, 16 Boul. Moulins, tel. 93 50 65 25, 36 r.

Montauban
***Mapotel Ingres, 10 Avenue Mayenne, tel. 63 63 36 01, 31 r., SP
**Midi, 12 rue Notre-Dame, tel. 63 63 17 23, 63 r.

Montbéliard
**Joffre, 34 bis Avenue Mar.-Joffre, tel. 81 94 44 64, 47 r.

Montélimar
***Parc Chabaud, 18 Avenue d'Aygu, tel. 75 01 65 66, 22 r.
**Sphinx, 19 Boul. Desmarais, tel. 75 01 86 64, 25 r.

Montpellier
L****Mapotel Métropole, 3 rue Clos-René, tel. 67 58 11 22, 84 r.
***Novotel, 125 bis Avenue Palavas, tel. 67 64 04 04, 97 r., SP
**L'Hôtel, 6 & 8 rue J.-Ferry, tel. 67 58 88 75, 55 r.

Mont-St-Michel
***Mère Poulard, tel. 33 60 14 01, 27 r.
**Mouton Blanc, tel. 33 60 14 08, 20 r.

Moulins
***Paris, 21 rue Paris, tel. 70 44 00 58, 27 r.
**Parc, 31 Avenue Gén.-Leclerc, tel. 70 44 12 25, 28 r.

Mulhouse
***Altéa, 4 Place Gén.-de-Gaulle, tel. 89 46 01 23, 96 r.
***Bourse, 14 rue Bourse, tel. 89 56 18 44, 50 r.

**Bâle, 19-21 Passage Central, tel. 89 46 19 87, 32 r.
**Touring, 10 rue Moulin, tel. 89 45 32 84, 30 r.
**Wir, 1 Porte Bâle, tel. 89 56 13 22, 39 r.

Munster

**Deux Sapins, 49 rue 9 Zouaves, tel. 89 77 33 96, 19 r.

Nancy

****Grand Hôtel, 2 Place Stanislas, tel. 83 35 03 01, 42 r.
***Altéa Thiers, 11 rue R.-Poincaré, tel. 85 35 61 01, 119 r.
***Europe, 5 rue Carmes, tel. 83 35 52 10, 80 r.
**Albert 1er-Astoria, 2 rue Armée-Patton, tel. 83 40 31 24, 132 r.
**Central, 6 rue R.-Poincaré, tel. 83 32 21 24, 68 r.

Nantes

L****Sofitel, Rue A.-Millerand, tel. 40 47 61 03, 100 r., SP
***L'Hôtel, 6 rue Henry-IV, tel. 40 29 30 31, 31 r.
***Jules Verne, 3 rue Covedic, tel. 40 35 74 50, 65 r.
***Pullman Beaulieu, 3 rue Dr-Zamenhof, tel. 40 47 10 58, tel. 150 r.
**Colonies, 5 rue Chapeau-Rouge, tel. 40 48 79 76, 39 r.
**Grand Hôtel, 2 rue Santeuil, tel. 40 73 46 68, 43 r.
**Graslin, 1 rue Piron, tel. 40 69 72 91, 47 r.
**Trois Marchands, 26 rue A.-Brossard, tel. 40 47 62 00, 64 r.

Narbonne

***Motel d'Occitanie, Avenue de la Mer, tel. 68 65 23 71, 55 r., SP
**Lion d'Or, 39 Avenue P.-Sémard, tel. 68 32 06 92,27 r.

Neuf-Brisach

**Cerf, 11 rue Strasbourg, tel. 89 72 56 03, 30 r.

Neufchâteau

**St-Christophe, Route de Dijon, tel. 29 94 16 28, 36 r.

Nevers

***Loire, Quai Médine, tel. 86 61 50 92, 58 r.
**Clèves, 8 rue St-Didier, tel. 86 61 15 87, 15 r.

Nice

L****Beach Régency, 223 Prom. des Anglais, tel. 93 83 91 51, 322 r., SP
L****Negresco, 37 Prom. des Anglais, tel. 93 88 39 51, 130 r.
****Beau Rivage, 24 rue St-François, tel. 93 80 80 70, 118 r.
****Méridien Nice, 1 Prom. des Anglais, tel. 93 82 25 25, 305 r., SP
****Sofitel-Splendid, 50 Boul. Victor-Hugo, tel. 93 88 69 54, 116 r., SP
***Ambassador, 8 Avenue Suède, tel. 93 87 90 19, 45 r.
***Atlantic, 12 Boul. Victor-Hugo, tel. 93 88 40 15, 123 r.
***Lausanne, 36 rue Rossini, tel. 93 88 85 94, 40 r.
***Locarno, 4 Avenue Baumettes, tel. 93 96 28 00, 48 r.
***Malmaison Mapotel, 48 Boul. Victor-Hugo, tel. 93 87 62 56, 50 r.
***Napoléon, 8 rue Grimaldi, tel. 93 87 70 07, 84 r.
***West-End, 31 Prom. des Anglais, tel. 93 88 79 91, 100 r.
***Windsor, 11 rue Dalpozzo, tel. 93 88 59 35, 63 r., SP
**Harvey, 18 Avenue Suède, tel. 93 88 73 73, 62 r.
**Idéal Séjour, 12 rue Maccarani, tel. 93 87 72 14, 24 r.
**King George's, 15 rue Grimaldi, tel. 93 87 73 61, 30 r.
**Nouvel Hôtel, 19 bis Boul. Victor-Hugo, tel. 93 87 15 00, 60 r.
**Star, 14 rue Biscarra, tel. 93 85 19 03, 19 r.
**Suisse, 15 Quai Rauba-Capeu, tel. 93 62 33 00, 42 r.
**Touring, 5 rue Russie, tel. 93 88 70 15, 19 r.
**Trianon, 15 Avenue Auber, tel. 93 88 30 69, 32 r.

Nîmes

****Imperator Concorde, Place A.-Briand, tel. 66 21 90 30, 65 r.
***Mercure, 113 Chemin de l'Hostellerie, tel. 66 84 14 55, 98 r., SP
***Novotel, 124 Chemin de l'Hostellerie, tel. 66 84 60 20, 96 r., SP
***Tuileries, 22 rue Roussy, tel. 66 21 31 15, 10 r.
**Amphithéâtre, 4 rue Arènes, tel. 66 67 28 51, 21 r.
**Ibis, Chemin de l'Hostellerie, tel. 66 38 00 65, 108 r., SP
**Milan, 17 Avenue Feuchères, tel. 66 29 29 90, 33 r.
**Nimotel, Centre Hôtelier, tel. 66 38 13 84, 162 r., SP

Noirmoutier

***Général d'Elbée, 2 Quai Gaspard, tel. 51 39 10 29, 30 r., SP
**Fleur de Sel, Rue Saulnier, tel. 51 39 21 59, 35 r., SP

Hôtel de Crillon in the Place de la Concorde, Paris

Noyon **Grillon, 37–39 rue St-Eloi, tel. 44 09 14 18, 34 r.

Obernai ***Parc, 169 rue Gén.-Gouraud, tel. 88 95 50 08, 50 r., SP
**Vosges, 5 Place de la Gare, tel. 88 95 53 78, 20 r.

Oloron-Ste-Marie **Béarn, 4 Place G.-Clemenceau, tel. 59 39 00 99, 28 r.

Orange ***Altéa Orange, Route Caderousse, tel. 90 34 24 10, 99 r., SP
**Glacier, 46 Cours A.-Briand, tel. 90 34 02 01, 28 r.

Orléans ****Sofitel Orléans, 44–46 Quai Barentin, tel. 36 62 17 39, 109 r., SP
***Cèdres, 17 rue Mar.-Foch, tel. 38 62 22 92, 35 r.
***Orléans, 6 rue A.-Crespin, tel. 38 53 35 34, 18 r.
***St-Aignan, 3 Place Gambetta, tel. 38 53 15 35, 27 r.
**Marguerite, 14 Place Vieux-Marché, tel. 38 53 74 32, 25 r.
**St-Jean, 19 rue Porte-St-Jean, tel. 38 53 63 32, 27 r.
**St-Martin, 52 Boul. A.-Martin, tel. 38 62 47 47, 22 r.
**Sanotel, 16 Quai St-Laurent, tel. 38 54 47 65, 50 r.

Orthez ***Château des Trois Poètes, on N117, tel. 59 69 16 20, 10 r.
**Climat de France, Rue Soulor, tel. 59 69 28 77, 24 r.

Paris ****de Crillon, 10 Place de la Concorde, tel. 44 71 15 00, 163 r.
****Grand Hôtel Inter Continental, 2 rue Scribe, tel. 40 07 32 32, 515 r.
****Lotti, 7 rue Castiglione, tel. 42 60 37 34, 133 r.
****Pavillon de la Reine, 28 Place des Vosges, tel. 42 77 96 40, 55 r.
****Plaza-Athénée, 25 Avenue Montaigne, tel. 47 23 78 33, 211 r.
****Pont Royal Best Western, 7 rue Montalembert, tel. 45 44 38 27, 78 r.
****Ritz, 15 Place Vendôme, tel. 42 60 38 30, 187 r.
****Westminster, 15 rue de la Paix, tel. 42 61 57 46, 102 r.
***Anjou Lafayette Best Western, 4 rue Ribouté, tel. 42 46 83 44, 39 r.

***Atlantide République, 114 Boul. R.-Lenoir, tel. 43 38 29 29, 27 r.
***Beaubourg, 11 rue S.-Le-Franc, tel. 42 74 34 24, 28 r.
***Bourdonnais, 111 Avenue Bourdonnais, tel. 47 05 45 42, 60 r.
***Cayré Copatel, 4 Boul. Raspail, tel. 45 44 36 88, 126 r.
***de l'Elysée, 12 rue Saussaies, tel. 42 65 29 25, 32 r.
***Gotty, 11 rue Trévise, tel. 47 70 12 90, 44 r.
***Kléber, 7 rue Belloy, tel. 47 23 80 22, 23 r.
***Lutétia, 45 Boul. Raspail, tel. 49 54 46 46, 276 r.
***Mercure Paris Bercy, 6 Boul. V.-Auriol, tel. 45 82 48 00, 89 r.
***Mercure Paris Montmartre, 3 rue Caulaincourt, tel. 42 94 17 17, 308 r.
***Montana-Tuileries, 12 rue St-Roch, tel. 42 60 35 10, 25 r.
***de Neuville, 3 rue Verniquet, tel. 43 80 26 30, 28 r.
***Novotel Paris les Halles, Place M.-de-Navarre, tel. 42 21 31 31, 285 r.
***Pullman St-Honoré, 15 rue Boissy-d'Anglas, tel. 42 66 93 62, 112 r.
***Quality Inn Paris Rive Gauche, 92 rue Vaugirard, tel. 42 22 00 56, 134 r.
***Le Relais St-Germain, 9 Carrefour de l'Odéon, tel. 43 29 12 05, 11 r.
***Renoir, 39 rue Montparnasse, tel. 43 21 72 50, 29 r.
**Bel'Hôtel, 20 rue Pouchet, tel. 46 27 34 77, 30 r.
**Charing Cross, 39 rue Pasquier, tel. 42 87 41 04, 31 r.
**des Ducs d'Anjou, 1 rue Ste-Opportune, tel. 42 36 92 24, 38 r.
**Le Fondary, 30 rue Fondary, tel. 45 75 14 75, 20 r.
**Ibis Paris Lafayette, 122 rue Lafayette, tel. 45 23 27 27, 70 r.
**Inter-Hotel du Vieux Saule, 6 rue Picardie, tel. 42 72 01 14, 31 r.
**Jardin des Plantes, Rue Linné, tel. 47 07 06 20, 33 r.
**Keppler, 12 rue Keppler, tel. 47 20 65 05, 49 r.
**Lindbergh, 5 rue Chomel, tel. 47 48 35 53, 26 r.
**du Midi, 114 Avenue Daumesnil, tel. 43 07 72 03, 36 r.
**Palma, 77 Avenue Gambetta, tel. 46 36 13 65, 32 r.

Pau

***Bristol, 3 rue Gambetta, tel. 59 27 72 98, 24 r.
**Atlantic, 222 Avenue J.-Mermoz, tel. 59 32 38 24, 31 r.

Périgueux

***Bristol,, 37 rue A.-Gadaud, tel. 53 08 75 90, 28 r.
**Régina, 14 rue D.-Papin, tel. 53 08 40 44, 46 r.

Perpignan

***France, 6 Quai S.-Carnot, tel. 68 34 92 81, 35 r.
***Mondial, 40 Boul. Clemenceau, tel. 68 34 23 40, 41 r.
**Aragon, 17 Boul. Brutus, tel. 68 54 04 46, 33 r.
**Athéna, 1 rue Queya, tel. 68 34 37 63, 37 r.
**Christina, 50 Cours Lassus, tel. 68 35 24 61, 37 r.

Plombières-les-Bains

***Grand Hôtel, 2 Avenue Etats-Unis, tel. 29 66 00 03, 114 r.
**Modern, Avenue Th.-Gautier, tel. 29 66 04 02, 47 r.

Poitiers

****France, 28 rue Carnot, tel. 49 41 32 01, 87 r.
***Royal Poitou, 215 Route de Paris (N10), tel. 49 01 72 86, 32 r.
**Climat de France, Rue Frères-Lumière, tel. 49 61 38 75, 70 r.
**Ibis Sud, Avenue 8-Mai-1945, tel. 49 53 13 13, 117 r.

Pontarlier

***Commerce, 18 rue Dr-Grenier, tel. 81 39 14 09, 30 r.
**Grand Hôtel Poste, 55 rue République, tel. 81 39 18 12, 22 r.

Pontoise

****Novotel, tel. 30 30 39 47, 196 r., SP
***Ibis, 28 Avenue Grouettes, tel. 34 22 11 44, 80 r.

Port-Grimaud

****Giraglia, Grand'Rue, tel. 94 56 31 33, 48 r.
***Port, Place du Marché, tel. 94 56 36 18, 20 r.

Port Leucate

**Motel Etoile du Sud, tel. 68 86 03 31, 81 r., SP

Le Puy

****Christel, 15 Boul. A.-Clair. tel. 71 02 24 44, 30 r.
***Régina, 34 Boul. Mar.-Fayolle, tel. 71 09 14 71, 40 r.
**Licorn' Hôtel, 25 Avenue C.-Dupuy, tel. 71 02 46 22, 44 r., SP

Quiberon	****Sofitel-Thalassa, Pointe de Goulvars, tel. 97 50 20 00, 116 r., SP ***Ker Noyal, Chemin des Dunes, tel. 97 50 08 41, 102 r. **Bellevue, Rue Tiviec, tel. 97 50 16 28, 42 r., SP
Quimper	***Griffon, 131 Route Bénodet, tel. 98 90 33 33, 48 r., SP **La Tour d'Auvergne, 13 rue Reguaires, tel. 98 95 81 70, 45 r.
Reims	****Boyer Les Crayères, 64 Boul. H.-Vasnier, tel. 26 82 80 80, 19 r. ***Altéa Champagne, 31 rue P.-Doumer, tel. 26 88 53 54, 115 r. ***Crystal, 86 Place D.-d'Erlon, tel. 26 88 44 44, 28 r. ***Paix, 9 rue Buirette, tel. 26 40 04 08, 105 r., SP **Ardenn, 8 rue Caqué, tel. 26 47 42 38, 14 r. **Univers, 41 Boul. Foch, tel. 26 88 68 08, 41 r. **Welcome, 29-31 rue Buirette, tel. 26 47 39 39, 68 r. **Libergier, 20 rue Libergier, tel. 26 47 28 46, 17 r.
Remiremont	**Poste, 67 rue Gén.-de-Gaulle, tel. 29 62 55 67, 21 r.
Rennes	***Altéa Parc du Colombier, 1 rue Cap.-Maignan, tel. 99 31 54 54, 140 r. ***Anne de Bretagne, 12 rue Tronjolly, tel. 99 31 49 49, 42 r. ***Novotel Rennes-Alma, Avenue Canada, tel. 99 50 61 32, 98 r., SP ***Président, 27 Avenue Janvier, tel. 99 65 42 22, 34 r. **Angelina, 1 Quai Lamennais, tel. 99 79 29 66, 27 r. **Astrid, 32 Avenue L.-Barthou, tel. 99 30 82 38, 30 r. **Garden, 3 rue Duhamel, tel. 99 65 45 06, 24 r. **Sévigné, 47 Avenue Janvier, tel. 99 67 27 55, 46 r.
Ribeauvillé	L****Clos St-Vincent, Route Bergheim, tel. 89 73 67 65, 11 r. **Tour, 1 rue de la Mairie, tel. 89 73 72 73, 32 r.
Rocamadour	***Beau Site, Rue R.-le-Preux, tel. 65 33 63 08, 55 r. **Belvédère, at L'Hospitalet, tel. 65 33 63 25, 18 r.
La Rochelle	***Les Brises, Chemin Digue Richelieu, tel. 46 43 89 37, 46 r. ***France-Angleterre, 22-24 rue Gargoulleau, tel. 46 41 34 66, 76 r. **St-Jean d'Acre, 4 Place Chaîne, tel. 46 41 73 33, 57 r. **St-Nicolas, 13 rue Sardinière, tel. 46 41 71 55, 76 r.
Rodez	***Tour Maje, Boul. Gally, tel. 65 68 34 68, 45 r. **Midi-Dauty, 1 rue Béteille, tel. 65 68 02 07, 34 r.
Ronchamp	***Ronchamp, 1 rue Neuve, tel. 84 20 60 35, 21 r. **Carrer, at Le Rhien, tel. 82 20 62 32, 20 r.
Roscoff	***Brittany, Boul. Ste-Barbe, tel. 98 69 70 78, 17 r., SP **Talabardon, Place de l'Eglise, tel. 98 61 24 95, 38 r.
Rouen	****Pullman Albane, Rue Croix-de-Fer, tel. 35 98 06 98, 121 r. ***Dieppe, Place B.-Tissot, tel. 35 71 96 00, 42 r. **Astrid, 121 rue Jeanne-d'Arc, tel. 35 71 75 88, 40 r. **Normandie, 19 rue Bec, tel. 35 71 55 77, 23 r. **Québec, 18-24 rue Québec, tel. 35 70 09 38, 38 r. **Viking, 21 Quai du Havre, tel. 35 70 34 95, 37 r.
Roussillon	***Mas de Garrigon, Route St-Saturnin-d'Apt, tel. 90 05 63 22, 8 r., SP **Résidence des Ocres, Route Gordes, tel. 90 05 60 50, 16 r.
Royan	***France, Place Renaissance, tel. 46 05 02 29, 38 r. **Vialard, 23 Boul. A.-Briand, tel. 46 05 84 22, 23 r.
Le Rozier	**Grand Hôtel Voyageurs, tel. 65 62 60 09, 21 r.
Les Sables d'Olonne	***Atlantic, 5 Promenade Godet, tel. 51 95 37 71, 30 r., SP **Chêne Vert, 5 rue Bauduère, tel. 51 32 09 47, 30 r.

Saint-Claude
**St-Hubert, 3 Place St-Hubert, tel. 84 45 10 70, 30 r.

Saint-Denis
**Fimotel, 20 rue J.-Saulnier, tel. 48 09 48 10, 60 r.

Saint-Dié
**France, 1 rue Dauphine, tel. 29 56 32 61, 11 r.

Sainte-Enimie
**Burlatis, Rue Combe, tel. 66 48 52 30, 18 r.

Saint-Emilion
****Hostellerie Plaisance, Place Clocher, tel. 57 24 72 32, 11 r.
***Logis des Remparts, Rue Guadet, tel. 57 24 70 43, 15 r.
**Auberge de la Commanderie, Rue Guadet, tel. 57 24 70 19, 15 r.

Saintes
***Relais du Bois St-Georges, Rue Royan, tel. 46 93 50 99, 30 r., SP
**Bouquets, Route Rochefort, tel. 46 74 04 47, 35 r.

Saintes-Maries-de-la-Mer
****Pont des Bannes, Route d'Arles, tel. 90 47 81 09, 25 r., SP
***Galoubet, Route de Cacharel, tel. 90 97 82 17, 20 r., SP
**Lou Marquès, tel. 90 47 82 89, 14 r.

Saint-Etienne
***Altéa Parc de l'Europe, Rue Wuppertal, tel. 77 25 22 75, 120 r.
***Astoria, Rue H.-Déchaud, tel. 77 25 09 56, 33 r.
***Midi, 19 Boul. Pasteur, tel. 77 57 32 55, 33 r.
***Terminus du Forez, 31 Av. Denfert-Rochereau, tel. 77 32 48 47, 66 r.
**Carnot, 11 Boul. J.-Janin, tel. 77 74 27 16, 24 r.
**Central, 3 rue Blanqui, tel. 77 32 31 86, 25 r.
**Cheval Noir, 11 rue F.-Gillet, tel. 77 33 41 72, 46 r.
**Touring Continental, 10 rue F.-Gillet, tel. 77 32 58 43, 25 r.

Saint-Germain-en-Laye
L****Pavillon Henri-IV, 21 rue Thiers, tel. 34 51 62 62, 42 r.

Saint-Jean-de-Luz
L****Chantaco, at Chantaco golf course, tel. 59 26 14 76, 20 r.
***Basque, Rond-Point Ste-Barbe, tel. 59 26 04 24, 23 r.
**Petit Trianon, 56 Boul. Victor-Hugo, tel. 59 26 11 90, 26 r.

Saint-Malo
***Central, B.P. 142, tel. 99 40 87 70, 46 r.
***Elisabeth, 2 rue Cordiers, tel. 99 56 24 98, 17 r.
**Bristol-Union, 4 Place Poissonnerie, tel. 99 40 83 36, 27 r.
**Quic en Groigne, 8 rue d'Estrées, tel. 99 40 86 81, 15 r.

Saint-Nazaire
***Berry, 1 Place de la Gare, tel. 40 22 42 61, 27 r.
**Europe, 2 Place Martyrs-de-la-Résistance, tel. 40 22 49 87, 39 r.

Saint-Nizier-du-Moucherotte
**Le Concorde, tel. 76 53 42 61, 31 r.

Saint-Omer
***Le Bretagne, 2 Place Vainquai, tel. 21 38 25 78, 41 r.
**St-Louis, 25 rue d'Arras, tel. 21 38 35 21, 30 r.

Saint-Quentin
***Grand Hôtel, 6 rue Dachery, tel. 23 62 69 77, 24 r.
**Paix-Albert 1er, 3 Place 8-Octobre, tel. 23 62 77 62, 82 r.

Saint-Rémy-de-Provence
****Château des Alpilles, on D31, tel. 90 92 03 33, 17 r., SP
***Hostellerie du Vallon de Valrugues, Chemin C.-Cigalo, tel. 90 92 04 40, 24 r., SP
**Canto Cigalo, Chemin C.-Cigalo, tel. 90 92 14 28, 20 r.

Saint-Tropez
L****Byblos, Av. P.-Signac, tel. 94 97 00 04, 70 r., SP
***Yaca, 3 Boul. Aumale, tel. 94 97 11 79, 22 r., SP
**Hélios, Port Pilon, tel. 94 97 00 64, 30 r.

Salers
**Beffroi, Rue Beffroi, tel. 71 40 70 11, 11 r.

Salon-de-Provence
****Abbaye de Ste-Croix, Route Val Cuech, tel. 90 56 50 11, 24 r., SP
**Midi, 518 Allées Craponne, tel. 90 53 34 67, 27 r.

Sancerre	**Panoramic, Remparts Augustins, tel. 48 54 22 44, 57 r.
Sarlat	***La Madeleine, 1 Place Petite-Rigaudie, tel. 53 59 10 41, 19 r. **St-Albert & Montaigne, 2 Place Pasteur, tel. 53 59 01 09, 61 r.
Sarrebourg	**France, 3 Av. France, tel. 87 03 21 47, 50 r.
Saumur	***Budan, 3 Quai Carnot, tel. 41 51 28 76, 80 r. **Roi René, 94 Av. Gén.-de-Gaulle, tel. 41 67 45 30, 38 r.
Sedan	**Europe, 5 Place de la Gare, tel. 24 27 18 71, 23 r.
Sélestat	***Vaillant, Place République, tel. 88 92 09 46, 47 r.
Senlis	**Ibis, on N325, tel. 44 53 70 50, 50 r.
Sens	***Paris/Poste, 97 rue République, tel. 86 65 17 43, 26 r. **Résidence R. Binet, 20 rue R.-Binet, tel. 86 95 21 50, 33 r.
Sète	***Grand Hôtel, 17 Quai de-Lattre-de-Tassigny, tel. 67 74 71 77, 47 r. **Orque Bleue, 10 Quai A.-Herber, tel. 67 74 72 13, 30 r.
Sisteron	**Grand Hôtel Cours, Place de l'Eglise, tel. 92 61 04 51, 50 r. **Tivoli, Place Tivoli, tel. 92 61 15 16, 19 r.
Soissons	***Picardie, 6 rue Neuve, tel. 23 53 34 10, 33 r. **Motel des Lions, Route de Reims, tel. 23 73 29 83, 28 r.
La Souterraine	**Porte St-Jean, 2 rue des Bains, tel. 55 63 03 83, 14 r.
Strasbourg	L****Grand Hôtel, 12 Place de la Gare, tel. 88 32 46 90, 90 r. L****Hilton International, Avenue Herrenschmidt, tel. 88 37 10 10, 246 r. L****Régent Contades, 8 Avenue Liberté, tel. 88 36 26 26,32 r. L****Sofitel, 4 Place St-Pierre-le-Jeune, tel. 88 32 99 30, 158 r. L****Terminus Gruber, 10 Place de la Gare, tel. 88 32 87 00, 70 r. ***France, 20 rue Jeu-des-Enfants, tel. 88 32 37 12, 70 r. ***Monopole Métropole, 16 rue Kuhn, tel. 88 32 11 94, 94 r. ***Novotel, Quai Kléber, tel. 88 22 10 99, 97 r. ***Des Rohan, 17 rue Maroquin, tel. 88 32 85 11, 36 r. **Continental, 14 rue Marie-Kuss, tel. 88 22 28 07, 48 r. **Royal, 3 rue Marie-Kuss, tel. 88 32 28 71, 52 r. **St-Christophe, 2 Place de la Gare, tel. 88 22 30 30, 70 r.
Sully-sur-Loire	**Pont de Sologne, 21 Porte Sologne, tel. 38 36 26 34, 24 r.
Tarascon	***Provence, 7 Boul. Victor-Hugo, tel. 90 91 06 43, 11 r. **Terminus, Place Col.-Berrurier, tel. 90 91 18 95, 20 r.
Tarbes	***Foch, 18 Place Verdun, tel. 62 93 71 58, 30 r. ***Henri IV, 7 Avenue P.-Barère, tel. 62 34 01 68, 22 r.
Thann	**Kléber, 39 rue Kléber, tel. 89 37 13 66, 25 r.
Thonon-les-Bains	***Savoie/Léman, 2 Boul. Corniche, tel. 50 71 13 80, 31 r. **Alpazur, 8 Avenue Gén.-Leclerc, tel. 50 71 37 25, 26 r.
Tignes	***Ski d'Or, Val Claret, tel. 79 06 51 60, 22 r. **Campanules, Lac de Tignes, tel. 79 06 34 36, 36 r.
Toul	**Villa Lorraine, 15 rue Gambetta, tel. 83 43 08 95, 29 r.
Toulon	***Altéa Tour Blanche, Boul. Amiral-Vence, tel. 94 24 41 57, 92 r. ***La Corniche, 1 Littoral F.-Mistral, tel. 94 41 39 53, 22 r.

***Grand Hôtel, 4 Place Liberté, tel. 94 22 59 50, 45 r.
**Amirauté, 4 rue A.-Guiol, tel. 94 22 19 67, 64 r.
**Dauphiné, 10 rue Berthelot, tel. 94 92 20 28, 57 r.
**Maritima, 9 rue Gimelli, tel. 94 92 39 33, 48 r.
**Nouvel Hôtel, 224 Boul. Tessé, tel. 94 89 04 22, 29 r.
**Terminus, 7 Boul. Tessé, tel. 94 89 23 54, 40 r.

Toulouse

****Altéa Wilson, 7 rue Labéda, tel. 61 21 21 75, 91 r.
****Concorde, 16 Boul. Bonrepos, tel. 61 62 48 60, 97 r., SP
***Grand Hôtel de l'Opéra, 1 Place Capitole, tel. 61 21 82 66, 46 r., SP
***Mercure St-Georges, Rue St-Jérome, tel. 61 23 11 77, 170 r.
***Paris Best Western, 18 Allées J.-Jaurès, tel. 61 62 98 30, 40 r.
***Victoria, 76 rue Bayard, tel. 61 62 50 90, 78 r.
**Star, 17 rue Baqué, tel. 61 47 45 15, 17 r.
**Taur, 2 rue Taur, tel. 61 21 17 54, 17 r.
**Touristic, 25 Place Victor-Hugo, tel. 61 23 14 55, 38 r.

Tours

***Bordeaux, 3 Place Mar.-Leclerc, tel. 47 05 40 32, 56 r.
***Central, 21 rue Berthelot, tel. 47 05 46 44, 42 r.
***Royal, 65 Avenue Grammont, tel. 47 64 71 78, 35 r.
***Univers, 5 Boul. Heurteloup, tel. 47 05 37 12, 86 r.
**Châteaux de la Loire, 12 rue Gambetta, tel. 47 05 10 05, 32 r.
**Criden, 65 Boul. Heurteloup, tel. 47 20 81 14, 32 r.
**Europe, 12 Place Mar.-Leclerc, tel. 47 05 42 07, 53 r.
**Mirabeau, 89 bis Boul. Heurteloup, tel. 47 05 24 60, 25 r.

Troyes

***Grand Hôtel, 4 Avenue Mar.-Joffre, tel. 25 79 90 90, 100 r.
***Poste, 35 Avenue E.-Zola, tel. 25 73 05 05, 26 r.
**Champenois, 15 rue P.-Gauthier, tel. 25 76 16 05, 26 r.

Tulle

***Le Limouzi, 16 Quai République, tel. 55 26 42 00, 50 r.
**Gare, 25 Avenue W.-Churchill, tel. 55 20 04 04, 13 r.

Uzerche

**Teyssier, Rue Pont Turgot, tel. 55 73 10 05, 17 r.

Uzès

***Entraigues, 8 rue Calade, tel. 66 22 32 68, 17 r.
**St-Geniès, Route St-Ambroix, tel. 66 22 29 99, 18 r.

Vaison-la-Romaine

***Beffroi, Rue de l'Evêché, tel. 90 36 04 71, 21 r.
**Burrhus, 2 Place Montfort, tel. 90 36 00 11, 14 r.

Val-d'Isère

****Sofitel, tel. 79 06 08 30, 48 r., SP
***Savoyarde, tel. 79 06 01 55, 45 r.
**La Galise, tel. 79 06 05 04, 37 r.

Valençay

****Espagne, 9 rue du Château, tel. 54 00 00 02, 10 r.
**Lion d'Or, Place du Marché, tel. 54 00 00 87, 15 r.

Valenciennes

***Grand Hôtel, 8 Place de la Gare, tel. 27 46 32 01, 91 r.
**Notre Dame, 1 Place Abbé-Thellier-de-Poncheville, tel. 27 42 30 00, 40 r.

Vannes

***Aquarium, Parc du Golfe, tel. 97 40 44 52, 48 r.
**Image Ste-Anne, 8 Place Libération, tel. 97 63 27 36, 32 r.

Vence

L****Château St-Martin, Route Coursegoules, tel. 93 58 02 02, 15 r., SP
***Floréal, 440 Avenue Rhin et Danube, tel. 93 58 64 40, 43 r., SP
**Mas de Vence, 583 Avenue E.-Hugues, tel. 93 58 06 16, 41 r., SP

Vendôme

**Vendôme, 15 Faubourg Chartrain, tel. 54 77 02 88, 35 r.

Verdun

***Hostellerie du Coq Hardi, 8 Avenue Victoire, tel. 29 86 36 36, 40 r.
**Montaulbain, 4 rue Vieille-Prison, tel. 29 86 00 47, 10 r.

Vernon	***D'Evreux le Relais Normand, 7 Place d'Evreux, tel. 32 21 16 12, 20 r. **Strasbourg, 6 Place d'Evreux, tel. 32 51 23 12, 23 r.
Versailles	L****Trianon Palace, 1 Boul. de la Reine, tel. 39 50 34 12, 110 r. ***Bellevue Best Western, 12 Avenue Sceaux, tel. 39 50 13 41, 24 r. **Printania, 7 bis rue Montbauron, tel. 39 50 44 10, 30 r.
Vichy	****Aletti Thermal Palace, 3 Place J.-Aletti, tel. 70 31 78 77, 57 r. ****Pavillon Sévigné, 10-12 Place Sévigné, tel. 70 32 16 22, 57 r. ***Paix, 13 rue Parc, tel. 70 98 20 56, 80 r. ***Régina, 4 Avenue Thermale, tel. 70 98 20 95, 90 r. **Venise, 25 Avenue A.-Briand, tel. 70 31 83 23, 26 r.
Vienne	***Résidence de la Pyramide, 41 Quai Riondet, tel. 74 53 16 46, 15 r. **Poste, 47 Cours Romestang, tel. 74 85 02 04, 42 r.
Villard-de-Lans	***Eterlou, Route de Grenoble, tel. 76 95 17 65, 24 r., SP **Pré Fleuri, Avenue A.-Pietri, tel. 76 95 10 96, 18 r.
Vittel	***Angleterre, Rue Charmey, tel. 29 08 08 42, 62 r. **Beauséjour, 160 Avenue Tilleuls, tel. 29 08 09 34, 37 r.
Wissembourg	**Walck, 2 rue Walck, tel. 88 94 06 44, 15 r.

Information

Outside France

United Kingdom

French Government Tourist Office
178 Piccadilly
London W1V 0AL
tel. (071) 491 7622

Monaco Govenment Tourist and Convention Office
3–18 Chelsea Garden Market
Chelsea Harbour, London SW10 0XE
tel. (071) 352 9962

Andorra Tourist Delegation
63 Westover Road
London SW18 2RF
tel. (081) 874 4806

United States

French Government Tourist Office
610 Fifth Avenue, Suite 222
New York NY 10020–2452
tel. (212) 757 1125

645 N. Michigan Avenue
Chicago IL 60611–2967
tel. (312) 337 6301

9454 Wilshire Boulevard
Beverly Hills CA 90212–2967
tel. (310) 271 7838

Cedar Maple Plaza
2305 Cedar Springs Road
Suite 205
Dallas TX 75201
tel. (214) 720 4010

Canada

Représentation Française du Tourisme
1981 Avenue McGill Collège
Suite 490, Montréal, Québec H3A 2W9
tel. (514) 288 4264

French Government Tourist Office
30 St Patrick Street
Suite 700, Toronto, Ontario M5T 3A3
tel. (416) 593 4723

In France

Central Office

Maison de la France
8 Avenue de l'Opéra, F-75001 Paris
tel. (1) 42 96 10 23

Abbeville

Office de Tourisme
1 Place Amiral Courbet, F-80100 Abbeville
tel. 22 24 27 92

Agde

Office de Tourisme
Espace Molière, F-34300 Agde
tel. 67 94 29 68

Aigues-Mortes

Office de Tourisme
Porte de la Gardette, F-30220 Aigues-Mortes
tel. 66 53 73 00

Aix-en-Provence

Office de Tourisme
Place Gén.-de-Gaulle, F-13100 Aix-en-Provence
tel. 42 26 02 93

Aix-les-Bains

Office de Tourisme
Place M.-Mollard, F-73100 Aix-les-Bains
tel. 79 35 05 92

Ajaccio

Office de Tourisme
1 Place Foch, F-20000 Ajaccio
tel. 95 21 40 87

Albertville

Office de Tourisme
1 rue Bugeaud, F-73200 Albertville
tel. 79 32 04 22

Albi

Office de Tourisme
Place Ste-Cécile, F-81000 Albi
tel. 63 54 22 30

Alençon

Office de Tourisme
Maison d'Ozé, F-61000 Alençon
tel. 33 26 11 36

L'Alpe d'Huez

Office de Tourisme
Place Paganon, F-38750 L'Alpe d'Huez
tel. 76 80 35 41

Amboise

Office de Tourisme
Quai Gén.-de-Gaulle, F-37400 Amboise
tel. 47 57 01 37

Amélie-les-Bains-Palalda

Office de Tourisme
Quai du 8 Mai 1945, F-66110 Amélie-les-Bains-Palalda
tel. 68 39 01 98

Amiens

Office de Tourisme
Rue J.-Catelas, F-80000 Amiens
tel. 22 91 79 28

Les Andelys	Syndicat d'Initiative 24 rue Philippe-Auguste, F-27700 Les Andelys tel. 32 54 41 93
Andorra la Vella	Sindicat d'Iniciativa Calle Dr-Vilanova, Andorra la Vella tel. 20 21 4
Anduze	Syndicat d'Initiative Plan de Brie, F-30140 Anduze tel. 66 61 98 17
Angers	Office de Tourisme Place Kennedy, F-49051 Angers tel. 41 88 69 93
Angoulême	Office de Tourisme 2 Place St-Pierre, F-16000 Angoulême tel. 45 95 16 84
Annecy	Office de Tourisme 1 rue J.-Jaurès, F-74000 Annecy tel. 50 45 00 33
Antibes	Maison du Tourisme 11 Place Gén.-de-Gaulle, F-06600 Antibes tel. 93 33 95 64
Arbois	Office de Tourisme Avenue la Mairie, F-39600 Arbois tel. 84 37 47 37
Arcachon	Office de Tourisme Place F.-Roosevelt, F-33120 Arcachon tel. 56 83 01 69
Argentan	Office de Tourisme Place du Marché, F-61200 Argentan tel. 33 67 12 48
Argentat	Office de Tourisme Avenue Pasteur, F-19400 Argentat tel. 55 28 16 05
Arles	Office de Tourisme Esplanade des Lices, F-13200 Arles tel. 90 96 40 28
Arras	Office de Tourisme Hôtel de Ville, F-62000 Arras tel. 21 51 26 95
Aubusson	Syndicat d'Initiative Rue Vieille, F-23200 Aubusson tel. 55 66 32 12
Aurillac	Office de Tourisme Place Square, F-15000 Aurillac tel. 71 48 46 58
Autun	Office de Tourisme 3 Avenue Ch.-de-Gaulle, F-71400 Autun tel. 85 52 20 34

Auxerre
Office de Tourisme
1–2 Quai de la République, F-89000 Auxerre
tel. 86 52 06 19

Avignon
Office de Tourisme
41 Cours J.-Jaurès, F-84000 Avignon
tel. 90 82 65 11

Ax-les-Thermes
Office de Tourisme
Place du Breilh, F-09110 Ax-les-Thermes
tel. 61 64 20 64

Azay-le-Rideau
Syndicat d'Initiative
Place Europe, F-37190 Azay-le-Rideau
tel. 47 45 44 40

Bagnères-de-Bigorre
Office de Tourisme
3 Allée Tournefort, F-65200 Bagnères-de-Bigorre
tel. 62 95 50 71

Bagnères-de-Luchon
See Luchon

Bar-le-Duc
Office de Tourisme
5 rue Jeanne D'Arc, F-55000 Bar-le-Duc
tel. 29 79 11 13

Barr
Office de Tourisme
Avenue la Mairie, F-67140 Barr
tel. 88 08 66 65

Bastia
Office de Tourisme
Place St-Nicolas, F-20200 Bastia
tel. 95 31 00 89

La Baule
Office de Tourisme
8 Place Victoire, F-44504 La Baule
tel. 40 24 34 44

Bayeux
Office de Tourisme
1 rue Cuisiniers, F-14400 Bayeux
tel. 31 92 16 26

Bayonne
Office de Tourisme
Place Liberté, F-64100 Bayonne
tel. 59 59 31 31

Beaugency
Office de Tourisme
28 Place Martroi, F-45190 Beaugency
tel. 38 44 54 42

Beaune
Office de Tourisme
opposite Hôtel-Dieu, F-21200 Beaune
tel. 80 22 24 51

Beauvais
Office de Tourisme
Rue Beauregard, F-60000 Beauvais
tel. 44 45 08 18

Belfort
Office de Tourisme
Passage de France, F-90000 Belfort
tel. 84 28 12 23

Bergerac
Office de Tourisme
97 rue Neuve-d'Argenson, F-24100 Bergerac
tel. 53 57 03 11

Besançon Office de Tourisme
2 Place 1ère-Armée-Française, F-25000 Besançon
tel. 81 80 92 55

Béziers Office de Tourisme
27 rue 4-Septembre, F-34500 Béziers
tel. 67 49 24 19

Biarritz Office de Tourisme
Square d'Ixelles, F-64200 Biarritz
tel. 59 24 20 24

Blois Office de Tourisme
3 Avenue J.-Laigret, F-41000 Blois
tel. 54 74 06 49

Bordeaux Office de Tourisme
12 Cours 30-Juillet, F-33080 Bordeaux
tel. 56 44 28 41

Boulogne-sur-Mer Office de Tourisme
Quai de la Poste, F-62200 Boulogne-sur-Mer
tel. 21 31 68 38

Bourganeuf Syndicat d'Initiative
Tour Lastic, F-23400 Bourganeuf
tel. 56 64 12 20

Bourg-en-Bresse Office de Tourisme
6 Avenue d'Alsace-Lorraine, F-01000 Bourg-en-Bresse
tel. 74 22 49 40

Bourges Office de Tourisme
21 rue Victor-Hugo, F-18000 Bourges
tel. 48 24 75 33

Brest Office de Tourisme
1 Place Liberté, F-29200 Brest
tel. 98 44 24 96

Briançon Office de Tourisme
Porte de Pignerol, F-05100 Briançon
tel. 92 21 08 50

Brioude Office de Tourisme
Place Champanne, F-43100 Brioude
tel. 71 74 97 49

Caen Office de Tourisme
Place St-Pierre, F-14300 Caen
tel. 31 86 27 65

Cagnes-sur-Mer Office de Tourisme
6 Boul. Mar.-Juin, F-06800 Cagnes-sur-Mer
tel. 93 20 61 64

Cahors Office de Tourisme
Place A.-Briand, F-46000 Cahors
tel. 66 35 09 56

Calais Office de Tourisme
12 Boul. Clemenceau, F-62100 Calais
tel. 21 96 62 40

Calvi
Office Municipal du Tourisme
Port de Plaisance, F-20260 Calvi
tel. 95 65 16 67

Cambrai
Office de Tourisme
48 rue de Noyon, F-59400 Cambrai
tel. 27 78 36 15

Cannes
Office de Tourisme
Esplanade Prés-Georges Pompidou, F-06400 Cannes
tel. 93 39 01 01

Carcassonne
Office de Tourisme
15 Boul. Camille-Pelletan, F-11012 Carcassonne
tel. 68 25 07 04

Carnac
Office de Tourisme
Avenue Druides, F-56340 Carnac
tel. 97 52 13 52

Carpentras
Office de Tourisme
170 Avenue J.-Jaurès, F-84200 Carpentras
tel. 90 63 00 78

Cauterets
Office de Tourisme
Place de l'Hôtel-de-Ville, F-66110 Cauterets
tel. 62 92 50 27

Cerbère
Syndicat d'Initiative
Front de Mer, F-66290 Cerbère
tel. 68 88 42 36

Céret
Syndicat d'Initiative
1 Avenue G.-Clémenceau, F-66400 Céret
tel. 68 87 00 53

Cergy-Pontoise
Office de Tourisme
6 Place Petit-Martroy, F-95300 Pontoise
tel. 30 38 24 25

Châlons-sur-Marne
Office de Tourisme
3 Quai des Arts, F-51000 Châlons-sur-Marne
tel. 26 65 17 89

Chambéry
Office de Tourisme
24 Boul. de la Colonne, F-73000 Chambéry
tel. 79 33 42 47

Chamonix
Office de Tourisme
Place Triangle-de-l'Amitié, F-74400 Chamonix
tel. 50 53 00 24

Chantilly
Office de Tourisme
23 Avenue Mar.-Joffre, F-60500 Chantilly
tel. 44 57 08 58

Chartres
Office de Tourisme
Place de la Cathédrale, F-28000 Chartres
tel. 37 21 50 00

Châteaudun
Office de Tourisme
1 rue de Luynes, F-28200 Châteaudun
tel. 37 45 22 46

Information

Chenonceaux	Syndicat d'Initiative Rue du Château, F-37150 Chenonceaux tel. 47 23 94 45
Cherbourg	Maison du Tourisme 2 Quai Alexandre-III, F-50100 Cherbourg tel. 33 43 52 02
Chinon	Office de Tourisme 12 rue Voltaire, F-37500 Chinon tel. 47 93 17 85
Clermont-Ferrand	Office de Tourisme 69 Boul. Gergovia, F-63000 Clermont-Ferrand tel. 73 93 30 20
Cluny	Office de Tourisme Rue Mercière, F-71250 Cluny tel. 85 59 05 34
Cognac	Office de Tourisme 19 Place J.-Monnet, F-16100 Cognac tel. 45 82 10 71
Collioure	Office de Tourisme Place 18-Juin, F-66190 Collioure tel. 68 82 15 47
Colmar	Office de Tourisme 4 rue Unterlinden, F-68000 Colmar tel. 89 20 68 92
Compiègne	Office de Tourisme Place de l'Hôtel-de-Ville, F-60321 Compiègne tel. 44 40 01 00
Condom	Syndicat d'Initiative Place Bossuet, F-32100 Condom tel. 62 28 00 80
Cordes	Syndicat d'Initiative Marie, F-81170 Cordes tel. 63 56 00 52
Corsica	See Ajaccio
Coutances	Office de Tourisme Place Georges Leclerc, F-50200 Coutances tel. 33 45 17 79
Dax	Office de Tourisme Place Thiers, F-40100 Dax tel. 58 90 20 00
Deauville	Office de Tourisme Place de la Mairie, F-14800 Deauville tel. 31 88 21 43
Dieppe	Office de Tourisme Quai du Carénage, F-76200 Dieppe tel. 35 84 11 77
Digne-les-Bains	Office de Tourisme Le Rond-Point, F-04000 Digne-les-Bains tel. 92 31 42 73

Dijon
Office de Tourisme
Place d'Arcy, F-21022 Dijon
tel. 80 43 42 12

Dinan
Office de Tourisme
6 rue de l'Horloge, F-22100 Dinan
tel. 96 39 75 40

Dinard
Office de Tourisme
2 Boul. Féart, F-35800 Dinard
tel. 99 46 94 12

Divonne-les-Bains
Office de Tourisme
Rue des Bains, F-01220 Divonne-les-Bains
tel. 50 20 01 22

Douai
Office de Tourisme
70 Place d'Armes, F-59500 Douai
tel. 27 88 26 79

Dunkirk (Dunkerque)
Office de Tourisme
Le Beffroi, rue de l'Admiral Ronarch, F-59140 Dunkerque
tel. 28 66 79 21

Elne
Office de Tourisme
Place de la République, F-66200 Elne
tel. 68 22 05 07

Epernay
Office de Tourisme
7 Avenue Champagne, F-51200 Epernay
tel. 26 55 33 00

Epinal
Office de Tourisme
13 rue de la Comédie, F-88000 Epinal
tel. 29 82 53 32

Espalion
Office de Tourisme
Boul. J.-Poulenc, F-12500 Espalion
tel. 65 44 10 63

Etretat
Office de Tourisme
Place M.-Guillard, F-76790 Etretat
tel. 35 27 05 21

Evian-les-Bains
Office de Tourisme
Place d'Allinges, F-74500 Evian-les-Bains
tel. 50 75 04 26

Evreux
Office de Tourisme
1 Place Gén.-de-Gaulle, F-27000 Evreux
tel. 32 24 04 43

Les Eyzies-de-Tayac
Syndicat d'Initiative
Place de la Mairie, F-24620 Les Eyzies-de-Tayac
tel. 53 06 97 05

Fécamp
Maison du Tourisme
113 rue Alexandre le Grand, F-76400 Fécamp
tel. 35 28 51 01

Figeac
Office de Tourisme
Place Vival, F-46100 Figeac
tel. 65 34 06 25

Foix	Office de Tourisme 45 Cours G.-Fauré, F-09000 Foix tel. 61 65 12 12
Fontainebleau	Office de Tourisme 31 Place N.-Bonaparte, F-77300 Fontainebleau tel. 64 22 25 68
Font-Romeu	Office de Tourisme Avenue E.-Brousse, F-66120 Font-Romeu tel. 68 30 02 74
Fréjus	Office de Tourisme Rue J.-Jaurès, F-83600 Fréjus tel. 94 51 54 14
Gap	Office de Tourisme 12 rue Faure de Serre, F-05000 Gap tel. 92 51 57 03
Gérardmer	Office de Tourisme Place des Déportés, F-88400 Gérardmer tel. 29 63 08 74
Gien	Office de Tourisme Centre Anne-de-Beaujeu, F-45500 Gien tel. 38 67 25 28
La Grande-Motte	Office de Tourisme Place de la Marie, F-34280 La Grande-Motte tel. 67 29 03 37
Grasse	Office de Tourisme 3 Place Foux, F-06130 Grasse tel. 93 36 03 56
Grenoble	Maison du Tourisme 14 rue de la République, F-38019 Grenoble tel. 76 54 34 36
Guebwiller	Office de Tourisme 5 Place St-Léger, F-68500 Guebwiller tel. 89 76 10 63
Haguenau	Office de Tourisme Place de la Gare, F-67500 Haguenau tel. 88 93 70 00
Le Havre	Office de Tourisme Forum Hôtel de Ville, F-76059 Le Havre tel. 35 21 22 88
Honfleur	Office de Tourisme Place A.-Boudin, F-14600 Honfleur tel. 31 89 23 30
Hyères	Office de Tourisme Rotonde J.-Salusse, Avenue Belgique, F-83400 Hyères tel. 94 65 18 55
Juan-les-Pins	Maison du Tourisme 51 Boul. Ch.-Guillaumont, F-06160 Juan-les-Pins tel. 93 61 04 98

Kaysersberg

Office de Tourisme
Avenue la Mairie, F-68240 Kaysersberg
tel. 89 78 22 78

Laon

Office de Tourisme
Place du Parvis, F-02000 Laon
tel. 23 20 28 62

Leucate

Syndicat d'Initiative
Centre Polyvalent, F-11370 Leucate
tel. 68 40 91 31

Lille

Office de Tourisme
Place Rihour, F-59002 Lille
tel. 20 30 81 00

Limoges

Office de Tourisme
Boulevard Fleurus, F-87000 Limoges
tel. 55 34 46 87

Lisieux

Office de Tourisme
11 rue d'Alençon, F-14100 Lisieux
tel. 31 62 08 41

Loches

Office de Tourisme
Place Wermelskirchen, F-37600 Loches
tel. 47 59 07 98

Lons-le-Saunier

Office de Tourisme
1 rue Pasteur, F-39000 Lons-le-Saunier
tel. 84 24 65 01

Lourdes

Office de Tourisme
Place Champ-Commun, F-65100 Lourdes
tel. 62 94 15 64

Luchon

Office de Tourisme
Allées Etigny, F-31110 Luchon
tel. 61 79 21 21

Lunéville

Office de Tourisme
Au Château, F-54300 Lunéville
tel. 83 74 06 55

Luz-St-Sauveur

Office de Tourisme
Place 8-Mai, F-65120 Luz-St-Sauveur
tel. 62 92 81 60

Lyons (Lyon)

Office de Tourisme
Place Bellecour, F-69214 Lyon
tel. 78 42 25 75

Le Mans

Office de Tourisme
Hôtel des Ursulines, Rue Etoile, F-72000 Le Mans
tel. 43 28 17 22

Marseilles (Marseille)

Office de Tourisme
4 Canebiére, F-13001 Marseille
tel. 91 54 91 11

Megève

Office de Tourisme
Rue de la Poste, F-74120 Megève
tel. 50 21 27 28

Mende	Syndicat d'Initiative Boul. H.-Bourillon, F-48000 Mende tel. 66 65 02 69
Menton	Office de Tourisme Palais de l'Europe 8 Avenue Boyer, F-06500 Menton tel. 93 57 57 00
Metz	Office de Tourisme Place d'Armes, F-57007 Metz tel. 87 75 65 21
Moissac	Office de Tourisme Place Durand-de-Bredon, F-82200 Moissac tel. 63 04 01 85
Molsheim	Office de Tourisme Place de l'Hôtel-de-Ville, F-67120 Molsheim tel. 88 38 11 61
Monaco	See Monte Carlo
Montauban	Office de Tourisme Ancien Collège, Place Prax, F-82000 Montauban tel. 63 63 60 60
Montbéliard	Office de Tourisme 1 rue H.-Mouhot, F-25200 Montbéliard tel. 81 94 45 60
Monte-Carlo	Direction du Tourisme et des Congrès 2A Boul. Moulins, MC-98030 Monte-Carlo tel. 92 16 61 66
Montélimar	Office de Tourisme Allées Champ-de-Mars, F-26200 Montélimar tel. 75 01 00 20
Montpellier	Office de Tourisme 78 Avenue Pirée, F-34000 Montpellier tel. 67 22 06 16
Mont-St-Michel	Office de Tourisme Corps de Garde des Bourgeois, F-50116 Mont-St-Michel tel. 33 60 14 30
Moulins	Office de Tourisme Place de l'Hôtel-de-Ville, F-03000 Moulins tel. 70 44 14 14
Mulhouse	Office de Tourisme 9 Avenue Mar.-Foch, F-68100 Mulhouse tel. 89 45 68 31
Munster	Office de Tourisme Place du Marché, F-68140 Munster tel. 89 77 31 80
Nancy	Office de Tourisme 14 Place Stanislas, F-54000 Nancy tel. 83 35 22 41

Nantes
Office de Tourisme
Place Commerce, F-44005 Nantes
tel. 40 47 04 51

Narbonne
Office de Tourisme
Place R.-Salengro, F-11100 Narbonne
tel. 68 65 15 60

Neuf-Brisach
Office de Tourisme
Place d'Armes, F-68600 Neuf-Brisach
tel. 89 72 56 66

Neufchâteau
Syndicat d'Initiative
Marie, F-88300 Neufchâteau
tel. 29 94 14 75

Nevers
Office de Tourisme
31 rue du Rempart, F-58000 Nevers
tel. 86 59 07 03

Nice
Office de Tourisme
Avenue Thiers, F-06000 Nice
tel. 93 87 07 07

Nîmes
Office de Tourisme
6 rue Auguste, F-30000 Nîmes
tel. 66 67 29 11

Noirmoutier (Ile de Noirmoutier)
Office de Tourisme
Route du Pont, F-85330 Noirmoutier-en-l'Ile
tel. 51 39 80 71

Noyon
Office de Tourisme
Place de l'Hôtel-de-la-Ville, F-60400 Noyon
tel. 44 44 21 88

Obernai
Office de Tourisme
Chapelle du Beffroi, F-67210 Obernai
tel. 88 95 64 13

Oléron (Ile d'Oléron)
Office de Tourisme
Place de la République, F-17480 Le Château-d'Oloron
tel. 46 47 60 51

Oloron-Ste-Marie
Office de Tourisme
Place de la Résistance, F-64400 Oloron-Ste-Marie
tel. 59 39 98 00

Orange
Office de Tourisme
Cours A.-Briand, F-84100 Orange
tel. 90 34 70 88

Orléans
Office de Tourisme
Place Albert-1er, F-45000 Orléans
tel. 38 53 05 95

Orthez
Office de Tourisme
Maison Jeanne-d'Albret, F-64300 Orthez
tel. 59 69 02 75

Paris
Office de Tourisme et des Congrès
127 Avenue des Champs-Elysées, F-75008 Paris
tel. 49 52 53 54

Pau	Office de Tourisme Place Royale, F-64000 Pau tel. 59 27 27 08
Périgueux	Syndicat d'Initiative 26 Place Francheville, F-24000 Périgueux tel. 53 53 10 63
Perpignan	Office de Tourisme Palais des Congrès, Place A.-Lanoux tel. 68 66 30 30
Perros-Guirec	Office de Tourisme 21 Place de l'Hôtel-de-la-Ville, F-22700 Perros-Guirec tel. 96 23 21 15
Plombières-les-Bains	Office de Tourisme Rue Stanislas, F-88370 Plombières-les-Bains tel. 29 66 01 30
Poitiers	Office de Tourisme 8 rue Grandes-Ecoles, F-86000 Poitiers tel. 49 41 21 24
Pontarlier	Office de Tourisme 56 rue de la République, F-25300 Pontarlier tel. 81 46 48 33
Pontoise	See Cergy-Pontoise
Pornic	Office de Tourisme Quai du Commandant l'Herminier, F-44210 Pornic tel. 40 82 04 40
Port-Barcarès	Office de Tourisme Front de Mer, F-66420 Port-Barcarès tel. 68 86 16 56
Provins	Office de Tourisme Place H.-de Balzac, F-77160 Provins tel. 64 00 16 65
Le Puy-en-Velay	Office de Tourisme Place du Breuil, F-43000 Le Puy-en-Velay tel. 71 09 38 41
Quiberon	Office de Tourisme 7 rue Verdun, F-56170 Quiberon tel. 97 50 07 84
Quimper	Office de Tourisme Place Résistance, F-29000 Quimper tel. 98 53 04 05
Ré (Ile de Ré)	Syndicat d'Initiative Place Carnot, F-17590 Ars-en-Ré tel. 46 29 46 09
Reims	Office de Tourisme 2 rue Guillaume-de-Machault, F-51100 Reims tel. 26 47 25 69
Remiremont	Office de Tourisme 2 Place H.-Utard, F-88200 Remiremont tel. 29 62 23 70

Rennes

Office de Tourisme
Pont de Nemours, F-35025 Rennes
tel. 99 79 01 98

Ribeauvillé

Office de Tourisme
Grand' Rue, F-68150 Ribeauvillé
tel. 89 73 62 22

Rocamadour

Office de Tourisme
Avenue la Mairie, F-46500 Rocamadour
tel. 65 33 62 59

La Rochelle

Office de Tourisme
Place de la Petite Sirène, F-17000 La Rochelle
tel. 46 41 14 68

Rodez

Office de Tourisme
Place Foch, F-12000 Rodez
tel. 65 68 02 27

Roscoff

Maison du Tourisme
46 rue Gambetta, F-29680 Roscoff
tel. 98 61 12 13

Rosheim

Syndicat d'Initiative
Avenue la Mairie, F-67560 Rosheim
tel. 88 50 75 38

Rouen

Office de Tourisme
25 Place de la Cathédrale, F-76008 Rouen
tel. 35 71 41 77

Royan

Office de Tourisme
Palais des Congrès, F-17200 Royan
tel. 46 38 65 11

Le Rozier

Syndicat d'Initiative
F-48150 Le Rozier
tel. 65 62 60 89

Les Sables-d'Olonne

Office de Tourisme
Rue Mar.-Leclerc, F-85100 Les Sables-d'Olonne
tel. 51 32 03 28

Saint-Claude

Office de Tourisme
1 Avenue Belfort, F-39200 Saint-Claude
tel. 84 45 34 24

Saint-Denis

Office de Tourisme
2 rue Légion-d'Honneur, F-93200 Saint-Denis
tel. 42 43 33 55

Saint-Dié

Office de Tourisme
31 rue Thiers, F-88100 Saint-Dié
tel. 29 55 17 62

Sainte-Enimie

Office de Tourisme
Marie, F-48210 Sainte-Enimie
tel. 66 48 53 44

Saint-Emilion

Office de Tourisme
Place Créneaux, F-33330 Saint-Emilion
tel. 57 24 72 03

Saintes	Office de Tourisme 62 Cours National, F-17100 Saintes tel. 46 74 23 82
Saintes-Maries-de-la-Mer	Office de Tourisme Avenue Van Gogh, F-13460 Saintes-Maries-de-la-Mer tel. 90 47 82 55
Saint-Etienne	Office de Tourisme Place Roannelle, F-42000 Saint-Etienne tel. 77 25 12 14
Saint-Germain-en-Laye	Office de Tourisme 38 rue Au Pain, F-78100 Saint-Germain-en-Laye tel. 34 51 05 12
Saint-Jean-de-Luz	Office de Tourisme Place Mar.-Foch, F-64500 Saint-Jean-de-Luz tel. 59 26 03 16
Saint-Malo	Office de Tourisme Esplanade St-Vincent, F-35400 Saint-Malo tel. 99 56 64 48
Saint-Nazaire	Office de Tourisme Place F.-Blancho, F-44600 Saint-Nazaire tel. 40 22 40 65
Saint-Nizier-du-Moucherotte	Syndicat d'Initiative F-38250 Saint-Nizier-du-Moucherotte tel. 76 53 40 60
Saint-Omer	Office de Tourisme Boul. P.-Guillain, F-62500 Saint-Omer tel. 21 98 70 00
Saint-Paul	Office de Tourisme Maison Tour, Rue Grande, F-06570 Saint-Paul tel. 93 32 86 95
Saint-Quay-Portrieux	Office de Tourisme 17 bis rue Jeanne d'Arc, F-22410 Saint-Quay-Portrieux tel. 96 70 40 64
Saint-Quentin	Office de Tourisme Espace St.-Jacques, 14 rue Sellerie, F-02100 Saint-Quentin tel. 23 67 05 00
Saint-Rémy-de-Provence	Office de Tourisme Place J.-Jaurès. F-13210 Saint-Rémy-de-Provence tel. 90 92 05 22
Saint-Tropez	Office de Tourisme Quai J.-Jaurès, F-83990 Saint-Tropez tel. 94 97 45 21
Salins-les-Bains	Syndicat d'Initiative Place Salines, F-39110 Salins-les-Bains tel. 84 73 01 34
Salon-de-Provence	Office de Tourisme 56 Cours Gimon, F-13300 Salon-de-Provence tel. 90 56 27 60

Sancerre
Syndicat d'Initiative
Hôtel de Ville, F-18300 Sancerre
tel. 48 54 00 26

Sarlat-la-Canéda
Office de Tourisme
Place de la Liberté, F-24200 Sarlat-la-Canéda
tel. 53 59 27 67

Sarrebourg
Office de Tourisme
Chapelle des Cordeliers, F-57400 Sarrebourg
tel. 87 03 11 82

Saumur
Office de Tourisme
Place Bilange, F-49415 Saumur
tel. 41 51 03 06

Sedan
Office de Tourisme
Parking du Château, F-08200 Sedan
tel. 24 27 73 73

Sélestat
Office de Tourisme
La Commanderie, Boul. Gén.-Leclerc, F-67600 Sélestat
tel. 88 92 02 66

Senlis
Office de Tourisme
Place Parvis-Notre-Dame, F-60300 Senlis
tel. 44 53 06 40

Sens
Office de Tourisme
Place J.-Jaurès, F-89100 Sens
tel. 86 65 19 49

Sète
Office de Tourisme
60 Grand' Rue Mario-Roustan, F-34200 Sète
tel. 67 74 71 71

Sisteron
Office de Tourisme
Hôtel de Ville, F-04200 Sisteron
tel. 92 61 12 03

Soissons
Office de Tourisme
1 Avenue Gén.-Leclerc, F-02200 Soissons
tel. 23 53 08 27

La Souterraine
Syndicat d'Initiative
Place de la Gare, F-23300 La Souterraine
tel. 55 63 10 06

Strasbourg
Office de Tourisme
17 Place de la Cathédrale, F-67082 Strasbourg
tel. 88 52 28 22

Sully-sur-Loire
Office de Tourisme
Place Gén.-de-Gaulle, F-45600 Sully-sur-Loire
tel. 38 36 23 70

Tarascon
Office de Tourisme
59 rue des Halles, F-13150 Tarascon
tel. 90 91 03 52

Tarbes
Syndicat d'Initiative
3 Cours Gambetta, F-65000 Tarbes
tel. 62 51 30 31

Thann	Office de Tourisme 6 Place Joffre, F-68800 Thann tel. 89 37 96 20
Thonon-les-Bains	Office de Tourisme Place du Marché, F-74200 Thonon-les-Bains tel. 50 71 55 55
Tignes	Office de Tourisme Au Lac, F-73320 Tignes tel. 79 06 15 55
Toul	Office de Tourisme Parvis de la Cathédrale, F-54200 Toul tel. 83 64 11 69
Toulon	Office de Tourisme 8 Avenue Colbert, F-83000 Toulon tel. 94 22 08 22
Toulouse	Office de Tourisme Donjon du Capitole, F-31000 Toulouse tel. 61 11 02 22
Tours	Office de Tourisme Place Mar.-Leclerc, F-37042 Tours tel. 47 05 58 08
Troyes	Office de Tourisme 16 Boul. Carnot, F-10014 Troyes tel. 25 73 00 36
Tulle	Office de Tourisme Quai Baluze, F-19000 Tulle tel. 55 26 59 61
Uzerche	Office de Tourisme Place Lunade, F-19140 Uzerche tel. 55 73 15 71
Uzès	Office de Tourisme Avenue de la Libération, F-30700 Uzès tel. 66 22 68 88
Vaison-la-Romains	Office de Tourisme Place Chanoine-Sautel, F-84110 Vaison-la-Romaine tel. 90 36 02 11
Val d'Isère	Office de Tourisme Maison de Val d'Isère, F-73150 Val d'Isère tel. 79 06 10 83
Valençay	Office de Tourisme Hôtel de Ville, F-36600 Valençay tel. 54 00 14 33
Valenciennes	Office de Tourisme 1 rue Askièvre, F-59300 Valenciennes tel. 27 46 22 99
Vannes	Office de Tourisme 1 rue Thiers, F-56000 Vannes tel. 97 47 24 34

Vence
Office de Tourisme
Place Grand-Jardin, F-06140 Vence
tel. 93 58 06 38

Vendôme
Office de Tourisme
47-49 rue de la Poterie, F-41100 Vendôme
tel. 54 77 05 07

Verdun
Office de Tourisme
Place de la Nation, F-55100 Verdun
tel. 29 86 14 18

Vernon
Office de Tourisme
36 rue Carnot, F-27200 Vernon
tel. 32 51 39 60

Versailles
Office de Tourisme
7 rue Réservoirs, F-78000 Versailles
tel. 39 50 36 22

Vichy
Office de Tourisme
19 rue du Parc, F-03200 Vichy
tel. 70 98 71 94

Villard-de-Lans
Office de Tourisme
Place Mure-Ravaud, F-38250 Villard-de-Lans
tel. 76 95 10 38

Vitré
Office de Tourisme
Promenade St-Yves, F-35500 Vitré
tel. 99 75 04 46

Vittel
Syndicat d'Initiative
Avenue Bouloumié, F-88800 Vittel
tel. 29 08 08 88

Wissembourg
Office de Tourisme
Place de la République, F-67160 Wissembourg
tel. 88 94 10 11

Insurance

General

Visitors are strongly advised to ensure that they have adequate holiday insurance including loss or damage to luggage, loss of currency and jewellery.

Health

British citizens, like nationals of other European Community countries, are entitled to obtain medical care under the French health services on the same basis as French people. This means that they must pay the cost of treatment and medicine but are reimbursed 75% of the cost of medical or dental treatment and 40–70% of most prescribed medicines through the local sickness insurance office (*caisse primaire d'assurance-maladie*). Before leaving home they should obtain form E111 from post offices, which certifies their entitlement to insurance cover and must be presented to the sickness insurance office when seeking reimbursement. It is nevertheless advisable, even for EC nationals, to take out some form of short-term health insurance providing complete cover and possibly avoiding delays. Nationals of non-EC countries should certainly have insurance cover.

Vehicles

Visitors travelling by car should be ensure that their insurance is comprehensive and covers use of the vehicle in France.

See also Travel Documents.

Language

French developed out of Vulgar Latin, the colloquial form of classical Latin, which was spoken by the Celtic peoples of Gaul after their conquest by the Romans. Although incorporating many words of Celtic and later of Germanic origin, it preserved its basically Latin structure, and was for centuries the most important of the Romance languages, widely spoken in educated circles throughout Europe and used in diplomatic intercourse. Although it is the mother tongue of no more than 80 million people it is still one of the leading languages of the world, taught in schools all over the world and used over large areas as the language of commerce and communication. Although English is widely spoken in France, particularly by those concerned in any way with the tourist trade, visitors will get more out of their holiday if they know at least some French. A small dictionary or phrase-book will be found helpful; the following paragraphs of this Guide can give only the essential minimum of vocabulary.

Provençal

In southern France Provençal, a language which is also derived from Latin but differs considerably from French, is still spoken by many people. The language of the south became known as the *langue d'oc* – hence the name of the southern province of Languedoc – as distinct from the *langue d'oïl* spoken in the north; the two terms come from the different forms of the word for "yes" (modern French *oui).*

The principal characteristics of Provençal are the maintenance of *a* in an open syllable (*pra,* compared with French *pré,* from Latin *pratum*); the change of this *a* to *ié* where French has *é (marchié,* compared with French *marché,* from Latin *mercatum*); the existence of four terminal vowels (*a, e, i* and *o,* with Provençal *a* and *e* corresponding to French *e*); the ending *-o* in the first person of the verb; the regional distinction between nominative and accusative; and the development of certain sounds peculiar to Provençal.

Other languages

In Alsace and parts of Lorraine a dialect of German *(Elsässerditsch)* is widely spoken; in Corsica a Central Italian dialect peculiar to the island; in Brittany the Breton language *(Brezonnek),* an offshoot of the British branch of the Celtic languages; and in the extreme south-west of France the non-Indo-European Basque language *(Euskara).*

Pronunciation of French

Characteristic features are the placing of the stress towards the end of the word and the frequent nasalisation of vowels.

Vowels (always pronounced without the diphthongisation found in English): *ai* like English *ay; ais* an open *e* as in "bed"; *é* like *ay; è* and *ê* an open *e; an, en, em* at the end of a syllable like a nasalised *on* (not quite *ong); un, im, in, ein* at the end of a syllable like a nasalised *un* (not quite *ung); eu* a little like the *u* in "fur"; *oi, oy* like *wa; ou* like *oo; u* a sound obtained by pronouncing *ee* with rounded lips.

Consonants: *c* before *e, i* or *y* and *ç* before other vowels, like *s; c* before *a, o* or *u* like *k;* j and *g* before *e, i* or *y,* like *zh; g* before *a, o* or *u* like a hard English *g; ch* like *sh; gn* usually like *ny* in "canyon"; *h* always silent; *ll* between vowels often palatalised to a consonantal *y* sound, but sometimes a light *l* (e.g. in *elle*); *q, qu* like *k.*

The following letters are usually silent at the end of a word (and often also at the end of a syllable): *d, e, r* (only after *e*), *s, t, x, z.*

Numbers

0 zéro
1 un, une
2 deux
3 trois
4 quatre
5 cinq
6 six
7 sept
8 huit
9 neuf

10 dix
11 onze
12 douze
13 treize
14 quatorze
15 quinze
16 seize
17 dix-sept
18 dix-huit
19 dix-neuf
20 vingt
21 vingt et un
22 vingt-deux
30 trente
40 quarante
50 cinquante
60 soixante
70 soixante-dix
71 soixante et onze
80 quatre-vingt(s)
81 quatre-vingt-un
90 quatre-vingt-dix
91 quatre-vingt-onze
100 cent
101 cent un
153 cent cinquante trois
200 deux cent(s)
300 trois cent(s)
400 quatre cent(s)
500 cinq cent(s)
1000 mille
1001 mille un
2000 deux mille
1,000,000 un million

Ordinals

1st premier, première
2nd deuxième second(e)
3rd troisième
4th quatrième
5th cinquième
6th sixième
7th septième
8th huitième
9th neuvième
10th dixième
11th onzième
12th douzième
100th centième

Fractions

½ demi(e)   ⅓ tiers   ¼ quart   ¾ trois quarts

Useful Expressions

When addressing anyone it is usual to add the polite *Monsieur, Madame* or *Mademoiselle,* and any request or enquiry should be accompanied by *s'il vous plaît* ("please").

Good morning, good day!	Bonjour!
Good evening!	Bonsoir!
Good night!	Bonne nuit!
Goodbye	Au revoir
Do you speak English?	Parlez-vous anglais?
I do not understand	Je ne comprends pas
Yes	Oui
No	Non
Please	S'il vous plaît
Thank you	Merci
Yesterday	Hier
Today	Aujourd'hui
Tomorrow	Demain
Help!	Au secours!
Have you a single room?	Avez-vous une chambre à un lit?
Have you a double room?	Avez-vous une chambre à deux lits?
Have you a room with private bath?	Avez-vous une chambre avec bain?
How much does it cost?	Combien (est-ce que) ça coûte?
Quel est le prix de . . .?	
Please wake me at 6	Veuillez me réveiller à six heures
Where is the lavatory?	Où sont les toilettes?
Where is the chemist's?	Où est la pharmacie?

Where is the post office?	Où est la poste?
Where is there a doctor?	Où y a-t-il un médecin?
Where is there a dentist?	Où y a-t-il un dentiste?
Is this the way to the station?	Est-ce le chemin de la gare?

Months, Days of the Week, Festivals

Months	January	Janvier
	February	Février
	March	Mars
	April	Avril
	May	Mai
	June	Juin
	July	Juillet
	August	Août
	September	Septembre
	October	Octobre
	November	Novembre
	December	Décembre
Days of the week	Sunday	Dimanche
	Monday	Lundi
	Tuesday	Mardi
	Wednesday	Mercredi
	Thursday	Jeudi
	Friday	Vendredi
	Saturday	Samedi
	Day	Jour, journée
	Public holiday	Jour de fête
Festivals	New Year	Nouvel An
	Easter	Pâques
	Ascension	Ascension
	Whitsun	Pentecôte
	Corpus Christi	Fête-Dieu
	Assumption	Assomption
	All Saints	Toussaint
	Christmas	Noël
	New Year's Eve	La Saint-Sylvestre

Food and Drink

See the section on Food and Drink on page 535.

Road and Traffic Signs

Attention!	Caution
Au pas!	Dead slow
Bouchon	Tailback
Brouillard	Fog
Centre ville	To town centre
Chantier	Road works
Danger (de mort)	Danger (of death)
Déviation	Diversion
Douane	Customs
Fin de limitation de vitesse	End of speed restriction
Frontière	Frontier
Garage	Parking; passing place
Gravier, gravillons	Loose stones, gravel

Halte!	Stop
Impasse	No through road; cul-de-sac
Limitation de vitesse	Speed restriction
Passage interdit!	No entry, no thoroughfare
Passage protégé	You have priority at junction ahead
Poids lourds	Heavy loads
Priorité à droite	Traffic coming from right has priority
Prudence!	Drive with care
Ralentir, ralentissez!	Reduce speed now
Route barrée	Road closed
Sens unique	One-way street
Serrez à droite	Keep in to the right
Sortie de camions	Trucks crossing
Tenez vos distances!	Keep your distance
Toutes directions	All directions
Travaux	Road works
Verglas	Black ice
Virage (dangereux)	(Dangerous) bend
Voie unique	Single-lane traffic
Zone bleue	Parking only with parking disc
Zone rouge	"Red zone": parking prohibited
Mise en fourrière immédiate	Parked cars may be towed away

Rail and Air Travel

Airport	Aéroport
All aboard!	En voiture!
Arrival	Arrivée
Baggage	Bagages
Baggage check	Bulletin de bagages
Bus station	Gare routière
Couchette	Couchette
Departure	Départ
Flight	Vol
Halt	Arrêt
Information	Information, renseignements
Lavatory	Toilette(s)
Left luggage office	Consigne
Line (railway)	Voie
Luggage	Bagages
Non-smoking	Non-fumeurs
Platform	Quai
Porter	Porteur
Restaurant-car	Wagon-restaurant
Sleeping-car	Wagon-lit
Smoking	Fumeurs
Station	Gare
Stewardess	Hôtesse (de l'air)
Stop	Arrêt
Ticket	Billet, ticket
Ticket collector	Contrôleur
Ticket window	Guichet
Timetable	Horaire
Train	Train
Waiting room	Salle d'attente
Window seat	Coin fenêtre

At the Post Office

Address	Adresse

Express	Exprès
Letter	Lettre
Letter-box	Boîte à lettres
Parcel	Paquet, colis
Postcard	Carte postale
Poste restante	Poste restante
Postman	Facteur
Registered	Recommandé
Small packet	Petit paquet
Stamp	Timbre(-poste)
Telegram	Télégramme
Telephone	Téléphone
Telex	Télex

Topographical Terms

Abbaye	Abbey
Aiguille	Pinnacle, crag
Anse	Bay
Archevêché	Archbishop's palace
Archipel	Archipelago
Arènes	Amphitheatre
Auberge	Inn
Autoroute	Motorway
Avenue	Avenue
Bac	Ferry
Baie	Bay
Bain	Bath(s)
Banlieue	Suburb(s)
Barrage	Dam
Basilique	Church (usually one of particular dignity)
Bassin	Dock; ornamental lake, pond
Belvédère	Viewpoint
Bibliothèque	Library
Bois	Wood
Boulevard	Boulevard, avenue
Bourse	(Stock) exchange
Butte	Low hill, bluff
Calvaire	Calvary
Camping	Camping site
Capitainerie	Harbourmaster's office
Carrefour	Road intersection
Carrière	Quarry
Cascade	Waterfall
Cathédrale	Cathedral
Causse	Limestone plateau
Cave	Cellar
Caverne	Cave
Chaîne	Chain, range (of hills)
Chalet	Chalet; mountain hut
Champ	Field
Chaos	Tumble of rocks
Chapelle	Chapel
Chartreuse	Charterhouse
Château	Castle, country house, manor-house
Château-fort	(Fortified) castle
Chemin	Road, track
Chemin de fer	Railway
Cime	Peak, summit
Cimetière	Cemetery

Citadelle	Citadel
Cité	City (often the old part of a town)
Cité universitaire	University residence(s)
Clocher	(Bell-)tower
Cloître	Cloister
Clos	Enclosure, field, vineyard
Cluse	Gorge
Col	Pass
Collégiale	Collegiate church
Colline	Hill
Colonne	Column
Combe	Valley, combe
Comté	County
Corniche	Corniche road (along side of hill)
Côte	Coast; slope (of hill)
Côté	Side
Coteau	Slope, hillside
Cour	Courtyard
Cours	Avenue
Cours d'eau	River, watercourse
Couvent	Convent, religious house
Crête	Crest, ridge (of hill)
Défilé	Defile, gorge
Dent	Crag, pinnacle (of mountain)
Dolmen	Megalithic tomb
Dôme	Dome; rounded hill
Donjon	Keep
Ecluse	Lock (on canal)
Ecole	School
Ecole normale	Teachers' training college
Embouchure	Estuary, mouth (of river)
Escalier	Staircase
Est	East
Estuaire	Estuary
Etablissement thermal	Spa establishment
Etang	Pond, lake
Evêché	Bishop's palace
Falaise	Cliff
Faubourg	Suburb, outer district of town
Fleuve	River (flowing into sea)
Fontaine	Fountain
Forêt	Forest
Forêt domaniale	State forest
Fort	Fort
Forteresse	Fortress
Fosse	Pit; grave
Fossé	Ditch; moat
Gare	Railway station
Gare routière	Bus station
Gave	Mountain stream (in Pyrenees)
Glacier	Glacier
Golf	Golf-course
Golfe	Gulf, bay
Gorge	Gorge
Gouffre	Chasm, swallowhole
Grotte	Cave
Gué	Ford
Halle	Market hall
Hameau	Hamlet
Hauteur	Height, hill
Hippodrome	Racecourse
Hôpital	Hospital

Horloge	Clock
Hôtel	Hotel; aristocratic mansion
Hôtel de ville	Town hall
Ile	Island
Ilot	Islet
Impasse	Cul-de-sac
Jardin	Garden
Jardin des plantes	Botanic garden
Lac	Lake
Lagune	Lagoon
Lande	Heath
Logis	Lodging
Lycée	Grammar school
Mairie	Town hall
Maison	House
Manoir	Manor-house
Maquis	Scrub(land)
Marais	Marsh, bog
Marché	Market
Mare	Pool
Marécage	Marsh, bog
Mas	Farmhouse (in Provence)
Menhir	Standing stone
Mer	Sea
Monastère	Monastery
Monnaie	Mint
Mont	Mount(ain)
Montagne	Mountain
Moulin	Mill
Mur, muraille	Wall
Musée	Museum
Nef	Nave (of church)
Nez	Nose, cape
Nord	North
Oratoire	Oratory
Ouest	West
Palais	Palace
Palais de justice	Law courts
Parc	Park
Passerelle	Footbridge
Pays	Country
Phare	Lighthouse
Pic	Peak
Piscine	Swimming pool
Place	Square
Plage	Beach
Plaine	Plain
Plâteau	Plateau
Pointe	Cape, point; peak (of hill)
Pont	Bridge
Porche	Porch
Port	Port, harbour
Portail	Doorway
Porte	Door
Poste	Post office
Prairie, pré	Meadow
Presqu'île	Peninsula
Prieuré	Priory
Promontoire	Promontory
PTT	Post office
Puits	Well
Quai	Quay; embankment

Quartier	Quarter, district (of a town)
Rade	Anchorage, roadsteads
Refuge	Traffic island; mountain hut
Remparts	Ramparts
Rivière	River (not flowing into sea)
Roc, roche, rocher	Rock
Rond-point	Roundabout
Route	Road
Ru	Stream
Rue	Street
Ruisseau	Stream
Sable	Sand
Saline	Salt-pan
Salle	Hall, room
Saut	Waterfall
Sente, sentier	Path
Source	Spring; source of river
Square	Public square with gardens
Stade	Stadium
Station	Resort; station
Station thermale	Spa, health resort
Sud	South
Syndicat d'initiative	Tourist information office
Téléférique	Cableway
Télésiège	Chair-lift
Téléski	Ski-lift
Temple	Temple; Protestant church
Thermes	Baths
Tombe, tombeau	Tomb
Torrent	Mountain stream
Tour	Tower
Trésor	Treasure, treasury
Tribunal	Law court
Trottoir	Pavement
Trou	Hole
Tunnel	Tunnel
Université	University
Val, vallée, vallon	Valley
Viaduc	Viaduct
Village	Village
Ville	Town

Leisure Parks and Fun Pools

Modern leisure facilities, entertainment parks and fun pools are springing up all over France. The following is a selection from the many leisure parks and pools listed by the Syndicat National des Parcs de Loisirs et d'Attraction (for address, see below):

Leisure parks in Paris
1 Jardin d'Acclimatation, Bois de Boulogne
Planète Magique, Théâtre de la Gaîté Lyrique, 3 bus rue Papin
Parisbas, 3 rue Dantin
Aquafun, 58 rue Corvisart
Parc Floral de Paris, 16 Route de la Brasserie
Aquaboulevard, 4-6 rue Louis-Armand
Parc Océanique Cousteau, Forum des Halles
(entrance on Bourse du Commerce side)

Leisure parks round Paris
2 Parc Astérix, Plailly (38 km/24 miles north)

Mirapolis adventure park

Mirapolis, Cergy-Pontoise (30 km/19 miles north-west)
Euro Disneyland, Marne-la-Vallée (30 km/19 miles east)
Parc de St-Vrain, St-Vrain, nr Arpajon (34 km/21 miles south)
Babyland, St-Pierre-du-Perray, Corbeil (30 km/19 miles south-east)
Parc Aquatique, Levallois-Perret (north-west)
Aqualand, Gif-sur-Yvette, nr Roissy (20 km/12 miles south-east)
Réserve Africaine et Parc Zoologique et de Loisirs, Thiory (west of Paris, on D11)
Le Pays France Miniature, Elancourt (not far from the Versailles Palace)

Leisure parks elsewhere in France

3 Blockhaus d'Eperlecques, Moulle (south-west of Dunkirk)

4 Bal Loisirs, Tournehem-sur-la-Hem, nr Nordausques (25 km/15 miles south of Calais)

5 Bagatelle, Merlimont (between Le Touquet and Berck, on D940)

6 Aqualand, Le Touquet

7 Agora, Berck

8 Aqualand, Marquenterre, Fort-Mahon-Plage (13 km/8 miles north-west of Rue, 40 km/25 miles north of Abbeville)

9 Le Moulin de la Tour, Dennebrœucq, nr Fauquembergues (22 km/14 miles south-west of St-Omer)

10 La Chanterelle, Verlinghem (7 km/4 miles north-west of Lille)

11 Forest Hill Nauticlub, Marcq-en-Barœul (between Lille and Roubaix)

12 Lillom, Château d'Isenghien, Lomme (5 km/3 miles from Lille)

13 Le Fleury, Wavrechain (18 km/11 miles south-west of Valenciennes)

14 Le Tiffany's, Anzouville-sur-Saône, Bacqueville-en-Caux (19 km/12 miles south-west of Dieppe)

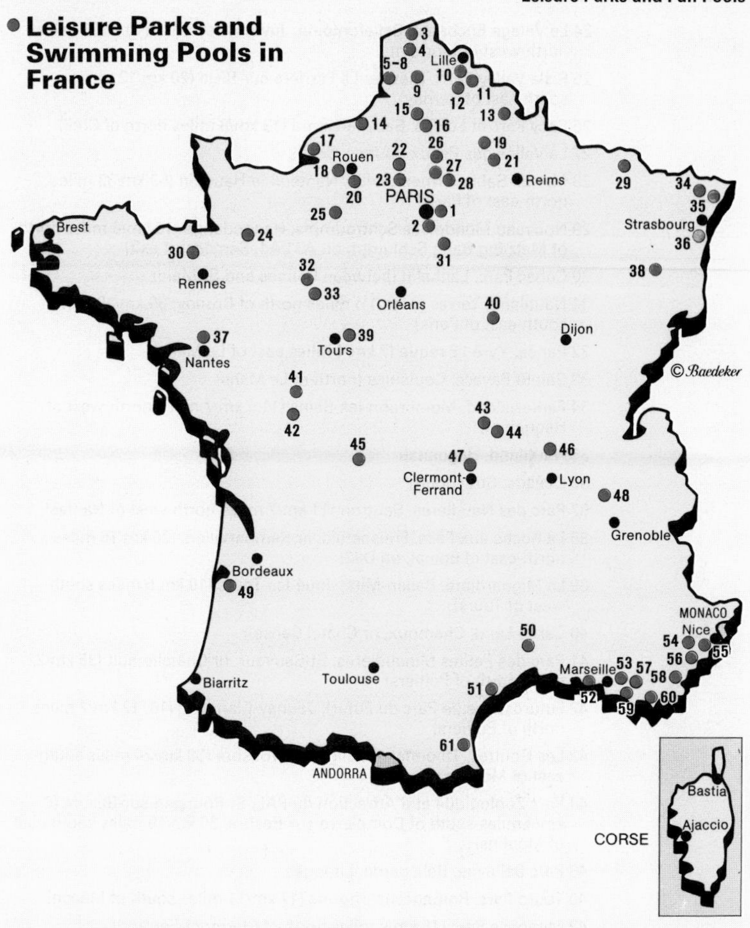

15 Grottes de Naours, 13 km/8 miles north of Amiens

16 Jules Verne, Amiens

17 Canyon Park, Epretot, nr St-Romain-de-Colbosc (20 km/12 miles east of Le Havre)

18 Parc du Bocasse, Clères (25 km/15 miles north of Rouen)

19 Domaine des Isles, Offoy (20 km/12 miles west of St-Quentin)

20 Parc Océade, Rouen

21 Fort de Vendeuil and Parc du Fort de Vendeuil, Vendeuil, La Fère (24 km/15 miles north of Laon)

22 Parc d'Hérouval, Chaumont-en-Vexin (8 km/5 miles east of Gisors)

23 Le Bois d'Hérouval, Monjavoult (9 km/6 miles south of Gisors)

24 Le Village Enchanté, Bellefontaine, Juvigny-le-Tertre (10 km/6 miles north-west of Mortain)

25 Risle Valley Parc, Thevray-La Ferrière-sur-Risle (20 km/12 miles south-east of Bernay)

26 Sacy Parc et Loisirs, Sacy-le-Grand (13 km/8 miles north of Creil)

27 La Vallée des Peaux Rouges, Senlis

28 Mer de Sable, Ermenonville, Nanteuil-le-Haudoin (53 km/33 miles north-east of Paris)

29 Nouveau Monde des Schtroumpfs, Hagondange (10 km/6 miles north of Metz Big Bang Schlumpf, on A31/A4, Semécourt exit)

30 Cobac Parc, Lanhelin (between Rennes and St-Malo)

31 Nautiland, Yerres (2 km/1½ miles north of Brunoy, 30 km/19 miles south-east of Paris)

32 Papéa, Yvré-l'Evêque (7 km/4 miles east of Le Mans)

33 Sainte-Pavace, Coulaines (north of Le Mans)

34 Fantasialand, Morsbronn-les-Bains (11.5 km/7 miles north-west of Haguenau)

35 Nautiland, Haguenau

36 Océade, Strasbourg

37 Parc des Naudières, Sautron (11 km/7 miles north-west of Nantes)

38 La Roche aux Fées, Fraispetuis, nr Rambervillers (26 km/16 miles north-east of Epinal, on D32)

39 La Mignardière, Ballan-Miré, Joué-lès-Tours (10 km/6 miles south-west of Tours)

40 Cardo Land, Chamoux, nr Châtel Censoir

41 Parc des Petites Minaudières, St-Sauveur, nr Châtellerault (35 km/22 miles north of Poitiers)

42 Futuroscope (le Parc du Futur), Jaunay-Clan (on N10, 12 km/7 miles north of Poitiers)

43 Les Gouttes, Thionne, nr Jaligny-sur-Besbre (38 km/24 miles south-east of Moulins)

44 Parc Zoologique et d'Attraction du PAL, St-Pourçain-sur-Besbre (6 km/4 miles south of Dompierre-sur-Besbre, 30 km/19 miles south-east of Moulins)

45 Parc Bellevue, Bellegarde, Limoges

46 Touro Parc, Romanèche-Thorins (17 km/11 miles south of Mâcon)

47 Mirabelle Parc (15 km/9 miles north of Clermont-Ferrand)

48 Avenir Land, Les Avenières (17 km/9 miles north-east of La Tour-du-Pin, on D40, 55 km/34 miles east of Lyons)

49 Préhisto Parc, Les Eyzies-de-Tayac

50 Aquacity, Gujan-Mestras (10 km/6 miles from Arcachon)

51 Nauticlub, Nímes

52 Aqualand, Cap d'Agde

53 Aquacity, Pennes-Mirabeau (between Marseilles and Aix-en-Provence)

54 Aquacity, Septèmes-les-Vallons (12 km/7 miles north of Marseilles)

55 Parc de St-Paul, St-Paul (9 km/6 miles north of Cagnes-sur-Mer)

56 Zygofolis, Crémat, nr Nice

57 Aquaplash (Marineland), Antibes

58 Corral, Cuges-les-Pins (26 km/16 miles east of Marseilles)

59 Aquatica, Fréjus

60 Aqualand, St-Cyr-sur-Mer (9 km/6 miles east of La Ciotat)

61 Aquatica, Hyères

62 Aquacity de St-Cyprien, St-Cyprien (13 km/8 miles south-east of Perpignan)

63 Aqua-Cymé Gliss, Porticcio (south of Ajaccio, Corsica)

Information

Syndicat National des Parcs de Loisirs et d'Attraction (SNPLA)
F-62156 Merlimont
tel. 21 94 60 33

Medical Assistance

French medical services are excellent, and the country is well supplied with doctors, many of them able to speak English. British visitors to France will find it helpful to obtain a free booklet prepared by the Department of Health, and available from post offices – "Health Advice For Travellers" (containing form E111), which gives information about health precautions and how to get urgent medical treatment when abroad.

See also Insurance.

Military Cemeteries

Information about the many British and Commonwealth military cemeteries of the two world wars in France can be obtained from the Commonwealth War Graves Commission, 2 Marlow Road, Maidenhead, Berks, SL6 7DX, tel. (0628) 34221. The Commission publishes maps showing the location of cemeteries in northern France and will help to trace particular graves. Help and advice can also be obtained from the Commission's office in France: Rue Angèle-Richard, 62217 Beaurains (Pas-de-Calais), tel. 21 71 03 24.

Motoring

Roads

France is served by a dense network of roads, and even minor roads are usually in excellent condition.

Motorways

The motorways *(autoroutes)* which have been developed in recent years now have a total length of some 6920 km/4300 miles. They are marked by blue and white road signs. Apart from a few short sections round large towns they are subject to toll charges *(péage)*. Tolls can be paid by most credit cards.
The principal motorways are those which radiate from Paris and those along the Mediterranean coast. The most important are the following:
North: A1 Paris–Lille (Autoroute du Nord)
East: A4 Paris–Metz–Strasbourg (Autoroute de l'Est)
South-east and south: A6–A7 Paris–Lyons–Marseilles (Autoroute du Soleil)
South-west: A11 Paris–Nantes (L'Océane)
South-west and south: A10 Paris–Bordeaux (L'Aquitaine)
Mediterranean: A8 Aix-en-Provence–Menton (La Provençale)
A9 Orange–Narbonne (La Languedocienne)
Mediterranean–Atlantic:
A61–A62 Narbonne–Toulouse–Bordeaux (Autoroute des Deux Mers)
North-west: A13 Paris–Caen (Autoroute de Normandie)

Routes nationales

Most of the traffic, however, is still carried by the excellently engineered *routes nationales* (national highways), of which there are some 30,000 km/19,000 miles. These are marked by red and white kilometre stones bearing the number of the road, prefixed by the letter N. Frequently these have only three lanes for traffic in both directions, the middle lane being used for overtaking. France's extensive network of roads means that as a rule they are not too crowded, though there may be considerable holdups during the holiday season on the main roads radiating from Paris. Alternative routes on less crowded roads, described as *Itinéraires Bis* or *Emeraudes*, are signposted in green and white.

Routes départementales

Roads of lesser importance, the *routes départementales,* have yellow and white kilometre stones bearing a number prefixed by the letter D. The most important of these departmental roads are just as good as the *routes nationales.* Due regard should be paid to signs indicating road conditions, such as *Chaussée déformée* (uneven road surface).
Information about road and traffic conditions can be obtained by ringing Inter-services Routes (CNIR), (1) 48 94 33 33 (24-hour service).

Rule of the road

As in the rest of continental Europe, vehicles travel on the right, with overtaking on the left.

Seat belts

Seat belts must be worn by the driver and front- and back-seat passengers. Children under 10 are not allowed to sit in the front seat of a car unless in a specially approved fitted seat facing backwards.

Priority

In general, certainly in built-up areas, priority at road junctions belongs to traffic coming from the right, and warnings are often given by the sign *Priorité à droite.* Important main roads are given priority over side roads, indicated by the sign *Passage protégé* before junctions. On roundabouts traffic on the roundabout has priority over traffic entering it: this is a change introduced within the last few years, and there is frequently a reminder before roundabouts, *Vous n'avez pas la priorité* or *Cedez le passage.*

Lights

In built-up areas with adequate street lighting sidelights only should be used. At night all vehicles should drive with dipped headlights; the main beam should be flashed as a warning signal instead of using the horn.
French cars are required to have headlights which emit a yellow beam. This is not obligatory for visitors' cars, but it is recommended: it is a simple matter to fit amber lens converters or to use an amber coating. For right-hand drive cars it is necessary to fix beam deflectors on the vehicle's headlights. It is also strongly advised to carry a complete spare-bulb kit as it is an offence to drive with faulty lights.

Speed limits

The present speed limits in France are:

motorways (toll): 130 km/80 miles per hour, when wet 110 km/68 miles per hour; there is a *minimum* speed limit of 80 km/49 miles per hour in the outside lane on a level stretch of motorway during good daytime visibility

dual-carriageways and non-toll motorways: 110 km/68 miles per hour, when wet 100 km/62 miles per hour

Paris ring road (*périphérique*) and urban stretches of motorway: 80 km/ 49 miles per hour

national and departmental roads: 90 km/55 miles per hour, when wet 80 km/49 miles per hour

built-up areas: 50 km/31 miles per hour

In fog, with visibility down to 50 metres/55 yards, the speed limit is 50 km/ 31 miles per hour

Drivers who have held a licence for less than a year are limited to 90 km/ 55 miles per hour.

Drinking and driving

Driving under the influence of drink is regarded very seriously in France, and the traffic police frequently carry out random checks with the breathalyser *(alcootest)*. It is an offence to drive with 0.08% of blood alcohol, and if a driver is found to be considerably above the limit the penalties are severe, even when no traffic offence has been committed.

Parking

As a rule there are adequate parking facilities (sometimes guarded by attendants) at the main tourist sights; a fee is usually charged. Parking is permitted on the left-hand side of the road in built-up areas, but in narrow streets it may be prohibited on either side alternately (either on alternate days or in each half of a month). This is indicated by the sign *Stationnement alterné,* with an indication of the pattern of alternation – on even-numbered days *(jours pairs)* on one side and odd-numbered days *(jours impairs)* on the other, or on days 1-15 and 16-31.

Zone bleue

In town centres there are often designated "blue zones" *(zones bleues)*, within which a parking disc must be displayed. Discs can be purchased from the police or obtained free from tourist offices, motoring organisations and some commercial firms.

Zone grise

In addition to the ordinary parking meters in towns in designated "grey zones" (*zones grises*) there are now also *horodateurs*. These machines, centrally situated in parking areas, issue tickets which must be displayed behind the windscreen.

Zone verte

In town centres there may be "green zones" (*zones vertes*), in some parts of which parking is forbidden.

Route rouge

In Paris it is completely forbidden to park, or even stop, on a "red route" (*route rouge*).

Motor caravans

Many public car parks, particularly in town centres and on coast roads, exclude motor caravans. The ban is usually enforced by a horizontal bar at the entrance limiting the height to 1.90–2 metres (6–6½ feet).

Breakdown assistance

If you break down on a motorway you can call for help from one of the emergency telephones alongside the road. Elsewhere dial 17 for Police Secours. Motorists covered by the AA Five Star Service who cannot obtain local assistance should ring the English-speaking AA Continental Emergency Centre in Lyons (the call is free anywhere in France: details upon acceptance of premium).

Petrol

Prices of premium *(super)* 98 octane, and standard *(ordinaire, normale)* 90 octane, petrol are much the same in France as in Britain; diesel fuel *(gazole, gas-oil)* tends to be dearer.

Lead-free petrol

Lead-free petrol *(sans plomb),* both standard (95 octane) and super (98 octane), is available throughout France.

Museums

France has more than 2000 museums covering every conceivable field of interest, in particular archaeology and history, technology and classical and modern art. Paris, of course, takes a leading place, with France's four largest museums as well as spectacular special exhibitions, but the museums elsewhere in France have been steadily increasing in importance.

Museums

The lists of museums given below are merely a selection. The numbers refer to the map on page 596.

Information

Further information can be obtained from:
Direction des Musées de France
Palais du Louvre
F-75001 Paris
tel. (1) 42 60 39 26

Museums in Paris

1 Musée du Louvre (painting and sculpture of different countries and periods)
Centre Georges Pompidou (contemporary art; special exhibitions)
Musée d'Orsay (French art of 19th and 20th centuries)
Musée Picasso
Musée National Auguste Rodin
Musée National des Thermes et de l'Hôtel de Cluny (medieval art and culture)
Musée d'Art Moderne de la Ville de Paris (modern art)
Musée de l'Homme (ethnology)
Musée Guimet (art of East Asia and the Far East)
Musée National d'Histoire Naturelle (natural history)
Musée National des Techniques (technology)
Musée de la Marine (maritime museum)

Museums around Paris

2 Fontainebleau, Musée National du Château de Fontainebleau (furniture)
Sèvres, Musée National de Céramique (ceramics)
Le Bourget, Musée de l'Air et de l'Espace (history of aviation; at airport)
St-Germain-en-Laye, Musée des Antiquités Nationales (archaeology)
Musée du Prieuré (art)
Bièvres, Musée Français de la Photographie (history of photography)
Beauvais, Galerie Nationale de la Tapisserie et d'Art Textile (tapestries and textiles)
Ecouen, Musée National de la Renaissance (Renaissance art)
Nemours, Musée de Préhistoire de l'Ile-de-France (prehistory and early historical period)
Magny-les-Hameaux, Musée National des Granges de Port-Royal (museum of Jansenism)
Senlis, Musée de la Vénerie (hunting)

Museums elsewhere in France

3 St-Omer, Musée de l'Hotel Sandelin (art and ceramics)
4 Lille, Musée des Beaux-Arts (art)
5 Villeneuve-d'Ascq, Musée d'Art Moderne (modern art)
6 Douai, Musée de la Chartreuse (art)
7 Rouen, Musée le Secq des Tournelles (artistic metalwork)
Musée des Beaux-Arts et de la Céramique (art and ceramics)
Musée Départemental des Antiquities de la Seine Maritime (local antiquities)
8 Amiens, Musée de Picardie (art and history)
9 St-Quentin, Musée Antoine Lecuyer (art)
10 Bayeux, Musée de la Tapisserie (the Bayeux Tapestry)
11 Reims, Musée St-Remi (archaeology and history)
Musée St-Denis (art)
12 Metz, Musée d'Art et d'Histoire (art and history)
13 Strasbourg, Musée des Beaux-Arts (art)
Musée de l'Oeuvre Notre-Dame (applied art, history)
Musée Alsacien (folk art and traditions)
Musée Historique (history)

14 Caen, Musée des Beaux-Arts (art)
Musée de Normandie (history)
15 Nancy, Musée de l'Ecole de Nancy (art, applied art)
Musée des Beaux-Arts (art)
Musée Lorrain (ethnology, art, history)
16 Douarnenez, Musée du Bateau (shipping, fishing)
17 Rennes, Musée de Bretagne (ethnology)
Musée des Beaux-Arts (art)
18 Orléans, Musée des Beaux-Arts (art)
19 Colmar, Musée d'Unterlinden (art)
20 Quimper, Musée des Beaux-Arts (art)
Musée Départemental Breton (history)
21 Le Mans, Musée de Tesse (art)
22 Mulhouse, Musée National de l'Automobile (Schlumpf Collection of vintage cars)
Musée du Chemin de Fer (railways)
Musée de l'Impression sur Etoffes (printed fabrics)
23 Dijon, Musée des Beaux-Arts (art)
Musée Archéologique (archaeology)
24 Angers, Galerie David d'Angers (art)
Musée des Beaux-Arts (art)
Musée Turpin de Crissé (mainly oriental art)
25 Autun, Musée Rolin (archaeology and art)
26 Besançon, Musée des Beaux-Arts et d'Archéologie (art and archaeology)
27 Nantes, Musée des Beaux-Arts (art)
Musée du Château (applied arts, folk art, seafaring, industrial)
Musée Thomas Dobrée (medieval art)
Musée d'Histoire Naturelle (natural history)
Musée Jules Verne
28 Mouilleron-en-Pareds, Musée des Deux Victoires (Georges Clemenceau)
Musée du Maréchal de Lattre de Tassigny
29 Meursault, Archéodrome (ethnology)
30 Les Sables-d'Olonne, Musée de l'Abbaye Ste-Croix (modern art)
31 Poitiers, Musée Ste-Croix (ethnology, art)
32 Moulins, Musée d'Art et d'Archéologie (art and archaeology)
33 Ile d'Aix, Musée Napoléonien
Musée Africain
34 Lyons, Musée de la Civilisation Gallo-Romaine (Gallo-Roman antiquities)
Musée Historique des Tissus (woven fabrics, carpets)
Musée des Beaux-Arts et d'Art Contemporain (art, including contemporary art)
Musée d'Art Décoratif (decorative art)
35 St-Etienne, Musée d'Art Moderne (modern art)
Musée d'Art et d'Industrie (art and industry)
36 Grenoble, Musée Dauphinois (ethnology)
Musée de Peinture et de Sculpture (painting and sculpture)
37 Bordeaux, Musée des Arts Décoratifs (decorative arts)
Musée des Beaux-Arts (art)
Musée d'Aquitaine (history)
38 Les Eyzies-de-Tayac, Musée National de Préhistoire (prehistory)
39 Cabrerets, Domaine de Cuzals, Musée de Plein Air du Quercy (open-air museum of ethnology and history)
40 Montauban, Musée Ingres
41 Albi, Musée Toulouse Lautrec
42 Avignon, Musée du Petit Palais (art)
Musée Calvet (art)
43 St-Paul-de-Vence, Fondation Maeght (modern art)
44 Nice, Musée National Message Biblique Marc Chagall
Musée des Beaux-Arts (art)

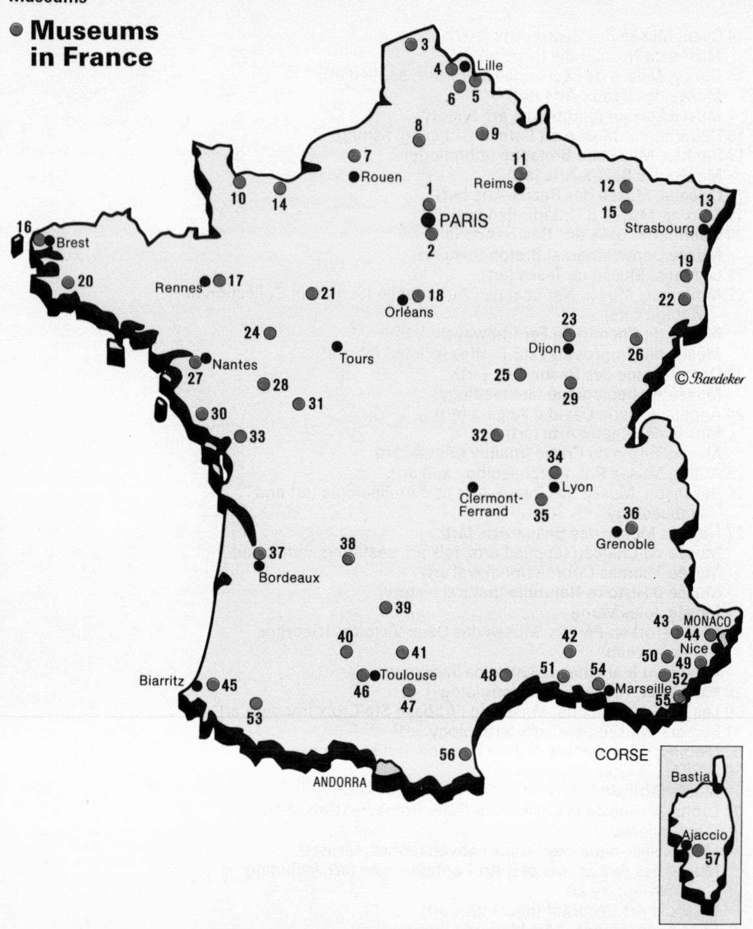

Musée Archéologique (archaeology)
Musée Matisse
Musée d'Art Naïf (naive art)
Musée d'Art Moderne et d'Art Contemporain
45 Bayonne, Musée Bonnat (art)
46 Toulouse, Musée des Augustins (art and history)
Musée Paul Dupuy (applied arts)
Musée Georges Labit (Oriental and Egyptian art)
Musée St-Raymond (archaeology)
47 Castres, Musée Goya
48 Montpellier, Musée Fabre (art)
49 Antibes, Musée Picasso
50 Biot, Musée Fernand Léger
51 Arles, Musée Camarguais (history)
Musée Lapidaire Païen (pagan art)

Musée Lapidaire Chrétien (Christian art)
Musée Réattu (art)
Musée Arlaten (folk art and traditions)
52 Vallauris, Musée Pablo Picasso
53 Pau, Musée National du Château (art and history)
54 Marseilles, Musée d'Histoire de Marseille (local history)
Musée des Beaux-Arts (art)
Centre de la Vieille Charité (archaeology)
Musée Cantini (modern art)
55 St-Tropez, Musée de l'Annonciade (modern art)
56 Perpignan, Musée Hyacinthe Rigaud (art)
Musée Catalan (history)
57 Ajaccio (Corsica), Musée de la Maison Bonaparte

National Parks, Nature Parks and Nature Reserves

National Parks (Parcs Nationaux)

1 Parc National de la Vanoise
Administrative office: Chambéry (Savoie)
Area: 52,839 hectares/130,568 acres
Situation: between the high valleys of the Isère and the Arc in Savoy, at altitudes between 1250 and 3850 m (4100 and 12,650 ft)
Activities: photo safaris, climbing, ski trekking, guided walks

2 Parc National des Ecrins
Administrative office: Gap (Hautes-Alpes)
Area: 91,800 hectares/226,842 acres
Situation: in départements of Isère and Hautes-Alpes, with Pelvoux hunting reserve, at altitudes between 800 and 1400 m (2600 and 4600 ft)
Activities: climbing, walking, cycle tours

3 Parc National des Cévennes
Administrative office: Florac (Lozère)
Area: 91,279 hectares/225,555 acres
Situation: in départements of Lozère, Gard and Ardèche
Activities: walking, ski trekking, water sports, caving, ecological museum

4 Parc National du Mercantour
Administrative office: Nice (Alpes-Maritimes)
Area: 68,500 hectares/169,267 acres
Situation: North of St-Martin-Vésubie, between the Maritime Alps and the Italian frontier
Activities: walking, climbing, caving

5 Parc National de Port-Cros
Administrative office: Hyères (Var)
Area: 675 hectares (plus 1800 hectares underwater)/1668 acres (plus 4448 acres underwater)
Situation: the Ile de Port-Cros and the sea-bed round it; also forests and estates on the Ile de Porquerolles
Activities: walking, swimming, underwater observation

6 Parc National des Pyrénées
Administrative office: Tarbes (Hautes-Pyrénées)
Area: 45,707 hectares/112,944 acres
Situation: South-west of Tarbes, near the Spanish frontier, at altitudes between 1100 and 3300 m (3600 and 10,800 ft)
Activities: walking, pony-trekking, climbing, fishing

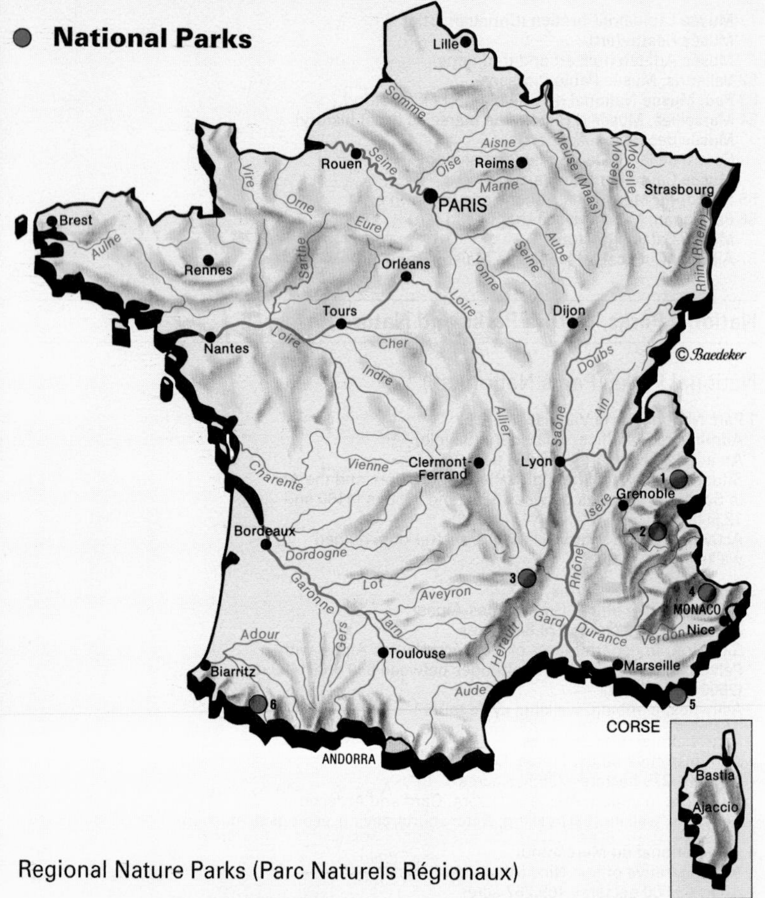

Regional Nature Parks (Parc Naturels Régionaux)

Several of these parks have an ecological museum *(écomusée).*

Parc du Nord–Pas-de-Calais (Nord, Pas-de-Calais). Area: 145,850 hectares/360,403 acres. Activities: walking, riding, water sports

Parc de Brotonne (Seine-Maritime, Eure). Area: 58,000 hectares/143,321 acres. Activities: walking, riding

Parc des Marais du Cotentin et du Bessin (Manche, Calvados). Area: 120,000 hectares/296,526 acres. Activities: birdwatching

Parc d'Armorique (Finistère). Area: 112,000 hectares/276,758 acres. Activities: riding, shooting, fishing

Parc Normandie-Maine (Manche, Mayenne, Orne, Sarthe). Area: 224,880 hectares/555,690 acres. Activities: walking, riding

Parc de la Haute-Vallée de Chevreuse (Yvelines). Area: 25,630 hectares/63,333 acres. Activities: walking, riding

Parc de la Montagne de Reims (Marne). Area: 50,480 hectares/124,739 acres. Activities: walking, fishing, speleology

Parc de la Forêt d'Orient (Aube). Area: 70,050 hectares/173,097 acres. Activities: riding, fishing, water sports

Parc de Lorraine (Meuse, Moselle, Meurthe-et-Moselle). Area: 200,000 hectares/494,210 acres. Activities: water sports, shooting, fishing

Parc des Vosges du Nord (Bas-Rhin, Moselle). Area: 119,175 hectares/294,497 acres. Activities: water sports, canoeing

Parc des Ballons des Vosges (Haut-Rhin, Haute-Saône, Vosges, Terretoire de Belfort). Area: 280,000 hectares/691,894 acres. Activities: walking

Parc du Haut-Jura (Jura, Doubs, Ain). Area: 75,675 hectares/186,997 acres. Activities: walking, speleology

Parc du Morvan (Saône-et-Loire, Côte-d'Or, Nièvre, Yonne). Area: 196,120 hectares/484,622 acres. Activities: riding, canoeing, shooting, fishing

Parc de la Brenne (Indre). Area: 167,200 hectares/413,160 acres. Activities: birdwatching

Parc de Brière (Loire-Atlantique). Area: 40,000 hectares/98,842 acres. Activities: walking, botanical excursions

Parc du Marais-Poitevin, Val de Sèvre and Vendée (Charente-Maritime, Deux-Sèvres, Vendée). Area: 190,000 hectares/469,500 acres. Activities: tours

Parc des Volcans d'Auvergne (Puy-de-Dôme, Cantal). Area: 393,000 hectares/971,123 acres. Activities: climbing, canoeing, speleology

Parc du Livradois-Forez (Haute-Loire, Puy-de-Dôme). Area: 300,000 hectares/741,315 acres. Activities: walking, riding

Parc du Pilat (Loire, Rhône). Area: 62,280 hectares/153,897 acres. Activities: riding

Parc du Vercors (Isère, Drôme). Area: 172,240 hectares/425,614 acres. Activities: walking, riding, speleology

Parc du Queyras (Hautes-Alpes). Area: 60,330 hectares/149,078 acres. Activities: riding, climbing, canoeing

Parc du Lubéron (Vaucluse, Alpes-de-Haute-Provence). Area: 142,000 hectares/350,889 acres. Activities: riding

Parc de la Camargue (Bouches-du-Rhône). Area: 85,000 hectares/210,039 acres. Activities: riding

Parc du Haut-Languedoc (Hérault, Tarn). Area: 145,000 hectares/358,302 acres. Activities: riding, canoeing

Parc des Landes de Gascogne (Gironde, Landes). Area: 290,000 hectares/716,604 acres. Activities: riding, canoeing

Parc de la Corse (Corsica). Area: 332,500 hectares/821,624 acres. Activities: walking

Nature Reserves (Réserves Naturelles)

There are 113 officially recognised nature reserves in France, some of which have nature trails and discovery trails. The arrangements for access differ from area to area.

Information

Fédération des Parcs Naturels de France
4 rue de Stockholm, F-75008 Paris
tel. (1) 42 94 90 84

Newspapers and Periodicals

British newspapers are usually available in the larger French towns on the day of publication; elsewhere they may be a day late. A wide range of English-language periodicals and magazines is also available.

Opening Times

Museums

All national museums, with the exception of Versailles, the Trianon Palace and the Musee d'Orsay, are closed on Tuesdays and public holidays; municipal museums generally close on Mondays. As a rule no visitors are admitted within half an hour of closing time.

Sights

Museums, châteaux, excavation sites and some churches are closed at lunch-time (though there are many exceptions to this during the main holiday season).
Sightseers should not of course look round churches during services.
See also Business Hours

Parks

See Gardens, Leisure Parks, National Parks

Passports

See Travel Documents

Post and Telephone

Opening times

Post offices are open Monday to Friday from 8 a.m. to 7 p.m. (sometimes with a break for lunch), on Saturday from 8 a.m. to 12 noon. Opening times of small offices in rural areas may vary.

Stamps

Stamps (*timbres-poste*) can be bought in tobacconists' shops (*bureaux de tabac*) as well as in post offices.

Postage rates

Letters within France cost 2.50 F; to Britain and other EC countries (up to 20 grams) also 2.50 F; to the United States and Canada (air mail, up to 10 grams) 3.70 F.

Telephone

Public pay phones can be used for trunk and international as well as local calls. Coin-operated phones usually take ½, 1, 2, 5 and 10 franc coins; increasing numbers of pay phones, however, are now operated by phone cards *(télécartes)*, obtainable from post offices and some tobacconists, Telecom offices, SNCF (railway) kiosks and other counters (look for the sign "Télécarte en vente ici").
A daytime telephone call to Britain will cost about 4.50 F per minute, to the United States or Canada about 9.50 F; there are reduced rates in the evening and at weekends.

Dialling codes

For calls to Britain dial 19 44, to the United States and Canada 19 1; the zero prefixed to a local dialling code should be omitted.
For calls from Britain to France dial 010 33 (+1 for Paris), from the United States or Canada 011 33 (+1 for Paris).
Within France, dialling codes now form part of the subscriber's number, except for Paris (Île de France) where a 1 precedes the number, followed by 16 if telephoning **to** Paris from the provinces of France (**from** Paris to the provinces precede the number by 16 only).

Public Holidays

Fixed holidays

January 1st: New Year's Day (Jour de l'An)
May 1st: Labour Day (Fête du Travail)

May 8th: Armistice Day 1945
July 14th: National Day (Fête Nationale), commemorating the taking of the Bastille
August 15th: Assumption (Assomption)
November 1st: All Saints' (Toussaint)
November 11th: Armistice Day 1918
December 25th: Christmas (Noël)

Movable holidays

Easter Monday (Lundi de Pâques)
Ascension
Whit Monday (Lundi de Pentecôte)

Holidays in Alsace

Good Friday (Vendredi Saint)
December 26th

Radio and Television

Radio

British radio programmes can be received in France on long and medium as well as short waves (BBC World Service).
During the holiday season some French stations – e.g. Radio Alsace on Strasbourg 2, Radio France and Radio Provence (from Marseilles, Avignon, Briançon, Digne, Gap and Toulon) – transmit daily programmes in English for the benefit of visitors.

Television

Since television transmitters have a relatively short range, it is not usually possible to receive British television programmes in France, except in areas near Britain. French television uses a different system and British portable colour television sets cannot receive French programmes; black and white sets may be able to receive them however.

Rail Services

SNCF

The French railways, offering high standards of service and comfort, are run by a State corporation, the Société Nationale des Chemins de Fer Français (SNCF). The main routes are served by EuroCity trains (EC), fast express trains and through expresses *(rapides)*. See map on page 602.

Head office

Direction Générale
10 Place de Budapest
F-75436 Paris Cédex 09
Tel. (1) 45 82 60 00

Offices abroad

French Railways, 179 Piccadilly, London W1V 0BA. Tel. (071) 493 9731

610 Fifth Avenue, New York NY 10020. Tel. (212) 582 2816

2121 Ponce de Leon Boulevard, Coral Gables FL 33134. Tel. (305) 445 8648

11 East Adams Street, Chicago Il 60603. Tel. (312) 427 8691

9465 Wilshire Boulevard, Beverly Hills CA 90212. Tel. (213) 272 7967

360 Post Street, San Francisco CA 94102. Tel. (415) 982 1993

1500 Stanley Street, Montreal H3A 1R3, P.Q. Tel. (514) 288 8255

TGV

Since 1981 France has had the Train à Grande Vitesse (TGV), which provides the fastest regular train service in the world, travelling at speeds of

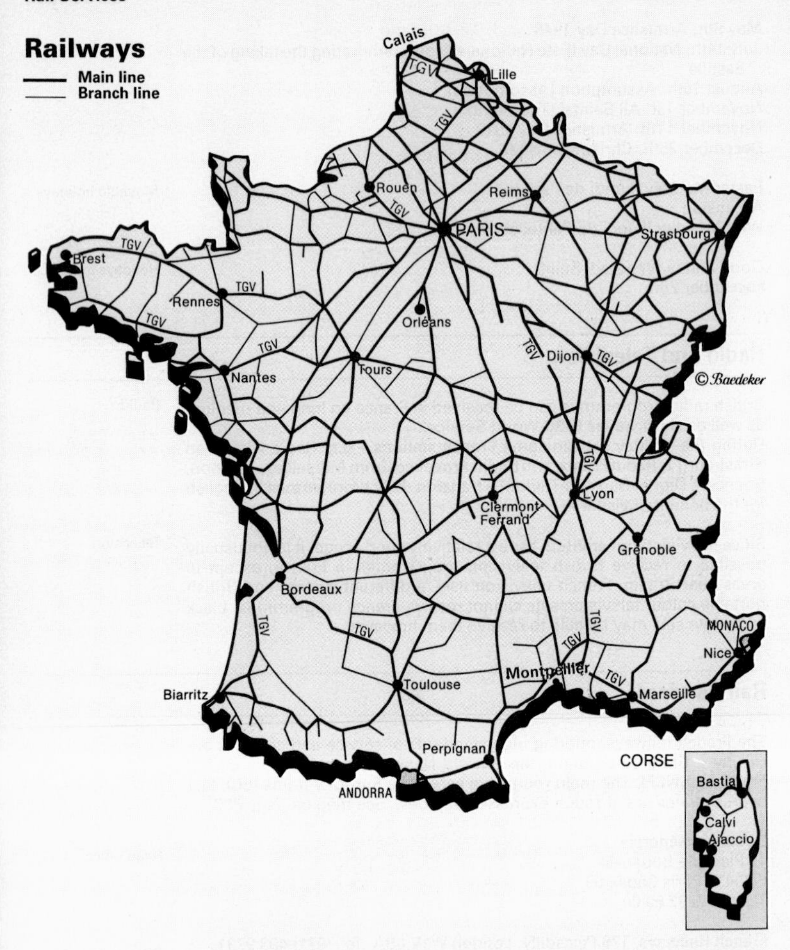

300 km/186 miles an hour. The TGV network, radiating from Paris, comprises the "TGV Sud-Est" serving the south-east. "TGV Atlantique" serving the south-west, and "TGV Nord Europe" to Lille and Calais to connect with the Channel Tunnel services beginning in 1994. With plans for a "TGV-Est" service for eastern France and for the routes to be inter-linked, the TGV network is designed to cover the whole of France into the next century.

Motorail

French Railways run car sleeper services from the Channel ports (Calais and Dieppe) and from Lille, Nantes, Paris, Rouen and Seclin (near Lille) to towns in the south, west and east of France. Information from SNCF offices (above).

Tickets

Tickets are not checked at the entrance to the platform. Passengers must themselves validate (*composter*) their ticket in a date-stamping machine at the entrance, and failure to do so entails a surcharge of 20%.

Rail services in Corsica

Since 1983 the Corsican railways have been run by the SNCF, but have preserved their own fare structure. Tickets can only be bought locally. Ferries to Corsica: see Getting to France.

Concession Fares

Concession fares for holidaymakers are mostly available only within the so-called *période bleue*, sometimes also the *période blanche:* that is, outside the the busiest periods. There are usually time limits on reduced-price tickets.

Euro Domino

A Euro Domino pass for France offers unlimited travel on 3, 5 or 10 days in the period of a month. There is a 25% reduction on the cost of a pass for those under 26.

Billet Séjour

The *Billet Séjour*, offering a reduction of 25%, is available to all passengers making a return journey or a round trip of not less than 1000 kilometres, and staying part of a Sunday.

Children

Children under 4 accompanied by adults travel free; between 4 and 12 they pay half fare.

Young people

There are reduced fares for school-children and students (up to the age of 26) holding an Inter-Rail card (unlimited second class travel for a month), the Carrissimo card (reductions of 20 to 50% on a specified number of journeys), or the Euro Domino pass (see above).

Families

The *Kiwi* card, for children under 16, gives a 50% reduction for the child (under 4's free) and up to 4 persons travelling with them. The card can only be purchased in France and is valid for a year.

Senior citizens

The *Carte Vermeil* entitles persons over 60 to reductions on journeys. There are two types: *Carte Vermeil Quatre Temps* gives a 50% reduction on 4 journeys, and *Carte Vermeil Plein Temps* a 50% reduction on unlimited journeys in EC and other European countries. Both cards are valid for a year.

Disabled

A booklet available from French Railways, "Guide Pratique Voyageur: Supplément à l'intention des personnes à mobilité réduite" gives information about special offers and reductions for the disabled.

Restaurants

Abbeville

Au Châteaubriant, 1 Place Hôtel-de-Ville, tel. 22 24 08 23

Aigues-Mortes

Arcades, 23 Boul. Gambetta, tel. 66 53 81 13

Aix-en-Provence

Capucin, 7 ter rue Mignet, tel. 42 20 69 77
Clos de la Violette, 10 Avenue Violette, tel. 42 23 30 71
Vendôme, 2 bis Avenue N.-Bonaparte, tel. 42 26 01 00
Vieille Auberge, 63 rue Espariat, tel. 42 27 17 41

Aix-les-Bains

Brasserie Poste, 32 Avenue Victoria, tel. 79 35 00 65

Ajaccio

L'Amore Piattu, 8 Place Ch.-de-Gaulle, tel. 95 51 00 53
Côte d'Azur, 12 Cours Napoléon, tel. 95 21 50 24
À Tinella, 85 rue Fesch, tel. 95 21 50 24

Albertville

Chez Uginet, Pont Adoubes, tel. 79 32 00 50

Albi

Jardin des Quatre Saisons, 19 Boul. Strasbourg, tel. 63 60 77 76
Tilbury, tel. 63 55 41 90

Amboise

Auberge du Mail, 32 Quai Gén.-de-Gaulle, tel. 47 57 60 39
Le Manoir St-Thomas, Place Richelieu, tel. 47 57 22 52

Restaurants

	Les Marissons, 68 rue Marissons, tel. 22 92 96 66 Le Mermoz, 7 rue J.-Mermoz, tel. 22 91 50 63
Anduze	Auberge du Fer à Cheval, tel. 66 85 02 80
Angers	L'Entrecôte, Avenue Joxé, tel. 41 43 71 77 Le Logis, 17 rue St-Laud, tel. 41 87 44 15 Le Quéré, 9 Place Ralliement, tel. 41 87 64 94 Le Toussaint, 7 Place Kennedy, tel. 41 87 46 20
Angoulême	Halles, 11 rue Massillon, tel. 45 92 65 24 Le Margaux, 25 rue Genève, tel. 45 92 58 98
Annecy	*Auberge de l'Eridan, 7 Avenue Chavoires, tel. 50 66 22 04 L'Amandier, 6 Avenue Mandallaz, tel. 50 51 74 50 Le Pré de la Danse, 16 rue J.-Mermoz, tel. 50 23 70 41
Antibes	L'Armoise, 2 rue Touraque, tel. 93 34 71 10 Auberge Provençale, Place Nationale, tel. 93 34 13 24 Les Vieux Murs, Avenue Amiral-de-Grasse, tel. 93 34 06 73
Arcachon	Chez Baron, 15 rue Prof.-Jolyet, tel. 56 83 29 96 Patio, 10 Boul. Plage, tel. 56 83 02 72
Argentan	Renaissance, 20 Avenue 2e-Division-Blindée, tel. 33 36 14 20
Arles	Côté Cour, Rue A.-Pichot, tel. 90 49 77 76 Hostellerie des Arènes, 62 rue Refuge, tel. 90 96 13 05 Vaccarès, Place Forum, tel. 90 96 06 17
Arras	La Faisanderie, 45 Grand'Place, tel. 21 48 20 76
Aurillac	Quatre Saisons, 10 rue Champeil, tel. 71 64 89 19
Autun	Hostellerie Vieux Moulin, Porte Arroux, tel. 85 52 10 90
Auxerre	Jardin Gourmand, 56 Boul. Vauban, tel. 86 51 53 52
Avignon	*Hiély, 5 rue République, tel. 90 86 17 07 Brunel, 46 rue Balance, tel. 90 85 24 83 Le Vernet, 58 rue Vernet, tel. 90 86 64 53
Azay-le-Rideau	Aigle d'Or, tel. 47 45 24 58
Banyuls-sur-Mer	Le Sardinal, Place Reig, tel. 68 88 30 07
Barr	A la Couronne, 4 rue Boulangers, tel. 88 08 25 83
Bastia	Bistrot du Port, Rue Posta Vecchia, tel. 95 32 19 83 Chez Assunta, Place Neuve-Fontaine, tel. 95 31 67 06
Bayonne	Beluga, 15 rue Tonneliers, tel. 59 25 52 13
Beaune	Rotisserie La Paix, 47 Faubourg Madeleine, tel. 80 22 33 33
Beauvais	A la Côtelette, 8 rue Jacobins, tel. 44 45 04 42
Belfort	Hostellerie du Château Servin, 9 rue Gén.-Négrier, tel. 84 21 41 85 Le Pot au Feu, 27 bis Grande Rue, tel. 84 28 57 84 Thiers, 9 rue Thiers, tel. 84 28 10 24
Bergerac	Le Cyrano, 2 Boul. Montaigne, tel. 53 57 02 76

Le Chaland, Promenade Micaud, tel. 81 80 61 61 Mungo Park, 11 rue J.-Petit, tel. 81 81 28 01 Poker d'As, 14 Square St-Amour, tel. 81 81 42 49 Tour de la Pelote, 41 Quai Strasbourg, tel. 81 82 14 58	**Besançon**
Le Framboisier, 33 Avenue Prés.-Wilson, tel. 67 62 62 57 L'Olivier, 12 rue Boïeldieu, tel. 67 28 86 64	**Béziers**
Belle Epoque, 10 Avenue Victor-Hugo, tel. 59 24 66 06 Café de Paris, 5 Place Bellevue, tel. 59 24 19 53	**Biarritz**
Bocca d'Or, 15 rue Haute, tel. 54 78 04 74 Rendez-vous des Pêcheurs, 27 rue Foix, tel. 54 74 67 48	**Blois**
Le Bistrot du Clavel, 44 rue Ch.-Domercq, tel. 56 92 91 52 Le Chapon Fin, 5 rue Montesquieu, tel. 56 79 10 10 Le Rouzic, 34 Cours Chapeau-Rouge, tel. 56 44 39 11 Le Vieux Bordeaux, 27 rue Buhan, tel. 56 52 94 36	**Bordeaux**
La Matelote, 80 Boul. Ste-Beuve, tel. 21 30 17 97	**Boulogne-sur-Mer**
Jacques Guy, 19 Place Bernard, tel. 74 45 29 11	**Bourg-en-Bresse**
Jacques Coeur, 3 Place Coeur, tel. 48 70 12 72 Le Jardin Gourmand, 15 bis Avenue E.-Renan, tel. 48 21 35 91	**Bourges**
Frère Jacques, 15 bis rue Lyon, tel. 98 44 38 65 Le Poulbot, 26 rue Aiguillon, tel. 98 44 19 08 Le Vatel, 23 rue Fautras, tel. 98 44 51 02	**Brest**
Le Péché Gourmand, 2 Route de Gap, tel. 92 20 11 02	**Briançon**
La Bourride, 15 rue Vaugueux, tel. 31 93 50 76 Le Chalut, 3 rue Vaucelles, tel. 31 52 01 06 L'Ecaille, 13 rue de Geole, tel. 31 86 49 10 St-Andrew's, 9 Quai Juillet, tel. 31 86 26 80	**Caen**
La Réserve, 91 Boul. Plage, tel. 93 31 00 17	**Cagnes-sur-Mer**
Le Balandre, 5 Avenue Ch.-de-Freycinet, tel. 65 30 01 97	**Cahors**
Le Channel, 3 Boul. Résistance, tel. 21 34 42 30 La Duchesse, 44 rue Duc-de-Guise, tel. 21 97 59 69	**Calais**
L'Escargot, 10 rue Gén.-de-Gaulle, tel. 27 81 24 54	**Cambrai**
Le Festival, 52 Boul. Croisette, tel. 93 38 04 81 La Mirabelle, 24 rue St-Antoine, tel. 93 38 72 75 Rescator, 7 rue Mar.-Joffre, tel. 93 39 44 57 Villa Dionysos, 7 rue Marceau, tel. 93 38 79 73	**Cannes**
Languedoc, 32 Allée léna, tel. 68 25 22 17 La Marquière, 13 rue St-Jean, tel. 68 71 52 00	**Carcassonne**
Lann Roz, 12 Avenue Poste, tel. 97 52 10 48	**Carnac**
Rapière du Comtat, 47 Boul. du Nord, tel. 90 67 20 03	**Carpentras**
Hostellerie La Fruitière, tel. 62 92 52 04	**Cauterets**
Le Zinc, Place Touleuses, tel. 30 30 42 90	**Cergy-Pontoise**
Chaumière, 14 rue Denfert-Rochereau, tel. 79 33 16 26 La Vanoise, 6 Place de la Gare, tel. 79 69 02 78	**Chambéry**

Restaurants

Chamonix	Eden, tel. 50 53 06 40 La Tartiffle, 87 rue Moulins, tel. 50 53 20 02
Chantilly	Relais Condé, 42 Avenue Mar.-Joffre, tel. 44 57 05 75
Chartres	Buisson Ardent, 10 rue au Lait, tel. 37 34 04 66 La Vieille Maison, 5 rue au Lait, tel. 37 34 10 67
Châteaudun	La Rose, 12 rue Lambert-Licors, tel. 37 45 21 83
Cherbourg	Grandgousier, 21 rue Abbaye, tel. 33 53 19 43
Chinon	Au Plaisir Gourmand, 2 rue Parmentier, tel. 47 93 20 48
Clermont-Ferrand	Le Brezou, 51 rue St-Dominique, tel. 73 93 56 71 Clavé, 10 rue St-Adjutor, tel. 73 36 46 30 Truffe d'Argent, 1 rue H.-Michel, tel. 73 93 22 42 Vacher et Brasserie Gare Routière, 69 Boul. Gergovia, tel. 73 93 13 32
Cognac	Pigeons Blancs, 110 rue J.-Brisson, tel. 45 82 16 36
Collioure	La Balette, Route de Port-Vendres, tel. 68 82 05 07
Colmar	* Schillinger, 16 rue Stanislas, tel. 89 41 43 17 Da Alberto, 24 rue Marchands, tel. 89 23 37 69 Fer Rouge, 53 Grand'Rue, tel. 89 41 37 24
Compiègne	Hostellerie Royal Lieu, 9 rue Senlis, tel. 44 20 10 24
Corsica	See Ajaccio
Dax	Bois de Boulogne, tel. 58 74 23 32
Deauville	Ciro's, Promenade Planches, tel. 31 68 18 10
Dieppe	La Mélie, 2 Grande Rue Pollet, tel. 35 84 21 19
Dijon	* Jean-Pierre Billoux, 14 Place Darcy, tel. 80 30 11 00 Thibert, 10 Place Wilson, tel. 80 67 74 64 La Toison d'Or,18 rue Ste-Anne, tel. 80 30 73 52 Le Vinarium, 23 Place Bossuet, tel. 80 30 36 23
Dinan	Mère Pourcel, 3 Place Merciers, tel. 96 39 03 80
Dinard	Prieuré, 1 Place Gén.-de-Gaulle, tel. 99 46 13 74
Divonne-les-Bains	Champagne, Avenue Genève, tel. 50 20 13 13
Douai	Au Turbotin, 9 rue Massue, tel. 27 87 04 16
Dunkirk (Dunkerque)	Aux Ducs de Bourgogne, 29 rue Bourgogne, tel. 28 66 78 69 Richelieu, Place de la Gare, tel. 28 66 52 13
Epernay	Le Manoir de Champagne, 19 Avenue Champagne, tel. 26 55 04 45
Epinal	Les Abbesses, 23 rue Louvière, tel. 29 82 53 69
Espalion	Le Méjane, 8 rue Méjane, tel. 65 48 22 37
Etretat	L'Escale, Place Mar.-Foch, tel. 35 27 03 69
Evian-les-Bains	La Toque Royale, at Casino, tel. 50 75 03 78

Restaurant	City
France, 29 rue St-Thomas, tel. 32 39 09 25	**Evreux**
Viking, 63 Boul. Albert-1er, tel. 35 29 22 92	**Fécamp**
Camp du Drap d'Or, 21 rue N.-Peyrevidal, tel. 61 02 87 87	**Foix**
François 1er, 3 rue Royale, tel. 64 22 24 68	**Fontainebleau**
Le Vieux Four, 57 rue Grisolle, tel. 94 51 56 38	**Fréjus**
La Roseraie, tel. 92 51 43 08	**Gap**
Bonne Auberge de Martimprey, Col de Martimprey, tel. 29 63 19 08	**Gérardmer**
Beau Site et La Poularde, 13 Quai Nice, tel. 38 67 36 05	**Gien**
Amphitryon, 16 Boul. Victor-Hugo, tel. 93 36 58 73	**Grasse**
Le Berlioz, 4 rue Strasbourg, tel. 76 56 22 39 L'Escalier, 6 Place Lavalette, tel. 76 54 66 16 Manoir des Dauphins, 48 Cours Libération, tel. 76 48 00 06 Poularde Bressane, 12 Place P.-Mistral, tel. 76 87 08 90	**Grenoble**
Barberousse, 8 Place Barberousse, tel. 88 73 31 09	**Haguenau**
Cambridge, 90 rue Voltaire, tel. 35 42 50 24 Guimbarde, 61 rue L.-Brindeau, tel. 35 42 15 36 Le Monaco, 16 rue Paris, tel. 35 42 21 01 Le Petit Bedon, 39 rue L.-Brindeau, tel. 35 41 36 81	**Le Havre**
Cheval Blanc, Quai Passagers, tel. 31 89 39 87	**Honfleur**
Auberge de l'Esterel, 21 rue Iles, tel. 93 61 08 67	**Juan-les-Pins**
Chambard, Rue Gén.-de-Gaulle, tel. 89 47 10 17	**Kaysersberg**
La Petite Auberge, 45 Boul. Brossolette, tel. 22 23 02 44	**Laon**
*Le Flambard, 79 rue Angleterre, tel. 20 51 00 06 *Le Restaurant, 1 Place Sébastopol, tel. 20 57 05 05 La Coquille, 60 rue St-Etienne, tel. 20 54 29 82 La Devinière, 61 Boul. Louis, tel. 20 52 74 64	**Lille**
Champlevé, 1 Place Wilson, tel. 55 34 43 34 Deux Atres, 17 rue Gén.-Bessol, tel. 55 79 64 54 Petits Ventres, 20 rue Boucherie, tel. 55 33 34 02 Pré St-Germain, 28 rue Loi, tel. 55 34 15 17	**Limoges**
Ferme du Roy, tel. 31 31 33 98	**Lisieux**
Cheval Rouge, 47 rue Lecourbe, tel. 84 47 20 44	**Lons-le-Saunier**
Auberge Maurice Prat, 22 Avenue A.-Béguère, tel. 62 94 01 53 L'Ermitage, Place Mgr-Laurence, tel. 62 94 08 42	**Lourdes**
Le Voltaire, 8 Avenue Voltaire, tel. 83 74 07 09	**Lunéville**
*Paul Bocuse, Pont de Collonges, tel. 78 22 01 40 *Vettard, 7 Place Bellecour, tel. 78 42 07 59 Fédora, 249 rue M.-Merieux, tel. 78 69 46 26 *Léon de Lyon, 1 rue Pleney, tel. 78 28 11 33 Mère Brazier, 12 rue Royale, tel. 78 28 15 49	**Lyons**

Restaurants

Le Mans	La Ciboulette, 14 rue Vielle-Porte, tel. 43 24 65 67 Feuillantine, 19 bis rue Foisy, tel. 43 24 00 38 Le Grenier à Sel, 26 Place Eperon, tel. 43 23 26 30 La Grillade, 1 bis rue C.-Blondeau, tel. 43 24 21 87
Marseilles	Chez Caruso, 158 Quai Port, tel. 91 90 94 04 Damaro, 19 Place Lenche, tel. 91 56 10 04 Jambon de Parme, 67 rue Le-Palud, tel. 91 54 37 98 Michel, 6 rue Catalans, tel. 91 52 30 63
Megève	Auberge Les Griottes, Route Nationale, tel. 50 93 05 94
Menton	Chez Mireille-l'Ermitage, 1080 Promenade Soleil, tel. 93 35 77 23
Metz	Le Bouquet Garni, 10 rue Pasteur, tel. 87 66 85 97 La Dinanderie, 2 rue Paris, tel. 87 30 14 40 Maire, 1 rue Pont-des-Morts, tel. 87 32 43 12 Ville de Lyon, 7 rue Piques, tel. 87 36 07 01
Monaco	See Monte Carlo
Montauban	Ambroisie, 41 rue Comédie, tel. 63 66 27 40 Chapon Fin, 1 Place St-Orens, tel. 63 63 12 10
Montbéliard	Tour Henriette, 59 Faubourg Besançon, tel. 81 91 03 24
Monte Carlo	Louis XV, Hôtel de Palais, Place Casino, tel. 92 16 30 01 Le Grill, Hôtel de Paris, Place Casino, tel. 92 16 30 02 Polpetta, 2 rue Paradis, tel. 93 50 67 84 Le Saint Benoît, 10 ter Avenue de la Costa, tel. 93 25 02 34
Montpellier	Chandelier, 3 rue Leenhardt, tel. 67 92 61 62 Le Louvre, 2 rue Vieille, tel. 67 60 59 37 Le Ménestrel, Place Préfecture, tel. 67 60 62 51
Moulins	Jacquemart, 10 Place Hôtel de Ville, tel. 70 44 32 58
Mulhouse	Auberge de la Tonnelle, 61 rue Mar.-Joffre, tel. 89 54 25 77 Aux Caves du Vieux Couvent, 23 rue Couvent, tel. 89 46 29 79 Poste, 7 rue Gén.-de-Gaulle, tel. 89 44 07 71
Nancy	Capucin Gourmand, 31 rue Gambetta, tel. 83 35 26 98 La Chine, 31 rue Ponts, tel. 83 30 13 89 Le Goéland, 27 rue Ponts, tel. 83 35 17 25 Nouveaux Abattoirs, 4 Boul. Austrasie, tel. 83 35 46 25
Nantes	Le Bouchon, 7 rue Bossuet, tel. 40 20 08 44 Le Gavroche, 139 rue Hauts-Pavés, tel. 40 76 22 49 Les Maraîchers, 21 rue Fouré, tel. 40 47 06 51 San Francisco, 3 Chemin Bateliers, tel. 40 49 59 42
Narbonne	Alsace, 2 Avenue P.-Sémard, tel. 68 65 10 24
Nevers	Auberge Porte du Croux, 17 rue Porte-du-Croux, tel. 86 57 12 71
Nice	Ane Rouge, 7 Quai Deux-Emmanuel, tel. 93 89 49 63 Chantecler, 37 Promenade Anglais, tel. 93 88 39 51 Les Dents de la Mer, 2 rue St-François-de-Paule, tel. 93 80 99 16 La Merenda, 4 rue Terrasse
Nîmes	Alexandre, at Garons, tel. 66 70 08 99 Le Lisita, 2 Boul. Arènes, tel. 66 67 29 15

Tour d'Argent Restaurant in Paris

Le Magister, 5 rue Nationale, tel. 66 76 11 00
Mas des Abeilles, tel. 66 38 28 57

Noirmoutier
Grand Four, 1 rue Cure, tel. 51 39 12 24

Noyon
Alliés, 5 Boul. Mony, tel. 44 44 01 89

Obernai
Ami Fritz, at Ottrott-le-Haut, tel. 88 95 80 81

Oléron (Ile d'Oléron)
La Perrotine, at harbour, tel. 46 47 01 01

Orange
Parvis, 3 Cours Poutoules, tel. 90 34 82 00
L'Antre de Cybèle, 6 rue Pont-Neuf, tel. 90 34 09 52

Orléans
Le Bigorneau, 54 rue Turcies, tel. 38 68 01 10
La Crémaillère, 34 rue N.-D.-de-Recouvrance, tel. 38 53 49 17
Jean, 64 rue Ste-Catherine, tel. 38 53 40 87
Lautrec, 28 Place Châtelet, tel. 38 54 09 54

Paris
*L'Ambroisie, 9 Place des Vosges, tel. 42 78 51 45
*Le Divellec, 107 rue Université, tel. 45 51 91 96
*L'Espadon (Hôtel Ritz), 15 Place Vendôme, tel. 42 60 38 30
*La Tour d'Argent, 15 Quai Tournelle, tel. 43 54 23 31
Charlot Roi des Coquillages, 12 Place Clichy, tel. 48 74 49 64
La Couronne, 5 rue Berri, tel. 45 63 78 49
Jacques Hébert, 38 rue S.-Mercier, tel. 45 57 77 88
La Marbouille, 41 rue Trois-Frères, tel. 42 64 49 15
Le Petit Colombier, 42 rue Acacias, tel. 43 80 28 54
Au Pressoir, 257 Avenue Daumesnil, tel. 43 44 38 21
Le Récamier, 4 rue Récamier, tel. 45 48 86 58
Relais d'Auteuil, 31 Boul. Murat, tel. 46 51 09 54

Pau
Fin Gourmet, facing station, tel. 59 27 47 71
Pierre, 16 rue L.-Barthou, tel. 59 27 76 86

Restaurants

Périgueux	L'Oison, 31 rue St-Front, tel. 53 09 84 02 La Flambée, 2 rue Montaigne, tel. 53 53 23 06
Perpignan	Le Bourgogne, 63 Avenue Mar.-Leclerc, tel. 68 34 96 05 Brasserie Vauban, 29 Quai Vauban, tel. 68 51 05 10 Le Quai, 37 Quai Vauban, tel. 68 35 31 14
Poitiers	Armes d'Obernai, 19 rue A.-Ranc, tel. 49 41 16 33 Maxime, 4 rue St-Nicolas, tel. 49 41 09 55 St-Hilaire, 65 rue E.-Renaudot, tel. 49 41 15 45
Port-Grimaud	La Tartane, tel. 94 56 38 32
Provins	Le Médiéval, 6 Place H.-de-Balzac, tel. 64 00 01 19
Le Puy-en-Velay	Bateau Ivre, 5 rue Portail-d'Avignon, tel. 71 09 67 10 Sarda, 12 rue Chênebouterie, tel. 71 09 58 94
Quiberon	Le Relax, 25 Boul. Castero, tel. 97 50 12 84
Quimper	Le Capucin Gourmand, 19 rue Réguaires, tel. 98 95 43 12 Le Parisien, 13 rue J.-Jaurès, tel. 98 90 35 29
Reims	Le Florence, 43 Boul. Foch, tel. 26 47 12 70 Foch, 37 Boul. Foch, tel. 26 47 48 22 Le Forum, 34 Place Forum, tel. 26 47 56 87 Vonelly, 13 rue Gambetta, tel. 26 47 22 00
Ribeauvillé	Vosges, 2 Grand' Rue, tel. 89 73 61 39
Riquewihr	Auberge Schoenenbourg, 2 rue Piscine, tel. 89 47 92 28
La Rochelle	*Richard Coutanceau, Plage de la Concurrence, tel. 46 41 48 19 La Marmite, 14 rue St-Jean-du-Pérot, tel. 46 41 17 03 Les Quatre Sergents, 49 rue St-Jean-du-Pérot, tel. 46 41 35 80
Rosheim	Auberge Cerf, 120 rue Gén.-de-Gaulle, tel. 88 50 40 14
Rouen	Bertrand Warin, 9 rue Pie, tel. 35 89 26 69 Dufour, 67 rue St-Nicolas, tel. 35 71 90 62 Gill, 60 rue St-Nicolas, tel. 35 71 16 14 P'tits Parapluies, 45 rue Bourg-l'Abbé, tel. 35 88 55 26
Roussillon	La Tarasque, tel. 90 05 63 86
Royan	Trois Marmites, 37 Avenue Ch.-Regazzoni, tel. 46 38 66 31
Les Sables d'Olonne	Le Clipper, 19 bis Quai Guiné, tel. 51 32 03 61
Saint-Denis	Grill St-Denis, 59 rue Strasbourg, tel. 48 27 61 98 Mets du Roy, 4 rue Boulangerie, tel. 48 20 89 74
Saintes	Logis Santon, 54 Cours Genêt, tel. 46 74 20 14
Saintes-Maries-de-la-Mer	Brûleur de Loup, tel. 90 97 83 31
Saint-Etienne	*Pierre Gagnaire, 3 rue G.-Teissier, tel. 77 37 57 93 Le Gratin, 30 rue St-Jean, tel. 77 32 32 60 La Loco, 29 Avenue Denfert-Rochereau, tel. 77 32 48 47 Monte Carlo, 19 bis Cours Victor-Hugo, tel. 77 32 43 63
Saint-Germain-en-Laye	Des Coches, 7 rue Coches, tel. 39 73 66 40

Restaurant	Town
Auberge Kaiku, 17 rue République, tel. 59 26 13 20	**Saint-Jean-de-Luz**
Duchesse Anne, 5 Place Guy-la-Chambre, tel. 99 40 85 33 Delaunay, 6 rue Ste-Barbe, tel. 99 40 92 46	**Saint-Malo**
Bon Accueil, 39 rue Marceau, tel. 40 22 07 05 Moderne, 46 rue Anjou, tel. 40 22 55 88	**Saint-Nazaire**
La Truye qui File, 8 rue Bleuets, tel. 21 38 41 34	**Saint-Omer**
Le Pichet, 6 Boul. Gambetta, tel. 23 62 03 67 Le Riche, 10 rue Toiles, tel. 23 62 33 53	**Saint-Quentin**
Marceau, 13 Boul. Marceau, tel. 90 92 37 11	**Saint-Rémy-de-Provence**
Le Chabichou, Avenue Foch, tel. 94 54 80 00 Leï Mouscardïns, at end of harbour, tel. 94 97 01 53	**Saint-Tropez**
Robin, 1 Boul. G.-Clemenceau, tel. 90 56 06 53	**Salon-de-Provence**
Tour, Place Halle, tel. 48 54 00 81	**Sancerre**
Mathis, 7 rue Gambetta, tel. 87 03 21 67	**Sarrebourg**
Délices du Château, tel. 41 67 65 60	**Saumur**
Edel, 7 rue Serruriers, tel. 88 92 86 55	**Sélestat**
Rôtisserie de Formanoir, 17 rue Châtel, tel. 44 53 04 39	**Senlis**
Auberge de la Vanne, 176 Route de Lyon, tel. 86 65 13 63	**Sens**
La Palangrotte, Rampe P.-Valéry, tel. 67 74 80 35	**Sète**
Avenue, 35 Avenue Ch.-de-Gaulle, tel. 23 53 10 76	**Soissons**
*Burehiesel, Parc de l'Orangerie, tel. 88 61 62 24 *Le Crocodile, 10 rue Outre, tel. 88 32 13 02 Ami Schutz, 1 rue Ponts-Couverts, tel. 88 32 76 98 Zimmer, 8 rue Temple-Neuf, tel. 88 32 35 01	**Strasbourg**
Hostellerie Grand Sully, Boul. Champ-de-Foire, tel. 38 36 27 56	**Sully-sur-Loire**
L'Amphitryon, 38 rue Larrey, tel. 62 34 08 99 L'Isard, 70 Avenue Mar.-Joffre, tel. 62 93 06 69	**Tarbes**
Le Prieuré, 68 Grande Rue, tel. 50 71 31 89	**Thonon-les-Bains**
La Belle Epoque, 31 Avenue Victor-Hugo, tel. 83 43 23 41	**Toul**
La Ferme, 6 Place L.-Blanc, tel. 94 41 43 74 Au Sourd, 10 rue Molière, tel. 94 92 28 52	**Toulon**
*Les Jardins de l'Opéra, 1 Place Capitole, tel. 61 23 07 76 *Vanel, 22 rue M.-Fontvieille, tel. 61 21 51 82 Brasserie Beaux-Arts, 1 Quai Daurade, tel. 61 21 12 12 Orsi "Bouchon Lyonnais", 13 rue Industrie, tel. 61 62 97 43	**Toulouse**
*Barrier, 101 Avenue Tranchée, tel. 47 54 20 39 L'Atlantic, 59 rue Commerce, tel. 47 64 78 41 Bigarade, 122 rue Colbert, tel. 47 05 48 81 Les Tuffeaux, 19 rue Lavoisier, tel. 47 47 19 89	**Tours**

Troyes	Le Bourgogne, 40 rue Gén.-de-Gaulle, tel. 25 73 02 67 Théâtre, 35 rue J.-Lebocey, tel. 25 73 18 47 Le Valentino, Cour Rencontre, tel. 25 73 14 14
Tulle	Toque Blanche, Place M.-Brigouleix, tel. 55 26 75 41
Vaison-la-Romaine	Le Bateleur, Place Th.-Aubanel, tel. 90 36 28 04
Valençay	Chêne Vert, tel. 54 00 06 54
Valenciennes	L'Alberoi, tel. 27 46 86 30
Vannes	Le Richemont, Place de la Gare, tel. 97 42 61 41
Vence	Auberge des Seigneurs, Place Frêne, tel. 93 58 04 24
Vendôme	Petit Bilboquet, Route de Tours, tel. 54 77 16 60
Vernon	Les Fleurs, 71 rue Carnot, tel. 32 51 16 80
Versailles	*Les Trois Marches, 3 rue Colbert, tel. 39 50 13 21 Potager du Roy, 1 rue Mar.-Joffre, tel. 39 50 35 34 Rescatore, 27 Avenue St-Cloud, tel. 39 50 23 60
Vichy	Escargot qui Tète, 84 rue Paris, tel. 70 31 22 88 Violon d'Ingres, 22 Place J.-Epinat, tel. 70 98 97 70
Vienne	Bec Fin, 7 Place St-Maurice, tel. 74 85 76 72 Magnard, 45 Cours Brillier, tel. 74 85 10 43
Villard-de-Lams	Le Dauphin, Avenue Alliés, tel. 76 95 15 56
Vitré	Taverne de l'Ecu, 12 rue Beaucherie, tel. 99 75 11 09
Wissembourg	Ange, Rue République, tel. 88 94 12 11

Shopping and Souvenirs

Craft products

Among the things to look for in France are the many attractive local craft products – pottery and ceramics (in Normandy, Provence, etc.), wooden articles (particularly items made from olive-wood), lace from Brittany, basketwork and wickerwork. Interesting antiques can occasionally be found.

Paris

Paris is famed for its fashion shops, book and record shops and antique dealers.

Provence

Perfumes and herb essences (lavender, etc.) are a speciality of Provence, particularly of Grasse – though the main brands are to be found all over France. Provençal fabrics (for example in the form of scarves or bags) are also favourite souvenirs.

Food and drink

Many of France's culinary specialities (see Food and Drink) can be bought in bottled or canned form, and make very acceptable presents. If you think of taking back wine from a wine-producing region it is advisable to ask the advice of the producer – either a small grower, who is likely to promote his wares with the offer of a free tasting (*dégustation gratuite*), or a large cooperative winery (*cave coopérative*).

On the duty-free allowances for the import of wine see Customs Regulations. If you want to take in larger quantities duty will be payable, but there is still likely to be a worthwhile saving over prices at home.

Son et Lumière

During the summer season there are many Son et Lumière performances in châteaux and other places of particular interest to tourists. These usually present a kind of historical pageant, with theatrical lighting effects, of events connected with particular buildings. Some places increasing costs have led to a reduction in the programme of shows. It is advisable, therefore, to enquire locally about Son et Lumière performances in the area.

Souvenirs

See Shopping and Souvenirs

Sport

Canal and river cruising

See entry

Canoeing

There are plenty of peaceful stretches of water in France, but also many areas of wild water which call for high standards of fitness and experience.

Information:
Fédération Française de Canoë–Kayak
87 Quai de la Marne, F-94340 Joinville-de-Pont
tel. (1) 48 89 39 989

Diving

France has long taken a leading place in the field of scuba diving, oceanography and underwater archaeology. The Mediterranean coasts and Corsica are still the favoured places for these activities, though the immediate coastal areas have lost much of their marine fauna as a result of overfishing and pollution. On the Atlantic coast careful regard must be paid to the tides and currents. For underwater hunting a permit (obtainable from local diving clubs) is required.

Information:
Fédération Française d'Etudes et de Sports Sous-Marins
24 Quai de la Rive-Neuve, F-13007 Marseille
tel. 91 33 99 31

The Federation's "Annuaire Officiel" lists diving clubs and training courses.

Fishing

Fishing is perhaps the Frenchman's favourite recreation, and the country's numerous rivers, streams and lakes offer ample scope for coarse fishing, spinning and fly-fishing. Fishing waters are classified into two categories, category 1 being mainly salmon and trout, category 2 mainly other species. A special stamp (*supplément*) is required for the former category, the ordinary *timbre de base* for the latter. Fishing regulations and close seasons vary from area to area and for the different types of water. To fish in public water (*eaux libres*) it is necessary to obtain a permit from the local angling club (*société de pêche*); for private water (*eaux closes*) the permission of the owner or tenant must be obtained.

A well-tended golf course in Touraine

Information:
Fédération Française de Pêche au Coup
20 rue Emile-Zola, F-93120 La Courneuve
tel. (1) 48 34 45 01

Sea-fishing from the shore is free to all (maximum of two rods per person); but there are certain closed areas, about which enquiry should be made. Special regulations apply to fishing from boats or with nets.

Information:
Fédération Française des Pêcheurs en Mer
Village Vacances FACAF, F-40600 Biscarosse
tel. 58 78 28 35

Flying

See entry

Golf

Although golf is becoming increasingly popular in France, it still retains something of its exclusive character. There are more than 130 golf clubs belonging to the association known as France Golf International, and over 460 courses, 30 of them in the Paris region alone, as well as the so-called "Plan Vert" centres with practice areas open to the public.
Many travel operators and other organisations offer golfing holidays and golf coaching courses.

Information:
France Golf International, Maison de la France
8 avenue de l'Opéra, F-75001 Paris, tel. (1) 42 96 10 23

An annual publication, "Golf in France" lists golf-courses, etc. and a map of touristic golf courses is also available.

Riding

There are opportunities for riding practically everywhere in France. Many private agencies offer riding lessons and pony trekking. In many places horse-drawn carriages can be hired.

Information:
Fédération Française d'Equitation
Délégation Nationale au Tourisme Equestre (ANTE)
Ile St-Germain, 170 Quai Stalingrad
F-92130 Issy-les-Moulineaux.
tel. (1) 46 48 83 93

Sailing

There are facilities for sailing on the inland lakes and round the coasts of France, particularly in the Mediterranean. There are boats for hire, sailing clubs and sailing schools (sailing, cruising in coastal waters and on the open sea, wind-surfing) in many places.

Information:
Fédération Française de la Voile
55 Avenue Kléber, F-75784 Paris Cédex 16
tel. (1) 45 53 68 00

Shooting

With its varied topography France offers ample scope for the sportsman – deer, wild pig, pheasants, wild duck, hares, etc.
Foreigners who desire to shoot in France must have a shooting permit (*permis de chasse*) or a shooting licence (*licence de chasse*) (valid for 48 hours), which can be obtained from the Prefecture of the département on presentation of a game licence from the visitor's own country. A shooting insurance must be taken out in France; and an applicant for a shooting permit must also produce a police certificate of character.

Information:
Office National de la Chasse
BP 236, F-75822 Paris, tel. (1) 44 15 17 17

Surfing and wind-surfing

Surfing – a sport which originally came from Polynesia – is practised on the Atlantic coast between the Gironde estuary and the Spanish frontier, the only area where the incoming tide creates the necessary waves.
Wind-surfing is now practised almost everywhere, but mainly in Aquitaine and Brittany, where the wind conditions are right. Regard must always be had to currents and offshore winds. In some coastal resorts flags are flown as warning signals for wind-surfers.

Tennis

The fact that tennis is one of France's most popular sports is due partly to the activity of the Fédération Française de Tennis (FFT), but is also attributable to the prestige of the major tournaments, like the French Open international championship in the Roland-Garros stadium in Paris, held annually at the end of May/early June.
Information about special tennis-playing holidays can be obtained from the various departmental tourist organisations and from advertisements in tennis magazines.

Information:
Fédération Française de Tennis
Stade Roland-Garros
2 Avenue Gordon-Bennett, F-75016 Paris
tel. (1) 47 43 48 00

Walking

See entry

Water-skiing

There are water-skiing clubs in most seaside resorts, which can give information about local conditions.

Information:
Fédération Française de Ski Nautique
16 rue Clément-Marot, F-75008 Paris
tel. (1) 47 20 05 00

Winter sports

See entry

Taking the Cure

France's medicinal springs were already being used for curative purposes in Roman times. There are now something like 1200 springs used in the treatment of a wide range of conditions in a hundred or so spas (which are often identified by the addition of "les Bains" to their name. Most of these resorts, which are often also popular holiday centres, have preserved an agreeable flavour of earlier days.

See map on page 618.

Spas

1 Bagnoles-de-l'Orne (Orne).
Altitude: 222 m/730 ft. Circulatory disorders

2 Forges-les-Eaux (Seine-Maritime).
Altitude: 175 m/575 ft. Circulatory disorders

3 Enghien-les-Bains (Seine-et-Oise).
Altitude: 46 m/150 ft. Respiratory passages, lymphatic disorders

4 St-Amand-les-Eaux (Nord).
Altitude: 17 m/55 ft. Rheumatism, bones and joints.

5 Niederbronn (Bas-Rhin).
Altitude: 192 m/630 ft. Rheumatism, bones and joints.

6 Pechelbronn (Bas-Rhin).
Altitude: 150 m/490 ft. Rheumatism, bones and joints.

7 Morsbronn (Bas-Rhin).
Altitude: 183 m/600 ft. Rheumatism, bones and joints.

8 Bourbonne-les-Bains (Haute-Marne).
Altitude: 270 m/885 ft. Rheumatism, bones and joints.

9 Contrexéville (Vosges).
Altitude: 337 m/1105 ft. Kidneys, urinary organs.

10 Vittel (Vosges).
Altitude: 335 m/1100 ft. Kidneys, urinary organs.

11 Bains-les-Bains (Vosges).
Altitude: 350 m/1150 ft. Circulatory disorders.

12 Plombières-les-Bains (Vosges).
Altitude: 424 m/1390 ft. Digestive organs.

13 Bussang (Vosges).
Altitude: 600 m/1970 ft. Circulatory disorders.

14 Luxeuil-les-Bains (Haute-Savoie).
Altitude: 300 m/985 ft. Gynaecological conditions.

15 La Roche-Posay (Vienne).
Altitude: 75 m/245 ft. Skin diseases.

16 Pouques-les-Eaux (Nièvre).
Altitude: 200 m/650 ft. Digestive organs.

17 Bourbon-l'Archambault (Allier).
Altitude: 260 m/850 ft. Rheumatism, bones and joints.

18 St-Honoré-les-Bains (Nièvre).
Altitude: 300 m/985 ft. Respiratory passages, lymphatic disorders.

19 Bourbon-Lancy (Saône-et-Loire).
Altitude: 240 m/790 ft. Rheumatism, bones and joints.

20 Maizières (Côte-d'Or).
Altitude: 350 m/1150 ft. Rheumatism, bones and joints.

21 Lons-le-Saunier (Jura).
Altitude: 255 m/835 ft.
Respiratory passages, rheumatism, lymphatic disorders.

22 Salins-les-Bains (Jura).
Altitude: 354 m/1160 ft. Respiratory passages, lymphatic disorders.

23 Besançon (Doubs).
Altitude: 242 m/795 ft.
Gynaecological conditions, respiratory passages.

24 Rochefort (Charente-Maritime).
Altitude: 5 m/16 ft. Rheumatism, bones and joints.

25 Saujon (Charente-Maritime).
Altitude: 7 m/23 ft. Nervous system.

26 Evaux-les-Bains (Creuse).
Altitude: 460 m/1510 ft. Rheumatism, bones and joints.

27 Néris-les-Bains (Allier).
Altitude: 350 m/1150 ft. Nervous system.

28 Châteauneuf-les-Bains (Puy-de-Dôme).
Altitude: 390 m/1280 ft. Rheumatism, bones and joints.

29 Châtelguyon (Puy-de-Dôme).
Altitude: 400 m/1310 ft. Digestive organs.

30 Vichy (Allier).
Altitude: 283 m/930 ft. Digestive organs.

31 Sail-les-Bains (Loire).
Altitude: 300 m/985 ft. Skin diseases.

32 La Bourboule (Puy-de-Dôme).
Altitude: 850 m/2790 ft. Respiratory passages, lymphatic disorders.

33 Royat (Puy-de-Dôme).
Altitude: 450 m/1475 ft. Circulatory disorders.

34 Le Mont-Dore (Puy-de-Dôme).
Altitude: 1050 m/3445 ft. Respiratory passages, lymphatic disorders.

35 St-Nectaire (Puy-de-Dôme).
Altitude: 700 m/2300 ft. Kidneys, urinary organs.

36 Montrond-les-Bains (Loire).
Altitude: 370 m/1215 ft. Digestive organs.

37 Charbonnières-les-Bains (Rhône).
Altitude: 250 m/820 ft. Circulatory disorders.

38 Divonne-les-Bains (Ain).
Altitude: 500 m/1640 ft. Digestive organs.

39 Thonon-les-Bains (Haute-Savoie).
Altitude: 430 m/1410 ft. Kidneys, urinary organs.

40 Evian-les-Bains (Haute-Savoie).
Altitude: 376 m/1234 ft. Kidneys, urinary organs.

41 St-Gervais-les-Bains (Haute-Savoie).
Altitude: 850 m/2790 ft. Skin diseases.

42 Aix-les-Bains (Savoie).
Altitude: 250 m/820 ft. Rheumatism, bones and joints.

43 Aix-les-Bains-Marlioz (Savoie).
Altitude: 280 m/920 ft. Respiratory passages, lymphatic disorders.

44 Challes-les-Eaux (Savoie).
Altitude: 310 m/1020 ft. Respiratory passages, rheumatism.

45 Allevard (Isère).
Altitude: 475 m/1560 ft. Respiratory passages, lymphatic disorders.

46 Uriage-les-Bains (Isère).
Altitude: 414 m/1360 ft. Skin diseases.

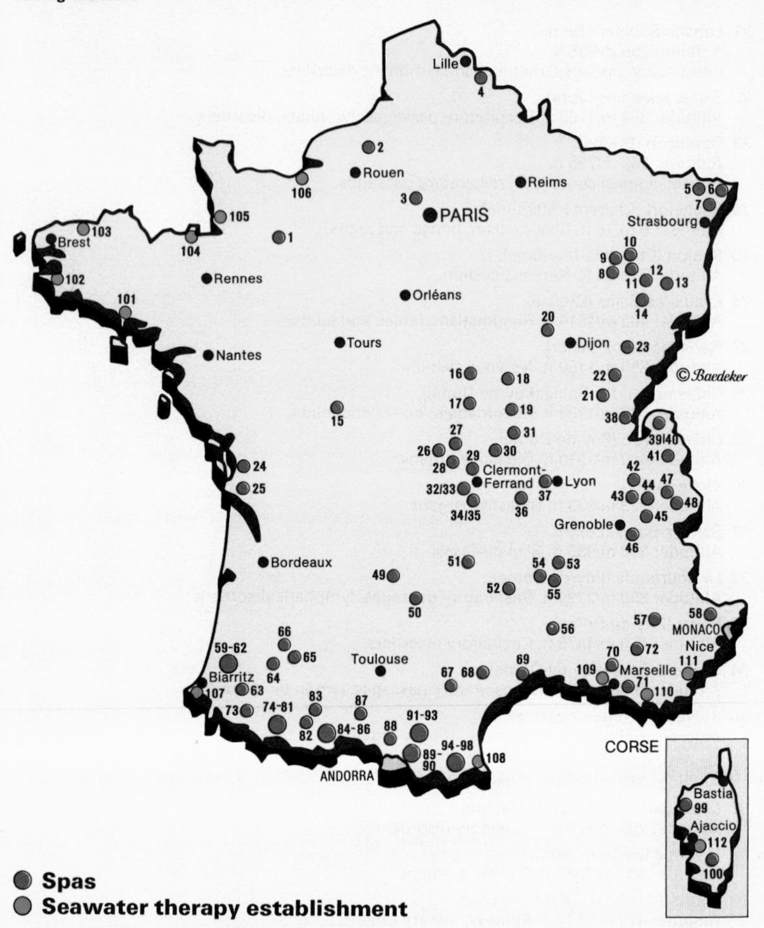

47 La Léchère-les-Bains (Savoie).
Altitude: 440 m/1440 ft. Circulatory disorders.

48 Brides-les-Bains (Savoie).
Altitude: 600 m/1970 ft. Metabolic disorders.

Salins-des-Brides (Savoie).
Altitude: 550 m/1800 ft. Rheumatism, bones and joints.

49 Miers-Alvignac (Lot).
Altitude: 360 m/1180 ft. Digestive organs.

50 Cransac (Aveyron).
Altitude: 292 m/960 ft. Rheumatism, bones and joints.

51 Chaudes-Aigues (Cantal).
Altitude: 750 m/2460 ft. Rheumatism, bones and joints.

52 Bagnols-les-Bains (Lozère).
Altitude: 913 m/2995 ft. Circulatory disorders.

53 St-Laurent-les-Bains (Ardèche).
Altitude: 840 m/2755 ft. Rheumatism, bones and joints.

54 Neyrac-les-Bains (Ardèche).
Altitude: 390 m/1280 ft. Skin diseases.

55 Vals-les-Bains (Ardèche).
Altitude: 250 m/820 ft. Metabolic disorders.

56 Les Fumades-les-Bains (Gard).
Altitude: 200 m/655 ft. Respiratory passages, lymphatic disorders.

57 Digne (Basses-Alpes).
Altitude: 650 m/2130 ft. Rheumatism, bones and joints.

58 Berthemont-les-Bains (Alpes-Maritimes).
Altitude: 950 m/3120 ft.
Respiratory passages, rheumatism, lymphatic disorders.

59 Préchacq-les-Bains (Landes).
Altitude: 20 m/65 ft. Rheumatism, bones and joints.

60 Dax (Landes).
Altitude: 12 m/40 ft. Rheumatism, bones and joints.

61 Tercis-les-Bains (Landes).
Altitude: 65 m/215 ft. Skin diseases.

62 Saubusse-les-Bains (Landes).
Altitude: 85 m/280 ft. Kidneys, urinary organs.

63 Salies-de-Béarn (Basses-Pyrénées).
Altitude: 54 m/175 ft. Gynaecological conditions

64 Eugénie-les-Bains (Landes).
Altitude: 85 m/280 ft. Kidneys, urinary organs.

65 Castera-Verduzan (Gers).
Altitude: 119 m/390 ft. Digestive organs.

66 Barbotan (Gers).
Altitude: 130 m/425 ft. Circulatory disorders.

67 Lamalou-les-Bains (Hérault).
Altitude: 200 m/650 ft. Nervous system.

68 Avène-les-Bains (Hérault).
Altitude: 300 m/980 ft. Skin diseases.

69 Balaruc-les-Bains (Hérault).
Altitude: 2 m/7 ft. Rheumatism, bones and joints.

70 Aix-en-Provence (Bouches-du-Rhône).
Altitude: 177 m/580 ft. Circulatory disorders.

71 Camoins-les-Bains (Bouches-du-Rhône).
Altitude: 250 m/820 ft.
Respiratory passages, lymphatic disorders.

72 Gréoux-les-Bains (Basses-Alpes).
Altitude: 400 m/1300 ft. Rheumatism, bones and joints.

73 St-Christau (Basses-Pyrénées).
Altitude: 330 m/1080 ft. Skin diseases.

74 Les Eaux-Chaudes (Basses-Pyrénées).
Altitude: 675 m/2215 ft.
Respiratory passages, lymphatic disorders.

75 Les Eaux-Bonnes (Basses-Pyrénées).
Altitude: 750 m/2460 ft.
Respiratory passages, lymphatic disorders.

76 Barzun (Hautes-Pyrénées).
Altitude: 1235 m/4050 ft. Respiratory passages.

77 Cauterets (Hautes-Pyrénées).
Altitude: 1000 m/3280 ft.
Respiratory passages, lymphatic disorders.

78 Argelès-Gazost (Hautes-Pyrénées).
Altitude: 460 m/1510 ft. Circulatory disorders.

79 St-Sauveur-les-Bains (Hautes-Pyrénées).
Altitude: 730 m/2395 ft. Gynaecological conditions.

80 Beaucens-les-Bains (Hautes-Pyrénées).
Altitude: 480 m/1575 ft. Rheumatism, bones and joints.

81 Barèges (Hautes-Pyrénées).
Altitude: 1240 m/4070 ft. Rheumatism, bones and joints.

82 Bagnères-de-Bigorre (Hautes-Pyrénées).
Altitude: 550 m/1805 ft. Nervous system.

83 Capvern (Hautes-Pyrénées).
Altitude: 450 m/1475 ft. Kidneys, urinary organs.

84 Luchon (Haute-Garonne).
Altitude: 630 m/2070 ft.
Respiratory passages, lymphatic disorders.

85 Barbazan (Haute-Garonne).
Altitude: 450 m/1475 ft. Digestive organs.

86 Encausse-les-Thermes (Haute-Garonne).
Altitude: 362 m/1190 ft. Digestive organs.

87 Salies-du-Salat (Haute-Garonne).
Altitude: 300 m/980 ft.
Respiratory passages, lymphatic disorders.

88 Ussat-les-Bains (Ariège).
Altitude: 486 m/1595 ft. Nervous system.

89 Ax-les-Thermes (Ariège).
Altitude: 720 m/2360 ft. Rheumatism, bones and joints.

90 Alet-les-Bains (Aude).
Altitude: 206 m/675 ft. Digestive organs.

91 Escouloubre-les-Bains (Aude).
Altitude: 911 m/2990 ft.
Respiratory passages, rheumatism, lymphatic disorders.

92 Ginoles-les-Bains (Aude).
Altitude: 350 m/1150 ft. Kidneys, urinary organs.

93 Rennes-les-Bains (Aude).
Altitude: 310 m/1020 ft. Rheumatism, bones and joints.

94 Molitg-les-Bains (Pyrénées-Orientales).
Altitude: 450 m/1475 ft. Skin diseases.

95 Vernet-les-Bains (Pyrénées-Orientales).
Altitude: 650 m/2130 ft. Rheumatism, bones and joints.

96 La Preste-les-Bains (Pyrénées-Orientales).
Altitude: 1130 m/3710 ft. Kidneys, urinary organs.

97 Amélie-les-Bains (Pyrénées-Orientales).
Altitude: 230 m/755 ft. Rheumatism, bones and joints.

98 Le Boulou (Pyrénées-Orientales).
Altitude: 78 m/255 ft. Digestive organs.

99 Guagno-les-Bains (Corse-du-Sud).
Altitude: 430 m/1410 ft. Rheumatism, bones and joints.

100 Isolaccio-di-Fiamorbo-Pietrapola (Haute-Corse).
Rheumatism, bones and joints.

Sea-Water Treatment Establishments

101 Quiberon (Morbihan).
Institut de Thalassothérapie de Quiberon.

102 Douarnenez-Tréboul (Finistère).
Centre de Cure Marine de la Baie de Tréboul-Douarnenez.

103 Roscoff (Finistère).
Institut Marin Rock-Roum.

104 St-Malo-Paramé (Ille-et-Vilaine).
Thermes Marins de St-Malo-Paramé.

105 Granville (Manche).
Centre de Thalasso-Réadaptation Fonctionnelle "Le Normandy".

106 Trouville (Calvados).
Cures Marines de Trouville.

107 Biarritz (Pyrénées-Atlantiques).
Institut de Thalassothérapie.

108 Collioure (Pyrénées-Orientales)
Centre Hélio-Marin de Réadaptation Fonctionnelle "Mer-Air-Soleil"

109 Marseilles (Bouches-du-Rhône)
Balnéothérapie Marseillaise

110 Toulon (Var)
Centre de Cures Marines de Toulon

111 St-Raphaël (Var)
Institut Marin "La Calanco"

112 Porticcio (Corse-du-Sud)
Institut de Thalassothérapie

Information:
Fédération Thermale et Climatique Française
16 rue de l'Estrapade, F-75005 Paris
tel. (1) 34 25 11 85

Telephones

See Post and Telephone

Television

See Radio and Television

Time

France observes Central European Time, one hour ahead of Greenwich Mean Time. Summer Time (from the last Sunday in March to the last Sunday in September) is two hours ahead of GMT.

Tipping

Cafés and restaurants

The menu should indicate whether a service charge is included (*service compris*) or not (*service non compris*). The charge is 15%. An additional tip is always welcome.

Tipping

Cinemas and theatres	The usher or usherette expects 2 francs per person.
Hairdressers	A men's hairdresser gets 10%. In ladies' hairdressing saloons the hairdresser and hair-washer get 5 francs and the hair-washer and manicurist 10 francs.
Hotels	The porter gets 5 or 10 francs per item of luggage on arrival and departure. It is usual to leave up to 10 francs a day for the chambermaid.
Lavatory attendants	In theatres and restaurants at least 5 francs is paid to the attendant, elsewhere 2 francs.
Lock-keepers	Lock-keepers on inland waterways are accustomed to get a tip for their services.
Museums and châteaux	The guide showing a party round should get 5 francs per person.
Porters	Porters should be given a tip of 5 francs or so (depending on the amount of luggage) in addition to the official charge.
Taxis	Taxi drivers get 10–15% of the fare.

Travel Documents

Passport	Visitors from Britain, other EC countries, the United States and Canada require only a valid passport (a British Visitor's Passport is acceptable) for a stay of up to 3 months in France.
Car documents	British driving licences and car registration documents are accepted in France. Although nationals of EC countries do not need an international insurance certificate (green card), it is desirable to have one, since otherwise only third-party cover is provided. All foreign cars must display an oval nationality plate.

Walking

Walking in the Vosges	The densest network of well maintained and waymarked footpaths in France is in the Vosges, where the Club Vosgien has done pioneering work in developing the system and producing maps and guides.
Information	Club Vosgien, M. Roland Leonhard 79 Route de Colmar, F-67100 Strasbourg tel. 88 34 30 00
Long-distance trails in France	Walking is becoming increasingly popular in the Jura, the Massif Central, the Alps, the Ile-de-France and Brittany as well as in the Vosges. France now has more than 25,000 km/15,500 miles of long-distance trails (*sentiers de grande randonnée*), waymarked in white and red and identified by numbers prefixed by GR. The Comité National des Sentiers de Grande Randonnée published a series of guides to the different routes, with information about features of interest and accommodation.
Information	Comité National des Sentiers de Grande Randonnée 9 Avenue George V, F-75008 Paris tel. (1) 47 23 62 32
European long-distance trails	European long-distance trail E2 runs south from the Luxembourg border through Lorraine and continues through the Vosges; then through the Jura and the Alps, running roughly parallel to the Swiss and Italian frontiers, to end at Nice.

European long-distance trail E3 runs east from the Atlantic coast at Royan via Limoges and Clermont-Ferrand, turns north, crosses the Loire and runs east of Paris to the Luxembourg border.
European long-distance trail E4 begins at Bourg-Madame on the French-Spanish frontier, descends the northern slopes of the Pyrenees and continues by way of Carcassonne into the Cévennes; then runs high above the Ardèche gorge and through the Vercors, continuing by way of Grenoble and Chambéry to the Swiss frontier.

Climbing and hill walking

There is good climbing and walking not only in the high Alps and Pyrenees but in lower hills all over France. The Club Alpin Français has branches in many French towns.

Information

Club Alpin Français
24 Avenue Laumière, F-75019 Paris
tel. (1) 42 02 75 94

When to Go

France likes to call itself the "land of four seasons"; and it is true that with its varied pattern of landscape, extending from the Channel coast by way of the Pyrenees and the Alps to the Côte d'Azur and the island of Corsica, and its consequent variety of climate, France offers attractions to visitors at every time of year. It is worth remembering, however, that accommodation is usually more easily and cheaply available outside the main holiday season (July and August).
For detailed information about climate see page 14.

Spring

Spring is a good time to visit Alsace, the châteaux in the Loire valley, Provence, the Côte d'Azur (particularly between Cannes and Menton), the Basque coast and the coasts of Corsica, where there is good bathing early in the year.

Summer

In summer there is a wide choice: the Vosges, the Jura, Auvergne, the Cévennes and the Tarn gorges, the Pyrenees, the Alps, inland Corsica, the coastal regions and resorts of Nord-Pas-de-Calais, Normandy and Brittany, the Atlantic coast between Les Sables-d'Olonne and Royan, the Côte d'Argent and the Basque coast, the whole of the Mediterranean coast and Corsica.

Autumn

Autumn is the time to visit Burgundy and the other wine-growing regions on the fringes of the Vosges and round Bordeaux; but all the areas mentioned above are attractive, particularly in early autumn.

Winter

In winter the upland and mountain regions – particularly, of course, the Alps, but also the Pyrenees, Auvergne, the Cévennes and the Jura – offer excellent skiing, and the winter resorts on the Riviera and in Corsica attract many visitors with their mild climate.

Paris

Paris has something to offer at every time of year. In winter it has its brilliantly lit streets, its theatres and concerts; in spring and autumn the surrounding countryside is at its most beautiful; and in summer, when many Parisians are away from Paris on holiday, visitors may have an opportunity of exploring the city at a more leisurely pace.

Wine

Types of Grape

(Source: Comité National des Vins de France, Paris)

Aligoté. – A regional grape grown in Burgundy.

Aramon. – A regional grape grown in Languedoc.

Auxerrois. – A regional grape grown round Cahors.

Breton: see Cabernet Franc.

Cabernet Franc. – A grape which produces the great Bordeaux wines. Also grown in the Loire valley under the name of Breton and used in making the red wines of Bourgeuil, Chinon and Saumur-Champigny.

Cabernet-Sauvignon. – A grape grown in the Bordeaux region, particularly in Médoc and Graves, which produces 50–70% of the great wines of the area. It makes full-bodied, full-coloured red wines rich in tannic acid which improve with age.

In Anjou it is used along with Cabernet Franc to produce semi-dry rosé wines.

Cardinal. – A favourite table grape.

Carignan. – The principal grape of the Mediterranean region. Along with Grenache and Cinsaut it produces substantial highly coloured red wines of high alcohol content which improve with age.

Chardonnay. – A grape used in the great white wines of Burgundy (Montrachet, Meursault, Chablis, Pouilly-Fuissé) and Champagne (Blanc de Blancs). It produces light, fruity, transparent wines.

Chasselas. – Used in Alsace, under the name of Gutedel, to produce light white wines. Also a good table grape.

Chenin. – Also known as Pineau de la Loire. Grown in Anjou and Touraine, it produces in some years full-bodied but mild white wines.

Cinsaut. – A grape grown in the Mediterranean region which produces delicate, soft, aromatic wines.

Clairette. – A white grape grown in the south of France. It produces wines of high alcohol content which tend to take on a taste of "age". Also a table grape.

Cot. – A regional grape grown in the Loire valley.

Folle Blanche. – Also known as Gros Plant du Pays Nantais. An even older grape than Melon, it came from the Charente and Gers; it was formerly used to produce cognac and armagnac in the Nantes area.

Gamay. – This black grape with white juice does best on the granitic soils of Beaujolais. The wines it yields are light, fruity and palatable. It is also used in Auvergne wines.

Gewürztraminer. – A grape grown in Alsace which produces a strong, full-bodied white wine with a delicate bouquet and full aroma.

Grauklevner: see Tokay.

Grenache. – Grown in the south of France (Châteauneuf du Pape; dessert wines of Banyuls and Rivesaltes). In combination with Cinsaut, Mourvèdre and Syrah it produces the delicate wines of Languedoc.

Grolleau. – A regional grape grown in the Loire valley.

Gros Plant du Pays Nantais: see Folle Blanche.

Gutedel: see Chasselas.

Jacquère. – A regional grape grown in Savoy.

Knipperlé. – A regional grape grown in Alsace. Little aroma.

Maccabéo. – A regional grape grown in Roussillon.

Malbec. – A regional grape grown in the Bordeaux area.

Malvoisie. – A regional grape grown in Roussillon.

Manseng. – A regional grape grown in the Pyrenean foreland area.

Mauzac. – A regional grape grown round Gaillac and Limoux.

Melon. – Formerly grown in Burgundy, it is now used to produce fresh, dry, fruity white Muscadet in the Nantes area.

Merlot. – A black grape which is used to supplement the Cabernet grapes of the Bordeaux area. It is the dominant element in Pomerol and St-Emilion, giving fire and fullness to the wine.

Meunier. – A regional grape grown in Champagne.

Mondeuse. – A regional grape grown in Savoy.

Mourvèdre. – A grape grown in the southern Côtes du Rhône (Châteauneuf du Pape), east of the Rhône (Coteaux du Tricastin, Côtes du Ventoux) and the Côtes de Provence. It is found at its best round Bandol, giving the wine distinction and keeping quality.

Muscadelle. – A regional grape grown in the Bordeaux area.

Muscat. – There are many kinds of muscatel grapes, used both as table grapes and for the production of wine, which all have a strong and unmistakable aroma of muscatel but produce very different kinds of wine:

Muscat d'Alsace is a dry fruity wine.

Muscat de Hambourg is both a table grape and a wine grape, particularly in southern and south-western France.

Muscat Doré à Petits Grains (small-berried golden muscatel) produces the famous dessert wines Muscat de Frontignan, Muscat de Rivesaltes, Muscat de Lunel and Muscat de Beaumes de Venise.

In the Die area, east of the Rhône, Muscat is used along with Clairette to produce a popular sparkling wine, Clairette de Die.

Muscat d'Alexandrie is used in Roussillon to produce excellent dessert wines.

Nielluccio. – A regional grape grown in Corsica.

Pécoul-Touar. – A regional grape grown in Provence.

Picpoul. – A regional grape grown in Languedoc.

Pineau de la Loire: see Chenin.

Pinot Blanc. – Grown in Alsace, under the name of Weissklevner or Weissburgunder, to produce a dry, flowery white wine.

Pinot Gris: see Tokay.

Pinot Noir. – Produces the great red wines of Burgundy. Also grown in Champagne. It is also found in Alsace under the name of Spätburgunder, in the Mâconnais and in the rosé wines of Sancerre and Alsace.

Poulsard. – Typical of the Jura, where it is used in combination with Trousseau, Pinor or Chardonnay to produce red and rosé wines.

Riesling. – The best known of the grapes grown in Alsace, it produces a distinguished dry white wine, fruity and with a delicate bouquet.

Roussanne. – A regional grape grown in the Rhône valley.

Roussette. – A regional grape grown in Savoy.

Sauvignon. – An excellent white grape which produces wines of some distinction. It is found particularly in the Bordeaux area (Graves) and the Loire valley.

Savagnin. – A late ripening grape which is sometimes not harvested until November. It gives the "ice wines" or *vins jaunes* (yellow wines) of the Jura, Château-Chalon, L'Etoile, Arbois and Côtes du Jura their distinctive character.

Sciaccarello. – A regional grape grown in Corsica.

Semillon. – The commonest white grape of the Bordeaux area, the basis for the great white wines of Bordeaux, either dry like Graves or sweet like Sauternes, Barsac, etc.

Spätburgunder: see Pinot Noir.

St-Emilion des Charentes: see Ugni Blanc.

Sylvaner. – Grown in Alsace to produce fresh, fruity white wines.

Syrah. – An aromatic grape grown in the northern Côtes du Rhône (red Hermitage, Cornas). The wine has a beautiful ruby colour and a characteristic tang. Syrah is also used to add quality to the wines of Languedoc.

Tannat. – A regional grape grown in the Pyrenean foreland area.

Terret. – A regional grape grown in Languedoc.

Tibouren. – A regional grape grown in Provence.

Tokay. – Grown in Alsace, where it is also known as Grauklevner or Pinot Gris. It produces a full-bodied dry white wine.

Tressot. – A regional grape grown in Burgundy.

Ugni Blanc. – This grape is widely grown in Provence, and gives the wines of southern Languedoc the tannic acid which they often lack. It is also used in western France, under the name of St-Emilion des Charentes, to produce cognac.

Vermentino. – A regional grape grown in Corsica.

Viognier. – A regional grape grown in the Rhône valley.

Weissburgunder, Weissklevner: see Pinot Blanc.

The Language of the Wine Label

Appellation (d'origine) controlée (AOC)	An indication of the place of origin (the right to which is strictly controlled)
Blanc de Blancs	A white wine (particularly a sparkling wine) made from white grapes fermented without their skins
Brut	Extra dry (of champagne or quality sparkling wines)
Cave, caveau	Wine cellar; wine-making establishment
Cépage	Type of vine
Château	Wine-making establishment (only for quality wines)

Clos	Vineyard
Cuvée	Blending
Domaine	"Estate": wine-making establishment (quality wines only)
Méthode champenoise	The "champagnisation" of wine by natural fermentation in bottle
Mis(e) en bouteille	Bottled, bottling
Nouveau	A young, fresh red wine
Sigille	Seal of quality
Vendange tardive	Late-gathered grapes
Vin délimité de qualité supérieure (VDQS)	A wine of high quality from a particular area
Vin de pays	Local wine, country wine
Vin de table	Table wine

French Wines at a Glance

(Source: Comité National des Vins de France, Paris)

See map of French wine-growing areas on p. 627.

NAME	AREA	COLOUR	CHARACTERISTICS	YEARS IN CELLAR	DRINKING TEMP. (°C/F)
Alsace	Alsace	white	dry, distinguished	2-5	10/50
		rosé	dry, light	2-5	10/50
Arbois	Jura	white	dry, flowery	2-8	10/50
		red	vigorous, elegant	5-10	16/61
Banyuls	Languedoc-Roussillon	red	a fruity dessert wine, semi-sweet to sweet	6-15	5/41
Beaujolais	Burgundy	red	light, palatable	1-2	12/54
Beaune	Burgundy	red	full-bodied, elegant	6-12	16/61
Bergerac	SW France	white	from dry to sweet	2-5	8-6/46-43
		rosé	dry, light	1-2	10/50
		red	vigorous, elegant	3-6	18/64
Blanquette de Limoux	Languedoc-Roussillon	white	a light sparkling wine, from extra dry (brut) to sweet (doux)	3-5	6/43
Bordeaux	Bordeaux	white	mostly sweet, fruity	4-6	6/43
		red	vigorous, slightly dry	5-10	18/64
Bourgogne (Burgundy)	Burgundy	white	dry, distinguished	2-5	10/50
		red	full-bodied, rich bouquet	5-10	16/61
Cahors	SW France	red	very full-bodied, dry	5-10	16/61
Chablis	Burgundy	white	dry, distinguished	3-15	10/50
Champagne	Champagne	white	an elegant sparkling wine	1-4	6/43
Châteauneuf du Pape	Rhône valley	red	very full-bodied	3-8	16/61
Clairette de Die	Rhône valley	white	a light sparkling wine, from extra-dry (brut) to a sweet muscatel taste	1-2	6/43
Corbières	Languedoc-Roussillon	red	full-bodied	2-3	16/61
Côteaux Champenois	Champagne	white	dry, distinguished	1-3	10/50
		red	vigorous, elegant	2-5	18/64
Côteaux du Languedoc	Languedoc-Roussillon	rosé	dry, semi-light	2-3	10/50
		red	vigorous, fresh	2-3	16/61
Cóte de Beaune	Burgundy	red	full-bodied, elegant	6-12	16/61

NAME	AREA	COLOUR	CHARACTERISTICS	YEARS IN CELLAR	DRINKING TEMP. (°C/F)
Côtes de Provence	Provence/ Côte d'Azur	rosé	dry, vigorous	1-2	10/50
		red	vigorous, fresh	2-5	16/61
Côtes du Jura	Jura	white	dry, flowery	2-5	10/50
		rosé	dry, light	1-2	10/50
		red	vigorous, elegant	5-10	16/61
Côtes du Rhône	Rhône valley	red	full-bodied, rich bouquet	2-3	16/61
Côtes du Roussillon	Languedoc-Roussillon	white	dry, distinguished	2-5	10/50
		rosé	dry, vigorous	1-2	10/50
		red	full-bodied	3-5	16/61
Côtes du Ventoux	Rhône valley	red	vigorous, fresh	2-3	16/61
Crémant d'Alsace	Alsace	white	a light sparkling wine, from extra dry (brut) to sweet (doux)	1-4	6/43
Crémant de Bourgogne	Burgundy	white	a light sparkling wine, from extra dry (brut) to sweet (doux)	1-4	6/43
Crémant de Loire	Loire valley	white	a light sparkling wine, from extra dry (brut) to sweet (doux)	1-4	6/43
Crozes-Hermitage	Rhône valley	red	full-bodied, elegant	3-10	16/61
Entre-deux-Mers	Bordeaux	white	dry, fresh	2-3	8/46
Fitou	Languedoc-Roussillon	red	full-bodied, rich bouquet	3-6	16/61
Gaillac	SW France	white	dry, fresh	1-2	8/46
		white	sparkling	1-2	6/43
		rosé	dry, fresh	1-2	10/50
		red	vigorous, fresh	2-5	16/61
Gevrey-Chambertin	Burgundy	red	full-bodied, rich bouquet	8-15	16/61
Gigondas	Rhône valley	red	full-bodied	3-5	16/61
Graves	Bordeaux	white	dry, distinguished	5-10	10/50
		red	full-bodied, elegant	7-15	18/64
Graves de Vayres	Bordeaux	white	sweet, fruity	4-6	6/43
Graves Supérieures	Bordeaux	white	sweet, flowery	5-10	6/43
Jurançon	SW France	white	dry, distinguished	2-5	10/50
Mâcon	Burgundy	white	dry, fruity	1-3	10/50
		rosé	dry, semi-light	1-2	10/50
		red	light, fruity	2-3	12/54
Médoc	Bordeaux	red	full-bodied, elegant	5-10	18/64
Meursault	Burgundy	white	dry, distinguished	5-20	10/50
Minervois	Languedoc-Roussillon	red	full-bodied	2-3	16/61
Monba-zillac	SW France	white	sweet, well rounded	5-15	6/43
Muscadet	Loire valley	white	dry, fresh	1-3	8/46
Muscat d'Alsace	Alsace	white	dry, distinguished, muscatel taste	2-4	10/50
Muscat de Rivesaltes	Languedoc-Roussillon	white	a sweet dessert wine with a muscatel taste	2-3	5/41
Pomerol	Bordeaux	red	full-bodied, rich bouquet	10-20	16/61
Rivesaltes	Languedoc-Roussillon	white	a sweet dessert wine	6-10	5/41
Rosé d'Anjou	Loire valley	rosé	sweet, fruity	1-1	8/46
St-Emilion	Bordeaux	red	full-bodied, rich bouquet	10-20	16/61
Sancerre	Loire valley	white	dry, distinguished	1-2	10/50
Saumur	Loire valley	white	semi-dry	1-5	10/50
		white	sparkling	1-4	6/43
Sauternes	Bordeaux	white	sweet, well rounded	10-20	6/43
Tavel	Rhône valley	rosé	dry, full-bodied	1-2	10/50

NAME	AREA	COLOUR	CHARACTERISTICS	YEARS IN CELLAR	DRINKING TEMP. (°C/F)
Touraine	Loire valley	white	dry to sweet	1-10	8-6/46-43
		red	light, flowery	1-5	12/54
Vin de Corse	Corsica	rosé	dry, full-bodied	3-6	10/50
		red	very full-bodied	3-6	16/61
Vin de Pays	Languedoc-Roussillon Corsica	red rosé white	light, fruity	1-2	12/54
Vin de Savoie	Savoy	white	dry, fruity	2-5	10/50
		rosé	dry, light	1-2	10/50
		red	semi-light, flowery	2-5	12/54
Vouvray	Loire valley	white	sweet, well rounded	1-25	6/43
		white	sparkling wine	1-4	6/43

Information

Zwicker and Edelzwicker are blended wines made in Alsace. Both are white wines, fresh and aromatic in character. They should not be drunk too cold.

Centre de Documentation et de Dégustation du Vin
45 rue de Liancourt, F-75014 Paris
tel. (1) 43 27 67 21

Académie du Vin
25 rue Royale, F-75008 Paris
tel. (1) 42 65 09 85

L'Invitation à Découvrir
(Villa des Entrepreneurs), F-75015 Paris
tel. (1) 45 79 89 12

Musée du Vin
Rue Charles-Dickens, F-75116 Paris
tel. (1) 45 25 63 26

Winter Sports

Facilities for winter sports in France are extensive and varied. Since development of the necessary infrastructure for winter sports began only in the mid 1960s, there are many well equipped modern resorts. There are now more than 400 winter sports centres, with 3500 cableways and lifts (only Austria has more) in huge skiing areas with guaranteed snow.

Today there is a choice between well planned modern resorts like Lac de Tignes, gigantic skiing metropolises like La Plagne (which can accommodate 30,000 visitors), traditional winter sports resorts which have developed from existing communities, like the fashionable Mégève and Chamonix, and numbers of modest places favoured by weekend skiers.

The carefully planned development has produced excellent accommodation, ski-lifts, recreation and après-ski facilities to meet all the needs of winter sports enthusiasts – though it should be mentioned that a skiing holiday is not exactly inexpensive.

The resorts between Lake Geneva and the Côte d'Azur are, of course, particularly popular because of the large skiing areas they offer, the excellent snow prospects, the short waiting-times for the numerous lifts and the southern sun – particularly in the Alpes Maritimes. Considerably less crowded than the Alps are the Pyrenees, which also offer good skiing, for example at Font-Romeu, Bagnères or Cauterets.

Langlauf skiing

There are now increasing numbers of langlauf trails – which offer long ski treks through country untroubled by mass tourism – in the Vercors, the Massif Central, the Vosges and the Jura as well as in the other skiing areas.

Information

Fédération Française de Ski
50 rue Marquisats, BP 2451, F-74011 Annecy Cedex
tel. 50 51 40 34

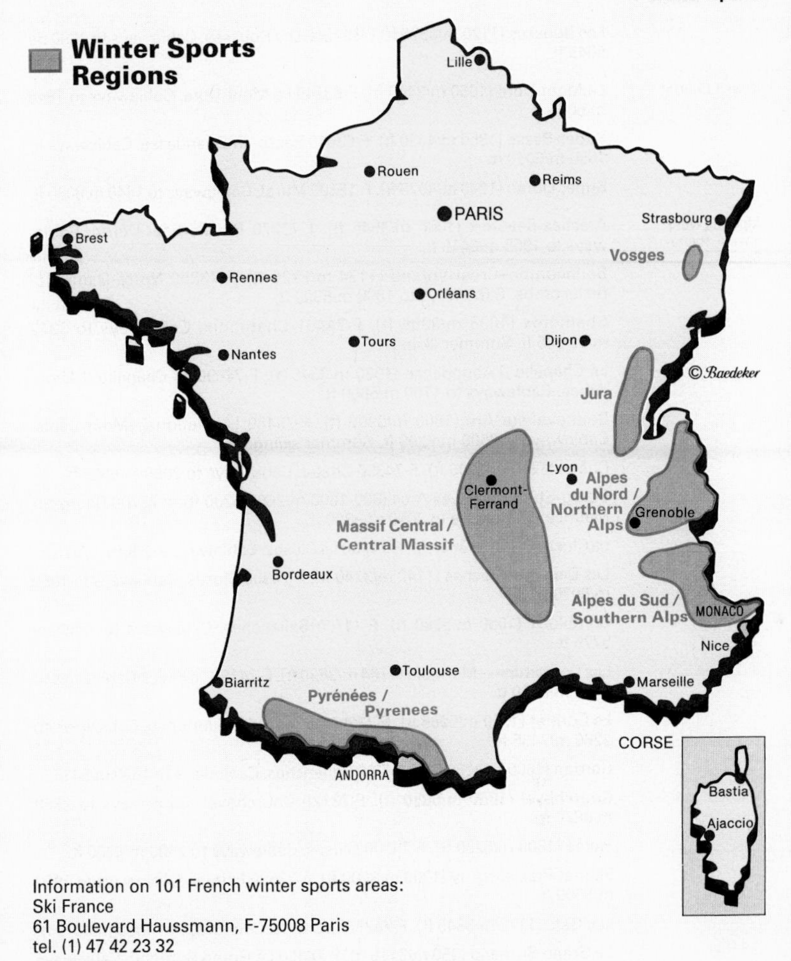

Information on 101 French winter sports areas:
Ski France
61 Boulevard Haussmann, F-75008 Paris
tel. (1) 47 42 23 32

Ski France operates a snow bulletin (mid-December to mid-April)
tel. (1) 42 66 64 28 (24-hours)

Winter Sports Areas

See map above

Vosges

La Bresse (630 m/2070 ft). F-88250 La Bresse. Cableways to 1300 m/4265 ft.

Gérardmer (666 m/2185 ft). F-884400 Gérardmer. Cableways to 1113 m/3650 ft.

Jura

Métabief–Mont d'Or (1000 m/3280 ft). F-25370 Les Hôpitaux Neufs. Cableways to 1430 m/4690 ft.

Les Rousses (1120 m/3675 ft) F-392200 Les Rousses. Cableways to 1690 m/5545 ft.

Massif Central

Le Mont-Dore (1050 m/3445 ft). F-63240 Le Mont-Dore. Cableways to 1846 m/6055 ft

Super-Besse (1350 m/4430 ft). F-63610 Besse-en-Chandesse. Cableways to 1850 m/6070 ft.

Super Lioran (1240 m/4070 ft). F-15300 Murat. Cableways to 1840 m/6035 ft.

Alpes du Nord
Savoie, Haute-Savoie

Arèches-Beaufort (1080 m/3545 ft). F-73270 Beaufort-sur-Doron. Cableways to 1955 m/6415 ft.

Bellecombe–Crest-Voland (1134 m/3720 ft). F-73850 Notre-Dame-de-Bellecombe. Cableways to 1800 m/5900 ft.

Chamonix (1035 m/3395 ft). F-74401 Chamonix. Cableways to 3842 m/12,605 ft. Summer skiing.

La Chapelle d'Abondance (1020 m/3345 ft). F-74690 La Chapelle d'Abondance. Cableways to 1700 m/5600 ft.

Bonneval-sur-Arc (1800 m/5900 ft). F-73480 Lanslebourg–Mont-Cenis. Cableways to 2500 m/8200 ft. Summer skiing.

Châtel (1200 m/3900 ft). F-74390 Châtel. Cableways to 2080 m/6825 ft.

Bourg-St-Maurice–Les Arcs (800-1600 m/2600-5200 ft). F-73700 Bourg-St-Maurice. Cableways to 3000 m/9800 ft.

La Clusaz (1100 m/3600 ft). F-74200 La Clusaz. Cableways to 2400 m/7875 ft.

Les Carroz d'Araches (1140 m/3740 ft). F-74300 Cluses. Cableways to 1850 m/6070 ft.

Combloux (1000 m/3280 ft). F-74700 Sallanches. Cableways to 1760 m/5775 ft.

Les Contamines–Montjoie (1164 m/3820 ft). F-74190 Le Fayet. Cableways to 2487 m/8160 ft.

Le Corbier (1550 m/5085 ft). F-73300 St-Jean-de-Maurienne. Cableways to 2266 m/7435 ft.

Cordon (1000 m/3280 ft). F-74700 Sallanches. Cableways to 1650 m/5415 ft.

Courchevel (1850 m/6070 ft). F-73120 Courchevel. Cableways to 2700 m/8860 ft.

Flaine (1600 m/5250 ft). F-74300 Cluses. Cableways to 2500 m/8200 ft.

Flumet-Praz-sur-Arly (1000 m/3280 ft). F-73590 Flumet. Cableways to 1800 m/5900 ft.

Les Gets (1172 m/3845 ft). F-74260 Les Gets. Cableways to 1850 m/6070 ft.

Le Grand Bornand (950 m/3115 ft). F-74450 Le Grand Bornand. Cableways to 1850 m/6070 ft.

Les Houches (1008 m/3310 ft). F-74310 Les Houches. Cableways to 1900 m/6235 ft.

Megève (1113 m/3650 ft). F-74120 Megève. Cableways to 2040 m/6700 ft.

Les Menuires (1810 m/5940 ft). F-73440 St-Martin-de-Belleville. Cableways to 3010 m/9875 ft. Summer skiing

Méribel-les-Allues (1600 m/5250 ft). F-73550 Méribel-les-Allues. Cableways to 2700 m/8860 ft.

Morzine-Avoriaz (1000 m/3280 ft). F-74110 Morzine. Cableways to 2460 m/8070 ft.

La Plagne (1970 m/6465 ft). F-73210 Aime. Cableways to 3250 m/10,660 ft. Summer skiing.

Pralognan-la-Vanoise (1410 m/4625 ft). F-73710 Pralognan-la-Vanoise. Cableways to 2265 m/7430 ft.

St-François–Longchamp (1450 m/4760 ft). F-73130 La Chambre. Cableways to 2200 m/7220 ft.

St-Gervais–Le Bettex (900 m/2950 ft). F-74170 St-Gervais-les-Bains. Cableways to 1950 m/6400 ft.

Samoens (720 m/2360 ft). F-74340 Samoens. Cableways to 2125 m/6970 ft.

Tignes (2100 m/6890 ft). F-73320 Tignes. Cableways to 3016 m/9895 ft. Summer skiing.

Val-Cenis (1450 m/4760 ft). F-73480 Lanslebourg–Mont-Cenis. Cableways to 2540 m/8335 ft.

Val-d'Isère (1850 m/6070 ft). F-73150 Val-d'Isère. Cableways to 3254 m/10,675 ft. Summer skiing.

Valloire (1450 m/4760 ft). F-73450 Valloire. Cableways to 2450 m/8040 ft. Summer skiing.

Thollon-les Memises (1000 m/3280 ft). F-74500 Evian. Cableways to 1982 m/6595 ft.

Alpes du Nord
Isère

Alpe d'Huez (1860 m/6100 ft). F-38750 Alpe d'Huez. Cableways to 3350 m/10,990 ft. Summer skiing.

Autrans (1050 m/3445 ft). F-38880 Autrans. Cableways to 1630 m/53500 ft.

Chamrousse (1650 m/5415 ft). F-38410 Uriage. Cableways to 2250 m/7380 ft.

Les Deux-Alpes (1650 m/5415 ft). F-38520 Bourg-d'Oisans. Cableways to 3166 m/10,390 ft. Summer skiing.

St-Pierre-de-Chartreuse (900 m/2950 ft). F-38380 St-Laurent-du-Pont. Cableways to 1700 m/5580 ft.

Villard-de-Lans (1050 m/3445 ft). F-38250 Villard-de-Lans. Cableways to 1929 m/6330 ft.

Alpes du Sud

Auron (1600 m/5250 ft). F-06660 St-Etienne-de-Tinée. Cableways to 2417 m/7930 ft.

Beuil-les-Launes (1410 m/4625 ft). F-06470 Guillaumes. Cableways to 2010 m/6595 ft.

La Colmiane–Valdeblore (1500 m/4920 ft). F-06420 St-Sauveur-sur-Tinée. Cableways to 1800 m/5950 ft.

La Foux-d'Allos (1800 m/5905 ft). F-04260 Allos. Cableways to 2600 m/8530 ft.

Isola 2000 (2010 m/6595 ft). F-06420 St-Sauveur-sur-Tinée. Cableways to 2450 m/8040 ft.

Montgenèvre (1860 m/6100 ft). F-05100 Briançon. Cableways to 2600 m/8530 ft.

Orcières Merlette (1815 m/5955 ft). F-05170 Orcières. Cableways to 2655 m/8710 ft.

Les Orres (1550 m/5085 ft). F-05200 Embrun. Cableways to 2770 m/9090 ft.

Pra-Loup (1628 m/5340 ft). F-04400 Barcelonnette. Cableways to 2502 m/8210 ft.

La Sauze–Super-Sauze (1400 m/4595 ft). F-04400 Barcelonnette. Cableways to 2400 m/7875 ft.

Superdévoulu (1500 m/4920 ft). F-05250 St-Etienne-en-Dévoulu. Cableways to 2500 m/8200 ft.

Valberg (1600 m/5250 ft). F-06470 Guillaumes. Cableways to 2010 m/6595 ft.

Vars (1650 m/5415 ft). F-05600 Guillestre. Cableways to 2580 m/8465 ft.

Pyrenees

Ax-les-Thermes (1400 m/4595 ft). F-09110 Ax-les-Thermes. Cableways to 2300 m/7545 ft.

Barèges (1230 m/4035 ft). F-65120 Luz-St-Sauveur. Cableways to 2000 m/6560 ft.

Cauterets Lys (937 m/3075 ft). F-65110 Cauterets. Cableways to 2300 m/7545 ft. Summer skiing.

Font-Romeu (1750 m/5740 ft). F-66120 Font-Romeu. Cableways to 2215 m/7265 ft.

Gourette les Eaux-Bonnes (1400 m/4595 ft). F-64440 Laruns. Cableways to 2400 m/7875 ft.

La Mongie (1750 m/5740 ft). F-65200 Bagnères-de-Bigorre. Cableways to 2360 m/7745 ft.

St-Lary–Soulan (1700 m/5580 ft). F-65170 St-Lary. Cableways to 2380 m/7810 ft.

Les Agudes (1600 m/5250 ft). F-31110 Bagnères-de-Luchon. Cableways to 2400 m/7875 ft.

Les Angles-Formiguères (1600 m/5250 ft). F-66210 Mont-Louis. Cableways to 2370 m/7775 ft.

Among the resorts in the Pyrenees La Mongie is particularly to be recommended; it has magnificent descents, ski-lifts and cableways.

Youth Hostels (auberges de jeunesse)

There are two French youth hostel associations, LFAJ with 300 hostels and FUAJ with 250. They can be used by foreign visitors with an international youth hostel card (obtainable from the youth hostel association in their own country). Advance booking is advisable in July and August; the maximum stay permitted during the main holiday season is usually three nights.

Information

Ligue Française pour les Auberges de la Jeunesse (LFAJ)
38 Boulevard Raspail, F-75007 Paris
tel. (1) 45 48 69 84

Fédération Unie des Auberges de Jeunesse (FUAJ)
27 rue Pajol, F-75018 Paris
tel. (1) 42 41 59 00

Index

The Most Important Places of Tourist Interest at a Glance

Continued from page 6

The places listed on pages 6 and 638 are merely a selection of the principal sights – places of interest in themselves or for attractions in the surrounding area. There are, of course, innumerable other sights throughout France, to which attention is drawn by one or more stars.